MAWLI BĪ

Celebration ermissibility

MAWLID AL-NABĪ

Celebration and Permissibility

Shaykh-ul-Islam
Dr Muhammad Tahir-ul-Qadri

TRANSLATED BY

Muhammad Imran Sulaiman & Waqas Ahmed Amin

Author: Dr Muhammad Tahir-ul-Qadri

Published by
Minhaj-ul-Quran Publications
292–296 Romford Road
Forest Gate, E7 9HD
London (UK)

All proceeds from the books, literature and audio-visual media (all multimedia) delivered by Dr Muhammad Tahir-ul-Qadri are entirely donated to Minhaj-ul-Quran International (MQI).

Translation and Editorial Team
Muhammad Imran Sulaiman, Waqas Ahmed Amin, Dr Maya Naz & M Farooq Rana

Acknowledgements
We would like to thank and show our appreciation to Mujtaba Tariq (USA), Haji Fiaz Ahmed (Nelson) and all others who contributed to make this project successful.

A catalogue record for this book is available from the British Library.

Library of Congress Control Number: 2013952866

ISBN–13: 978–1–908229–14–4 (hbk)
ISBN–13: 978–1–908229–24–3 (pbk)

www.minhaj.org | www.minhajuk.org
www.minhajpublications.com

First published January 2014

Printed by Mega Printing, Turkey

بِسْمِ ٱللَّهِ ٱلرَّحْمَٰنِ ٱلرَّحِيمِ

In the name of God, Most Compassionate, Ever-Merciful

﴿قُلْ بِفَضْلِ ٱللَّهِ وَبِرَحْمَتِهِۦ فَبِذَٰلِكَ فَلْيَفْرَحُوا۟ هُوَ خَيْرٌ مِّمَّا يَجْمَعُونَ﴾

Say: (All this) is due to the bounty and mercy of Allah (bestowed upon you through raising Muhammad ﷺ as the exalted Messenger). So the Muslims should rejoice over it. This is far better than (all that affluence and wealth) that they amass. [Qur'ān 10:58]

Saying of the Prophet ﷺ

«دَعْوَةُ أَبِي إِبْرَاهِيمَ، وَبُشْرَى عِيسَى؛ وَرَأَتْ أُمِّي أَنَّهُ يَخْرُجُ مِنْهَا نُورٌ أَضَاءَتْ مِنْهَا قُصُورُ الشَّامِ».

I am the answer to my father Ibrāhīm's supplication and the glad-tidings of ʿĪsā ﷺ. (Upon my birth,) my dear mother witnessed light emanating from her (blessed body) which illuminated the palaces of Syria. [Aḥmad b. Ḥanbal]

Shaykh-ul-Islam Dr Muhammad Tahir-ul-Qadri

Shaykh-ul-Islam Dr Muhammad Tahir-ul-Qadri was born in 1951 in the city of Jhang, Pakistan, hailing from a family of Islamic saints, scholars and teachers. His formal religious education was initiated in Medina at the age of 12 in Madrasa al-ʿUlūm al-Sharʿiyya, a traditional school situated in the blessed house of the Companion of the Prophet Muhammad ﷺ, Abū Ayyūb al-Anṣārī ؓ. He completed the traditional studies of classical and Arabic sciences under the tutelage of his father and other eminent scholars of the time. He continued to travel around the Islamic world in the pursuit of sacred knowledge, and studied under many famous scholars of Mecca, Medina, Syria, Baghdad, Lebanon, the Maghreb, India and Pakistan, and received around five hundred authorities and chains of transmission from them in hadith and classical Islamic and spiritual sciences. Amongst them is an unprecedented, unique and highly honoured chain of authority which connects him, through four teachers, to Shaykh ʿAbd al-Razzāq, the son of Sayyidunā Shaykh ʿAbd al-Qādir al-Jīlānī al-Ḥasanī al-Ḥusaynī (of Baghdad), al-Shaykh al-Akbar Muḥyī al-Dīn b. al-ʿArabī [(the author of *al-Futūḥāt al-Makkiyya*) (Damascus)] and Imam Ibn Ḥajar al-ʿAsqalānī, the great hadith authority of Egypt. Through another chain he is linked to Imam Yūsuf b. Ismāʿīl al-Nabhānī directly via only one teacher. His chains of transmission are published in two of his thabts (detailed list): *al-Jawāhir al-Bāhira fī al-Asānīd al-Ṭāhira* and *al-Subul al-Wahabiyya fī al-Asānīd al-Dhahabiyya*.

In the academic sphere, Dr Qadri received a First Class Honours Degree from the University of the Punjab in 1970. After earning his MA in Islamic studies with University Gold Medal in 1972 and achieving his LLB in 1974, Dr Qadri began to practise law in the district courts of Jhang. He moved to Lahore in 1978 and joined the University of the Punjab as a lecturer in law and completed his doctorate in Islamic Law. He was later appointed as a professor of Islamic Law and was head of the department of Islamic legislation for LLM.

Dr Qadri was also a jurist advisor to the Federal Shariat Court and Appellate Shariah Bench of the Supreme Court of Pakistan and advisor on the development of Islamic Curricula to the Federal Ministry of Education. Within a short span of time, Dr Qadri emerged as one of the Pakistan's leading Islamic jurists and scholars and one of the world's most renowned and leading authorities on Islam. A prolific author, researcher and orator, Dr Qadri has written around one thousand books, of which more than four hundred and fifty have been published, and has delivered over six thousand lectures (in Urdu, English and Arabic) on a wide range of subjects.

Shaykh-ul-Islam Dr Muhammad Tahir-ul-Qadri issued a historic fatwa on the vital matter of suicide bombings and terrorism carried out in the name of Islam. It is regarded as a significant and historic step, the first time that such an explicit and unequivocal decree against the perpetrators of terror has been broadcast so widely. The original fatwa was written in Urdu, and amounts to 600 pages of research and references from the Qur'ān, hadith, the opinions of the Companions ﷺ, and the widely accepted classical texts of Islamic scholarship. This historic work has been published in English and Indonesian, while translation into Arabic, Norwegian, Danish, Hindi and other major languages is also in process. Islamic Research Academy of Jamia al-Azhar Egypt wrote a detailed description of the fatwa and verified its contents as well.

Dr Qadri is also the founder and head of Minhaj-ul-Quran International (MQI), an organisation with branches and centres in more than ninety countries around the globe; he is the chairman of the Board of Governors of Minhaj University Lahore, which is chartered by the Government of Pakistan; he is the founder of Minhaj Education Society, which has established more than 600 schools and colleges in Pakistan; and he is the chairman of Minhaj Welfare Foundation, an organization involved in humanitarian and social welfare activities globally.

Transliteration Key

ا/آ/ى	ā	ظ	ẓ
ب	b	ع	ʿ
ت	t	غ	gh
ث	th	ف	f
ج	j	ق	q
ح	ḥ	ك	k
خ	kh	ل	l
د	d	م	m
ذ	dh	ن	n
ر	r	ه	h
ز	z	و	w/ū
س	s	ي	y/ī
ش	sh	ة	a
ص	ṣ	ء	ʾ
ض	ḍ	أ	a
ط	ṭ	إ	i

Formulaic Arabic Expressions

(*Subḥānahū wa taʿālā*) an invocation to describe the Glory of Almighty Allah: 'the Exalted and Sublime'

(*Ṣalla-llāhu ʿalayhi wa ālihī wa sallam*) an invocation of God's blessings and peace upon the Prophet Muhammad and his family: 'God's blessings and peace be upon him and his family'

(*ʿAlayhis-salām*) an invocation of God's blessings and peace upon a Prophet or an angel: 'May peace be upon him'

(*ʿAlayhas-salām*) an invocation of God's blessings and peace upon a Prophet's mother, wife, daughter and other pious woman: 'May peace be upon her'

(*ʿAlayhimus-salām*) an invocation of God's blessings and peace upon two Prophets or two angels: 'May peace be upon both of them'

(*ʿAlayhimus-salām*) an invocation of God's blessings and peace upon three or more Prophets: 'May peace be upon them'

(*Raḍiya-llāhu ʿanhu*) an invocation of God's pleasure with a male Companion of the Prophet: 'May God be pleased with him'

(*Raḍiya-llāhu ʿanhā*) an invocation of God's pleasure with a female Companion of the Prophet: 'May God be pleased with her'

(*Raḍiya-llāhu ʿanhumā*) an invocation of God's pleasure with two Companions of the Prophet: 'May God be pleased with both of them'

(*Raḍiya-llāhu ʿanhum*) an invocation of God's pleasure with more than two Companions of the Prophet: 'May God be pleased with them'

Contents

Preface 1

Chapter 1

Mawlid al-Nabī ﷺ and the Signs of Islam: A Historical Perspective 15

1.1 The Significance of 'Remembrance' as the Qur'ān's Scheme of Guidance 17

1.2 The Abrahamic Religion 19

Section 1

In Remembrance of the Prophets: The Five Ritual Prayers 23

1.3 The Fajr Ritual Prayer: In Remembrance of Prophet Ādam ﷺ 25

1.4 The Ẓuhr Ritual Prayer: In Remembrance of Prophet Ibrāhīm ﷺ 25

1.5 The ʿAṣr Ritual Prayer: In Remembrance of Prophet ʿUzayr ﷺ 26

1.6 The Maghrib Ritual Prayer: In Remembrance of Prophet Dāwūd ﷺ 26

1.7 The ʿIshā Ritual Prayer: In Remembrance of Prophet Muhammad ﷺ 26

Section 2

In Remembrance of the Prophets: The Rites of Pilgrimage 29

1.8 The Iḥrām: In Remembrance of the Prophets' Attire for Pilgrimage 32

1.9 Talbiya: In Remembrance of Ibrāhīm's Call to Pilgrimage and its Reply 35

1.10 Ṭawāf: In Remembrance of the Sunna of Prophets 40
1.11 Raml: In Remembrance of the Manner in which the Prophet ﷺ and his Companions Performed the Ṭawāf 43
1.12 Iḍṭibāᶜ: The Sunna of the Last Messenger ﷺ 46
1.13 Kissing the Black Stone: In Remembrance of the Practice of Allah's Beloved 48
1.14 Maqām Ibrāhīm: In Remembrance of Prophet Ibrāhīm ﷺ 49
1.15 Saᶜy between al-Ṣafā and al-Marwa: In Remembrance of the Sunna of Hājar ﷺ 52
1.15.1 Well of Zam Zam: Raison D'être for its Name 55
1.16 ᶜArafāt, Muzdalifa and Minā: In Remembrance of Prophet Ādam ﷺ 56
1.17 Combining the Prayers at ᶜArafāt and Muzdalifa: Sunna of Prophet Muhammad ﷺ 58
1.18 Animal Sacrifice: In Remembrance of Ismāᶜīl 60
1.18.1 Sacrificial Animals: One of the Signs of Allah 61
1.19 The Ritual Casting of Stones: The Sunna of Prophet Ibrāhīm ﷺ 61
1.19.1 An Objection 65
1.19.2 Our Reply to this Objection 66

Chapter 2

Remembering Events of Joy and Sorrow 69

2.1 On Commemorating the Day of Mūsā ﷺ 72
2.2 On Commemorating the Day of Nūḥ ﷺ 73
2.3 The Day of Islam's Completion: A Day of Festivity (ᶜĪd) 73
2.4 The Prophet's Instruction whilst Passing-by al-Ḥijr 74
2.4.1 The Prohibition of Drinking Water from the Well of Thamūd at al-Ḥijr 75
2.4.2 The Injunction of Drinking Water from the Well Connected to Ṣāliḥ's She-Camel 76
2.4.3 In Remembrance of Prophet Ṣāliḥ's She-Camel 77

2.4.4 Expressing Sorrow whilst Remembering the Punishment Inflicted on Thamūd 78
2.4.5 The Prophet's Own Action whilst Passing by al-Ḥijr 81
2.4.5.1 Points to Consider 82
2.5 Remembering the Punishment of the People of the Elephants and Swiftly Passing through the Valley of Muḥassir 84
2.6 ʿUmar's Expression of Remorse 87

Chapter 3

Remembering the *Mawlid* of Prophets ﷺ: A Qurʾānic Analysis 89

3.1 Background to the Mawlūd 91
3.2 Remembering the Prophets ﷺ: A Divine Practice 91
3.3 The Significance of the Mawlid of Prophets ﷺ 99
3.3.1 The Mawlid of Prophet Ādam ﷺ 100
3.3.2 The Mawlid of Prophet Mūsā ﷺ 102
3.3.3 The Mawlid of Maryam ﷺ 105
3.3.4 The Mawlid of Yaḥyā ﷺ 108
3.3.5 The Mawlid of ʿĪsā ﷺ 112
3.3.6 The Mawlid of the Chosen-One Prophet Muhammad ﷺ 115
3.4 From the Mawlid of the Prophets to the Mawlid of Prophet Muhammad ﷺ 120

Chapter 4

Evidence from the Qurʾān on *Mawlid al-Nabī* ﷺ 123

4.1 Evidence from the Commemoration of the Qurʾān's Descent 126
4.1.1 Comparison between Layla al-Qadr and the Night of His Birth 128
4.2 Evidence from the Commemoration of Receiving a Blessing 133

4.3 Evidence from the Celebration of Independence 134
4.3.1 An Important Requirement for the Continuation of Civilisation 136
4.4 Expressing Happiness on a Blessing is the Sunna of Prophets 137
4.4.1 An Important Point to Consider 138
4.5 The Divine Injunction on Celebrating Mawlid al-Nabī ﷺ 138
4.5.1 Qurʾānic Philosophy Concealed in the Word Qul [Say] 139
4.5.1.1 The Indispensability of Believing in the Messenger ﷺ before Believing in Allah 141
4.5.1.2 An Injunction's Importance and Significance Increases with the Word 'Say' 142
4.5.2 The Prophet ﷺ: The Blessing of Allah ﷻ and His Mercy 142
4.5.2.1 An Interesting Intellectual Point 143
4.5.2.2 Interpreting the Qurʾān through the Qurʾān 143
4.5.2.2.1 The Meaning of "And Allah is Most Bountiful" 148
4.5.2.2.2 The Meaning of Faḍl According to Leading Exegetes 149
4.5.2.2.3 The Meaning of Faḍl and Raḥma According to Leading Exegetes 153
4.5.2.2.4 The View of Ashraf ʿAlī Thānwī 156
4.5.3 Why we Should Celebrate Faḍl and Raḥma 158
4.5.4 The Purpose of the Semantic Use of Restriction within the Verse 159
4.5.5 The Wisdom Behind the Use of the Words "So In That" 160
4.5.6 Showing Gratitude at the Individual and Communal Level 161
4.5.7 The Use of Many Emphases in This Verse 162
4.5.8 The Exegesis of "This is far better than all that they amass" 164
4.6 The Celebration of Mawlid al-Nabī ﷺ is to Show Gratitude for the Exalted Blessing 165

4.7 Why is it Necessary to Express Gratitude on a Blessing? 166
4.8 The Prevalent Methods of Expressing Gratitude 167
4.8.1 Remembering and Mentioning the Blessing 167
4.8.2 Worship and Servitude 168
4.8.3 Proclaiming the Blessing 169
4.8.3.1 How Should We Proclaim the Blessing? 170
4.8.4 To Celebrate as a Festivity [ʿĪd] 171

Chapter 5

Evidence from the Hadith on *Mawlid al-Nabī* ﷺ 173

5.1 The Evidence of Commemorating Yawm ʿĀshūrāʾ 175
5.1.1 Celebrating the Day of Mūsā ﷺ 176
5.1.2 The Prophet's Commemoration is on Account of His Connection to Mūsā ﷺ 179
5.1.3 The Jews Commemorated Yawm ʿĀshūrāʾ as a Day of Festivity (ʿĪd) 179
5.1.4 The Evidence of al-ʿAsqalānī for Mawlid al-Nabī ﷺ 182
5.2 The Evidence of Commemorating the Day of Nūḥ ﷺ 185
5.3 The Evidence of Commemorating the Day of Changing the Kaʿba's Covering 186
5.4 The Evidence of Commemorating the Day of Islam's Completion as an ʿĪd 189
5.5 The Excellence of Friday: The Day of Ādam's Creation 194
5.5.1 Friday: the Day of Invoking Blessings and Salutations 197
5.6 The Importance of ʿĪsā's Birthplace and its Visitation 199
5.7 The Prophet ﷺ Commemorated his own Birthday by Fasting 199
5.8 The Prophet ﷺ Commemorated his own Birthday by Sacrificing an Animal 201

5.9 A Disbeliever's Punishment is Lightened on Account of His Happiness on the Prophet's Birth 205
5.9.1 Why is a Disbeliever's Punishment Lightened? 213
5.9.2 An Objection and its Reply 216
5.9.3 An Admonition 217

Chapter 6

The Position of the Hadith-Scholars & Imams on Celebrating *Mawlid al-Nabī* ﷺ 221

6.1 Ḥujja al-Dīn Imam Muḥammad b. Ẓufar al-Makkī (497–565 AH) 223
6.2 Shaykh Muʿīn al-Dīn ʿUmar b. Muḥammad al-Mallā (b. 570 AH) 224
6.3 Ibn al-Jawzī (510–579 AH) 225
6.4 Abū al-Khaṭṭāb b. Diḥya al-Kalbī (544–633) 227
6.5 Shams al-Dīn al-Jazarī (d. 660 AH) 227
6.6 Imam Abū Shāma (599–665 AH) 229
6.7 Imam Ṣadr al-Dīn Mawhūb b. ʿUmar al-Jazarī (d. 665 AH) 230
6.8 Imam Ẓahīr al-Dīn Jaʿfar al-Taznatī (d. 682 AH) 231
6.9 Ibn Taymiyya (661–728 AH) 232
6.10 Imam Abū ʿAbd Allāh b. al-Ḥājj al-Mālikī (d. 737 AH) 233
6.11 Imam Shams al-Dīn al-Dhahabī (673–748 AH) 238
6.12 Imam Kamāl al-Dīn al-Adfawī (685–748 AH) 240
6.13 Taqī al-Dīn Abū al-Ḥasan al-Subkī (683–756 AH) 241
6.14 ʿImād al-Dīn b. Kathīr (701–774 AH) 242
6.14.1 The Celebration of Mawlid al-Nabī ﷺ held by Abū Saʿīd al-Muẓaffar (Saladin's brother in-law) 243
6.15 Burhān al-Dīn b. Jamāʿa (725–790 AH) 247
6.16 Zayn al-Dīn b. Rajab al-Ḥanbalī (736–795 AH) 248
6.17 Walī al-Dīn Abū Zurʿa al-ʿIrāqī (762–826 AH) 249
6.18 Shams al-Dīn Muḥammad al-Dimashqī (777–842 AH) 250

6.19 Ibn Ḥajar al-ʿAsqalānī (773–852 ah) 251
6.20 Imam Shams al-Dīn al-Sakhāwī (831–902 ah) 254
6.21 Imam Jalāl al-Dīn al-Suyūṭī (849–911 ah) 255
6.22 Shihāb al-Dīn Abū al-ʿAbbās al-Qasṭallānī (851–923 ah) 258
6.23 Naṣīr al-Dīn b. al-Ṭabbākh 260
6.24 Jamāl al-Dīn b. ʿAbd al-Raḥmān al-Kattānī 261
6.25 Imam Yūsuf b. ʿAlī b. Zarīq al-Shāmī 262
6.26 Muhammad b. Yūsuf al-Ṣāliḥī al-Shāmī (d. 942 ah) 263
6.27 Ibn al-Ḥajar al-Haytamī al-Makkī (909–973 ah) 264
6.28 Muhammad b. Jār Allāh b. Ẓahīra al-Ḥanafī (d. 986 ah) 265
6.29 Quṭb al-Dīn al-Ḥanafī (d. 988 ah) 266
6.30 The Research of Mullā ʿAlī al-Qārī (d. 1014 ah) 267
6.31 Mujaddid Alf Thānī (971–1034 ah) 271
6.32 Imam ʿAlī b. Ibrāhīm al-Ḥalabī (975–1044 ah) 271
6.33 Shaykh ʿAbd al-Ḥaqq Muḥaddith al-Dihlawī (958–1052 ah) 272
6.34 Imam Muhammad al-Zurqānī (1055–1122 ah) 274
6.35 Shāh ʿAbd al-Raḥīm al-Dihlawī (1054–1131 ah) 276
6.36 Shaykh Ismāʿīl al-Ḥaqqī (1063–1137 ah) 277
6.37 Shāh Walī Allāh Muḥaddith al-Dihlawī (1114–1174 ah) 277
6.38 Shāh ʿAbd al-ʿAzīz Muḥaddith al-Dihlawī (1159–1239 ah) 278
6.39 ʿAbd Allāh b. Muhammad b. ʿAbd al-Wahhāb al-Najdī (1165–1242 ah) 279
6.40 Shāh Aḥmad Saʿīd Mujaddidī al-Dihlawī (d. 1277 ah) 280
6.41 Muftī Muhammad ʿInāyat Aḥmad al-Kākawrawī (1228–1279 ah) 281
6.42 Aḥmad ʿAlī Sahāranpūrī (d. 1297 ah) 282
6.43 Sayyid Aḥmad b. Zaynī al-Daḥlān (1233–1304 ah) 283

6.44 ᶜAbd al-Ḥayy Lakhnawī (1264–1304 AH) 284
6.45 Nawāb Siddīq Ḥasan Khān Bhopālī (d. 1307 AH) 285
6.46 Ḥājī Imdād Allāh Muhājir al-Makkī (1233–1317 AH) 285
6.47 Nawāb Waḥīd al-Zamān (d. 1338 AH) 288
6.48 Yūsuf b. Ismāᶜīl al-Nabhānī (1265–1350 AH) 288
6.49 Dr. Muhammad Iqbāl (1294–1357 AH) 290
6.50 Ashraf ᶜAlī Thānwī (1280–1362 AH) 292
6.51 Muftī Rashīd Aḥmad Ludhyānwī (b. 1341 AH) 294
6.52 Muftī Muhammad Maẓhar Allāh al-Dihlawī 295
6.53 The Research of Shaykh Muhammad Riḍā al-Miṣrī 295
6.54 The Unanimous Opinion of the Scholars of Deoband 298
6.55 The History of Mawlid Celebrations in the Muslim World 300
6.55.1 The Celebration of Mawlid al-Nabī ﷺ in Mecca 302
6.55.1.1 Eyewitness Accounts of the Mawlid in Mecca 308
6.55.2 The Celebration of Mawlid al-Nabī ﷺ in Medina 310
6.55.3 The Celebration of Mawlid al-Nabī ﷺ in Egypt and the Levant 311
6.55.4 The Celebration of Mawlid al-Nabī ﷺ in Qaws 314
6.55.5 The Celebration of Mawlid al-Nabī ﷺ in Andalusia and Rome 315
6.55.6 The Celebration of Mawlid al-Nabī ﷺ in the Indian Subcontinent 315
6.56 Significant Literature on the Mawlid 318

Chapter 7
Why the First Generation of Muslims did not Celebrate the *Mawlid* 341

7.1 The Prophet's Passing Away was Extremely Painful for the Companions ﷺ 343
7.1.1 Human Nature Does Not Allow One to Openly Express Joy During Times of Sadness 344
7.2 The Immense Grief was an Impediment to the Expression of Joy amongst the First Generation 344
7.2.1 Separation from the Prophet ﷺ: The Cause of Abū Bakr's Death 345
7.2.2 ʿUmar's Reaction to the Prophet's Demise 346
7.2.3 The Grief of Fāṭima al-Zahrāʾ ﷺ 349
7.2.4 The Grief of Anas b. Mālik ﷺ 355
7.2.5 The Grief of Bilāl b. Rabāḥ ﷺ 357
7.2.6 The Grief of ʿAbd Allāh b. ʿUmar ﷺ 362
7.2.7 The Grief of ʿAbd Allāh b. Zayd and the Loss of his Eyesight 362
7.2.8 More Narrations on the Companions' Grief 363
7.2.9 The Grief of the Animals that Served the Prophet ﷺ 365
7.3 Joy and Sorrow were Equally Felt in the Month of Rabīʿ al-Awwal 366
7.4 As Time Passed, Joy Prevailed Over Grief 366
7.5 The Prophet's Birth and His Passing Away are Both a Mercy 367
7.6 The Prophet's Passing Away is a Source of Intercession for His Community 368
7.7 To be Grateful for a Blessing is Allah's Decree 369
7.8 We Are in Receipt of His Blessings, so Why the Sorrow? 370
7.9 The Prophet's Prophecy is Established till the Day of Judgment 372
7.10 Expressing Joy is not an Innovation: it is Human Nature 372
7.11 It was not the Culture of the First Generation to Celebrate Events 376
7.11.1 The Migration to Medina 376
7.11.2 The Constitution of Medina 378

7.11.3 The Day of Badr 378

7.11.4 The Conquest of Mecca 378

7.11.5 The Night of Destiny: The Night of the Qurʾān's Descent 379

7.11.6 New Requirements for a New Age 379

Chapter 8

The Formative Constituents of *Mawlid al-Nabī* ﷺ 381

Section 1

Holding Gatherings and Congregations 385

8.1 The Prophet ﷺ Making Mention of his Creation which Took Place before his Birth 387

8.2 The Prophet ﷺ Organised a Gathering for the Mention of his Birth 388

8.3 Organising Special Gatherings for the Mention of Virtues and Excellence 392

Section 2

Relating the Prophet's Biography and Virtues 397

8.4 Mentioning the Rulings of the Sharia 399

8.5 Mentioning the Prophetic Natural Talent and Conduct 399

8.6 Mentioning the Prophet's Physical Traits 400

8.7 Mentioning the Prophet's Excellent Virtues and Exceptionality 401

8.8 Mentioning the Accounts of His Blessed Birth and the Spiritual Signs and Sublimity that Took Place 404

Section 3

Reciting Odes and Poems in Praise of the Prophet ﷺ 407

8.9 Poetic Praise of the Prophet ﷺ in the Qurʾān 409

8.10 The Prophet ﷺ Himself Listened to Odes in His Honour 421

8.10.1 Listening to Poetic Praise from Ḥassān b. Thābit ﷺ 421
8.10.2 Listening to Poetic Praise from al-Aswad b. Sarīʿ 424
8.10.3 Listening to Poetic Praise from ʿAbd Allāh b. Rawāḥa 425
8.10.4 Listening to Poetic Praise from ʿĀmir b. Akwaʿ in an Open Gathering 427
8.10.5 Listening to Poetic Praise from ʿAbbās b. ʿAbd al-Muṭṭalib 428
8.10.6 Listening to Poetic Praise from Kaʿb and the Gifting of the Cloak 430
8.10.7 Listening to Poetic Praise from Nābigha al-Jaʿdī 432
8.10.8 The Girls of Medina Recited Poetic Praise with Hand Drums (Daff) 433
8.10.9 Imam al-Būṣīrī's Recovery and His Receiving the Prophet's Cloak as a Gift 434
8.11 A List of the Noble Companions who Recited Poetry in Honour of the Prophet ﷺ 436

Section 4

Sending Salutations and Invoking Peace on the Prophet ﷺ 443

8.12 Salutations on the Prophet ﷺ is the Sunna of Almighty Allah and His Decree 445
8.13 The Significance of Sending Salutations of Peace [Salām] 447
8.14 The Perpetual Independent Status of Sending Salutations of Peace 452
8.14.1 Acceptance of one's Praise for Allah is through the Means of Sending Salutations on the Prophet ﷺ 454
8.14.2 The Salutations of Peace in the Tashahhud 455
8.14.3 The Prophet's Injunction on Sending Salām after Ṣalāt 457
8.15 Salutations Reaching the Prophet ﷺ 457

8.15.1 Invocations of Peace and Blessings Reach the Prophet ﷺ Directly 458
8.15.2 The Holy Prophet ﷺ Listens to the Invocations and Salutations Directly 460
8.15.3 The Prophet ﷺ Replies to the Salutations 462
8.15.4 The Angels Invoke Peace and Blessings on the Prophet ﷺ 462

Section 5
Qiyām (The Ritual Standing) 466

8.16 Is the Ritual Standing (Qiyām) Exclusive to Allah? 469
8.16.1 The Different Positions of Prayer are not Worship Per Se 470
8.16.2 If the Standing Position is Worship, Then What About the Other Positions? 471
8.16.3 In Which Way is the Ritual Standing Worship? 472
8.17 The Ritual Standing (Qiyām) in Light of the Sunna is Permissible 472
8.18 The Classifications of the Ritual Standing (Qiyām) 473
8.18.1 Standing to Welcome Someone (Qiyām li al-Istiqbāl) 473
8.18.2 Standing out of Love (Qiyām li al-Maḥabba) 475
8.18.3 Standing out of Joy (Qiyām li al-Farḥa) 476
8.18.4 Standing Out of Veneration (Qiyām li al-Taʿẓīm) 478
8.18.4.1 The Difference between Qiyām li al-Istiqbāl and Qiyām li al-Taʿẓīm 478
8.18.4.2 The Companions' Practice of Standing for the Prophet ﷺ Out of Veneration 479
8.18.4.3 The Ritual Prayer is for Allah; the Iqāma is for the Prophet ﷺ 481
8.18.5 Standing for Human Dignity (Qiyām li al-Ikrām al-Insānī) 489

8.18.6 Standing for Remembrance (Qiyām li al-Dhikr) 492
8.18.6.1 The Prophet's Remembrance is Allah's Remembrance 493
8.18.7 Standing to Invoke Peace and Blessings (Qiyām li al-Ṣalāt wa al-Salām) 494
8.18.7.1 The Meaning of Ṣalāt: Invocation of Peace and Blessings 496
8.18.7.2 The Literal Meaning of the Word Ṣalāt 497
8.18.7.3 Applying the Literal Meaning of Ṣalāt 498
8.18.8 Standing During the Mawlid is not Held to Receive the Prophet ﷺ 501
8.18.9 The Ritual Standing for the Mawlid in Essence is for Happiness and Joy 503
8.18.10 Prohibition of Qiyām: Its Causes 505

Section 6

Arranging Lighting 507

8.19 The Stars Descended Like Fireworks 510
8.20 Candle Lighting in Mecca on the Occasion of the Prophet's Birth 511

Section 7

Distributing Food 515

8.21 The Excellent Virtue of Feeding Others in the Qur'ān 517
8.22 Encouragement of Feeding Others in the Hadith 519

Section 8

Mawlid Processions 523

Chapter 9

Various Aspects of *Mawlid al-Nabī* ﷺ: A Brief Overview 529

9.1 Sharia Aspect 532

9.1.1 Remembrance of Allah's Favours 532
9.1.2 Commemorating the Day of the Table-Spread's Descent as an ʿĪd 534
9.2 Historical Aspect 535
9.3 Cultural Aspect 538
9.4 Instructional Aspect 541
9.4.1 The Fundamental Responsibility of Parents 542
9.4.2 Food for Thought 542
9.4.3 A Strategy for Safeguarding Faith 542
9.5 Daʿwa Aspect 543
9.6 Motivational Aspect 544
9.6.1 The External and Internal Facets of Deeds 545
9.6.2 The Essence of Good Deeds is Love for the Prophet ﷺ 547
9.7 Spiritual Aspect 549

Chapter 10

Is Celebrating *Mawlid al-Nabī* ﷺ a *Bidʿa*? 551

10.1 The Literal Meaning of Bidʿa 553
10.1.1 Confirmation of its Meaning from the Qurʾān 554
10.2 The Technical Meaning of Bidʿa 555
10.3 Is Every Aspect of Local Culture Bidʿa? 556
10.3.1 The Cultural Norms of the Companions ﵃ 557
10.3.2 The Cultural Demonstrations of Mawlid al-Nabī ﷺ 557
10.3.2.1 The Mawlid Processions Belong to Culture 558
10.3.2.2 Invoking Blessings on the Prophet ﷺ while Standing Belongs to Culture 559
10.3.2.3 Arranging Decorations on the Mawlid Belongs to Culture 559
10.4 The True Meaning of Bidʿa 561
10.4.1 Removal of Misconceptions and the Correct Understanding of 'Fa Huwa Radd' 562

10.5 Inventing Something in the Religion: Its Intended Meaning in the Prophet's Era 564
10.6 The New Matters (Muḥdathāt al-Umūr) that Arose in the Era of the Rightly Guided Caliphs 571
10.6.1 The Transgression of False Attribution of Prophethood was Declared an Innovation 571
10.6.2 The Transgression of Apostasy was Declared an Innovation 571
10.6.3The Transgression of the Deniers of Alms-due was Declared an Innovation 571
10.6.4 The Transgression of the Khawārij was Declared an Innovation 572
10.6.4.1 In Our Age, What is the Correct Application of Labelling Something an 'Invented Matter' (Muḥdathāt al-Umūr)? 574
10.7 The Concept of Innovation in Light of the Reports of the Companions 576
10.7.1 The Compilation of the Qur'ān and the Practice of the Shaykhayn 577
10.7.2 The Initiation of the Tarāwīḥ Ritual Prayer in Congregation 578
10.7.3 The Second Ādhān before the Friday Congregational Prayer 580
10.8 The Concept of Innovation and Some Contemporary Examples 580
10.8.1 The Establishment of an Islamic State 580
10.8.2 The Construction of Mosques 581
10.8.3 Translating and Interpreting the Qur'ān 581
10.9 The Category of Innovation According to the Scholars 582
10.9.1 Imam al-Shāfiʿī (150–204 ah) 582
10.9.2 ʿIzz al-Dīn b. ʿAbd al-Salām (577–660 ah) 583
10.9.3 Mullā ʿAlī al-Qārī al-Ḥanafī (d. 1014 ah) 584
10.9.3.1 Every Innovation is an Error: The Correct Understanding 585
10.10 The Categories of Innovation 586

10.10.1 The Subcategories of the Praiseworthy Innovation 586
10.10.1.1 Obligatory Innovation (al-Bidʿa al-Wājiba) 587
10.10.1.2 Commendable Innovation (al-Bidʿa al-Mustaḥabba/ al-Bidʿa al-Mustaḥsana) 587
10.10.1.3 Discretionary Innovation (al-Bidʿa al-Mubāḥa) 588
10.10.2 The Subcategories of the Blameworthy Innovation 588
10.10.2.1 Forbidden Innovation (al-Bidʿa al-Muḥarrama) 588
10.10.2.2 Reprehensible Innovation (al-Bidʿa al-Makrūha) 589
10.10.3 Evidence for the Categorisation of Innovation in Light of the Hadith 589
10.11 Mawlid al-Nabī ﷺ has its Basis in the Qurʾān and Hadith 591
10.12 The Majority of the Prophet's Community Cannot Agree upon an Error 592
10.13 Understanding the True Spirit of the Religion is Essential 595

Chapter 11

Doctrinal Issues Related to *Mawlid al-Nabī* ﷺ 599

11.1 Employing the Term: Mīlād al-Nabī ﷺ 601
11.1.1 The Usage of the Word Mīlād in the Books of Arabic Linguistics 602
11.1.2 The Usage of the Word Mīlād in the Books of Hadith and Sīra 602
11.1.3 The Usage of the Word Mīlād in Literary Works 605
11.2 Mawlid al-Nabī ﷺ is an ʿĪd of Happiness: Not an ʿĪd of Sharia 606
11.3 The Hadith-Scholars' Approach in Recounting the Prophet's Merits and the Mawlid al-Nabī 609

11.3.1 IMAM AL-TIRMIDHĪ'S APPROACH IN ARRANGING THE CHAPTERS OF KITĀB AL-MANĀQIB 612
11.4 THE HISTORIANS' APPROACH IN RECOUNTING THE PROPHET'S MERITS AND THE MAWLID AL-NABĪ ﷺ 614
11.5 DEMANDING EVIDENCE FROM THE SHARIA FOR MAWLID AL-NABĪ ﷺ 616
11.6 CELEBRATING MAWLID AL-NABĪ ﷺ IS AN ACT OF TAWḤĪD 620
11.7 SPENDING ON MAWLID AL-NABĪ ﷺ IS NOT EXTRAVAGANCE 621
11.8 ARRANGEMENTS FOR THE DISPLAY OF THE MAGNIFICENCE AND GRANDEUR OF ISLAM 622
11.9 THE REQUIREMENTS FOR HOLDING GATHERINGS OF MAWLID AL-NABĪ ﷺ 624
11.10 ASPECTS WHICH REQUIRE REFORMING 627
11.11 THE NECESSITY OF ABSTAINING FROM EXCESSES 629

BIBLIOGRAPHY 633

INDICES 663
INDEX OF QURʾĀNIC VERSES 665
INDEX OF HADITH REPORTS AND NARRATIONS 675
GENERAL INDEX 685

Preface

THE CELEBRATION OF *MAWLID AL-NABĪ* ﷺ IS THE EXPRESSION OF joy and happiness upon the blessed and historic birth of the most exalted Prophet ﷺ. It is such a praiseworthy act that even a disbeliever like Abū Lahab gains benefit. If the punishment of a staunch disbeliever, like Abū Lahab, is lightened every Monday due to his rejoicing upon the Prophet's birth, what then would be the reward of a Muslim who commemorates this day throughout his life?

The Prophet ﷺ, the chief of the created beings, would himself honour Mondays, the day of his blessed birth. As a means of showing gratitude, he would fast this day as it was the day when he became known to the inhabitants of the earth. By doing so, he was acting upon the divine command of expressing gratitude, since it was due to his gracious existence that everything was created.

The celebration of *Mawlid al-Nabī* ﷺ encourages participants to engage in important duties, such as invoking peace and blessings upon the most exalted Messenger ﷺ—it creates an atmosphere of yearning and desire in the heart. Sending salutations upon him, according to the Sharia, is an act that accumulates immense reward, and thus, the majority amongst the *Umma* has considered *mawlid* to be a meritorious act.

The gatherings of *mawlid* fulfil the role of reiterating the importance of the *sīra* and reinvigorating the spirit of the love of Almighty Allah's Messenger ﷺ. It is for this reason that the gatherings of *mawlid* contain recollections and accounts of the prophetic role model, his virtues, characteristics, and miracles.

A fundamental aim of *Mawlid al-Nabī* ﷺ is to attain love and proximity of the Prophet ﷺ and to revive the believer's relationship with his most revered person—this *per se* revives the very goal of the Sharia. Acknowledging his virtues and perfection increases one's faith in Almighty Allah and belief in prophethood. Revering the Holy Prophet ﷺ is the first fundamental requirement of *īmān* (faith).

The demonstration of joy and jubilation, expressed through the celebration of *Mawlid al-Nabī* ﷺ, holding gatherings of *dhikr* (Allah's remembrance) and relating prophetic odes, in addition to serving food, is one of the greatest methods of showing gratitude to Almighty Allah. By sending His Messenger ﷺ to us, Almighty Allah entitled us to become recipients of boundless benevolence, and this is why He reminds us of this most excellent gift.

Like the way the superiority of *Ramaḍān* has been decreed by Almighty Allah above other months, due to the Qurʾān being revealed therein, the month of *Rabīʿ al-Awwal* also possesses distinction in that this is the month in which the one who brought us the Qurʾān was born. This month, on account of the blessed birth of Allah's Messenger ﷺ, is more virtuous than all the other months.

In fact, the night in which the most exalted Prophet ﷺ was born is even loftier than *Layla al-Qadr* (the Night of Destiny). The virtue of *Layla al-Qadr* lies in the initiation of the Qurʾānic revelation and the descent of angels. However, had it not been for him upon whose heart the Qurʾān was revealed, we would not have received any divine scripture, *Layla al-Qadr* or the very religion of Islam. All such blessings were achieved through the means of Prophet Muhammad ﷺ. Therefore, the night of his blessed birth is superior to the Night of Destiny.

Almighty Allah has conferred countless and unlimited favours upon humankind. These favours are without bounds and will continue forever. Each blessing is as great as the other. Despite this, Almighty Allah does not boast His favours. He has bestowed us the delight of tasting a vast selection of food, but He does not recall His favours. He refreshes us with a variety of drinks, but again He does not boast of His favours. The alternating system of day and night as a means of organising our time allows us to take rest and to fulfil our needs in life; the land, sea and sky have all been made subservient to us; we have been appointed as the *crème de la crème* of creation and granted respect and honour, but Almighty Allah does not recall His favours. We have been blessed with parents, siblings and offspring; from the far reaches of this universe to the deepest depths of our inner selves, we have been granted with bounties which are beyond the understanding of our intellect, but in spite of this, Almighty Allah, being the Lord of the Worlds, does not boast of His favours and benevolence. However, there is one such blessing that Almighty Allah has sent for humanity, concerning whom He openly and expressly recalls His favour and benevolence. He has made the believers aware of this, stating:

﴿لَقَدْ مَنَّ ٱللَّهُ عَلَى ٱلْمُؤْمِنِينَ إِذْ بَعَثَ فِيهِمْ رَسُولًا مِّنْ أَنفُسِهِمْ يَتْلُوا۟ عَلَيْهِمْ ءَايَٰتِهِۦ وَيُزَكِّيهِمْ وَيُعَلِّمُهُمُ ٱلْكِتَٰبَ وَٱلْحِكْمَةَ وَإِن كَانُوا۟ مِن قَبْلُ لَفِى ضَلَٰلٍ مُّبِينٍ ١٦٤﴾

Indeed, Allah has conferred a great favour on the believers that He raised amongst them (the most Eminent) Messenger ﷺ from amongst themselves, who recites to them His Revelations, purifies them, and educates them on the Book and Wisdom though, before that, they were in manifest error.[1]

In Islam, expressing gratitude to Almighty Allah for His blessing is a mark of servitude. The rationale behind this has been mentioned in the Qur'ān:

﴿وَإِذْ تَأَذَّنَ رَبُّكُمْ لَئِن شَكَرْتُمْ لَأَزِيدَنَّكُمْ ۖ وَلَئِن كَفَرْتُمْ إِنَّ عَذَابِى لَشَدِيدٌ ٧﴾

And (recall) when your Lord proclaimed: If you are thankful, I shall certainly increase (My blessings on) you, and if you are ungrateful, then My torment is surely severe.[2]

This verse explains that the acknowledgement of favours leads to the acquisition of additional blessings. Expressing gratitude is not specific to this *Umma*—it has also been enjoined on the

[1] Qur'ān 3:164.

[2] Qur'ān 14:7.

previous *Ummas*. For instance, the Children of Israel [Banū Isrāʾīl] are reminded of that blessing through which they attained supremacy over all nations and were emancipated from the tyranny of Pharaoh:

﴿وَإِذْ نَجَّيْنَـٰكُم مِّنْ ءَالِ فِرْعَوْنَ يَسُومُونَكُمْ سُوٓءَ ٱلْعَذَابِ يُذَبِّحُونَ أَبْنَآءَكُمْ وَيَسْتَحْيُونَ نِسَآءَكُمْ ۚ وَفِى ذَٰلِكُم بَلَآءٌ مِّن رَّبِّكُمْ عَظِيمٌ ﴿٤٩﴾﴾

And (also recall) when We delivered you from Pharaoh's people, who used to inflict severe torment upon you: they slaughtered your sons and kept your daughters alive. There was an arduously terrible trial in it from your Lord.[1]

This verse explains that freedom from slavery is such a huge blessing that it is incumbent upon succeeding generations to show gratitude for it. From this, it can be derived that the emancipation of a nation should be taken without hesitation, as a God-given gift that must be appreciated. This verse is a testament to the fact that recounting blessings in an organised manner, by expressing joy and happiness, is essential so that forthcoming generations appreciate the value of this blessing and realise its importance.

Generally, man appreciates Almighty Allah's blessings throughout the year; yet, through the vicissitudes of time when a significant day arrived, wherein an entire community was favoured by Him, the manifestation of happiness automatically resulted in a collective celebration. The Qurʾān relates that when the Children of Israel were delivered from Pharaoh's oppression and safely entered the valley in Sinai, crossing the tides of the River Nile, they encountered severe heat and drought—so a cloud was made to shade them. This was one such blessing about which the Qurʾān states:

﴿وَظَلَّلْنَا عَلَيْكُمُ ٱلْغَمَامَ وَأَنزَلْنَا عَلَيْكُمُ ٱلْمَنَّ وَٱلسَّلْوَىٰ ۖ﴾

[1] Qurʾān 2:49.

And (recall) when We cast the shade of clouds over you (in the Tīha valley) and sent down for you manna and quails.[1]

The Qur'ān, in several places whilst mentioning very specific blessings, decrees that the accounts of the day (in which a blessing was granted) be commemorated (as a day of festivity). This also was the practice of the prophets. When ʿĪsā ﷺ supplicated for a table of heavenly food for his community, he prayed in the following manner:

﴿ٱللَّهُمَّ رَبَّنَآ أَنزِلْ عَلَيْنَا مَآئِدَةً مِّنَ ٱلسَّمَآءِ تَكُونُ لَنَا عِيدًا لِّأَوَّلِنَا وَءَاخِرِنَا وَءَايَةً مِّنكَ﴾

O Allah, our Lord, send down to us from heaven the table spread (with bounties) so that (the day of its descent) becomes (ʿīd) *a festival day for us, and for our predecessors (as well as our) successors, and that (the table-spread) comes as a sign from You.*[2]

In this verse, the Qur'ān has provided us with the concept, as is demonstrated in this prophetic example, that the day upon which a divine blessing descends should be commemorated as a day of thanksgiving. The verse further indicates that expressing happiness on receiving a certain blessing is only expressed by those who are associated with that prophet upon whom that blessing was granted.

Another common method of thanking Almighty Allah for His blessings is that, as well as expressing happiness, one describes Almighty Allah's favours in the presence of others. Expressing gratitude to Almighty Allah in this way is also proven from the Qur'ān:

﴿وَأَمَّا بِنِعْمَةِ رَبِّكَ فَحَدِّثْ ﴿١١﴾﴾

And proclaim (well) the bounties of your Lord.[3]

---

[1] Qur'ān 2:57.

[2] Qur'ān 5:114.

[3] Qur'ān 93:11.

First there was the injunction of remembering the favour and blessing bestowed by Almighty Allah in that the blessing should be reminisced with the heart and tongue; but this remembrance is not for anyone, except for Almighty Allah alone. After this, the injunction of mentioning the blessing has been given in which a person openly mentions the blessing in the presence of others so that its significance is evident to the people. It should be noted here that the remembrance is in relation to Almighty Allah, whilst mentioning it is in relation to the creation so that as many people can be engaged in its recollection. The Qurʾān states:

﴿فَٱذۡكُرُونِيٓ أَذۡكُرۡكُمۡ وَٱشۡكُرُواْ لِي وَلَا تَكۡفُرُونِ ١٥٢﴾

So remember Me, I shall remember you. And always be thankful to Me and never be ungrateful to Me.[1]

In other words, do not simply recall My favours (on an individual basis); instead, mention them in an atmosphere of gratitude whereby people also hear of them. An additional manner of expressing thankfulness is to hold celebrations in the form of a festivity (*ʿīd*). Former communities, on the day on which they received a particular blessing, would consider that day as a day of festivity and celebration. The Qurʾān relates the supplication of ʿĪsā ﷺ, which is as follows:

﴿ٱللَّهُمَّ رَبَّنَآ أَنزِلۡ عَلَيۡنَا مَآئِدَةٗ مِّنَ ٱلسَّمَآءِ تَكُونُ لَنَا عِيدٗا لِّأَوَّلِنَا وَءَاخِرِنَا وَءَايَةٗ مِّنكَۖ﴾

O Allah, our Lord, send down to us from heaven the table spread (with bounties) so that (the day of its descent) becomes (ʿīd) *a festival day for us, and for our predecessors (as well as our) successors, and that (the table-spread) comes as a sign from You.*[2]

---

1 Qurʾān 2:152.

2 Qurʾān 5:114.

Here, the receiving of a temporal blessing, such as the table-spread, is being mentioned as a day of festivity (ʿ*īd*). Even today, Christians observe Sunday as the day when this blessing descended upon them. Can a blessing like the table-spread be equal to the sending of the Prophet ﷺ? Countless blessings like that can be sacrificed for the sake of the most esteemed blessing, our Prophet Muhammad ﷺ.

It is narrated in *Ṣaḥīḥ al-Bukhārī* that a Jew said to ʿUmar ؓ that if the verse, ﴿*Today I have perfected your Dīn (Religion) for you*﴾ had been revealed in the Torah, the Jews would have taken that day as a day of festivity (ʿ*īd*). In reply to this, ʿUmar ؓ said that he remembers well the day and place of the revelation of this verse: it was the day of Pilgrimage on the plains of ʿArafa, and a Friday (and both of these days are days of festivity [ʿ*īd*]).[1]

A question arises: if the day when the verse concerning the perfection of the religion is revealed can be regarded as a day of festivity (ʿ*īd*), why then can the day when the Benefactor of Humanity was born not be considered so? This query, in relation to the virtue of the day of Friday, invites thoughtful people to ponder.

It is also mentioned in the prophetic traditions that Allah's Messenger ﷺ sacrificed a goat in commemoration of his birth and distributed its meat amongst guests. According to Anas ؓ, the most exalted Prophet ﷺ performed an ʿ*aqīqa* [a ceremonial sacrifice for a new-born baby] after the declaration of prophethood. Imam al-Suyūṭī (911–849 AH), using this prophetic tradition as evidence, argues that ʿAbd al-Muṭṭalib, the Prophet's ﷺ grandfather, performed ʿ*aqīqa* on the seventh day after his birth, and the ʿ*aqīqa* is only required once in a lifetime. Therefore, it is apparent that the prophetic action was not an ʿ*aqīqa*, rather it was an act of

[1] Narrated by al-Bukhārī in *al-Ṣaḥīḥ*: *Kitāb al-Īmān* [The Book of Faith], chapter: 'Increase and decrease of faith', 1:25 §45; Muslim in *al-Ṣaḥīḥ*: *Kitāb al-Tafsīr* [The Book of Exegesis], 4:2313 §3017; al-Tirmidhī in *al-Jāmiʿ al-Ṣaḥīḥ*: *Abwāb tafsīr al- Qurʾān* [Chapters on the Qurʾānic exegesis], chapter: 'Sūra al-Māʾida', 5:250 §3043; and al-Nasāʾī in *al-Sunan*: *Kitāb al-Īmān* [The Book of Faith], chapter: 'Increase and decrease of faith', 8:114 §5012.

hospitality which he ﷺ did out of commemoration of his birth.¹

It is unfathomable to imagine a divine blessing greater than the Prophet ﷺ. The unequivocal joy and happiness that has been expressed can be gathered from historic accounts. In the books of prophetic virtues and characteristic, there is a plenitude of examples that clearly demonstrate Almighty Allah's pleasure on the birth of His Beloved Messenger ﷺ.

There are anecdotes in that throughout the entire year in which the Prophet ﷺ was born, amazing and inexplicable occurrences were witnessed. The special mercy of Almighty Allah showered upon those blessed hours that the world was yearning for—waiting in its anticipation for centuries until finally, when the appointed moment arrived, Almighty Allah, the Creator of the Universe, manifested into this earthly realm the Jewel of Creation; and He ﷻ put on such a display of light that the horizons of the east and west were illuminated.

ʿUthmān b. Abī al-ʿĀṣ ؓ states that his mother informed him:

شَهِدْتُ آمِنَةَ لَمَّا وُلِدَ رَسُولُ اللهِ ﷺ، فَلَمَّا ضَرَبَهَا الْمَخَاضُ، نَظَرْتُ إِلَى النُّجُومِ تَدَلَّى، حَتَّى إِنِّي لَأَقُولُ إِنَّهَا لَتَقَعَنَّ عَلَيَّ، فَلَمَّا وَلَدَتْ، خَرَجَ مِنْهَا نُورٌ أَضَاءَ لَهُ الْبَيْتُ الَّذِي نَحْنُ فِيهِ، وَالدَّارُ، فَمَا شَيْءٌ أَنْظُرُ إِلَيْهِ إِلَّا نُورٌ.

> I was present with Āmina ؓ at the moment of the birth of Allah's Messenger ﷺ. When it was the time of delivery, I saw the stars drawing near to the extent that I felt that they would fall on me. When she gave birth, such a light emitted from her, illuminating the house in which we were in and its enclosure, so that there was not a thing except that I saw light.²

---

¹ For further details refer to the fifth chapter of this book.

² Narrated by al-Shaybānī in *al-Āḥād wa al-Mathānī*, 6:29 §3210 (Umm ʿUthmān b. Abī al-ʿĀṣ); al-Ṭabarānī in *al-Muʿjam al-kabīr*, 25:147 & 186, §355 & 457; al-Māwardī in *Aʿlām al-Nabuwwa*, p. 247; al-Ṭabarī

Abū Umāma narrates that he asked the Prophet, 'O Allah's Messenger, what was the beginning of your affair?' The Prophet replied:

«دَعْوَةُ أَبِي إِبْرَاهِيمَ، وَبُشْرَى عِيسَى؛ وَرَأَتْ أُمِّي أَنَّهُ يَخْرُجُ مِنْهَا نُورٌ أَضَاءَتْ مِنْهَا قُصُورُ الشَّامِ.»

I am the answer to my father Ibrāhīm's supplication and the glad-tidings of ʿĪsā. (Upon my birth,) my dear mother witnessed light emanating from her (blessed body) which illuminated the palaces of Syria.[1]

---

in *Tārīkh al-umam wa al-mulūk*, 1:454; al-Bayhaqī in *Dalāʾil al-Nabuwwa wa maʿrifa aḥwāl Ṣāḥib al-Sharīʿa*, 1:111; Abū Nuʿaym in *Dalāʾil al-Nabuwwa*, p.135 §76; Ibn al-Jawzī in *al-Muntaẓam fī tārīkh al-umam wa al-mulūk*, 2:247; Ibn ʿAsākir in *Tārīkh Dimashq al-kabīr*, 3:79 & in *al-Sīra al-Nabawiyya*, 3:46; Ibn Kathīr in *al-Bidāya wa al-nihāya*, 2:264; al-Haythamī in *Majmaʿ al-zawāʾid wa manbaʿ al-fawāʾid*, 8:220; Ibn Rajab al-Ḥanbalī in *Laṭāʾif al-maʿārif fīmā li-mawāsim al-ʿām min al-waẓāʾif*, p. 173; and al-ʿAsqalānī in *Fatḥ al-Bārī*, 6:583.

[1] Narrated by Aḥmad b. Ḥanbal in *al-Musnad*, 5:262 §22315; Ibn Ḥibbān in *al-Ṣaḥīḥ*, 14:313 §6404 relates with these words in another lengthy narration with a different chain of transmission; al-Bukhārī in *al-Tārīkh al-kabīr*, 5:342 §7807/1736, relates these words with a different chain of transmission in a lengthy narration; al-Bukhārī in *al-Tārīkh al-awsaṭ*, 1:13 §33, relates these words with a different chain of transmission in a lengthy narration; Ibn Abī Usāma in *al-Musnad*, 2:867 §927; al-Rūyānī in *al-Musnad*, 2:209 §1267; Ibn al-Jaʿd in *al-Musnad*, 492 §3428; al-Ṭayālasī in *al-Musnad*, 155 §1140; al-Ṭabarānī in *al-Muʿjam al-kabīr*, 8:175 §7729; al-Ṭabarānī in *Musnad al-shāmiyyīn*, 2:402 §1582; al-Daylamī in *al-Firdaws bi-maʾthūr al-khiṭāb*, 1:46 §113; al-Lālkaʾī in *Iʿtiqād ahl al-sunna wa al-jamāʿa*, 1:422-3 §1404; Abū Nuʿaym in *Ḥilya al-awliyāʾ wa ṭabaqāt al-aṣfiyāʾ*, 6:90; Ibn al-Jawzī in *al-Muntaẓam fī tārīkh al-mulūk wa al-umam*, 2:248; Ibn ʿAsākir in *al-Sīra al-Nabawiyya*, 1:127; Ibn Kathīr in *al-Bidāya wa al-nihāya*, 2:275, 306 & 322; al-Haythamī in *Majmaʿ al-zawāʾid wa manbaʿ al-fawāʾid*, 8:222, states Imam Aḥmad has narrated it with a fine (ḥasan) chain of transmission; and al-Suyūṭī in *Kifāyat al-ṭālib al-labīb fī khaṣāʾiṣ al-Ḥabīb*, 1:79.

Regarding the incidents surrounding the birth of her beloved son, Āmina ؓ stated:

لَـمَّـا فَصَلَ مِنِّي خَرَجَ مَعَهُ نُورٌ أَضَاءَ لَهُ مَا بَيْنَ الْـمَشْرِقِ إِلَى الْـمَغْرِبِ.

When he (the chief of the created beings, the Holy Prophet ﷺ), appeared, a light was emitted with him that whatever was between the east and west was illuminated.[1]

In another tradition, Āmina ؓ mentions that light radiated from her to the extent that she witnessed the palaces and market places of Bosra, in Syria—she could even see the necks of the camels travelling there.[2]

The hadith-scholars have established the legality of celebrating *Mawlid al-Nabī* from the hadiths of *ʿĀshūrāʾ*. *Yawm al-ʿĀshūrāʾ* is commemorated by Jews: it is the day of deliverance when Mūsā ؑ and the Children of Israel escaped from the despotism of Pharaoh. Thus it was an independence day, which they commemorated by

[1] Narrated by Ibn Saʿd in *al-Ṭabaqāt al-kubrā*, 1:102; Ibn al-Jawzī in *Ṣafwa al-ṣafwa*, 1:52; Ibn ʿAsākir in *al-Sīra al-Nabawiyya*, 3:46; Ibn Kathīr in *al-Bidāya wa al-nihāya*, 2:264; Ibn Rajab al-Ḥanbalī in *Laṭāʾif al-maʿārif fīmā li-mawāsim al-ʿām min al-waẓāʾif*, p. 172; al-Suyūṭī in *Kifāyat al-ṭālib al-labīb fī khaṣāʾiṣ al-Ḥabīb* ﷺ, 1:79; and al-Ḥalabī in *Insān al-ʿuyūn fī sīra al-Amīn al-Maʾmūn*, 1:83.

[2] Narrated by Ibn Saʿd in *al-Ṭabaqāt al-kubrā*, 1:102; al-Ṭabarānī in *al-Muʿjam al-kabīr*, 24:214 §545; Ibn Ḥibbān in *al-Ṣaḥīḥ*, 14:313 §6404; ʿAbd al-Razzāq in *al-Muṣannaf*, 5:318; al-Dārimī in *al-Sunan*, 1:20 §13; al-Shaybānī in *al-Āḥād wa al-Mathānī*, 3:56 §1369; al-Ḥākim in *al-Mustadrak*, 2:673 §4230; al-Ḥaythamī states in *Majmaʿ al-zawāʾid* (8:222) that Imam Aḥmad and al-Ṭabarānī narrate this tradition, and the one narrated by Imam Aḥmad has a fine (*ḥasan*) chain of transmission; al-Ḥaythamī in *Mawārid al-ẓamʾān ilā zawāʾid Ibn Ḥibbān*, 512 §2093; Ibn Isḥāq in *al-Sīra al-Nabawiyya*, 1:97 & 103; Ibn Hishām in *al-Sīra al-Nabawiyya*, 160; Ibn Athīr in *al-Kāmil fī al-tārīkh*, 1:459; al-Ṭabarī in *Tārīkh al-umam wa al-mulūk*, 1:455; Ibn ʿAsākir in *Tārīkh Dimashq al-kabīr*, 1:171–2; Ibn ʿAsākir in *Tārīkh Dimashq al-kabīr*, 3:466 & in *al-Sīra al-Nabawiyya*, 3:46; Ibn Kathīr in *al-Bidāya wa al-nihāya*, 2:264 & 275; Ibn Rajab al-Ḥanbalī in *Laṭāʾif al-maʿārif fīmā li-mawāsim al-ʿām min al-waẓāʾif*, p.173; al-Suyūṭī in *Kifāyat al-ṭālib al-labīb fī khaṣāʾiṣ al-Ḥabīb* ﷺ, 1:78; al-Ḥalabī in *Insān al-ʿuyūn fī sīra al-Amīn al-Maʾmūn*, 1:83; and Aḥmad b. Zaynī al-Daḥlān, *al-Sīra al-Nabawiyya*, 1:46.

fasting as a means of showing gratitude. After the migration, the Prophet ﷺ witnessed this practice of the Jews living in Medina and stated, 'I am closer to Moses ﷺ than them (in terms of my being a prophet)'. Hence, as an expression of gratitude, the Prophet ﷺ began fasting on *Yawm al-ʿĀshūrā'* and ordered his Companions ﷺ to follow suit.[1]

There are numerous narrations on this from which it can be inferred that if the Jews can express happiness upon the day of their prophet's victory and freedom, then we, as Muslims, ought to demonstrate similar feelings upon *Mawlid al-Nabī* ﷺ, given that the Mercy to the Worlds ﷺ came to redeem humankind from the shackles of oppression and injustice:

﴿وَيَضَعُ عَنْهُمْ إِصْرَهُمْ وَٱلْأَغْلَٰلَ ٱلَّتِي كَانَتْ عَلَيْهِمْ﴾

And he removes from them their heavy burdens and yokes (i.e., shackles) weighing upon them (due to their acts of disobedience and blesses them with freedom).[2]

On a final note, what blessing could be greater for a believer in this world than when the month of the most exalted Prophet's ﷺ blessed birth comes—when the believer feels that every other happiness in comparison to it is worthless? The true happiness is the pleasure of expressing joy and delight upon the arrival

---

[1] Narrated by al-Bukhārī in *al-Ṣaḥīḥ*: *Kitāb al-Ṣawm* [The Book of Fasting], chapter: 'The fast of *Yawm al-ʿĀshūrā'*', 2:704 §1900; al-Bukhārī in *al-Ṣaḥīḥ*: *Kitāb al-Anbiyā'* [The Book of Prophets], chapter: 'Allah's statement: Has the news of Mūsā reached you', 3:1244 §3216; al-Bukhārī in *al-Ṣaḥīḥ*: *Kitāb Faḍā'il al-Ṣaḥāba* [The Book of the virtues of the Companions], chapter: 'The Jews coming to the Prophet when he arrived in Medina', 3:1434 §3727; Muslim in *al-Ṣaḥīḥ*: *Kitāb al-Ṣiyām* [The Book of Fasting], chapter: 'The fast of *Yawm al-ʿĀshūrā'*', 2:795–6 §1130; Abū Dāwūd in *al-Sunan*: *Kitāb al-Ṣawm* [The Book of Fasting], chapter: 'The fast of *Yawm al-ʿĀshūrā'*', 2:326 §2444; Ibn Mājah in *al-Sunan*: *Kitāb al-Ṣiyām* [The Book of Fasting], chapter: 'The fast of *Yawm al-ʿĀshūrā'*', 1:552 §1734; Aḥmad b. Ḥanbal in *al-Musnad*, 1:291 & 336 §2644 & 3112; and Abū Yaʿlā in *al-Musnad*, 4:441 §2567.

[2] Qur'ān 7:157.

of Allah's Messenger ﷺ. The communities that went before us were obliged to show thankfulness and express joy upon gaining blessings of lesser significance that were confined to a particular time and place. On the other hand, the emergence of this grandest eternal and perpetual blessing, the most exalted Messenger ﷺ, is a continuous source of grace and benefit to all. Muslims should therefore be an embodiment of unlimited thankfulness whilst exhibiting emotions of high spirit and cheerfulness.

The Qurʾān, in a most eloquent style, has enjoined humanity to honour and revere the embodiment of mercy, blessing, and grace, bestowed upon them in the form of the most benevolent Prophet Muhammad ﷺ, who dispelled centuries of darkness and shattered the barriers of hatred and animosity that had divided people into scattered tribes. Almighty Allah says:

﴿وَٱذۡكُرُواْ نِعۡمَتَ ٱللَّهِ عَلَيۡكُمۡ إِذۡ كُنتُمۡ أَعۡدَآءٗ فَأَلَّفَ بَيۡنَ قُلُوبِكُمۡ
فَأَصۡبَحۡتُم بِنِعۡمَتِهِۦٓ إِخۡوَٰنٗا﴾

> *But call to mind the blessing of Allah upon you when you were enemies (one to another). Then He created the bond of love amongst your hearts, and by His blessing you became brothers.*[1]

This mending of broken hearts and reconciliation of human brotherhood is a glorious achievement that history shall fail to match. Therefore, articulating feelings of elation and indebtedness, and expressing gratitude to Almighty Allah upon the birth of the Chosen One ﷺ, more so than for any other gain, is mandatory upon the *Umma*.

Muhammad Tahir-ul-Qadri

---

[1] Qurʾān 3:103.

Chapter 1

Mawlid al-Nabī ﷺ and the Signs of Islam: A Historical Perspective

OUR CONVICTIONS, PERSONAL DEVELOPMENT, AND SPIRITUAL life revolve around the concept of *dhikr*—which is 'to remind', 'remember' and 'commemorate through acts of remembrance'. Our daily dealings, discourse, understanding, and all affairs of our life are limited to the knowledge which we have obtained and preserved in our minds. In this way, every step of our existence has been etched in our memories and it is these memories that guide our proceedings in life. For instance, the nature of our relationships is subject to our recollections with the person in question; and it is on this basis that our behaviour and conduct is moulded. Without the faculty of memory, we cannot make judgments about a thing: we would not even be able to distinguish friend from foe. Our life would be in total disarray. Thus, our conscious awareness is intrinsically dependant on our memories and recollections.

1.1 The Significance of 'Remembrance' as the Qurʾān's Scheme of Guidance

The foundation of Qurʾānic guidance, bestowed upon humankind, is based upon the order to 'remind'. Accordingly, the individual who believes in Almighty Allah and His Final Messenger ﷺ should simultaneously express faith in the former and present guidance sent by Almighty Allah. The Qurʾān states:

﴿وَٱلَّذِينَ يُؤْمِنُونَ بِمَآ أُنزِلَ إِلَيْكَ وَمَآ أُنزِلَ مِن قَبْلِكَ وَبِٱلْـَٔاخِرَةِ هُمْ يُوقِنُونَ﴾

And those who believe in (all) that which has been revealed to you and that which was revealed before you, and also have (perfect) faith in the Hereafter.[1]

[1] Qurʾān 2:4.

Here, on the basis of 'remembrance', attesting belief in former scriptures and subsequently preserving that remembrance throughout one's life has been described as an essential ingredient for the completion of faith.

Whenever somebody intends to perform an action, he does so according to the information he has retained. Emotions such as love, fear, humility and submission are shaped by the memories that we recall. Although these are sentiments relating to the heart, if it were not for the mental processes which take place, they simply would not exist. Hence, memory is such a huge blessing from Almighty Allah.

When the polytheists were invited to true faith, they would typically reply that 'we are content to adhere to the religion of our forefathers.' In other words, they were unwilling to sever their roots. In the following verse, such disbelievers are reminded that their ancestors perished because they chose the wrong path, and thus, they ought to accept the invitation to truth that their predecessors were invited to. However, they rejected Almighty Allah and His Messenger ﷺ, and they themselves perished as a result. The Qur'ān states:

﴿فَأَنجَيْنَٰهُ وَٱلَّذِينَ مَعَهُۥ بِرَحْمَةٍ مِّنَّا وَقَطَعْنَا دَابِرَ ٱلَّذِينَ كَذَّبُوا۟ بِـَٔايَٰتِنَا ۖ وَمَا كَانُوا۟ مُؤْمِنِينَ ﴿٧٢﴾﴾

Then We emancipated him and those who were on his side by Our Mercy, and cut the roots of those who denied Our Revelations. And they were those who would never have believed.[1]

In this verse, the disbelievers are being 'reminded' that their ancestors chose the wrong path, and thus consequently were destroyed; therefore they should heed to the guidance which was sent and not repeat the same mistake. Similarly, Muslims are also obliged to believe in the revelations which were sent to previous prophets and messengers, as they contains the same message as

[1] Ibid., 7:72.

the Qur'ān. Hence, it is as important to affirm former divinely revealed scriptures as it is to affirm the Qur'ān.

1.2 THE ABRAHAMIC RELIGION

Remembering the prophets that went before us and affirming their prophethood is an indispensable part of our faith. For this reason, the Qur'ān, in several passages, accordingly refers to Islam as the 'Religion of Ibrāhīm ﷺ':

1. ﴿وَمَن يَرۡغَبُ عَن مِّلَّةِ إِبۡرَٰهِـۧمَ إِلَّا مَن سَفِهَ نَفۡسَهُۥۚ وَلَقَدِ ٱصۡطَفَيۡنَٰهُ فِي ٱلدُّنۡيَاۖ وَإِنَّهُۥ فِي ٱلۡأٓخِرَةِ لَمِنَ ٱلصَّٰلِحِينَ﴾

1. *And who turns away from the religion of Ibrāhīm except he who has engaged himself in foolishness? And surely, We did choose him in the worldly life, and certainly in the Hereafter (too) he will be amongst the high-ranking intimate companions.*[1]

2. ﴿وَقَالُواْ كُونُواْ هُودًا أَوۡ نَصَٰرَىٰ تَهۡتَدُواْۗ قُلۡ بَلۡ مِلَّةَ إِبۡرَٰهِـۧمَ حَنِيفٗاۖ وَمَا كَانَ مِنَ ٱلۡمُشۡرِكِينَ﴾

2. *And (the People of the Book) say: 'Become Jews or Christians, then you will be guided aright.' Say: '(Nay,) the truth is that we have embraced the religion of Ibrāhīm who, far from every falsehood, turned absolutely to Allah alone. And he was not of the polytheists.'*[2]

3. ﴿قُلۡ صَدَقَ ٱللَّهُۗ فَٱتَّبِعُواْ مِلَّةَ إِبۡرَٰهِيمَ حَنِيفٗاۖ وَمَا كَانَ مِنَ ٱلۡمُشۡرِكِينَ﴾

3. *Say: 'Allah has proclaimed the truth, so follow the Religion of Ibrāhīm who, rejecting every evil, devoted himself wholly to Allah. And he was not one of the polytheists.*[3]

---

[1] Ibid., 2:130.

[2] Ibid., 2:135.

[3] Ibid., 3:95.

4. ﴿وَمَنْ أَحْسَنُ دِينًا مِّمَّنْ أَسْلَمَ وَجْهَهُۥ لِلَّهِ وَهُوَ مُحْسِنٌ وَٱتَّبَعَ مِلَّةَ إِبْرَٰهِيمَ حَنِيفًا ۗ وَٱتَّخَذَ ٱللَّهُ إِبْرَٰهِيمَ خَلِيلًا﴾

4. *And with regard to adopting the Religion, who can be better than the one who submits his whole being entirely to Allah, whilst he also holds spiritual excellence, and persistently follows the Dīn (Religion) of Ibrāhīm, a devotee (to Allah and) upright? And Allah had taken Ibrāhīm for a sincere and intimate friend. (So, he also becomes Allah's friend by virtue of his spiritual affiliation to Ibrāhīm.)*[1]

5. ﴿قُلْ إِنَّنِى هَدَىٰنِى رَبِّىٓ إِلَىٰ صِرَٰطٍ مُّسْتَقِيمٍ دِينًا قِيَمًا مِّلَّةَ إِبْرَٰهِيمَ حَنِيفًا ۚ وَمَا كَانَ مِنَ ٱلْمُشْرِكِينَ﴾

5. *Say: 'Verily, my Lord has guided me to the straight path. (This is the path of) the well-founded Religion, the path followed by Ibrāhīm single-mindedly devoted to Allah, turning aside from every falsehood. And he was not of the polytheists.'*[2]

6. ﴿ثُمَّ أَوْحَيْنَآ إِلَيْكَ أَنِ ٱتَّبِعْ مِلَّةَ إِبْرَٰهِيمَ حَنِيفًا ۖ وَمَا كَانَ مِنَ ٱلْمُشْرِكِينَ﴾

6. *Then, (O Glorious Beloved,) We sent down Revelation to you: Follow the Religion of Ibrāhīm, who was at variance with every falsehood, and was not of those who associate partners with Allah.*[3]

7. ﴿وَجَٰهِدُوا۟ فِى ٱللَّهِ حَقَّ جِهَادِهِۦ ۚ هُوَ ٱجْتَبَىٰكُمْ وَمَا جَعَلَ عَلَيْكُمْ فِى ٱلدِّينِ مِنْ حَرَجٍ ۚ مِّلَّةَ أَبِيكُمْ إِبْرَٰهِيمَ ۚ هُوَ سَمَّىٰكُمُ ٱلْمُسْلِمِينَ مِن

[1] Ibid., 4:125.

[2] Ibid., 6:161.

[3] Ibid., 16:123.

قَبْلُ وَفِى هَٰذَا لِيَكُونَ ٱلرَّسُولُ شَهِيدًا عَلَيْكُمْ وَتَكُونُوا۟ شُهَدَآءَ عَلَى ٱلنَّاسِ ۚ فَأَقِيمُوا۟ ٱلصَّلَوٰةَ وَءَاتُوا۟ ٱلزَّكَوٰةَ وَٱعْتَصِمُوا۟ بِٱللَّهِ هُوَ مَوْلَىٰكُمْ ۖ فَنِعْمَ ٱلْمَوْلَىٰ وَنِعْمَ ٱلنَّصِيرُ﴾

7. And strive hard in the way of Allah (for the establishment of peace and human dignity) such a striving as is due to Him. He has chosen you, and has not laid upon you any hardship or constriction (in the matter of) Religion. This is the Religion of your father, Ibrāhīm. He (Allah) has named you Muslims in the previous (Books) as well as in this (Holy Qur'ān) so that this (final) Messenger may be a witness over you and you be witnesses over mankind. So, (to sustain this status) establish the Prayer, pay Zakāt (the Alms-due) and hold fast to (the embrace of) Allah. He (alone) is your Helper (Patron). So what an excellent Patron and what an excellent Helper is He![1]

The aforementioned verses command that one must remain steadfast to the Religion of Ibrāhīm ﷺ. Before interpreting the visions of his two fellow prisoners, Prophet Yūsuf ﷺ conveyed his religious observance as such:

﴿وَٱتَّبَعْتُ مِلَّةَ ءَابَآءِىٓ إِبْرَٰهِيمَ وَإِسْحَٰقَ وَيَعْقُوبَ﴾

And I follow the Religion of my father and forefathers: Ibrāhīm, Isḥāq and Ya'qūb.[2]

In this verse, the remembrance of earlier messengers, that is to mention the accounts of the messengers and their communities, is being formulated as one of the central tenets of the religion; and this is a practice of the prophets. The Qur'ān states:

﴿إِنَّآ أَوْحَيْنَآ إِلَيْكَ كَمَآ أَوْحَيْنَآ إِلَىٰ نُوحٍ وَٱلنَّبِيِّـۧنَ مِنۢ بَعْدِهِۦ﴾

[1] Ibid., 22:78.

[2] Ibid., 12:38.

> *(O Beloved!) Indeed, We have sent Revelation to you as We sent it to Nūḥ and (other) Messengers after him.*[1]

Recalling the accounts of the prophets of previous communities and knowing the Religion of Ibrāhīm ﷺ is a source of illumination for the hearts and minds of the believers—it guides their each and every step.

The subject of 'remembrance' is a vast topic, and an entire book would have to be dedicated to it. The Qur'ān, in recognising the fact that commemoration impacts upon various stages of a person's life, frequently draws our attention towards it. With regards to this issue, it should be sufficient for us to examine the words which the Qur'ān uses in relation to remembrance. The word *dhikr* has appeared in the Qur'ān approximately 267 times and has come with the meaning of 'remembering', 'reminding' and 'preserving'; it has also been used to express advice and admonition—the Qur'ān itself is referred to as '*al-Dhikr*'. The term *nisyān*, contrarily, is employed in certain places as the opposite of *dhikr*; it means 'to forget', 'to cause to forget', 'to disregard something as insignificant', and 'to abandon something'.[2]

The teachings revealed by Almighty Allah through the ages, for man's guidance, are in essence one and the same; yet, due to the distortion at the hands of people, the original message was lost. The Qur'ān, in order to consolidate its guidance, reiterates its message over and over again; even the commandments within the Qur'ān recur frequently, albeit from a different perspective, in order to stay fresh in the mind of the reader. In this way, it serves the purpose of creating a feeling for its significance, thus making one conscious of abiding by its rulings.

Bearing this in mind, the following chapter will explore how matters of worship are related to the commemoration of prophetic endeavours. Furthermore, it will explain how events of joy and remorse in the lives of prophets revive feelings of humility, love and reverence within us.

---

[1] Ibid., 4:163.

[2] Al-Farāhīdī, *Kitāb al-ʿAyn*, 7:304–5; Ibn Manẓūr, *Lisān al-ʿArab*, 15:322–3; and Fayrūz Ābādī, *al-Qāmūs al-muḥīṭ*, 4:398.

Section 1

In Remembrance of the Prophets: The Five Ritual Prayers

THE MAJORITY OF MUSLIMS, ON THE BASIS OF *MAWLID AL-Nabī*, commemorate the 12th of *Rabīʿ al-Awwal*. They express their ecstatic love and devotion for the Mercy to the Worlds, our venerable master, Prophet Muhammad ﷺ, in their own particular way. Commemorating such incidents is a matter which is firmly established as one of the signs of Islam.

The foundational pillar of Islam lies in the establishment of the five prescribed ritual prayers. It is an individual obligation upon every Muslim and is the distinguishing factor between faith and disbelief. These prayers are in essence a commemoration of acts of gratitude to Almighty Allah which were performed by prophets at various times. Almighty Allah valued these acts so much that He ordained these voluntary prayers to be performed compulsorily by the *Umma* of Prophet Muhammad ﷺ.

Imam al-Ṭaḥāwī (229–331 AH), concerning the five prescribed ritual prayers, transmits a statement of Imam Muhammad b. ʿĀʾisha in his book, *Sharḥ maʿānī al-āthār*, in which he states:

1.3 The *Fajr* Ritual Prayer: In Remembrance of Prophet Ādam عليه السلام

إِنَّ آدَمَ عليه السلام لَـمَّـا تِيبَ عَلَيْهِ عِنْدَ الْفَجْرِ، صَلَّى رَكْعَتَيْنِ، فَصَارَتِ الصُّبْحَ.

When Ādam's عليه السلام repentance was accepted at dawn, he offered two cycles of ritual prayer (in order to show gratitude); thus it became the *fajr* ritual prayer.

1.4 The *Ẓuhr* Ritual Prayer: In Remembrance of Prophet Ibrāhīm عليه السلام

وَفُدِيَ إِسْحَاقُ عِنْدَ الظُّهْرِ فَصَلَّى إِبْرَاهِيمُ عليه السلام أَرْبَعًا، فَصَارَتِ الظُّهْرَ.

Ibrāhīm ﷺ performed four cycles of prayer upon being blessed with Isḥāq ﷺ in the afternoon; thus it became the *ẓuhr* ritual prayer.

1.5 The ʿ*Aṣr* Ritual Prayer: In Remembrance of Prophet ʿUzayr ﷺ

وَبُعِثَ عُزَيْرٌ ﷺ، فَقِيْلَ لَهُ: كَمْ لَبِثْتَ؟ فَقَالَ: يَوْمًا أَوْ بَعْضَ يَوْمٍ. فَصَلَّى أَرْبَعَ رَكَعَاتٍ، فَصَارَتِ الْعَصْرَ.

ʿUzayr ﷺ was resurrected (after a century) and was asked: 'How long did you remain (in this state)?' He replied, 'A day or part thereof.' Thereafter, he offered four cycles of ritual prayer, and this became the ʿ*aṣr* ritual prayer.

1.6 The *Maghrib* Ritual Prayer: In Remembrance of Prophet Dāwūd ﷺ

وَقَدْ قِيْلَ: غُفِرَ لِعُزَيْرٍ ﷺ وَغُفِرَ لِدَاوُدَ ﷺ عِنْدَ الْـمَغْرِبِ، فَقَامَ فَصَلَّى أَرْبَعَ رَكَعَاتٍ فَجَهِدَ فَجَلَسَ فِي الثَّالِثَةِ، فَصَارَتِ الْـمَغْرِبُ ثَلَاثاً.

It is narrated that Prophets ʿUzayr ﷺ and Dāwūd ﷺ were granted forgiveness at sunset. They intended to perform four cycles, but due to weakness and tiredness, they sat in the third cycle (being unable to complete the ritual prayer). Thus, the *maghrib* ritual prayer consisted of three cycles.

1.7 The ʿ*Ishā*ʾ Ritual Prayer: In Remembrance of Prophet Muhammad ﷺ

وَأَوَّلُ مَنْ صَلَّى الْعِشَاءَ الْآخِرَةَ، نَبِيُّنَا مُحَمَّدٌ ﷺ.

> The first person to perform the ʿishāʾ prayer—the final ritual prayer of the day—was our Prophet Muhammad ﷺ.[1]

These two and four cycles of ritual prayer which were performed by the esteemed Apostles as means of expressing gratitude to Almighty Allah for His grace and mercy serve as acts of remembrance in honour of these prophetic endeavours. Thus, throughout the day, Almighty Allah, through the performance of these ritual prayers, has placed continual reminders for us in memory of His prophets and messengers.

On a similar note, Ibn ʿĀbidīn al-Shāmī (1244–1306 AH) in his book, *Radd al-muḥtār ʿalā durr al-mukhtār*, writes:

قِيْلَ: اَلصُّبْحُ صَلَاةُ آدَمَ، وَالظُّهْرُ لِدَاوُدَ، وَالْعَصْرُ لِسُلَيْمَانَ، وَالْمَغْرِبُ لِيَعْقُوبَ، وَالْعِشَاءُ لِيُونُسَ عليهم السلام، وَجُمِعَتْ فِي هَذِهِ الْأُمَّةِ.

> It is said: The *fajr* ritual prayer is the prayer of Ādam ﷺ; the *ẓuhr* prayer is the prayer of Dāwūd ﷺ; the *ʿaṣr* prayer is the prayer of Sulaymān ﷺ; the *maghrib* prayer is the prayer of Yaʿqūb ﷺ; and the *ʿishāʾ* prayer is the prayer of Yaḥyā ﷺ—and all of these prayers have been gathered together in this Community (*Umma*).[2]

Those sanctified moments, wherein the prophets turned to their Lord in a state of gratitude, humility and submission, were decreed by Almighty Allah as acts of worship, which became means by which the Community of the Final Messenger ﷺ could attain Almighty Allah's proximity and His unlimited mercy. These accepted acts of worship performed by those eminent Apostles, through the intermediation of our Prophet ﷺ, were bestowed upon this Community as an everlasting act of remembrance. What could

---

[1] Reported by al-Ṭaḥāwī in *Sharḥ maʿānī al-āthār*: *Kitāb al-Ṣalāh* [The Book of Ritual Prayer], chapter: 'The middle prayer, i.e. the ritual prayers', 1:226 §1014.

[2] Ibn ʿĀbidīn, *Radd al-muḥtār ʿalā durr al-mukhtār ʿalā tanwīr al-abṣār*, 1:351.

be a greater proof of the importance of commemoration in religious affairs that the most central pillar amongst the pillars of Islam, i.e. the five prescribed ritual prayers, is in its practical manifestation an act of remembrance of the prophets?

Thus, we can conclude that the commemoration of actions or incidents, which have attained acceptance in the divine court, is not merely permissible, rather it is the very basis of the thought and philosophy of Islam. The celebration of *Mawlid al-Nabī* is the commemoration of the birth of Almighty Allah's Beloved, the Best of Creation and the Leader of the Prophets ﷺ. It is but one example of a celebration that is absolutely permissible and in total accordance with the decree of Almighty Allah.

Section 2

In Remembrance of the Prophets عليهم السلام: The Rites of Pilgrimage

AFTER THE DECLARATION OF FAITH AND THE RITUAL PRAYER, Pilgrimage *(ḥajj)* is the third most important pillar of Islam. The basic obligation of the Pilgrimage and its rites are in reality the observations of the heroic events in the lives of Ibrāhīm, Ismāʿīl and Hājar.

The commemoration of their displays of steadfastness, perseverance, and sacrifice were made compulsory by Almighty Allah upon the *Umma* as acts of worship. Throughout the world, the *Umma*, in their millions, assemble at Mecca each year to remember these endeavours, thereby attaining Allah's pleasure. Almighty Allah has forever preserved the memory of these devotional acts which were performed with utmost love and sincerity by His blessed servants, and He proclaimed them to be amongst His signs.

Upon entering the precincts of the Sacred Mosque in Mecca, feelings of love are stirred up and tears begin to flow profusely, resulting in contentment of the heart. Stepping into the holy vicinity, the servants of God circumambulate the House of Almighty Allah and passionately proceed toward the Black Stone, flocking towards it in spite of the huge crowd, striving to touch and kiss it. Then the servant goes forth to perform the *saʿy* (the ritual walking between the mountains of *al-Ṣafā* and *al-Marwa*). On the 9th of *Dhū al-Ḥijja*, every pilgrim departs to the plain of *ʿArafāt*; here the *ẓuhr* and *ʿaṣr* ritual prayers are combined. At *Muzdalifa*, the *maghrib* and *ʿishāʾ* ritual prayers are combined together in the time of *ʿishā*. Thereafter, at *Minā*, the *ramy* (the ritual casting of stones) is performed, followed by a ceremonial sacrifice.

There are no rational justifications for the performance of these rituals: these performances are simply a reflection of passion and devotion. The intellect may repeatedly call into question the logical consistency of these rituals, but no rational explanation can be given which may provide a satisfactory answer. On the other hand, if the same query were to be posed at the level of one's emotion (passion), the answer would be that the rationale behind these rites of Pilgrimage is a hidden indication of affection.

Almighty Allah ordained the dedication of His noble servants so much that He prescribed that these endeavours be commemorated as ritual worship until the Day of Judgment. The repetition of these endeavours, in the form of Pilgrimage rites, is an act in which some divinely favoured servant is reminisced. The Pilgrimage is, in essence, an act of remembrance.

This chapter will reveal how the Pilgrimage rites are in reality tributes in memory of the actions, worship, and activities of these blessed prophets of Almighty Allah. Similarly, the actions performed by Ibrāhīm and Hājar عليهما السلام were performed in such a way that Almighty Allah had honoured it so that the community of the Final Prophet ﷺ would perform these actions as Pilgrimage. These rites of Pilgrimage, which are performed between the 8th and 13th of *Dhū al-Ḥijja*, are briefly explained below:

1.8 The *Iḥrām*: In Remembrance of the Prophets' Attire for Pilgrimage

Concerning the rites of Pilgrimage (*ḥajj*) and Visitation (*ʿumra*), donning the *iḥrām* is of particular significance; wearing it is imperative for the one who circumambulates the Sacred House, the *Kaʿba*. These two sheets of cloth form the same dress which was worn by Almighty Allah's prophets during Pilgrimage. Almighty Allah loved this attire so much that He made it obligatory for the pilgrims to remove their conventional clothing and to don these two sheets. By dressing in the same two sheets, pilgrims from every corner of the world are imitating the practice of seventy prophets who wore the *iḥrām* in their respective eras. The following are traditions which elucidate this matter:

1. Abū Mūsā al-Ashʿarī رضي الله عنه narrates that the Prophet ﷺ said:

«لَقَدْ مَرَّ بِالصَّخْرَةِ مِنَ الرَّوْحَاءِ سَبْعُوْنَ نَبِيًّا، مِنْهُمْ مُوْسَى نَبِيُّ اللهِ، حُفَاةً، عَلَيْهِمُ الْعَبَاءُ، يَؤُمُّوْنَ بَيْتَ اللهِ الْعَتِيْقِ.»

> Seventy Prophets passed by the rocks of *al-Rawḥā* (a valley between Mecca and Medina)—amongst them being Mūsā ﷺ, the Prophet of Allah ﷻ—barefoot, wrapped in a cloth, proceeding to the Ancient House of Allah ﷻ.[1]

2. Concerning the *iḥrām* of Mūsā ﷺ, ʿAbd Allāh b. Masʿūd ﷺ reports that the Prophet ﷺ said:

«كَأَنِّي أَنْظُرُ إِلَى مُوْسَى بْنِ عِمْرَانَ فِي هَذَا الْوَادِي مُحْرِمًا بَيْنَ قَطَوَانِيَّتَيْنِ.»

> It is as though I am looking at Mūsā b. ʿImrān ﷺ in this valley wearing two *qaṭwānī* (white) robes.[2]

3. Imam al-Azraqī (b. 223 AH) was the first author to compile a book on the history of Mecca, called *Akhbār Makka wa mā jāʾa fīhā min al-āthār*. He relates with his own chain of narration that ʿAbd Allāh b. Masʿūd ﷺ said:

لَقَدْ سَلَكَ فَجَّ الرَّوْحَاءِ سَبْعُوْنَ نَبِيًّا حُجَّاجًا، عَلَيْهِمْ لِبَاسُ الصُّوفِ.

> Seventy Prophets have trodden the mountainous path of *al-Rawḥā* as pilgrims; upon them were garments of wool (*ṣūf*).[3]

---

[1] Narrated by Abū Yaʿlā in *al-Musnad*, 13:201 & 255 §7231 & 7271; Abū Yaʿlā in *al-Musnad*, 7:262 §4275 also narrates from Anas b. Mālik; Daylamī in *al-Firdaws bi-maʾthūr al-khiṭāb*, 3:433 §5328; Abū Naʿīm in *Ḥilya al-awliyāʾ wa ṭabaqāt al-aṣfiyāʾ*, 1:260; al-Mundhirī in *al-Targhīb wa al-tarhīb min al-ḥadīth al-sharīf*, 2:118 §1739 states that there are no criticism on the chain of transmission of this tradition; Ibn ʿAsākir in *Tārīkh Dimashq al-kabīr*, 21:166; and al-Ḥaythamī in *Majmaʿ al-zawāʾid wa manbaʿ al-fawāʾid*, 3:220.

[2] Narrated by Abū Yaʿlā in *al-Musnad*, 9:27 §5093; al-Ṭabarānī in *al-Muʿjam al-kabīr*, 10:142 §10,255; al-Ṭabarānī in *al-Muʿjam al-awsaṭ*, 6:308 §6487; Abū Naʿīm in *Ḥilya al-awliyāʾ wa ṭabaqāt al-aṣfiyāʾ*, 4:189; al-Mundhirī in *al-Targhīb wa al-tarhīb min al-ḥadīth al-sharīf*, 2:118 §1740 states that Abū Yaʿlā and al-Ṭabarānī narrate this with a fine (*ḥasan*) chain of transmission; al-Ḥaythamī in *Majmaʿ al-zawāʾid wa manbaʿ al-fawāʾid*, 3:221 states that Abū Yaʿlā and Ṭabarānī narrate this with a fine (*ḥasan*) chain of transmission.

[3] Narrated by al-Azraqī in *Akhbār Makka wa mā jāʾa fīhā min al-āthār*, 1:71–72.

4. Concerning Prophet Mūsā's ﷺ attire on the occasion of *ḥajj*, the student of ʿAbd Allāh b. ʿAbbās and ʿAbd Allāh b. ʿUmar ؓ, Mujāhid b. Jubayr states:

> حَجَّ مُوسَى النَّبِيُّ ﷺ عَلَى جَمَلٍ أَحْمَرَ، فَمَرَّ بِالرَّوْحَاءِ، عَلَيْهِ عَبَاءَتَانِ قَطَوَانِيَّتَانِ، مُتَّزِراً بِأَحَدِهِمَا مُرْتَدِيًا بِالْأُخْرَى، فَطَافَ بِالْبَيْتِ.

> Prophet Mūsā ﷺ performed Pilgrimage on a red camel. He passed by *al-Rawḥā* wearing two *qaṭawānī* (white) cloaks: one was used as a lower-garment and the other was wrapped around the body. He circumambulated the Kaʿba.[1]

5. In another narration, the *iḥrām* of Prophets Hūd and Ṣāliḥ ﷺ has also been mentioned. ʿAbd Allāh b. ʿAbbās ؓ reports that whilst the Prophet ﷺ passed by ʿAsfān valley during the *ḥajj* season, he asked, 'O Abū Bakr, which valley is this?' Abū Bakr ؓ replied, 'It is the ʿAsfān valley.' The Prophet ﷺ said:

> «لَقَدْ مَرَّ بِهِ هُودٌ وَصَالِحٌ عَلَى بَكَرَاتٍ حُمْرٍ خُطُمُهَا اللِّيفُ، أُزُرُهُمُ الْعَبَاءُ، وَأَرْدِيَتُهُمُ النِّمَارُ، يُلَبُّونَ يَحُجُّونَ الْبَيْتَ الْعَتِيقَ.»

> Hūd and Ṣāliḥ ﷺ passed by this valley, riding on young red camels whose halters were of palm fibres. Their loin-cloth was a cloak and their outer garment was a black and white striped robe. They were performing the Pilgrimage to the Sacred House (the Kaʿba) whilst proclaiming the *talbiya* (the declaration of service).[2]

From these traditions, it can be seen that the prophets would don plain robes when performing the Pilgrimage; they would

---

[1] Ibid., 1:67.
[2] Narrated by Aḥmad b. Ḥanbal in *al-Musnad*, 1:232; al-Bayhaqī in *Shuʿab al-īmān*, 3:440 §4003 also narrates a similar narration concerning Mūsā; and al-Mundhirī in *al-Targhīb wa al-tarhīb min al-ḥadīth al-sharīf*, 2:117 §1737.

perform the Pilgrimage solely for the pleasure of Almighty Allah. Their garment would consist of two sheets: one as a loincloth, and the other as an outer garment.

This garment was so pleasing to Almighty Allah that till the Day of Judgment, it was made incumbent to be worn by the pilgrims: donning one's conventional attire during the Pilgrimage was made prohibited. In normal circumstances, offering the ritual prayer bareheaded is considered a blemish and contrary to the Sunna, but in the Pilgrimage this is not the case. In the state of *iḥrām,* every pilgrim is present in the vicinity of the Sacred House, the *Kaᶜba*, with their heads uncovered. To have one's head uncovered there is a symbol of humility and humbleness, and this is most commendable according to Almighty Allah.

Alongside this, acts such as clipping the nails, cutting the hair, and trimming the moustache have also been prohibited[1] so that outwardly, in every respect, the pilgrim is in accordance with the precedent set by the prophets of Almighty Allah.

1.9 *Talbiya*: In Remembrance of Ibrāhīm's Call to Pilgrimage and its Reply

Whether performing the Pilgrimage (*ḥajj*) or Visitation (*ᶜumra*), the pilgrim, upon wearing the *iḥrām*, with utmost sincerity and humility supplicates to Allah with the following words:

لَبَّيْكَ اللَّهُمَّ لَبَّيْكَ، لَبَّيْكَ لَا شَرِيْكَ لَكَ لَبَّيْكَ، إِنَّ الْحَمْدَ وَالنِّعْمَةَ لَكَ وَالْمُلْكَ، لَا شَرِيْكَ لَكَ.

> Here I am, O Lord! Here I am! There is none worthy of worship except You. Here I am! Verily all praise, blessings and sovereignty belong to You. None is worthy of worship except You.[2]

---

[1] Al-Kāsānī, *Badāʾiᶜ al-ṣanāʾiᶜ fī tartīb al-sharāʾiᶜ*, 2:198.

[2] Narrated by al-Bukhārī in *al-Ṣaḥīḥ*: *Kitāb al-Ḥajj* [The Book of Pilgrimage], chapter: '*talbiya*', 2:561 §1474; al-Bukhārī in *al-Ṣaḥīḥ*: *Kitāb al-Libās* [The Book of Garments], chapter: 'Gumming the hair', 5:2213 §5571; Muslim in *al-Ṣaḥīḥ*: *Kitāb al-Ḥajj* [The Book of Pilgrimage],

This *talbiya* is recited in the Sacred Mosque during the Pilgrimage (*ḥajj*) and Visitation (*ʿumra*), yet few people are aware of its origin. It is actually a reply to Ibrāhīm's call upon completing the construction of the *Kaʿba*, on Allah's order, some four thousand years ago. Concerning this, the Qurʾān states:

﴿وَأَذِّن فِي ٱلنَّاسِ بِٱلْحَجِّ يَأْتُوكَ رِجَالًا وَعَلَىٰ كُلِّ ضَامِرٍ يَأْتِينَ مِن كُلِّ فَجٍّ عَمِيقٍ﴾

Enjoin people with the Pilgrimage and they shall flock to you, on foot and riding from every corner.[1]

In the prophetic traditions, it states that Ibrāhīm ﷺ climbed mount *Abū Qubays* and proclaimed to all humanity that they should come to Almighty Allah's house for Pilgrimage.[2]

Beyond time and space, this call was made to reach every place where people resided. In fact, all the souls in the spiritual world which were yet to be born perceived this announcement; whoever replied to this call with '*labbayk* (I am here!)' was granted the ability to perform the Pilgrimage and permission to visit Almighty Allah's house—as proven in the following traditions:

1. ʿAbd Allāh b. ʿAbbās ؓ reports:

---

chapter: 'the *talbiya*: its description and timing' 2:841–842 §1184; al-Tirmidhī in *al-Jāmiʿ al-Ṣaḥīḥ: Kitāb al-Ḥajj* [The Book of Pilgrimage], chapter: 'What has been related concerning the *talbiya*', 3:187–188 §825–826; Abū Dāwūd in *al-Sunan: Kitāb al-Manāsik* [The Book of Pilgrimage Rites], chapter: 'How the *talbiya* is performed', 2:162 §1812; al-Nasāʾī in *al-Sunan: Kitāb Manāsik al-Ḥajj* [The Book of Pilgrimage Rites], chapter: 'How the *talbiya* is performed', 5:159–160 §2747–2750; and Ibn Mājah in *al-Sunan: Kitāb al-Manāsik* [The Book of Pilgrimage Rites], chapter: 'The *talbiya*', 2:974 §2918.

[1] Qurʾān 22:27.

[2] Narrated by Ibn Abī Ḥātim al-Rāzī in *Tafsīr al-Qurʾān al-ʿaẓīm*, 8:2487–2488; Ibn Jawzī in *Zād al-masīr fī ʿilm al-tafsīr*, 5:423; al-Suyūṭī in *al-Durr al-manthūr fī al-tafsīr bi al-maʾthūr*, 6:32; and Ibn ʿAjība in *al-Baḥr al-madīd fī tafsīr al-Qurʾān al-majīd*, 4:410.

لَمَّا بَنَى إِبْرَاهِيْمُ الْبَيْتَ أَوْحَى اللهُ إِلَيْهِ أَنْ أَذِّنْ فِي النَّاسِ بِالْحَجِّ. قَالَ: فَقَالَ إِبْرَاهِيْمُ: أَلَا! إِنَّ رَبَّكُمْ قَدِ اتَّخَذَ بَيْتًا وَأَمَرَكُمْ أَنْ تَحُجُّوهُ، فَاسْتَجَابَ لَهُ مَا سَمِعَهُ مِنْ حَجَرٍ أَوْ شَجَرٍ أَوْ أَكَمَةٍ أَوْ تُرَابٍ: لَبَّيْكَ اللَّهُمَّ لَبَّيْكَ.

When Ibrāhīm ﷺ constructed the *Kaᶜba*, Almighty Allah inspired Him to call humankind to Pilgrimage. Ibrāhīm ﷺ announced, 'Your Lord has appointed a house and ordered you to make Pilgrimage to it. There was not a rock, tree, hill or soil that heard the call, except that it replied, 'I am here, O Allah! I am here!'[1]

2. ᶜAbd Allāh b. ᶜAbbās ﷺ states:

لَمَّا فَرَغَ إِبْرَاهِيْمُ عليه السلام مِنْ بِنَاءِ الْبَيْتِ الْعَتِيْقِ، قِيْلَ لَهُ: أَذِّنْ فِي النَّاسِ بِالْحَجِّ، قَالَ: رَبِّ، وَمَا يَبْلُغُ صَوْتِي، قَالَ: أَذِّنْ وَعَلَيَّ الْبَلَاغُ، قَالَ: فَقَالَ إِبْرَاهِيْمُ: يَا أَيُّهَا النَّاسُ! كُتِبَ عَلَيْكُمُ الْحَجُّ إِلَى الْبَيْتِ الْعَتِيْقِ. قَالَ: فَسَمِعَهُ مَا بَيْنَ السَّمَاءِ إِلَى الْأَرْضِ، أَلَا تَرَى أَنَّ النَّاسَ يَجِيْئُوْنَ مِنْ أَقَاصِي الْأَرْضِ يُلَبُّوْنَ.

When Ibrāhīm ﷺ completed the construction of the *Kaᶜba,* it was said to him, 'Call people for the Pilgrimage.' He said, 'O my Lord, my voice will not reach.' Almighty Allah said: 'Raise the call and We shall make the creation hear it.' Ibrāhīm ﷺ said, 'O people! Almighty Allah has ordained pilgrimage upon you.' The narrator adds: 'Everything between the heavens and the earth heard

[1] Narrated by al-Ḥakim, in *al-Mustadrak ᶜalā al-ṣaḥīḥayn*, 2:601 §4026; al-Bayhaqī, in *al-Sunan al-kubrā*, 5:176 §9613; al-Bayhaqī, in *Shuᶜab al-īmān*, 3:439 §3998; al-Ṭabarī, in *Tārīkh al-umam wa al-mulūk*, 1:156; Mujāhid, in *al-Tafsīr*, 2:422; al-Jaṣṣāṣ, in *Aḥkām al-Qurʾān*, 5:63; al-Ṭabarī, in *Jāmiᶜ al-bayān fī tafsīr al-Qurʾān*, 17:144; and al-Ṣuyūṭī, in *al-Durr al-manthūr fī al-tafsīr bi al-maʾthūr*, 6:32.

this announcement. Do you not see how people from the furthest corners of the earth come reciting the *talbiya* (in response to this call)?'[1]

3. Regarding the verse of the Qur'ān, ﴾*And enjoin people with the Pilgrimage*﴿, ᶜAbd Allāh b. ᶜAbbās ؓ says:

قَامَ إِبْرَاهِيْمُ خَلِيْلُ اللهِ عَلَى الْـحَجَرِ، فَنَادَى: يَا أَيُّهَا النَّاسُ! كُتِبَ عَلَيْكُمُ الْـحَجُّ. فَأَسْمَعَ مَنْ فِـي أَصْلَابِ الرِّجَالِ وَأَرْحَامِ النِّسَاءِ فَأَجَابَهُ مَنْ آمَنَ مِـمَّنْ سَبَقَ فِـي عِلْمِ اللهِ أَنْ يَحُجَّ إِلَى يَوْمِ الْقِيَامَةِ: لَبَّيْكَ اَللَّهُمَّ لَبَّيْكَ.

Ibrāhīm ؑ, the intimate friend of Allah, stood upon a rock and exclaimed, 'O people! The Pilgrimage has been prescribed upon you.' All those in the loins of men and the wombs of women were made to hear this call, and the believers who, in the pre-eternal knowledge of Allah, were destined to perform the Pilgrimage until the Day of Judgment answered (the call) by saying, 'Here I am, O Lord! Here I am!'[2]

4. Abū Hurayra ؓ states that the Prophet ﷺ said:

---

[1] Narrated by Ibn Abī Shayba, in *al-Muṣannaf*, 6:329 §31818; al-Ḥākim, in *al-Mustadrak ᶜalā al-ṣaḥīḥayn*, 2:421 §3464; al-Bayḥaqī, in *al-Sunan al-kubrā*, 5:176 §9614; al-Maqdasī in *al-Aḥādīth al-mukhtāra*, 10:20–21; al-Ṭabarī, in *Jāmiᶜ al-bayān fī tafsīr al-Qur'ān*, 17:144 also narrates it from Saᶜīd b. Jubayr; al-Ṣuyūṭī, in *al-Durr al-manthūr fī al-tafsīr bi al-ma'thūr*, 6:32; al-Ṣuyūṭī, in *al-Durr al-manthūr fī al-tafsīr bi al-ma'thūr*, 6:233 also narrates it from Saᶜīd b. Jubayr; al-Shawkānī, in *Fatḥ al-Qadīr*, 3:450; and Ālūsī, in *Rūḥ al-maᶜānī fī Tafsīr al-Qur'ān al-ᶜaẓīm wa al-sabᶜ al-mathānī*, 17:143.

[2] Narrated by al-Ṭabarī, in *Jāmiᶜ al-bayān fī tafsīr al-Qur'ān*, 17:144; al-Ṣuyūṭī, in *al-Durr al-manthūr fī al-tafsīr bi al-ma'thūr*, 6:33; al-Ṭabarī, in *Tārīkh al-umam wa al-mulūk*, 1:157; and al-ᶜAsqalānī, in *Fatḥ al-Bārī*, 6:406.

«لَـمَّـا فَرَغَ إِبْرَاهِيْمُ عليه السلام مِنْ بِنَاءِ البَيْتِ أَمَرَهُ اللهُ أَنْ يُنَادِيَ فِي الْـحَجِّ، فَقَامَ عَلَى الْـمَنَارِ، فَقَالَ: يَا أَيُّـهَا النَّاسُ! إِنَّ رَبَّكُمْ قَدْ بَنَى لَكُمْ بَيْتًا فَحُجُّوْهُ وَأَجِيْبُوْا اللهَ تعالى، قَالَ: فَأَجَابُوْهُ فِيْ أَصْلَابِ الرِّجَالِ وَأَرْحَامِ النِّسَاءِ: أَجَبْنَاكَ. أَجَبْنَاكَ لَبَّيْكَ اَللَّهُمَّ لَبَّيْكَ، قَالَ: فَكُلُّ مَنْ حَجَّ الْيَوْمَ فَهُوَ مِـمَّنْ أَجَابَ إِبْرَاهِيْمَ عَلَى قَدْرِ مَا لَبَّى.»

> When Ibrāhīm ﷺ completed the construction of the *Kaʿba*, Allah ﷻ commanded him to call for the Pilgrimage. So he ascended onto a tower and shouted, 'O people! Your Lord has made a house for you, so perform the Pilgrimage and answer unto Allah. All those in the loins of men and the wombs of woman answered saying, 'We answer You! We answer You! Here I am, O Lord! Here I am!' The narrator adds: Whoever performs the Pilgrimage today, he is amongst those who answered Ibrāhīm's call according to the number of times he made the *talbiya*.[1]

The call of *labbayk* was proclaimed for a single moment thousands of years ago, but this heavenly melody is heard from all directions. By chanting this, the pilgrims bring to mind this incident in relation to Prophet Ibrāhīm ﷺ. This proves that recalling past events (in our thought) is in accordance with the teachings of Islam. Likewise, through the celebration of *Mawlid al-Nabī* ﷺ, we reminisce the birth of our Beloved Prophet ﷺ and express happiness on his arrival. The Holy Prophet ﷺ is remembered through gatherings, consisting of the recitation of odes in his praise and other commendable deeds.

---

[1] Narrated by al-Fākahī, in *Akhbār Makka fī qadīm al-dahr wa ḥadīthihī*, 1:446 §973; The tradition has been reported briefly from Mujāhid b. Jubayr in the following books: Ibn Abī Shayba, in *al-Muṣannaf*, 6:330 §31,826; al-Ṭabarī, in *Jāmiʿ al-bayān fī tafsīr al-Qurʾān*, 17:145; Ibn ʿAbd al-Barr, in *al-Tamhīd limā fī al-muwaṭṭā min al-maʿānī wa al-asānīd*, 15:131; and al-Zaylaʿī in *Naṣb al-rāya li-aḥādīth al-hidāya*, 3:23.

1.10 ṬAWĀF: IN REMEMBRANCE OF THE SUNNA OF PROPHETS ﷺ

Circumambulating the Kaʿba seven times is known as *ṭawāf*. Performing the *ṭawāf* is the practice (Sunna) of the Prophets. This is explained further in the following traditions:

1. ʿAbd Allāh b. ʿAbbās ؓ relates:

فَكَانَ أَوَّلُ مَنْ أَسَّسَ الْبَيْتَ وَصَلَّى فِيهِ وَطَافَ بِهِ آدَمُ ﷺ.

The first person to lay the foundation of the Kaʿba, to pray in it and circumambulate it was Prophet Ādam ﷺ.[1]

2. Imam Muḥammad b. Isḥāq states that he was informed that Prophet Ādam ﷺ felt sad upon being unable to find a heavenly atmosphere on earth whereupon he could pray. So Almighty Allah (by means of the angels) constructed the Holy Sanctuary for Ādam ﷺ and commanded him to reside therein. Ādam ﷺ headed towards Mecca and Almighty Allah caused water to spring forth from the spot where he rested. And when he reached Mecca:

فَأَقَامَ بِهَا يَعْبُدُ اللهَ عِنْدَ ذَلِكَ الْبَيْتِ وَيَطُوفُ بِهِ، فَلَمْ تَزَلْ دَارَهُ حَتَّى قَبَضَهُ اللهُ بِهَا.

He settled therein, worshipping Allah besides that House and circumambulating it. This place remained his residence until Allah took his soul.[2]

3. ʿUmar b. al-Khaṭṭāb ؓ asked Kaʿb al-Aḥbār ؓ about the House of Almighty Allah. Kaʿb al-Aḥbār ؓ said, 'Allah ﷻ sent down the Kaʿba enfolded in a diamond with Ādam ﷺ and informed him: 'O Ādam ﷺ! I have sent down My house with you. It shall be

---

[1] Narrated by al-Azraqī in *Akhbār Makka wa mā jāʾa fīhā min al-āthār*, 1:36, 40; and al-Suyūṭī, in *al-Durr al-manthūr fī al-tafsīr bi al-maʾthūr*, 1:313.

[2] Narrated by al-Azraqī in *Akhbār Makka wa mā jāʾa fīhā min al-āthār*, 1:39; Ibn ʿAsākir in *Tārīkh Dimashq al-kabīr*, 7:425; and al-Maqdasī in *al-Badʾ wa al-tārīkh*, 4:82.

circumambulated and the prayer offered beside it just as is done at my ᶜ*Arsh*.' The angels descended along with the house and laid its foundation stones and built it.

فَكَانَ آدَمُ عليه السلام يَطُوْفُ حَوْلَهُ كَمَا يُطَافُ حَوْلَ الْعَرْشِ، وَيُصَلِّي عِنْدَهُ كَمَا يُصَلَّى عِنْدَ الْعَرْشِ.

> Ādam ﷺ used to circumambulate it, as the ᶜ*Arsh* is circumambulated. And he would offer the prayer beside it, as he used to offer the prayer beside the ᶜ*Arsh*.[1]

4. With the exception of Ādam ﷺ, numerous other Prophets performed the *ṭawāf*. Concerning this, the eminent successor (*tābiᶜī*), Mujāhid b. Jubayr, states:

حَجَّ خَمْسَةٌ وَسَبْعُوْنَ نَبِيًّا، كُلُّهُمْ قَدْ طَافَ بِالْبَيْتِ.

> Seventy-five Prophets performed the Pilgrimage; all of them circumambulated the House.[2]

Circumambulating the *Kaᶜba* seven times is also the practice (Sunna) of the Prophets.

5. ᶜAbd Allāh b. ᶜAbbās ﷺ reports:

حَجَّ آدَمُ عليه السلام وَطَافَ بِالْبَيْتِ سَبْعًا.

> Ādam ﷺ performed the Pilgrimage and circumambulated the House seven times.[3]

---

[1] Narrated by al-Azraqī in *Akhbār Makka wa mā jāʾa fīhā min al-āthār*, 1:39.

[2] Narrated by al-Azraqī in *Akhbār Makka wa mā jāʾa fīhā min al-āthār*, 1:67–68; al-Fākahī, in *Akhbār Makka fī qadīm al-dahr wa ḥadīthihī*, 4:268 §2599; and Aḥmad b. Ḥanbal, in *al-ᶜIlal wa maᶜrifa al-rijāl*, 3:193 §4831.

[3] Narrated by al-Azraqī in *Akhbār Makka wa mā jāʾa fīhā min al-āthār*, 1:45; and al-Ṣuyūṭī, in *al-Durr al-manthūr fī al-tafsīr bi al-maʾthūr*, 1:320.

6. Imam ʿAbd Allāh b. Abī Sulaymān said:

طَافَ آدَمُ عليه السلام سَبْعًا بِالْبَيْتِ حِيْنَ نَزَلَ.

Ādam ﷺ circumambulated the house seven times when he descended.[1]

7. Imam Muhammad b. Isḥāq writes regarding the *ṭawāf* of Ibrāhīm and Ismāʿīl ﷺ:

لَـمَّـا فَرَغَ إِبْرَاهِيْمُ خَلِيْلُ الرَّحْمَنِ مِنْ بِنَاءِ الْبَيْتِ الْـحَرَامِ، جَاءَهُ جِبْرِيْلُ فَقَالَ: طُفْ بِهِ سَبْعًا، فَطَافَ بِهِ سَبْعًا هُوَ وَإِسْمَـاعِيْلُ.

When Ibrāhīm ﷺ, the intimate friend of Allah, completed the construction of the Sanctified House, Jibrāʾīl ﷺ came to him and said, 'Circumambulate it seven times.' So, Ibrāhīm ﷺ and Ismāʿīl ﷺ circumambulated it seven times.[2]

The Final Messenger, Prophet Muhammad ﷺ preserved the practice of previous Prophets by also circumambulating the *Kaʿba* seven times.

8. ʿUmar b. al-Khaṭṭāb ﷺ narrates:

قَدِمَ النَّبِيُّ ﷺ فَطَافَ بِالْبَيْتِ سَبْعًا.

The Prophet ﷺ entered (Mecca) and circumambulated the House seven times.[3]

[1] Narrated by al-Azraqī in *Akhbār Makka wa mā jāʾa fīhā min al-āthār*, 1:43.

[2] Narrated by al-Azraqī in *Akhbār Makka wa mā jāʾa fīhā min al-āthār*, 1:65; and al-Qurṭubī in *al-Jāmiʿ li-aḥkām al-Qurʾān*, 2:129.

[3] Narrated by al-Bukhārī in *al-Ṣaḥīḥ*: *Kitāb al-Ḥajj* [The Book of Pilgrimage], chapter: 'The one who offers the two cycles of the post-*ṭawāf* ritual prayer behind the *Maqām Ibrāhīm*', 2:588 §1547; al-Bukhārī in *al-Ṣaḥīḥ*: *Kitāb al-Ḥajj* [The Book of Pilgrimage], chapter: 'What it related concerning the *saʿy* between *al-Ṣafā* and *al-Marwa*', 2:593 §1563; al-Bukhārī in *al-Ṣaḥīḥ*:

9. Jābir b. ʿAbd Allāh ﷺ states:

أَنَّ النَّبِيَّ ﷺ حِينَ قَدِمَ مَكَّةَ طَافَ بِالْبَيْتِ سَبْعًا.

When the Prophet ﷺ entered Mecca, he circumambulated the House seven times.[1]

It can be clearly deduced from these reports that performing the *ṭawāf* (with its seven circuits) is to follow in the footsteps of the prophets; through its performance we revive their remembrance.

1.11 *Raml*: In Remembrance of the Manner in which the Prophet ﷺ and his Companions Performed the *Ṭawāf*

Performing the *ṭawāf* is one of the most important aspects of the Pilgrimage. The male pilgrims are commanded to carry out the first three circuits of the *ṭawāf* somewhat haughtily. Technically, this is referred to as *raml*. Generally speaking, walking haughtily is a sign of arrogance and it is despised by Almighty Allah[2]; but, during the

---

Kitāb al-Ḥajj [The Book of Pilgrimage], chapter: 'When the to take off the *iḥrām* after the *ʿumra*', 2:636 §1700; and Muslim in *al-Ṣaḥīḥ*: *Kitāb al-Ḥajj* [The Book of Pilgrimage], chapter: 'What is necessitated upon the one who activates *iḥrām* for *ḥajj*', 2:906 §1234.

[1] Narrated by al-Tirmidhī in *al-Jāmiʿ al-Ṣaḥīḥ*: *Kitāb al-Ḥajj* [The Book of Pilgrimage], chapter: 'What it related concerning starting at *al-Ṣafā* before *al-Marwa*', 3:216 §862; al-Tirmidhī in *al-Jāmiʿ al-Ṣaḥīḥ*: *Abwāb al-Tafāsīr* [The Chapters of Exegeses], chapter: '*Sūra al-Baqara*', 5:210 §2967; al-Nasāʾī in *al-Sunan*: *Kitāb Manāsik al-Ḥajj* [The Book of Pilgrimage Rites], chapter: 'The statement after the two cycles of the post-*ṭawāf* ritual prayer', 5:235 §2961; Ibn Khuzayma in *al-Ṣaḥīḥ*, 4:170 §2620; and al-Ṭabarānī in *al-Muʿjam al-ṣaghīr*, 1:126 §187.

[2] Ḥāritha b. Wahb al-Khuzāʿī ﷺ reports that the Prophet ﷺ said:

«أَلَا أُخْبِرُكُمْ بِأَهْلِ الْجَنَّةِ؟ كُلُّ ضَعِيفٍ مُتَضَعِّفٍ، لَوْ أَقْسَمَ عَلَى اللهِ لَأَبَرَّهُ. أَلَا أُخْبِرُكُمْ بِأَهْلِ النَّارِ؟ كُلُّ عُتُلٍّ جَوَّاظٍ مُسْتَكْبِرٍ.»

Shall I not inform you of the people of Paradise? All who are weak

Pilgrimage, the opposite is the case.

The underlying wisdom in this is that after the emigration to Medina, the Muslims became weak and slender after many relentless struggles. When returning to Mecca to perform the Visitation (*ʿumra)*, the year following the Treaty of *Ḥudaybiyya*, their weakness began to show on their bodies. The disbelievers of Mecca noticed that the Muslims were sluggish in performing the *ṭawāf*, and so they taunted them saying that after departing from Mecca, the Muslims had become so frail that they were unable to even walk properly. Consequently, the esteemed Messenger ﷺ ordered the noble Companions ؓ to march pompously to remove this deliberation from the minds of the infidels. Though no non-Muslim remained in Mecca after its conquest, the *ṭawāf* procedure has remained as such for centuries.

---

and thought to be weak. If they were to take an oath by Allah ﷻ, Allah ﷻ would carry it out. Shall I not tell you about the people of the Hellfire? All those who are coarse, domineering, and arrogant.

Narrated by al-Bukhārī in *al-Ṣaḥīḥ*: *Kitāb al-Tafsir* [The Book of Exeges], chapter: '*Sūra Nūn wa al-Qalam*', 4:1870 §4634; al-Bukhārī in *al-Ṣaḥīḥ*: *Kitāb al-Adab* [The Book of Proprieties], chapter: 'Arrogance', 5:2255 §5723; and Muslim in *al-Ṣaḥīḥ*: *Kitāb al-Janna wa Ṣifa Naʿīmihā wa Ahlihā* [The Book of the Description and People of Paradise], chapter: 'The arrogant will enter the Hellfire and the weak will enter Paradise', 4:2190 §2853.

Abū Hurayra ؓ reports that the Prophet ﷺ said:

«يَقُولُ اللهُ ﷻ: الْكِبْرِيَاءُ رِدَائِي وَالْعَظَمَةُ إِزَارِي، فَمَنْ نَازَعَنِي وَاحِدًا مِنْهُمَا أَلْقَيْتُهُ فِي النَّارِ.»

Allah ﷻ states: Greatness is My cloak and pride is My robe. Whoever tries to remove any of these from Me, I shall cast him into the Hellfire.

Narrated by Ibn Abī Shayba, in *al-Muṣannaf*, 5:329 §26,579; al-Ṭabarānī in *al-Muʿjam al-awsaṭ*, 3:352 §3380 reports this from ʿAlī ؓ; al-Qaḍāʿī in *Musnad al-shihāb*, 2:331 §1464; al-Bayhaqī in *Shuʿab al-īmān*, 6:380 §8157.

Imam Muslim, in his *al-Ṣaḥīḥ*, in *Kitāb al-Ḥajj* [The Book of Pilgrimage], under the chapter, *Istiḥbāb al-raml fī al-ṭawāf wa al-ʿumra wa fī al-ṭawāf al-awwal min al-ḥajj* [The desirability of *raml* in the *ṭawāf* of *ʿumra* and the first *ṭawāf* of *ḥajj*], on this subject relates many Prophetic traditions which are as following:

1. ʿAbd Allāh b. ʿAbbās ﷺ states that the Holy Prophet ﷺ and his noble Companions ﷺ became weak after an epidemic struck Medina. They arrived in Mecca (for *ʿumra* the year after the Treaty of *Ḥudaybiyya*) whereupon the leaders of the polytheists said to their people, 'A people shall come to you who have been left frail after illness.' After hearing this, the residents of Mecca sat beside the Black Stone. So when the Muslims arrived:

وَأَمَرَهُمُ النَّبِيُّ ﷺ أَنْ يَرْمُلُوا ثَلَاثَةَ أَشْوَاطٍ، وَيَمْشُوا مَا بَيْنَ الرُّكْنَيْنِ لِيَرَى الْمُشْرِكُونَ جَلَدَهُمْ. فَقَالَ الْمُشْرِكُونَ: هَؤُلَاءِ الَّذِينَ زَعَمْتُمْ أَنَّ الْحُمَّى قَدْ وَهَنَتْهُمْ، هَؤُلَاءِ أَجْلَدُ مِنْ كَذَا وَكَذَا.

The Prophet ﷺ ordered them (i.e., the Companions) to perform three circuits haughtily and to walk between the two corners (i.e., the Yemeni corner and the Black Stone) so that the polytheists would see their sturdiness. (Upon observing this spectacle,) the polytheists exclaimed, 'Do you expect us to believe that these people have become weak due to sickness? They are very strong and free from what you claim!'[1]

2. ʿAbd Allāh b. ʿAbbās ﷺ clearly states in another tradition:

---

[1] Narrated by Muslim in *al-Ṣaḥīḥ*: *Kitāb al-Ḥajj* [The Book of Pilgrimage], chapter: 'The desirability of *raml* in the *ṭawāf* of *ʿumra* and the first *ṭawāf* of *ḥajj*', 2:923 §1266; al-Bukhārī in *al-Ṣaḥīḥ*: *Kitāb al-Ḥajj* [The Book of Pilgrimage], chapter: 'How was the *raml* initiated', 2:581 §1525; Aḥmad b. Ḥanbal in *al-Musnad*, 1:294; and al-Bayhaqī in *al-Sunan al-kubrā*, 5:82 §9056.

إِنَّمَا سَعَى رَسُولُ اللهِ ﷺ بِالْبَيْتِ وَبَيْنَ الصَّفَا وَالْمَرْوَةِ لِيُرِيَ الْمُشْرِكِينَ قُوَّتَهُ.

Allah's Messenger ﷺ walked quickly around the House and between *al-Ṣafā* and *al-Marwa* in order to display his strength to the polytheists.[1]

3. Abū Ṭufayl ʿĀmir b. Wāthila ﷺ narrates from ʿAbd Allāh b. ʿAbbās ﷺ that:

إِنَّ رَسُولَ اللهِ ﷺ قَدِمَ مَكَّةَ، فَقَالَ الْمُشْرِكُونَ: إِنَّ مُحَمَّدًا وَأَصْحَابَهُ لَا يَسْتَطِيعُونَ أَنْ يَطُوفُوا بِالْبَيْتِ مِنَ الْهُزَالِ وَكَانُوا يَحْسُدُونَهُ. قَالَ: فَأَمَرَهُمْ رَسُولُ اللهِ ﷺ أَنْ يَرْمُلُوا ثَلَاثًا وَيَمْشُوا أَرْبَعًا.

Allah's Messenger ﷺ entered Mecca and the polytheists said, 'Muḥammad and his followers are unable to circumambulate the house due to emaciation.' They used to be envious of him. Thus, the esteemed Messenger ﷺ commanded them to perform the *raml* in three circuits and to walk in four.[2]

1.12 *Iḍṭibāʿ*: The Sunna of the Last Messenger ﷺ

During the *ṭawāf*, to place the *iḥrām* under the right armpit and to

---

[1] Narrated by al-Bukhārī in *al-Ṣaḥīḥ*: *Kitāb al-Ḥajj* [The Book of Pilgrimage], chapter: 'What it related concerning the *saʿy* between *al-Ṣafā* and *al-Marwa*', 2:594 §1562; Muslim in *al-Ṣaḥīḥ*: *Kitāb al-Ḥajj* [The Book of Pilgrimage], chapter: 'The desirability of *raml* in the *ṭawāf* of *ʿumra* and the first *ṭawāf* of *ḥajj*', 2:923 §1266; al-Tirmidhī in *al-Jāmiʿ al-Ṣaḥīḥ*: *Kitāb al-Ḥajj* [The Book of Pilgrimage], chapter: 'What it related concerning the *saʿī* between *al-Ṣafā* and *al-Marwa*', 3:217 §863; al-Nasāʾī in *al-Sunan al-kubrā*, 2:405 §3941; al-Ḥumaydī in *al-Musnad*, 1:232 §497; and al-Bayhaqī in *al-Sunan al-kubrā*, 5:82 §9057–9058.

[2] Reported by Muslim in *al-Ṣaḥīḥ*: *Kitāb al-Ḥajj* [The Book of Pilgrimage], chapter: 'The desirability of *raml* in the *ṭawāf* of *ʿumra* and the first *ṭawāf* of *ḥajj*', 2:921–922 §1264; Ibn Ḥibbān in *al-Ṣaḥīḥ*, 9:154 §3845; and al-Bayhaqī in *al-Sunan al-kubrā*, 5:100 §9161.

place both its ends on the left shoulder is called *iḍṭibāʿ*.[1]

As has been explained, the most exalted Prophet ﷺ, as a display of strength and awe, commanded his noble Companions to perform the *raml*. Alongside this, the most exalted Prophet ﷺ also ordered the *iḍṭibāʿ* during the *ṭawāf*—he himself led by example. To adhere to this beloved Sunna is binding upon all who travel for the Pilgrimage (*ḥajj*) and Visitation (*ʿumra*). Pilgrims continuously commemorate this practice of their beloved Prophet ﷺ.

1. ʿAbd Allāh b. ʿAbbās ؓ states:

أَنَّ رَسُولَ اللهِ ﷺ وَأَصْحَابَهُ اعْتَمَرُوا مِنَ الْجِعْرَانَةِ، فَرَمَلُوا بِالْبَيْتِ وَجَعَلُوا أَرْدِيَتَهُمْ تَحْتَ آبَاطِهِمْ، قَدْ قَذَفُوهَا عَلَى عَوَاتِقِهِمُ الْيُسْرَى.

Allah's Messenger ﷺ and his Companions ؓ performed the Visitation (*ʿumra*) from *Jiʿrāna*. They performed the *raml* around the House and placed their cloaks under their armpit and cast it over their left shoulder.[2]

2. Yaʿlā b. Umayya states:

طَافَ النَّبِيُّ ﷺ مُضْطَبِعًا بِبُرْدٍ أَخْضَرَ.

The Prophet ﷺ performed the *ṭawāf* with *iḍṭibāʿ*, wearing a green cloak.[3]

---

[1] Ibn Manẓūr, *Lisān al-ʿArab*, 8:216.

[2] Reported by Abū Dāwūd in *al-Sunan*: *Kitāb al-Manāsik* [The Book of Pilgrimage Rites], chapter: 'The *iḍṭibāʿ* in the *ṭawāf*', 2:177 §1884; Aḥmad b. Ḥanbal in *al-Musnad*, 1:306; al-Ṭabarānī in *al-Muʿjam al-kabīr*, 12:62 §12,478; Bayhaqī in *al-Sunan al-kubrā*, 5:79 §9038–9039; and al-Maqdasī in *al-Aḥādīth al-mukhtāra*, 10:207–208 §213–215.

[3] Reported by Abū Dāwūd in *al-Sunan*: *Kitāb al-Manāsik* [The Book of Pilgrimage Rites], chapter: 'The *iḍṭibāʿ* in the *ṭawāf*', 2:177 §1883; al-Tirmidhī in *al-Jāmiʿ al-Ṣaḥīḥ*: *Kitāb al-Ḥajj* [The Book of Pilgrimage], chapter: 'What it related concerning the Prophet performing the *ṭawāf* with *iḍṭibāʿ*.', 3:214 §859; Ibn Mājah in *al-Sunan*: *Kitāb al-Manāsik* [The Book of Pilgrimage Rites], chapter: 'The *iḍṭibāʿ*', 2:984 §2954; al-Dārimī, in *al-Sunan*, 2:65 §1843; and al-Bayhaqī in *al-Sunan al-kubrā*, 5:79 §9035.

3. Al-Ṭībī explains the wisdom behind the *iḍṭibāʿ*:

إِنَّمَـا فَعَلَ ذَلِكَ إِظْهَارًا لِلتَّشَجُّعِ، كَالرَّمَلِ فِي الطَّوَافِ.

> It was only done as a gesture of courage, as is the case of *raml* in the *ṭawāf*.[1]

In our time, fourteen centuries have lapsed since any disbeliever was in Mecca, yet we are still required to perform the *iḍṭibāʿ* in imitation of the Sunna of the Holy Prophet ﷺ and his noble Companions. By following in their footsteps, our hearts and minds are enlightened, thereby preparing us to stand firm against any such falsehood today.

1.13 Kissing the Black Stone: In Remembrance of the Practice of Allah's Beloved

One of the reasons why the Black Stone (*al-ḥajr al-aswad*) is deemed sacred is because Angel Jibrāʾīl ﷺ brought it from paradise.[2] The prophets would kiss and greet (*istislām*) this stone in accordance to the command of Almighty Allah. The Final Prophet ﷺ, following the Sunna of his predecessor Ibrāhīm ﷺ, placed the Black Stone in its place with his own blessed hands and kissed it with his pure lips. Thus, this became a ritual of the Pilgrimage. The only reason why believers kiss it today is due to the fact that Prophet Muhammad ﷺ did so.

This fact is substantiated from the statement of ʿUmar b. al-Khaṭṭāb ﷺ, who once, whilst performing the *ṭawāf*, stood opposite the Black Stone and said:

---

[1] ʿAẓīm Ābādī, *ʿAwn al-maʿbūd ʿalā sunan Abī Dāwūd*, 5:236, and Mubārakpūrī, *Tuḥfat al-aḥwadhī fī sharḥ jāmiʿ Tirmidhī*, 3:506.

[2] Reported by al-Azraqī in *Akhbār Makka wa mā jāʾa fīhā min al-āthār*, 1:62,64 & 325; Ibn Abī Shayba, in *al-Muṣannaf*, 3:275 §14,146; Ibn al-Jaʿd, in *al-Musnad*, p.148 §940; al-Fākahī, in *Akhbār Makka fī qadīm al-dahr wa ḥadīthihī*, 1:91 §25; and al-Ḥaythamī in *Majmaʿ al-zawāʾid wa manbaʿ al-fawāʾid*, 3:242.

إِنِّـي أَعْلَمُ أَنَّكَ حَجَرٌ لَا تَضُرُّ وَلَا تَنْفَعُ، وَلَوْلَا أَنِّـي رَأَيْتُ النَّبِيَّ ﷺ يُقَبِّلُكَ مَا قَبَّلْتُكَ.

> I know full well that you are just a stone. You do not harm nor benefit anyone. Had I not seen the Prophet ﷺ kiss you, I would never do so.[1]

According to another narration, ʿUmar ﷺ stated:

إِنَّمَـا أَنْتَ حَجَرٌ، وَلَوْلَا أَنِّـي رَأَيْتُ رَسُولَ اللهِ ﷺ قَبَّلَكَ مَا قَبَّلْتُكَ.

> You are merely a stone. Had I not seen Allah's Messenger ﷺ kiss you, I would never do so.[2]

After saying this, ʿUmar ﷺ proceeded forward to kiss the Black Stone (*al-ḥajr al-aswad*).

This event highlights the fact that the noble Companions only kissed the Black Stone because they wanted to follow in the footsteps of their most exalted Prophet ﷺ—this was an act of remembrance on their part. And till the Day of Judgment, this Sunna shall remain.

1.14 *Maqām Ibrāhīm*: In Remembrance of Prophet Ibrāhīm ﷺ

---

[1] Reported by al-Bukhārī in *al-Ṣaḥīḥ*: *Kitāb al-Ḥajj* [The Book of Pilgrimage], chapter: 'What it mentioned concerning the Black Stone', 2:579 §1520; al-Bukhārī in *al-Ṣaḥīḥ*: *Kitāb al-Ḥajj* [The Book of Pilgrimage], chapter: '*Raml* in the Pilgrimage and Visitation', 2:582 §1528; al-Bukhārī in *al-Ṣaḥīḥ*: *Kitāb al-Ḥajj* [The Book of Pilgrimage], chapter: 'Kissing the Black Stone', 2:583 §1532; Muslim in *al-Ṣaḥīḥ*: *Kitāb al-Ḥajj* [The Book of Pilgrimage], chapter: 'The desirability of kissing the Black Stone during the *ṭawāf*', 2:925 §1270; Ibn Mājah in *al-Sunan*: *Kitāb al-Manāsik* [The Book of Pilgrimage Rites], chapter: 'Greeting the Black Stone', 2:981 §2943; al-Nasāʾī in *al-Sunan al-kubrā*, 2:400 §3918; and Aḥmad b. Ḥanbal in *al-Musnad*, 1:46 §325.

[2] Reported by Mālik, in *al-Muwaṭṭā*: *Kitāb al-Ḥajj* [The Book of Pilgrimage], chapter: 'Kissing the Black Stone corner in the greeting,' 1:367 §818; and Aḥmad b. Ḥanbal in *al-Musnad*, 1:53 §380.

Maqām (station) linguistically refers to a place where one's foot is placed.[1] There are various opinions about the *Maqām Ibrāhīm*. The majority of the scholars and exegetes (based on the opinions of Jābir b. ʿAbd Allāh, ʿAbd Allāh b. ʿAbbās and Qatāda, et al.) believed that *Maqām Ibrāhīm* is the name of the stone that is located in this place. Two cycles of supererogatory ritual prayer are offered there. This is the most authentic opinion.[2]

A tradition related by Imam al-Bukhārī (194–256 AH) elaborates upon the above narration explaining that at the time of constructing the *Kaʿba*, Ismāʿīl ﷺ would assemble the stones and Ibrāhīm ﷺ would craft the walls. When the walls were built quite high, Ibrāhīm ﷺ stood upon this stone (*Maqām Ibrāhīm*) in order to be able to reach the top and complete the structure.[3]

Another tradition states that whenever Ibrāhīm ﷺ struggled to carry the stones brought by Ismāʿīl ﷺ, he would stand upon the *Maqām Ibrāhīm*, and it would lift him off the ground and transport him around the building until the *Kaʿba* was completed.[4]

Anas ﷺ reports that ʿUmar ﷺ requested the Holy Prophet ﷺ saying:

يَا رَسُوْلَ اللهِ! لَوِ اتَّخَذْتَ مِنْ مَّقَامِ إِبْرَاهِيْمَ مُصَلًّى.

> O Messenger of Allah ﷺ! If only you would take *Maqām Ibrāhīm* as a place of prayer.

---

[1] Al-Farāhīdī, *Kitāb al-ʿAyn*, 5:232; Fayrūz Ābādī, *al-Qāmūs al-muḥīṭ*, 4:170; Ibn Manẓūr, *Lisān al-ʿArab*, 12:498; and al-Zabīdī, *Tāj al-ʿurūs min jawāhir al-qāmūs*, 17:592.

[2] Narrated by al-Ṭabarī, in *Jāmiʿ al-bayān fī tafsīr al-Qurʾān*, 1:537; al-Qurṭubī in *al-Jāmiʿ li-aḥkām al-Qurʾān*, 2:112; al-Rāzī in *al-Tafsīr al-kabīr*, 4:45; al-Ālūsī, in *Rūḥ al-maʿānī fī tafsīr al-Qurʾān wa sabʿ al-mathānī*, 1:379; and al-ʿAsqalānī, in *Fatḥ al-Bārī*, 1:499.

[3] Narrated by al-Bukhārī in *al-Ṣaḥīḥ*: *Kitāb al-Anbiyāʾ* [The Book of the Prophets], chapter: 'Rushing back: to walk quickly,' 3:1235 §3184; ʿAbd al-Razzāq, in *al-Muṣannaf*, 5:110 §9107; al-Ṭabarī, in *Jāmiʿ al-bayān fī tafsīr al-Qurʾān*, 1:550; Ibn Kathīr, in *al-Tafsīr al-Qurʾān al-ʿaẓīm*, 1:178; and al-Qazwīnī, in *al-Tadwīn fī akhbār Qazwīn*, 1:105.

[4] Al-Azraqī, *Akhbār Makka wa mā jāʾa fīhā min al-āthār*, 1:58 and 2:33.

Upon this, the verse was revealed:

﴿وَٱتَّخِذُواْ مِن مَّقَامِ إِبۡرَٰهِـۧمَ مُصَلًّى﴾

Make the place, where Ibrāhīm ﷺ *stood, a place of Prayer.*[1]

Almighty Allah's Messenger ﷺ immediately acted upon this by praying behind *Maqām Ibrāhīm*.[2]

Jābir b. ᶜAbd Allāh ﷺ narrates that when we approached the Sacred House with Allah's Messenger ﷺ, he performed the *ṭawāf* (three circuits with *raml* and four circuits in the normal manner). Subsequently, he advanced towards the *Maqām Ibrāhīm* and recited the verse, 'Make the place, where Ibrāhīm ﷺ stood, a place of Prayer'. He then stood between the *Kaᶜba* and *Maqām Ibrāhīm* and offered two cycles of ritual prayer.[3]

Almighty Allah ordained the stone upon which Ibrāhīm ﷺ stood to build the *Kaᶜba* as a place of prayer as this was the desire of a prominent Companion, ᶜUmar ﷺ. This stone was blessed as the most gracious Prophet ﷺ prayed besides it. Until the Day of Judgment, it is imperative (*wājib*) upon all Muslims circumambulating the *Kaᶜba* to offer two cycles of ritual prayer besides *Maqām Ibrāhīm*; failing to do so will result in one's *ṭawāf* being incomplete—if no space is available, it is permissible to pray elsewhere, although praying near the station is recommended.[4]

---

[1] Qurʾān 2:125.

[2] Narrated by al-Bukhārī in *al-Ṣaḥīḥ*: *Kitāb al-Tafsīr* [The Book of Exegeses], chapter: 'Allah's statement: "*Make the place, where Ibrāhīm stood, a place of Prayer*" 4:1629 §4213; al-Tirmidhī in *al-Jāmiᶜ al-Ṣaḥīḥ*: *Abwāb al-Tafsīr* [The Chapters of Exegeses], chapter: '*Sūra al-Baqara*', 5:206 §2960; Ibn Mājah in *al-Sunan*: *Kitāb Iqāma al-Ṣalāh wa al-Sunna Fīhā* [The Book of establishing the prayer and the *sunna* therein], chapter: 'The *Qibla*', 1:322 §1008; al-Nasāʾī in *al-Sunan al-kubrā*, 6:289 §10,998; Ibn Ḥibbān in *al-Ṣaḥīḥ*, 15:319 §6896; and Aḥmad b. Ḥanbal in *al-Musnad*, 1:36 §250.

[3] Narrated by Muslim in *al-Ṣaḥīḥ*: *Kitāb al-Ḥajj* [The Book of Pilgrimage], chapter: 'The Prophet's Pilgrimage', 2:887 §1218.

[4] Al-Sarkhaṣī, *Kitāb al-Mabsūṭ*, 4:12; al-Kāsānī, *Badāʾiᶜ al-ṣanāʾiᶜ fī tartīb*

Since the footprint of Ibrāhīm ﷺ exists on this stone, Muslims shall forever revere it and perform supererogatory ritual prayers besides it to revive the memory of Prophet Ibrāhīm's efforts in erecting the *Kaʿba*.

1.15 *Saʿy* between *al-Ṣafā* and *al-Marwa*: In Remembrance of the Sunna of Hājar ﷺ

There are actions performed by Almighty Allah's chosen servants that apparently do not look like acts of worship and were not performed with the intention of worship (*ʿibāda*), yet Almighty Allah treasured them to the extent that He declared them to be a part of a collective form of worship.

An example is that of Hājar ﷺ, who ran between *al-Ṣafā* and *al-Marwa*, desperately searching for water for her infant, Ismāʿīl ﷺ. Almighty Allah loved this act so much that He decreed that the pilgrims should pace between the two mountains as a component of the Pilgrimage; technically, this is referred to as *saʿy*. Its performance is imperative (*wājib*) in both the Pilgrimage (*ḥajj*) and Visitation (*ʿumra*).

It must be borne in mind that during the seven circuits of the *saʿy*, no specific recitation from the Qurʾān or invocation (*dhikr*) has been prescribed. One is permitted to recite whatever they want from the Qurʾān; or, one can invoke blessings upon the Holy Prophet ﷺ. Even if nothing is known by memory, then merely repeating Almighty Allah's glorious name or the declaration of faith is sufficient. Otherwise, a person could simply perform the *saʿy* in total silence.

Imam al-Bukhārī (256–194AH) and numerous other exegetes and hadith-scholars have recorded several traditions in relation to the story behind the significance of *al-Ṣafā* and *al-Marwa*. One example is as follows:

ʿAbd Allāh b. ʿAbbās ﷺ states that Ibrāhīm ﷺ took Hājar and Ismāʿīl ﷺ from Syria to Mecca. At the time, Mecca was uninhabited and no source of water was in sight. Ibrāhīm ﷺ left his wife and son

---

al-sharāʾiʿ, 2:148; al-Samarqandī, *Tuḥfa al-Fuqahāʾ*, 1:402; and Ibn Nujaym, *al-Baḥr al-rāʾiq sharḥ kanz al-daqāʾiq*, 2:356.

besides the House of Almighty Allah and provided them with some water and dates. As he departed, Hājar ؓ exclaimed, 'Where are you going, Ibrāhīm? Are you leaving us in this deserted valley?' She asked this question repeatedly, but Ibrāhīm ؑ did not turn to look at her. Hence, Hājar ؓ asked 'Are you leaving us because Almighty Allah commanded you to do so?' He replied in the affirmative. And Hājar ؓ said, 'If this is the case, then He will not abandon us.'

Hājar ؓ then sat at this place whilst Ibrāhīm ؑ went on his way until he was out of sight. When he reached a place called *Thaniya*, he raised his hands and supplicated:

﴿رَّبَّنَآ إِنِّيٓ أَسۡكَنتُ مِن ذُرِّيَّتِي بِوَادٍ غَيۡرِ ذِي زَرۡعٍ عِندَ بَيۡتِكَ ٱلۡمُحَرَّمِ رَبَّنَا لِيُقِيمُواْ ٱلصَّلَوٰةَ فَٱجۡعَلۡ أَفۡـِٔدَةٗ مِّنَ ٱلنَّاسِ تَهۡوِيٓ إِلَيۡهِمۡ وَٱرۡزُقۡهُم مِّنَ ٱلثَّمَرَٰتِ لَعَلَّهُمۡ يَشۡكُرُونَ﴾

O our Lord! Verily, I have settled my offspring (Ismāʿīl) in the barren valley (of Mecca) in the close vicinity of Your Sacred House, O our Lord, so that they may establish Prayer. So make the hearts of the people incline towards them with love and fondness, and provide for them (all kinds of) fruits as sustenance so that they may remain grateful.[1]

ʿAbd Allāh b. ʿAbbās ؓ states:

وَجَعَلَتْ أُمُّ إِسْمَاعِيْلَ تُرْضِعُ إِسْمَاعِيْلَ، وَتَشْرَبُ مِنْ ذَلِكَ الْمَاءِ، حَتَّى إِذَا نَفِدَ مَا فِي السِّقَاءِ عَطِشَتْ وَعَطِشَ ابْنُهَا. وَجَعَلَتْ تَنْظُرُ إِلَيْهِ يَتَلَوَّى، أَوْ قَالَ: يَتَلَبَّطُ، فَانْطَلَقَتْ كَرَاهِيَةَ أَنْ تَنْظُرَ إِلَيْهِ، فَوَجَدَتِ الصَّفَا أَقْرَبَ جَبَلٍ فِي الْأَرْضِ يَلِيْهَا، فَقَامَتْ عَلَيْهِ، ثُمَّ اسْتَقْبَلَتِ الْوَادِيَ تَنْظُرُ هَلْ تَرَى أَحَداً فَلَمْ تَرَ أَحَداً، فَهَبَطَتْ مِنَ الصَّفَا حَتَّى إِذَا بَلَغَتِ الْوَادِيَ

[1] Qurʾān 14:37.

رَفَعَتْ طَرْفَ دِرْعِهَا، ثُمَّ سَعَتْ سَعْيَ الْإِنْسَانِ الْمَجْهُوْدِ حَتَّى جَاوَزَتِ الْوَادِيَ، ثُمَّ أَتَتِ الْمَرْوَةَ فَقَامَتْ عَلَيْهَا وَنَظَرَتْ هَلْ تَرَى أَحَدًا فَلَمْ تَرَ أَحَدًا، فَفَعَلَتْ ذَلِكَ سَبْعَ مَرَّاتٍ.

Hājar ﷺ started breastfeeding her child and drinking the water until the container was empty. She and her child became thirsty. Hājar ﷺ observed her infant writhing (or kicking) his legs on the ground due to intense thirst. She could not bear seeing him in this state. *Al-Ṣafā* was the closest hill, so she climbed it and looked across the valley in order to try and find people. When she could not locate anyone, she hastened across the valley to *al-Marwa* and climbed it. She did this seven times.

ʿAbd Allāh b. ʿAbbās ﷺ narrates that the Noble Prophet ﷺ said:

«فَذَلِكَ سَعْيُ النَّاسِ بَيْنَهُمَا.»

This is the reason why people perform *saʿy* between these two hills.[1]

Almighty Allah cherished His dear servant's devotion so much that He counted them amongst His signs:

﴿إِنَّ ٱلصَّفَا وَٱلْمَرْوَةَ مِن شَعَآئِرِ ٱللَّهِ﴾

Verily the hills of al-Ṣafā and al-Marwa are from amongst

[1] Narrated by al-Bukhārī in *al-Ṣaḥīḥ*: *Kitāb al-Anbiyāʾ* [The Book of the Prophets], chapter: 'Allah's statement: Take Ibrāhīm's station as a place of prayer,' 3:1228–1229 §3184; al-Nasāʾī in *al-Sunan al-kubrā*, 5:100 §8379; ʿAbd al-Razzāq, in *al-Muṣannaf*, 5:105–106 §9107; al-Bayhaqī in *al-Sunan al-kubrā*, 5:100 §8379; al-Nasāʾī in *Faḍāʾil al-Ṣaḥāba*, 1:82 §273; al-Qurṭubī in *al-Jāmiʿ li-aḥkām al-Qurʾān*, 9:368–369; and Ibn Kathīr, in *al-Tafsīr al-Qurʾān al-ʿaẓīm*, 1:177.

the signs of Allah.[1]

This incident occurred some four thousand years ago. The valley and hills in question no longer exist in their original form, and the apprehensions of that beloved maidservant of God are no longer an immediate concern. Regardless of this, the pilgrims perform the *saʿy* between the two hills as enjoined by Almighty Allah. And all of this is done to commemorate Hājar's concern for her son, Ismāʿīl ﷺ, and her uneasy and troubled state.

1.15.1 Well of *Zam Zam*: *Raison D'Être* for its Name

When Ismāʿīl ﷺ struck his heels on the ground owing to excessive thirst, by the will of Almighty Allah, a spring of water gushed out from the ground. Hājar ﷺ feared that Ismāʿīl ﷺ may be harmed by the immense rush of water, so she exclaimed, '*zam zam* (stop, stop)!' Thereafter, the pressure of the surging water eased, and thus it has since been referred to as *Zam zam*.

This spring is a divine gift to pilgrims that has been flowing for millennia. It is customary to drink it standing, in a state of ritual ablution, whilst facing the direction of the *qibla*; this particular ruling is owing to its link to Ismāʿīl ﷺ.[2] *Zam zam* is the best water on the face of the earth and is also a cure for many illnesses.

The aforementioned points prove that Islam does not simply recommend commemorating past events, but in certain situations makes it compulsory. *Mawlid al-Nabī* must be viewed from the same angle. Prophet Muhammad ﷺ is the source of Almighty Allah's mercy, grace and favour upon the world. Expressing gratitude upon *Mawlid al-Nabī* ﷺ, whereby one's love for him

---

[1] Qurʾān 2:158.

[2] Narrated by al-Bukhārī in *al-Ṣaḥīḥ*: *Kitāb al-Ḥajj* [The Book of Pilgrimage], chapter: 'What has been related concerning *Zam zam*,' 2:590 §1556; al-Bukhārī in *al-Ṣaḥīḥ*: *Kitāb al-Ashriba* [The Book of Beverages], chapter: 'To drink standing,' 5:2130 §5294; Muslim in *al-Ṣaḥīḥ*: *Kitāb al-Ashriba* [The Book of Beverages], chapter: 'Drinking *Zam zam* whilst standing', 3:1601–1602 §2027; and al-ʿAynī, in *ʿUmda al-qārī sharḥ Ṣaḥīḥ al-Bukhārī*, 9:277.

and obedience to him is strengthened, is the basis upon which this celebration is initiated.

1.16 *ʿArafāt*, *Muzdalifa* and *Minā*: In Remembrance of Prophet Ādam ﷵ

Pilgrims reside at *ʿArafāt* on the 9th of *Dhū al-Ḥijja*. It is interesting to note that no specific worship has been enjoined there: simply being present at *ʿArafāt* is sufficient to fulfil the obligation of *ḥajj*. *ʿArafāt* reminds us of the reunion between Ādam and Ḥawwāʾ ﷵ which took place on the 9th of *Dhū al-Ḥijja*, as is proven from the following prophetic traditions:

1. ʿAbd Allāh b. ʿAbbās ﷺ said:

أُهْبِطَ آدَمُ ﷵ بِالْـهِنْدِ وَحَوَّاءُ بِجَدَّةَ، فَجَاءَ فِي طَلَبِهَا حَتَّى اجْتَمَعَا، فَازْدَلَفَتْ إِلَيْهِ حَوَّاءُ فَلِذَلِكَ سُمِّيَتِ الْـمُزْدَلِفَةَ، وَتَعَارَفَا بِعَرَفَاتٍ فَلِذَلِكَ سُمِّيَتْ عَرَفَاتٍ، وَاجْتَمَعَا بِجَمْعٍ فَلِذَلِكَ سُمِّيَتْ جَمْعًا.

> Ādam ﷵ descended to India whilst Ḥawwāʾ ﷵ to Jeddah. Ādam ﷵ sought her until they were finally reunited. Ḥawwāʾ ﷵ came to him and thus she was referred to as the 'one who draws near (*Muzdalifa*)'. Husband and wife recognised one another at *ʿArafāt* and thus its name (a place where one recognises another). They came together at *Jamʿ*, hence its name (a place of union).[1]

2. Ādam ﷵ descended on mount '*Nawdh*' in the Indian Subcontinent, whereas Ḥawwāʾ ﷵ was sent to Jeddah. Ibn Saʿd (168–230 AH), al-Ṭabarī (264–310 AH), and al-Nawawī (631–677 AH) were of the view that Ādam ﷵ met his wife at *ʿArafāt*, hence the name.[2]

3. Al-Qurṭubī (284–380 AH) writes in *al-Jāmiʿ li-aḥkām al-*

---

[1] Al-Ṭabarī, *Tārīkh al-umam wa al-mulūk*, 1:79; Ibn al-Athīr, *al-Kāmil fī al-tārīkh*, 1:34; Ibn Saʿd, *al-Ṭabaqāt al-kubrā*, 1:39; and Ibn ʿAsākir in *Tārīkh Dimashq al-kabīr*, 69:109.

[2] Al-Ṭabarī, *Tārīkh al-umam wa al-mulūk*, 1:79; Ibn Saʿd, *al-Ṭabaqāt al-kubrā*, 1:35–36; and al-Nawawī, *Tahdhīb al-asmāʾ wa al-lughāt*, 3:237.

Qurʾān:

أَنَّ آدَمَ لَـمَّـا هَبَطَ وَقَعَ بِالْـهِنْدِ، وَحَوَّاءُ بِجِدَّةَ، فَاجْتَمَعَا بَعْدَ طُوْلِ الطَّلَبِ بِعَرَفَاتٍ يَوْمَ عَرَفَةَ وَتَعَارَفَا، فَسُمِّيَ الْيَوْمُ عَرَفَةَ وَالْـمَوْضِعُ عَرَفَاتٍ، قَالَهُ الضَّحَّاكُ.

Ādam ﷺ descended to the Indian Subcontinent and Ḥawwāʾ ﷺ to Jeddah. They eventually met each other at *ʿArafāt* on the day of *ʿArafa*. Therefore, this day became known as *ʿArafa* and the place as *ʿArafāt*. This is the statement of al-Ḍaḥḥāk.[1]

4. Concerning the naming of *al-Muzdalifa*, Ibn Ḥajar al-ʿAsqalānī (773–852 AH), Yāqūt al-Ḥamawī (B. 626 AH) and al-Shawkānī (1173–1250 AH) write:

وَسُمِّيَتِ الْـمُزْدَلِفَةُ جَمْعاً، لِأَنَّ آدَمَ اجْتَمَعَ فِيْهَا مَعَ حَوَّاءَ، وَازْدَلَفَ إِلَيْهَا أَيْ دَنَا مِنْهَا.

Al-Muzdalifa is referred to as '*Jamʿ*' because Ādam joined Ḥawwāʾ ﷺ therein and was in close proximity to her.[2]

5. Concerning the naming of *Minā*, ʿAbd Allāh b. ʿAbbās ﷺ states:

إِنَّمَـا سُمِّيَتْ مِنىً مِنىً لِأَنَّ جِبْرِيْلَ ﷺ حِيْنَ أَرَادَ أَنْ يُفَارِقَ آدَمَ ﷺ، قَالَ لَهُ: تَـمَنَّ. قَالَ: أَتَـمَنَّى الْـجَنَّةَ. فَسُمِّيَتْ مِنًى لِأُمْنِيَّةِ آدَمَ ﷺ.

Minā was named so since when Jibrāʾīl ﷺ intended to separate from Ādam ﷺ, he asked whether he desired

[1] Al-Qurṭubī, *al-Jāmiʿ li-aḥkām al-Qurʾān*, 2:415.

[2] Al-ʿAsqalānī, in *Fatḥ al-Bārī*, 3:523; Yāqūt al-Ḥamawī, *Muʿjam al-Buldān*, 5:121; and al-Shawkānī, *Nayl al-awṭār sharḥ muntaqā al-akhbār*, 1:423.

anything. Ādam ﷺ replied, 'Paradise'. This is why it is named *Minā*—due to the desire of Ādam ﷺ.[1]

Just as the ritual casting of stones (*ramy*), the *saʿy* and the *talbiya* are acts of commemoration in honour of Allah's blessed servants, similarly *ʿArafāt* and *Muzdalifa* are honoured as being places where Ādam and Ḥawwāʾ ﷺ met after a long period of time. It must be stressed that '*ʿArafāt*' and '*Muzdalifa*' literally mean 'recognition'[2] and 'proximity'[3], respectively. Reflect upon how Almighty Allah revives the memory of this momentous reunion annually on the 9th of *Dhū al-Ḥijja* by obliging the attendance of pilgrims there.

1.17 Combining the Prayers at *ʿArafāt* and *Muzdalifa*: Sunna of Prophet Muhammad ﷺ

Muslims, in accordance to the will of Almighty Allah, always perform their ritual prayers in their prescribed times. Yet at the plain of *ʿArafāt,* the pilgrims combine the *ẓuhr* and *ʿaṣr* ritual prayers. This is only because the beloved Prophet ﷺ offered these ritual prayers together, and so it became enjoined on the pilgrims to do the same. Likewise, the pilgrims will combine the *maghrib* and *ʿishā* ritual prayers when the sun sets; the pilgrims do not offer the ritual prayer straight away, but they wait till they reach *Muzdalifa*. This is substantiated by the following traditions:

1. The hadith-scholars quote a lengthy narration from Jābir b. ʿAbd Allāh ﷺ in relation to the Holy Prophet's ﷺ farewell pilgrimage. They have unambiguously stated that the Holy Prophet ﷺ performed the *ẓuhr* and *ʿaṣr* ritual prayers together at *ʿArafāt* with one *adhān* and two *iqāmas*, and the same was done with the

---

[1] Al-Azraqī, *Akhbār Makka wa mā jāʾa fīhā min al-āthār,* 2:180; al-Nawawī, *Tahdhīb al-asmāʾ wa al-lughāt*, 3:333; and al-Qurṭubī, *al-Jāmiʿ li-aḥkām al-Qurʾān*, 3:7.

[2] Al-Farāhīdī, *Kitāb al-ʿayn*, 2:121; and Ibn Manẓūr, *Lisān al-ʿArab*, 9:236 & 242.

[3] Al-Khiṭābī, *Gharīb al-ḥadīth*, 2:24; and Ibn Manẓūr, *Lisān al-ʿArab*, 9:138.

maghrib and *ʿishā*ʾ ritual prayers at *Muzdalifa*.[1]

2. Imam Jaʿfar al-Ṣādiq ؑ narrates from his father Imam al-Bāqir ؑ:

أَنَّ النَّبِيَّ ﷺ صَلَّى الظُّهْرَ وَالْعَصْرَ بِأَذَانٍ وَاحِدٍ بِعَرَفَةَ وَلَمْ يُسَبِّحْ بَيْنَهُمَا، وَإِقَامَتَيْنِ وَصَلَّى الْمَغْرِبَ وَالْعِشَاءَ بِجَمْعٍ بِأَذَانٍ وَاحِدٍ وَإِقَامَتَيْنِ وَلَمْ يُسَبِّحْ بَيْنَهُمَا.

The Prophet ﷺ offered the *ẓuhr* and *ʿasr* ritual prayers, with one *ādhān* and two *iqāmas*, at *ʿArafāt*. He did not recite any glorification of Allah (*al-tasbīḥ*) in between them. He offered the *maghrib* and *ʿishā* ritual prayers combined with one *ādhān* and two *iqāmas* and he did not recite any glorifications between them.[2]

3. ʿAbd Allāh b. Masʿūd ؓ said:

مَا رَأَيْتُ رَسُولَ اللهِ ﷺ صَلَّى صَلَاةً إِلَّا لِمِيقَاتِهَا إِلَّا صَلَاتَيْنِ: صَلَاةَ الْمَغْرِبِ وَالْعِشَاءِ بِجَمْعٍ.

I have never seen Allah's Messenger ﷺ perform the prayer except at its prescribed time, save two prayers: the *maghrib* and *ʿishā* ritual prayers combined.[3]

---

[1] Narrated by Muslim in *al-Ṣaḥīḥ*: *Kitāb al-Ḥajj* [The Book of Pilgrimage], chapter: 'The Prophet's Pilgrimage', 2:886–892 §1217; and Abū Dāwūd in *al-Sunan*: *Kitāb al-Manāsik* [The Book of Pilgrimage Rites], chapter: 'Description of the Prophet's Pilgrimage', 2:185 §1905.

[2] Narrated by Abū Dāwūd in *al-Sunan*: *Kitāb al-Manāsik* [The Book of Pilgrimage Rites], chapter: 'Description of the Prophet's Pilgrimage', 2:186 §1906; and al-Bayhaqī in *al-Sunan al-kubrā*, 1:400 §1741.

[3] Narrated by Muslim in *al-Ṣaḥīḥ*: *Kitāb al-Ḥajj* [The Book of Pilgrimage], chapter: 'Desirability of offering the Morning Prayer when it is dark on the Day of *Naḥr* at *Muzdalifa*', 2:938 §1289; and al-Bukhārī in *al-Ṣaḥīḥ*: *Kitāb al-Ḥajj* [The Book of Pilgrimage], chapter: 'When to offer the *fajr* ritual prayer at *jamʿ* (*Muzdalifa*),' 2:904 §1598.

Although the Qur'ān has ordained the ritual prayer to be performed at its prescribed time[1], during the Pilgrimage, at *ʿArafāt* and *Muzdalifa*, there is an exception to this general rule. This is because it is the practice of the beloved Prophet ﷺ.

1.18 Animal Sacrifice: In Remembrance of Ismāʿīl

The pilgrims, in the performance of their pilgrimage rites, and the Muslims around the globe commemorate the Sunna of Prophet Ibrāhīm by sacrificing an animal on *ʿīd al-aḍḥā*. This sacrifice in essence is an act of remembrance of Ibrāhīm's readiness to sacrifice his beloved son, Ismāʿīl , for the pleasure of Almighty Allah. This sacrifice was so dearly valued that the pilgrims were enjoined to sacrifice an animal annually at the pilgrimage. Not only the pilgrims, but each and every Muslim who has the ability to do so is required to slaughter an animal for the sake of Almighty Allah.

Imam Ḥasan al-Baṣrī (21–110 AH) states:

مَا فُدِيَ إِسْمَاعِيْلُ إِلَّا بِتَيْسٍ كَانَ مِنَ الأُرْوِيِّ أُهْبِطَ عَلَيْهِ مِنْ ثَبِيْرٍ، وَمَا يَقُوْلُ اللهُ: ﴿وَفَدَيْنَٰهُ بِذِبْحٍ عَظِيمٍ﴿١٠٧﴾﴾ لِذَبِيْحَتِهِ فَقَطْ، وَلَكِنَّهُ الذَّبْحُ عَلَى دِيْنِهِ فَتِلْكَ السُّنَّةُ إِلَى يَوْمِ الْقِيَامَةِ، فَاعْلَمُوْا أَنَّ الذَّبِيْحَةَ تَدْفَعُ مَيْتَةَ السُّوْءِ فَضَحُّوْا عِبَادَ اللهِ.

Ismāʿīl's ransom was the slaughtering of a big, healthy ram at *Thabīr* Valley (Mount Mecca). In regards to this, Allah states, ﴾*We ransomed him with a big sacrifice*﴿. This sacrifice specifies the slaughter of the ram as the substitute to Ismāʿīl's sacrifice. Despite this, the *Umma* is required to slaughter an animal annually until the Day of Judgment. (Imam Ḥasan al-Baṣrī addressed the listeners,) 'So you should know that this sacrifice keeps the deceased away from harm, hence you should perform the sacrifice, O people!'[2]

---

[1] Qur'ān 4:103.

[2] Narrated by al-Ṭabarī, *Tārīkh al-umam wa al-mulūk*, 1:167; al-Ṭabarī, in

This act is undoubtedly a celebration of Ibrāhīm ☬ and Ismāʿīl's huge sacrifice so that the believers will hopefully remain connected to the essence of this religion and thereby be ready to surrender their wealth and lives for the sake of Almighty Allah's pleasure.

1.18.1 Sacrificial Animals: One of the Signs of Allah

Although animals are slaughtered worldwide, any creature sacrificed in commemoration of Ismāʿīl ☬ is unique. They are distinctively referred to as the signs of Almighty Allah:

﴿وَٱلْبُدْنَ جَعَلْنَٰهَا لَكُم مِّن شَعَٰٓئِرِ ٱللَّهِ﴾

The animals of sacrifice have been prescribed as signs of Allah for you.[1]

Today, this Sunna of Ibrāhīm ☬ is being relived through the sacrificing of animals. It is a good deed and a means of attaining Almighty Allah's pleasure.

1.19 The Ritual Casting of Stones: The Sunna of Prophet Ibrāhīm ☬

For three days, the pilgrims reside at *Minā*, and they stone the pillars known as the *jamarāt*. This action is in commemoration of Prophet Ibrāhīm ☬.

ʿAbd Allāh b. ʿAbbās ☬ narrates that Allah's Messenger ﷺ said:

«إِنَّ جِبْرِيلَ ذَهَبَ بِإِبْرَاهِيمَ إِلَى جَمْرَةِ الْعَقَبَةِ، فَعَرَضَ لَهُ الشَّيْطَانُ، فَرَمَاهُ بِسَبْعِ حَصَيَاتٍ فَسَاخَ. ثُمَّ أَتَى الْجَمْرَةَ الْوُسْطَى، فَعَرَضَ لَهُ الشَّيْطَانُ، فَرَمَاهُ بِسَبْعِ حَصَيَاتٍ فَسَاخَ. ثُمَّ أَتَى الْجَمْرَةَ الْقُصْوَى، فَعَرَضَ لَهُ

Jāmiʿ al-bayān fī tafsīr al-Qurʾān, 23:87–88; and al-Fākahī, in *Akhbār Makka fī qadīm al-dahr wa ḥadīthihi*, 5:124.

[1] Qurʾān 22:36.

الشَّيْطَانُ، فَرَمَاهُ بِسَبْعِ حَصَيَاتٍ فَسَاخَ.»

Jibrā᾿īl ﷺ took Ibrāhīm ﷺ to *Jamra al-ʿAqaba* whereupon Satan emerged. Ibrāhīm ﷺ cast seven pebbles in his direction upon which Satan fell to the ground. Ibrāhīm ﷺ then proceeded to *Jamra al-Wusṭā* whereupon Satan emerged (for a second time). Ibrāhīm ﷺ cast seven pebbles in his direction upon which Satan fell to the ground. Ibrāhīm ﷺ then proceeded to *Jamra al-Quṣwā* whereupon Satan emerged (for the third time). Ibrāhīm ﷺ cast seven pebbles in his direction upon which Satan fell to the ground.[1]

ʿAbd Allāh b. ʿAbbās ﷺ himself said:

إِنَّ إِبْرَاهِيمَ لَـمَّـا أُمِرَ بِالْـمَنَاسِكِ... ذَهَبَ بِهِ جِبْرِيلُ إِلَى جَمْرَةِ الْعَقَبَةِ فَعَرَضَ لَهُ شَيْطَانٌ، قَالَ يُونُسُ: الشَّيْطَانُ فَرَمَاهُ بِسَبْعِ حَصَيَاتٍ حَتَّى ذَهَبَ، ثُمَّ عَرَضَ لَهُ عِنْدَ الْـجَمْرَةِ الْوُسْطَى، فَرَمَاهُ بِسَبْعِ حَصَيَاتٍ. قَالَ قَدْ ﴿تَلَّهُۥ لِلْجَبِينِ﴾ وَعَلَى إِسْمَاعِيلَ قَمِيصٌ أَبْيَضُ، وَقَالَ: يَا أَبَتِ، إِنَّهُ لَيْسَ لِي ثَوْبٌ تُكَفِّنُنِي فِيهِ غَيْرُهُ، فَاخْلَعْهُ حَتَّى تُكَفِّنَنِي فِيهِ فَعَالَـجَهُ لِيَخْلَعَهُ، فَنُودِيَ مِنْ خَلْفِهِ ﴿أَن يَٰٓإِبْرَٰهِيمُ ١٠٤ قَدْ صَدَّقْتَ ٱلرُّءْيَآ﴾. فَالْتَفَتَ إِبْرَاهِيمُ، فَإِذَا هُوَ بِكَبْشٍ أَبْيَضَ أَقْرَنَ أَعْيَنَ، قَالَ ابْنُ عَبَّاسٍ: لَقَدْ رَأَيْتُنَا نَبِيعُ هَذَا الضَّرْبَ مِنَ الْكِبَاشِ، قَالَ: ثُمَّ ذَهَبَ بِهِ جِبْرِيلُ إِلَى الْـجَمْرَةِ الْقُصْوَى، فَعَرَضَ لَهُ الشَّيْطَانُ، فَرَمَاهُ بِسَبْعِ حَصَيَاتٍ حَتَّى ذَهَبَ.

[1] Narrated by Aḥmad b. Ḥanbal in *al-Musnad*, 1:306; al-Ḥākim in *al-Mustadrak*, 1:638 §1713; al-Bayhaqī in *al-Sunan al-kubrā*, 5:153 §9475; al-Maqdasī in *al-Aḥādīth al-mukhtāra*, 10:283 §296; Mundhirī in *al-Targhīb wa al-tarhīb min al-ḥadīth al-sharīf*, 2:134 §1807; and Ḥaythamī in *Majmaʿ al-zawā᾿id wa manbaʿ al-fawā᾿id*, 3:259.

> When Ibrāhīm ﷺ was ordered to carry out the rites of Pilgrimage, Jibrāʾīl ﷺ took him to *Jamra al-ʿAqaba*, whereupon Satan emerged. Ibrāhīm ﷺ cast seven pebbles at him until he fled. Satan then appeared at *Jamra al-Wusṭā* and was again met with seven stones. (ʿAbd Allāh b. ʿAbbās ﷺ recited the verse,) ﴾*Ibrāhīm ﷺ laid him down on his forehead*﴿.[1] Ismāʿīl ﷺ was wearing a white shirt. He said, 'My dear father, I have no cloth that could be used as a burial shroud, so please remove this shirt from my body so that you can use it to bury me in.' Ibrāhīm ﷺ was on the verge of removing it when a voice was heard from the unseen, ﴾*O Ibrāhīm! (How wonderfully) have you made your dream really true!*﴿ [2] Ibrāhīm ﷺ turned around and saw a beautiful, large-eyed, white ram. ʿAbd Allāh b. ʿAbbās ﷺ said, 'We used to sell this type of ram in the same place.'' He continued, 'Jibrāʾīl ﷺ guided Ibrāhīm ﷺ to *Jamra al-Quṣwā*, whereupon Satan emerged. Ibrāhīm ﷺ again threw seven stones towards him until he fled.[3]

Ibrāhīm ﷺ, whilst directing seven stones at Satan, would simultaneously proclaim Almighty Allah's greatness (*al-takbīr*). In support of this, Mujāhid b. Jubayr (d. 104 AH) states:

خَرَجَ بِإِبْرَاهِيْمَ جِبْرِيْلُ، فَلَمَّـا مَرَّ بِجَمْرَةِ الْعَقَبَةِ إِذَا بِإِبْلِيْسَ عَلَيْهَا، فَقَالَ جِبْرِيْلُ: كَبِّرْ وَارْمِهِ، ثُمَّ ارْتَفَعَ إِبْلِيْسُ إِلَى الْـجَمْرَةِ الْوُسْطَى، فَقَالَ لَهُ جِبْرِيْلُ: كَبِّرْ وَارْمِهِ، ثُمَّ ارْتَفَعَ إِبْلِيْسُ إِلَى الْـجَمْرَةِ الْقُصْوَى، فَقَالَ لَهُ جِبْرِيْلُ: كَبِّرْ وَارْمِهِ.

---

[1] Qurʾān 37:103.

[2] Ibid., 37:104–105.

[3] Narrated by Aḥmad b. Ḥanbal in *al-Musnad*, 1:297; al-Ṭabarānī in *al-Muʿjam al-kabīr*, 10:268 §10,628; al-Bayhaqī in *al-Sunan al-Kubrā*, 5:153–154; Ḥaythamī in *Majmaʿ al-zawāʾid wa manbaʿ al-fawāʾid*, 3:259; al-Ṭabarī, in *Jāmiʿ al-bayān fī tafsīr al-Qurʾān*, 23:80; and Ibn Kathīr, in *al-Tafsīr al-Qurʾān al-ʿaẓīm*, 4:16.

> Ibrāhīm ﷷ went with Jibrāʾīl ﷷ. When he passed *Jamra al-ʿAqaba*, Satan emerged. Jibrāʾīl ﷷ said, 'Say the *takbīr* and stone him.' Satan then appeared at *Jamra al-Wusṭā* and Jibrāʾīl ﷷ said, 'Say the *takbīr* and stone him.' Satan then appeared at *Jamra al-Quṣwā* and Jibrāʾīl ﷷ said, 'Say the *takbīr* and stone him.[1]

Casting pebbles at Satan is not only the Sunna of Prophet Ibrāhīm ﷷ, but it is also the Sunna of Prophet Ādam ﷷ. Imam al-Kalbī writes:

إِنَّمَا سُمِّيَتِ الْجِمَارُ، الْجِمَارَ لِأَنَّ آدَمَ ﷷ كَانَ يَرْمِي إِبْلِيْسَ فَيُجْمِرُ مِنْ بَيْنِ يَدَيْهِ.

> *Jimār* (the place where the stone is cast) is named as such, as Ādam ﷷ would pelt Iblīs as he who would hasten away before him.[2]

This action, which took place at the hands of Almighty Allah's beloved servant thousands of years ago, was so pleasing to Almighty Allah that the *Umma* was ordained to re-enact it (in the form of pilgrimage rites). It became a necessary part of the Pilgrimage; without it, the Pilgrimage remains incomplete.

This action is not void of meaning and purpose, as it teaches us three things:

(i) A continuation of the Sunna of prophets.

(ii) Through the replication of these acts, sentiments of love and obedience to the prophets are expressed.

(iii) By pelting the pillars which represent the devil, Muslims express their hatred for Satan.

The whole sum of this entire discussion is that expressing emotions by bringing to mind a certain historic incident is not only permissible in the Sharia, but it is also one of the customs laid by Almighty Allah. In light of this, if today Muslims were to

---

[1] Narrated by al-Azraqī in *Akhbār Makka wa mā jāʾa fīhā min al-āthār,* 1:68.

[2] Ibid., 2:181.

express their joy and happiness upon the blessed birth of Allah's Messenger ﷺ in the form of religious gatherings, then doing so would be perfectly valid.

These celebrations serve to strengthen our personal relationship with the beloved Prophet ﷺ and are means of increasing our love and faith in him. To remember the beloved and to be annihilated in his love are states which are valued in the sight of Almighty Allah. With sincere intentions, travelling to the Holy Sanctuary for the Pilgrimage keeps alive our remembrance of Prophet Ibrāhīm ﷺ, and as a result, Almighty Allah forgives our minor and major sins.[1] Comparatively, what then would be the recompense of the Muslim who conveys salutations upon the greatest Prophet ﷺ and strengthens the connection of love with him through the celebration of *Mawlid al-Nabī* ﷺ? After all, isn't love of the Prophet ﷺ the essence of faith?

1.19.1 AN OBJECTION

There are some people who do not celebrate *Mawlid al-Nabī* ﷺ. Their objection is that celebrating the Prophet's ﷺ birth is not important, but obeying him is—after all, the purpose of his sending was to guide us and to instruct us in the Sharia. Thus, our sole concern should be to follow his teachings by living our lives in accordance to the Qur'ān and Sunna whilst advising others to

---

[1] Abū Hurayra ؓ narrates that the Prophet ﷺ said:

«مَنْ حَجَّ للهِ فَلَمْ يَرْفُثْ وَلَمْ يَفْسُقْ، رَجَعَ كَيَوْمِ وَلَدَتْهُ أُمُّهُ.»

Whoever performs the Pilgrimage, and commits no indecency or offence, he will return (purified from sin) like the day his mother gave birth to him.

> Narrated by al-Bukhārī in *al-Ṣaḥīḥ*: *Kitāb al-Ḥajj* [The Book of Pilgrimage], chapter: 'The merits of an accepted Pilgrimage,' 2:553 §1449; Ibn al-Jaʿd in *al-Musnad*, p.141 §896; Ibn Mundah in *al-Īmān*, p.392 §230; al-Maqdisī in *Faḍāʾil al-Aʿmāl*, p.81 §347; and al-Ṭabarī, in *Jāmiʿ al-bayān fī tafsīr al-Qurʾān*, 2:277.

do the same. According to the objectors, celebrating *mawlid* and investing one's efforts in it is pointless and a waste of time.

1.19.2 Our Reply to this Objection

Our point of view is that there is no denying of the fact that the most exalted Prophet ﷺ was sent to bless us with the light of guidance in the form of his Sunna, and Islam as a complete way of life. In this respect, there is no difference of opinion. Following in the footsteps of the most exalted Prophet ﷺ and living our lives in accordance to the teaching of Islam is binding on us. And we, by the grace of Almighty Allah, have struggled, intellectually and practically, for the establishment of Islam. Where we disagree is on the importance and significance of *Mawlid al-Nabī* ﷺ, and this is a different matter altogether.

There is no discussion here on adhering to and following the Sunna of the Prophet ﷺ, as this is one important aspect of the religion. However, there are other aspects too. The religion does not solely comprise actions, but also emotions, such as love and adoration; and it is with this aspect that the celebration of *Mawlid al-Nabī* ﷺ is related.

Almighty Allah conferred an extremely great blessing on humanity by raising His beloved Messenger ﷺ amongst us. The day in which he was born is a day of immense happiness and joy, and a day of showing gratitude. Almighty Allah has showered His bounty and mercy upon us in the form of the blessed Prophet ﷺ. This is why expressing gratitude by celebrating the day of his birth is of great merit. This is one important point which cannot be ignored.

There are events, which took place many millennia before us, in which there is a message. Take the Pilgrimage rites for example; at first glance, there is no correlation between the various rites. Apparently, these were different events which have now passed. What lessons can these events hold for us in the practical sense? From this, we can deduce that Islam is affirming both realities: it holds significant the aspects of the religious teaching which are related to the divine rulings, as this is the requirement for establishing the religion; and it also holds important the emotional aspect which plays a role in our lives by keeping historic memories alive in our hearts and mind. In essence, Islam takes a two-angle approach to past incidents: the practical approach and the emotional approach.

Expressing unrelenting happiness on the birth of the Prophet ﷺ is in respect to its historical, cultural, and spiritual significance. That is, this incident should not be forgotton as it should be kept alive in our hearts. For this reason, on the occasion of *Mawlid al-Nabī* ﷺ, there is an atmosphere of joy and happiness, so that this incident is given the respect that it deserves.

In the pages that precede us, it is clear that the rites of Pilgrimage are in reality related to events which are linked to the lives of Almighty Allah's blessed servants. These events are commemorated as His signs. If there is no dispute on this, then there should be no objection to celebrating *Mawlid al-Nabī* ﷺ.

Chapter 2

Remembering Events of Joy and Sorrow

THE BIRTH OF THE MOST EXALTED PROPHET ﷺ IS THE MOST magnificent occurrence in history. It is the day in which the Mercy to the Worlds ﷺ came. In expressing joy and happiness, no day can be greater than it. Happiness and despair, tranquillity and fear, and hope and disappointment are those aspects of human life which shape one's mind-set at the individual and collective level. Almighty Allah, by bestowing favours upon bygone nations, made them prosperous with the wealth of happiness and ease whilst threatening them with His punishment and making an example of them if they were ungrateful to Him and disobedient.

Guidance is related to the psychological reality of man. Until the seed of sincerity flowers in a person's heart, one's actions will fail to bear fruits. When a person attains spiritual states, and his heart and mind become enlightened, the light of guidance descends on him; and with this light, he travels through life's journey with strides.

To benefit from these states, one must acknowledge that the source of those states comes down to one's connections. In the absence of his son, Prophet Yaʿqūb ﷺ lost his eye-sight on account of grief. This prophet of Almighty Allah was absorbed in a state of sorrow. But when Prophet Yūsuf ﷺ sent his shirt to be placed over his father's eyes, Yaʿqūb's grief was replaced with happiness and his eye-sight returned. His state went from one of patience to gratitude. This all came down to connections, as the shirt was connected to Prophet Yūsuf ﷺ.

Similarly, in our lives, there are incidents which revolve around such connections. There are items in our homes which have been passed down from generation to generation; such items are preserved as artefacts—even touching them brings back memories. Likewise, our feelings of joy and sorrow are related to such connections, and it is from these connections that our inner states are spawned and cultivated.

There are several anecdotes in the prophetic traditions in which the most exalted Prophet ﷺ, through his own practice, imparted on this *Umma* the lesson to re-enact historic incidents by imitating the states of joy and sorrow. If we reflect carefully upon these anecdotes, we shall see that the states of joy and sorrow are a result of a certain connection, which in turn is tied to a certain person. Some of these anecdotes which have been reported in the prophetic traditions are mentioned below:

2.1 On Commemorating the Day of Mūsā ﷺ

When the most exalted Prophet ﷺ migrated to Medina, he questioned the Jews who were residing there about their fasting on the 10th of *Muḥarram*. They replied that this is the day when Almighty Allah granted Mūsā ﷺ victory by drowning Pharaoh and his army. It was the day when the Children of Israel were delivered from Pharaoh's tyranny and oppression. For this reason, Mūsā ﷺ, expressed his gratitude to Almighty Allah and fasted on that day, and so we fast on this day too. The Holy Prophet ﷺ hearing this replied that I am closer to Mūsā ﷺ than you (in terms of both being Allah's prophets). Thereafter, the Holy Prophet ﷺ would fast on the 10th of *Muḥarram* whilst ordering his Companions to do the same.[1]

From this, it is clear that the Children of Israel, on this national occasion, expressed their happiness by fasting as a way of commemorating this day; the Prophet ﷺ, as a means of expressing

---

[1] Narrated by al-Bukhārī in *al-Ṣaḥīḥ*: *Kitāb al-Ṣawm* [The Book of Fasting], chapter: 'The fast of *Yawm ʿĀshūrā*'', 2:704 §1900; al-Bukhārī in *al-Ṣaḥīḥ*: *Kitāb al-Anbiyāʾ* [The Book of Prophets], chapter: 'Allah's statement: Has the news of Moses reached you', 3:1244 §3216; al-Bukhārī in *al-Ṣaḥīḥ*: *Kitāb Faḍāʾil al-Ṣaḥāba* [The Book of the virtues of the Companions], chapter: 'The Jews coming to the Prophet when he arrived in Medina', 3:1434 §3727; Muslim in *al-Ṣaḥīḥ*: *Kitāb al-Ṣiyām* [The Book of Fasting], chapter: 'The fast of *Yawm ʿĀshūrā*'', 2:795–796 §1130; Abū Dāwūd in *al-Sunan*: *Kitāb al-Ṣawm* [The Book of Fasting], chapter: 'The fast of *Yawm ʿĀshūrā*'', 2:326 §2444; Ibn Mājah in *al-Sunan*: *Kitāb al-Ṣiyām* [The Book of Fasting], chapter: 'The fast of *Yawm ʿĀshūrā*'', 1:552 §1734; Aḥmad b. Ḥanbal in *al-Musnad*, 1:291 & 336 §2644 & 3112; and Abū Yaʿlā in *al-Musnad*, 4:441 §2567.

his happiness for that occasion, likewise commemorated this day by fasting.

2.2 On Commemorating the Day of Nūḥ ﷺ

Imam Aḥmad b. Ḥanbal (164–241 AH) and Ḥāfiẓ Ibn Ḥajar al-ʿAsqalānī (773–852 AH) relate another significant aspect of *Yawm ʿĀshūrāʾ* from Abū Hurayra ؓ in that *Yawm ʿĀshūrāʾ* is the day wherein Almighty Allah blessed Nūḥ ﷺ and his Companions—it was the day on which they descended from the ark on Mount Judi. From then on, Nūḥ ﷺ and his Companions expressed their gratitude to Almighty Allah, and it was commemorated by succeeding generations as a significant day of reverence. On this day, the most exalted Prophet ﷺ would keep a fast and command his noble Companions to do so as well.[1]

2.3 The Day of Islam's Completion: A Day of Festivity (ʿĪd)

Kaʿb al-Aḥbār ؓ narrates that he said to ʿUmar b. al-Khaṭṭāb ؓ: 'I know a people had this verse been revealed upon them, they would have taken that day as a day of festivity (*ʿīd*). ʿUmar ؓ enquired: 'And which verse is this?' And Kaʿb ؓ replied:

﴿ٱلْيَوْمَ أَكْمَلْتُ لَكُمْ دِينَكُمْ وَأَتْمَمْتُ عَلَيْكُمْ نِعْمَتِي وَرَضِيتُ
لَكُمُ ٱلْإِسْلَٰمَ دِينًا﴾

Today I have perfected your Dīn (Religion) for you, and have completed My Blessing upon you, and have chosen for you Islam (as) Dīn (a complete code of life).[2]

ʿUmar ؓ remarked:

---

[1] Narrated by Aḥmad b. Ḥanbal in *al-Musnad*, 2:359–360 §8702; and al-ʿAsqalānī, in *Fatḥ al-Bārī*, 4:247.

[2] Qurʾān 5:3.

إِنِّي لَأَعْرِفُ فِي أَيِّ يَوْمٍ أُنْزِلَتْ: ﴿ٱلْيَوْمَ أَكْمَلْتُ لَكُمْ دِينَكُمْ﴾، يَوْمَ جُمُعَةٍ وَيَوْمَ عَرَفَةَ، وَهُمَا لَنَا عِيْدَانِ.

I know the day in which the verse, ﴿*Today I have perfected your Dīn for you*﴾ was revealed: it was the day of *ʿArafa* and a Friday; and they are both (already) days of *ʿĪd* for us.[1]

Here, it was Kaʿb ﵁ who articulated his thoughts that the day on which this glad tiding was received should be taken as a day of *ʿĪd*; and it was ʿUmar ﵁ who approved and verified it. From this, it can be learnt that in our national and communal life, there are events which have a significant impact that should be commemorated in the form of an *ʿĪd*; this is not contradictory to the spirit of the Qurʾān and Sunna. Rather, it is a recommended act which is of national and communal importance.[2]

2.4 The Prophet's Instruction whilst Passing-by *al-Ḥijr*

In the year 9 AH, during the expedition to *Tabūk*, the Muslim army passed by two wells which belong to the people of *Thamūd*. Concerning that place, the Holy Prophet ﷺ stated that this was the place where the community of Prophet Ṣāliḥ ﵇ slaughtered the she-camel, and as a result, they were punished by Almighty Allah. The Messenger ﷺ only allowed his noble Companions to obtain water from one of the wells in order to fulfil their needs whilst prohibiting them from drawing water from the other.

The well from which the Holy Prophet ﷺ ordered his noble Companions to draw water was the same well from which the she-camel would drink. The she-camel had her allocated day, but the people of *Thamūd* were unable to bear this, so they hamstrung and killed her.

---

[1] Al-Ṭabaranī, *al-Muʿjam al-Awsaṭ*, 1:253 §830; al-ʿAsqalānī, in *Fatḥ al-Bārī*, 1:105 §45; and Ibn Kathīr, in *al-Tafsīr al-Qurʾān al-ʿaẓīm*, 2:14.

[2] For further details on commemorating incidents of joy, refer to the fifth chapter of this book.

This incident occurred centuries ago, and undoubtedly, the well by then had changed; but despite this, Allah's Messenger ﷺ gave it much importance. This well was connected to Ṣāliḥ's she-camel, and on account of its blessings, the Holy Prophet ﷺ instructed his noble Companions to draw water from it. As for the well which was used by the people of *Thamūd*, the Holy Prophet ﷺ forbade his noble Companions from using its water, as they were the ones who were sounded the warning of Almighty Allah's chastisement. On this act of treachery (of killing the she-camel), Almighty Allah sent down His punishment, and they were annihilated as a result. With this in mind, the Holy Prophet ﷺ prohibited them from making use of its water.

Prior to the announcement of this sanction, a group of noble Companions had unknowingly utilised water from the wells of *Thamūd*. Upon hearing the announcement, they entreated to the Holy Prophet ﷺ; they said that they had already used its waters, as they did not know that it was prohibited. The Holy Prophet ﷺ bade them to dispose the water and the foodstuff, which they prepared, and to replace it with water from the well which was connected to the she-camel.

The following are Prophetic traditions which elaborate this further:

2.4.1 THE PROHIBITION OF DRINKING WATER FROM THE WELL OF *THAMŪD* AT *AL-ḤIJR*

ʿAbd Allāh b. ʿUmar ؓ narrates:

أَنَّ رَسُولَ اللهِ ﷺ لَمَّا نَزَلَ الْحِجْرَ فِي غَزْوَةِ تَبُوكَ، أَمَرَهُمْ أَنْ لَا يَشْرَبُوا مِنْ بِئْرِهَا وَلَا يَسْتَقُوا مِنْهَا. فَقَالُوا: قَدْ عَجَنَّا مِنْهَا وَاسْتَقَيْنَا، فَأَمَرَهُمْ أَنْ يَطْرَحُوا ذَلِكَ الْعَجِينَ، وَيُهَرِيقُوا ذَلِكَ الْمَاءَ.

On the expedition to *Tabūk*, Allah's Messenger ﷺ stopped at *al-Ḥijr*, he ordered the Companions not to drink from its wells or draw water from them. (Some of the Companions) said, 'We have kneaded the dough from it and have drawn its water (to fill our water-skins).' The Prophet ﷺ instructed them to throw away the dough and pour away the water.[1]

2.4.2 The Injunction of Drinking Water from the Well Connected to Ṣāliḥ's She-Camel

ʿAbd Allāh b. ʿUmar ؓ narrates that some people accompanying Allah's Messenger ﷺ at *al-Ḥijr* (*Thamūd*'s native land) drew water from its wells using it to prepare the dough and fill their water-skins.

فَأَمَرَهُمْ رَسُولُ اللهِ ﷺ أَنْ يُهَرِيقُوا مَا اسْتَقَوْا مِنْ بِئْرِهَا، وَأَنْ يَعْلِفُوا الْإِبِلَ الْعَجِينَ، وَأَمَرَهُمْ أَنْ يَسْتَقُوا مِنْ الْبِئْرِ الَّتِي كَانَتْ تَرِدُهَا النَّاقَةُ.

Allah's Messenger ﷺ ordered the Companions to pour away the water which they drew from its well; and to feed the dough to the camels. And he ordered them to draw water from the well belonging to the she-camel.[2]

ʿAbd Allāh b. ʿUmar ؓ reports that in the year of the expedition to *Tabūk*, the Muslims camped by the ruins of *Thamūd*. They had filled their utensils with its waters, prepared the dough, and cooked the meat.

---

[1] Narrated by al-Bukhārī in *al-Ṣaḥīḥ*: *Kitāb al-Anbiyā*ʾ [The Book of the Prophets], chapter: 'Allah's statement: And to *Thamūd* their brother, Ṣāliḥ', 3:1236–1237 §3198; al-Qurṭubī in *al-Jāmiʿ li-aḥkām al-Qurʾān*, 10:46; al-Baghawī in *Muʿālim al-tanzīl*, 2:178; Ibn Ḥazm in *al-Muḥallā*, 1:220; and al-ʿAsqalānī, in *Taghlīq al-taʿlīq*, 4:19.

[2] Narrated by al-Bukhārī in *al-Ṣaḥīḥ*: *Kitāb al-Anbiyā*ʾ [The Book of the Prophets], chapter: 'Allah's statement: And to *Thamūd* their brother, Ṣāliḥ', 3:1237 §3199; Muslim in *al-Ṣaḥīḥ*: *Kitāb al-Zuhd* [The Book of Renunciation], chapter: 'Enter not the dwelling of those who wronged themselves', 4:2286 §2981; Ibn Ḥibbān in *al-Ṣaḥīḥ*, 14:82 §6202; al-Bayhaqī in *al-Sunan al-kubrā*, 1:235 §1050; and al-Qurṭubī in *al-Jāmiʿ li-aḥkām al-Qurʾān*, 10:46.

فَأَمَرَهُمْ رَسُولُ اللهِ ﷺ فَأَهَرَاقُوا الْقُدُورَ وَعَلَفُوا الْعَجِينَ الإِبِلَ، ثُمَّ ارْتَحَلَ بِهِمْ حَتَّى نَزَلَ بِهِمْ عَلَى الْبِئْرِ الَّتِي كَانَتْ تَشْرَبُ مِنْهَا النَّاقَةُ. وَنَهَاهُمْ أَنْ يَدْخُلُوا عَلَى الْقَوْمِ الَّذِينَ عُذِّبُوا، قَالَ: إِنِّي أَخْشَى أَنْ يُصِيبَكُمْ مِثْلُ مَا أَصَابَهُمْ، فَلَا تَدْخُلُوا عَلَيْهِمْ.

> Allah's Messenger ﷺ (when he became aware of this) bade them (to dispose of that water); and they emptied their utensils and fed the camels the dough. Then he brought them to the well from which the she-camel used to drink. He prohibited them from entering (the homes) of those who were punished, saying, 'I fear that what afflicted them may be afflicted on you, so do not enter upon them.'[1]

It is interesting to note that this water *per se* was not unfit for use—according to the Sharia, this water was pure. Simply because this water was connected to a people who were punished for killing the she-camel, the Holy Prophet ﷺ forbade his Companions from using it. In contrast to this, the other well was connected to Prophet Ṣāliḥ's she-camel; and on account of its connection, it was honoured and declared a source of grace and blessing.

2.4.3 In Remembrance of Prophet Ṣāliḥ's She-Camel

The points mentioned above clearly demonstrate that any blessing which is connected to a prophet or messenger is established permanently. Respecting such connections and obtaining blessings from them is a lesson which is being imparted by the Holy Prophet ﷺ himself. It is certainly worth noting that the well in question is the well from which Prophet Ṣāliḥ's she-camel drank; Prophet Ṣāliḥ ﷺ has not been mentioned as drinking from it.

Millennia have passed, and Allah knows best how much the

[1] Narrated by Aḥmad b. Ḥanbal in *al-Musnad*, 2:117 §5984; and Ibn Ḥibbān in *al-Ṣaḥīḥ*, 14:83 §6203. Imam Aḥmad's narration fulfils the conditions set by Imam al-Bukhārī and Imam Muslim.

water has changed since or whether the water drank by the she-camel is still the same; but, the only certain thing is the connection between the she-camel, attributed to one of Allah's prophets, and the well. This connection is held in such high esteem that even after such a lapse of time, its water is respected and its blessings intact.

2.4.4 Expressing Sorrow whilst Remembering the Punishment Inflicted on *Thamūd*

A long time has passed since the people of *Thamūd* last walked on the face of the earth; not a single trace of them remains. The fate that befell them is now long gone. Yet Allah's Messenger ﷺ forbade his noble Companions from entering their dwellings and instructed them to pass by their ruins in a state of grief whilst shedding tears, as though the chastisement was still befalling upon them.

ʿAbd Allāh b. ʿUmar ؓ narrates that the Prophet ﷺ said:

«لَا تَدْخُلُوا مَسَاكِنَ الَّذِينَ ظَلَمُوا أَنْفُسَهُمْ، إِلَّا أَنْ تَكُونُوا بَاكِينَ أَنْ يُصِيبَكُمْ مَا أَصَابَهُمْ.»

> Do not enter the dwellings of those who wronged themselves except in a tearful state, lest the same castigation comes upon you.[1]

The Holy Prophet's ﷺ instruction, with regards to this ill-fated community, was to pass by their ruins in sorrow whilst shedding tears. The most compassionate Prophet ﷺ, through his noble Companions, is giving this *Umma* advice that when recounting the anecdotes of perished nations, we should recount them in a way that one should express humility before Almighty Allah so that

---

[1] Narrated by al-Bukhārī in *al-Ṣaḥīḥ*: *Kitāb al-Anbiyāʾ* [The Book of the Prophets], chapter: 'Allah's statement: And to *Thamūd* their brother, Ṣāliḥ', 3:1237 §3200–3201; Muslim in *al-Ṣaḥīḥ*: *Kitāb al-Zuhd* [The Book of Renunciation], chapter: 'Enter not the dwelling of those who wronged themselves', 4:2285–2286 §2980; Aḥmad b. Ḥanbal in *al-Musnad*, 2:96; Ibn Ḥibbān in *al-Ṣaḥīḥ*, 14:80 §6199; and al-Rūyānī in *al-Musnad*, 2:407 §1409.

His punishment may not afflict us as it afflicted them. Though apparently, such was not the case as the Prophet's ﷺ blessed presence is deterrence from such a thing happening, but even then they were instructed to create within themselves states and feelings of grief and sorrow. This is the lesson that we can learn from this prophetic tradition.

This topic is related to the feelings and emotions of the heart and soul. Imam Muslim has transmitted this narration in his '*al-Ṣaḥīḥ*' in the book, '*Kitāb al-Raqā'iq*' [The book of renunciation and softening the heart]. The Imam wanted to convey the message that this topic is related to those deeds and actions which have a spiritualising effect on one's heart and soul. By mentioning anecdotes of this kind, a special feeling or emotion is created inside a person, which results in one changing their life at the spiritual level. If there was no psychological or spiritual benefit to one's soul, then why would the most compassionate Prophet ﷺ feel the need of instructing his noble Companions to recreate the experience? He would not order them to do something which had no effect on purifying and rectifying their internal state. The fact that the most compassionate Prophet ﷺ instructed them to do this means that these states invariably have an effect.

ʿAbd Allāh b. ʿUmar ؓ narrates that the Prophet ﷺ said:

«لَا تَدْخُلُوا عَلَى هَؤُلَاءِ الْمُعَذَّبِينَ إِلَّا أَنْ تَكُونُوا بَاكِينَ؛ فَإِنْ لَمْ تَكُونُوا بَاكِينَ، فَلَا تَدْخُلُوا عَلَيْهِمْ لَا يُصِيبُكُمْ مَا أَصَابَهُمْ.»

Do not enter upon these people afflicted with punishment except in a tearful state. If you are unable to be tearful, then do not enter upon them, lest the same castigation comes upon you.[1]

[1] Narrated by al-Bukhārī in *al-Ṣaḥīḥ*: *Kitāb al-Masājid* [The Book of Mosques], chapter: 'The ritual prayer in places of punishment', 1:167 §423; al-Bukhārī in *al-Ṣaḥīḥ*: *Kitāb al-Magāzī* [The Book of Military Expeditions], chapter: 'The Prophet's encampment at *al-Ḥijr*', 4:1609 §4158; Muslim in *al-Ṣaḥīḥ*: *Kitāb al-Zuhd* [The Book of Renunciation], chapter: 'Enter not the dwelling of those who wronged themselves', 4:2285

The Holy Prophet ﷺ is forbidding his noble Companions from entering the dwellings of *Thamūd* as though they are still living there. This is because these people were made an example of by Almighty Allah for the crime they committed in killing the she-camel. Even though this incident took place a long time ago, it is the most compassionate Prophet ﷺ who is giving the order to bring to mind this divine retribution and to create within oneself fear of Almighty Allah.

The most exalted Prophet ﷺ enjoined his noble Companions to envisage the punishment of Almighty Allah so that a state would befall them that would make them weep when they pass by their ruins. And if they were unable to do so, then they were instructed not to enter its valleys. Some of the Companions entreated to the Holy Prophet ﷺ, asking what they should do if they could not bring themselves to tears. Replying to this, ʿAbd Allāh b. ʿUmar ؓ narrates that the Prophet ﷺ said:

«فَإِنْ لَـمْ تَبْكُوا فَتَبَاكَوْا، خَشْيَةَ أَنْ يُصِيبَكُمْ مِثْلُ مَا أَصَابَهُمْ.»

> If you are unable to weep, then endeavour to weep fearing that what afflicted them may afflict you.[1]

Weeping is better; but if one is unable to weep, one should try to bring it on by impersonating someone who is. The whole point of this is that by imagining Almighty Allah's punishment, one is brought to a state fear, and as a result, one is humbled before Him, seeking His refuge. This incident took place long ago and its moments have passed, but despite this, the Holy Prophet ﷺ is reminiscing it by reliving its memory with his noble Companions.

---

§2980; al-Bayhaqī in *al-Sunan al-kubrā*, 2:451; and ʿAbd b. Ḥumayd, in *al-Musnad*, 1:255 §798.

[1] Ibn Kathīr in *al-Bidāya wa al-nihāya*, 1:138; Ibn Kathīr, in *al-Tafsīr al-Qurʾān al-ʿaẓīm*, 2:557; and al-ʿAsqalānī, in *Fatḥ al-Bārī*, 6:380.

2.4.5 The Prophet's Own Action whilst Passing by *al-Ḥijr*

Whilst passing by the dwellings of *Thamūd*, the chief of the created beings, the Prophet ﷺ paced hastily, sheltering himself with his cloak, and imagining that the punishment was descending at that moment.

ᶜAbd Allāh b. ᶜUmar ؓ narrates:

ثُمَّ تَقَنَّعَ بِرِدَائِهِ وَهُوَ عَلَى الرَّحْلِ.

The Prophet ﷺ sheltered himself with his cloak whilst seated on his riding animal.[1]

ᶜAbd Allāh b. ᶜUmar ؓ also reports:

لَـمَّـا مَرَّ النَّبِيُّ ﷺ بِالْـحِجْرِ، قَالَ: «لَا تَدْخُلُوا مَسَاكِنَ الَّذِينَ ظَلَمُوا أَنْفُسَهُمْ أَنْ يُصِيبَكُمْ مَا أَصَابَهُمْ، إِلَّا أَنْ تَكُونُوا بَاكِينَ.» ثُمَّ قَنَّعَ رَأْسَهُ وَأَسْرَعَ السَّيْرَ حَتَّى أَجَازَ الْوَادِيَ.

When the Prophet ﷺ passed by *al-Ḥijr*, he said, "Do not enter the dwellings of those who wronged themselves, lest the same castigation comes upon you—pass by them in a tearful state." Then he sheltered his blessed head, and paced hastily until he passed the way.[2]

---

[1] Narrated by al-Bukhārī in *al-Ṣaḥīḥ*: *Kitāb al-Anbiyā*ʾ [The Book of the Prophets], 'Allah's statement: And to *Thamūd* their brother, Ṣāliḥ', 3:1237 §3200; Aḥmad b. Ḥanbal in *al-Musnad*, 2:66; al-Nasāʾī in *al-Sunan al-kubrā*, 6:373 §11,270; and Ibn Mubārak in *al-Zuhd*, p.543 §1556.

[2] Narrated by al-Bukhārī in *al-Ṣaḥīḥ*: *Kitāb al-Magāzī* [The Book of Military Expeditions], chapter: 'The Prophet's encampment at *al-Ḥijr*', 4:1609 §4157; Muslim in *al-Ṣaḥīḥ*: *Kitāb al-Zuhd* [The Book of Renunciation], chapter: 'Enter not the dwelling of those who wronged themselves', 4:2286 §2980; ᶜAbd al-Razzāq, in *al-Muṣannaf*, 1:415 §1624; and al-Bayhaqī in *al-Sunan al-kubrā*, 2:451.

The Prophet's sheltering his head whilst making a speedy flight past the valley, as well as his commanding his noble Companions to be in a tearful state, are actions which contain for us much wisdom.

2.4.5.1 Points to Consider

The following points can be derived from these prophetic traditions:

Firstly, we should keep in mind that the very presence of the most powerful Prophet ﷺ is a source of Almighty Allah's mercy and a deterrent against His wrath and punishment; thus, there was not a single iota of possibility that the punishment could have descended upon them whilst the Holy Prophet ﷺ was physically present in their midst. Furthermore, the expedition consisted of the Prophet's noble Companions who had set out in the way of Almighty Allah—there was not a single disbeliever amongst them, God-forbid. There has never been a better company on the face of the earth, throughout history. Is it fathomable that Almighty Allah would send His punishment upon such noble personalities?

At that time, the people of *Thamūd*, who committed the grave injustice of hamstringing the she-camel, no longer existed. Despite this, the most compassionate Prophet ﷺ gave counsel to his noble Companions that they should envisage the punishment descending, and they should recreate the experience of fear and apprehension in their hearts and minds. Thus, every Companion wept bitterly and expressed remorse as though the punishment was actually going to descend.

Secondly, another important point is that the noble Companions were not alone in this expedition: the chief of the created beings, the esteemed Prophet ﷺ, was with them. In this regard, Almighty Allah states:

﴿وَمَا كَانَ ٱللَّهُ لِيُعَذِّبَهُمْ وَأَنتَ فِيهِمْ﴾

Allah shall not punish a people whilst you (the Prophet) are amongst them.[1]

[1] Qur'ān 8:33.

Despite being aware of this glad-tiding, the noble Companions recalled the fate of *Thamūd* and brought themselves to submission out of fear of Almighty Allah. By doing this, they implemented the Holy Prophet's teachings and fulfilled one of the requirements of Islam, namely that one expresses happiness on occasions of joy, and grief on occasions of sorrow. In order to create a psychological atmosphere in the heart and mind, one should reminisce the emotions that are expected from the event. A place has been made for this in order to develop such emotions and feelings in one's heart.

It should be noted that there is a great difference between feeling something naturally and creating a feeling for something. When a person has firm belief and his connection is strong, his states of emotions arise on impulse. This can only be attained through truly realising one's servitude to Allah's Messenger ﷺ. When it is an occasion of sorrow, one's tears fall effortlessly on account of sadness; and if it is an occasion of joy, one naturally breaks into a smile out of happiness and delight. To reminisce past incidents in such a way is in exact accordance with the Prophet's ﷺ intent, and this has been proven from the traditions.

Finally, one last point is that the most compassionate Prophet ﷺ did not only instruct his noble Companions to pass by the valley in a tearful state, but the Prophet ﷺ himself passed by it while sheltering his blessed head with his cloak and pacing swiftly on his camel. One would have felt that it was as if the Holy Prophet ﷺ was fleeing far away from these people who were on the brink of annihilation.

Why did the Holy Prophet ﷺ feel the need for this, in spite of the fact that this incident took place many millennia ago? The most exalted Prophet's station in the sight of Almighty Allah is such that wherever he went, blessings would descend, and punishment would be averted. The Prophet ﷺ himself is a paragon of mercy and an intercessor for mankind. The one for whose sake Almighty Allah averts His punishment—how can he be embroiled in fear of it? Thinking such a thing is not possible, even a person with the weakest *Īmān* (faith) would not think that. Therefore, if the Prophet ﷺ fled from this valley in that state, it was only to teach this *Umma* a lesson.

2.5 Remembering the Punishment of the People of the Elephants and Swiftly Passing through the Valley of *Muḥassir*

There is a difference of opinion regarding the location of *Muḥassir* valley: one opinion is that it is a region close to *Muzdalifa*[1]; another opinion, according to Faḍl b. ʿAbbās 🌺, is that it is in *Minā*[2]. Reconciling these two opinions, ʿAbd al-Ḥaqq Muḥaddith al-Dihlawī states that the reality is that *Muḥassir* valley is in fact an area between *Minā* and *Muzdalifa*.[3] The entire vicinity of *Muzdalifa* is a place where pilgrims are stationed, but they are prohibited from being stationed at *Muḥassir* valley[4], as it falls outside of its vicinity.

On the 10th of *Dhū al-Ḥijja*, just before sunrise (in the time left to offer two cycles of ritual prayer), the pilgrims, whilst reciting the *talbiya*, depart from *Muzdalifa* for *Minā*; and when they approach the valley of *Muḥassir*, they are to quicken their pace and travel swiftly whilst simultaneously seeking refuge in Almighty Allah from His punishment.[5]

Why is this so? The reason for this is that prior to the Holy Prophet's birth, Abraha intended to destroy the *Kaʿba* with an army of elephants. When he reached the *Muḥassir* valley with

---

[1] Yāqūt Ḥamawī, *Muʿjam al-Buldān*, 1:449.

[2] Narrated by Muslim in *al-Ṣaḥīḥ*: *Kitāb al-Ḥajj* [The Book of Pilgrimage], chapter: 'The duration the pilgrim recites the talbiya' 2:931 §1282; al-Nasāʾī in *al-Sunan*: *Kitāb Manāsik al-Ḥajj* [The Book of Pilgrimage Rites], chapter: 'Order on being calm when travelling from *ʿArafa*', 5:285 §3020; al-Nasāʾī in *al-Sunan al-kubrā*, 2:434 §4056; Aḥmad b. Ḥanbal in *al-Musnad*, 1:210 §1796; and al-Bayhaqī in *al-Sunan al-kubrā*, 5:127 §9316.

[3] ʿAbd al-Ḥaqq al-Dihlawī, *Ashʿat al-lumʿāt sharḥ mishkāt al-maṣābīḥ*, 2:345.

[4] Narrated by Aḥmad b. Ḥanbal in *al-Musnad*, 4:82 §16,797; Ibn Ḥibbān in *al-Ṣaḥīḥ*, 9:166 §3854; al-Shaybānī in *Kitāb al-Mabsūṭ*, 2:422; Ibn Abī Shayba in *al-Muṣannaf*, 3:246 §13884–13885; al-Daylamī in *al-Firdaws bi-maʾthūr al-khiṭāb*, 3:44 §4113; al-Bayhaqī in *al-Sunan al-kubrā*, 9:295 §19,021; al-Ṭabarānī, *al-Muʿjam al-kabīr*, 2:138 §1583; al-Haythamī in *Majmaʿ al-zawāʾid wa manbaʿ al-fawāʾid*, 3:251; and al-Haythamī in *Majmaʿ al-zawāʾid wa manbaʿ al-fawāʾid*, 4:25.

[5] Wahba al-Zuḥaylī, *al-Fiqh al-Islāmī wa adillatuhu*, 3:2168.

his ill-intent, the wrath of Almighty Allah descended upon him; a flock of birds annihilated him and his army by dropping pieces of stone at them.[1] This incident is recorded in *Sūra al-Fīl* (the chapter of the elephants):

﴿أَلَمْ تَرَ كَيْفَ فَعَلَ رَبُّكَ بِأَصْحَٰبِ ٱلْفِيلِ ۝١ أَلَمْ يَجْعَلْ كَيْدَهُمْ فِى تَضْلِيلٍ ۝٢ وَأَرْسَلَ عَلَيْهِمْ طَيْرًا أَبَابِيلَ ۝٣ تَرْمِيهِم بِحِجَارَةٍ مِّن سِجِّيلٍ ۝٤ فَجَعَلَهُمْ كَعَصْفٍ مَّأْكُولٍ ۝٥﴾

Have you not seen how your Lord dealt with those who had elephants? Did He not thwart their crafty designs? And He sent on to them (ambient) swarms of birds. Which pelted them with stone-hard slugs. Then (Allah made them perish) like chewed-up chaff.[2]

It was for this reason, whilst performing the rites of Pilgrimage, the most compassionate Prophet ﷺ ordered his noble Companions to pass through the *Muḥassir* valley swiftly. Their behaviour was quite telling, as though punishment was about to descend: a punishment which in fact had descended on Abraha and his army long ago. Despite this, the Holy Prophet ﷺ instructed his noble Companions to imbibe in themselves a state of Almighty Allah's fear; and the Holy Prophet ﷺ himself did the same, and he travelled through the valley at speed.

ʿAlī رضي الله عنه described the most exalted Prophet's state whilst he passed through the *Muḥassir* valley:

---

[1] Ibn Hishām, *al-Sīra al-Nabawiyya*, p. 65–67; Ibn Athīr, *al-Kāmil fī al-tārīkh*, 1:442–447; al-Suhaylī, *al-Rawḍ al-unuf fī tafsīr al-sīra al-nabawiyya li-Ibn Hishām*, 1:117–126; Ibn al-Wardī, *Tatimma al-mukhtaṣar fī akhbār al-bashr*, 1:92; Ibn Kathīr, *al-Bidāya wa al-nihāya*, 2:101–110; al-Qasṭallānī, *al-Mawāhib al-ladunya*, 1:99–104; al-Ṣāliḥī, *Subul al-hudā wa al-rashād fī sīra khayr al-ʿibād*, 1:217–222; and al-Zurqānī, *Sharḥ al-mawāhib al-ladunya*, 1:156–166.

[2] Qurʾān 105:1–5.

ثُمَّ أَفَاضَ حَتَّى انْتَهَى إِلَى وَادِي مُحَسِّرٍ، فَقَرَعَ نَاقَتَهُ فَخَبَّتْ حَتَّى جَاوَزَ الْوَادِيَ فَوَقَفَ.

He continued until he reached to the valley of *Muḥassir*. Then he took to the reigns of his camel, and it proceeded rashly till it passed through the valley. Then he stopped.[1]

ʿAbd al-Ḥaqq Muḥaddith al-Dihlawī (958–1052 AH) writes:

مستحب ست شتاب رفتن ازین وادی، واگر پیاده است تیز رَود، واگر سوار است تیز راند.

It is recommended that one goes through this valley speedily, whether on foot or riding.[2]

Why did the Holy Prophet ﷺ order his noble Companions to travel through this valley quickly? There are no flocks of birds present, nor showers of stones. The answer is that this was an action from which we can learn a lesson concerning admonition and warning, and the importance of giving rise to one's spiritual state. This pacing through the valley has become a Sunna until the Day of Judgment, and the pilgrims are commanded to pass through it quickly.

There is one purpose behind this—that past incidents should be remembered in one's heart, with their awareness firmly imprinted in the mind. The above mentioned Prophetic traditions affirm this; historical incidents such as these hold an important place in the teachings of Islam.

---

1 Narrated by al-Tirmidhī in *al-Jāmiʿ al-Ṣaḥīḥ*: *Kitāb al-Ḥajj* [The Book of Pilgrimage], chapter: 'What has been related that the whole of *ʿArafa* is a place of standing', 3:232§885; Aḥmad b. Ḥanbal in *al-Musnad*, 1:75 §562; Ibn Khuzayma in *al-Ṣaḥīḥ*, 4:272 §2861; al-Bazzār in *al-Baḥr al-Zukhār*, 2:165 §532; and Abū Yaʿlā in *al-Musnad*, 1:264 §312.

2 ʿAbd al-Ḥaqq al-Dihlawī, *Ashʿat al-lumʿāt sharḥ mishkāt al-maṣābīḥ*, 2:324.

2.6 ʿUmar's Expression of Remorse

Feeling emotions of joy and sorrow on one's memories is natural; their expression can be seen on the face. When a moment of happiness arises, one's face lights up; but if it is a time of grief, then tears flow from the eyes. In connection to this, there is an incident relating to ʿUmar b. al-Khaṭṭāb ﷺ:

ʿAbd al-Raḥmān b. Abī Layla ﷺ narrates:

> أَمَّنَا عُمَرُ بْنُ الْـخَطَّابِ ﷺ فِي الْفَجْرِ، فَقَرَأَ سُوْرَةَ يُوْسُفَ، حَتَّى إِذَا انْتَهَى إِلَى قَوْلِهِ: ﴿وَٱبْيَضَّتْ عَيْنَاهُ مِنَ ٱلْحُزْنِ فَهُوَ كَظِيمٌ﴾ بَكَى حَتَّى سَالَتْ دُمُوْعُهُ، ثُمَّ رَكَعَ.
>
> ʿUmar ﷺ lead us in the *fajr* prayer. He recited *Sūra Yūsuf*, until he reached the verse, ﴾*And his eyes turned white due to misery. And he was suppressing his sorrow*﴿ ʿUmar ﷺ wept until his tears flowed; then he went into the bowing position.[1]

Ibn Abzī said:

> صَلَّيْتُ خَلْفَ عُمَرَ، فَقَرَأَ سُوْرَةَ يُوْسُفَ حَتَّى إِذَا بَلَغَ ﴿وَٱبْيَضَّتْ عَيْنَاهُ مِنَ ٱلْحُزْنِ فَهُوَ كَظِيمٌ﴾ وَقَعَ عَلَيْهِ الْبُكَاءُ، فَرَكَعَ.
>
> I performed the ritual prayer behind ʿUmar ﷺ. He recited *Sūra Yūsuf* till he reached the verse, ﴾*And his eyes turned white due to misery.*﴿ Crying overcame him, and then he went into the bowing position.[2]

In these traditions, we can see that ʿUmar ﷺ expressed sorrow

---

[1] Narrated by al-Shaybānī, *Kitāb al-ḥujja ʿalā ahl al-Madīna*, 1:113 & 115–116; and al-Ṭaḥāwī, *Sharḥ maʿānī al-āthār*: *Kitāb al-Ṣalā* [The Book of Ritual Prayer], chapter: 'The time in which one performs the *fajr* ritual prayer, i.e. its timing', 1:233 §1051.

[2] Ibn Qudāma, *al-Mughnī*, 1:335.

at Prophet Yaʿqūb's grief. In the books of Prophetic traditions and Qurʾānic exegesis, there are numerous examples of this kind which prove that the essence of faith lies in the state of one's heart—possessing this state bestows a believer with its sweetness. Even affirming one's faith in the most exalted Prophet ﷺ is, in its essence, an act relating to a believer's heart; his obedience and following originates from one's love for him. His blessed birth is declared in the Qurʾān as the greatest benevolence upon mankind[1]. How can this favour be appreciated? How can the arrival of Allah's Messenger ﷺ be given what it deserves in honour and veneration? How can one's deep love for the beloved Prophet ﷺ be expressed? The answer to all these questions takes us in one direction and that is the expression of joy and happiness on the occasion of *Mawlid al-Nabī* ﷺ. On this auspicious occasion, we arrange gatherings and become emotional in his love; each and every step we take, we take in his obedience.

The whole sum of this discussion is that expressing joy or sorrow at past events and bringing on that state in oneself falls within the ambit of the Sunna of Allah's Messenger ﷺ. Though fourteen centuries have passed since the birth of our Prophet ﷺ, we still express our happiness by remembering the occasion of his blessed birth. The reason why we exert efforts in celebrating his blessed birth is that the Prophet ﷺ, on incidents that took place thousands of years before, enjoined his Companions to remember past events and to relive the experience of those incidents. Hence it is the Sunna of the Prophet ﷺ and his Companions.

The Prophet's blessed arrival to this world is Almighty Allah's greatest mercy; it is a bounty and the greatest act of benevolence. It is a momentous occasion for this community. Every Muslim is required to bring on the states of happiness and joy and to feel the jubilation and excitement felt by Āmina ؓ. Being of the community of the most exalted Prophet ﷺ, it is binding on us that the memory of this 1400 year old incident should be kept alive in our hearts through the celebration of *Mawlid al-Nabī* ﷺ.

---

[1] Qurʾān 3:164.

Chapter 3

Remembering the *Mawlid* of Prophets عليهم السلام: A Qurʾānic Analysis

IN THE PRECEDING CHAPTERS, WE HAVE PROVIDED AN ANALYSIS on how the various signs of Islam, which have become binding on the Muslim community in the form of ritual worship, are acts of remembrance of the prophets. If the lives of the prophets can be remembered through acts of worship, why cannot the blessed arrival of the most exalted Prophet ﷺ be commemorated? A close reading of the Qurʾān will reveal that relating the incidents surrounding the birth of Almighty Allah's close-servants is a divine practice. In this chapter, we will see how the Qurʾān makes mention of the birth of the prophets.

3.1 Background to the *Mawlūd*

The imams and hadith-scholars amongst the Arabs have written many books on the topic of the Holy Prophet's ﷺ birth. In their customary usage, this genre of literature is known as '*mawlid*', '*mawālīd*', or '*mawlūd*'. In the Arab world, the majority of the Muslims in the month of *Rabīʿ al-Awwal* have a widespread tradition of holding gatherings for its recitation wherein they mention the historic events surrounding the blessed birth of the Holy Prophet ﷺ. In Medina, Mecca, Syria, Egypt, Iraq, Oman, Jordan, United Arab Emirates, Kuwait, Libya and Morocco, as well as every country in the world, there are recitations of the *mawlūd* which have been authored by the imams and hadith-scholars. To make mention of the incidents surrounding the Prophet's birth is known amongst Urdu speakers as '*mīlād nāma*'.

3.2 Remembering the Prophets ﷺ: A Divine Practice

In the minds of certain 'modernists', there is a perception that the blessed birth of the most exalted Prophet ﷺ is a transpired incident, so what then is the need for its remembrance? In their view, it is his life and noble conduct that should be remembered. Such a mindset is totally incompatible with the Qur'ān's outlook; and hence addressing it is necessary so that its confusion is removed.

An analysis of the Qur'ān and hadith informs us that remembering Allah's beloved and chosen people is not only an act of worship, it is the very practice (Sunna) of Almighty Allah. In the Qur'ān, Almighty Allah makes mention of the births and lives of His special and chosen servants, and its recitation was made by the most esteemed Prophet ﷺ many times. Therefore, on the basis of this, remembering the incidents surrounding the blessed birth of the most esteemed Prophet ﷺ in detail comes under the practice of Almighty Allah and His Messenger ﷺ.

To make mention of their accounts is such a great source of blessing that its reality is open for all to see. In various places, the accounts of the prophets and their communities have been relayed in great detail, but in some places, it is not uncommon to find that the remembrance of the prophets and the righteous has been made the main item of speech.

1. In *sūra al-Anʿām*, Almighty Allah, whilst making mention of the prophets, states:

﴿وَإِسْمَٰعِيلَ وَٱلْيَسَعَ وَيُونُسَ وَلُوطًا ۚ وَكُلًّا فَضَّلْنَا عَلَى ٱلْعَٰلَمِينَ ﴿٨٦﴾ وَمِنْ ءَابَآئِهِمْ وَذُرِّيَّٰتِهِمْ وَإِخْوَٰنِهِمْ ۖ وَٱجْتَبَيْنَٰهُمْ وَهَدَيْنَٰهُمْ إِلَىٰ صِرَٰطٍ مُّسْتَقِيمٍ ﴿٨٧﴾﴾

> *And (We guided) Ismāʿīl, al-Yasaʿ, Yūnus and Lūṭ (too). And We exalted all of them above all the people (of their time). And also of their ancestors and descendants and their brothers (We honoured some with similar excellence) and We chose them (for Our special favour and eminence) and guided them to the straight road.*[1]

2. The 14th chapter of the Qur'ān has been named after Almighty Allah's intimate friend, Prophet Ibrāhīm ﷺ. In this chapter, his

[1] Qur'ān 6:86–87.

two sons, Ismāʿīl and Isḥāq ﷺ, have been mentioned:

﴿ٱلْحَمْدُ لِلَّهِ ٱلَّذِى وَهَبَ لِى عَلَى ٱلْكِبَرِ إِسْمَٰعِيلَ وَإِسْحَٰقَ ۚ إِنَّ رَبِّى لَسَمِيعُ ٱلدُّعَآءِ﴾

All praise belongs to Allah alone, Who has bestowed upon me (two sons) in old age, Ismāʿīl and Isḥāq. Indeed, my Lord is the All-Hearer of prayer.[1]

3. *Sūra Maryam* is replete with the mention of Allah's favoured servants; there is an uninterrupted remembrance of prophets in it. Almighty Allah commences the chapter with the supplication of Zakariyyā ﷺ:

﴿ذِكْرُ رَحْمَتِ رَبِّكَ عَبْدَهُۥ زَكَرِيَّآ ﴿٢﴾ إِذْ نَادَىٰ رَبَّهُۥ نِدَآءً خَفِيًّا ﴿٣﴾﴾

This is an account of the mercy of your Lord (bestowed) upon His (chosen) servant Zakariyyā, when he called upon his Lord in a low voice (charged with politeness and submissiveness).[2]

4. Almighty Allah states:

﴿وَحَنَانًا مِّن لَّدُنَّا وَزَكَوٰةً ۖ وَكَانَ تَقِيًّا﴾

And (blessed him) with sympathy and tenderness and purity and virtuousness from Our kind presence, and he was very God-fearing.[3]

5. Almighty Allah states:

﴿وَٱذْكُرْ فِى ٱلْكِتَٰبِ مَرْيَمَ إِذِ ٱنتَبَذَتْ مِنْ أَهْلِهَا مَكَانًا شَرْقِيًّا﴾

---

[1] Ibid., 14:39.

[2] Ibid., 19:2–3.

[3] Ibid., 19:13.

And, (O My Esteemed Beloved,) recite the account of Maryam in the Book (the Holy Qur'ān) when she separated from her family (adopting seclusion for worship and) moved to the eastern house.[1]

6. Almighty Allah states:

﴿وَٱذۡكُرۡ فِي ٱلۡكِتَٰبِ إِبۡرَٰهِيمَۚ إِنَّهُۥ كَانَ صِدِّيقٗا نَّبِيًّا﴾

And recite the account of Ibrāhīm in the Book (the Holy Qur'ān). Surely, he was a Prophet blessed with truthfulness.[2]

7. Almighty Allah states:

﴿وَٱذۡكُرۡ فِي ٱلۡكِتَٰبِ مُوسَىٰٓۚ إِنَّهُۥ كَانَ مُخۡلَصٗا وَكَانَ رَسُولٗا نَّبِيًّا﴾

And recite the account of Mūsā in (this Holy) Book. Surely, (getting rid of the grip of self,) he had become exalted and was a Messenger and Prophet.[3]

8. Almighty Allah states:

﴿وَٱذۡكُرۡ فِي ٱلۡكِتَٰبِ إِسۡمَٰعِيلَۚ إِنَّهُۥ كَانَ صَادِقَ ٱلۡوَعۡدِ وَكَانَ رَسُولٗا نَّبِيّٗا ۝٥٤ وَكَانَ يَأۡمُرُ أَهۡلَهُۥ بِٱلصَّلَوٰةِ وَٱلزَّكَوٰةِ وَكَانَ عِندَ رَبِّهِۦ مَرۡضِيّٗا ۝٥٥﴾

And recite the account of Ismāʿīl in (this) Book. Surely, he was true to (his) promise and was a Messenger and Prophet. And he used to enjoin on his family Prayer and Zakat (the Alms-due), and (held) the station of marḍiyya in the presence of his Lord (i.e., his Lord was well-pleased with him).[4]

---

[1] Ibid., 19:16.

[2] Ibid., 19:41.

[3] Ibid., 19:51.

[4] Ibid., 19:54–55.

9. Concerning Idrīs ﷺ, Almighty Allah states:

﴿وَٱذْكُرْ فِى ٱلْكِتَٰبِ إِدْرِيسَ ۚ إِنَّهُۥ كَانَ صِدِّيقًا نَّبِيًّا ﴿٥٦﴾ وَرَفَعْنَٰهُ مَكَانًا عَلِيًّا ﴿٥٧﴾﴾

And mention in the Book the account of Idrīs. Verily, he was a Prophet possessing the truth. And We raised him to a lofty station.[1]

10. In the same way, *sūra al-Anbiyā'* is also replete with accounts of Prophets. From verse 50 onwards, there are unremitting accounts which start with the following words:

﴿وَهَٰذَا ذِكْرٌ مُّبَارَكٌ أَنزَلْنَٰهُ ۚ أَفَأَنتُمْ لَهُۥ مُنكِرُونَ﴾

This (Qur'ān) is the Most Blessed Admonition which We have revealed. Do you deny it?[2]

11. Giving the title of the 'most blessed remembrance (*al-dhikr al-mubārak*), the subsequent verse commences making mention of the Father of Prophets, Ibrāhīm ﷺ:

﴿وَلَقَدْ ءَاتَيْنَآ إِبْرَٰهِيمَ رُشْدَهُۥ مِن قَبْلُ وَكُنَّا بِهِۦ عَٰلِمِينَ﴾

And surely, We awarded Ibrāhīm understanding and guidance (commensurate with his rank) well before, and We knew full well his (competence and capability).[3]

12. After giving a detailed account, there is mention of Prophets Lūṭ, Isḥāq and Ya'qūb ﷺ. This mention ends with the words:

﴿وَكُلًّا جَعَلْنَا صَٰلِحِينَ﴾

---

[1] Ibid., 19:56–57.

[2] Ibid., 21:50.

[3] Ibid., 21:51.

And We made all of them pious.[1]

13. Then in verse 73, further details are given concerning their standing:

﴿وَجَعَلْنَٰهُمْ أَيِمَّةً يَهْدُونَ بِأَمْرِنَا وَأَوْحَيْنَآ إِلَيْهِمْ فِعْلَ ٱلْخَيْرَٰتِ وَإِقَامَ
ٱلصَّلَوٰةِ وَإِيتَآءَ ٱلزَّكَوٰةِ ۖ وَكَانُوا۟ لَنَا عَٰبِدِينَ﴾

And We made them the leaders (of mankind) who guided (people) by Our command, and We sent to them Revelation (giving commands) to do good deeds, establish Prayer and pay Zakat (the Alms-due). And all of them were Our devoted worshippers.[2]

14. Verses 76–84 make mention of Prophets Nūḥ, Dāwūd, Sulaymān and Ayyūb عليهم السلام. This remembrance ends with the mention of Prophet Ayyūb عليه السلام:

﴿فَٱسْتَجَبْنَا لَهُۥ فَكَشَفْنَا مَا بِهِۦ مِن ضُرٍّ ۖ وَءَاتَيْنَٰهُ أَهْلَهُۥ وَمِثْلَهُم مَّعَهُمْ
رَحْمَةً مِّنْ عِندِنَا وَذِكْرَىٰ لِلْعَٰبِدِينَ﴾

So We granted his prayer, and We removed the misery that was afflicting him. And We (also) gave him back his family, and (bestowed upon him) the like of them along with them. This is an exceptional mercy from Us, and advice for those who are devoted to Our worship, (that is how Allah rewards patience and gratitude).[3]

15. Then in the next verse, Prophets Ismāʿīl, Idrīs, and Dhū al-Kifl عليهم السلام are mentioned:

﴿وَإِسْمَٰعِيلَ وَإِدْرِيسَ وَذَا ٱلْكِفْلِ ۖ كُلٌّ مِّنَ ٱلصَّٰبِرِينَ ﴿٨٥﴾ وَأَدْخَلْنَٰهُمْ فِى
رَحْمَتِنَآ ۖ إِنَّهُم مِّنَ ٱلصَّٰلِحِينَ ﴿٨٦﴾﴾

[1] Ibid., 21:72.

[2] Ibid., 21:73.

[3] Ibid., 21:84.

And (also recall) Ismāʿīl, and Idrīs and Dhū al-Kifl. They were all steadfast men of patience. And We admitted them to (the embrace of) Our mercy. Surely, they were of the pious.[1]

16. After this, verses 87–90 mention Prophets Yūnus (known by the epithet of Dhū al-Nūn), Zakariyyā and Yaḥyā ﷺ; this remembrance ends with a mention of their spiritual states:

﴿إِنَّهُمْ كَانُوا۟ يُسَٰرِعُونَ فِى ٱلْخَيْرَٰتِ وَيَدْعُونَنَا رَغَبًا وَرَهَبًا ۖ وَكَانُوا۟ لَنَا خَٰشِعِينَ﴾

Surely, they (all) used to hasten in (doing) pious deeds and used to call on Us (feeling) eager, fond, fearful and frightened, and used to humble before Our presence in tearful submissions.[2]

17. Almighty Allah then explains the purpose behind His making mention of these blessed and favoured servants:

﴿إِنَّ فِى هَٰذَا لَبَلَٰغًا لِّقَوْمٍ عَٰبِدِينَ﴾

Surely, there is for the devoted worshippers a guarantee and sufficient provision in this (Qur'ān of achieving the objective).[3]

18. This whole chapter has been an uninterrupted remembrance of Allah's esteemed servants, but its climax comes with the mention of the king of all the beloveds and the mercy of all the worlds, our Prophet Muhammad ﷺ. This remembrance of Allah's favoured servants comes to an end with the following statement:

﴿وَمَآ أَرْسَلْنَٰكَ إِلَّا رَحْمَةً لِّلْعَٰلَمِينَ﴾

---

[1] Ibid., 21:85–86.

[2] Ibid., 21:90.

[3] Ibid., 21:106.

And, (O Esteemed Messenger,) We have not sent you but as a mercy for all the worlds.[1]

19. After this, no other prophet is mentioned, as this remembrance of love has reached its climax. After the remembrance of the most exalted Prophet ﷺ, the chapter comes to a close with the remembrance of Almighty Allah:

﴿قَٰلَ رَبِّ ٱحۡكُم بِٱلۡحَقِّۗ وَرَبُّنَا ٱلرَّحۡمَٰنُ ٱلۡمُسۡتَعَانُ عَلَىٰ مَا تَصِفُونَ﴾

(Our Beloved) submitted: My Lord, judge (between us) with truth, and Our Lord is Ever-Merciful and He is the One Whose help is sought against the (heart-rending) words which, (O disbelievers,) you utter.[2]

20. In *sūra Ṣād*, Almighty Allah states:

﴿وَٱذۡكُرۡ إِسۡمَٰعِيلَ وَٱلۡيَسَعَ وَذَا ٱلۡكِفۡلِۖ وَكُلّٞ مِّنَ ٱلۡأَخۡيَارِ﴾

And (also) mention Ismāʿīl and al-Yasaʿ and Dhū al-Kifl. And all of them were of the chosen ones.[3]

From these five chapters, only a few verses have been selected; otherwise, the Qurʾān is abounding with such passages in which Almighty Allah makes mention of His beloved servants. In these passages, their spiritual struggle and efforts are remembered; the words of supplication spoken by these favoured ones and the context in which they were spoken and its style have all been narrated. Furthermore, as well as the divine favours they received, their steadfastness and excellence have also been mentioned. In sum, no facet of their life has been left out, and one is continuously reminded that these remembrances are exclusively for the ones who are steadfast in Almighty Allah's worship and obedience.

Anyone who wishes to adopt Almighty Allah's worship and

---

[1] Ibid., 21:107.

[2] Ibid., 21:112.

[3] Ibid., 38:48.

obedience as a means of attaining His pleasure and close-proximity should take these remembrances as a source of aspiration. This is the reason why, from the time of the noble Companions until the present-day, in every age, the recollection of the accounts of the life of the chief of the created beings, the Holy Prophet, ﷺ has been the characteristic of the believers. The imams, hadith-scholars, and the divine friends of Almighty Allah have held, according to their own temperament, gatherings for the remembrance of the Holy Prophet ﷺ; and in every era, hundreds of volumes have been authored and compiled in line with this divine practice.

One of the characteristics of the Qur'ān is that the accounts relating to the births of the prophets have been narrated by Almighty Allah. In this respect, recounting the *mawlid* is in fact Allah's Sunna.

3.3 THE SIGNIFICANCE OF THE *MAWLID* OF PROPHETS ﷺ

The birth of a loved one is a joyous occasion for any person. From this, we can see that birthdays have a special significance; moreover, importance increases when the occasion is connected to a prophet. The birth of prophets is, in of itself, amongst the greatest blessings of Almighty Allah. A nation, through the birth of its prophet, is bestowed all other blessings. The final Prophet ﷺ in particular is the gateway to guidance and divine revelation; through him, we were bestowed with the Qur'ān and the month of *Ramaḍān*. In fact, all the blessings we have received come down to that enlightened and blissful dawn in the month of *Rabīʿ al-Awwal* in which our Beloved ﷺ arrived. Thus, to be merry on his birth and to celebrate it, is a sign of one's faith and a reflection of one's personal, heartfelt attachment to the Prophet ﷺ.

The Qur'ān, whilst making mention of the birth of some of the prophets, demarcates that day for its significance and merits:

1. Concerning the birth of Yaḥyā ؑ, Almighty Allah states:

﴿وَسَلَامٌ عَلَيْهِ يَوْمَ وُلِدَ وَيَوْمَ يَمُوتُ وَيَوْمَ يُبْعَثُ حَيًّا﴾

> *And peace be on Yaḥyā, the day he was born, the day he dies, and the day he will be raised up alive!*[1]

2. In the Qurʾān, the following statement is attributed to Prophet ʿĪsā ﷺ:

﴿وَٱلسَّلَٰمُ عَلَيَّ يَوۡمَ وُلِدتُّ وَيَوۡمَ أَمُوتُ وَيَوۡمَ أُبۡعَثُ حَيّٗا﴾

> *And peace be upon me on the day of my birth, the day of my demise and the day I shall be raised up alive!*[2]

3. On the blessed birth of the most revered Prophet ﷺ, Almighty Allah takes oath saying:

﴿لَآ أُقۡسِمُ بِهَٰذَا ٱلۡبَلَدِ ۝١ وَأَنتَ حِلُّۢ بِهَٰذَا ٱلۡبَلَدِ ۝٢ وَوَالِدٖ وَمَا وَلَدَ ۝٣﴾

> *I swear by this city (Mecca), (O My Esteemed Beloved,) because you are residing in it. (O My Esteemed Beloved!) By (your) father (Ādam or Ibrāhīm) and by those who are born.*[3]

If the day in which a prophet is born has no special significance in the Qurʾān and Sunna, why then has this day been singled out for the invoking of blessings and the taking of oath? It is clear that this day is significant, as Almighty Allah has made mention of it. The following is a selection of the accounts of the *mawlid* of a number of prophets, mentioned in the Qurʾān:

3.3.1 The *Mawlid* of Prophet Ādam ﷺ

From amongst Almighty Allah's favoured servants, the creation of the father of mankind, Ādam ﷺ, is the first to be mentioned in the Qurʾān:

---

[1] Ibid., 19:15.

[2] Ibid., 19:33.

[3] Ibid., 90:1–3.

﴿وَإِذْ قَالَ رَبُّكَ لِلْمَلَـٰٓئِكَةِ إِنِّى جَاعِلٌ فِى ٱلْأَرْضِ خَلِيفَةً﴾

And (recall) when your Lord said to the angels: I am about to place My vicegerent on the earth.[1]

Almighty Allah mentioned the *mawlid* of Ādam ﷺ before his creation, as related in the following verses. When Ādam ﷺ was created in his human form, the angels were commanded to prostrate to him; but Iblīs was insolent and was thus made an outcast. The full account of this incident surrounding Ādam's creation is given below:

﴿وَإِذْ قَالَ رَبُّكَ لِلْمَلَـٰٓئِكَةِ إِنِّى خَـٰلِقٌۢ بَشَرًا مِّن صَلْصَـٰلٍ مِّنْ حَمَإٍ مَّسْنُونٍ ۝٢٨ فَإِذَا سَوَّيْتُهُۥ وَنَفَخْتُ فِيهِ مِن رُّوحِى فَقَعُوا۟ لَهُۥ سَـٰجِدِينَ ۝٢٩ فَسَجَدَ ٱلْمَلَـٰٓئِكَةُ كُلُّهُمْ أَجْمَعُونَ ۝٣٠ إِلَّآ إِبْلِيسَ أَبَىٰٓ أَن يَكُونَ مَعَ ٱلسَّـٰجِدِينَ ۝٣١﴾

And (recall) when your Lord said to the angels: I am about to create a human organism from old (and) black stinking, resounding mud. So when I accomplish the perfection of his (physical) constitution into his real being and breathe My (divine) spirit into (the inner self of) this (human physical) organism, then fall down prostrate before him. So, (no sooner did the light of Allah's effulgence illumine the human organism than) all the angels fell down in prostration together, except Iblīs. He refused to join those who prostrated themselves.[2]

In numerous places in the Qur'ān, Ādam ﷺ is mentioned in detail—not just his creation, but various aspects of his life, such as his abode in Paradise, the angels' thoughts on his creation, the accursed Satan's objections and his failing to prostrate to him,

[1] Ibid., 2:30.

[2] Ibid., 15:28–31.

have all been mentioned in detail. With relation to the creation of man, all verses that have been mentioned in this regard are all associated to Prophet Ādam ﷺ; this is what is known as Prophet Ādam's *mawlid* or *mawlūd*.

3.3.2 The *Mawlid* of Prophet Mūsā ﷺ

Mūsā ﷺ is that glorious prophet who was sent to challenge Pharaoh (a cruel and tyrannical ruler who made claims to divinity). Almighty Allah, by sending Mūsā ﷺ, protected the Children of Israel from Pharaoh's oppression and treachery; resultantly, Pharaoh was drowned, and had thus become a sign of admonition and a lesson for humanity. When Pharaoh's soothsayers informed him that a child was to be born who would one day overturn his kingdom, Pharaoh reacted by increasing the scale of his oppression. He ordered the killing of infant boys and left the girls alive. It was in such circumstances that Mūsā ﷺ was born, as mentioned by Almighty Allah in various passages of the Qurʾān.

Sūra al-Qaṣaṣ commences with this story which comprises 50 verses. The first 5 passages are reserved for Prophet Mūsā ﷺ. Below are the first 14 verses of *sūra al-Qaṣaṣ* in which Almighty Allah makes mention of his birth up to his youth, thereby substantiating the fact that recounting the *mawlid* of prophets is a Sunna of Almighty Allah:

﴿طسٓمٓ ١ تِلۡكَ ءَايَٰتُ ٱلۡكِتَٰبِ ٱلۡمُبِينِ ٢ نَتۡلُواْ عَلَيۡكَ مِن نَّبَإِ مُوسَىٰ
وَفِرۡعَوۡنَ بِٱلۡحَقِّ لِقَوۡمٖ يُؤۡمِنُونَ ٣ إِنَّ فِرۡعَوۡنَ عَلَا فِي ٱلۡأَرۡضِ وَجَعَلَ أَهۡلَهَا
شِيَعٗا يَسۡتَضۡعِفُ طَآئِفَةٗ مِّنۡهُمۡ يُذَبِّحُ أَبۡنَآءَهُمۡ وَيَسۡتَحۡيِۦ نِسَآءَهُمۡۚ إِنَّهُۥ
كَانَ مِنَ ٱلۡمُفۡسِدِينَ ٤ وَنُرِيدُ أَن نَّمُنَّ عَلَى ٱلَّذِينَ ٱسۡتُضۡعِفُواْ فِي ٱلۡأَرۡضِ
وَنَجۡعَلَهُمۡ أَيِمَّةٗ وَنَجۡعَلَهُمُ ٱلۡوَٰرِثِينَ ٥ وَنُمَكِّنَ لَهُمۡ فِي ٱلۡأَرۡضِ وَنُرِيَ
فِرۡعَوۡنَ وَهَٰمَٰنَ وَجُنُودَهُمَا مِنۡهُم مَّا كَانُواْ يَحۡذَرُونَ ٦ وَأَوۡحَيۡنَآ إِلَىٰٓ أُمِّ
مُوسَىٰٓ أَنۡ أَرۡضِعِيهِۖ فَإِذَا خِفۡتِ عَلَيۡهِ فَأَلۡقِيهِ فِي ٱلۡيَمِّ وَلَا تَخَافِي وَلَا تَحۡزَنِيٓۖ

إِنَّا رَآدُّوهُ إِلَيْكِ وَجَاعِلُوهُ مِنَ ٱلْمُرْسَلِينَ ﴿٧﴾ فَٱلْتَقَطَهُۥٓ ءَالُ فِرْعَوْنَ لِيَكُونَ
لَهُمْ عَدُوًّا وَحَزَنًا ۗ إِنَّ فِرْعَوْنَ وَهَـٰمَـٰنَ وَجُنُودَهُمَا كَانُوا۟ خَـٰطِـِٔينَ ﴿٨﴾ وَقَالَتِ
ٱمْرَأَتُ فِرْعَوْنَ قُرَّتُ عَيْنٍ لِّى وَلَكَ ۖ لَا تَقْتُلُوهُ عَسَىٰٓ أَن يَنفَعَنَآ أَوْ نَتَّخِذَهُۥ
وَلَدًا وَهُمْ لَا يَشْعُرُونَ ﴿٩﴾ وَأَصْبَحَ فُؤَادُ أُمِّ مُوسَىٰ فَـٰرِغًا ۖ إِن كَادَتْ لَتُبْدِى
بِهِۦ لَوْلَآ أَن رَّبَطْنَا عَلَىٰ قَلْبِهَا لِتَكُونَ مِنَ ٱلْمُؤْمِنِينَ ﴿١٠﴾ وَقَالَتْ لِأُخْتِهِۦ
قُصِّيهِ ۖ فَبَصُرَتْ بِهِۦ عَن جُنُبٍ وَهُمْ لَا يَشْعُرُونَ ﴿١١﴾ ۞ وَحَرَّمْنَا عَلَيْهِ
ٱلْمَرَاضِعَ مِن قَبْلُ فَقَالَتْ هَلْ أَدُلُّكُمْ عَلَىٰٓ أَهْلِ بَيْتٍ يَكْفُلُونَهُۥ لَكُمْ
وَهُمْ لَهُۥ نَـٰصِحُونَ ﴿١٢﴾ فَرَدَدْنَـٰهُ إِلَىٰٓ أُمِّهِۦ كَىْ تَقَرَّ عَيْنُهَا وَلَا تَحْزَنَ وَلِتَعْلَمَ
أَنَّ وَعْدَ ٱللَّهِ حَقٌّ وَلَـٰكِنَّ أَكْثَرَهُمْ لَا يَعْلَمُونَ ﴿١٣﴾ وَلَمَّا بَلَغَ أَشُدَّهُۥ
وَٱسْتَوَىٰٓ ءَاتَيْنَـٰهُ حُكْمًا وَعِلْمًا ۚ وَكَذَٰلِكَ نَجْزِى ٱلْمُحْسِنِينَ ﴿١٤﴾ ﴾

Ṭā, Sīn, Mīm *(Only Allah and the Messenger know the real meaning). These are the Verses of the enlightening Book. (O Esteemed Beloved!) We recite to you from the true account of Mūsā and Pharaoh for those who have believed. Certainly, Pharaoh had become an arrogant rebel (i.e., a tyrannical despot) in the land, and he had divided the citizens of his (state) into (various) sects (and groups). He had oppressed and weakened one of these groups (the population comprising the Children of Israel). He used to kill their sons (to crush their future strength), and let their women live (to increase their number without men and spread immorality and indecency amongst them). Surely, he was one of those who rouse disruption. And We wanted to do favour to the people who had been weakened in the land (through oppression, exploitation and deprivation of rights and freedom) and make them leaders (of the oppressed people) and inheritors (of the throne of the kingdom); And to give them governance and power in the land and show Pharaoh and Haman and their armies (the revolution) that they used to fear. And We revealed to the heart of the mother of Mūsā: Suckle him on, but when you fear (for his life), put him afloat into the river, and be not afraid (of this situation) nor grieve. Surely, We shall bring him back to you and shall make him one of Our Messengers. Then Pharaoh's family picked him up (from the river) so that (by the will of Allah) he proved for them an enemy and (a cause of) grief. Surely, Pharaoh, Haman and their armies were the evildoers. And the wife of Pharaoh said (on seeing Mūsā): (This child) is coolness of eyes for me and for you; do not kill him. He may perhaps bring us benefit or we may adopt him as a son. And they were unaware (of the outcome of this plan). And the heart of Mūsā's mother felt empty (of patience). And she would nearly have disclosed the secret (owing to her impatience), had We not energised her heart with the strength of peace and patience so that she might remain one of the firm believers (in Allah's promise). And (Mūsā's mother) said to his sister: Follow him (to be aware of him). So she watched him from a distance, but they were (completely) unaware. And We had in advance prohibited him from the feed of wet nurses. So (Mūsā's sister) said: Shall I tell you about a family who will bring up this (child) for you and will (also) be his well-wisher? So (this way) We returned Mūsā to his mother so that her eyes might keep cool and so that she might not feel grieved and in order that she might know (with certitude) that Allah's promise is true but most of the people do not know. And when Mūsā reached his maturity and (the age of) moderation and stability, We honoured him with the command (of Prophethood) and knowledge and wisdom. And that is how We reward the righteous.*[1]

[1] Ibid., 28:1–14.

In these 14 verses, the following have been mentioned by Almighty Allah: the incidents prior to the birth of Mūsā ﷺ, the moment of his birth, his being placed in the basket by Allah's command, his being taken to the palace of Pharaoh and finally his return to his mother to be suckled up to his prime. This is the *mawlid* of Mūsā ﷺ.

3.3.3 THE *MAWLID* OF MARYAM ﷺ

Almighty Allah has made mention of the *mawlid* of Maryam ﷺ, who is not a prophet, but a pious woman, a saint, and the noble mother of a chosen prophet, ʿĪsā ﷺ. Before relating the account of her *mawlid*, Almighty Allah first mentions some of His prophets and the nobility of their descendants:

﴿إِنَّ ٱللَّهَ ٱصۡطَفَىٰٓ ءَادَمَ وَنُوحٗا وَءَالَ إِبۡرَٰهِيمَ وَءَالَ عِمۡرَٰنَ عَلَى ٱلۡعَٰلَمِينَ ٣٣
ذُرِّيَّةَۢ بَعۡضُهَا مِنۢ بَعۡضٖۗ وَٱللَّهُ سَمِيعٌ عَلِيمٌ ٣٤﴾

Verily, Allah chose Ādam, and Nūḥ, and the family of Ibrāhīm and the family of ʿImrān (in dignity) above all the people of the world. They are all one race, descendants of one another. And Allah is All-Hearing, All-Knowing.[1]

After this introduction, the *mawlid* of Maryam ﷺ begins. Some may object that since the Qur'ān has solely mentioned past events, how can one claim this to be a *mawlid*? Those making this objection should understand that those things which are for the purpose of teaching and guidance have a limited scope, i.e. only those things which are relevant to the topic need to be mentioned; as for those things which are not relevant, there would be no need for it to form part of the Qur'ānic teaching. The following verses recount the *mawlid* of Maryam ﷺ; they are not placed for any particular teaching or guidance, but are simply a recollection of the story of her birth. Almighty Allah states:

---

[1] Ibid., 3:33–34.

﴿إِذْ قَالَتِ ٱمْرَأَتُ عِمْرَٰنَ رَبِّ إِنِّى نَذَرْتُ لَكَ مَا فِى بَطْنِى مُحَرَّرًا فَتَقَبَّلْ مِنِّىٓ ۖ إِنَّكَ أَنتَ ٱلسَّمِيعُ ٱلْعَلِيمُ ۝٣٥ فَلَمَّا وَضَعَتْهَا قَالَتْ رَبِّ إِنِّى وَضَعْتُهَآ أُنثَىٰ وَٱللَّهُ أَعْلَمُ بِمَا وَضَعَتْ وَلَيْسَ ٱلذَّكَرُ كَٱلْأُنثَىٰ ۖ وَإِنِّى سَمَّيْتُهَا مَرْيَمَ وَإِنِّىٓ أُعِيذُهَا بِكَ وَذُرِّيَّتَهَا مِنَ ٱلشَّيْطَٰنِ ٱلرَّجِيمِ ۝٣٦﴾

And (recall) when the wife of ʿImrān said: O my Lord, I vow purely to You what is in my womb, freeing him (from other obligations). So, accept (this offering) from me. You are indeed All-Hearing, All-Knowing. So when she delivered a baby girl, she submitted: Lord, I have given birth but to a female child. But Allah knew best what she had given birth to. (She said:) And the boy (that I prayed for) could never (be) like the girl (that Allah has blessed me with); and I have named her Maryam (the worshipper); and, surely, I commit her and her children to Your protection against (the mischief of) Satan, the outcast.[1]

This is a beautiful account of the birth of Maryam ﷺ, which has been related by Almighty Allah. The following verses relate her childhood when she was brought up under the care of Zakariyyā ﷺ. During that time, the blessings which Almighty Allah had bestowed and the out-of-season fruits she received have been mentioned. Using the place of her residence as a mediation (*wasīla*), Zakariyyā ﷺ entreated to Almighty Allah, supplicating for offspring, and Almighty Allah gave him the glad tidings of Yaḥyā ﷺ:

﴿فَتَقَبَّلَهَا رَبُّهَا بِقَبُولٍ حَسَنٍ وَأَنۢبَتَهَا نَبَاتًا حَسَنًا وَكَفَّلَهَا زَكَرِيَّا ۖ كُلَّمَا دَخَلَ عَلَيْهَا زَكَرِيَّا ٱلْمِحْرَابَ وَجَدَ عِندَهَا رِزْقًا ۖ قَالَ يَٰمَرْيَمُ أَنَّىٰ لَكِ هَٰذَا ۖ قَالَتْ هُوَ مِنْ عِندِ ٱللَّهِ ۖ إِنَّ ٱللَّهَ يَرْزُقُ مَن يَشَآءُ بِغَيْرِ حِسَابٍ﴾

[1] Ibid., 3:35–36.

So, her Lord graciously accepted her (Maryam) with excellent acceptance and brought her up immaculately and entrusted her guardianship to Zakariyyā. Every time Zakariyyā entered her chamber of worship, he found with her (novel and uncommon) food items. He inquired: O Maryam, wherefrom have these things come for you? She replied: This (sustenance) comes from Allah. Verily, Allah provides sustenance without measure to whom He wills.[1]

The verses above are related to Maryam's childhood and upbringing. However, it does not end there; Almighty Allah further explains even the minor details of how the religious leaders argued amongst themselves regarding who should be given the responsibility to care for Maryam عليها السلام:

﴿وَإِذْ قَالَتِ ٱلْمَلَـٰٓئِكَةُ يَـٰمَرْيَمُ إِنَّ ٱللَّهَ ٱصْطَفَىٰكِ وَطَهَّرَكِ وَٱصْطَفَىٰكِ عَلَىٰ
نِسَآءِ ٱلْعَـٰلَمِينَ ﴿٤٢﴾ يَـٰمَرْيَمُ ٱقْنُتِى لِرَبِّكِ وَٱسْجُدِى وَٱرْكَعِى مَعَ ٱلرَّٰكِعِينَ ﴿٤٣﴾
ذَٰلِكَ مِنْ أَنۢبَآءِ ٱلْغَيْبِ نُوحِيهِ إِلَيْكَ ۚ وَمَا كُنتَ لَدَيْهِمْ إِذْ يُلْقُونَ أَقْلَـٰمَهُمْ
أَيُّهُمْ يَكْفُلُ مَرْيَمَ وَمَا كُنتَ لَدَيْهِمْ إِذْ يَخْتَصِمُونَ ﴿٤٤﴾﴾

And (remember) when the angels said: O Maryam, surely Allah has chosen you and has blessed you with purity and has exalted you today over all the women of the world. O Maryam! Obey your Lord consistently with utmost humbleness, prostrate yourself, and bow down in worship along with those who bow down. (O Beloved!) These are the tidings of the unseen which We reveal to you. But (at that time) you were not present with them when they were casting their pens (by way of a draw to determine) which of them should take care of Maryam. Nor were you with them when they were disputing with one another.[2]

---

[1] Ibid., 3:37.

[2] Ibid., 3:42–44.

This was the *mawlid* of Maryam عليها السلام along with which seemingly minor details have been related, such as the religious leaders casting their pens, drawing lots and disputing with one another—none of these details apparently have any connection with teaching or guidance. On the other hand, speaking of the details and virtues of the blessed birth of the Holy Prophet ﷺ is a means by which faith is perfected and completed; and it is a means by which we can adhere to Allah's Sunna. If only people would understand that if the *mawlid* of a pious, saintly lady has been mentioned in the Qur'ān, then why not make mention of the *mawlid* of the beloved Prophet ﷺ? To make mention of the beautiful Prophet's *mawlid* is in no way an innovation; rather, it is an act of true faith and the essence of monotheism.

3.3.4 The *Mawlid* of Prophet Yaḥyā عليه السلام

Almighty Allah has mentioned the *mawlid* of Yaḥyā عليه السلام in detail. When Zakariyyā عليه السلام was taking care of Maryam عليها السلام, he supplicated to Almighty Allah at her place of residence taking it as a source of mediation (*wasīla*). Concerning this Almighty Allah states:

﴿هُنَالِكَ دَعَا زَكَرِيَّا رَبَّهُۥ ۖ قَالَ رَبِّ هَبْ لِى مِن لَّدُنكَ ذُرِّيَّةً طَيِّبَةً ۖ إِنَّكَ
سَمِيعُ ٱلدُّعَآءِ (٣٨) فَنَادَتْهُ ٱلْمَلَٰٓئِكَةُ وَهُوَ قَآئِمٌ يُصَلِّى فِى ٱلْمِحْرَابِ أَنَّ ٱللَّهَ
يُبَشِّرُكَ بِيَحْيَىٰ مُصَدِّقًۢا بِكَلِمَةٍ مِّنَ ٱللَّهِ وَسَيِّدًا وَحَصُورًا وَنَبِيًّا مِّنَ
ٱلصَّٰلِحِينَ (٣٩) قَالَ رَبِّ أَنَّىٰ يَكُونُ لِى غُلَٰمٌ وَقَدْ بَلَغَنِىَ ٱلْكِبَرُ وَٱمْرَأَتِى
عَاقِرٌ ۖ قَالَ كَذَٰلِكَ ٱللَّهُ يَفْعَلُ مَا يَشَآءُ (٤٠) قَالَ رَبِّ ٱجْعَل لِّىٓ ءَايَةً ۖ قَالَ
ءَايَتُكَ أَلَّا تُكَلِّمَ ٱلنَّاسَ ثَلَٰثَةَ أَيَّامٍ إِلَّا رَمْزًا ۗ وَٱذْكُر رَّبَّكَ كَثِيرًا وَسَبِّحْ
بِٱلْعَشِىِّ وَٱلْإِبْكَٰرِ (٤١)﴾

At the same place, Zakariyyā supplicated his Lord. He submitted: 'O my Lord, bless me, out of Your Grace, with a virtuous and pure offspring. Surely, You alone hear the supplication. Whilst he was still standing in the chamber offering the Prayer (or supplicating), the angels called out to him: 'Indeed, Allah gives you the good news of (a son) Yaḥyā, who shall confirm Allah's Word (i.e., ʿĪsā), and he will be a leader, well-protected against (temptation for) women, and a Prophet from amongst (Our) exceptionally pious servants. (Zakariyyā) submitted: 'O my Lord, how shall I have a son when old age has already overtaken me, and my wife is (also) barren?' He said: 'The same way as Allah does whatever He wills. Zakariyyā submitted: 'O my Lord, fix a sign for me.' Allah said: 'The sign for you is that for three days you will not be able to communicate to the people except by gestures. And remember your Lord abundantly and glorify Him persistently, evening and morning.[1]

It should be clear that Yaḥyā ﷺ was not yet born: only Zakariyyā's supplication was accepted. Even before his birth, Almighty Allah mentioned some of his virtues. Furthermore in *sūra Maryam*, his birth is mentioned in full, whereas the first passage has been reserved for Prophet Yaḥyā's *mawlid*. This mention commences as follows:

﴿كٓهيعٓصٓ ۝١ ذِكْرُ رَحْمَتِ رَبِّكَ عَبْدَهُۥ زَكَرِيَّآ ۝٢﴾

'Kāf, Hā, Yā, ʿAyn, Ṣād. *(Only Allah and the Messenger [blessings and peace be upon him] know the real meaning.) This is an account of the mercy of your Lord (bestowed) upon His (chosen) servant Zakariyyā.*'[2]

From these verses, it can be learnt that mentioning the birth of a prophet (i.e., *mawlid*) has been expressed in the Qur'ān as Almighty Allah's mercy. If the mentioning of the *mawlid* of Prophet Yaḥyā ﷺ is to mention the mercy of Almighty Allah, then why cannot the mentioning of the *mawlid* of the Holy Prophet ﷺ also be Almighty Allah's mercy? What mercy could be greater

[1] Ibid., 3:38–41.

[2] Ibid., 19:1–2.

than the one who is sent as a mercy for all the worlds? Hence, rationally and logically speaking, mentioning the *mawlid* of the Prophet ﷺ is to mention the mercy of Almighty Allah.

The Qurʾān further goes on to mention the *mawlid* of Prophet Yaḥyā ﷺ as a mercy in the following way:

﴿إِذۡ نَادَىٰ رَبَّهُۥ نِدَآءً خَفِيّٗا ٣ قَالَ رَبِّ إِنِّي وَهَنَ ٱلۡعَظۡمُ مِنِّي وَٱشۡتَعَلَ
ٱلرَّأۡسُ شَيۡبٗا وَلَمۡ أَكُنۢ بِدُعَآئِكَ رَبِّ شَقِيّٗا ٤ وَإِنِّي خِفۡتُ ٱلۡمَوَٰلِيَ مِن
وَرَآءِي وَكَانَتِ ٱمۡرَأَتِي عَاقِرٗا فَهَبۡ لِي مِن لَّدُنكَ وَلِيّٗا ٥ يَرِثُنِي وَيَرِثُ
مِنۡ ءَالِ يَعۡقُوبَۖ وَٱجۡعَلۡهُ رَبِّ رَضِيّٗا ٦ يَٰزَكَرِيَّآ إِنَّا نُبَشِّرُكَ بِغُلَٰمٍ ٱسۡمُهُۥ
يَحۡيَىٰ لَمۡ نَجۡعَل لَّهُۥ مِن قَبۡلُ سَمِيّٗا ٧ قَالَ رَبِّ أَنَّىٰ يَكُونُ لِي غُلَٰمٞ وَكَانَتِ
ٱمۡرَأَتِي عَاقِرٗا وَقَدۡ بَلَغۡتُ مِنَ ٱلۡكِبَرِ عِتِيّٗا ٨ قَالَ كَذَٰلِكَ قَالَ رَبُّكَ هُوَ
عَلَيَّ هَيِّنٞ وَقَدۡ خَلَقۡتُكَ مِن قَبۡلُ وَلَمۡ تَكُ شَيۡـٔٗا ٩ قَالَ رَبِّ ٱجۡعَل لِّيٓ ءَايَةٗۖ
قَالَ ءَايَتُكَ أَلَّا تُكَلِّمَ ٱلنَّاسَ ثَلَٰثَ لَيَالٖ سَوِيّٗا ١٠ فَخَرَجَ عَلَىٰ قَوۡمِهِۦ مِنَ
ٱلۡمِحۡرَابِ فَأَوۡحَىٰٓ إِلَيۡهِمۡ أَن سَبِّحُواْ بُكۡرَةٗ وَعَشِيّٗا ١١ يَٰيَحۡيَىٰ خُذِ ٱلۡكِتَٰبَ
بِقُوَّةٖۖ وَءَاتَيۡنَٰهُ ٱلۡحُكۡمَ صَبِيّٗا ١٢ وَحَنَانٗا مِّن لَّدُنَّا وَزَكَوٰةٗۖ وَكَانَ تَقِيّٗا ١٣ وَبَرَّۢا
بِوَٰلِدَيۡهِ وَلَمۡ يَكُن جَبَّارًا عَصِيّٗا ١٤ وَسَلَٰمٌ عَلَيۡهِ يَوۡمَ وُلِدَ وَيَوۡمَ يَمُوتُ وَيَوۡمَ
يُبۡعَثُ حَيّٗا ١٥﴾

When he called upon his Lord in a low voice (charged with politeness and submissiveness). He submitted: O my Lord, my bones have grown tender and (my) head has turned white like a flame due to old age and, O my Lord, I have never been unblessed when supplicating You. And I fear my (disbelieving) relatives (may ruin the blessing of Dīn [Religion]) after my (soul departs) and my wife (too) is barren. So bless me from Your presence with an heir (son), (The one) who should be my heir (of divine blessing) and also the heir of (the chain of Prophethood from) the Children of Yaʿqūb. And, O my Lord, You (also) make him a recipient of Your Pleasure. (Allah said:) O Zakariyyā, indeed We give you the good news of a son whose name shall be Yaḥyā. We have not given this name to anyone before him. (Zakariyyā) submitted: My Lord, how can there be a son to me whilst my wife is barren, and I have shrivelled (into extreme debility) on account of old age? (He) said: (Don't be amazed.) It will be the same way. Your Lord said: It is easy for Me (to create a son). Certainly, I created you (too) before, whilst you were (just) nothing. (Zakariyyā) submitted: My Lord, set a sign for me. He said: Your sign is that, despite good health, you shall not be able to speak to the people for three nights (and days). Then (Zakariyyā) came out from his worshipping chamber to his people and conveyed to them (i.e., made them understand) by gestures to glorify (Allah) morning and evening. O Yaḥyā! Hold fast to (Our) Book (the Torah). And We granted him wisdom and vision (Prophethood) whilst yet a child, and (blessed him) with sympathy and tenderness and purity and virtuousness from Our kind presence, and he was very Godfearing. (He was) greatly righteous (and dutiful) to his parents and was neither disobedient nor arrogant (like common boys). And peace be on Yaḥyā, the day he was born, the day he dies, and the day he will be raised up alive![1]

The first passage has completely been allocated for the *mawlid* of Yaḥyā ﷺ, in which his birth is mentioned and the supplication Zakariyyā ﷺ had made for him. Almighty Allah gave the glad tidings of Yaḥyā's birth, and when Zakariyyā ﷺ expressed his amazement, Almighty Allah mentioned His omnipotence. In sum, the dialogue which took place between him (Zakariyyā ﷺ) and Almighty Allah has been fully disclosed in the Qur'ān in detail. Thereafter, some aspects relating to Yaḥyā's spiritual stature and some exclusive facets of his life are mentioned. After relating the

---

1 Ibid., 19:3–15.

incidents of his blessed birth and life, it then comes to a close with the sending of peace on the day of his birth, death, and his raising on the Day of Judgment. The Qurʾān's recollection of these events only serve the purpose of instilling awareness of the significance of the *mawlid* of Prophet Yaḥyā عليه السلام in our minds. This is the *mawlid* of Yaḥyā عليه السلام as mentioned in the Qurʾān.

3.3.5 The *Mawlid* of Prophet ʿĪsā عليه السلام

After making mention of the *mawlid* of Maryam عليها السلام, the *mawlid* of her son, Prophet ʿĪsā عليه السلام, is mentioned. A whole passage has been dedicated to the *mawlid* of ʿĪsā, in which the glad tidings of his birth were given to his noble mother before he was born. On this, the Qurʾān states:

﴿إِذْ قَالَتِ ٱلْمَلَٰٓئِكَةُ يَٰمَرْيَمُ إِنَّ ٱللَّهَ يُبَشِّرُكِ بِكَلِمَةٍ مِّنْهُ ٱسْمُهُ ٱلْمَسِيحُ
عِيسَى ٱبْنُ مَرْيَمَ وَجِيهًا فِى ٱلدُّنْيَا وَٱلْءَاخِرَةِ وَمِنَ ٱلْمُقَرَّبِينَ ۝٤٥ وَيُكَلِّمُ
ٱلنَّاسَ فِى ٱلْمَهْدِ وَكَهْلًا وَمِنَ ٱلصَّٰلِحِينَ ۝٤٦ قَالَتْ رَبِّ أَنَّىٰ يَكُونُ لِى وَلَدٌ
وَلَمْ يَمْسَسْنِى بَشَرٌ ۖ قَالَ كَذَٰلِكِ ٱللَّهُ يَخْلُقُ مَا يَشَآءُ ۚ إِذَا قَضَىٰٓ أَمْرًا فَإِنَّمَا
يَقُولُ لَهُۥ كُن فَيَكُونُ ۝٤٧﴾

When the angels said: 'O Maryam, surely, Allah gives you glad tidings of a (particular) Word from Him named the Messiah, ʿĪsā, the son of Maryam, who would be eminent and exalted, (both) in this world and in the Hereafter, and would be of those who are exceptionally intimate servants of Allah blessed with His nearness. And he will talk to the people (alike) both in the cradle and in ripe years, and he will be one of the most pious servants (of Allah).' Maryam submitted: 'O my Lord, how shall I have a son when no man has ever touched me?' He said: 'Just as Allah creates what He pleases. When He decides (to do) some work, He just gives it the command Be, and it becomes.[1]

[1] Ibid., 3:45–47.

After discussing ʿĪsā's *mawlid* in detail, further accounts are given, such as how Jibrāʾīl ﵇ blew the spirit into Maryam ﵇ and how she became expectant after that. At the time of delivery, even the pain felt by Maryam ﵇ is mentioned, and how Almighty Allah let flow a stream of water and provided her with dates in order to alleviate her pain. The moments of his birth, the incidents which took place afterwards (when she was accused and criticised), and the reply given by Prophet ʿĪsā ﵇ whilst he was still in the cradle have all been mentioned in the Qurʾān by Almighty Allah:

﴿وَٱذۡكُرۡ فِي ٱلۡكِتَٰبِ مَرۡيَمَ إِذِ ٱنتَبَذَتۡ مِنۡ أَهۡلِهَا مَكَانٗا شَرۡقِيّٗا ١٦
فَٱتَّخَذَتۡ مِن دُونِهِمۡ حِجَابٗا فَأَرۡسَلۡنَآ إِلَيۡهَا رُوحَنَا فَتَمَثَّلَ لَهَا بَشَرٗا سَوِيّٗا ١٧
قَالَتۡ إِنِّيٓ أَعُوذُ بِٱلرَّحۡمَٰنِ مِنكَ إِن كُنتَ تَقِيّٗا ١٨ قَالَ إِنَّمَآ أَنَا۠ رَسُولُ
رَبِّكِ لِأَهَبَ لَكِ غُلَٰمٗا زَكِيّٗا ١٩ قَالَتۡ أَنَّىٰ يَكُونُ لِي غُلَٰمٞ وَلَمۡ يَمۡسَسۡنِي
بَشَرٞ وَلَمۡ أَكُ بَغِيّٗا ٢٠ قَالَ كَذَٰلِكِ قَالَ رَبُّكِ هُوَ عَلَيَّ هَيِّنٞۖ وَلِنَجۡعَلَهُۥٓ ءَايَةٗ
لِّلنَّاسِ وَرَحۡمَةٗ مِّنَّاۚ وَكَانَ أَمۡرٗا مَّقۡضِيّٗا ٢١ ۞فَحَمَلَتۡهُ فَٱنتَبَذَتۡ بِهِۦ مَكَانٗا
قَصِيّٗا ٢٢ فَأَجَآءَهَا ٱلۡمَخَاضُ إِلَىٰ جِذۡعِ ٱلنَّخۡلَةِ قَالَتۡ يَٰلَيۡتَنِي مِتُّ قَبۡلَ
هَٰذَا وَكُنتُ نَسۡيٗا مَّنسِيّٗا ٢٣ فَنَادَىٰهَا مِن تَحۡتِهَآ أَلَّا تَحۡزَنِي قَدۡ جَعَلَ رَبُّكِ
تَحۡتَكِ سَرِيّٗا ٢٤ وَهُزِّيٓ إِلَيۡكِ بِجِذۡعِ ٱلنَّخۡلَةِ تُسَٰقِطۡ عَلَيۡكِ رُطَبٗا جَنِيّٗا ٢٥
فَكُلِي وَٱشۡرَبِي وَقَرِّي عَيۡنٗاۖ فَإِمَّا تَرَيِنَّ مِنَ ٱلۡبَشَرِ أَحَدٗا فَقُولِيٓ إِنِّي نَذَرۡتُ
لِلرَّحۡمَٰنِ صَوۡمٗا فَلَنۡ أُكَلِّمَ ٱلۡيَوۡمَ إِنسِيّٗا ٢٦ فَأَتَتۡ بِهِۦ قَوۡمَهَا تَحۡمِلُهُۥۖ قَالُواْ
يَٰمَرۡيَمُ لَقَدۡ جِئۡتِ شَيۡـٔٗا فَرِيّٗا ٢٧ يَٰٓأُخۡتَ هَٰرُونَ مَا كَانَ أَبُوكِ ٱمۡرَأَ
سَوۡءٖ وَمَا كَانَتۡ أُمُّكِ بَغِيّٗا ٢٨ فَأَشَارَتۡ إِلَيۡهِۖ قَالُواْ كَيۡفَ نُكَلِّمُ مَن كَانَ
فِي ٱلۡمَهۡدِ صَبِيّٗا ٢٩ قَالَ إِنِّي عَبۡدُ ٱللَّهِ ءَاتَىٰنِيَ ٱلۡكِتَٰبَ وَجَعَلَنِي نَبِيّٗا ٣٠
وَجَعَلَنِي مُبَارَكًا أَيۡنَ مَا كُنتُ وَأَوۡصَٰنِي بِٱلصَّلَوٰةِ وَٱلزَّكَوٰةِ مَا دُمۡتُ حَيّٗا ٣١

وَبَرًّا بِوَالِدَتِي وَلَمْ يَجْعَلْنِي جَبَّارًا شَقِيًّا ﴿٣٢﴾ وَالسَّلَامُ عَلَيَّ يَوْمَ وُلِدتُّ وَيَوْمَ
أَمُوتُ وَيَوْمَ أُبْعَثُ حَيًّا ﴿٣٣﴾ ذَٰلِكَ عِيسَى ابْنُ مَرْيَمَ ۚ قَوْلَ الْحَقِّ الَّذِي فِيهِ
يَمْتَرُونَ ﴿٣٤﴾ مَا كَانَ لِلَّهِ أَن يَتَّخِذَ مِن وَلَدٍ ۖ سُبْحَانَهُ ۚ إِذَا قَضَىٰ أَمْرًا فَإِنَّمَا
يَقُولُ لَهُ كُن فَيَكُونُ ﴿٣٥﴾

And, (O My Esteemed Beloved,) recite the account of Maryam in the Book (the Holy Qurʾān) when she separated from her family (adopting seclusion for worship and) moved to the eastern house. So she adopted veiling from them (the family and the people so that the absolute divine beauty unveils Himself). Then We sent towards her Our Spirit (the angel, Jibrāʾīl), who appeared before her in complete form of a human being. (Maryam) said: 'I seek refuge with the Most Gracious (Lord) from you if you fear (Allah).' (Jibrāʾīl) said: 'I am only a messenger from your Lord. (I have come) to bestow upon you a pure son.' (Maryam) said: 'How can there be a son to me, whereas no man has even touched me, nor am I unchaste?' (Jibrāʾīl) said: '(Do not wonder.) It will be the same way. Your Lord says: 'This (work) is easy for Me, and (the objective is) that We may make him a sign for the people and mercy from Us. And it is a matter (already) decreed.'' So Maryam conceived him and positioned herself at a remote site, aloof (from the people). Then the birth pangs drove her to the trunk of a palm-tree. She said (in anxiety): 'Would that I had died before this and had become totally forgotten!?' Then (Jibrāʾīl or ʿĪsā himself) called out to her from beneath her: 'Grieve not. Surely your Lord has made a water spring flow under you (or has created and laid under you an exalted human being). And shake the trunk of the date-palm towards you. It will shed fresh ripe dates upon you. So eat and drink and cool (your) eyes (with the sight of your beautiful, lovely baby). Then if you see any man, say (to him by gestures): I have vowed a fast (of silence) to the Most Gracious (Lord), so I shall just not talk to any human being today.' Then, carrying (the baby in her lap), she came to her people. They said: 'O Maryam, surely you have brought quite an amazing thing! O sister of Hārūn! Neither was your father a bad man, nor was your mother an unchaste woman?' On this Maryam pointed to (the baby). They said: 'How can we talk to him who is (yet) an infant in the cradle?' (The infant himself) spoke out: 'I am indeed a servant of Allah. He has given me the Book and has raised me as a Prophet. And wherever I may reside, He has made me an embodiment of blessing. And He has enjoined upon me Prayer and Zakāt (the Alms-due) as long as I am alive. And (He has made me) treat my mother with excellence and has not made me disobedient and ill-fated. And peace be upon me on the day of my birth, the day of my demise and the day I shall be raised up alive!' Such is ʿĪsā, the son of Maryam. (That is) the truth about which these people doubt. It is not Allah's Glory that He should take (to Himself anyone as) a son. Holy and Glorified is He (above this). When He decrees any matter, He only says to it: Be, and it becomes.[1]

3.3.6 THE *MAWLID* OF THE CHOSEN-ONE PROPHET MUHAMMAD ﷺ

In the preceding pages, the *mawlid* of the prophets have been mentioned; in these accounts, it is Almighty Allah Himself who is the narrator. The purpose of the Qur'ān narrating the incidents surrounding the birth of the prophets, their miracles and blessings, and making mention of His favours upon them is to show that this is a practice (Sunna) of Allah; it is the Qur'ān's position that these verses should be recited over and again. A question can be raised that the Qur'ān mentions the *mawlid* of other prophets, but has the *mawlid* of our Prophet Muhammad ﷺ been mentioned? The reply

[1] Ibid., 19:16–35.

to this is in the affirmative: the blessed birth of the most exalted Prophet ﷺ has been mentioned in the Qurʾān.

A close-reading of the Qurʾān makes this point clear that by making mention of the birth of the prophets, Almighty Allah has made famous their prestige. If one observes the Qurʾān, one will see that the *mawlid* of other prophets have simply been limited to the narration of the events surrounding their births; whereas on the other hand, the Holy Prophet's status is set apart with distinction—Almighty Allah does not only take an oath on the city of his birth, but He also takes an oath on his forefathers and ancestors:

﴿لَآ أُقْسِمُ بِهَٰذَا ٱلْبَلَدِ ۝١ وَأَنتَ حِلٌّۢ بِهَٰذَا ٱلْبَلَدِ ۝٢ وَوَالِدٍ وَمَا وَلَدَ ۝٣﴾

I swear by this city (Mecca), (O My Esteemed Beloved,) because you are residing in it. (O My Esteemed Beloved!) By (your) father (Ādam or Ibrāhīm) and by those who are born.[1]

In Mecca, there is the House of Allah, the Black Stone, the area for performing the *ṭawāf*, *multazam*, *Maqām Ibrāhīm*, the well of *zam zam*, *al-Ṣafā* and *al-Marwa*; but, Almighty Allah did not take an oath for any of these. Rather, Almighty Allah takes an oath on Mecca because it was the abode of His beloved, and then He takes an oath on the forefathers and ancestors of the beloved Prophet ﷺ. It is an important point to take note that Almighty Allah does not take an oath on anyone's birth, except the birth of the beloved Prophet ﷺ.

Concerning the Prophet's sending, Almighty Allah states:

﴿كَمَآ أَرْسَلْنَا فِيكُمْ رَسُولًا مِّنكُمْ يَتْلُواْ عَلَيْكُمْ ءَايَٰتِنَا وَيُزَكِّيكُمْ وَيُعَلِّمُكُمُ ٱلْكِتَٰبَ وَٱلْحِكْمَةَ وَيُعَلِّمُكُم مَّا لَمْ تَكُونُواْ تَعْلَمُونَ﴾

Likewise, We have sent you (Our) Messenger (blessings and peace be upon him) from amongst yourselves who recites to you Our Revelations and purifies and sanctifies

[1] Ibid., 90:1–3.

(your hearts and ill-commanding selves) and teaches you the Book and inculcates in you logic and wisdom and enlightens you (on the mysteries of spiritual gnosis and divine truth) which you did not know.[1]

﴿لَقَدْ مَنَّ ٱللَّهُ عَلَى ٱلْمُؤْمِنِينَ إِذْ بَعَثَ فِيهِمْ رَسُولًا مِّنْ أَنفُسِهِمْ﴾

Indeed, Allah conferred a great favour on the believers that He raised amongst them (the most eminent) Messenger (blessings and peace be upon him) from amongst themselves, who recites to them His Revelations, purifies them, and educates them on the Book and Wisdom though, before that, they were in manifest error.[2]

﴿يَـٰٓأَيُّهَا ٱلنَّاسُ قَدْ جَآءَكُمُ ٱلرَّسُولُ بِٱلْحَقِّ مِن رَّبِّكُمْ فَـَٔامِنُوا۟ خَيْرًا لَّكُمْ﴾

O humankind! Indeed, this Messenger (blessings and peace be upon him) has come to you with the truth from your Lord. So believe (in him) for your own good.[3]

﴿يَـٰٓأَهْلَ ٱلْكِتَـٰبِ قَدْ جَآءَكُمْ رَسُولُنَا يُبَيِّنُ لَكُمْ كَثِيرًا مِّمَّا كُنتُمْ تُخْفُونَ مِنَ ٱلْكِتَـٰبِ وَيَعْفُوا۟ عَن كَثِيرٍ ۚ قَدْ جَآءَكُم مِّنَ ٱللَّهِ نُورٌ وَكِتَـٰبٌ مُّبِينٌ﴾

O People of the Book! Indeed there has come to you Our Messenger who (clearly) unfolds to you many such things from the Book as you have been concealing and who overlooks many of (your) wrongs (too). There has indeed come to you a light from Allah (i.e., Muhammad

---

[1] Ibid., 2:151.

[2] Ibid., 3:164.

[3] Ibid., 4:170.

[blessings and peace be upon him]) and an Enlightening Book (i.e., the Holy Qur'ān).[1]

﴿يَٰٓأَهۡلَ ٱلۡكِتَٰبِ قَدۡ جَآءَكُمۡ رَسُولُنَا يُبَيِّنُ لَكُمۡ عَلَىٰ فَتۡرَةٖ مِّنَ ٱلرُّسُلِ أَن تَقُولُواْ مَا جَآءَنَا مِنۢ بَشِيرٖ وَلَا نَذِيرٖۖ فَقَدۡ جَآءَكُم بَشِيرٞ وَنَذِيرٞۗ وَٱللَّهُ عَلَىٰ كُلِّ شَيۡءٖ قَدِيرٞ﴾

O People of the Book! Indeed, Our (Last) Prophet has come to you (at the juncture) when (the chain of) Messengers succession is breaking off, and he expounds to you (Our commands and injunctions) with ample clarity, (because) you may (by way of excuse) say: There has come to us no Bearer of good news or a Warner. (Now this excuse of yours has also lost ground because) undoubtedly, (the Final) Bearer of glad tidings and Warner has come to you, and Allah has absolute power over everything.[2]

﴿لَقَدۡ جَآءَكُمۡ رَسُولٞ مِّنۡ أَنفُسِكُمۡ عَزِيزٌ عَلَيۡهِ مَا عَنِتُّمۡ حَرِيصٌ عَلَيۡكُم بِٱلۡمُؤۡمِنِينَ رَءُوفٞ رَّحِيمٞ﴾

Surely, a (Glorious) Messenger from amongst yourselves has come to you. Your suffering and distress (becomes) grievously heavy on him (blessings and peace be upon him). (O humankind,) he is ardently desirous of your (betterment and guidance. And) he is most (deeply) clement and merciful to the believers.[3]

﴿وَمَآ أَرۡسَلۡنَٰكَ إِلَّا رَحۡمَةٗ لِّلۡعَٰلَمِينَ﴾

---

[1] Ibid., 5:15.

[2] Ibid., 5:19.

[3] Ibid., 9:128.

And, (O Esteemed Messenger,) We have not sent you but as a mercy for all the worlds.[1]

﴿هُوَ ٱلَّذِى بَعَثَ فِى ٱلْأُمِّيِّـۧنَ رَسُولًا مِّنْهُمْ يَتْلُوا۟ عَلَيْهِمْ ءَايَـٰتِهِۦ وَيُزَكِّيهِمْ وَيُعَلِّمُهُمُ ٱلْكِتَـٰبَ وَٱلْحِكْمَةَ وَإِن كَانُوا۟ مِن قَبْلُ لَفِى ضَلَـٰلٍ مُّبِينٍ﴾

He is the One Who sent a (Glorious) Messenger (blessings and peace be upon him) amongst the illiterate people from amongst themselves who recites to them His Revelations and cleanses and purifies them (outwardly and inwardly) and teaches them the Book and wisdom. Indeed they were in open error before (his most welcome arrival).[2]

﴿إِنَّآ أَرْسَلْنَآ إِلَيْكُمْ رَسُولًا﴾

Surely, We have sent towards you a Messenger (blessings and peace be upon him).[3]

In the verses above, there is mention of the Prophet's arrival and this in essence is the remembrance of his blessed birth. If one contemplates these verses deeply, it can be understood that Almighty Allah's mentioning of the birth of His beloved is for the whole of humanity: along with the believers, the people of the book, the disbelievers and the polytheists have been included. Everyone is being made aware that Allah's beloved is coming; his arrival is being declared a mercy and blessing for the whole of the universe. Almighty Allah is holding the remembrance of His beloved's arrival in such high esteem that no one can claim that it is a trivial matter.

Through these verses, Almighty Allah is teaching the *Umma* that the remembrance of the Prophet's blessed birth is binding on coming generations. In light of this, the mind-set which belittles the need for remembering the birth of the Prophet ﷺ can be taken

---

[1] Ibid., 21:107.

[2] Ibid., 62:2.

[3] Ibid., 73:15.

as being tantamount to rejecting the dozens of verses in which the birth of the prophets are mentioned. When we remember Prophet Muhammad ﷺ in the context of his *mawlid*, we are emulating the Sunna of Almighty Allah and are thus being obedient to His commands. If one carefully reads these verses in which the births of Almighty Allah's favoured servants are mentioned, it will be known that these stories do not contain any particular teaching or guidance (which can directly be implemented in our lives); instead, they are narrations, the purpose of which is to remember the *mawlid* of the prophets.

3.4 From the *Mawlid* of the Prophets to the *Mawlid* of Prophet Muhammad ﷺ

Almighty Allah holds the remembrance of the *mawlid* of His favoured servants in such high esteem that even the thoughts that came into the minds of these people have been mentioned. For example, when one reads the *mawlid* of Yaḥyā ﷺ, when Zakariyyā ﷺ entered the convent of Maryam ﷺ finding out-of-season fruits there, he made a supplication praying for offspring. And then when he was given glad-tidings of a righteous son, a thought naturally came to his mind as to how he could have a son when he was an old man and his wife was barren. Consequently, he questioned Almighty Allah about this—the Qurʾān has mentioned this incident and its subsequent reply.

Likewise, a reading of the *mawlid* of ʿĪsā ﷺ is extremely faith refreshing as well thought-provoking. Upon reading some of the minor details that have been related, one can only stop to think what was the need of mentioning such details. For example: mentioning the pain felt by Maryam ﷺ and her feelings of apprehension to the extent she exclaimed that she wished she had died before this or had been forgotten. Every minute detail has been mentioned from the moment Jibrāʾīl ﷺ made his presence to the birth of ʿĪsā ﷺ. By mentioning such details, Almighty Allah is creating awareness amongst the *Umma* that just as the Qurʾān has mentioned the *mawlid* of various prophets in detail, in the same way when the time comes to mentioning the *mawlid* of the most beloved servant of Almighty

Allah, our master Muhammad ﷺ, it too should be mentioned in a similar fashion. One should mention the accounts of his enlightened birth from the loins of Prophet Ādam ﷺ to the loins of ʿAbd Allāh ﷺ, until he came to the lap of Āmina ﷺ and subsequently was fostered by Ḥalīma al-Saʿdiya ﷺ. These events should be mentioned in such detail that all accounts, blessings, and miracles witnessed should be mentioned. This is the Sunna of Almighty Allah and the position adopted by the Qurʾān. The *mawlid* of other prophets have been mentioned through the means of revelation by our beloved Prophet ﷺ; and quite apparently, the mention of the *mawlid* of our esteemed Prophet ﷺ is to be done by the generations to come, as there will be no prophet after him. For this reason, his remembrance will have to be made by this *Umma*.

The *mawlid* of the Prophet ﷺ is the mention of those incidents which took place before and at the time of his auspicious birth. It is the mention of how the light (*nūr*) of the Holy Prophet ﷺ transferred from Ādam ﷺ to ʿAbd Allāh ﷺ, through the loins of pious men and the wombs of righteous women; and how through his birth, Almighty Allah bestowed manifold blessings upon humanity. Throughout the year, odes are recited in praise of the Prophet ﷺ but when the month of *Rabīʿ al-Awwal* arrives, a new life is breathed into this love, and special gatherings are held in his honour. On this occasion, some people recall the Prophet's beautiful tresses and cheeks, and others recall his heart-warming smile and his strolling in the streets of Mecca; some speak about the splendour of the Green Dome, others about the golden enclosures of his sacred tomb, the streets of Medina and its beauty. The memories of his noble mother Āmina ﷺ and his foster mother Ḥalīma refresh the scenes of Mecca fourteen centuries ago. In this month poems are sung in his love, and his remembrance is made. When the birth of the Prophet ﷺ is mentioned, the believers hearing these passionate poems feel that their dormant love for him awakens.

In the pages that have passed, we have shown how the Qurʾān has mentioned the *mawlid* of other prophets. These pages are a refutation to the one who questions the importance of mentioning the incidents surrounding the Prophet's birth. If after reading these verses one still thinks that these things are of no importance, then such a person is making an objection against the explicit text of the Qur'ān, and this only points to his own lack of knowledge and his misunderstanding. Through this Qur'ānic analysis, it is important to understand that making mention of the *mawlid* of the most exalted Prophet ﷺ is a Sunna of Almighty Allah; and until the Day of Judgment, it will be adopted by those who possess deep love for the beloved Prophet ﷺ in their hearts.

So how should this remembrance be made? Almighty Allah Himself explained this. By mentioning the events surrounding his auspicious birth, we are complying with the Sunna of Almighty Allah as He is the One who mentioned the *mawlid* of other prophets. We have explained that when Almighty Allah mentions the *mawlid* of the prophets in the Qur'ān, He does not overlook even the most minute detail. In this way, keeping this Sunna of Almighty Allah in mind in relation to remembering the Prophet ﷺ, we should mention his creation, his being a light (*nūr*), and his birth; we should make mention of his noble ancestry, his exclusive attributes and the miraculous events that took place when the Beloved ﷺ made his arrival to this world.

When the occasion arises, we commence this remembrance from Ādam ﷺ and go to Ibrāhīm ﷺ, then Ismā'īl ﷺ, and then to 'Abd Allāh ﷺ. After this, we mention how the Prophet ﷺ came to Āmina ﷺ and was looked after by Ḥalīma ﷺ, so that the delight of its remembrance brings ease to our hearts and forever imprints its virtue in our minds. The gatherings in which the birth of the Holy Prophet ﷺ is commemorated are the gatherings in which his prophethood is mentioned. Therefore, to say that holding such gatherings is impermissible—God forbid—is incorrect. The evidence from the Qur'ān and Sunna on the permissibility of celebrating *Mawlid al-Nabī* ﷺ and its constituent elements are contained in the subsequent chapters.

Chapter 4

Evidence from the Qurʾān on *Mawlid al-Nabī* ﷺ

DESTINY HAS DECREED SOME THINGS SUPERIOR TO OTHERS. Certain days and locations hold distinction over other days and locations in different respects. Similarly, some people have been given superiority over other people by Almighty Allah, such as Allah's raising some Messengers above others in rank:

﴿تِلْكَ ٱلرُّسُلُ فَضَّلْنَا بَعْضَهُمْ عَلَىٰ بَعْضٍ﴾

Of all these Messengers (whom We sent) We have exalted some above others.[1]

In the same way, Almighty Allah has preferred certain moments, days, and months over other moments, days, and months. Concerning the reason for the virtue of the month of *Ramaḍān*, the Qur'ān states:

﴿شَهْرُ رَمَضَانَ ٱلَّذِىٓ أُنزِلَ فِيهِ ٱلْقُرْءَانُ﴾

The month of Ramaḍān *(is the month) in which the Qur'ān has been sent down as guidance.*[2]

In this blessed month, there is a night (i.e., *Layla al-Qadr*) which possesses superiority over all other nights on account of the Qur'ān being revealed therein:

﴿إِنَّآ أَنزَلْنَـٰهُ فِى لَيْلَةِ ٱلْقَدْرِ﴾

Surely, We sent down this (Holy Qur'ān) during the Night of Destiny.[3]

---

[1] Qur'ān 2:253.

[2] Ibid., 2:185.

[3] Ibid., 97:1.

In a similar fashion, despite other holy sites, Almighty Allah only takes oath on the city of Mecca, thereby giving it superiority over other cities. The reason for this is that the Holy Prophet ﷺ spent most of his life in this city:

﴿لَآ أُقْسِمُ بِهَٰذَا ٱلْبَلَدِ ۝١ وَأَنتَ حِلٌّۢ بِهَٰذَا ٱلْبَلَدِ ۝٢﴾

> *I swear by this city (Mecca), (O My Esteemed Beloved,) because you are residing in it.*[1]

Likewise, after Islam and *īmān*, the basis of honour and merit amongst humanity is the criterion of piety (*taqwā*). Almighty Allah says:

﴿إِنَّ أَكْرَمَكُمْ عِندَ ٱللَّهِ أَتْقَىٰكُمْ﴾

> *Surely, the most honourable amongst you in the sight of Allah is he who fears Allah the most.*[2]

In sum, there are various verses in the Qurʾān in which Almighty Allah makes clear the sacredness of various things and the reasons for their superiority. Just as *Layla al-Qadr* is superior to a thousand months, the month of *Rabīʿ al-Awwal* also holds distinction in a similar way, because the one who brought us the Qurʾān was born in this month. This is the felicitous month in which Almighty Allah showered His blessings upon the believers by sending His most beloved Messenger ﷺ to them. Therefore, on account of the Prophet's blessed birth, the month of *Rabīʿ al-Awwal* is superior to all other months. If it is described as the month of his *mawlid*, it would be more fitting.

4.1 Evidence from the Commemoration of the Qurʾān's Descent

The Qurʾān is Allah's speech, and being one of His attributes, it possesses the quality of oneness. Its revelation is a great blessing

---

[1] Ibid., 90:1–2.

[2] Ibid., 49:13.

for mankind: through its light, man has been salvaged from the darkness of ignorance and has been bestowed honour and dignity. The Qurʾān was brought to us through a special human being: its light has been brought to us by a light. Almighty Allah says:

﴿قَدْ جَآءَكُم مِّنَ ٱللَّهِ نُورٌ وَكِتَـٰبٌ مُّبِينٌ﴾

There has indeed come to you a light from Allah (i.e., Muhammad ﷺ) and an Enlightening Book (i.e., the Holy Qurʾān).[1]

Through the knowledge of the Qurʾān, mankind has been made recipient of unending favours—what then would be the greatness of that man upon whom the Qurʾān was revealed? What would be the status of that person through whose teachings, vast treasures of knowledge and wisdom and the fountainhead of guidance were bestowed on mankind; upon whose heart Allah's revelation descended, and through whose beautiful conduct, he was declared its teacher? Who can grasp the loftiness of his station? The truth is that the Qurʾān in its totality is a collection of the beautiful remembrances of Allah's Messenger ﷺ; it is a recollection of his perfect character, his virtues and uniqueness amongst creation. No wonder Iqbāl wrote:

زِ قرآن پیش خود آئین آویز

دگرگون گشت از خویش بگریز

O believer! Read the Qurʾān to improve your character.
Yearn for him whose portrayal you perceive through the Qurʾān.[2]

We must therefore be grateful for such an immense blessing; this is one of the most important requirements for believing in it and having love for it. Yet this gratitude is incomplete without

---

[1] Ibid.,5:15.

[2] Iqbāl, *Kulliyāt: Armighān-e-Ḥijāz*, p.816.

appreciating the one through whose intermediation we became its recipients. For this reason, on the night in which the Qurʾān was revealed we hold gatherings to celebrate and remember the virtues of Almighty Allah's final revelation and its teaching; so why should we not do the same on the night in which that eminent personality was born through whose blessing we became the recipients of the Qurʾān? The night of his blessed birth should be commemorated, *a fortiori*, with much more concern.

4.1.1 Comparison between *Layla al-Qadr* and the Night of His Birth

The Qurʾān, a book in which the Prophet's ﷺ exemplary moral character is mentioned and his traits beautifully described, made on account of its revelation, a single night in the month of *Ramaḍān* superior in rank to a thousand months. This sacred night is the Night of Destiny (*Layla al-Qadr*) in which the Preserved Tablet (*al-Lawḥ al-Maḥfūẓ*) descended to the lower heavens. Almighty Allah made this night a means of achieving the esteemed rank for all the people until the Day of Judgment, and this night was declared the jewel in the crown amongst the nights. If this is true of the Qurʾān's descent, what would one say about him for whose sake the whole of creation came into existence, the one who enlightened the cosmos with perpetuating love and mercy and is the possessor of the Qurʾān? What esteem would the night of his birth hold in Almighty Allah's sight? Man's intellect is incapacitated to think what that might be.

The merit of *Layla al-Qadr* is because it is the night of the revelation of the Qurʾān and the descent of angels. But had it not been for the Holy Prophet ﷺ, there would not have been any revelation nor any *Layla al-Qadr*—even the whole of creation would not have come into origination. In reality, all of these blessings are because of the blessed birth of our Prophet ﷺ. Thus, were we to say that the night of his birth is superior to the Night of Destiny, it would be no exaggeration. By declaring the Night of Destiny to be greater than a thousand months, Almighty Allah has appointed a fixed limit to its virtue; on the other hand, the virtue of the night of his birth is beyond the limits of perception. However, it should be kept in mind that though the virtue of the night of his birth is greater, one should perform much worship on *Layla al-Qadr*, as the rewards which have been stipulated in the worship on this night is more, and this is established in the Qur'ān and hadith.

The imams and hadith-scholars have discussed the virtues of certain nights, such as the night of the 15th of *Shaʿbān*, *Layla al-Qadr*, the nights of *ʿīd al-Fiṭr* and *yawm ʿArafa*, and the night of his birth. Many amongst them have declared the night of his birth greater than *Layla al-Qadr*. Imam al-Qasṭallānī (923–851 AH), Shaykh ʿAbd al-Ḥaqq Muḥaddith al-Dihlawī (1052–958 AH), Imam al-Zurqānī (1122–1055 AH), and Imam al-Nabhānī (d. 1350 AH) all clearly state this.

1. Imam al-Qasṭallānī, concerning this, writes:

إِذَا قُلْنَا بِأَنَّهُ عَلَيْهِ الصَّلَاةُ وَالسَّلَامُ وُلِدَ لَيْلاً، فَأَيُّمَا أَفْضَلُ: لَيْلَةُ الْقَدْرِ أَوْ لَيْلَةُ مَوْلِدِهِ ﷺ؟ أُجِيْبُ: بِأَنَّ لَيْلَةَ مَوْلِدِهِ عَلَيْهِ الصَّلَاةُ وَالسَّلَامُ أَفْضَلُ مِنْ لَيْلَةِ الْقَدْرِ مِنْ وُجُوْهٍ ثَلَاثَةٍ:

أَحَدُهَا: أَنَّ لَيْلَةَ الْـمَوْلِدِ لَيْلَةُ ظُهُوْرِهِ ﷺ، وَلَيْلَةُ الْقَدْرِ مُعْطَاةٌ لَّهُ، وَمَا شَرُفَ بِظُهُوْرِ ذَاتِ الْـمُشْرِفِ مِنْ أَجْلِهِ أَشْرَفُ مِـمَّـا شَرُفَ بِسَبَبِ مَا أُعْطِيَهُ، وَلَا نِزَاعَ فِيْ ذَلِكَ، فَكَانَتْ لَيْلَةُ الْـمَوْلِدِ - بِهَذَا الْإِعْتِبَارِ - أَفْضَلُ.

الثَّانِي: أَنَّ لَيْلَةَ الْقَدْرِ شَرُفَتْ بِنُزُوْلِ الْـمَلَائِكَةِ فِيْهَا، وَلَيْلَةُ الْـمَوْلِدِ شَرُفَتْ بِظُهُوْرِهِ ﷺ فِيْهَا. وَمِـمَّنْ شَرُفَتْ بِهِ لَيْلَةُ الْـمَوْلِدِ أَفْضَلُ مِـمَّنْ شَرُفَتْ بِهِ لَيْلَةُ الْقَدْرِ، عَلَى الْأَصَحِّ الْـمُرْتَضَى (أَيْ عِنْدَ جُمْهُوْرِ أَهْلِ السُّنَّةِ) فَتَكُوْنُ لَيْلَةُ الْـمَوْلِدِ أَفْضَلَ.

اَلثَّالِثُ: لَيْلَةُ الْقَدْرِ وَقَعَ التَّفَضُّلُ فِيْهَا عَلَى أُمَّةِ مُحَمَّدٍ ﷺ، وَلَيْلَةُ الْـمَوْلِدِ الشَّرِيْفِ وَقَعَ التَّفَضُّلُ فِيْهَا عَلَى سَائِرِ الْـمَوْجُوْدَاتِ، فَهُوَ الَّذِي بَعَثَهُ اللهُ

تَعَالَى رَحْمَةً لِّلْعَالَـمِيْنَ، فَعَمَّتْ بِهِ النِّعْمَةُ عَلَى جَمِيْعِ الْـخَلَائِقِ، فَكَانَتْ لَيْلَةُ الْـمَوْلِدِ أَعَمَّ نَفْعاً، فَكَانَتْ أَفْضَلَ مِنْ لَيْلَةِ الْقَدْرِ بِهَذَا الِاعْتِبَارِ.

Saying that he was born in the night, which then of the two nights is superior: the Night of Destiny, or the night of his birth? My reply is that the night of his birth is superior to the Night of Destiny in three respects:

Firstly, the night of his birth is the night of his exalted appearance, whereas the Night of Destiny was bestowed upon him. That (night) which has been honoured by the manifestation of the cause of its honour is greater than that which was honoured on account of the thing which was bestowed because of him—and on this there is no dispute. Therefore, the night of his birth, in this respect, is greater.

Secondly, the Night of Destiny is honoured because the angels descend on that night, whilst the night of his birth is honoured because it is the night of his appearance. Since he is superior to the the angels, the night of *Mawlid al-Nabī* ﷺ is superior to the Night of Destiny. And according to the most reliable and approved verdict (i.e., the majority of the *Ahl al-Sunna*), the night of his birth is superior.

Thirdly, the virtue which occurs on the Night of Destiny is (exclusively) for the Community of Muhammad ﷺ, whilst the night of his birth, the virtue which occurred in it, is for everything in existence. It is he who was raised by Almighty Allah as a mercy for all the worlds; thus, the blessing is inclusive of the whole creation, and the night of his birth is of broader benefit. Therefore, it is superior to the Night of Destiny in this respect.[1]

---

[1] Al-Qasṭallānī, *al-Mawāhib al-ladunya bi al-minaḥ al-Muḥammadiyya*, 1:145; ʿAbd al-Ḥaqq al-Dihlawī, *Mā thabata min al-Sunna fī ayyām al-sana*, p.59–60; al-Zurqānī, *Sharḥ al-mawāhib al-ladunya bi al-minaḥ al-Muḥammadiyya*, 1:255–256; and al-Nabhānī, *Jawāhir al-biḥār fī faḍāʾil al-Nabī al-Mukhtār*, 3:424.

2. Imam al-Ṭaḥāwī (239–321 AH) transmits the opinions of some Shāfiʿī scholars:

أَنَّ أَفْضَلَ اللَّيَالِي لَيْلَةُ مَوْلِدِهِ ﷺ، ثُمَّ لَيْلَةُ الْقَدْرِ، ثُمَّ لَيْلَةُ الْإِسْرَاءِ وَالْـمِعْرَاجِ، ثُمَّ لَيْلَةُ عَرَفَةَ، ثُمَّ لَيْلَةُ الْـجُمُعَةِ، ثُمَّ لَيْلَةُ النِّصْفِ مِنْ شَعْبَانَ، ثُمَّ لَيْلَةُ الْعِيْدِ.

> The most superior night (in virtue) is the night of his birth, followed by the Night of Destiny, then the night of his night journey and ascension, followed by the night of *ʿArafa*, then the night of Friday, then the night of 15th of *Shaʿbān*, and then the night of *ʿĪd*.[1]

3. Imam al-Nabhānī (d. 1350 AH), in his well acclaimed masterpiece, *al-Anwār al-Muḥammadiyya fī al-mawāhib al-laduniyya* (p. 28), writes:

وَلَيْلَةُ مَوْلِدِهِ ﷺ أَفْضَلُ مِنْ لَيْلَةِ الْقَدْرِ.

> The night of his birth is superior to the Night of Destiny.

4. Muhammad ʿAbd al-Ḥayy Farangī Maḥallī Lakhnawī (1264–1304 AH), replying to the question whether the night of the Prophet's birth is superior or the Night of Destiny, writes:

> The superiority of *Layla al-Qadr* over all other nights is established from the texts and proven in several ways:
> 1. On this night, the Spirit and the angels descend to the earth.
> 2. From dusk till dawn, Allah's special manifestation (*tajallī*) descends to the lower heavens.
> 3. The Qurʾān descended from the Preserved Tablets (*al-Lawḥ al-Maḥfūẓ*) to the lower heavens on this night.

[1] Ibn ʿĀbidīn, *Radd al-muḥtār ʿalā durr al-mukhtār ʿalā tanwīr al-abṣār*, 2:511; al-Shirwānī, *Ḥāshiyya ʿalā tuḥfat al-muḥtāj bi-sharḥ al-minhāj*, 2:405; and al-Nabhānī, *Jawāhir al-biḥār fī faḍāʾil al-Nabī al-Mukhtār*, 3:426.

And on account of these merits, the *Umma* of Prophet Muhammad ﷺ has been given solace in that this one night amounts to more than a thousand months of worship. Almighty Allah states:

﴿لَيۡلَةُ ٱلۡقَدۡرِ خَيۡرٞ مِّنۡ أَلۡفِ شَهۡرٖ﴾

The Night of Destiny is better than a thousand months (in merit, blessings, reward and recompense).[1]

Staying awake in this night has also been emphasised in the hadith. Some of the hadith-scholars have preferred the night of *Mawlid al-Nabī* ﷺ over *Layla al-Qadr*; their position is not that worship on the night of *Mawlid al-Nabī* ﷺ is equal to that of *Layla al-Qadr*, because reward and punishment can only be established from a definitive text (*al-naṣṣ al-qaṭʿī*). Rather, the night of his most esteemed birth is superior to the Night of Destiny on account of its own distinction in the sight of Almighty Allah.[2]

The virtue of *Layla al-Qadr* is that on this night, the Qurʾān descended as well as the angels. On the other hand, the person of Prophet Muhammad ﷺ is so outstanding that it was upon him that the Qurʾān was revealed, and 70,000 angels constantly make visitation to his sacred tomb, circumambulating it, and sending their salutations on the Prophet ﷺ in the morning, with another 70,000 doing the same in the evening. This practice will continue until the Day of Judgment, and any angel who was blessed to make a visitation to the Prophet's sacred tomb once will not get a second chance to do so again.[3] The angels descend, entering the Prophet's

---

[1] Qurʾān 97:3.

[2] ʿAbd al-Ḥayy al-Lakhnawī, *Majmūʿa al-fatāwā*, 1:86–87.

[3] Ibn Mubārak in *al-Zuhd*, p.558 §1600; al-Dārimī in *al-Sunan*, 1:57 §94; al-Qurṭubī in *al-Tadhkira fī umūr aḥwāl al-mawtā wa umūr al-ākhira*, chapter: 'The Prophet's resurrection from his grave,' p.213–214; al-Najjār in *al-Radd ʿalā man yaqūl al-Qurʾān makhlūq*, p.63 §89; Ibn Ḥibbān in

court as humble servants. Their descent makes *Layla al-Qadr* superior to a thousand months, and yet the superiority of the night in which the honourable Prophet ﷺ came cannot be comprehended or imagined—countless months be sacrificed for that night of *Mawlid al-Nabī* ﷺ.

Another important point to keep in mind is that the virtue of *Layla al-Qadr* is exclusively for the believers, whereas *Mawlid al-Nabī* ﷺ is not only for the believers, but for the whole of mankind.

4.2 Evidence from the Commemoration of Receiving a Blessing

Almighty Allah has also bestowed His blessings on past communities, and in return, they expressed their thankfulness to Him through acts of celebration by making the day in which they received that blessing a day of festivity (*ʿīd*). The underlying purport of this example is to show that past communities, according to their customs and tradition, have been commemorating specific days; it is a practice which the Qur'ān endorses.[1] Thus, if previous communities expressed gratitude for minor blessings, is it not then

al-ʿAẓama, 3:1018–1019 §537; al-Azdī in *Faḍl al-ṣalāt ʿalā al-Nabī*, p.92 §101; al-Bayhaqī in *Shuʿab al-īmān*, 3:492–493 §4170; Abū Nuʿaym in *Ḥilya al-awliyā' wa ṭabaqāt al-aṣfiyā'*, 5:390; Ibn Jawzī in *al-Wafā' bi-aḥwāl al-Muṣṭafā*, p.833 §1578; Ibn al-Qayyim in *Jalā' al-afhām fī al-ṣalāt wa al-salām ʿalā Khayr al-anām*, p.68 §129; al-Samhūdī in *Wafā' al-wafā' bi-akhbār dār al-Muṣṭafā'*, 2:559; al-Qasṭallānī in *al-Mawāhib al-ladunya bi al-minaḥ al-Muḥammadiyya*, 4:625; al-Suyūṭī in *Kifāya al-ṭālib al-labīb fī khaṣā'iṣ al-Ḥabīb*, 2:376; al-Ṣāliḥī in *Subul al-hudā wa al-rashād fī sīra Khayr al-ʿibād*, 12:452–453; and al-Zurqānī in *Sharḥ al-mawāhib al-ladunya bi al-minaḥ al-Muḥammadiyya*, 12:283–284.

1

﴿ٱللَّهُمَّ رَبَّنَآ أَنزِلْ عَلَيْنَا مَآئِدَةً مِّنَ ٱلسَّمَآءِ تَكُونُ لَنَا عِيدًا لِّأَوَّلِنَا وَءَاخِرِنَا وَءَايَةً مِّنكَ﴾

O Allah, our Lord, send down to us from heaven the table spread (with bounties) so that (the day of its descent) becomes (ʿīd) *a festival day for us, and for our predecessors (as well as) our successors, and that (the table-spread) comes as a sign from You.* [Qur'ān 5:114]

all the more necessary for us to show our gratitude to Allah for being the recipients of the most significant blessing ever? Almighty Allah Himself has commanded us to do this:

﴿وَٱذۡكُرُواْ نِعۡمَتَ ٱللَّهِ عَلَيۡكُمۡ إِذۡ كُنتُمۡ أَعۡدَآءٗ فَأَلَّفَ بَيۡنَ قُلُوبِكُمۡ
فَأَصۡبَحۡتُم بِنِعۡمَتِهِۦٓ إِخۡوَٰنٗا﴾

But call to mind the blessing of Allah upon you when you were enemies (one to another). Then He created the bond of love amongst your hearts, and by His blessing you became brothers.[1]

What a wonderful act of benevolence without doubt that Almighty Allah, through His beloved Messenger ﷺ, united the hearts of those who were embroiled in the heat of conflict and discord. Those who were once thirsty for the blood of their brother were now bonded together. In reality, this blessing was received on account of the Prophet's raising amongst humankind: his very being is the source of this blessing. The Prophet's ﷺ arrival to this universe and the gratitude expressed by those who were reformed from their warring demeanours simply by bringing belief in him necessitates that on the occasion of the Holy Prophet's birth, we become the embodiment of thankfulness, expressing our gratitude to Almighty Allah.

4.3 Evidence from the Celebration of Independence

Remembering Almighty Allah's blessings through acts of gratitude is not only binding on the Community of Prophet Muhammad ﷺ, it has also been enjoined on previous communities. Almighty Allah commanded the Children of Israel, saying:

﴿يَٰبَنِيٓ إِسۡرَٰٓءِيلَ ٱذۡكُرُواْ نِعۡمَتِيَ ٱلَّتِيٓ أَنۡعَمۡتُ عَلَيۡكُمۡ وَأَنِّي فَضَّلۡتُكُمۡ
عَلَى ٱلۡعَٰلَمِينَ﴾

---

[1] Qur'ān 3:103.

O Children of Ya'qūb! Recall those favours that I bestowed upon you, and that I exalted you above all the people (of your age). [1]

Likewise, in other verses, Almighty Allah recounts His favours upon the Children of Israel:

﴿وَإِذْ نَجَّيْنَٰكُم مِّنْ ءَالِ فِرْعَوْنَ يَسُومُونَكُمْ سُوٓءَ ٱلْعَذَابِ﴾

And (also recall) when We delivered you from Pharaoh's people, who used to inflict severe torment upon you: they slaughtered your sons and kept your daughters alive. There was an arduously terrible trial in it from your Lord.[2]

From the above Qur'ānic verses, the following point can be derived that a nation's independence is a great blessing. The Children of Israel were ordered to show gratitude to Almighty Allah for being freed from captivity. The independence of our nation from the imperialism of the British Raj and the formation of a new Islamic state in the form of Pakistan is a great blessing from Almighty Allah. When we celebrate our independence day annually on the 14th of August, it becomes binding on us to commemorate this blessing in light of the Qur'ān's injunction of expressing gratitude to Almighty Allah.

Similarly, it is evident from the text of the Qur'ān that each year, commemorating the occasion of one's national independence and expressing gratitude in various other ways is not merely a worldly or political affair, but a religious one; failing to accept this is to depart from Allah's command. In each age, century, and era, there is a global culture; and every country, nation, and tribe has its own historical references which they commemorate as days of thanksgiving or merriment. There is not a country or place on this world in which there is not a festival of either religious or national significance. Jewish, Christian, Buddhist, Hindu, and even secular

---

[1] Ibid., 2:47.

[2] Ibid., 2:49.

nations, maintaining their cultural heritage and traditions have days of celebration. Almighty Allah has instructed the Muslims to observe His days (*ayyām Allāh*). The Prophet's person is for us the fountainhead of guidance in our lives, and the source of our culture and civilisation. In the backdrop of today's globalised monolithic culture, commemorating *Mawlid al-Nabī* ﷺ is of central importance for the flourishing of our Islamic identity.

4.3.1 An Important Requirement for the Continuation of Civilisation

In the verses quoted above, where the recalling of a favour is concerned, it is evident that the Qur'ān is referring to a specific incident. However, the requirement of showing gratitude is that Almighty Allah's blessing is remembered all the time, and that its memory is not erased from one's mind so that one is continually thanking Almighty Allah for it. It is, however, an accepted reality that, along with keeping that blessing in mind throughout the year, when the anniversary of that event comes, spontaneously, one's joy increases many folds. This is because it is an inevitable part of human nature as well as a cultural necessity that the exact time is remembered specifically and amply celebrated. Expressing happiness and joy on a blessing, in an organised fashion and as a means of showing gratitude, is necessary so that succeeding generations are aware of that blessing and know the significance of that day. It is only in such a way that a civilisation can preserve itself and its culture without being lost into the annals of history.

If we are unable to be grateful to Almighty Allah for His blessings and incapable of transmitting our most important traditions to the coming generations, then it will not be long before they will become unmindful of those blessings, and the significance of that day in which that blessing was attained becomes negligible in their estimation. Thus, the divine imperative necessitates that throughout the year, gratitude should be expressed to Almighty Allah, but when that specific day comes (the day when independence was attained), special preparations should be made for the expression of happiness and joy in the form of a celebration so that succeeding generations may come to know the importance of that day.

In the light of this discussion, if expressing gratitude for one's independence is established from the Qur'ān, how can it be then that expressing happiness on the Holy Prophet's birth is not permissible when he is the reason for the creation of the universe? It is through his mediation that all other blessings were attained.

4.4 EXPRESSING HAPPINESS ON A BLESSING IS THE SUNNA OF PROPHETS

When ʿĪsā ﷺ requested Almighty Allah to grant his community a table-spread from heaven, he supplicated in the following manner:

﴿ٱللَّهُمَّ رَبَّنَآ أَنزِلْ عَلَيْنَا مَآئِدَةً مِّنَ ٱلسَّمَآءِ تَكُونُ لَنَا عِيدًا لِّأَوَّلِنَا
وَءَاخِرِنَا وَءَايَةً مِّنكَ﴾

O Allah, our Lord, send down to us from heaven the table spread (with bounties) so that (the day of its descent) becomes (ʿīd) *a festival day for us, and for our predecessors (as well as) our successors, and that (the table-spread) comes as a sign from You.*[1]

In this verse, the Qur'ān, through the words of this Prophet, has given the concept that the day in which Allah's blessing descends that day should be commemorated as a day of festivity (*ʿīd*)—this is a commendable way of expressing gratitude for a blessing. The words, ﴾*for our predecessors*﴿, and ﴾*(as well as) our successors*﴿, indicate that after the reception of that blessing, there will be those who will come in the earlier periods of that community, and there will be those who will come in the latter periods; so those who come in the earlier periods should commemorate through acts of festivity (*ʿīd*), and those who come in the latter period should follow in a similar vein.

[1] Ibid., 5:114.

4.4.1 An Important Point to Consider

In the verse, there is the personal pronoun, 'our', in the words 'our predecessors' and 'our successors', which is indicative that this blessing will only be appreciated by those who are from amongst 'us'; whereas those who are not from 'us', they have no reason to join in the celebration. Here, the Qur'ān has placed a criterion for the states of people. That was the community of Prophet ʿĪsā ﷺ, whilst this is the community of Prophet Muhammad ﷺ. The same criterion has been placed on us in that when it is the month of *Rabīʿ al-Awwal*, on the day in which the Holy Prophet ﷺ was born, we should see who bears witness of being associated with that blessing and who does not. When the time of *Mawlid al-Nabī* ﷺ arrives, if, instead of joy, one feels agitated or doubts creep into mind, then it is a clear sign of a deficiency in one's *īmān*, and subsequently one should repent to Almighty Allah. This is because it is such a dangerous malady that warding it off is of overriding importance for the one who wishes to preserve his religion. How can it be that one makes claim to the Holy Prophet ﷺ, of being from his community, and yet does not express happiness upon his birth?

Demanding evidence for *Mawlid al-Nabī* ﷺ and debating for its impermissibility nullifies the requirements of faith, namely to love and honour the chief of all mankind, the Holy Prophet ﷺ. Love needs no evidence. When the blessed month of his birth arrives, a believer's heart should be in a state of joy, eagerness, and happiness. He should be filled with so much excitement that all other merriments are worthless, as true happiness is to be joyous upon his birth. He should feel that there cannot be a day more delightful than this, and he is unable to imagine any greater joy in this universe.

4.5 The Divine Injunction on Celebrating *Mawlid al-Nabī* ﷺ

One of the accepted means by which one can be grateful to Almighty Allah for His mercy and blessing is to expressively announce one's happiness and joy. And what blessing can be greater than *Mawlid al-Nabī* ﷺ? This is such a great blessing that Almighty Allah Himself has enjoined on us to be joyful on this occasion:

﴿قُلْ بِفَضْلِ ٱللَّهِ وَبِرَحْمَتِهِۦ فَبِذَٰلِكَ فَلْيَفْرَحُوا۟ هُوَ خَيْرٌ مِّمَّا يَجْمَعُونَ﴾

Say: (All this) is due to the bounty and mercy of Allah (bestowed upon you through raising Muhammad ﷺ as the exalted Messenger). So the Muslims should rejoice over it. This is far better than (all that affluence and wealth) that they amass.[1]

In this verse, Almighty Allah is addressing the beloved Prophet ﷺ that his noble Companions, and in turn the whole *Umma*, should be informed that Almighty Allah's blessing which has descended upon them in the form of Prophet Muhammad ﷺ should be celebrated jubilantly as much as possible. The obtaining of this blessing is a communal one, and so it should be celebrated by the community on a collective basis. As the injunction is to rejoice, this can only be done either by commemorating the blessing as a day of festivity (*ʿīd*), or by holding a celebration. This verse is therefore clear in its inference that the Muslims should commemorate the day of his birth by taking it as a day of happiness and joy (i.e., as a day of *ʿīd*). In relation to this, there are some important points which are listed below:

4.5.1 Qur'ānic Philosophy Concealed in the Word *Qul* [Say]

In the Qur'ān, Almighty Allah has addressed certain groups of people, e.g. when addressing mankind, He says, 'O people'; when addressing the believers, He says, 'O you who believe', and in other places when issuing a ruling, He employs the word 'say'. By issuing the command 'say', Almighty Allah is making an announcement by using the intermediation of His most beloved and venerable Prophet ﷺ.

The word 'say' is in the imperative conjugation. One of the

[1] Ibid., 10:58.

Qur'ānic maxims is that wherever the word 'say' is introduced, it is indicative of an important and fundamental reality of the religion. For example, when Almighty Allah announces His lordship and whilst explaining the correct understanding of His divine oneness, He states:

﴿قُلْ هُوَ ٱللَّهُ أَحَدٌ﴾

(O Esteemed Messenger!) Proclaim: He is Allah, Who is the One.[1]

Similarly, when explaining the purpose of servitude (which is to attain the love of Almighty Allah) and the means by which it is obtained, an injunction has been given for obedience to the Prophet ﷺ:

﴿قُلْ إِن كُنتُمْ تُحِبُّونَ ٱللَّهَ فَٱتَّبِعُونِى يُحْبِبْكُمُ ٱللَّهُ﴾

(O Beloved!) Say: If you love Allah, follow me. Allah will then take you as (His) beloved, and forgive you your sins for you, and Allah is Most Forgiving, Ever-Merciful.[2]

Likewise, for the expression of perfect servitude and outlining the philosophy of one's life, death, worship, and sacrifice for the sake of Almighty Allah, it states:

﴿قُلْ إِنَّ صَلَاتِى وَنُسُكِى وَمَحْيَاىَ وَمَمَاتِى لِلَّهِ رَبِّ ٱلْعَٰلَمِينَ﴾

Say: My Prayer, my Ḥajj (Pilgrimage) and my sacrifice (together with the entire worship and servitude) and my life and my death are for Allah alone, the Lord of all the worlds.[3]

---

[1] Ibid., 112:1.

[2] Ibid., 3:31.

[3] Ibid., 6:162.

With regards to the philosophy of this Qur'ānic style, the following points are of particular interest:

4.5.1.1 The Indispensability of Believing in the Messenger ﷺ before Believing in Allah

There is no doubt that the Qur'ān is the speech of Almighty Allah, which has been conveyed verbatim by the Holy Prophet ﷺ. Despite this, to obtain Almighty Allah's love and proximity, and to outline the fundamental creed and actions of Islam, the Qur'ān has used the medium of the word 'say', which in essence means, 'O beloved! You inform them'. From this we can see that a person's belief in Almighty Allah's divine oneness and obedience to Him is through the means of the Holy Prophet ﷺ. Therefore, it is befitting that this announcement is made by the most exalted Prophet ﷺ. From this account, it should be noted that one's belief in the Messenger ﷺ comes before one's belief in Almighty Allah.

If someone believes in Almighty Allah without believing in the most exalted Messenger ﷺ, that person can be anything but a believer. To enter the fold of Islam, it is necessary to believe in Almighty Allah through the means of Prophet Muhammad ﷺ. Any claim of affirming Almighty Allah's oneness accompanied with a denial of prophethood is in of itself disbelief. Therefore, the word 'say' designates the philosophy that the most exalted Prophet ﷺ is the sole means by which Almighty Allah's divine oneness can be achieved; without it, there is no possibility of attaining proximity to Almighty Allah.

بمصطفیٰ برساں خویش را کہ دیں ہمہ اوست

اگر بہ او نرسیدی، تمام بولھبی است

Religion in essence is nothing but submission to the commands of al-Muṣṭafā ﷺ
Were we not to reach his door we would surely be at complete loss.[1]

[1] Iqbāl, *Kulliyāt: Armighān-e-Ḥijāz*, p.691.

4.5.1.2 An Injunction's Importance and Significance Increases with the Word '*Say*'

Almighty Allah's speech has been conveyed to mankind through the means of Prophet Muhammad ﷺ. There are certain points where it is necessary to bring to attention the importance and significance of a certain injunction. For this purpose, the word 'say' is employed. This is indicative of the Holy Prophet's authority as the intermediary to Almighty Allah. Undoubtedly, the usage of the word 'say' in the Qur'ān has many wisdoms, e.g., if we ponder over the verse, ﴾*Say: (All this) is due to the bounty and mercy of Allah. So the Muslims should rejoice over it*﴿, we can derive much wisdom. Almighty Allah could have revealed this verse without the word 'say': e.g., 'O people, in the bounty and mercy of Almighty Allah, rejoice', but He did not say this; instead, He said, 'O beloved, with your tongue, inform them that in the bounty and mercy of Allah they should rejoice'.

A question comes to mind: the one who bestowed this blessing is Almighty Allah, and the ones who are to express happiness are His servants, so why did He enjoin on the believers to celebrate His mercy and blessing through the blessed lips of the Prophet ﷺ? Almighty Allah could have simply instructed them Himself, as He did with former communities by recalling His favours upon them. The reply to this is contained in the verse itself: it is showing the believers that they received all of these blessings through the venerable person of the Prophet Muhammad ﷺ and his raising as Almighty Allah's Messenger.

4.5.2 The Prophet ﷺ: The Blessing of Allah ﷻ and His Mercy

In *sūra Yūnus*, verse 58, rejoicing on two things has been mentioned: the bounty (*faḍl*) of Almighty Allah and His mercy (*raḥma*). Why have the words 'bounty' and 'mercy' been mentioned separately here, and what do they mean?

From amongst the styles of the Qur'ān, one style is that when the words *faḍl* and *raḥma* are mentioned, they refer to the blessed person of the Prophet ﷺ—further evidence on this will be given later. First, we will look at what is meant by the words *faḍl* and *raḥma*.

4.5.2.1 AN INTERESTING INTELLECTUAL POINT

There are two things mentioned in this verse:

1. Allah's bounty (*faḍl*)
2. Allah's mercy (*raḥma*)

Between these two words, there is the particle *waw* (and), which is for conjunction. According to general principles of grammar, the words *faḍl* and *raḥma* have been mentioned separately, indicating that they are two different things. Therefore, as a way of referring to them both, the demonstrative pronoun, *dhālika* (that), should have been used in its dual form—but it is not, instead it comes in its singular form. If this principle were to have been adopted, the verse would have stated, '*the Muslims should rejoice over them*'; but as it was not, the verse instead states, ﴾*The Muslims should rejoice over it*﴿.

In English grammar, we say, 'Zayd and Bakr are in the room'; not, 'Zayd and Bakr *is* in the room.' When there are two people mentioned, we use the plural form to refer to them both. Likewise in the Arabic language, *dhālika* (that) is used for a singular person or thing; but when we want to refer to the dual or plural, we use the demonstrative pronouns, *dhānika* and *ūlā'ika*, respectively. Keeping this principle in mind, if we look back at the verse, we will see that the singular demonstrative pronoun, *dhālika*, is employed after the words, *faḍl* and *raḥma*.

What is the wisdom behind this? Has the Qur'ān changed its principles. No, this is not the case. We have to accept that at this place, the singular demonstrative pronoun has been employed because the words *faḍl* and *raḥma* are in reference to a single thing. From this Qur'ānic style, the following point should be properly understood that Almighty Allah has in essence placed His *faḍl* and *raḥma* in a single being, and it is on account of this venerable being that we are being commanded to rejoice.

4.5.2.2 INTERPRETING THE QUR'ĀN THROUGH THE QUR'ĀN

If we were to interpret the aforementioned verse in light of other verses of the Qurʾān (known as *tafsīr al-Qurʾān bi al-Qurʾān*), it will become clear as the light of day that Almighty Allah's bounty and mercy is indeed Prophet Muhammad ﷺ. The interpretation for the word *raḥma* can be found in *sūra al-Anbiyāʾ*, in which Almighty Allah bestows His last Prophet ﷺ the epithet, 'mercy for all the worlds'.

1. In the Qurʾān, the Prophet ﷺ is explicitly declared a mercy:

﴿وَمَآ أَرۡسَلۡنَٰكَ إِلَّا رَحۡمَةٗ لِّلۡعَٰلَمِينَ﴾

> *And, (O Esteemed Messenger,) We have not sent you but as a mercy for all the worlds.*[1]

The Holy Prophet ﷺ has been made a paragon of mercy for the whole of creation, consisting not only of this universe but of other realms too. His holy person is the embodiment of mercy, which has been sent for the guidance and wellbeing of humanity. Almighty Allah's bounty and mercy, in the form of Prophet Muhammad ﷺ, has been made manifest in this world.

2. The Qurʾān, in another place whilst declaring the Prophet ﷺ as Allah's mercy and blessing, states:

﴿فَلَوۡلَا فَضۡلُ ٱللَّهِ عَلَيۡكُمۡ وَرَحۡمَتُهُۥ لَكُنتُم مِّنَ ٱلۡخَٰسِرِينَ﴾

> *So, had there not been Allah's bounty and His mercy upon you, you would have been wrecked indeed.*[2]

3. In the following verse, it is patently proven that the Prophet ﷺ is Allah's mercy and blessing:

﴿وَلَوۡلَا فَضۡلُ ٱللَّهِ عَلَيۡكُمۡ وَرَحۡمَتُهُۥ لَٱتَّبَعۡتُمُ ٱلشَّيۡطَٰنَ إِلَّا قَلِيلٗا﴾

> *Had there not been Allah's favour to you and His mercy, certainly you would (all) have followed Satan except only*

---

[1] Qurʾān 21:107.

[2] Ibid., 2:64.

a few.[1]

In this verse, Almighty Allah is addressing the believers in general and the Companions in particular. Whilst declaring the Holy Prophet's coming and raising as His blessing, Almighty Allah states that had it not been for the Prophet ﷺ, most people would have followed Satan, and consequently fallen prey to infidelity and polytheism. This is purely Allah's benevolence that He sent His beloved as a source of guidance, thereby saving them from Satan's trickeries and deception.

4. In another verse, Almighty Allah clearly states this:

﴿لَقَدْ مَنَّ ٱللَّهُ عَلَى ٱلْمُؤْمِنِينَ إِذْ بَعَثَ فِيهِمْ رَسُولًا مِّنْ أَنفُسِهِمْ يَتْلُوا۟ عَلَيْهِمْ ءَايَٰتِهِۦ وَيُزَكِّيهِمْ وَيُعَلِّمُهُمُ ٱلْكِتَٰبَ وَٱلْحِكْمَةَ وَإِن كَانُوا۟ مِن قَبْلُ لَفِى ضَلَٰلٍ مُّبِينٍ﴾

> *Indeed, Allah conferred a great favour on the believers that He raised amongst them (the most eminent) Messenger ﷺ from amongst themselves, who recites to them His Revelations, purifies them, and educates them on the Book and Wisdom though, before that, they were in manifest error.*[2]

Prior to the raising of the Chosen Prophet ﷺ, the whole of mankind was drowning in the darkness of misguidance and ignorance. It was in such conditions that the Holy Prophet ﷺ was sent amongst mankind. Through the recitation of the Qur'ān and the promulgation of its teachings, mankind was emancipated from the bondage of mental slavery, from ignorance and misguidance, and the light of faith was placed in their hearts, illuminating their souls with the Prophetic teachings by which they attained peace of mind. This was such an immense act of compassion that Almighty Allah declared it as His greatest favour. The raising of the Holy Prophet ﷺ is such a great bestowal that the statement, ﴿*So the*

[1] Ibid., 4:83.

[2] Ibid., 3:164.

Muslims should rejoice over it﴾, endorses it fully—no matter how much the believers rejoice, it can never be enough. This rejoicing should not merely be felt, rather it is necessary to be expressed openly.

5. Almighty Allah again makes reference to the aforementioned qualities:

﴿هُوَ ٱلَّذِى بَعَثَ فِى ٱلْأُمِّيِّـۧنَ رَسُولًا مِّنْهُمْ يَتْلُوا۟ عَلَيْهِمْ ءَايَٰتِهِۦ وَيُزَكِّيهِمْ
وَيُعَلِّمُهُمُ ٱلْكِتَٰبَ وَٱلْحِكْمَةَ وَإِن كَانُوا۟ مِن قَبْلُ لَفِى ضَلَٰلٍ مُّبِينٍ﴾

> *He is the One Who sent a (Glorious) Messenger* ﷺ *amongst the illiterate people from amongst themselves who recites to them His Revelations and cleanses and purifies them (outwardly and inwardly) and teaches them the Book and wisdom. Indeed they were in open error before (his most welcome arrival).*[1]

This verse is telling us that our most venerable master, Prophet Muhammad ﷺ, is indeed that Messenger who came to purify mankind from the filth of misguidance and disbelief by reciting Almighty Allah's revelation to them. And it was he who cleansed their inner selves from internal impurities, and bestowed the light of knowledge and wisdom to them by which they attained the great gift of Almighty Allah's gnosis and His guidance. Otherwise, before this they were plainly in error. The Holy Prophet's arrival is indeed the manifestation of the light of divine guidance, and this is Almighty Allah's blessing and mercy. It is binding on the believers that they express their gratitude for this.

6. In the verse subsequent to it, Almighty Allah has included all coming generations, up till the Day of Judgment, within the fold of this blessing:

﴿وَءَاخَرِينَ مِنْهُمْ لَمَّا يَلْحَقُوا۟ بِهِمْ ۚ وَهُوَ ٱلْعَزِيزُ ٱلْحَكِيمُ ۝٣ ذَٰلِكَ فَضْلُ
ٱللَّهِ يُؤْتِيهِ مَن يَشَآءُ ۚ وَٱللَّهُ ذُو ٱلْفَضْلِ ٱلْعَظِيمِ ۝٤﴾

[1] Ibid., 62:2.

> *And (He has sent this Messenger for purification and education amongst) others of them also who have not yet joined these people (that are present now i.e., they will come after them in the time to come). And He is Almighty, Most Wise. This (arrival of the Holy Messenger* ﷺ *as well as his spiritual benevolence) is Allah's bounty which He grants whom He likes. And Allah is Most Bountiful.*[1]

In the aforementioned verse of *sūra al-Jumuʿa*, Almighty Allah first describes His Prophet ﷺ as a Messenger and thereafter designates him as His blessing. It is established from these verses that Almighty Allah has sent His beloved Prophet ﷺ as a Messenger for all creatures: no person, place or time has been made an exception to this.

Those who were blessed with his Companionship were placed in the first generation of this community, and it was within their midst that the Holy Prophet ﷺ was born. In the third verse of *sūra al-Jumuʿa*, the ﴾*others of them*﴿ have been mentioned, and they are the people who will come after the Prophet's physical appearance. It includes all people of other nationalities and civilisations who entered the fold of Islam and will continue to become the members of the Prophet's community, as the verse says ﴾*also who have not yet joined these people (that are present now i.e., they will come after them in the time to come)*﴿. As they are born in a different epoch to the Prophet ﷺ, they are considered to be amongst the latter generations who were not able to see and meet him directly.

After mentioning the raising of the most exalted Prophet ﷺ, Almighty Allah states, ﴾*That is Allah's bounty*﴿: this is in reference to the Prophet's person. It is as though Almighty Allah is saying that the birth of the beloved Prophet ﷺ—and his raising for those who came after him and later on the gnosis of him—is Almighty Allah's grace which He ﷻ grants to whom He wills. So, whoever is filled with immense love of His beloved Messenger ﷺ and venerates him is the one who is a recipient of Almighty Allah's bounty. Just

---

[1] Ibid., 62:3–4.

as Almighty Allah has bestowed His blessing on those who came in the period in which the Holy Prophet ﷺ was born, those who came after him will also be showered with His mercy and favours.

Before proceeding to give further explanations of verse 58 of *sūra Yūnus*, it is necessary that the notions given in verse 4 of *sūra al-Jumuʿa* are properly understood first. The following is an exegesis of this verse:

4.5.2.2.1 The Meaning of ﴾*And Allah is Most Bountiful*﴿

Almighty Allah, who is the Originator of the whole creation, is the owner of all greatness and magnitudes. In His bounty, He is most great indeed, and He has authority over all things. It is important to note this most pertinent point that Almighty Allah is the owner of the bounty: He himself is not the bounty. As a way of example, when enquiring about a certain house and who it belongs to, the reply will be that so and so person is the owner of the house. In light of Arabic grammar, this is known as *al-iḍāfa* (the genitive construct), which is used to indicate possession and comprises a determined noun, *muḍāf* (possessed), and a determining noun, *muḍāf ilayh* (possessor). Though they come together, they are essentially separate from one another, e.g., the book's owner; the possessor and possessed are separate to each other; they can never be the same thing. Another example is 'Allah's Messenger': the word 'Messenger' is the noun which is possessed, and the word 'Allah' is its possessor; so in light of this rule, neither the Messenger can be Allah, nor can Allah be the Messenger.

After understanding this point, let us look back to this verse again and apply this rule. In this verse, Almighty Allah states: ﴾*And Allah is the possessor of the great bounty*﴿. The words ﴾*possessor of the bounty*﴿ is a genitive construct. In light of grammar, the possessor and the possessed are always different from each other. Thus, it is understood that the 'bounty' and the 'possessor' are two different things. Almighty Allah is the owner of that bounty; He Himself is not the bounty, because the bounty is that thing which has been bestowed by Almighty Allah.

The question here is that if Almighty Allah is not the bounty, who then is the bounty? The answer to this is that the bounty is the Prophet's esteemed being, which Almighty Allah has sent as a mercy and guidance for the whole of mankind. In order to substantiate this point further, the following is a compilation of a number of authoritative exegeses which will make clear this ambiguity.

4.5.2.2.2 THE MEANING OF *FAḌL* ACCORDING TO LEADING EXEGETES

Sūra al-Jumuʿa, verse 4, has been revealed for the blessed arrival of the Prophet of mercy, Prophet Muhammad ﷺ. His blessed advent was for all mankind, and it was declared a blessing by Almighty Allah. If anyone wants to see this blessing in its embodiment, let him look at the Prophet ﷺ. This point itself is elaborated by the Qur'ān. The following is a selection of some key exegeses relating to this specific verse in question.

1. ʿAbd Allāh b. ʿAbbās ﷺ (D. 68 AH) states that the great bounty means:

﴿ذُو ٱلْفَضْلِ﴾ اَلْـمَنِّ ﴿ٱلْعَظِيمِ﴾ بِالْإِسْلَامِ وَالنُّبُوَّةِ عَلَى مُحَمَّدٍ، وَيُقَالُ: بِالْإِسْلَامِ عَلَى الْـمُؤْمِنِيْنَ، وَيُقَالُ: بِالرَّسُوْلِ وَالْكِتَابِ عَلَى خَلْقِهِ.

﴾*(And Allah) is Most Bountiful*﴿ refers to a blessing, which is Islam and the prophethood bestowed on Prophet Muhammad ﷺ. It is also said that it is Islam bestowed on the believers. And it is also said that it is the Prophet ﷺ and the Qur'ān which have been bestowed on creation.[1]

2. Al-Zamakhsharī (467–538 AH) writes:

﴿ذَٰلِكَ﴾ اَلْفَضْلُ الَّذِي أَعْطَاهُ مُحَمَّدًا وَهُوَ أَنْ يَّكُوْنَ نَبِيَّ أَبْنَاءِ عَصْرِهِ، وَنَبِيَّ أَبْنَاءِ الْعُصُوْرِ الْغَوَابِرِ، هُوَ ﴿فَضْلُ ٱللَّهِ يُؤْتِيهِ مَن يَشَآءُ﴾.

﴾*That*﴿ blessing which Almighty Allah has bestowed

---

[1] Fayrūz Ābādī, *Tanwīr al-miqbās min tafsīr Ibn ʿAbbās*, p.471.

> on Muhammad ﷺ, who is the Prophet of the people of his time [till the Day of Judgment] and the time that has passed: that ﴾is *Allah's bounty which He grants to whom He likes*﴿.[1]

3. Al-Ṭabrasī (b. 548 AH) states:

> ﴿وَٱللَّهُ ذُو ٱلۡفَضۡلِ ٱلۡعَظِيمِ﴾ ذُو الْـمَنِّ الْعَظِيْمِ عَلَى خَلْقِهِ بِبَعْثِ مُحَمَّدٍ.
>
> ﴾*And Allah is Most Bountiful*﴿, the owner of the great blessing upon his creation by raising Prophet Muhammad.[2]

That is: the most respectable Prophet's raising amongst mankind is a greatest blessing from Almighty Allah and an act of His benevolence.

4. Ibn al-Jawzī (510–579 AH) states:

> ﴿وَٱللَّهُ ذُو ٱلۡفَضۡلِ ٱلۡعَظِيمِ﴾ بِإِرْسَالِ مُحَمَّدٍ.
>
> ﴾*And Allah is Most Bountiful*﴿ by sending Prophet Muhammad ﷺ.[3]

That is: Almighty Allah's sending the most revered Prophet ﷺ to mankind is a very great blessing and reward.

5. Imam al-Nasafī (b. 710 AH) states:

> ﴿ذَٰلِكَ﴾ الْفَضْلُ الَّذِي أَعْطَاهُ مُحَمَّدًا ... وَهُوَ أَنْ يَكُوْنَ نَبِيَّ أَبْنَآءِ عَصْرِهِ وَنَبِيَّ أَبْنَآءِ الْعُصُوْرِ الْغَوَابِرِ.
>
> ﴾*That*﴿ blessing which Allah has bestowed on Muhammad... he is the prophet of the people of his time

---

[1] Al-Zamakhsharī, *al-Kashshāf ʿan ḥaqāʾiq ghawāmiḍ al-tanzīl wa ʿuyūn al-aqāwīl fī wujūh al-taʾwīl*, 4:530.

[2] Al-Ṭabrasī, *Majmaʿ al-bayān fī tafsīr al-Qurʾān*, 10:429.

[3] Ibn Jawzī, *Zād al-masīr fī ʿilm al-tafsīr*, 8:260.

[till the Day of Judgment] and the time that has passed.[1]

The blessed sending and raising of the most merciful Prophet ﷺ encompasses the whole of mankind in the fold of its mercy: all those who passed before him and all those yet to come till the Day of Judgment are included within its scope. This is the interpretation of the verse, ﴿*That is Allah's bounty which He grants to whom He likes*﴾ in which Imam al-Nasafī covers both meanings. Allah's statement, ﴿*And others of them also who have not yet joined these people*﴾ is inclusive of those who would come later, who would not be able to see him; the Prophet ﷺ is also a messenger for them, and they too are ordered to 'rejoice' on his coming to this world.
6. Imam al-Khāzin (741–678 AH), interpreting what the 'Great Bounty' is, states:

أَيْ عَلَى خَلْقِهِ حَيْثُ أَرْسَلَ فِيْهِمْ رَسُوْلَهُ مُحَمَّدًا ﷺ.

That is: upon the creation whereby Allah sent Muhammad ﷺ as a messenger amongst them.[2]

7. Abū Ḥayyān al-Andalusī (682–749 AH) states:

وَ ﴿ذَٰلِكَ﴾ إِشَارَةٌ إِلَى بِعْثَتِهِ ﷺ.

﴿*That*﴾ is indicative to his raising.[3]

8. Ibn Kathīr (701–774 AH) explains:

يَعْنِي مَا أَعْطَاهُ اللهُ مُحَمَّدًا ﷺ مِنَ النُّبُوَّةِ الْعَظِيْمَةِ، وَمَا خَصَّ بِهِ أُمَّتَهُ مِنْ بِعْثَتِهِ ﷺ.

That is: what Allah has bestowed on Muhammad ﷺ of the manifest prophethood, and the attributes bestowed

[1] Al-Nasafī, *Madārik al-tanzīl wa ḥaqā'iq al-ta'wīl*, 5:198.

[2] Al-Khāzin, *Lubāb al-ta'wīl fī ma'ānī al-tanzīl*, 4:265.

[3] Abū Ḥayyān, *Tafsīr al-baḥr al-muḥīṭ*, 8:265.

on his Community through his raising.[1]

Therefore, the Prophet's blessed arrival and his messengerhood are both great blessings of Almighty Allah.

9. Imam al-Suyūṭī (911–849 AH) states:

﴿ذَٰلِكَ فَضْلُ ٱللَّهِ يُؤْتِيهِ مَن يَشَآءُ﴾ اَلنَّبِيُّ وَمَنْ ذُكِرَ مَعَهُ.

﴿*That is Allah's bounty which He grants to whom He likes*﴾ refers to the Prophet ﷺ and those who are mentioned with him.[2]

10. Al-Ālūsī (1270–1217 AH) states:

﴿ذَٰلِكَ﴾ إِشَارَةٌ إِلَى مَا تَقَدَّمَ مِنْ كَوْنِهِ عَلَيْهِ الصَّلَاةُ وَالسَّلَامُ رَسُوْلاً فِي الْأُمِّيِّيْنَ وَمَنْ بَعْدَهُمْ مُعَلِّمًا مُزَكِّياً، وَمَا فِيْهِ مِنْ مَعْنَى الْبُعْدِ لِلتَّعْظِيْمِ أَيْ ذَلِكَ الْفَضْلُ الْعَظِيْمُ.

﴿*That*﴾ is indicative to what has passed, such as his being an exalted messenger amongst the unlettered people, those after them as a teacher and the one who purifies. The meaning of distance in it is for veneration, i.e., 'that great blessing'.[3]

11. Aḥmad Muṣṭafā al-Marāghī (1300–1372 AH) comments:

أَيْ وَإِرْسَالُ هَذَا الرَّسُوْلِ إِلَى الْبَشَرِ مُزَكِّياً مُطَهِّرًا لَّهُمْ، هَادِياً مُعَلِّماً، فَضْلٌ مِّنَ اللهِ، وَإِحْسَانٌ مِّنْهُ إِلَى عِبَادِهِ.

That is, the sending of this beloved Messenger ﷺ to mankind as the one who purifies and cleanses them as a

[1] Ibn Kathīr, *Tafsīr al-Qurʾān al-ʿaẓīm*, 4:364.

[2] Al-Suyūṭī, *Tafsīr al-Jalālayn*, p.553.

[3] Al-Ālūsī, *Rūḥ al-maʿānī fī Tafsīr al-Qurʾān al-ʿaẓīm wa al-Sabʿ al-Mathānī*, 28:94–95.

teacher and guide is a blessing from Almighty Allah, and an act of benevolence from Him to His servants.[1]

12. Al-Ṭanṭāwī al-Jawharī (D. 1359 AH), a contemporary and well-known exegete from Egypt, explains:

﴿وَٱللَّهُ ذُو ٱلْفَضْلِ ٱلْعَظِيمِ﴾ فَإِذَا كَانَ مُحَمَّدٌ قَدْ أَرْسَلْتُهُ إِلَيْكُمْ أَيُّهَا الأُمِّيُّونَ وَإِلَى مَنْ يَأْتِي بَعْدَكُمْ.

﴾*And Allah is Most Bountiful*﴿: it became the blessing upon you when I sent Muhammad ﷺ to you, O unlettered people, and to those who will come after you.[2]

It is evident from the above exegeses that the most exalted Prophet ﷺ is being declared without exception a blessing for everyone. Since it is established from a definitive text (*al-naṣṣ al-qaṭʿi*) that Almighty Allah is declaring His Prophet ﷺ as His blessing and mercy, then to celebrate *Mawlid al-Nabī* ﷺ under the command ﴾*So the Muslims should rejoice over it*﴿, is therefore in accordance with the divine ruling and the teaching of the Qur᾽ān.

4.5.2.2.3 THE MEANING OF *FAḌL* AND *RAḤMA* ACCORDING TO LEADING EXEGETES

In the previous pages, the verses of *sūra al-Jumuʿa* were explained. Now we will look at verse 58 of *sūra al-Yūnus* in order to better understand the meaning of the words *faḍl* and *raḥma* in light of selected exegeses of the Qur᾽ān:

1. Ibn al-Jawzī (510–579 AH) transmits the statement of ʿAbd Allāh b. ʿAbbās ﷺ:

إِنَّ ﴿فَضْلُ ٱللَّهِ﴾: الْعِلْمُ، وَرَحْمَتُهُ: مُحَمَّدٌ. رَوَاهُ الضَّحَّاكُ عَنِ ابْنِ عَبَّاسٍ.

﴾Allah's bounty﴿ is knowledge (i.e., the Qur᾽ān) and His

[1] Aḥmad al-Marāghī, *Tafsīr al-Qur᾽ān al-kārīm*, 10/28:96.

[2] Al-Ṭanṭāwī al-Jawharī, *al-Jawāhir fī tafsīr al-Qur᾽ān al-kārīm*, 24:175.

mercy is Prophet Muhammad ﷺ. Al-Ḍaḥḥāk reports it from ʿAbd Allāh b. ʿAbbās ؓ.¹

2. Abū Ḥayyān al-Andalusī (682–749 AH) reports:

وَقَالَ ابْنُ عَبَّاسٍ فِيمَا رَوَى الضَّحَّاكُ عَنْهُ: اَلْفَضْلُ: اَلْعِلْمُ، وَالرَّحْمَةُ: مُحَمَّدٌ

Al-Ḍaḥḥāk narrates that ʿAbd Allāh b. ʿAbbās ؓ said: the bounty is knowledge (i.e., the Qurʾān) and the mercy is Prophet Muhammad ﷺ.²

3. Imam al-Suyūṭī (849–911 AH), also reporting the statement of ʿAbd Allāh b. ʿAbbās ؓ, states:

وَأَخْرَجَ أَبُو الشَّيْخِ عَنِ ابْنِ عَبَّاسٍ فِي الْآيَةِ، قَالَ: فَضْلُ اللَّهِ: اَلْعِلْمُ، وَرَحْمَتُهُ: مُحَمَّدٌ. قَالَ اللهُ: ﴿وَمَآ أَرۡسَلۡنَٰكَ إِلَّا رَحۡمَةً لِّلۡعَٰلَمِينَ﴾.

Abū al-Shaykh reports from Ibn ʿAbbās ؓ that in this verse, Allah's bounty is knowledge (i.e., the Qurʾān) and His mercy is Prophet Muhammad ﷺ. Almighty Allah states: ⟨And, (O Esteemed Messenger,) We have not sent you but as a mercy for all the worlds³⟩.⁴

4. Imam al-Ālūsī (1217–1270 AH) states:

وَأَخْرَجَ أَبُو الشَّيْخِ عَنِ ابْنِ عَبَّاسٍ أَنَّ الْفَضْلَ: اَلْعِلْمُ، وَالرَّحْمَةُ: مُحَمَّدٌ، وَأَخْرَجَ الْخَطِيبُ وَابْنُ عَسَاكِرَ عَنْهُ تَفْسِيرَ الْفَضْلِ بِالنَّبِيِّ عَلَيْهِ الصَّلَاةُ وَالسَّلَامُ.

---

¹ Ibn Jawzī, Zād al-masīr fī ʿilm al-tafsīr, 4:40.
² Abū Ḥayyān, Tafsīr al-baḥr al-muḥīṭ, 5:171.
³ Qurʾān 21:107.
⁴ Al-Suyūṭī, al-Durr al-manthūr fī al-tafsīr bi al-maʾthūr, 4:330.

> Abū al-Shaykh reports from ʿAbd Allāh b. ʿAbbās ؓ that Allah's bounty is knowledge (i.e., the Qur᾿ān) and His mercy is Prophet Muhammad ﷺ. Al-Khaṭīb and Ibn ʿAsākir have both reported from him that the meaning of bounty is the Prophet ﷺ.[1]

From the above exegeses, it is quite clear that ʿAbd Allāh b. ʿAbbās ؓ interprets bounty as knowledge, and knowledge here means the Qur᾿ān. The following verse helps to substantiate this point of view:

﴿وَعَلَّمَكَ مَا لَمْ تَكُن تَعْلَمُ ۚ وَكَانَ فَضْلُ ٱللَّهِ عَلَيْكَ عَظِيمًا﴾

> *And Allah has revealed to you the Book and Wisdom and has bestowed upon you all that knowledge which you did not possess. Mighty indeed is Allah's bounty on you.*[2]

If the meaning of bounty in this verse is either knowledge or the Qur᾿ān, even then, through deeper implication of its meaning, we can see that it refers to the most exalted Prophet ﷺ—as it was through his intermediation that the Qur᾿ān was received. The leader of exegetes of this community, and the glorious Companion, ʿAbd Allāh b. ʿAbbās ؓ, is the one who has given us the insight that the most exalted Prophet ﷺ is Almighty Allah's bounty and mercy. In the same verse, the words, ﴾*So the Muslims should rejoice over it*﴿, provide us with the understanding of expressing happiness on the occasion of *Mawlid al-Nabī* ﷺ; it is the means by which one can rejoice on Almighty Allah's bounty and mercy—when looking at it like this, no intelligent Muslim can disagree. This exegesis has unravelled the secrets of the verse above and has established the point that expressing joy and happiness on Almighty Allah's bounty and mercy in the form of celebrating *Mawlid al-Nabī* ﷺ is Almighty Allah's decree.

Al-Ṭabrasī (B. 548 AH) states:

---

1 Al-Ālūsī, *Rūḥ al-maʿānī fī Tafsīr al-Qur᾿ān al-ʿaẓīm wa al-Sabʿ al-Mathānī*, 11:141.

2 Qur᾿ān 4:113.

وَمَعْنَى الْآيَةِ قُلْ لِهَؤُلَاءِ الْفَرِحِيْنَ بِالدُّنْيَا الْمُعْتَدِيْنَ بِهَا الْجَامِعِيْنَ لَهَا إِذَا فَرِحْتُمْ بِشَيْءٍ فَافْرَحُوْا بِفَضْلِ اللهِ عَلَيْكُمْ وَرَحْمَتِهِ لَكُمْ بِإِنْزَالِ هَذَا الْقُرْآنِ وَإِرْسَالِ مُحَمَّدٍ إِلَيْكُمْ فَإِنَّكُمْ تَحْصُلُوْنَ بِهِمَا نَعِيْمًا دَائِمًا مُقِيْمًا هُوَ خَيْرٌ لَّكُمْ مِنْ هَذِهِ الدُّنْيَا الْفَانِيَةِ... عَنْ قَتَادَةَ وَمُجَاهِدٍ وَغَيْرِهِمَا قَالَ أَبُوْ جَعْفَرٍ الْبَاقِرِ عليه السلام: ﴿فَضْلُ ٱللَّهِ﴾ رَسُوْلُ اللهِ ﷺ.

> The meaning of this verse is: Say to these people who are happy with the world, vying one another for it and garnering it, that if you are to rejoice over something, rejoice in Allah's bounty and mercy upon you by revealing this Qurʾān and sending Prophet Muhammad ﷺ to you. (And if you do this), you shall attain by them a permanent and eternal blessing, which is better for you than this fleeting world... Qatāda and Mujāhid both narrate that Abū Jaʿfar al-Bāqir states: ﴾*Allah's bounty*﴿ is the Messenger of Allah ﷺ.[1]

It can be understood from the explanation provided by the exegeses above that amongst the blessings bestowed by Almighty Allah, the greatest of these is the Qurʾān and the Prophet Muhammad ﷺ. What this means is that only these two things are worth rejoicing over. If one is to celebrate something, let one celebrate the day in which our beloved Prophet ﷺ was born, as there is no day greater.

4.5.2.2.4 The View of Ashraf ʿAlī Thānwī

As a side note, it is worth mentioning the point of view of Ashraf ʿAlī Thānwī (1280–1362 AH), who is a prominent scholar belonging to the *Deobandi* school of thought. Just as it has been mentioned previously that the words *faḍl* and *raḥma* are a reference to the Prophet ﷺ, Thānwī, in his book '*Mīlād al-Nabī* ﷺ' (which is a compilation of his lectures), likewise states that the Prophet ﷺ is

---

1 Al-Ṭabrasī, *Majmaʿ al-bayān fī tafsīr al-Qurʾān*, 5:177–178.

Allah's greatest blessing and most perfect bounty.[1]

---

[1] Ashraf ʿAlī Thānwī whilst declaring that the original meaning of the verse in question is in reference to the Qurʾān, explains:

> Now, let us look at other verses of the Qurʾān to see what is meant by those two words (i.e., bounty and mercy)? It should be known that these two words come up plentifully in the Qurʾān. Sometimes, both refer to a single meaning, and at other places, they refer to two different ones. Thus, in one verse, Allah ﷻ states:
>
> ﴿فَلَوْلَا فَضْلُ ٱللَّهِ عَلَيْكُمْ وَرَحْمَتُهُۥ لَكُنتُم مِّنَ ٱلْخَٰسِرِينَ﴾
>
> *So, had there not been Allah's bounty and His mercy upon you, you would have been wrecked indeed.* [Qurʾān 2:64]
>
> Here, according to majority of the exegetes, the words, *faḍl* and *raḥma*, refer to the Prophet's blessed being. In another verse, it states:
>
> ﴿وَلَوْلَا فَضْلُ ٱللَّهِ عَلَيْكُمْ وَرَحْمَتُهُۥ لَٱتَّبَعْتُمُ ٱلشَّيْطَٰنَ إِلَّا قَلِيلًا﴾
>
> *Had there not been Allah's favour to you and His mercy, certainly you would (all) have followed Satan except only a few.* [Qurʾān 4:83]
>
> Here too, the majority of the exegetes have said that the Prophet ﷺ is meant here.
>
> In some verses, bounty refers to a worldly blessing, whilst mercy refers to a religious one. Thus, according to all the exegesis, he is a worldly blessing and a religious blessing.

Ashraf ʿAlī Thānwī further states:

> In this verse, when looking at its context, we can see that it refers to the Qurʾān. However, if we were to take it as a general meaning, then the Qurʾān should be taken as one of the objects which is more appropriate. That is, *faḍl* and *raḥma* should refer to the Holy Prophet's blessed arrival. According to this understanding, all the blessings, whether they are worldly or religious, the Qurʾān including, are contained within this. This is because the Prophet's blessed being is the source of all other blessings, and the essence of all bounty and mercy. Thus, this is the most comprehensive explanation; and on the basis of this exegesis, the summary of this verse is that whether it be the existence of the Prophet's light (*nūr*) or his physical birth, one should express their happiness, as he is the means of all blessing. (Apart from other general blessing,) the most superior blessing is faith

The reason for this is that this can be understood from the inferred meaning of the text (*dalāla al-naṣṣ*), i.e., that the words *faḍl* and *raḥma* refer to the Holy Prophet ﷺ. Almighty Allah is enjoining on the believers to celebrate the Prophet of mercy, who is the source of all our worldly and religious blessing. If anyone wants to see Almighty Allah's bounty and mercy in its physical embodiment, let him look at the Prophet ﷺ, who was made the paragon of His blessing and mercy. Therefore, the blessing and mercy of Almighty Allah have been gathered together in a single being, which is the being of the Holy Prophet ﷺ, who was sent for all places and epochs without exception.

It can be understood from this injunction that this verse is demanding the believers to rejoice, and hence it is applicable to all Muslims. So, on the occasion of his auspicious birth, they should express their happiness and joy, and whilst observing the limits set by the Sharia, whatever bliss is rejoiced will be permissible.

4.5.3 Why we Should Celebrate *Faḍl* and *Raḥma*

Why has Almighty Allah, in *sūra Yūnus*, verse 58, enjoined on us to rejoice in His *faḍl* and *raḥma*? What is the cause on the basis of which Almighty Allah wants us to express happiness on receiving such a blessing? Before knowing this, it is important to understand that the words *faḍl* and *raḥma* have been expressed in a certain context. In various verses, the Qurʾān has explained the background to this, which has been mentioned in the discussion that precedes us.

Almighty Allah, by addressing the Muslims, is stating that had it not been for His *faḍl* and *raḥma* in the form of the arrival of His Beloved Messenger ﷺ, then all of you, if not most, would have been led astray or would have been destroyed in your obedience of Satan. Had the most exalted Prophet ﷺ not been sent to mankind, who then would have saved you from the darkness of misguidance

---

(*īmān*), which quite obviously was brought to us by the Prophet ﷺ. In conclusion, taking all the information into account, *faḍl* and *raḥma* are the Prophet's auspicious being. Thus, one can never do enough to express one's happiness and joy upon the existence of his blessed person. [Ashraf ʿAlī Thānwī, *Khuṭbāt Mīlād al-Nabī*, pp. 63–65.]

and error, freeing you from the shackles of disbelief and polytheism, taking you into the light of divine truth and guidance? Had it not been for our noble guide, mankind would have been plunged into the depths of anarchy, cruelty and oppression, and man's fundamental human rights would not have been preserved.

We have been enjoined to express happiness upon the arrival of that esteemed being who brought the light of Almighty Allah's guidance to mankind. His blessed arrival is the result of Almighty Allah showering us with His mercy and bounty. To show happiness and joy is a requirement of one's faith and is an expression of one's love for him.

4.5.4 THE PURPOSE OF THE SEMANTIC USE OF RESTRICTION WITHIN THE VERSE

The semantic use of restriction in the verse, ﴾*So the Muslims should rejoice over it*﴿, is of particular importance. Interpreting it, Imam Fakhr al-Dīn al-Rāzī (606–543 AH) states:

قَوْلُهُ: ﴿فَبِذَٰلِكَ فَلْيَفْرَحُواْ﴾ يُفِيْدُ الْحَصْرَ، يَعْنِيْ يَجِبُ أَنْ لَّا يَفْرَحُ الإِنْسَانُ إِلَّا بِذَلِكَ.

> Allah's statement, ﴾*So the Muslims should rejoice over it*﴿, there is the use of restriction, i.e., it is important that people do not rejoice, except in that.[1]

In this verse, al-Rāzī commentates that all expression of joy and happiness, which are not only permissible but are also required by the Sharia, are all included in this. It has also been stated that Allah's bounty and mercy should be celebrated to the highest degree.

Dear reader! Almighty Allah forbids any type of celebration in which there is ostentation. Almighty Allah does not like any display of happiness on worldly blessings where the celebration goes beyond the acceptable limits. He states:

---

[1] Al-Rāzī, *Mafātīḥ al-ghayb (tafsīr al-kabīr)*, 17:117.

﴿إِنَّ ٱللَّهَ لَا يُحِبُّ ٱلْفَرِحِينَ﴾

Verily, Allah does not like those who gloat.[1]

However, when it comes to His bounty and mercy, Almighty Allah makes an exception: when it comes to His bounty and mercy, one should rejoice wholly. Through His statement, ﴿*This is far better than (all that affluence and wealth) that they amass*﴾, we can see that those who celebrate *Mawlid al-Nabī* ﷺ by lighting candles, arranging processions and gatherings, and distributing food as a means of expressing joy and happiness (to show their love for the Prophet ﷺ), they are doing acts which are pleasing to Almighty Allah—this expenditure is better than all the wealth that they gather. So when the month of his birth arrives, from all directions there is enthusiasm in serving the beloved Prophet, which in turn creates an atmosphere of excitement. Even if every happiness and joy in this world was to be sacrificed for this blessed day, it would still not be enough. Its permissibility is proven from the text of the Qurʾān: Almighty Allah does not only pave the way for its celebration, but in the discussion to follow, we will see that celebrating this great blessing has been enjoined on us.

4.5.5 The Wisdom Behind the Use of the Words ﴿*So In That*﴾

With regards to this, an academic discussion has preceded us on the wisdom behind the use of the demonstrative pronoun, *that*. Here, we will discuss a few more points:

﴿قُلْ بِفَضْلِ ٱللَّهِ وَبِرَحْمَتِهِۦ فَبِذَٰلِكَ فَلْيَفْرَحُوا۟﴾

Say: (All this) is due to the bounty and mercy of Allah. So the Muslims should rejoice over it.[2]

If the demonstrative pronoun were to have been omitted in this verse, the meaning would still be understood. However, it serves to

[1] Qurʾān 28:76.

[2] Ibid., 10:58.

add emphasis so that our attention is not diverted to anything else. Additionally, it comes to indicate that expressing one's thankfulness is not limited to fasting, prostrating, or giving charity. These are acceptable ways to show our thankfulness. But the arrival of this esteemed blessing ﷺ, through whom we have received all blessings, is so immense that on this occasion it is recommended to celebrate it in the form of arranging gatherings, lightings, and processions, and to distribute food to the destitute. It is as though Almighty Allah wants us to express our feelings of happiness and joy in such a manner that our celebrations prove our gratitude to Him for sending His Beloved ﷺ to us.

4.5.6 Showing Gratitude at the Individual and Communal Level

It is commonly witnessed that when a child is born to someone or independence is achieved, the occasion is celebrated with great splendour. This celebration takes place at both the individual and communal level. Almighty Allah desires that when the day of the Holy Prophet's ﷺ esteemed birth arrives, the happiness we feel on this occasion should triumph all other joys.

It is clear that when arranging gatherings and processions for the purpose of celebrating his birth, one's money is invested in it. Some object to this, claiming that there is no benefit: would it have not been better to spend this money on the poor and destitute, or on mosques and schools? Let us address this scepticism by stating that spending on the things mentioned above is absolutely correct in its own place, but Almighty Allah has negated this scepticism by giving the *Umma*'s communal happiness greater priority. Almighty Allah has not prohibited us from giving charity for His sake. One should not back off by saying that this wealth should only be spent on some charity, as Almighty Allah refutes this notion by stating: ﴾*So the Muslims should rejoice*﴿ and then He goes on to clarify this, stating: ﴾*This is far better than all that they amass*﴿—i.e., to spend on the occasion of his birth is better than gathering one's wealth for another cause.

4.5.7 The Use of Many Emphases in This Verse

Regarding the number of emphases that are found in the verse enjoining the celebration of *Mawlid al-Nabī* ﷺ, very few commandments in the Qur'ān have been revealed with that many emphases in them. If we look into this verse in detail, we will find ten emphases:

1. ﴾*Qul*﴿: by commencing the verse with the word 'say', emphasis is created; it is a means of getting the listener's attention.
2. ﴾*Bi-faḍl Allāh*﴿ (*Due to the bounty of Allah*): A question arises as to what this bounty is. By creating this question in the mind, the listener anticipates an answer. This is another means of creating emphasis.
3. ﴾*Wa bi-raḥmatihī*﴿ (*And His Mercy*): this is the third emphasis by which a question is posed to the mind of the listener as to what this mercy is.
4. Mentioning the word *mercy* after the word *bounty* is also an emphasis.
5. The wisdom behind the word ﴾*fa*﴿ (*so*): it comes before the words ﴾*bi-dhālika*﴿ (*in that*) serving the purpose of creating emphasis in Arabic grammar.
6. ﴾*Bi-dhālika*﴿ (*in that*): using the distant demonstrative pronoun after the words *bounty* and *mercy* is also for emphasis.
7. The ﴾*fā*﴿ in the word ﴾*fa'l-yafraḥū*﴿ (*So the Muslims should rejoice*) has been added, which serves the purpose of emphasis.
8. The ﴾*lām*﴿ in the word ﴾*fa'l-yafraḥū*﴿ (*So the Muslims should rejoice*) is also for emphasis.
9. ﴾*Huwa khayr*﴿ (*It is far better*): the pronoun is for emphasis.
10. ﴾*Mimmā yajmaʿūn*﴿ (*than that they amass*): this is also for emphasis.

In this verse, Almighty Allah has placed ten emphases in which He enjoins us to rejoice on His bounty and mercy. Using so many emphases in common speech is atypical, but as this commandment is in relation to the beloved Prophet ﷺ, these many emphases are placed in order to further beautify it so that there is no possibility of denial. After these many emphases, ending the speech stating that rejoicing is better than all that they gather clearly shows how significant it is.

What impact is created by the repetition of these emphases? The answer to this question can be understood through an example: if a father commands his child to do something, he simply says: 'Do the following thing.' If the child is sensible, this command will be enough. But it is not uncommon to find the father say, 'Son, I am telling you to do the following thing.' Now, when the child hears this, he knows that his father is commanding him to do something important, due to the added stress in this command. Moreover, sometimes the father may emphasise his command even more, saying: 'Son, listen. I am specifically telling you to do the following thing urgently.' Now in this command, there are several emphases which suggest that the child has no choice but to listen to his father.

In the first command, not obeying the father would be disrespectful, but when the father adds the extra emphases to his command, it is as though he is saying: 'I want you to only do this'. If the child knowing this disobeys his father, then such a child is most unfortunate indeed. The purpose of this example is only to help us explain the issue at hand: what comparison is there between the father and the Glorious Sustainer of the World, Almighty Allah?

Almighty Allah is commanding the beloved Prophet ﷺ: 'O Beloved! Go and tell them on My behalf that the bounty and mercy which they have received in the form of Allah's final Messenger ﷺ should emphatically be rejoiced over as a means of expressing gratitude.' The only standard placed by Almighty Allah for the celebration of *Mawlid al-Nabī* ﷺ is to affirm that the beloved Prophet ﷺ is Allah's servant and Messenger: without trespassing this perimeter, no matter how much one celebrates, it can never be enough—and how can it be when Almighty Allah Himself has not placed any limits to its celebration?

Almighty Allah is indicating by His command that the amount of reward one will gain by expressing happiness cannot be surmised. And whatever preparations one is making for the life Hereafter is unlike the reward in Almighty Allah's sight that is attained by expressing one's joy in celebrating the Prophet's birth. Almighty Allah states:

﴿هُوَ خَيْرٌ مِّمَّا يَجْمَعُونَ﴾

This is far better than (all that affluence and wealth) that they amass.[1]

It is clear that if one does not expresses his feelings of happiness on the arrival of this bounty and mercy, the worship and religious endeavours of that person will be of no concern to Almighty Allah: to be happy that the beloved Prophet ﷺ was born (which is a sign that one has *imān*) is of greater consideration. Obviously, performing those acts of worship is compulsory, but along with it one must be happy with the arrival of Allah's beloved Messenger.

4.5.8 The Exegesis of ﴾*This is far better than all that they amass*﴿

The general meaning of this verse is that rejoicing in Allah's bounty and mercy is better than all that we can gather. The question here is, what can be gathered? The following two things can be gathered:

1. With regards to this life, money, wealth, and means can be gathered.
2. And with regards to the life Hereafter, righteous deeds such as prayer, fasting, charity, and pilgrimage can be gathered.

However, the Qur'ān does not specify any of these two, as the word, *mā* (*what*), is general (*ʿām*) in its indication, which can be inclusive of all the things we gather, whether they are for this life or the life Hereafter.

Keeping the two points in mind, the verse can be interpreted in the following way: People! If you gather the money and wealth of this world by buying land and houses or hoarding gold and silver, it is not better than the happiness you express upon the arrival of My beloved. And if you strive for the life Hereafter by performing much supererogatory prayers and fasting, so that the weight of your good deeds is heavy, even then it is not better than the gratitude you show through the celebration of the birth of the beloved Prophet ﷺ; because if you do not express happiness upon his exalted arrival, then you have not given your good deeds the rights they are due, as his arrival was the cause of you having

[1] Ibid., 10:58.

those deeds in the first place—the Qur'ān and every good action you perform, be it prayer, fasting, and charity, and your Islam and *imān*, are all on account of his holy person.

Yes, it is true that the one who bestows all of this is indeed Almighty Allah, but all of it came through the means of His Prophet ﷺ. Therefore, to express happiness on that exalted being, through whom we are bestowed all of these blessings, is to show gratitude to Almighty Allah; and this action should be performed more than anything.

4.6 The Celebration of *Mawlid al-Nabī* ﷺ is to Show Gratitude for the Exalted Blessing

Almighty Allah, the Creator of the Universe, has bestowed unlimited and unrestricted favours and blessings upon mankind. He has blessed us with food, drink, beauty, and comfort. He has maintained for us the system of day and night. He has permitted us to govern the world around us for our own benefit. Out of His attributes of mercy and forgiveness, He has honoured man to be the greatest amongst His creatures, and has moulded him into the best composition and form. He has bestowed us with family and extended relations. There are even blessings of which we are unaware, but despite all of this, He has not boasted of His blessings and favours upon us. This is because He is the most generous, and whether one believes in Him or not, He still blesses us with these favours. He grants, yet He does not boast. However, there is one such blessing which Almighty Allah has bestowed upon mankind, and He does not just mention it amongst His favours; He recalls it, and emphasises it with two particles of emphasis: *lām* and *qad*. Almighty Allah states:

﴿لَقَدْ مَنَّ ٱللَّهُ عَلَى ٱلْمُؤْمِنِينَ إِذْ بَعَثَ فِيهِمْ رَسُولًا مِّنْ أَنفُسِهِمْ﴾

Indeed, Allah conferred a great favour on the believers that He raised amongst them (the most eminent) Messenger ﷺ from amongst themselves.[1]

---

[1] Ibid., 3:164.

It is clear from this verse that Almighty Allah is saying: O people! It is the greatest favour upon you that I have made My most beloved creation to be born amongst you. Through him, your destiny changed for the better: from the darkness of misguidance, you became honoured with light. Therefore, you should know that there has never been a blessing greater than this. When I have sent My beloved to you, for whose sake the whole of creation was brought into existence, it is important being the Lord of the Worlds that I recall My favour upon you; lest you become ungrateful thinking that this blessing is like any other.

By recalling this favour, the interest of the *Umma* is kept in mind. The Qurʾān is making it clear to every monotheist that they should not be silent on Allah's greatest blessing, rather they should be thankful for this blessing by expressing their happiness and joy through acts of celebration.

4.7 Why is it Necessary to Express Gratitude on a Blessing?

It is a mark of servitude that one expresses gratitude for a blessing Almighty Allah bestows. In the Qurʾān, another wisdom has been given for its necessity. Almighty Allah states:

﴿لَئِن شَكَرْتُمْ لَأَزِيدَنَّكُمْ وَلَئِن كَفَرْتُمْ إِنَّ عَذَابِي لَشَدِيدٌ﴾

> *If you are thankful, I shall certainly increase (My blessings on) you, and if you are ungrateful, then My torment is surely severe.*[1]

Expressing gratitude on a blessing, according to this verse, is a means of attaining further blessings. That is, Almighty Allah bestows more on His servant when he is grateful. However, ungratefulness is such a repugnant act that there are severe warnings of Allah's punishment for the one who is guilty of it. It is for this reason that in order to be worthy of other divine favours, it is necessary that one shows their gratitude to Almighty Allah for the arrival of the

[1] Ibid., 14:7.

exalted Prophet ﷺ.

4.8 THE PREVALENT METHODS OF EXPRESSING GRATITUDE

To conclude this chapter, we will briefly point out the various methods of expressing gratitude for Allah's blessings in light of the Qur'ān. Showing one's thankfulness for the blessing of the Prophet's ﷺ arrival can be done in one of the following ways:

4.8.1 REMEMBERING AND MENTIONING THE BLESSING

In the Qur'ān, one of the methods of expressing gratitude to Almighty Allah is to remember His blessings. In *sūra al-Baqara*, it states:

﴿يَٰبَنِيٓ إِسۡرَٰٓءِيلَ ٱذۡكُرُواْ نِعۡمَتِيَ ٱلَّتِيٓ أَنۡعَمۡتُ عَلَيۡكُمۡ﴾

O Children of Yaʿqūb! Recall those favours that I bestowed upon you, and that I exalted you above all the people (of your age).[1]

In *sūra Āl ʿImrān*, Almighty Allah addresses mankind, saying:

﴿وَٱذۡكُرُواْ نِعۡمَتَ ٱللَّهِ عَلَيۡكُمۡ إِذۡ كُنتُمۡ أَعۡدَآءٗ فَأَلَّفَ بَيۡنَ قُلُوبِكُمۡ
فَأَصۡبَحۡتُم بِنِعۡمَتِهِۦٓ إِخۡوَٰنٗا﴾

Remember the favours of Allah upon you when you were disunited, so he joined your hearts in love. Thus you became brothers due to His Blessing.[2]

To remember the blessed birth of the Prophet ﷺ, his beauty, life, virtues and miracles and his exclusive attributes is one of the means of expressing gratitude to Almighty Allah. By remembering this glorious blessing we are only benefiting ourselves, as the Holy Prophet's remembrance is always being celebrated by Almighty

[1] Ibid., 2:47.

[2] Ibid., 3:103.

Allah. Every moment that passes, the Prophet's ﷺ remembrance is given a greater status than the moment that preceded it. Almighty Allah states:

﴿وَلَلْآخِرَةُ خَيْرٌ لَّكَ مِنَ الْأُولَىٰ﴾

> *Indeed, every following hour is a better (source of eminence and exaltation) for you than the preceding one.*[1]

﴿وَرَفَعْنَا لَكَ ذِكْرَكَ﴾

> *And We exalted for you your remembrance (by annexing it to Ours everywhere in the world and in the Hereafter).*[2]

From this, we can see that remembering the most exalted Prophet ﷺ is a benefit to ourselves and we are not doing a favour to anyone. Expressing our gratitude to Almighty Allah on the occasion of his birth is a means of bettering our lives in the Hereafter. Aḥmad Riḍā Khān (1272–1340 AH) beautifully states:

﴿وَرَفَعْنَا لَكَ ذِكْرَكَ﴾ کا ہے سایہ تجھ پر
بول بالا ہے ترا، ذکر ہے اونچا تیرا

The shade of wa rafaʿnā laka dhikrak *is upon you*
For your words and remembrance have been made lofty[3]

4.8.2 Worship and Servitude

Performing worship and showing one's servitude to Almighty Allah is another means by which gratitude can be expressed. Offering ritual prayer, fasting, performing pilgrimage, and paying the alms-due are a few of the best means of expressing gratitude to Almighty

---

[1] Ibid., 93:4.

[2] Ibid., 94:4.

[3] Aḥmad Riḍā Khān, *Ḥadāʾiq-e-Bakhshish*, 1:18.

Allah.

As a way of expressing one's gratitude, it is also recommended to give charity to the poor and destitute and to look after the orphans and needy.

4.8.3 Proclaiming the Blessing

Another method of showing gratitude is to make much mention of the blessing bestowed on us by Almighty Allah by expressing one's happiness and letting others know about it. The Qur'ān states:

﴿وَأَمَّا بِنِعْمَةِ رَبِّكَ فَحَدِّثْ﴾

And proclaim (well) the bounties of your Lord.[1]

In the previous page, an injunction was given for the remembrance of Allah's blessing, i.e., the blessing should be remembered in the heart, and mentioned by the tongue. However, this remembrance was not for others, but for Almighty Allah alone. But in the above mentioned verse, there is the injunction of proclaiming the blessing, which means that others should know of it. Thus, the basic difference between the two (remembrance and proclaiming the blessing) is that the former is solely in relation to Almighty Allah, whilst the latter is in relation to the creation. For instance, Almighty Allah states:

﴿فَاذْكُرُونِي أَذْكُرْكُمْ وَاشْكُرُوا لِي وَلَا تَكْفُرُونِ﴾

So remember Me, I shall remember you. And always be thankful to Me and never be ungrateful to Me.[2]

Here, to make remembrance simply means that Almighty Allah should be remembered, whilst proclamation is not solely a remembrance, but it is to express openly in such a way that the creation becomes aware of it, and that as many people as possible are included within the fold of this divine injunction.

---

1 Qur'ān 93:11.

2 Ibid., 2:152.

The greatest wisdom of 'proclaiming the blessing' is that others become aware of it. Thus, another difference between the two methods is that the former can be done solitarily, whilst the latter requires a congregation. In order to express gratitude for this blessing, great gatherings should be held to remember that manifest blessing so that as many people as possible can be associated with it.

4.8.3.1 How Should We Proclaim the Blessing?

It is a point of interest that upon receiving such a great blessing, like the auspicious birth of the Holy Prophet ﷺ, the *Umma* discharges its duty by proclaiming it. This is done by remembering the Prophet ﷺ, his virtues, noble character, his auspicious birth, beauty, and graceful manners by reciting odes in his praise and invoking blessings and salutations upon him. All of this falls under the interpretation of ﴾*And proclaim (well) the bounties of your Lord*﴿, and there are many ways in which this blessing can be remembered. If only one would ponder for a little, and realise that all the gatherings of *Mawlid al-Nabī* ﷺ are like this generally, and that mentioning these things holds significance in these gatherings.

A question may come to mind here: how are we to remember the *mawlid* of the Prophet ﷺ? What are the limits of his remembrance? How are we to praise him and express his merits and virtues? The answer to these questions is lucidly explained in an ode dedicated to the Prophet ﷺ, composed by Imam Sharaf al-Dīn al-Būṣīrī (608–696 AH):

دَعْ مَا ادَّعَتْهُ النَّصَارَى فِيْ نَبِيِّهِمْ

وَاحْكُمْ بِمَا شِئْتَ مَدْحًا فِيْهِ وَاحْتَكِمِ

فَانْسِبْ إِلَى ذَاتِهِ مَا شِئْتَ مِنْ شَرَفٍ

وَانْسِبْ إِلَى قَدْرِهِ مَا شِئْتَ مِنْ عِظَمِ

فَإِنَّ فَضْلَ رَسُوْلِ اللهِ لَيْسَ لَهُ

حَدٌّ فَيُعْرِبُ عَنْهُ نَاطِقٌ بِفَمِ

Leave what the Christians claimed about their Prophet (i.e., that he is God or the son of God).
Then decide what you wish in praise of him, and do so well.
And ascribe to his person what you want of honour; and to his standing what you want of greatness.
For indeed, the excellence of Allah's Messenger ﷺ has no limits that a speaker may express with his mouth.

On this basis, the odes recited in praise of the Holy Prophet ﷺ are all commendable, so long as a distinction is made between Almighty Allah and His Prophet ﷺ (i.e., it is compulsory to the maintain the difference that Almighty Allah is the Creator and the Prophet ﷺ is His creation and worshipful servant—this is a condition of faith.)

4.8.4 To Celebrate as a Festivity [ᶜĪd]

Apart from remembering the blessing and mentioning it, another means of expressing one's gratitude to Almighty Allah and showing thankfulness for His blessing is to express happiness through acts of celebration and festivity (*ᶜīd*). Former communities had also shown gratitude in this way (as mentioned previously). And it is also the practice (Sunna) of prophets, who took the day in which a special blessing descended upon them as an *ᶜīd*. ᶜĪsā ﷺ supplicated to Almighty Allah with the following words:

﴿رَبَّنَآ أَنزِلۡ عَلَيۡنَا مَآئِدَةً مِّنَ ٱلسَّمَآءِ تَكُونُ لَنَا عِيدًا لِّأَوَّلِنَا وَءَاخِرِنَا﴾

O Allah, our Lord, send down to us from heaven the table spread (with bounties) so that (the day of its descent) becomes (ᶜīd) *a festival day for us, and for our predecessors (as well as) our successors, and that (the table-spread) comes as a sign from You.*[1]

One should keep in mind that here upon receiving a temporal

[1] Ibid., 5:114.

blessing such as the table-spread, ʿĪsā ﷺ mentions it with the word *ʿīd*, and interestingly enough, even till today Christians, as an act of thanksgiving, honour Sundays as the day in which they received this blessing.

What comparison can there be between receiving a table-spread and the raising of our beloved Prophet ﷺ, the chief of the created beings? That was a temporal blessing, and here is a permanent one. The mercy of all the worlds, the Holy Prophet ﷺ, is a blessing for eternity: for this life and the life to come. How can there be a comparison between the two? A brief pause will give us some food for thought that we must question ourselves: are we giving this blessing the gratitude it truly deserves?

The point here is not to compare the blessed birth of the Prophet ﷺ and the table-spread. What is important here is to show this historic reality which is worthy of our attention. The Christians frequently express their gratitude on Sundays, as this was the day when the table-spread descended on them. Previous communities, upon receiving a blessing like the table-spread (the mention of which has been preserved in the Qurʾān), would celebrate through acts of festivity as is pleasing to Almighty Allah and in conformity with the practice (Sunna) of prophets. So if the prophets took the day in which they received a generic blessing as a day of festivity (*ʿīd*), what can possibly be wrong with taking *Mawlid al-Nabī* ﷺ as a celebration? His arrival to this world is such a great blessing through which we attained all other blessings. Why can we not express jubilation on the occasion of our Prophet's birth?

From the details provided in this chapter, it is self-evident that celebrating *Mawlid al-Nabī* ﷺ is established from the text of the Qurʾān. Any objection to this is indicative of one's own non-acquaintance with its teaching. Instead of disputing its permissibility and making it a point of contention, one should simply express their joy and happiness upon the blessed arrival of the exalted Prophet ﷺ and become the recipients of Allah's favour.

Chapter 5

Evidence from the Hadith on *Mawlid al-Nabī* ﷺ

IN THE PREVIOUS CHAPTER, THERE WAS A DETAILED DISCUSSION in light of the Qur'ān and its exegeses on the permissibility of commemorating *Mawlid al-Nabī* ﷺ. In this chapter, its permissibility will be proven from the hadith: an analysis of the legal status of expressing happiness and joy on the most gracious, most compassionate Prophet's blessed birth will be discussed.

5.1 The Evidence of Commemorating *Yawm ʿĀshūrā'*

The most exalted Prophet ﷺ is Allah's bounty and mercy; he is Allah's greatest benevolence upon mankind. It is binding on the *Umma* that they express gratitude to Almighty Allah for this greatest blessing. Almighty Allah loves those who are grateful to Him, and doing so is also the Sunna of the prophets.

There are several ways in which thankfulness can be expressed: at the individual level, a person can be thankful to Almighty Allah by offering supererogatory prayers and giving charity; but at the communal level, when a blessing has been bestowed on a people, thankfulness should be expressed collectively. As the Holy Prophet's ﷺ birth and raising was for the whole of mankind, it is necessary that gratitude for this widely encompassing blessing is expressed at the collective level. And whatever action is of a communal nature, it will be based according to the culture and tradition of that community.

The day of the Prophet's ﷺ birth is celebrated on a cultural basis, like an *ʿīd* (i.e., a day of festivity). The celebration of this auspicious occasion is founded and proven from the acts of thanksgiving practiced by former communities. What is to follow are hadiths relating to *Yawm ʿĀshūrā'*, which are used as evidence for the permissibility of celebrating *Mawlid al-Nabī* ﷺ.

5.1.1 Celebrating the Day of Mūsā

Yawm ʿĀshūrāʾ is the day upon which Mūsā was granted victory over Pharaoh. It was the day when the Children of Israel were delivered from his tyranny and oppression. Thus, it was Prophet Mūsā's victory day and the independence day of the Children of Israel. As an act of gratitude, Mūsā fasted this day.

When the Holy Prophet migrated to Medina, he saw the Jews fasting *Yawm ʿĀshūrāʾ*. He enquired about it and they answered him with the information provided above. Hearing this, the Holy Prophet replied, 'I have greater right (being a Prophet) to Mūsā than you.' Resultantly, the Holy Prophet , as a means of expressing gratitude to Almighty Allah for this blessing bestowed on Mūsā , fasted and commanded all of his noble Companions to fast too. Below are some hadiths concerning the fast of *Yawm ʿĀshūrāʾ*:

1. ʿAbd Allāh b. ʿAbbās narrates:

قَدِمَ النَّبِيُّ ﷺ الْمَدِينَةَ فَرَأَى الْيَهُودَ تَصُومُ يَوْمَ عَاشُورَاءَ، فَقَالَ: «مَا هَذَا؟» قَالُوا: هَذَا يَوْمٌ صَالِحٌ، هَذَا يَوْمٌ نَجَّى اللهُ بَنِي إِسْرَائِيلَ مِنْ عَدُوِّهِمْ، فَصَامَهُ مُوسَى. قَالَ: «فَأَنَا أَحَقُّ بِمُوسَى مِنْكُمْ. فَصَامَهُ وَأَمَرَ بِصِيَامِهِ.»

The Prophet came to Medina and saw the Jews fasting on *Yawm ʿĀshūrāʾ*. He asked, 'What is this?' They replied, 'This is a blessed day; this is the day when Allah saved the Children of Israel from their enemy. So Mūsā fasted it.' The Prophet said, 'I have greater right to Mūsā than you.' So he fasted it, and ordered fast on that day.[1]

2. In another chain of transmission, ʿAbd Allāh b. ʿAbbās narrates:

---

[1] Narrated by al-Bukhārī in *al-Ṣaḥīḥ*: *Kitāb al-Ṣawm* [The Book of Fasting], chapter: 'The fast of *Yawm ʿĀshūrāʾ*', 2:704 §1900; Aḥmad b. Ḥanbal in *al-Musnad*, 1:291 §2644; Abū Yaʿlā in *al-Musnad*, 4:441 §2567; and Ibn Kathīr, *Tafsīr al-Qurʾān al-ʿaẓīm*, 1:92.

لَـمَّـا قَدِمَ النَّبِيُّ ﷺ الْـمَدِينَةَ وَجَدَ الْيَهُودَ يَصُومُونَ عَاشُورَاءَ، فَسُئِلُوا عَنْ ذَلِكَ، فَقَالُوا: هَذَا الْيَوْمُ الَّذِي أَظْفَرَ اللهُ فِيهِ مُوسَى وَبَنِي إِسْرَائِيلَ عَلَى فِرْعَوْنَ، وَنَحْنُ نَصُومُهُ تَعْظِيمًـا لَهُ. فَقَالَ رَسُولُ اللهِ ﷺ: «نَحْنُ أَوْلَى بِمُوسَى مِنْكُمْ.» ثُمَّ أَمَرَ بِصَوْمِهِ.

When the Prophet ﷺ came to Medina, he found the Jews fasting on *Yawm ʿĀshūrā*ʾ; so they were asked about that. They replied, 'This is the day in which Allah granted victory to Mūsā ﷺ and the Children of Israel over Pharaoh. So we fast on that day out of honour of it.' The Prophet ﷺ said, 'We are more entitled to Mūsā ﷺ than you.' Then he recommended its fast.[1]

3. In another tradition, the Jews' reply and the Holy Prophet's command is transmitted in the following way:

هَذَا يَوْمٌ عَظِيمٌ أَنْجَى اللهُ فِيهِ مُوسَى وَقَوْمَهُ، وَغَرَّقَ فِرْعَوْنَ وَقَوْمَهُ، فَصَامَهُ مُوسَى شُكْرًا فَنَحْنُ نَصُومُهُ. فَقَالَ رَسُولُ اللهِ ﷺ: «فَنَحْنُ أَحَقُّ وَأَوْلَى بِمُوسَى مِنْكُمْ.» فَصَامَهُ رَسُولُ اللهِ ﷺ وَأَمَرَ بِصِيَامِهِ.

The Jews replied, 'This is a great day. On this day, Allah liberated Mūsā ﷺ and his people and drowned Pharaoh and his people. So Mūsā ﷺ fasted this day out of gratitude, and we fast it (too).' The blessed Prophet ﷺ said: 'We have greater right and are more entitled to Mūsā ﷺ than you.' So the Prophet ﷺ fasted that day and ordered its fast.[2]

---

[1] Narrated by al-Bukhārī in *al-Ṣaḥīḥ*: *Kitāb Faḍāʾil al-Ṣaḥāba* [The Book of the Virtues of the Companions], chapter: 'The Jews coming to the Prophet when he arrived in Medina', 3:1434 §3727; Muslim in *al-Ṣaḥīḥ*: *Kitāb al-Ṣiyām* [The Book of Fasting], chapter: 'The fast of *Yawm ʿĀshūrā*', 2:795 §1130; and Abū Dāwūd in *al-Sunan*: *Kitāb al-Ṣawm* [The Book of Fasting], chapter: 'The fast of *Yawm ʿĀshūrā*', 2:326 §2444.

[2] Narrated by Muslim in *al-Ṣaḥīḥ*: *Kitāb al-Ṣiyām* [The Book of Fasting], chapter: 'The fast of *Yawm ʿĀshūrā*', 2:796 §1130; al-Bukhārī in *al-Ṣaḥīḥ*:

From the aforementioned traditions, it can be understood that the Children of Israel were subject to Pharaoh's tyranny and oppression, which made it difficult for them to observe their religion. However, on account of Mūsā's perseverance, the day finally dawned when the Children of Israel were able to escape from their enslavement, resulting in the annihilation of Pharaoh and his army. In this way, the Children of Israel were freed from persecution and were bestowed with the favour of victory and independence from Almighty Allah. Thus, Mūsā عليه السلام, as a means of expressing his gratitude, kept a fast on that day, and the Children of Israel observed that day as well by fasting; and even till today, this day is celebrated as a day of deliverance and independence. The Holy Prophet ﷺ also honoured this day by fasting, on account of his connection to Prophet Mūsā عليه السلام, and he ordered the Muslims to do the same. Imam al-Ṭaḥāwī (229–321 AH) states that it is clear that the Holy Prophet ﷺ fasted in order to express his gratitude to Almighty Allah for giving Mūsā عليه السلام dominance over Pharaoh.[1]

There is an important point to take note here: if the Jews can celebrate the day in which their prophet received victory and independence, why then can the Muslims not honour the day in which their beloved Prophet ﷺ was born? The Holy Prophet ﷺ, who is the master of all the prophets, was sent to mankind as Almighty Allah's bounty and mercy; through him, man was emancipated from the bonds of inequity and injustice. Almighty Allah states:

﴿وَيَضَعُ عَنْهُمْ إِصْرَهُمْ وَٱلْأَغْلَٰلَ ٱلَّتِى كَانَتْ عَلَيْهِمْ﴾

And he removes from them their heavy burdens and yokes (i.e., shackles) weighing upon them (due to their acts of disobedience and blesses them with freedom).[2]

---

*Kitāb al-Anbiyā*ʾ [The Book of Prophets], chapter: 'Allah's statement: Has the news of Mūsā reached you', 3:1244 §3216; Ibn Mājah in *al-Sunan*: *Kitāb al-Ṣiyām* [The Book of Fasting], chapter: 'The fast of *Yawm ʿĀshūrā*', 1:552 §1734; Aḥmad b. Ḥanbal in *al-Musnad*, 1:336 §3112.

[1] Al-Ṭaḥāwī in *Sharḥ maʿānī al-āthār*: *Kitāb al-Ṣawm* [The Book of Fasting], chapter: 'The fast of *Yawm ʿĀshūrā*', 2:132 §3209.

[2] Qurʾān 7:157.

The most compassionate Prophet's arrival to this world was a means by which mankind would be delivered from injustice. His birth was such an auspicious moment that the whole of creation became engaged in its celebration. For a believer, it is the most important happiness in his life: it is an extremely great act of benevolence which Almighty Allah has bestowed on the *Umma*. It is a day which is worthy of all respect and honour, and in turn, we should become the embodiment of thankfulness and gratitude. Every permissible means possible should be exhausted with all-consuming love and veneration for the purpose of giving this day its due.

5.1.2 The Prophet's Commemoration is on Account of His Connection to Mūsā ﷺ

Another point can be deduced from the hadiths above that the Holy Prophet ﷺ commemorated the day by fasting on account of his connection to Mūsā ﷺ. From this, we can learn that commemorating a significant day is itself a practice (Sunna) of the chosen Prophet ﷺ. For the believer, what day can be greater in significance than the day of his birth? Thus, commemorating the day of his birth falls within the ambit of the Sunna, and by doing so, one is following in the footstep of the chosen Prophet ﷺ.

5.1.3 The Jews Commemorated *Yawm ʿĀshūrāʾ* as a Day of Festivity (*ʿĪd*)

In the minds of some people, an objection may be raised that the Jews commemorated their independence day, i.e., *Yawm ʿĀshūrāʾ*, by fasting, whilst *Mawlid al-Nabī* ﷺ on the other hand is commemorated as an *ʿīd*, as no one fasts on this day.

In reply to this objection, to commemorate a blessed occasion as a day of happiness is a Sunna of the Holy Prophet ﷺ. So long as it is kept within the bounds of the Sharia, it can be commemorated in any manner. If the Jews kept a fast on that day, in no way does this negate the fact that thankfulness can be expressed in various other ways, because gratitude is not limited to fasting alone. Moreover, the above inference that thankfulness can only be expressed through fasting, cannot be made from these sources. The reality is that the Jews on this occasion of merriment kept fasts as an additional act of virtue.

Prior to Islam, *Yawm ʿĀshūrāʾ* was commemorated as an *ʿīd* amongst Arabs, but their celebration was for a different purpose, which will be explained later. When the Holy Prophet ﷺ settled in Medina, he found that the Jews as well as fasting on *Yawm ʿĀshūrāʾ* also took that day as a day of festivity (*ʿīd*). This is substantiated by the following hadiths:

1. Imam al-Bukhārī (194–256 AH) narrates that Abū Mūsā al-Ashʿarī ؓ reports:

كَانَ يَوْمُ عَاشُورَاءَ تَعُدُّهُ الْيَهُودُ عِيدًا، قَالَ النَّبِيُّ ﷺ: «فَصُومُوهُ أَنْتُمْ».

The Jews used to consider *Yawm ʿĀshūrāʾ* as an *ʿīd*. (Ordering the Muslims,) the Prophet ﷺ said, 'You should fast this day.'[1]

2. Imam Muslim (206–261 AH) also narrates from Abū Mūsā al-Ashʿarī ؓ:

كَانَ يَوْمُ عَاشُورَاءَ يَوْمًا تُعَظِّمُهُ الْيَهُودُ وَتَتَّخِذُهُ عِيدًا. فَقَالَ رَسُولُ اللهِ ﷺ: «صُومُوهُ أَنْتُمْ».

Yawm ʿĀshūrāʾ was a day venerated by the Jews; they took this day as an *ʿīd*. (Ordering the Muslims) the Prophet ﷺ said, 'You should fast this day.'[2]

Imam al-Ṭaḥāwī (229–321 AH) under this hadith states that the only reason why the Holy Prophet ﷺ ordered the Muslims to fast

---

[1] Narrated by al-Bukhārī in *al-Ṣaḥīḥ*: *Kitāb al-Ṣawm* [The Book of Fasting], chapter: 'The fast of *Yawm ʿĀshūrāʾ*', 2:704–705 §1901.

[2] Narrated by Muslim in *al-Ṣaḥīḥ*: *Kitāb al-Ṣiyām* [The Book of Fasting], chapter: 'The fast of *Yawm ʿĀshūrāʾ*', 2:796 §1131; al-Nasāʾī in *al-Sunan al-kubrā*, 2:159 §2848; al-Ṭaḥāwī in *Sharḥ maʿānī al-āthār*: *Kitāb al-Ṣawm* [The Book of Fasting], chapter: 'The fast of *Yawm ʿĀshūrāʾ*', 2:133 §3217; and al-Bayhaqī in *al-Sunan al-kubrā*, 4:289 §8197.

on *Yawm ʿĀshūrāʾ* is because the Jews used to fast on this day.
3. Imam Muslim (206–261 AH) narrates another tradition from Abū Mūsā al-Ashʿarī ؓ:

كَانَ أَهْلُ خَيْبَرَ يَصُومُونَ يَوْمَ عَاشُورَاءَ يَتَّخِذُونَهُ عِيدًا، وَيُلْبِسُونَ نِسَاءَهُمْ فِيهِ حُلِيَّهُمْ وَشَارَتَهُمْ. فَقَالَ رَسُولُ اللهِ ﷺ: «فَصُومُوهُ أَنْتُمْ.»

> The inhabitants of *Khaybar* used to fast on *Yawm ʿĀshūrāʾ* taking it as a day of *ʿīd*. They would adorn their womenfolk with their jewellery and (religious) symbols. (Ordering the Muslims,) the Prophet ﷺ said, 'You should fast this day.'[1]

From these hadiths narrated by Imam al-Bukhārī (194–256 AH) and Imam Muslim (206–261 AH), we can derive the following points:
1. *Yawm ʿĀshūrāʾ* was a day of victory for the Jews. For a very long time, they had been commemorating this day at the communal level as their day of *ʿīd*.
2. They honoured this day by taking it as an *ʿīd*. Their act of fasting was an additional means by which they expressed their thankfulness and gratitude.
3. This day was not confined to fasting; rather, it was only one aspect of the commemoration.
4. Analogously, if someone today objects, saying that celebrating *Mawlid al-Nabī* ﷺ without fasting is not permissible, such an objection will not be correct because it is not possible to infer this from the hadiths.

The Prophet ﷺ was already aware that the Jews took the day of *Yawm ʿĀshūrāʾ* as an *ʿīd*. This is why he never enquired about it and instead asked them why they were fasting on this day. They replied that it was out of respect and as an act of gratitude. And it

---

[1] Narrated by Muslim in *al-Ṣaḥīḥ*: *Kitāb al-Ṣiyām* [The Book of Fasting], chapter: 'The fast of *Yawm al-ʿĀshūrāʾ*', 2:796 §1131; Abū Nuʿaym in *al-Musnad al-mustakhraj ʿalā ṣaḥīḥ al-imām Muslim*, 3:212 §2575; al-Ismāʿīlī in *Muʿjam shuyūkh Abī Bakr al-Ismāʿīlī*, 3:722 §337; and al-ʿAsqalānī in *Fatḥ al-Bārī*, 4:248.

was upon this reply that the Holy Prophet ﷺ fasted on this day and commanded his Companions (رضي الله عنهم) to do so likewise.

5.1.4 The Evidence of al-ʿAsqalānī for *Mawlid al-Nabī* ﷺ

Ibn Ḥajar al-ʿAsqalānī (773–852 AH), using the aforementioned hadiths as evidence, has done some thorough research into the legal status of *Yawm ʿĀshūrāʾ* and has established from it the permissibility of celebrating *Mawlid al-Nabī* ﷺ. Imam Jalāl al-Dīn al-Suyūṭī (849–911 AH) has recorded his verdict:

وَقَدْ سُئِلَ شَيْخُ الإِسْلَامِ حَافِظُ الْعَصْرِ أَبُوالْفَضْلِ ابْنُ حَجَرٍ عَنْ عَمَلِ الْـمَوْلِدِ، فَأَجَابَ بِمَـا نَصَّهُ: قَالَ:

وَقَدْ ظَهَرَ لِيْ تَخْرِيْجُهَا عَلَى أَصْلٍ ثَابِتٍ، وَهُوَ مَا ثَبَتَ فِي الصَّحِيْحَيْنِ مِنْ: أَنَّ النَّبِيَّ ﷺ قَدِمَ الْـمَدِيْنَةَ، فَوَجَدَ الْيَهُوْدَ يَصُوْمُوْنَ يَوْمَ عَاشُوْرَاءَ، فَسَأَلَـهُمْ، فَقَالُوا: هُوَ يَوْمٌ أَغْرَقَ اللهُ فِيْهِ فِرْعَوْنَ، وَنَجَّى مُوْسَى، فَنَحْنُ نَصُوْمُهُ شُكْرًا لله تَعَالَى.

فَيُسْتَفَادُ مِنْهُ فِعْلُ الشُّكْرِ لله تَعَالَى عَلَى مَا مَنَّ بِهِ فِيْ يَوْمٍ مُّعَيَّنٍ مِنْ إِسْدَآءِ نِعْمَةٍ، أَوْ دَفْعِ نِقْمَةٍ، وَيُعَادُ ذَلِكَ فِي نَظِيْرِ ذَلِكَ الْيَوْمِ مِنْ كُلِّ سَنَةٍ.

وَالشُّكْرُ لله تَعَالَى يَحْصُلُ بِأَنْوَاعِ الْعِبَادَاتِ كَالسُّجُوْدِ وَالصِّيَامِ وَالصَّدَقَةِ وَالتِّلَاوَةِ، وَأَيُّ نِعْمَةٍ أَعْظَمُ مِنَ النِّعْمَةِ بِبُرُوْزِ هَذَا النَّبِيِّ ﷺ الَّذِي هُوَ نَبِيُّ الرَّحْمَةِ فِيْ ذَلِكَ الْيَوْمِ.

The *Ḥāfiẓ* of this era, *Shaykh al-Islām* Abu al-Faḍl b. Ḥajar al-ʿAsqalānī, was asked about the practice of *mawlid*, and he replied with the following statement:

It has come to my attention that there is an established basis for it, which can be found in the *Ṣaḥīḥayn* that the

> Prophet ﷺ entered Medina, and he found the Jews fasting *Yawm ʿĀshūrāʾ*. He asked them about it, and they replied, 'It is the day when Allah drowned Pharaoh and saved Mūsā ﷺ. So we fast this day out of gratitude to Allah.'
>
> The act of thanking Almighty Allah for a favour which He bestowed on a specific day, either by conferring a blessing or warding off tribulation and to bring up the likes of that day each year, can be deduced from it.
>
> Gratitude to Almighty Allah can be obtained through a variety of worships, such as prostrating, fasting, giving charity, and reciting the Qurʾān. And which blessing can be greater than the blessing of the appearance of this Prophet ﷺ, who is the prophet of mercy, on that day?[1]

Giving his reply, Ibn Ḥajar al-ʿAsqalānī (773–852 AH) grounds the celebration of *Mawlid al-Nabī* ﷺ in the hadiths contained in *Ṣaḥīḥ al-Bukhārī* and *Ṣaḥīḥ Muslim*. In these hadiths, the Holy Prophet ﷺ is confirming the practice of the Jews who expressed happiness through acts of festivity, showing their gratitude for the blessing which was bestowed upon them. Through the Prophet's approval, this practice holds the status of Sunna.

What day can be greater than the day when the Holy Prophet ﷺ arrived to this world? Why can *Mawlid al-Nabī* ﷺ not be celebrated as an *ʿīd*? Imam Jalāl al-Dīn al-Suyūṭī (849–911 AH) supports the verdict of Imam Ibn Ḥajar al-ʿAsqalānī (773–852 AH), which can be found in the compilation of his edicts called, *al-Ḥāwī li al-fatāwā* (p.205–206). Ibn Ḥajar al-ʿAsqalānī uses the fast of *ʿĀshūrāʾ* as evidence: despite the fact that the victory given to Mūsā ﷺ took place in an epoch long ago, the day of *ʿĀshūrāʾ* is singled out from the rest of the year as the blessed occasion for showing gratitude.

---

[1] Al-Suyūṭī, *Ḥusn al-maqṣid fī ʿamal al-mawlid*, p.63; al-Suyūṭī, *al-Ḥāwī li al-fatāwā*, pp. 205–206; al-Ṣāliḥī, *Subul al-hudā wa al-rashād fī sīra Khayr al-ʿibād*, 1:366; al-Zurqānī, *Sharḥ al-mawāhib al-ladunya bi al-minaḥ al-Muḥammadiyya*, 1:263; Aḥmad b. Zaynī al-Daḥlān, *al-Sīra al-Nabawiyya*, 1:54; and al-Nabhānī, *Ḥujja Allāh ʿalā al-ʿālimīn fī muʿjazāt Sayyid al-mursalīn*, p.237.

From this, we can see that though the event does not recur, the virtue of that day does; for example, Abū Lahab receives ease every Monday—the day of the Prophet's birth.

Prior to the obligation of fasting in *Ramaḍān*, the fast of *Yawm ʿĀshūrāʾ* was obligatory for Muslims.[1] When the fast of *Ramaḍān* became compulsory, its obligation was abrogated.[2] There may be confusion in the minds of some people that because its obligation is abrogated, its virtue has now ceased. The answer to this is that after fasting in *Ramaḍān* was made compulsory, the compulsion to fast in any other month no longer remained; despite this, the permissibility of fasting on *Yawm ʿĀshūrāʾ* has not been affected. This is because after abrogating the obligation of its fast, the Prophet ﷺ did not say, 'We no longer have any right to Mūsā ﷺ', compared to when declaring its obligation, he said, 'We have greater right to Mūsā ﷺ than you'.

Despite the abrogation of fasting on *Yawm ʿĀshūrāʾ*, there are still hadiths which can be found on its virtue. Fasting on this day was virtuous prior to its abrogation, and its virtue still remains intact after its abrogation; and it is an accepted fact that virtues are not abrogated. This is why the abrogation of fasting on *Yawm ʿĀshūrāʾ* does not have an impact on the inference made by Ibn Ḥajar al-ʿAsqalānī (773–852 AH).

---

[1] Al-Ṭaḥāwī in *Sharḥ maʿānī al-āthār*: *Kitāb al-Ṣawm* [The Book of Fasting], chapter: 'The fast of *Yawm ʿĀshūrā*', 2:129–132; and al-ʿAynī in *ʿUmda al-qārī sharḥ Ṣaḥīḥ al-Bukhārī*, 11:120.

[2] Imam al-Bukhārī (194–256 AH) narrates that ʿĀʾisha ﷺ reports:

كَانَ رَسُولُ اللهِ ﷺ أَمَرَ بِصِيَامِ يَوْمِ عَاشُورَاءَ، فَلَمَّا فُرِضَ رَمَضَانُ كَانَ مَنْ شَاءَ صَامَ وَمَنْ شَاءَ أَفْطَرَ.

Allah's Messenger ﷺ ordered the fast of *Yawm ʿĀshūrāʾ*. When *Ramaḍān* was obligated, one had a choice either to fast (*Yawm ʿĀshūrāʾ*) or not to fast (*Yawm ʿĀshūrāʾ*).

Narrated by al-Bukhārī in *al-Ṣaḥīḥ*: *Kitāb al-Ṣawm* [The Book of Fasting], chapter: 'The fast of *Yawm ʿĀshūrā*', 2:704§1897–1898.

If we have to accept that its virtue is abrogated, even then it does not affect our evidence for *Mawlid al-Nabī* ﷺ. This is because quite obviously, those who will be most happy on that day will be the ones who make the most claim to Mūsā ﷺ. The reason why the Holy Prophet ﷺ kept a fast on that day was to bring to attention the fact that if it is permissible to express gratitude on a prophet's victory, why would it not be permissible on the day in which a prophet was born? The Holy Prophet ﷺ out of his noble temperament would not expressly command his *Umma* to keep a fast on his birthday; instead he lead by example by fasting on Mondays, and even then he did not disclose its reason till someone asked him about it.

5.2 THE EVIDENCE OF COMMEMORATING THE DAY OF NŪḤ ﷺ

Imam Aḥmad b. Ḥanbal (164–241 AH) and Ḥāfiẓ Ibn Ḥajar al-ʿAsqalānī (773–852 AH) narrate a hadith from Abū Hurayra that *Yawm ʿĀshūrāʾ* is the day when Almighty Allah showered his grace and blessing on Prophet Nūḥ ﷺ and his people—it was the day when they descended onto Mount Judi safely. Nūḥ ﷺ and his community commemorated this day as a day of thanksgiving, and those who came later continued to honour this day.

Abū Hurayra ﷺ reports that when the most compassionate Prophet ﷺ asked the Jews about their fasting on *Yawm ʿĀshūrāʾ*, they, after mentioning the freedom of the Children of Israel and the drowning of Pharaoh, replied:

وَهَذَا يَوْمٌ اسْتَوَتْ فِيْهِ السَّفِيْنَةُ عَلَى الْـجُودِيِّ، فَصَامَهُ نُوْحٌ وَمُوْسَى عليهما السلام شُكْرًا لله تَعَالَى.

> And this is (also) the day when the ark settled (safely) on Mount Judi. So Nūḥ and Mūsā ﷺ fasted on this day out of gratitude to Allah.

Upon this, the most exalted Prophet ﷺ said:

«أَنَا أَحَقُّ بِمُوسَى وَأَحَقُّ بِصَوْمِ هَذَا الْيَوْمِ.»

> I have greater right to Mūsā ﷺ, and I have greater right to fast this day.[1]

Then the Holy Prophet ﷺ ordered his noble Companions to fast.

The survival of Prophet Nūḥ ﷺ, the second father of humanity, along with his followers, constituted the survival of humanity. His people commemorated that day and were forever grateful to Almighty Allah for it. From this we learn that any occasion upon which the believers attain security and freedom must be thanked at the collective level. This is an integral aspect of Islamic culture and civilisation. In this way, the blessed birthday of the beloved Prophet ﷺ will be a day of *ʿīd* for the believers until the Day of Judgment.

5.3 The Evidence of Commemorating the Day of Changing the *Kaʿba*'s Covering

During the age of ignorance, the *Quraysh* would keep a fast on *Yawm ʿĀshūrāʾ*, and they would commemorate that day as a day of *ʿīd*. Prior to migrating to Medina, the most gracious Prophet ﷺ would also commemorate this day by fasting. The reason for their honouring this day was because it was the day in which the *Kaʿba* was covered for the first time. This was the specific background for which the most exalted Prophet ﷺ, after migrating to Medina, asked the Jews about their fasting on *Yawm ʿĀshūrāʾ*.

1. Imam al-Bukhārī reports the statement of the mother of the believers, ʿĀʾisha ﷺ:

كَانَ يَوْمُ عَاشُورَاءَ تَصُومُهُ قُرَيْشٌ فِي الْجَاهِلِيَّةِ، وَكَانَ رَسُولُ اللهِ ﷺ يَصُومُهُ.

[1] Narrated by Aḥmad b. Ḥanbal in *al-Musnad*, 2:359–360 §8702; and al-ʿAsqalānī in *Fatḥ al-Bārī*, 4:247.

> The *Quraysh* used to fast *Yawm ʿĀshūrāʾ* during the days of ignorance; and the Prophet ﷺ used to fast it (too).[1]

When the *Kaʿba* was covered for the first time during the days of ignorance, it was the 10th of *Muḥarram*. Since that time, the inhabitants of Mecca would keep a fast on that day, each year, and they would commemorate it as an *ʿīd*. Their practice continued even after the Prophet's birth, and the Holy Prophet ﷺ himself fasted routinely on the day when the *Kaʿba* was covered.
2. Imam al-Bukhārī reports another statement from ʿĀʾisha رضي الله عنها:

كَانُوا يَصُومُونَ عَاشُورَاءَ قَبْلَ أَنْ يُفْرَضَ رَمَضَانُ وَكَانَ يَوْمًا تُسْتَرُ فِيهِ الْكَعْبَةُ، فَلَمَّا فَرَضَ اللهُ رَمَضَانَ قَالَ رَسُولُ اللهِ ﷺ: «مَنْ شَاءَ أَنْ يَصُومَهُ فَلْيَصُمْهُ وَمَنْ شَاءَ أَنْ يَتْرُكَهُ فَلْيَتْرُكْهُ.»

> They (the Arabs) used to fast *ʿĀshūrāʾ* prior to the obligation of *Ramaḍān*, as it used to be the day in which the *Kaʿba* was draped. When fasting in *Ramaḍān* became obligated, the Prophet ﷺ said, 'Whoever wants to fast it, let him fast; and whoever wants to leave it, let him leave it.'[2]

Ibn Ḥajar al-ʿAsqalānī (773–852 AH), giving his thoughts on this hadith, states:

---

[1] Narrated by al-Bukhārī in *al-Ṣaḥīḥ*: *Kitāb al-Ṣawm* [The Book of Fasting], chapter: 'The fast of *Yawm ʿĀshūrā*', 2:704 §1898; al-Bukhārī in *al-Ṣaḥīḥ*: *Kitāb al-Manāqib* [The Book of Virtues], chapter: 'The days of ignorance', 3:1393 §3619; Muslim in *al-Ṣaḥīḥ*: *Kitāb al-Ṣiyām* [The Book of Fasting], chapter: 'The fast of *Yawm ʿĀshūrā*', 2:792 §1125; al-Tirmidhī in *al-Jāmiʿ al-Ṣaḥīḥ*: *Kitāb al-Ṣawm* [The Book of Fasting], chapter: 'What has been related concerning the dispensation of fasting *Yawm ʿĀshūrā*', 3:127 §753.

[2] Narrated by al-Bukhārī in *al-Ṣaḥīḥ*: *Kitāb al-Ḥajj* [The Book of Pilgrimage], chapter: 'Allah's statement: Allah ﷻ has made the *Kaʿba* a sacred house,' 2:578 §1515; al-Ṭabarānī in *al-Muʿjam al-awsaṭ*, 7:278 §7495; al-Bayhaqī in *al-Sunan al-kubrā*, 5:159 §9513; and Ibn ʿAbd al-Barr, *al-Tamhīd limā fī al-muwaṭṭā min al-maʿānī wa al-asānīd*, 7:204.

فَإِنَّهُ يُفِيْدُ أَنَّ الْـجَاهِلِيَّةَ كَانُوْا يُعَظِّمُوْنَ الْكَعْبَةَ قَدِيْمًـا بِالسُّتُورِ وَيَقُومُونَ بِهَا.

> It can be understood that in the days of ignorance, they used to venerate the *Kaʿba*, since time immemorial, by covering it. This was a practice that they had established.[1]

Ibn Ḥajar al-ʿAsqalānī (773–852 AH), in another place, gives another reason:

أَمَّا صِيَامُ قُرَيْشٍ لِعَاشُوْرَاءَ فَلَعَلَّهُمْ تَلَقَّوْهُ مِنَ الشَّرْعِ السَّالِفِ، وَلِـهَذَا كَانُوْا يُعَظِّمُوْنَهُ بِكِسْوَةِ الْكَعْبَةِ فِيْهِ.

> As for the fast kept by *Quraysh* for *ʿĀshūrāʾ*, perhaps they received it from a previous Sharia and for this reason they used to venerate it by covering the *Kaʿba* on that day.[2]

Concerning the day of the draping of the *Kaʿba*, Imam al-Ṭabarānī (260–360 AH), in *al-Muʿjam al-kabīr* (5:138 §4876), transmits the statement of Zayd b. Thābit, who states:

لَيْسَ يَوْمُ عَاشُوْرَاءَ بِالْيَوْمِ الَّذِي يَقُوْلُهُ النَّاسُ، إِنَّمَـا كَانَ يَومٌ تُسْتَرُ فِيْهِ الْكَعْبَةُ وَكَانَ يَدُوْرُ فِي السَّنَةِ.

> *Yawm ʿĀshūrāʾ* is not the day which people presume. It is only the day in which the *Kaʿba* is covered; and this day used to rotate through the year.[3]

Venerating the day in which the *Kaʿba* is covered is a source of obfuscation for some people. They say that once the *Kaʿba* has been draped with its covering, what is the need for its veneration? This

---

[1] Al-ʿAsqalānī, *Fatḥ al-Bārī*, 3:455.

[2] Ibid., 4:246.

[3] Al-Haythamī, *Majmaʿ al-zawāʾid wa manbaʿ al-fawāʾid*, 3:187; al-ʿAsqalānī, *Fatḥ al-Bārī*, 4:248; and al-ʿAsqalānī, *Fatḥ al-Bārī*, 7:276.

statement is not correct, as the most exalted Prophet ﷺ was the one who honoured this day. Similarly, some people have a misgiving that the main purpose of the Prophet's raising was to teach us the Qurʾān and Sunna, and that his birthday was an incident which took place a long time ago; seeing that the Holy Prophet ﷺ has fulfilled his obligation, what then is the need of celebrating his birth? Is it not enough that we adhere to his Sunna and implement his teaching in our lives?

Before answering this question and other questions of this nature, it is necessary for all believers to be conscious of the Prophet's true stature: it is important first to bring to mind the purpose behind the Prophet's raising amongst mankind, the importance of his perfect exemplariness and the revelation of the Qurʾān; and the step by step development of Islamic civilisation from the moment of its inception.

The day in which the *Kaʿba* is covered repeats itself annually. The Arabs would honour that day on account of the *Kaʿba,* and so later it developed into an independent act of commemoration. It is for this reason that the day of *Mawlid al-Nabī* ﷺ, despite taking place many centuries ago, deserves honouring every time it comes up in the year; revering it and expressing happiness on that day is indispensable. Even Abū Lahab expressed his happiness on the occasion of the Prophet's birth by freeing his slave girl, Thuwayba, and resultantly, he received a lightening of his punishment every Monday. The Prophet ﷺ himself kept the practice of commemorating his birth alive. Therefore, to celebrate *Mawlid al-Nabī* ﷺ is not just permissible, is also established in the Sunna of the chosen Prophet ﷺ.

5.4 The Evidence of Commemorating the Day of Islam's Completion as an *ʿĪd*.

When the third verse of *sūra al-Māʾida*, ﴾*Today I have perfected your Dīn (Religion) for you*﴿, was revealed, the Jews made it an item of discussion with the Muslims. In the hadith which is to follow, a dialogue between a Jew and ʿUmar ﷺ is transmitted, which serves as evidence for the permissibility of celebrating *Mawlid al-Nabī* ﷺ:

1. Imam al-Bukhārī (194–256 AH) reports:

عَنْ عُمَرَ بْنِ الْخَطَّابِ أَنَّ رَجُلًا مِنَ الْيَهُودِ قَالَ لَهُ: يَا أَمِيرَ الْـمُؤْمِنِينَ، آيَةٌ فِي كِتَابِكُمْ تَقْرَءُونَهَا لَوْ عَلَيْنَا مَعْشَرَ الْيَهُودِ نَزَلَتْ لَاتَّخَذْنَا ذَلِكَ الْيَوْمَ عِيدًا. قَالَ: أَيُّ آيَةٍ؟ قَالَ: ﴿ٱلْيَوْمَ أَكْمَلْتُ لَكُمْ دِينَكُمْ وَأَتْمَمْتُ عَلَيْكُمْ نِعْمَتِي وَرَضِيتُ لَكُمُ ٱلْإِسْلَٰمَ دِينًا﴾. قَالَ عُمَرُ: قَدْ عَرَفْنَا ذَلِكَ الْيَوْمَ وَالْـمَكَانَ الَّذِي نَزَلَتْ فِيهِ عَلَى النَّبِيِّ ﷺ وَهُوَ قَائِمٌ بِعَرَفَةَ يَوْمَ جُمُعَةٍ.

ʿUmar b. al-Khaṭṭāb ☙ states that a Jewish man asked him, 'O commander of the faithful! There is a verse in your Holy book which you recite, had it been revealed upon us, the Jews, we would have taken that day as a day of festivity (ʿīd).' ʿUmar ☙ asked, 'And which verse is it?' He replied, ⟪Today I have perfected your Dīn (Religion) for you, and have completed My Blessing upon you, and have chosen for you Islam (as) Dīn (a complete code of life)⟫. ʿUmar ☙ said, 'Indeed, we know that day, and the place in which it was revealed on the Prophet ﷺ: he was standing in ʿArafa, on a Friday.'[1]

It is worthy to note here that the Jew remarked that had the verse of the perfection of the religion been revealed upon them, they would have taken that day as a day of festivity (ʿīd). They had

---

[1] Narrated by al-Bukhārī in *al-Ṣaḥīḥ*: *Kitāb al-Īmān* [The Book of Faith], chapter: 'The increase and decrease of faith,' 1:25 §45; al-Bukhārī in *al-Ṣaḥīḥ*: *Kitāb al-Maghāzī* [The Book of Military Expeditions], chapter: 'The farewell Pilgrimage,' 4:1600 §4145; al-Bukhārī in *al-Ṣaḥīḥ*: *Kitāb al-Tafsīr al-Qurʾān* [The Book of the Exegeses of the Qurʾān], chapter: 'Allah's statement: *Today I have perfected your Dīn (Religion) for you*,' 4:1683 §4330; al-Bukhārī in *al-Ṣaḥīḥ*: *Kitāb al-Iʿtiṣām bi al-Kitāb wa al-Sunna* [The Book of Adhering to the Qurʾān and *Sunna*], 6:2653 §6840; Muslim in *al-Ṣaḥīḥ*: *Kitāb al-Tafsīr* [The Book of Exegeses], 4:2313 §3017; al-Tirmidhī in *al-Jāmiʿ al-Ṣaḥīḥ*: *Abwāb al-Tafsīr al-Qurʾān* [The Chapters of the Exegeses of the Qurʾān], chapter: 'From *Sūra al-Māʾida*,' 5:250 §3043; and al-Nasāʾī in *al-Sunan*: *Kitāb al-Īmān* [The Book of Faith], chapter: 'The increase of faith,' 8:114 §5012.

a misconception that the Muslims took that day like any other. The answer to this should have been of this kind; however, ʿUmar ؓ instead said:

قَدْ عَرَفْنَا ذَلِكَ الْيَوْمَ، وَالْـمَكَانَ الَّذِي نَزَلَتْ فِيْهِ.

Indeed, we know that day, and the place in which it was revealed.

That day was a Friday and it was the occasion of Pilgrimage, on the plains of *ʿArafāt*. Apparently, there seems to be no correlation between the question and the answer; but in reality, ʿUmar's answer is totally in accordance with the question. By quoting the words *ʿArafa* and Friday, he gives a complete answer through allusion by saying that both of these two days are an *ʿīd* for the Muslims, i.e., this day is commemorated as an *ʿīd,* weekly and annually. This is why the Jew became silent and he did not repeat his question again, as ʿUmar ؓ had answered his question comprehensively.

Concerning Umar's reply, Ibn Ḥajar al-ʿAsqalānī (773–852 AH) states:

عِنْدِيْ أَنَّ هَذِهِ الرِّوَايَةَ اِكْتَفَى فِيْهَا بِالْإِشَارَةِ.

In my view, this narration suffices through allusion.[1]

2. Kaʿb al-Aḥbār, in one of his narrations, further elucidates ʿUmar's reply. He states that he said to ʿUmar ؓ that he knew a people had this verse been revealed upon them, they would have taken that day as a day of festivity (*ʿīd*). ʿUmar ؓ asked, 'And which verse is it?'. He replied:

﴿ٱلْيَوْمَ أَكْمَلْتُ لَكُمْ دِينَكُمْ وَأَتْمَمْتُ عَلَيْكُمْ نِعْمَتِي وَرَضِيتُ لَكُمُ ٱلْإِسْلَٰمَ دِينًا﴾

'Today I have perfected your Dīn (Religion) for you, and

[1] Al-ʿAsqalānī, *Fatḥ al-Bārī*, 1:105 §45.

have completed My Blessing upon you, and have chosen for you Islam (as) Dīn (a complete code of life).'[1]

ʿUmar ﷛ replied:

إِنِّي لَأَعْرِفُ فِي أَيِّ يَوْمٍ أُنْزِلَتْ: ﴿ٱلْيَوْمَ أَكْمَلْتُ لَكُمْ دِينَكُمْ﴾، يَوْمَ جُمُعَةٍ وَيَوْمَ عَرَفَةٍ، وَهُمَا لَنَا عِيْدَانِ.

Indeed, I know in which day the verse, ﴾*Today I have perfected your Dīn (Religion) for you*﴿, was revealed: it was a Friday and the day of *ʿArafa*; and they are both days of *ʿīd* for us.[2]

It can be established from the narration above that the Jew's point of view was correct, as it was confirmed by ʿUmar ﷛. Otherwise, he would have rejected it, stating that in our Sharia, the days of *ʿīd* have been fixed; this is why we cannot take this day as an *ʿīd*. But he did not say this. Instead he pointed out to the Jew that had this been bestowed upon you, you would have taken it as one day of *ʿīd*; we, however, have taken it as two days of *ʿīd*: the day of *ʿArafa* and Friday.

3. Supporting this view, there is an incident of ʿAbd Allāh b. ʿAbbās ﷛, reported by ʿAmmār b. Abī ʿAmmār, that he recited the verse, ﴾*Today I have perfected your Dīn (Religion) for you, and have completed My Blessing upon you, and have chosen for you Islam (as) Dīn (a complete code of life)*﴿, and a Jew came to him saying:

لَوْ أُنْزِلَتْ هَذِهِ عَلَيْنَا لَاتَّخَذْنَا يَوْمَهَا عِيْدًا.

Had this verse been revealed on us, we would have taken that day as an *ʿīd*.

ʿAbd Allāh b. ʿAbbās ﷛ replied:

---

[1] Qurʾān 5:3.

[2] Narrated by al-Ṭabarānī in *al-Muʿjam al-awsaṭ*, 1:253 §830; al-ʿAsqalānī, *Fatḥ al-Bārī*, 1:105 §45; and Ibn Kathīr, *Tafsīr al-Qurʾān al-ʿaẓīm*, 2:14.

فَإِنَّهَا نَزَلَتْ فِي يَوْمِ عِيْدَيْنِ: فِي يَوْمِ الْجُمُعَةِ وَيَوْمِ عَرَفَةَ.

> It was revealed on a day of two *ʿīds*: on a Friday and the day of *ʿArafa*.[1]

ʿAbd Allāh b. ʿAbbās ؓ did not reject the Jew's opinion, rather he endorsed it by saying that this verse was revealed on a Friday and the day of *ʿArafa*, and both of these two days are an *ʿīd* for the Muslims.

These hadiths affirm the concept that it is permissible to commemorate the day in which a blessing descends. Just as the day in which the verse concerning the perfection of the religion was revealed is being declared an *ʿīd*, in the same the way, the day in which the Prophet ﷺ, a mercy to the worlds, was born is also a day of *ʿīd*. To commemorate *Mawlid al-Nabī* ﷺ is the sweetness of faith. Before one comprehends this reality, it is imperative to realise that the founding pillar of faith is to love the Holy Prophet ﷺ. How can it be that you claim to have faith, and yet the condition of your faith does not allow you to express happiness upon the birth of your Prophet ﷺ?

The verse of *sūra al-Māʾida* was revealed on the most gracious Prophet ﷺ, and it came as a glad tiding and good news. The day in which this verse was revealed was marked as a day of two *ʿīds*: the *ʿīd* of Friday, and the *ʿīd* of *ʿArafa*. Therefore, it should not be difficult for the believers to understand this point that the day in which the final messenger was born, that day is the greatest day of the year. The majority of Muslims, by holding gatherings, express their happiness and are grateful to Almighty Allah for this eternal blessing—to express happiness on this day is a sign of *īmān*. The majority of Muslims have been honouring this day consistently, and on the 12th of *Rabīʿ al-Awwal*, they hold celebrations in its honour.

---

[1] Narrated by al-Tirmidhī in *al-Jāmiʿ al-Ṣaḥīḥ*: *Kitāb al-Tafsīr al-Qurʾān* [The Book of the Exegeses of the Qurʾān], chapter: 'From *Sūra al-Māʾida*', 5:250 §3044; al-Ṭabarānī in *al-Muʿjam al-kabīr*, 12:184 §12,835; al-Ṭabarī in *Jāmiʿ al-bayān fī tafsīr al-Qurʾān*, 6:82; al-Marūzī in *Taʿẓīm qadr al-ṣalāh*, 1:352 §354; Ibn Kathīr in *Tafsīr al-Qurʾān al-ʿaẓīm*, 2:14; and Ibn Mūsā al-Ḥanafī in *Muʿtaṣar al-mukhtaṣar*, 2:169.

Some people object, claiming that apart from ʿīd al-Fiṭr and ʿīd al-Aḍḥā, it is not permissible to use the term ʿīd for any other day. This objection can be refuted by the following statement of ʿAbd Allāh b. ʿAbbās ☙:

فَإِنَّهَا نَزَلَتْ فِي يَوْمِ عِيدَيْنِ: فِي يَوْمِ الْجُمُعَةِ وَيَوْمِ عَرَفَةَ.

It was revealed on a day of two ʿīds: on a Friday and the day of ʿArafa.

Some may say that the day of ʿArafa is in fact the day of ʿīd al-aḍḥā. Our response to this is that ʿUmar and ʿAbd Allāh b. ʿAbbās ☙ have both declared Friday also as a day of ʿīd. If Friday can be a day of ʿīd, according to the verdict of those most glorious Companions, then why can Mawlid al-Nabī ☙ not be a day of ʿīd? In fact, his birthday is the ʿīd of all ʿīds, because it was on account of his blessed being that we received the Qurʾān and were blessed with divine guidance.

5.5 The Excellence of Friday: The Day of Ādam's Creation

Friday, on account of its special importance and virtue, has been named the chief day of the week (*sayyid al-ayyām*). On this day, it is Sunna to take a bath, wear new clothes, and to apply scent. One is to leave aside business and go to the mosque to take part in the congregational prayer. The most gracious Prophet ☙ has enjoined his followers to invoke much blessing and salutations upon him on this day.

Aws b. Aws ☙ reports that the Prophet ☙ said:

«إِنَّ مِنْ أَفْضَلِ أَيَّامِكُمْ يَوْمَ الْجُمُعَةِ: فِيهِ خُلِقَ آدَمُ، وَفِيهِ قُبِضَ، وَفِيهِ النَّفْخَةُ، وَفِيهِ الصَّعْقَةُ: فَأَكْثِرُوا عَلَيَّ مِنَ الصَّلَاةِ فِيهِ، فَإِنَّ صَلَاتَكُمْ مَعْرُوضَةٌ عَلَيَّ.»

The finest of your days is the Day of Congregation (Friday), on which Ādam ﷺ was created and on which he died, on which the blast of the trumpet will sound [at the Resurrection] and on which the thunderbolt will strike. You must therefore invoke blessings upon me frequently on that day, for the blessing you invoke is presented to me.[1]

Friday is a day of ʿīd. Many great hadith scholars have reported this in their collections:

1. Ibn Mājah (209–273 AH) reports that ʿAbd Allāh b. ʿAbbās ؓ narrates that the Prophet ﷺ said:

«إِنَّ هَذَا يَوْمُ عِيدٍ جَعَلَهُ اللهُ لِلْمُسْلِمِينَ، فَمَنْ جَاءَ إِلَى الْجُمُعَةِ فَلْيَغْتَسِلْ، وَإِنْ كَانَ طِيبٌ فَلْيَمَسَّ مِنْهُ وَعَلَيْكُمْ بِالسِّوَاكِ.»

Indeed, this is the day of ʿīd. Allah made it for the Muslims. Whoever goes for the Friday (congregational prayers), let him bathe and, if possible, use some scent—the *miswāk* is binding upon you.[2]

---

[1] Narrated by Abū Dāwūd in *al-Sunan*: *Kitāb al-Ṣalāh* [The Book of Prayer], chapter: 'The excellence of Friday, the Day of Congregational prayer, and the night of Friday', 1:275 §1047; Abū Dāwūd in *al-Sunan*: *Abwāb al-Witr* [The Chapters of *Witr*], chapter: 'On repentance', 2:88 §1531; Ibn Mājah in *al-Sunan*: *Kitāb iqāma al-ṣalāh wa sunna fīhā* [The Book of Establishing the Prayer and the *Sunna* therein], chapter: 'The excellence of Friday', 1:345 §1085; al-Nasāʾī in *al-Sunan*: *Kitāb al-Jumʿa* [The Book of Friday], chapter: 'Increasing one's salutations upon the Prophet on Friday', 3:91 §1375; al-Nasāʾī in *al-Sunan al-kubrā*, chapter: 'The command to increase one's salutations upon the Prophet on Friday', 1:519 §1666; al-Dārimī in *al-Sunan*, 1:445 §1572; Ibn Abī Shayba in *al-Muṣannaf*, 2:253 §8697; al-Ṭabarānī in *al-Muʿjam al-kabīr*, 1:216 §589; al-Bayhaqī in *al-Sunan al-kubrā*, 3:248 §5789; al-Bayhaqī in *al-Sunan al-ṣughrā*, 1:372 §634; and Haythamī in *Mawārid al-ẓamʾān ilā zawāʾid Ibn Ḥibbān*, 1:146, §550.

[2] Narrated by Ibn Mājah in *al-Sunan*: *Kitāb iqāma al-ṣalāh* [The Book of Establishing the Prayer], chapter: 'Beautification on Friday', 1:349 §1098; al-Ṭabarānī in *al-Muʿjam al-awsaṭ*, 7:230 §7355; and Mundhirī in *al-Targhīb wa al-tarhīb min al-ḥadīth al-sharīf*, 1:286 §1058.

2. Aḥmad b. Ḥanbal (164–241 AH) reports that Abū Hurayra ؓ narrates that the Prophet ﷺ said:

«إِنَّ يَوْمَ الْـجُمُعَةِ يَوْمُ عِيدٍ، فَلَا تَجْعَلُوا يَوْمَ عِيدِكُمْ يَوْمَ صِيَامِكُمْ إِلَّا أَنْ تَصُومُوا قَبْلَهُ أَوْ بَعْدَهُ.»

> Friday is the day of *ʿīd*. Do not make your day of *ʿīd* a day of fasting, save that you fast the day before it or the day after it.[1]

3. Ibn Ḥibbān (270–354 AH) reports that Abū Awbar narrates:

كُنْتُ قَاعِدًا عِنْدَ أَبِي هُرَيْرَةَ إِذْ جَاءَهُ رَجُلٌ، فَقَالَ: إِنَّكَ نَهَيْتَ النَّاسَ عَنْ صِيَامِ يَوْمِ الْـجُمُعَةِ؟ قَالَ: مَا نَهَيْتُ النَّاسَ أَنْ يَصُومُوا يَوْمَ الْـجُمُعَةِ، وَلَكِنِّي سَمِعْتُ رَسُوْلَ اللهِ ﷺ يَقُوْلُ: «لَا تَصُومُوا يَوْمَ الْـجُمُعَةِ، فَإِنَّهُ يَوْمُ عِيْدٍ إِلَّا أَنْ تَصِلُوهُ بِأَيَّامٍ.»

> I was sitting with Abū Hurayra ؓ when a man came to him and said, 'You forbade people from fasting on Fridays.' He replied, 'I did not forbid people from fasting on Fridays, except that I heard Allah's Messenger ﷺ say, 'Do not fast on Fridays for it is a day of *ʿīd*, except that you join it with (other) days.''[2]

A question arises here: what is the cause for the merits of Friday—why has it been named the chief day of the week? The answer to this is contained in the hadiths that have just passed. The Holy Prophet ﷺ, giving the reason for the excellence of Friday, states:

---

[1] Narrated by Aḥmad b. Ḥanbal in *al-Musnad*, 2:303 & 532 §8012 & 10,903; Ibn Khuzayma in *al-Ṣaḥīḥ*, 3:315 & 318 §2161 & 2166; Ibn Rāhwayh in *al-Musnad*, 1:451 §524; and al-Ḥakim in *al-Mustadrak*, 1:603 §1595.

[2] Narrated by Ibn Ḥibbān in *al-Ṣaḥīḥ*, 8:375, §3610.

«فِيْهِ خُلِقَ آدَمُ.»

On this day, Ādam ﷺ was created.

Friday is the day in which the father of mankind, Ādam ﷺ, was created. It is the day of his *mawlid* and is declared an *ʿīd*: if Friday, being the day of Ādam's *mawlid*, can be honoured, why not the *mawlid* of the final Prophet ﷺ? One could say that the *mawlid* of Ādam ﷺ is commemorated because Ādam ﷺ was created in a special way, but this bears no effect on our discourse. This is because Ādam ﷺ was created on a Friday, and because he was created on a Friday that it became the chief day of the week, as it was the day of the creation of the first prophet and the father of mankind. On the basis of this, the day in which the Holy Prophet ﷺ was born is a day which can be called an *ʿīd* of *ʿīds*, as it is the day in which the mercy to all worlds came and the master of all the prophets.

5.5.1 Friday: the Day of Invoking Blessings and Salutations

The preparations that are made for Friday are like the ones made for the commemoration of *Mawlid al-Nabī* ﷺ, e.g., taking a bath, applying scent, and leaving one's business to partake in a congregation at the mosque. Apart from these, there are other preparations mentioned in the books of hadith. These extra preparations are in essence related to the most exalted Prophet ﷺ, such as invoking blessings and sending salutations upon him. This day has been chosen, as it is the day of the *mawlid* of Ādam ﷺ. As mentioned previously, the Prophet ﷺ said:

«فَأَكْثِرُوا عَلَيَّ مِنَ الصَّلَاةِ فِيْهِ.»

> You must therefore invoke blessings upon me frequently on that day.

This is the litany of the lovers: those who have true love for the most beloved Prophet ﷺ congregate on this day to invoke blessings and send salutations collectively. On this day, there are special gatherings of *Mawlid al-Nabī* ﷺ: circles of *ṣalāt* and *salām* are held. On one hand, this day is attributed to Ādam ﷺ as the day of his *mawlid*, and on the other hand, it is the day of invoking blessings and salutations on the Holy Prophet ﷺ. In one day, happiness is expressed for two prophets.

In the same hadith, the noble Companions asked:

يَا رَسُولَ اللهِ، وَكَيْفَ تُعْرَضُ صَلَاتُنَا عَلَيْكَ وَقَدْ أَرِمْتَ؟

O Messenger of Allah, how will the blessing we invoke be presented to you after your demise?

To this, the Holy Prophet ﷺ replied:

«إِنَّ اللهَ عَزَّ وَجَلَّ حَرَّمَ عَلَى الْأَرْضِ أَجْسَادَ الْأَنْبِيَاءِ.»

Indeed, Allah ﷻ has declared the bodies of the prophets forbidden to the earth.[1]

What this means is that the Holy Prophet ﷺ was informing his noble Companions that even after his physical departure from this world, he will still be alive with his body. So it is important that one makes a practice of invoking abundant blessings and salutations upon him on this day.

---

[1] Narrated by Abū Dāwūd in *al-Sunan*: *Kitāb al-Ṣalāh* [The Book of Prayer], chapter: 'The excellence of Friday, the Day of Congregational prayer, and the night of Friday', 1:275 §1047; Abū Dāwūd in *al-Sunan*: *Abwāb al-Witr* [The Chapters of *Witr*], chapter: 'On repentance', 2:88 §1531; Ibn Mājah in *al-Sunan*: *Kitāb iqāma al-ṣalāh wa sunna fīhā* [The Book of Establishing the Prayer and the Sunna therein], chapter: 'The excellence of Friday', 1:345 §1085; al-Nasāʾī in *al-Sunan*: *Kitāb al-Jumʿa* [The Book of Friday], chapter: 'Increasing one's salutations upon the Prophet on Friday', 3:91 §1375; al-Nasāʾī in *al-Sunan al-kubrā*, chapter: 'The command to increase one's salutations upon the Prophet on Friday', 1:519 §1666; al-Dārimī in *al-Sunan*, 1:445 §1572; Ibn Abī Shayba in *al-Muṣannaf*, 2:253 §8697; al-Ṭabarānī in *al-Muʿjam al-kabīr*, 1:216 §589; al-Bayhaqī in *al-Sunan al-kubrā*, 3:248 §5789; al-Bayhaqī in *al-Sunan al-ṣughrā*, 1:372 §634; and Haythamī in *Mawārid al-ẓamʾān ilā zawāʾid Ibn Ḥibbān*, 1:146, §550.

5.6 THE IMPORTANCE OF ᶜĪSĀ'S BIRTHPLACE AND ITS VISITATION

Anas b. Mālik ﷺ reports that when the most exalted Prophet ﷺ went on his Heavenly Ascension, Jibrāʾīl ﷺ halted at Bethlehem and told him to get off the Burrāq and offer prayer there. After completing the prayer, Jibrāʾīl ﷺ said to him:

أَتَدْرِي أَيْنَ صَلَّيْتَ؟ صَلَّيْتَ بِبَيْتِ لَحْمٍ حَيْثُ وُلِدَ عِيسَى ﷺ.

> Do you know where you prayed? You prayed at Bethlehem where ᶜĪsā ﷺ was born.[1]

It can be understood from this hadith that just as Friday is honoured as the day of Ādam's creation, Bethlehem is honoured, as it is the birthplace of ᶜĪsā ﷺ—both the time and place of a Prophet's birth is honoured. The most exalted Prophet ﷺ offered prayer at the place where ᶜĪsā ﷺ was born, which establishes the importance of venerating the birthplace of a prophet. This is why the lovers of the Holy Prophet ﷺ make visitations of the place where the Holy Prophet ﷺ was born. For a time, it was a practice of the inhabitants of Mecca that they used to lead processions from that place in commemoration of the *mawlid*. Moreover, if the place in which a prophet is born can be blessed, as established from the hadith above, then why not the moment of the Prophet's birth?

5.7 THE PROPHET ﷺ COMMEMORATED HIS OWN BIRTHDAY BY FASTING

On the legality of *Mawlid al-Nabī* ﷺ, the question may arise: Did the Prophet ﷺ himself give any specific instructions on commemorating

---

[1] Narrated by al-Nasāʾī in *al-Sunan*: *Kitāb al-Ṣalāh* [The Book of Prayer], chapter: 'The obligation of the prayer', 1:222 §450; al-Ṭabarānī in *Musnad al-shāmiyyīn*, 1:194 §341. In the following collections, this narration is reported by Shaddād b. Aws: al-Bazzār in *al-Baḥr al-zukhār* (*al-musnad*), 8:410 §3484; al-Ṭabarānī in *al-Muᶜjam al-kabīr*, 7:283 §7142; al-Haythamī in *Majmaᶜ al-zawāʾid wa manbaᶜ al-fawāʾid*, 1:73; and al-ᶜAsqalānī in *Fatḥ al-Bārī*, 7:199.

his birthday? The answer to this is in the affirmative. The most exalted Prophet ﷺ himself expressed happiness on his birthday as a means of expressing gratitude to Almighty Allah, and he encouraged his noble Companions to do so likewise. In the following narration, it is established that the Holy Prophet ﷺ used to fast on his *mawlid*.

Imam Muslim (206–261 AH) reports that Abū Qatāda al-Anṣārī ؓ narrates:

أَنَّ رَسُولَ اللهِ ﷺ سُئِلَ عَنْ صَوْمِ الِاثْنَيْنِ، فَقَالَ: «فِيهِ وُلِدْتُ وَفِيهِ أُنْزِلَ عَلَيَّ.»

> Allah's Messenger ﷺ was asked about fasting on Mondays. He said, 'That is the day in which I was born and the day in which I was raised (as a Prophet), or the day upon which the revelation descended upon me.'[1]

The speciality of Monday is because this is the blessed day in which the Holy Prophet ﷺ was born. In the Sharia, this day holds special importance and virtue. The Holy Prophet ﷺ himself kept fast on this day as an act of gratitude, and by doing so, this action holds the status of Sunna for his community. Even today, the believers all around the world keep fast on Mondays in order to observe this *Sunna*.

In Islam, birthdays hold special importance: those who claim that birthdays have no significance in Islam are uninformed of the teachings of the Sharia. The Holy Prophet ﷺ said, 'That is the day in which I was born,' and by doing so, he gave the concept of birthdays in Islam. The Qurʾān likewise makes mention of the

---

[1] Narrated by Muslim in *al-Ṣaḥīḥ*: *Kitāb al-Ṣiyām* [The Book of Fasting], chapter: 'The desirability of fasting three days in each month', 2:819 §1162; al-Bayhaqī in *al-Sunan al-kubrā*, 4:286 §38,182. The following narration contain the words, 'On this day prophethood descended upon me': al-Nasāʾī in *al-Sunan al-kubrā*, 2:146 §2777; Aḥmad b. Ḥanbal in *al-Musnad*, 5:296–297 §22,590–22,594; ʿAbd al-Razzāq in *al-Muṣannaf*, 4:296 §7865; Abū Yaʿlā in *al-Musnad*, 1:134 §144; al-Bayhaqī in *al-Sunan al-kubrā*, 4:300 §8259.

birthdays of prophets, which has been explained in one of the chapters that have preceded us. From this, it is clear that Almighty Allah highly esteems the birthdays of His prophets; when we look at it from this perspective, the *mawlid* of the Prophet ﷺ holds the highest degree. There are different ways in which this day can be commemorated, as established from the Qurʾān and Sunna. One way, as mentioned in the hadith above, is to keep a fast, but there are other methods, such as giving charity and distributing food. In the previous chapter, we have discussed the different ways in which one can express gratitude to Almighty Allah for a blessing.

5.8 The Prophet ﷺ Commemorated his own Birthday by Sacrificing an Animal

The Holy Prophet ﷺ commemorated his own birthday as a means of expressing gratitude to Almighty Allah. He sacrificed an animal on the occasion of his birthday and arranged a feast.

1. Imam Bayhaqī (384–458 AH) reports that Anas b. Mālik ؓ said:

إِنَّ النَّبِيَّ ﷺ عَقَّ عَنْ نَفْسِهِ بَعْدَ النُّبُوَّةِ.

The Prophet ﷺ performed an ʿaqīqa for himself after declaring his prophethood.[1]

2. Ḍiyāʾ al-Maqdisī (569–643 AH) reports that Anas b. Mālik ؓ said:

إِنَّ النَّبِيَّ ﷺ عَقَّ عَنْ نَفْسِهِ بَعْدَ مَا بُعِثَ نَبِيًّا.

The Prophet ﷺ performed an ʿaqīqa for himself after he was raised as a prophet.[2]

---

[1] Narrated by al-Bayhaqī in *al-Sunan al-kubrā*, 9:300 §43; al-Maqdisī in *al-Aḥādīth al-mukhtāra*, 5:205 §1833; al-Nawawī in *Tahdhīb al-asmāʾ wa al-lughāt*, 2:557 §962; al-ʿAsqalānī in *Fatḥ al-Bārī*, 9:595; al-ʿAsqalānī in *Tahdhīb al-tahdhīb*, 5:340 §661; and al-Mizzī in *Tahdhīb al-kamāl fī asmāʾ al-rijāl*, 16:32 §3523.

[2] Narrated by al-Maqdisī in *al-Aḥādīth al-mukhtāra*, 5:205 §1832; al-

3. ʿAbd Allāh b. ʿAbbās ﷺ narrates:

لَـمَّـا وُلِدَ النَّبِيُّ ﷺ عَقَّ عَنْهُ عَبْدُ الْـمُطَّلِبِ بِكَبْشٍ.

When the Prophet ﷺ was born, ʿAbd al-Muṭṭalib sacrificed a ram on his behalf.[1]

4. ʿAbd Allāh b. ʿAbbās ﷺ also narrates:

إِنَّ عَبْدَ الْـمُطَّلِبِ جَعَلَ لَهُ مَأْدُبَةً يَوْمَ سَابِعَةٍ.

ʿAbd al-Muṭṭalib prepared a banquet for him (i.e., his ʿ*aqīqa*) on the seventh day.[2]

There is no difference of opinion amongst the scholars that the Prophet's ʿ*aqīqa* was performed by his grandfather ʿAbd al-Muṭṭalib, on the seventh day after his birth. In light of the hadith, the ʿ*aqīqa* is the means by which a child is redeemed—how can it be possible that the Holy Prophet ﷺ would delay his own ʿ*aqīqa* for forty years? Samra b. Jundub ﷺ narrates that the Holy Prophet ﷺ said:

«الْغُلَامُ مُرْتَهَنٌ بِعَقِيقَتِهِ، يُذْبَحُ عَنْهُ يَوْمَ السَّابِعِ.»

A child is redeemed by its ʿ*aqīqa*. A sacrifice should be performed on its behalf on the seventh day.[3]

Ṭabarānī in *al-Muʿjam al-awsaṭ*, 1:298 §994; and al-Rūyānī in *Musnad al-Ṣaḥāba*, 2:386 §1371.

[1] Narrated by Ibn ʿAsākir in *Tārīkh Dimashq al-kabīr*, 3:32; al-Ḥalabī in *Insān al-ʿuyūn fī sīra al-Amīn al-Maʾmūn*, 1:128; and al-Suyūṭī in *Kifāyat al-ṭālib al-labīb fī khaṣāʾiṣ al-Ḥabīb* ﷺ, 1:134.

[2] Narrated by Ibn ʿAbd al-Barr, *al-Tamhīd limā fī al-muwaṭṭā min al-maʿānī wa al-asānīd*, 21:61; Ibn ʿAbd al-Barr in *al-Istiʿāb fī maʿrifa al-Aṣḥāb*, 1:51; Ibn Ḥibbān in *al-Thiqāt*, 1:42; al-Qurṭubī in *al-Jāmiʿ li-aḥkām al-Qurʾān*, 2:100; and Ibn al-Qayyim in *Zād al-maʿād fī hudā Khayr al-ʿibād*, 1:81.

[3] Narrated by al-Tirmidhī in *al-Jāmiʿ al-Ṣaḥīḥ*: *Kitāb al-Aḍāḥī* [The Book of Animal-Sacrifice], chapter: 'The ʿ*aqīqa*', 4:101 §1522; Abū Dāwūd in

One may ask, which *ʿaqīqa* did the Holy Prophet ﷺ perform after his prophethood? As the *ʿaqīqa* is not repeated twice, in this case, the Holy Prophet ﷺ slaughtered an animal as an expression of happiness on his birth; he arranged a feast to show gratitude to Almighty Allah. Some people may say that this was only an *ʿaqīqa* which was performed by the Holy Prophet ﷺ. If we were to take it as an *ʿaqīqa*, then the question is: what is an *ʿaqīqa*? The *ʿaqīqa* is in of itself an expression of happiness and a show of gratitude on the birth of a child. One may call it what they want, the concept is still the same that happiness is expressed on a person's birth.

Imam Jalāl al-Dīn al-Suyūṭī (849–911 AH) in his book, *Ḥusn al-maqṣid fī ʿamal al-mawlid* (p.64–65), supporting the evidence given by Ḥāfiẓ Ibn Ḥajar al-ʿAsqalānī (773–852 AH), provides an evidence of his own giving a strong base for the legality of celebrating *Mawlid al-Nabī* ﷺ. He writes:

وَظَهَرَ لِي تَخْرِيْجُهُ عَلَى أَصْلٍ آخَرَ، وَهُوَ مَا أَخْرَجَهُ الْبَيْهَقِيُّ، عَنْ أَنَسٍ رضي الله عنه أَنَّ النَّبِيَّ عَقَّ عَنْ نَفْسِهِ بَعْدَ النُّبُوَّةِ مَعَ أَنَّهُ قَدْ وَرَدَ أَنَّ جَدَّهُ عَبْدَ الْمُطَّلِبِ عَقَّ عَنْهُ فِيْ سَابِعِ وِلَادَتِهِ، وَالْعَقِيْقَةُ لَا تُعَادُ مَرَّةً ثَانِيَةً، فَيُحْمَلُ ذٰلِكَ عَلَى أَنَّ الَّذِي فَعَلَهُ النَّبِيُّ ﷺ إِظْهَارًا لِلشُّكْرِ عَلَى إِيْجَادِ اللهِ تَعَالَى إِيَّاهُ، رَحْمَةً لِّلْعَالَمِيْنَ وَتَشْرِيْفًا لِأُمَّتِهِ، كَمَا كَانَ يُصَلِّيْ عَلَى نَفْسِهِ، لِذٰلِكَ فَيَسْتَحِبُّ لَنَا أَيْضًا إِظْهَارُ الشُّكْرِ بِمَوْلِدِهِ بِاجْتِمَاعِ الإِخْوَانِ، وَإِطْعَامِ الطَّعَامِ، وَنَحْوِ ذٰلِكَ مِنْ وُجُوْهِ الْقُرُبَاتِ، وَإِظْهَارِ الْمَسَرَّاتِ.

There has come to light another basis (for its celebration), which has been reported by Imam Bayhaqī that Anas رضي الله عنه narrates that the Prophet ﷺ performed an *ʿaqīqa* for himself after declaring his prophethood, despite the fact that his grandfather, ʿAbd al-Muṭṭalib, performed his

---

al-Sunan: *Kitāb al-Ḍaḥāyā* [The Book of Animal-Sacrifice], chapter: 'The *ʿaqīqa*', 3:106 §2837; and Ibn Mājah in *al-Sunan*: *Kitāb al-Dhabāʾiḥ* [The Book of Animal-Slaughter], chapter: 'The *ʿaqīqa*', 2:1056 §3165.

> ʿ*aqīqa* on the seventh day after his birth. The ʿ*aqīqa* is not repeated for a second time. It can be derived from this that the action which the most exalted Prophet ﷺ performed was an expression of gratitude to Almighty Allah upon making him a mercy for all the worlds and an honour for his community. Therefore, it is recommended for us to show our gratitude and to express happiness by holding gatherings, distributing food, and performing other acts of devotion like it.[1]

Imam Jalāl al-Dīn al-Suyūṭī himself entertains the question and maintains that this in reality was not an ʿ*aqīqa*. Even if in the text it states that an ʿ*aqīqa* was performed, we should understand that the technical meaning of the term was not implied. It simply meant that an animal was sacrified to express happiness on the birth of the Holy Prophet ﷺ. The reason for this is that the Prophet's grandfather, ʿAbd al-Muṭṭalib, had already performed the ʿ*aqīqa* of the Prophet ﷺ on the seventh day after his birth. Imam Jalāl al-Dīn al-Suyūṭī, in order to reiterate his point, states that the ʿ*aqīqa* is performed only once in a lifetime—and not twice.

Someone may object saying that even if we were to admit that his ʿ*aqīqa* was performed by his grandfather, we cannot accept that, as it was done during the days of ignorance; this is why the Holy Prophet ﷺ repeated it. This is an objection which has no valid basis. If this objection were valid, then we would have to concede that the Prophet's marriage to Khadīja ﷺ would also have to be repeated—the *mahr* of which was paid by Abū Ṭālib. The ʿ*aqīqa* is simply an act of charity, whilst marriage is a contract between two spouses. If this objection is correct, then it would mean that the marital contract which took place between the Holy Prophet ﷺ and Sayyida Khadīja ﷺ would have to be renewed, as well as

[1] Al-Suyūṭī, *Ḥusn al-maqṣid fī ʿamal al-mawlid*, p.64–65; al-Suyūṭī, *al-Ḥāwī li al-fatāwā*, p.206; al-Ṣāliḥī, *Subul al-hudā wa al-rashād fī sīra Khayr al-ʿibād*, 1:367; al-Zurqānī, *Sharḥ al-mawāhib al-ladunya bi al-minaḥ al-Muḥammadiyya*, 1:263–264; and al-Nabhānī, *Ḥujja Allāh ʿalā al-ʿālimīn fī muʿjazāt Sayyid al-mursalīn*, p.237.

the *mahr*; but such was not the case. The reason why this objection fails is because any permissible action which took place in the days of ignorance is accepted by the Sharia; its enforcement only takes place after the revelation of its commandments.

In Islam, under the verse, ﴿*But that which has passed (before this command is forgiven)*﴾,[1] any wrong action that took place during the days of ignorance is forgiven; there is no need to make repentance from each sin individually. Likewise, all praiseworthy actions, such as marriage, *ᶜaqīqa*, and oaths for example, remain intact and are not nullified. This is why Imam al-Suyūṭī states that there is no need to repeat the *ᶜaqīqa* because there is no legal requirement for it in the Sharia. So from this whole discussion, it can be ascertained that the Holy Prophet ﷺ, after declaring his prophethood, sacrificed an animal as an expression of joy and happiness on his birth.

5.9 A Disbeliever's Punishment is Lightened on Account of His Happiness on the Prophet's Birth

From the previous evidence, it is clear that to commemorate *Mawlid al-Nabī* ﷺ is the Sunna of Almighty Allah, the most gracious Prophet ﷺ, and the noble Companions. This is why the hadith scholars and saints have elucidated its virtues and merits as expounded in the books of sīra and history. In this context, there is a famous incident which has been transmitted by Imam al-Bukhārī (194–256 AH) in *Kitāb al-Nikāḥ* of *al-Ṣaḥīḥ*. Before bringing this incident into discussion, it is important to establish an accepted principle from the Qurʾān, Sunna, and the consensus of the *Umma* that a disbeliever is not benefited by his actions in the Hereafter: there is no recompense for his good deeds, nor is his punishment alleviated. His good deeds are recompensed in this world.[2] The privilege of recompense in the Hereafter only belongs

---

[1] Qurʾān 4:22.

[2] Al-ᶜAsqalānī, *Fatḥ al-Bārī*, 9:145, and al-ᶜAynī, *ᶜUmda al-qārī sharḥ Ṣaḥīḥ al-Bukhārī*, 20:95.

Concerning this, the Qurʾān states:

to the Muslims, as they are the ones who have asserted true faith in Allah.[1]

﴿مَن كَانَ يُرِيدُ ٱلۡحَيَوٰةَ ٱلدُّنۡيَا وَزِينَتَهَا نُوَفِّ إِلَيۡهِمۡ أَعۡمَٰلَهُمۡ فِيهَا وَهُمۡ فِيهَا لَا يُبۡخَسُونَ ١٥ أُوْلَٰٓئِكَ ٱلَّذِينَ لَيۡسَ لَهُمۡ فِي ٱلۡأٓخِرَةِ إِلَّا ٱلنَّارُۖ وَحَبِطَ مَا صَنَعُواْ فِيهَا وَبَٰطِلٞ مَّا كَانُواْ يَعۡمَلُونَ ١٦﴾

Those who lust after the worldly life (only) with its beauty (and embellishment), We pay them back in full for their works here in this world, and their (worldly recompense) is not diminished in the least. They are the people for whom there is no (share) in the Hereafter except the Fire (of Hell). And (as for reward in the Hereafter) all (the works) they did in the world have come to nothing, and (all that) they used to do is null and void (because their account is cleared by paying them in full measure in the life of the world, and nothing remains in their balance for the Hereafter). (Qurʾān 11:15–16)

﴿وَٱلَّذِينَ كَفَرُوٓاْ أَعۡمَٰلُهُمۡ كَسَرَابِۭ بِقِيعَةٖ يَحۡسَبُهُ ٱلظَّمۡـَٔانُ مَآءً حَتَّىٰٓ إِذَا جَآءَهُۥ لَمۡ يَجِدۡهُ شَيۡـٔٗا وَوَجَدَ ٱللَّهَ عِندَهُۥ فَوَفَّىٰهُ حِسَابَهُۥۗ وَٱللَّهُ سَرِيعُ ٱلۡحِسَابِ﴾

And the deeds of the disbelievers are like a mirage in a vast barren field which the thirsty one deems to be water, until when he gets near it he finds it to be nothing. (Likewise, in the Hereafter) he will find Allah near him, but Allah fully paid him back (in the world). And Allah is Swift in taking account. (Qurʾān 24:39)

﴿وَقَدِمۡنَآ إِلَىٰ مَا عَمِلُواْ مِنۡ عَمَلٖ فَجَعَلۡنَٰهُ هَبَآءٗ مَّنثُورًا﴾

And (then) We shall turn to the deeds they (presumably) did (in life) and shall make them scattered dust particles. (Qurʾān 25:23)

[1] Concerning this, the Qurʾān states:

﴿يَسۡتَبۡشِرُونَ بِنِعۡمَةٖ مِّنَ ٱللَّهِ وَفَضۡلٖ وَأَنَّ ٱللَّهَ لَا يُضِيعُ أَجۡرَ ٱلۡمُؤۡمِنِينَ ١٧١ ٱلَّذِينَ ٱسۡتَجَابُواْ لِلَّهِ وَٱلرَّسُولِ مِنۢ بَعۡدِ مَآ أَصَابَهُمُ ٱلۡقَرۡحُۚ لِلَّذِينَ أَحۡسَنُواْ مِنۡهُمۡ وَٱتَّقَوۡاْ أَجۡرٌ عَظِيمٌ ١٧٢﴾

Now let us go to the narration reported by Imam al-Bukhārī. In this narration, there is a mention of one of the Prophet's uncles, Abū Lahab, who died a disbeliever. Abū Lahab expressed happiness on the occasion of the Holy Prophet's birth, and as a result, Almighty Allah benefitted him in the Hereafter, even though he was one of the bitterest enemies of Islam. This individual is extremely accursed that a complete chapter of the Qur'ān has been revealed in his condemnation:

﴿تَبَّتْ يَدَآ أَبِي لَهَبٍ وَتَبَّ ۝١ مَآ أَغْنَىٰ عَنْهُ مَالُهُۥ وَمَا كَسَبَ ۝٢
سَيَصْلَىٰ نَارًا ذَاتَ لَهَبٍ ۝٣﴾

They are filled with joy owing to the blessing (of divine disclosures of the nearness) of Allah and His bounty (the pleasures of meeting with Him), and (also) because Allah does not waste the reward of the believers. Those who submitted to the command of Allah and His Messenger (blessings and peace be upon him) even after sustaining injuries for those of them who possess spiritual excellence and are God-fearing, there is an immense reward. (Qur'ān 3:171–172)

﴿وَلَا نُضِيعُ أَجْرَ ٱلْمُحْسِنِينَ ۝٥٦ وَلَأَجْرُ ٱلْءَاخِرَةِ خَيْرٌ لِّلَّذِينَ ءَامَنُوا۟ وَكَانُوا۟ يَتَّقُونَ ۝٥٧﴾

And We waste not the reward of the pious. And certainly, the reward of the Hereafter is of greater value for those who believe and tread the path of Godwariness. (Qur'ān 12:56–57)

﴿إِنَّ ٱلَّذِينَ ءَامَنُوا۟ وَعَمِلُوا۟ ٱلصَّٰلِحَٰتِ إِنَّا لَا نُضِيعُ أَجْرَ مَنْ أَحْسَنَ عَمَلًا﴾

Indeed, those who believe and do pious deeds, We certainly do not waste the reward of the one who does pious deeds. (Qur'ān 18:30)

﴿وَٱلْعَٰقِبَةُ لِلْمُتَّقِينَ﴾

And good end is only for the Godfearing. [Qur'ān 7:128 & 28:83]

> *Perished be the two hands of Abū Lahab and be he perished himself (he has pointed his finger to Our Beloved)! Neither His (inherited) wealth nor his earned riches have given him any benefit. Soon he will tumble into the Flaming Fire.*[1]

This is a well-known incident which took place after the birth of the most gracious Prophet ﷺ, and it has been recorded in the books of hadith. Abū Lahab's slave girl, Thuwayba, was in the service of Āmina ؓ at the time of her delivery. When the most gracious Prophet ﷺ was born, she ran to inform Abū Lahab about the birth of his nephew. Hearing this good news, Abū Lahab was overwhelmed with happiness, and using the gesture of his two fingers, he freed Thuwayba.

Abū Lahab died without ever entering the fold of Islam. In this state, after his death, the Holy Prophet's uncle ʿAbbās ؓ saw him in a dream and enquired about his condition. He replied that he has been suffering from severe punishment day and night, but on Mondays, his punishment is lightened and water flows from his fingers, bringing him ease. The reason for this lightening of his punishment on Mondays is that upon hearing the news of the birth of his nephew, i.e., the Prophet Muhammad ﷺ, out of happiness, he freed his slave girl Thuwayba, using the gesture of his two fingers.

This incident has been reported by Zaynab b. Abī Salama ؓ, and many hadith-scholars have transmitted it. Imam al-Bukhārī, in his *al-Ṣaḥīḥ*, reports:

فَلَمَّا مَاتَ أَبُو لَهَبٍ أُرِيَهُ بَعْضُ أَهْلِهِ بِشَرِّ حِيبَةٍ، قَالَ لَهُ: مَاذَا لَقِيتَ؟ قَالَ أَبُو لَهَبٍ: لَمْ أَلْقَ بَعْدَكُمْ غَيْرَ أَنِّي سُقِيتُ فِي هَذِهِ بِعَتَاقَتِي ثُوَيْبَةَ.

When Abū Lahab died, some of his family members saw him (in a dream) in a dire state. They asked him, 'What has become of you?' Abū Lahab replied, 'I have not met (any good) after you, except that I am quenched (due to

[1] Qurʾān 111:1–3.

my act) through this (finger) due to my emancipation of Thuwayba (on account my happiness at the birth of Muhammad ﷺ).'[1]

Even though this narration is *mursal*[2], it is still accepted because

[1] Narrated by al-Bukhārī in *al-Ṣaḥīḥ*: *Kitāb al-Nikāḥ* [The Book of Marriage], chapter: 'And your mothers who fostered you', 5:1961 §4813; ʿAbd al-Razzāq in *al-Muṣannaf*, 7:478 §13,955; ʿAbd al-Razzāq in *al-Muṣannaf*, 9:26 §16,350; al-Marūzī in *al-Sunna*, p.82 §290; al-Bayhaqī in *al-Sunan al-kubrā*, 7:162 §13,701; al-Bayhaqī in *Shuʿab al-īmān*, 1:261 §281; al-Bayhaqī in *Dalāʾil al-Nabuwwa wa maʿrifa aḥwāl Ṣāḥib al-Sharīʿa* ﷺ, 1:149; Ibn Saʿd in *al-Ṭabaqāt al-kubrā*, 1:108; Ibn Abī Dunyā in *Kitāb al-manāmāt*, p.154 §263 has narrated this with a fine (*ḥasan*) chain of transmission; al-Baghawī in *Sharḥ al-Sunna*, 9:76 §2282; Ibn al-Jawzī in *Ṣafwa al-ṣafwa*, 1:62; al-Suhaylī in *al-Rawḍ al-unuf fī tafsīr al-sīrā al-Nabawiyya li-Ibn Hishām*, 3:98–99; al-Zaylaʿī in *Naṣb al-rāya li-aḥādīth al-hidāya*, 3:168; Ibn ʿAsākir in *Tārīkh Dimashq al-kabīr*, 67:171–172; Ibn Kathīr in *al-Bidāya wa al-nihāya*, 2:229–230; al-ʿAsqalānī in *Fatḥ al-Bārī*, 9:145; al-ʿAynī in *ʿUmda al-qārī sharḥ Ṣaḥīḥ al-Bukhārī*, 20:95; al-Shaybānī in *Ḥadāʾiq al-anwār*, 1:134; al-ʿĀmirī in *Sharḥ bahjat al-maḥāfil*, 1:41; and Anwar Shāh Kashmīrī in *Fayḍ al-Bārī ʿalā Ṣaḥīḥ al-Bukhārī*, 4:278.

[2] In the books of hadith principles, *mursal* is a hadith in which the chain of transmission ends at a successor (*tābiʿī*), i.e., the companion in this chain of transmission is not mentioned (al-Dhahabī, *al-Mūqiẓa*, p.38; Ibn Kathīr, *al-Bāʿith al-ḥathīth*, p.48; Ibn Ḥajar al-ʿAsqalānī, *Sharḥ nukhba al-fikr*, p.36–37; and al-Sakhāwī, *al-Ghāya fī sharḥ al-hidāya*, 1:272). Its ruling is that if the chain of transmission ends at an authoritative successor, the narration is accepted as evidence (al-Dhahabī, *al-Mūqiẓa*, p.39). According to three of the imams (Imam Abū Ḥanīfa, Imam Mālik and Imam Aḥmad b. Ḥanbal) and the majority of the hadith scholars, the *mursal* is accepted on the condition that the one omitting the name of the Companion is reliable and that he narrates from one who is reliable (al-Sakhāwī, *al-Ghāya fī sharḥ al-hidāya*, 1:273; Ibn Kathīr, *al-Bāʿith al-ḥathīth*, p.48; and ʿAbd al-Ḥaqq Muḥaddith al-Dihlawī, *Muqaddima fī uṣūl al-ḥadīth*, p.42–43). Their evidence is that a successor's connection is certain, and that a successor will not say, 'the Prophet ﷺ said', 'the Prophet ﷺ did', or 'the following happened in the presence of the Prophet ﷺ', unless they receive it from a reliable reporter.

Ibn Ḥajar al-ʿAsqalānī, in *Nuzha al-naẓr bi-sharḥ nukhba al-fikr* (p.37), writes:

> According to one statement of Imam Aḥmad and according to the Mālikī and Ḥanafī jurists, it is accepted unconditionally. According to Imam Shāfiʿī, if it can be supported from a different chain of

Imam al-Bukhārī (194–256 AH) has reported it in his *al-Ṣaḥīḥ*; and many great scholars of hadith have relied upon it, which is a testimony of its dependability. Moreover, this narration is not about the lawful and unlawful: its subject matter is about virtues. The scholars are well aware of the difference in the criteria required when proving issues of lawfulness and unlawfulness compared to issues of virtue.

The following is a collection of the verdicts of various scholars who took this narration as evidence for the celebration of *Mawlid al-Nabī* ﷺ:

1. Al-Ḥāfiẓ Shams al-Dīn Muhammad b. ʿAbd Allāh al-Jazarī (B. 660 AH), the author of *ʿUrf al-taʿrīf bi al-mawlid al-sharīf*, writes:

> فَإِذَا كَانَ أَبُوْلَـهَبٍ الْكَافِرُ الَّذِي نَزَلَ الْقُرْآنُ بِذَمِّهِ جُوْزِيَ فِي النَّارِ بِفَرَحِهِ لَيْلَةَ مَوْلِدِ النَّبِيِّ ﷺ بِهِ، فَمَـا حَالُ الْـمُسْلِمِ الْـمُوَحِّدِ مِنْ أُمَّةِ النَّبِيِّ ﷺ يَسُرُّ بِمَوْلِدِهِ، وَبَذَلَ مَا تَصِلُ إِلَيْهِ قُدْرَتُهُ فِي مَحَبَّتِهِ ﷺ؟ لَعَمْرِيْ إِنَّمَـا يَكُوْنُ جَزَآؤُهُ مِنَ اللهِ الْكَرِيْمِ أَنْ يُّدْخِلَهُ بِفَضْلِهِ جَنَّاتِ النَّعِيْمِ.

> If the disbeliever Abū Lahab, concerning whom the Qurʾān has revealed (a chapter) in his condemnation, is recompensed in the Hell-fire on account of his happiness on the night of the Prophet's birth, what then would be the state of a Muslim, a monotheist from the community of Prophet Muhammad ﷺ, who expresses happiness on his birth and expends of his abilities in his love? By my life, his reward will be from Allah, the Most Generous,

---

transmission, regardless whether that chain of transmission is connected or *mursal*, it will be accepted.

Mullā ʿAlī al-Qārī (D. 1014 AH), in *Sharḥ sharḥ nukhba al-fikr* writes:

> Ibn Jarīr relates that the consensus amongst the successors is that it is to be accepted. No report of rejection has come from them or the imams after them up to the beginning of the 200s, and they are the best generations which the Prophet ﷺ has borne witness to on their goodness.

that He will enter him by His grace into the Gardens.[1]

2. Al-Ḥāfiẓ Shams al-Dīn Muhammad b. Nāṣir al-Dīn al-Dimashqī (777–842 AH), in *Mawrid al-ṣādī fī mawlid al-hādī*, writes:

قَدْ صَحَّ أَنَّ أَبَا لَـهَبٍ يُخَفَّفُ عَنْهُ عَذَابُ النَّارِ فِي مِثْلِ يَوْمِ الْإِثْنَيْنِ لِإِعْتَاقِهِ ثُوَيْبَةَ سُرُوْرًا بِمِيْلَادِ النَّبِيِّ ﷺ.

It is correct that Abū Lahab's punishment in the Hell-fire is lightened on Mondays, due to his emancipation of Thuwayba out of happiness on the Prophet's birth.

Thereafter, the author relates some couplets on this:

إِذَا كَانَ هَذَا كَافِرًا جَآءَ ذَمُّهُ

وَتَبَّتْ يَدَاهُ فِي الْـجَحِيْمِ مُخَلَّدَا

أَتَى أَنَّهُ فِي يَوْمِ الْإِثْنَيْنِ دَائِمـًا

يُـخَفَّفُ عَنْهُ لِلسُّرُوْرِ بِأَحْـمَدَا

فَمَا الظَّنُّ بِالْعَبْدِ الَّذِي طُوْلَ عُمْرِهِ

بِأَحْـمَدَ مَسْرُوْراً وَمَاتَ مُوَحِّدَا

When this disbeliever, for whom condemnation came
Perished be the two hands in the Hell-fire forever
Came to him on Mondays, everlastingly
Reduction in his punishment owing to his pleasure

---

[1] Al-Suyūṭī, *al-Ḥāwī li al-fatāwā*, p.206; al-Suyūṭī, *Ḥusn al-maqṣid fī ʿamal al-mawlid*, p.65–66; al-Qasṭallānī, *al-Mawāhib al-ladunya bi al-minaḥ al-Muḥammadiyya*, 1:147; al-Zurqānī, *Sharḥ al-mawāhib al-ladunya bi al-minaḥ al-Muḥammadiyya*, 1:260–261; al-Ṣāliḥī, *Subul al-hudā wa al-rashād fī sīra Khayr al-ʿibād*, 1:366–367; and al-Nabhānī, *Ḥujja Allāh ʿalā al-ʿālimīn fī muʿjazāt Sayyid al-mursalīn*, p.237–238.

So what do you think of the servant who
Was pleased with Aḥmad and died a believer[1]

3. ʿAbd al-Ḥaqq Muḥaddith al-Dihlawī (958–1052 AH), contemplating on this narration, writes:

> This narration is evidence on the permissibility of celebrating *Mawlid al-Nabī* ﷺ and exhausting one's means on it. If Abū Lahab, concerning whom the Qurʾān has revealed (a chapter) in his condemnation, can have his punishment lightened on account of emancipating his slave girl, then what about the Muslim who is happy on the Prophet's birth and spends his wealth? And yes, innovations, such as unlawful singing and dancing and other prohibited acts, should be avoided; otherwise, one will be deprived of its blessings.[2]

4. ʿAbd al-Ḥayy Farangī Maḥallī Lakhnawī (1264–1304 AH) writes:

> Therefore, if a disbeliever like Abū Lahab, on account of his happiness on the Prophet's birth, can have his punishment lightened, then what about the Muslim who expresses happiness on his birth and spends what he can of his wealth in his love—will he not receive any reward? This is what Ibn Jawzī (510–579 AH) and ʿAbd al-Ḥaqq Muḥaddith Dihlawī (958–1052 AH) have written.[3]

5. Rashīd Aḥmad Ludhyānawī (d. 1341 AH) writes:

> If a condemned disbeliever like Abū Lahab has his punishment lightened on account of the happiness he expressed on the Prophet's blessed birth, then what about the Muslim who expresses happiness and expends

---

[1] Al-Suyūṭī, *al-Ḥāwī li al-fatāwā*, p.206; al-Suyūṭī, *Ḥusn al-maqṣid fī ʿamal al-mawlid*, p.66; and al-Nabhānī, *Ḥujja Allāh ʿalā al-ʿālimīn fī muʿjazāt Sayyid al-mursalīn*, p.238.

[2] ʿAbd al-Ḥaqq Muḥaddith al-Dihlawī, *Madārij al-nabuwwa*, 2:19.

[3] ʿAbd al-Ḥayy al-Lakhnawī, *Majmūʿa Fatāwā*, 2:282.

> of what he can of his wealth out of his love—will he not attain any reward?[1]

By using this incident of Thuwayba's emancipation as evidence, it is clear that this narration is authentic. It is also an evident proof for the permissibility of *Mawlid al-Nabī* ﷺ.

5.9.1 WHY IS A DISBELIEVER'S PUNISHMENT LIGHTENED?

From the above narrations, a question may arise: why is Abū Lahab's punishment lightened when the Qur'ān, hadith and the consensus of the community is explicit, that a disbeliever's action is not rewarded in the next life? The answer is that as this action was linked specifically to the Holy Prophet ﷺ, it was rewarded: Abū Lahab's emancipation of Thuwayba was done as an expression of happiness on the Holy Prophet's blessed birth; this is why Almighty Allah benefitted him in the Hereafter by lightening his punishment. It is clear that any good a disbeliever does in connection to the blessed Prophet ﷺ, it will not go unrewarded.

The lightening of Abū Lahab's punishment every Monday was not on account of his freeing Thuwayba. Rather, it was on account of the happiness he expressed on the Holy Prophet's birth. Almighty Allah is not concerned who the doer is, but for whom the action is done. It is of no concern that the one performing the action was a disbeliever like Abū Lahab, because Almighty Allah's love is exclusively for His esteemed Prophet ﷺ.

To substantiate this point further, the following are clarifications made by the hadith scholars:

1. Imam al-Bayhaqī (384–458 AH), in *Shuʿab al-īmān* on the Prophet's exclusivity, writes that even a disbeliever can be benefitted through his service to the Prophet ﷺ:

وَهٰذَا أَيْضًا لِأَنَّ الإِحْسَانَ كَانَ مَرْجِعُهُ إِلَى صَاحِبِ النُّبُوَّةِ، فَلَمْ يَضِعْ.

> And also this is because the (act of) benevolence is in reference to the Prophet ﷺ, and this is why it is not

[1] Ludhyānawī, *Aḥsan al-Fatāwā*, 1:347–348.

wasted.[1]

2. Imam al-Baghawī (436–516 AH) writes:

هَذَا خَاصٌّ بِهِ إِكْرَامًا لَهُ ﷺ.

This is exclusive to the Prophet ﷺ; it was done out of his honour.[2]

3. Imam al-Suhaylī (508–581 AH) has also taken this view:

قَالَ: مَا لَقِيْتُ بَعْدَكُمْ رَاحَةً، غَيْرَ أَنِّيْ سُقِيتُ فِيْ مِثْلِ هَذِهِ، وَأَشَارَ إِلَى النُّقْرَةِ بَيْنَ السَّبَابَةِ وَالإِبْهَامِ، بِعِتْقِي ثُوَيْبَةَ، وَفِيْ غَيْرِ الْبُخَارِيِّ إِنَّ الَّذِي رَآهُ مِنْ أَهْلِهِ هُوَ أَخُوْهُ الْعَبَّاسُ، قَالَ: مَكَثْتُ حَوْلاً بَعْدَ مَوْتِ أَبِيْ لَهَبٍ لَا أَرَاهُ فِيْ نَوْمٍ، ثُمَّ رَأَيْتُهُ فِيْ شَرِّ حَالٍ، فَقَالَ: مَا لَقِيْتُ بَعْدَكُمْ رَاحَةً إِلَّا أَنَّ الْعَذَابَ يُخَفَّفُ عَنِّي كُلَّ يَوْمِ اثْنَيْنِ. وَذَلِكَ أَنَّ رَسُوْلَ اللهِ ﷺ وُلِدَ يَوْمَ الاِثْنَيْنِ، وَكَانَتْ ثُوَيْبَةُ قَدْ بَشَّرَتْهُ بِمَوْلِدِهِ، فَقَالَتْ لَهُ: أَشَعَرْتُ أَنَّ آمِنَةَ وَلَدَتْ غُلَامًا لِأَخِيْكَ عَبْدِ اللهِ؟ فَقَالَ لَهَا: إِذْهَبِيْ، فَأَنْتِ حُرَّةٌ، فَنَفَعَهُ ذَلِكَ.

Abū Lahab said, 'I have not come across any ease after you, except that I am quenched from this—and he pointed to the web between his index finger and thumb—due to my emancipation of Thuwayba.' In sources other than *Ṣaḥīḥ al-Bukhārī*, the one who saw him from his relatives was his brother, ʿAbbās ؓ. He said, 'A whole year went by and I did not see Abū Lahab in a dream. Then I saw him in a dire state. He said, 'I have not come across any ease after you, except that the punishment is lightened for me every Monday.'' The reason for this is that the Holy Prophet ﷺ was born on a Monday. Thuwayba gave him

[1] Al-Bayhaqī, *Shuʿab al-īmān*, 1:261 §281.

[2] Al-Baghawī, *Sharḥ al-sunna*, 9:76.

glad tidings of the Prophet's birth, saying to him, 'Are you aware that Āmina ﵂ has given birth to a boy for your brother ʿAbd Allāh ﵁.' Hearing this, he said to her, 'Go! You are free.' This (expression of happiness on the Prophet's birth) is what had benefitted him.[1]

4. The leading exegete, Imam al-Qurṭubī (d. 671 AH), writes:

هَذَا التَّخْفِيْفُ خَاصٌّ بِهَذَا وَبِمَنْ وَرَدَ النَّصُّ فِيْهِ.

This lightening (of the punishment) is exclusive to this and whoever the texts have mentioned.[2]

5. The commentator of *Ṣaḥīḥ al-Bukhārī*, Imam al-Kirmānī (717–786 AH), writes:

يَحْتَمِلُ أَنْ يَكُوْنَ الْعَمَلُ الصَّالِحُ وَالْخَيْرُ الَّذِي يَتَعَلَّقُ بِالرَّسُوْلِ ﷺ مَخْصُوْصًا مِّنْ ذَالِكَ.

It is possible that the righteous deeds and good (a disbeliever does) which is associated with the Prophet ﷺ is exclusive in that respect.[3]

6. The commentator of *Ṣaḥīḥ al-Bukhārī*, Imam Badr al-Dīn al-ʿAynī (762–855 AH), writes:

يَحْتَمِلُ أَنْ يَكُوْنَ مَا يَتَعَلَّقُ بِالنَّبِيِّ ﷺ مَخْصُوْصًا مِّنْ ذَلِكَ.

It is possible that whatever is performed in connection to the Prophet ﷺ is exclusive in that respect.[4]

---

[1] Al-Suhaylī, *al-Rawḍ al-unuf fī tafsīr al-sīrā al-Nabawiyya li-Ibn Hishām*, 3:98–99.

[2] Al-ʿAynī, *ʿUmda al-qārī sharḥ Ṣaḥīḥ al-Bukhārī*, 20:95.

[3] Al-Kirmānī, *al-Kawākib al-darārī fī sharḥ Ṣaḥīḥ al-Bukhārī*, 19:79.

[4] Al-ʿAynī, *ʿUmda al-qārī sharḥ Ṣaḥīḥ al-Bukhārī*, 20:95.

7. Imam Jalāl al-Dīn al-Suyūṭī (849–911 AH) has espoused this position explicitly in his books, *Ḥusn al-maqṣid fī ʿamal al-mawlid* and *al-Ḥāwī li al-fatāwā*.
8. Imam ʿAbd al-Raḥmān b. Dabīʿ al-Shaybānī (866–944 AH) writes:

فَتَخْفِيْفُ الْعَذَابِ عَنْهُ إِنَّمَا هُوَ كَرَامَةُ النَّبِيِّ ﷺ.

> The lightening of his punishment was only out of honour for the Prophet ﷺ.[1]

From these explanations, it is clear that even the staunchest disbeliever like Abū Lahab, on account of the unintentional happiness he expressed on the Prophet's birth, is rewarded in the next life till the Day of Judgment. And it is only because of the association with the most esteemed Prophet ﷺ that a disbeliever is rewarded.

5.9.2 An Objection and its Reply

Some people object to this narration, saying that this incident took place in a dream and that ʿAbbās had not yet accepted Islam when he saw this dream —so why should it form any legal basis in the Sharia? The reply to this objection is as follows:

Firstly, when we make this incident a proof for the celebration of *Mawlid al-Nabī* ﷺ, we are not using Abū Lahab's statement as our basis; our basis is the statement of ʿAbbās.

Secondly, though this incident took place before ʿAbbās accepted Islam, there is no problem in using it as an evidence, because when ʿAbbās related this, he was a Muslim, and there is no second opinion on this. He narrated this as a Companion of the Prophet ﷺ. Therefore, this narration can be relied upon.

And finally, what greater evidence of its authority and acceptance can there be that a scholar of the likes of Imam al-Bukhārī (194–256 AH) has narrated it in his *al-Ṣaḥīḥ*. If according to Imam al-Bukhārī

[1] Al-Shaybānī, *Ḥadāʾiq al-anwār*, 1:134;.

this narration was not reliable, why would he include it in his collection of authentic hadith? He would have rejected it outright.

Apart from Imam al-Bukhārī, his teacher Imam ʿAbd al-Razzāq b. Hammām al-Ṣanʿānī (126–211 AH) also narrates it. Imam al-Marwazī (202–294 AH) narrates it in *al-Sunna*; Imam al-Bayhaqī (384–458 AH) narrates it in three of his collections: *al-Sunan al-kubrā*, *Shuʿab al-īmān*, and *Dalāʾil al-Nubuwwa wa maʿrifa aḥwāl Ṣāḥib al-Sharīʿa* ﷺ; Ibn Kathīr (701–774 AH) mentions it in *al-Bidāya wa al-nihāya*; Ibn Saʿd (168–230 AH) includes it in *al-Ṭabaqāt al-kubrā*; Imam al-Baghawī (436–512 AH) narrates it in *Sharḥ al-Sunna*; Ibn Jawzī (510–579 AH) mentions it in *Ṣafwa al-ṣafwa*; al-Suhaylī (508–581 AH) narrates it in *al-Rawḍ al-unuf fī tafsīr al-sīrā al-Nabawiyya li Ibn Hishām*; and Ibn ʿAsākir (499–571 AH) mentions it in *Tārīkh Dimashq al-kabīr*.

If this narration was not authentic, and the lightening of Abū Lahab's punishment on account of the happiness he expressed on the Prophet's birth was not accurate, then the above mentioned scholars and authorities would not have related it in their books. The scholars have not only accepted the narration, but they have relied on it, deriving intellectual points which need no further elucidation.

To summarise, in our view the fact that this narration was reported by ʿAbbās, recorded by Imam al-Bukhārī, and accepted by many hadith scholars is enough of an evidence this this report is authentic and reliable. From it, the permissibility of celebrating *Mawlid al-Nabī* ﷺ can be proven.

5.9.3 AN ADMONITION

From the above mentioned incident, the reality is that any action (even if it is minute) which is done for the sake of the Holy Prophet ﷺ holds a very great status in the sight of Almighty Allah, even if it is done by a non-Muslim. The believers, on the other hand, have been cautioned that even if they spent their whole lives doing good deeds, if they commit the slightest act of disrespect to the most exalted Prophet ﷺ, all their good deeds will be nullified. Allah, the Most High, states:

﴿يَٰٓأَيُّهَا ٱلَّذِينَ ءَامَنُواْ لَا تَرۡفَعُوٓاْ أَصۡوَٰتَكُمۡ فَوۡقَ صَوۡتِ ٱلنَّبِيِّ وَلَا تَجۡهَرُواْ لَهُۥ بِٱلۡقَوۡلِ كَجَهۡرِ بَعۡضِكُمۡ لِبَعۡضٍ﴾

O believers! Do not raise your voices above the voice of the Prophet ﷺ, and (also) do not speak to him so loud as you are loud when you speak to one another.[1]

Here, the Companions are being told to lower their voices, and while talking to one other, their voices should not be raised louder than the sweet voice of the most esteemed Prophet ﷺ. Almighty Allah Himself is teaching the noble Companions reverence for His Beloved ﷺ. The verse continues further and states that if one is not cautious in their behaviour with him, then the following warning should be kept in mind:

﴿أَن تَحۡبَطَ أَعۡمَٰلُكُمۡ وَأَنتُمۡ لَا تَشۡعُرُونَ﴾

(Lest) all your actions should come to nothing (including your faith), and you are not even aware (that your faith and all pious works have been wrecked).[2]

Here, neither Almighty Allah's oneness nor the Sunna of the Holy Prophet ﷺ are being rejected. There is no deviation from the Hereafter, the ritual prayer, fasting, alms-due, or Pilgrimage. This warning is only for a single act of raising one's voice above the voice of the most exalted Prophet ﷺ. Showing a lack of courtesy to the Prophet ﷺ results in all of one's good deeds coming to ruin.

In light of this discussion, it should be known that if on one hand there are millions of good deeds, but there is a minute act of disrespect occurring towards the most esteemed Prophet ﷺ, then the person will be deprived of the reward of all his deeds in the life Hereafter. And on the other hand, if a disbeliever who is an enemy of Islam and a denier of Almighty Allah's oneness performs a

---

[1] Qur'ān 49:2.

[2] Qur'ān 49:2.

single act in the reverence of the blessed birth of the most esteemed Prophet ﷺ, then he will be rewarded for this act in the purgatorial world and the world Hereafter:

ثابت ہوا کہ جملہ فرائض فروع ہیں

اَصل الاصول بندگی اس تاجور کی ہے

Established it is, all obligations are subordinate
The foundation of it all, is servitude to the Prophet[1]

The excellence and acceptance of man's endeavours is founded on the love for the Holy Prophet ﷺ. If there is no love for him, then any good deed performed is void of reward and remuneration from Almighty Allah. This is why the passionate people put forward their petition to the sacred court of the Holy Prophet ﷺ, saying:

اي كريمي كه آز خزانه غيب

گبر و ترسا وظيفه خور داری

دوستان را كجا كني محروم

تو كه با دشمن اين نظر داری

Oh the emblem of generosity! Your munificence is so vast
None are left thirsty from your open-heartedness
How could a lover ever be deprived from your blessed vision
When even a disbeliever is not left destitute by you[2]

It is clear from this chapter that celebrating *Mawlid al-Nabī* ﷺ is established from both the Prophet's speech and action. To commemorate his birth is not something against the Sharia; rather,

[1] Aḥmad Riḍā Khān, *Ḥadā'iq-e-Bakhshish*, 1:135.

[2] Saʿdī, *Kulliyāt* (*Gulistān*), p.66.

it is totally in accordance with the instructions dictated by Almighty Allah and His Messenger ﷺ—in fact, it is a requirement of Islam. Even the disbelievers are not deprived of its blessings. Therefore, if a sinful member of this community was to express happiness on the occasion of the Prophet's birth, how can it be that Almighty Allah will not reward him for it?

Chapter 6

The Position of the Hadith-Scholars & Imams on Celebrating *Mawlid al-Nabī* ﷺ

HAVING PRESENTED DETAILED EVIDENCE IN LIGHT OF THE Qur'ān and Sunna for the celebration of *Mawlid al-Nabī* ﷺ, in this chapter we shall provide the references of those imams who expressed their views concerning it. A historical perspective will be taken in that their views will be related in connection with various Islamic countries and times.

It is utterly wrong and opposed to reality to suggest that observing this act is a recent addition (*bidʿa*) to the religion, or that such practices were invented by the Muslims of the Indian Subcontinent. The reality is that *Mawlid al-Nabī* ﷺ is neither a custom which is exclusive to Pakistan and India, nor is it an innovation. The Muslims of the contemporary age are not the founders of this custom. In fact, *Mawlid al-Nabī* ﷺ is a joyful event that the inhabitants of the two Sacred Sanctuaries, Mecca and Medina, and the entire Arab world have been commemorating it for centuries. It was introduced to the non-Arab quarters of the Islamic world later.

The following are the views and verdicts of some of the leading Imams and hadith scholars regarding the commemoration of *Mawlid al-Nabī* ﷺ:

6.1 Ḥujja al-Dīn Imam Muḥammad b. Ẓufar al-Makkī (497–565 AH)

Ḥujja al-Dīn Imam Abū ʿAbd Allāh Muhammad b. ʿAbd Allāh b. Ẓufar al-Makkī (1104–1170 CE) narrates that it is mentioned in *al-Durr al-muntaẓim*:

وَقَدْ عَمِلَ الْمُحِبُّوْنَ لِلنَّبِيِّ ﷺ فَرَحاً بِمَوْلِدِهِ الْوَلَائِمَ، فَمِنْ ذَلِكَ مَا عَمِلَهُ
بِالْقَاهِرَةِ الْمُعِزِّيَّةِ مِنَ الْوَلَائِمِ الْكِبَارِ الشَّيْخُ أَبُو الْحَسَنِ الْمَعْرُوْفُ بِابْنِ

قُفْلٍ قَدَّسَ اللهُ تَعَالَى سِرَّهُ، شَيْخُ شَيْخِنَا أَبِي عَبْدِ اللهِ مُحَمَّدِ بْنِ النُّعْمَانِ، وَعَمِلَ ذٰلِكَ قَبْلُ جَمَالُ الدِّيْنِ الْعَجَمِيُّ الْهَمَذَانِيُّ. وَمِمَّنْ عَمِلَ ذٰلِكَ عَلَى قَدْرِ وُسْعِهِ يُوْسُفُ الْحَجَّارُ بِمِصْرَ، وَقَدْ رَأَى النَّبِيَّ ﷺ وَهُوَ يُحَرِّضُ يُوْسُفَ الْمَذْكُوْرَ عَلَى عَمَلِ ذٰلِكَ.

Out of their delight for his birth, the lovers of the Prophet ﷺ have organised banquets to celebrate it. One of them, in Cairo the honoured, is an incredible banquet organised by Shaykh Abū al-Ḥasan, known as Ibn Quful—may Allah Most High sanctify his secret. He is the teacher of our teacher, Abū ʿAbd Allāh Muhammad b. al-Nuʿmān. Before him, the *mawlid* celebration was organised by Jamāl al-Dīn al-ʿAjamī al-Hamadhānī. Others, such as Yūsuf al-Ḥajjār in Egypt, have strove to their utmost in organising them, and in fact he beheld the Prophet ﷺ [in a dream], encouraging him to continue.[1]

6.2 Shaykh Muʿīn al-Dīn ʿUmar b. Muhammad al-Mallā (b. 570 AH)

Shaykh Muʿīn al-Dīn Abū Ḥafṣ ʿUmar b. Ḥafṣ b. Khiḍar al-Irbilī al-Mūṣilī is well known by the title of al-Mallā. Amongst the inhabitants of Mosul, he was an extremely righteous, devoted, and learned individual.

وَكَانَ أَوَّلُ مَنْ فَعَلَ ذٰلِكَ بِالْمَوْصِلِ الشَّيْخُ عُمَرُ بْنُ مُحَمَّدٍ الْمُلَّا أَحَدُ الصَّالِحِيْنَ الْمَشْهُوْرِيْنَ، وَبِهِ اقْتَدَى فِي ذٰلِكَ صَاحِبُ إِرْبِلَ وَغَيْرُهُ رَحِمَهُمُ اللهُ تَعَالَى.

The first person to hold gatherings of *Mawlid al-Nabī* ﷺ in Mosul was Shaykh ʿUmar b. Muhammad al-Mallā, a man of acclaimed piety. The ruler of Irbil and others

[1] Al-Ṣāliḥī, *Subul al-hudā wa al-rashād fī sīra Khayr al-ʿibād*, 1:363.

followed him in this practice—may Allah ﷻ have mercy upon them.[1]

6.3 IBN AL-JAWZĪ (510–579 AH)

Jamāl al-Dīn Abū al-Faraj ᶜAbd al-Raḥmān b. ᶜAlī b. al-Jawzī (1116–1201 CE) was an author of many works. He compiled two books on the topic of *Mawlid al-Nabī* ﷺ:

1. *Bayān al-mīlād al-Nabawī*
2. *Mawlid al-ᶜurūs*

Ibn al-Jawzī states in *Bayān al-mīlād al-Nabawī*:

> لَا زَالَ أَهْلُ الْـحَرَمَيْنِ الشَّرِيْفَيْنِ وَمِصْرَ وَالْيَمَنِ وَالشَّامِ وَسَائِرُ بِلَادِ الْعَرَبِ مِنَ الْـمَشْرِقِ وَالْـمَغْرِبِ يَحْتَفِلُوْنَ بِمَجْلِسِ مَوْلِدِ النَّبِيِّ ﷺ، وَيَفْرَحُوْنَ بِقُدُوْمِ هِلَالِ شَهْرِ رَبِيْعِ الْأَوَّلِ وَيَهْتَمُّوْنَ اهْتِمَامًا بَلِيْغًا عَلَى السَّمَاعِ وَالْقِرَاءَةِ لِـمَوْلِدِ النَّبِيِّ ﷺ، وَيَنَالُوْنَ بِذَلِكَ أَجْرًا جَزِيْلًا وَفَوْزًا عَظِيْمًا.

> The people from the two Sacred Sanctuaries (Mecca and Medina), as well as Egypt, Yemen, the Levant, and the other Arab lands from east to west, continue to celebrate the birth of the Prophet ﷺ and express happiness when the new moon heralding *Rabīᶜ al-Awwal* appears. They go to great lengths in singing religious odes and reciting narrations of the Prophet's ﷺ blessed birth, and in all of this, they shall obtain a bountiful reward and mighty triumph.[2]

Ibn al-Jawzī in *Mawlid al-ᶜurūs* narrates:

---

[1] Abū Shāma, *al-Bāᶜith ᶜalā inkār al-bidᶜa wa al-ḥawādith*, p.24; al-Ṣāliḥī, *Subul al-hudā wa al-rashād fī sīra Khayr al-ᶜibād*, 1:365.

[2] Ibn al-Jawzī, *Bayān al-mīlād al-Nabawī*, p.58.

وَجَعَلَ لِـمَنْ فَرِحَ بِمَوْلِدِهِ حِجَابًا مِنَ النَّارِ وَسِتْرًا، وَمَنْ أَنْفَقَ فِي مَوْلِدِهِ دِرْهَمًا كَانَ الْـمُصْطَفَى ﷺ لَهُ شَافِعًا وَمُشَفَّعًا، وَأَخْلَفَ اللهُ عَلَيْهِ بِكُلِّ دِرْهَمٍ عَشْرًا.

فَيَا بُشْرَى لَكُمْ أُمَّةَ مُحَمَّدٍ لَقَدْ نِلْتُمْ خَيْرًا كَثِيرًا فِي الدُّنْيَا وَفِي الْأُخْرَى. فَيَا سَعْدُ مَنْ يَعْمَلُ لِأَحْمَدَ مَوْلِدًا فَيَلْقَى الْـهَنَاءَ وَالْعِزَّ وَالْـخَيْرَ وَالْفَخْرَ، وَيَدْخُلُ جَنَّاتِ عَدْنٍ بِتِيْجَانٍ دُرٍّ تَحْتَهَا خِلَعٌ خُضْرٌ.

> The one who rejoices upon his birth is veiled from the Hellfire. Whoever spends a *dirham* upon the *mawlid*, the Prophet ﷺ shall intercede for him whilst Allah ﷻ shall recompense him ten *dirhams* for each *dirham* spent.
>
> Glad tidings to you, O *Umma* of Muhammad ﷺ! Verily you have attained an abundance of goodness in this world and the next. Fortunate is he who partakes in the *mawlid* of the chosen Aḥmad ﷺ and thereby achieves bliss, prestige, blessing and pride. He shall enter the Garden of Eden, wearing a crown of pearls and garbed in green dress.[1]

Concerning the celebration of *Mawlid al-Nabī* ﷺ held by the king of Irbil, Abū Saʿīd al-Muẓaffar al-Kawkabarī and the great expenditure made by him, Ibn al-Jawzī remarks:

لَوْلَـمْ يَكُنْ فِيْ ذَلِكَ إِلَّا إِرْغَامُ الشَّيْطَانِ وَإِدْعَامُ أَهْلِ الْإِيْمَـانِ.

> It only enrages Satan and brings delight to the people of faith.[2]

In other words, the gatherings of *Mawlid al-Nabī* ﷺ bring humiliation to Satan whilst strengthening the believers.

---

1 Ibn al-Jawzī, *Mawlid al-ʿUrūs*, p.11.

2 Al-Ṣāliḥī, *Subul al-hudā wa al-rashād fī sīra Khayr al-ʿibād*, 1:363.

6.4 ABŪ AL-KHAṬṬĀB B. DIḤYA AL-KALBĪ (544–633 AH)

In his book, *Wafayāt al-aʿyān wa anbāʾ abnāʾ al-zamān* (3:448–450), the supreme judge Abū al-ʿAbbās Shams al-Dīn Aḥmad b. Muhammad b. Abī Bakr b. Khilkān makes mention of Ḥāfiẓ Abū al-Khaṭṭāb b. Diḥya al-Kalbī (544–633 AH):

كَانَ مِنْ أَعْيَانِ الْعُلَمَـاءِ، وَمَشَاهِيْرِ الْفُضَلَاءِ، قَدِمَ مِنَ الْـمَغْرِبِ، فَدَخَلَ الشَّامَ وَالْعِرَاقَ، وَاجْتَازَ بِإِرْبِلَ سَنَةَ أَرْبَعٍ وَسِتِّمِـائَةٍ، فَوَجَدَ مَلِكَهَا الْـمُعَظَّمَ مُظَفَّرَ الدِّيْنِ بْنَ زَيْنِ الدِّيْنِ يَعْتَنِي بِالْـمَوْلِدِ النَّبَوِيِّ، فَعَمِلَ لَهُ كِتَابَ «التَّنْوِيْرِ فِي مَوْلِدِ الْبَشِيْرِ النَّذِيْرِ» وَقَرَأَهُ عَلَيْهِ بِنَفْسِهِ، فَأَجَازَهُ بِأَلْفِ دِيْنَارٍ. قَالَ: وَقَدْ سَمِعْنَاهُ عَلَى السُّلْطَانِ فِي سِتَّةِ مَجَالِسَ، فِي سَنَةِ خَمْسٍ وَعِشْرِيْنَ وَسِتِّمِـائَةٍ.

> He was one of the eminent scholars of renown and people of virtue. He travelled from the Maghreb and entered the Levant and Iraq and passed through Irbil in 604 AH. He found that Irbil's ruler, the great king Muẓaffar al-Dīn b. Zayn al-Dīn, made elaborate plans to celebrate the Prophet's birth ﷺ, so he wrote a book for him called *al-Tanwīr fī Mawlid al-Bashīr al-Nadhīr* (Illumination on the birth of the Bearer of Glad Tidings and Warner). He read the book in al-Muẓaffar's presence and was awarded one thousand dinars. We heard it from the Sultan in six different gatherings in 625 AH.[1]

6.5 SHAMS AL-DĪN AL-JAZARĪ (D. 660 AH)

The leading reciter of the Qurʾān, Shams al-Dīn Muhammad b. ʿAbd Allāh al-Jazarī al-Shāfiʿī (B.1262 CE), writes in his compendium, *ʿUrf al-taʿrīf bi al-mawlid al-sharīf*:

---

[1] Al-Suyūṭī, *Ḥusn al-maqṣid fī ʿamal al-mawlid*, p.44–45; al-Suyūṭī, *al-Ḥāwī li al-fatāwā*, p.200; and al-Nabhānī, *Ḥujja Allāh ʿalā al-ʿālimīn fī muʿjazāt Sayyid al-mursalīn*, p.236–237.

وَقَدْ رُوِيَ أَبُوْلَـهَبٍ بَعْدَ مَوْتِهِ فِي النَّوْمِ، فَقِيْلَ لَهُ: مَا حَالُكَ؟ فَقَالَ: فِي النَّارِ، إِلَّا أَنَّهُ يُخَفَّفُ عَنِّي كُلَّ لَيْلَةِ اثْنَيْنِ، وَأَمُصُّ مِنْ بَيْنِ أُصْبُعَيْ هَاتَيْنِ مَاءً بِقَدْرِ هَذَا - وَأَشَارَ بِرَأْسِ إِصْبَعِهِ - وَإِنَّ ذَلِكَ بِإِعْتَاقِي لِثُوَيْبَةَ عِنْدَ مَا بَشَّرَتْنِي بِوِلَادَةِ النَّبِيِّ ﷺ وَبِإِرْضَاعِهَا لَهُ.

فَإِذَا كَانَ أَبُوْلَـهَبٍ الْكَافِرُ الَّذِي نَزَلَ الْقُرْآنُ بِذَمِّهِ جُوْزِيَ فِي النَّارِ بِفَرَحِهِ لَيْلَةَ مَوْلِدِ النَّبِيِّ ﷺ بِهِ، فَمَا حَالُ الْمُسْلِمِ الْمُوَحِّدِ مِنْ أُمَّةِ النَّبِيِّ ﷺ يَسُرُّ بِمَوْلِدِهِ، وَبَذَلَ مَا تَصِلُ إِلَيْهِ قُدْرَتُهُ فِي مَحَبَّتِهِ ﷺ؟ لَعَمْرِي إِنَّمَا يَكُوْنُ جَزَاؤُهُ مِنَ اللهِ الْكَرِيْمِ أَنْ يُدْخِلَهُ بِفَضْلِهِ جَنَّاتِ النَّعِيْمِ.

Abū Lahab was seen in a dream after his death. He was asked, 'What has become of you?' Abū Lahab replied, 'I am blazing in the hellfire. However, my punishment is lightened every Monday evening and so I am able to drink water from these finger tips [and he pointed to the tips of his index and middle finger]—and this is because I freed Thuwayba when she brought me the good news of the Prophet's birth and thus she was able to nurse him.'

If this is Abū Lahab, the disbeliever whom the Qur'ān condemned, and yet he is rewarded in the Fire because of the delight he felt on the night of the Prophet's birth ﷺ, what would be the status of a Muslim, a believer in Allah's Oneness, who is of the Prophet's *Umma* and who feels happiness during the occasion of his birth and spends what he can in celebration of his love and passion for him ﷺ? Certainly his reward from Allah the Most Generous is that He bestows upon him of His vast bounty and allows him to enter the Paradise of Delight![1]

---

1 Al-Suyūṭī, *al-Ḥāwī li al-fatāwā*, p.206; al-Suyūṭī, *Ḥusn al-maqṣid fī ʿamal al-mawlid*, p.65–66; al-Qasṭallānī, *al-Mawāhib al-ladunya bi al-minaḥ al-Muḥammadiyya,* 1:147; al-Zurqānī, *Sharḥ al-mawāhib al-ladunya bi al-minaḥ al-Muḥammadiyya*, 1:260–261; al-Ṣāliḥī, *Subul al-hudā wa al-rashād fī sīra Khayr al-ʿibād*, 1:366–367; and al-Nabhānī, *Ḥujja Allāh ʿalā*

He adds:

مِنْ خَوَاصِّهِ أَنَّهُ أَمَانٌ فِي ذٰلِكَ الْعَامِ، وَبُشْرَى عَاجِلَةٌ بِنَيْلِ الْبُغْيَةِ وَالْـمَرَامِ.

One of the unique qualities of the *mawlid* celebration that has been experienced is that it is a source of security for the entire year and an early glad tiding for every good thing that is sought after.[1]

6.6 IMAM ABŪ SHĀMA (599–665 AH)

Imam Abū Shāma ʿAbd al-Raḥmān b. Ismāʿīl (1202–1267 CE) is the shaykh of Imam al-Nawawī (631–677 AH/1233–1278 CE), the commentator of *Ṣaḥīḥ Muslim*. He writes in his book, *al-Bāʿith ʿalā inkār al-bidʿa wa al-ḥawādith*:

وَمِنْ أَحْسَنِ مَا ابْتُدِعَ فِي زَمَانِنَا مِنْ هٰذَا الْقَبِيْلِ مَا كَانَ يُفْعَلُ بِمَدِيْنَةِ إِرْبِلَ، جَبَرَهَا اللهُ تَعَالَى، كُلَّ عَامٍ فِي الْيَوْمِ الْـمُوَافِقِ لِيَوْمِ مَوْلِدِ النَّبِيِّ ﷺ مِنَ الصَّدَقَاتِ وَالْـمَعْرُوْفِ وَإِظْهَارِ الزِّيْنَةِ وَالسُّرُوْرِ، فَإِنَّ ذٰلِكَ مَعَ مَا فِيْهِ مِنَ الْإِحْسَانِ إِلَى الْفُقَرَاءِ مُشْعِرٌ بِمَحَبَّةِ النَّبِيِّ ﷺ، وَتَعْظِيْمِهِ وَجَلَالَتِهِ فِي قَلْبِ فَاعِلِهِ وَشُكْرِ اللهِ تَعَالَى عَلَى مَا مَنَّ بِهِ مِنْ إِيْجَادِ رَسُوْلِهِ الَّذِي أَرْسَلَهُ رَحْمَةً لِلْعَالَـمِيْنَ ﷺ وَعَلَى جَمِيْعِ الْأَنْبِيَاءِ وَالْـمُرْسَلِيْنَ.

One of the best things that have been inaugurated in our time is the celebration that takes place on the day corresponding to the anniversary of the Prophet's birth ﷺ. On that day, charity is gathered, good acts are performed, and fine raiment and happiness are displayed. Such actions, beyond being acts of kindness to the indigent, also indicate that the people have feelings of love, esteem, and exaltation for the Prophet ﷺ in their hearts, as well

al-ʿālimīn fī muʿjazāt Sayyid al-mursalīn, p.237–238.

[1] Al-Ṣāliḥī, *Subul al-hudā wa al-rashād fī sīra Khayr al-ʿibād*, 1:365–366.

as gratitude to Allah for having blessed them by creating His beloved Messenger whom He sent as a mercy unto the worlds ﷺ.[1]

Abū Shāma, praising the celebration of *Mawlid al-Nabī* ﷺ held by the king of Irbil, Abū Saʿīd al-Muẓaffar al-Kawkabarī, and the great expenditure made by him, remarks:

مِثْلَ هَذَا الْحُسْنِ يُنْدَبُ إِلَيْهِ وَيُشْكَرُ فَاعِلُهُ وَيُثْنَى عَلَيْهِ.

The likes of this goodness is recommended and its practitioner is appreciated and praised.[2]

6.7 Imam Ṣadr al-Dīn Mawhūb b. ʿUmar al-Jazarī (d. 665 AH)

The leading jurist of Egypt, Ṣadr al-Dīn Mawhūb b. ʿUmar al-Jazarī al-Shāfiʿī, writes:

هَذِهِ بِدْعَةٌ لَا بَأْسَ بِهَا، وَلَا تُكْرَهُ الْبِدَعُ إِلَّا إِذَا رَاغَمَتِ السُّنَّةَ، وَأَمَّا إِذَا لَمْ تُرَاغِمْهَا فَلَا تُكْرَهُ، وَيُثَابُ الْإِنْسَانُ بِحَسَبِ قَصْدِهِ فِي إِظْهَارِ السُّرُوْرِ وَالْفَرَحِ بِمَوْلِدِ النَّبِيِّ ﷺ.

وَقَالَ فِي مَوْضِعٍ آخَرَ: هَذَا بِدْعَةٌ، وَلَكِنَّهَا بِدْعَةٌ لَا بَأْسَ بِهَا، وَلَكِنْ لَا يَجُوْزُ لَهُ أَنْ يُسْأَلَ النَّاسُ بَلْ إِنْ كَانَ يَعْلَمُ أَوْ يَغْلِبُ عَلَى ظَنِّهِ أَنَّ نَفْسَ الْمَسْؤُوْلِ تَطِيْبُ بِمَا يُعْطِيْهِ فَالسُّؤَالُ لِذَلِكَ مُبَاحٌ أَرْجُوْ أَنْ لَا يَنْتَهِي إِلَى الْكَرَاهَةِ.

This [the commemoration of the *mawlid*] is a harmless innovation. Innovations are not considered offensive

---

[1] Abū Shāma, *al-Bāʿith ʿalā inkār al-bidʿa wa al-ḥawādith*, p.23–24; al-Ṣāliḥī, *Subul al-hudā wa al-rashād fī sīra Khayr al-ʿibād*, 1:365; al-Ḥalabī in *Insān al-ʿuyūn fī sīra al-Amīn al-Maʾmūn*, 1:84; Aḥmad b. Zaynī al-Daḥlān, *al-Sīra al-Nabawiyya*, 1:53; and al-Nabhānī, *Ḥujja Allāh ʿalā al-ʿālimīn fī muʿjazāt Sayyid al-mursalīn*, p.233.

[2] Al-Ṣāliḥī, *Subul al-hudā wa al-rashād fī sīra Khayr al-ʿibād*, 1:363.

unless they contend with a Sunna. And, so long as they do not contend with a Sunna, they are not considered offensive, and one is rewarded according to his intention in displaying happiness and delight in the celebration of the Prophet's birth ﷺ.

In another place, he said: Celebrating the *mawlid* is an innovation; however, it is an inoffensive innovation. That said, it is not permissible to ask people (for money to pay for its costs) unless one knows or is certain that the one asked gives money for it happily and willingly. It is allowed to ask such a person, and I would hope that it does not reach the level of offensiveness (*karāha*).[1]

6.8 IMAM ẒAHĪR AL-DĪN JAᶜFAR AL-TAZNATĪ (D. 682 AH)

Imam Ẓahīr al-Dīn Jaᶜfar b. Yaḥya b. Jaᶜfar al-Taznatī al-Shāfiᶜī (d.1283 AH) states:

هَذَا الْفِعْلُ لَـمْ يَقَعْ فِي الصَّدْرِ الْأَوَّلِ مِنَ السَّلَفِ الصَّالِحِ مَعَ تَعْظِيْمِهِمْ وَحُبِّهِمْ لَهُ إِعْظَاماً وَمَحَبَّةً لَا يَبْلُغُ جَمْعُنَا الْوَاحِدَ مِنْهُمْ وَلَا ذَرَّةً مِنْهُ، وَهِيَ بِدْعَةٌ حَسَنَةٌ إِذَا قَصَدَ فَاعِلُهَا جَمْعَ الصَّالِحِيْنَ وَالصَّلَاةَ عَلَى النَّبِيِّ ﷺ وَإِطْعَامَ الطَّعَامِ لِلْفُقَرَاءِ وَالْمَسَاكِيْنِ وَهَذَا الْقَدْرُ يُثَابُ عَلَيْهِ بِهَذَا الشَّرْطِ فِي كُلِّ وَقْتٍ.

This practice did not take place during the early period of the pious forebears, despite their immense reverence and love for the Prophet ﷺ. None of us, even if we all gathered together, can match the love and reverence of a single one amongst them—not even an atom's weight. It is a good innovation if the person who celebrates it intends to gather people of righteousness together to send prayers upon the Prophet ﷺ and feed the poor and indigent. So

[1] Ibid., 1:365–366.

long as it fits this description and meets these conditions, it will merit rewards at all times.[1]

6.9 Ibn Taymiyya (661–728 AH)

Taqī al-Dīn Aḥmad b. ʿAbd al-Ḥalīm b. ʿAbd al-Salām b. Taymiyya (1263–1328 CE) in his work, *Iqtiḍāʾ al-ṣirāṭ al-mustaqīm li-mukhālafa aṣḥāb al-jaḥīm*, writes:

وَكَذَلِكَ مَا يُحْدِثُهُ بَعْضُ النَّاسِ، إِمَّا مُضَاهَاةً لِلنَّصَارَى فِي مِيْلَادِ عِيْسَى ﵇، وَإِمَّا مَحَبَّةً لِلنَّبِيِّ ﷺ وَتَعْظِيْمًا. وَاللهُ قَدْ يُثِيْبُهُمْ عَلَى هَذِهِ الْمَحَبَّةِ وَالْاِجْتِهَادِ، لَا عَلَى الْبِدَعِ، مِنَ اتِّخَاذِ مَوْلِدِ النَّبِيِّ ﷺ عِيْدًا.

Likewise, that which has been introduced by some people, either in contest with the Christian celebration of Jesus' ﵇ birth, or out of love and honour of the Holy Prophet ﷺ, may be rewarded by Allah for the sake of this love and exertion—not for the innovation of taking the *mawlid* as a festivity.[2]

In another section of the book, the author writes:

فَتَعْظِيْمُ الْمَوْلِدِ وَاتِّخَاذُهُ مَوْسِمًا، قَدْ يَفْعَلُهُ بَعْضُ النَّاسِ، وَيَكُوْنُ لَهُ فِيْهِ أَجْرٌ عَظِيْمٌ؛ لِحُسْنِ قَصْدِهِ، وَتَعْظِيْمِهِ لِرَسُوْلِ اللهِ ﷺ، كَمَا قَدَّمْتُهُ لَكَ أَنَّهُ يَحْسُنُ مِنْ بَعْضِ النَّاسِ مَا يُسْتَقْبَحُ مِنَ الْمُؤْمِنِ الْمُسَدَّدِ.

So, to honour the *mawlid* and to take it as a season, as practiced by some, lies therein an immense reward due to the purity of intention and veneration of the Prophet ﷺ. As mentioned previously, some people may

---

[1] Ibid., 1:364.

[2] Ibn Taymiyya, *Iqtiḍāʾ al-ṣirāṭ al-mustaqīm li-mukhālafa aṣḥāb al-jaḥīm*, p.404.

consider commendable what the believers deem to be reprehensible.[1]

6.10 IMAM ABŪ ʿABD ALLĀH B. AL-ḤĀJJ AL-MĀLIKĪ (D. 737 AH)

Concerning the merits of *Mawlid al-Nabī* ﷺ, Imam Abū ʿAbd Allāh b. al-Ḥājj Muhammad b. Muhammad b. Muhammad al-Mālikī (B. 1336 CE) writes in his work, *al-Madkhal ilā tanmiya al-aʿmāl bi taḥsīn al-niyyāt wa al-tanbīh ʿalā kathīr min al-bidʿ al-muḥditha wa al-ʿawāʾid al-muntaḥila*:

أَشَارَ عَلَيْهِ الصَّلَاةُ وَالسَّلَامُ إِلَى فَضِيْلَةِ هَذَا الشَّهْرِ الْعَظِيْمِ بِقَوْلِهِ لِلسَّائِلِ الَّذِي سَأَلَهُ عَنْ صَوْمِ يَوْمِ الِاثْنَيْنِ، فَقَالَ لَهُ عَلَيْهِ الصَّلَاةُ وَالسَّلَامُ: «ذَلِكَ يَوْمٌ وُلِدْتُ فِيْهِ.»

فَتَشْرِيْفُ هَذَا الْيَوْمِ مُتَضَمِّنٌ لِتَشْرِيْفِ هَذَا الشَّهْرِ الَّذِي وُلِدَ فِيْهِ، فَيَنْبَغِي أَنْ نَحْتَرِمَهُ حَقَّ الِاحْتِرَامِ وَنُفَضِّلُهُ بِمَا فَضَّلَ اللهُ بِهِ الْأَشْهُرَ الْفَاضِلَةَ، وَهَذَا مِنْهَا لِقَوْلِهِ عَلَيْهِ الصَّلَاةُ وَالسَّلَامُ: «أَنَا سَيِّدُ وَلَدِ آدَمَ وَلَا فَخْرَ.» وَلِقَوْلِهِ عَلَيْهِ الصَّلَاةُ وَالسَّلَامُ: «آدَمُ وَمَنْ دُوْنَهُ تَحْتَ لِوَائِي.»

وَفَضِيْلَةُ الْأَزْمِنَةِ وَالْأَمْكِنَةِ بِمَا خَصَّهَا اللهُ تَعَالَى مِنَ الْعِبَادَاتِ الَّتِي تُفْعَلُ فِيْهَا، لِمَا قَدْ عُلِمَ أَنَّ الْأَمْكِنَةَ وَالْأَزْمِنَةَ لَا تَتَشَرَّفُ لِذَاتِهَا، وَإِنَّمَا يَحْصُلُ لَهَا التَّشْرِيْفُ بِمَا خُصَّتْ بِهِ مِنَ الْمَعَانِي. فَانْظُرْ رَحِمَنَا اللهُ وَإِيَّاكَ إِلَى مَا خَصَّ اللهُ تَعَالَى بِهِ هَذَا الشَّهْرَ الشَّرِيْفَ وَيَوْمَ الِاثْنَيْنِ. أَلَا تَرَى أَنَّ صَوْمَ هَذَا الْيَوْمِ فِيهِ فَضْلٌ عَظِيْمٌ لِأَنَّهُ ﷺ وُلِدَ فِيْهِ؟

فَعَلَى هَذَا فَيَنْبَغِي إِذَا دَخَلَ هَذَا الشَّهْرُ الْكَرِيْمُ أَنْ يُكَرَّمَ وَيُعَظَّمَ وَيُحْتَرَمَ الِاحْتِرَامَ اللَّائِقَ بِهِ وَذَلِكَ بِالِاتِّبَاعِ لَهُ ﷺ فِي كَوْنِهِ كَانَ يَخُصُّ الْأَوْقَاتِ

[1] Ibid., p.406.

الْفَاضِلَةَ بِزِيَادَةِ فِعْلِ الْبِرِّ فِيْهَا وَكَثْرَةِ الْـخَيْرَاتِ. أَلَا تَرَى إِلَى قَوْلِ الْبُخَارِيِّ: كَانَ رَسُوْلُ اللهِ ﷺ أَجْوَدَ النَّاسِ بِالْـخَيْرِ، وَكَانَ أَجْوَدَ مَا يَكُوْنُ فِي رَمَضَانَ. فَنَمْتَثِلُ تَعْظِيْمَ الْأَوْقَاتِ الْفَاضِلَةِ بِمَـا امْتَثَلَهُ عَلَى قَدْرِ اسْتِطَاعَتِنَا.

فَإِنْ قَالَ قَائِلٌ: قَدِ الْتَزَمَ عَلَيْهِ الصَّلَاةُ وَالسَّلَامُ فِي الْأَوْقَاتِ الْفَاضِلَةِ مَا الْتَزَمَهُ مِـمَّـا قَدْ عُلِمَ، وَلَـمْ يَلْتَزِمْ فِي هَذَا الشَّهْرِ مَا الْتَزَمَهُ فِي غَيْرِهِ. فَالْـجَوَابُ: أَنَّ الْـمَعْنَى الَّذِي لِأَجْلِهِ لَـمْ يَلْتَزِمْ عَلَيْهِ الصَّلَاةُ وَالسَّلَامُ إِنَّـمَـا هُوَ مَا قَدْ عُلِمَ مِنْ عَادَتِهِ الْكَرِيْمَةِ فِي كَوْنِهِ عَلَيْهِ الصَّلَاةُ وَالسَّلَامُ يُرِيْدُ التَّخْفِيْفَ عَنْ أُمَّتِهِ، وَالرَّحْمَةَ لَـهُمْ سِيَّمَـا فِيْمَـا كَانَ يَخُصُّهُ عَلَيْهِ الصَّلَاةُ وَالسَّلَامُ.

أَلَا تَرَى إِلَى قَوْلِهِ عَلَيْهِ الصَّلَاةُ وَالسَّلَامُ فِي حَقِّ حَرَمِ الْـمَدِيْنَةِ: «اَللَّهُمَّ! إِنَّ إِبْرَاهِيْمَ حَرَّمَ مَكَّةَ، وَإِنِّي أُحَرِّمُ الْـمَدِيْنَةَ بِمَـا حَرَّمَ بِهِ إِبْرَاهِيْمُ مَكَّةَ وَمِثْلَهُ مَعَهُ» ثُمَّ إِنَّهُ عَلَيْهِ الصَّلَاةُ وَالسَّلَامُ لَـمْ يُشَرِّعْ فِي قَتْلِ صَيْدِهِ وَلَا فِي قَطْعِ شَجَرِهِ الْـجَزَاءَ، تَخْفِيْفاً عَلَى أُمَّتِهِ وَرَحْمَةً لَـهُمْ، فَكَانَ عَلَيْهِ الصَّلَاةُ وَالسَّلَامُ يَنْظُرُ إِلَى مَا هُوَ مِنْ جِهَتِهِ... وَإِنْ كَانَ فَاضِلاً فِي نَفْسِهِ يَتْرُكُهُ لِلتَّخْفِيْفِ عَنْهُمْ.

The Prophet ﷺ indicated to the added virtue of this magnificent month when he responded to the person who asked him about fasting on Mondays. He ﷺ said, "That is the day in which I was born." Honoring this day includes honoring the month in which he was born, so it behooves us to hold it in the utmost esteem and reverence, and to prefer it as Allah has preferred the virtuous months—and this month is one of them because the Prophet ﷺ said, "I am the master of the children of Ādam, and that is no boast. Ādam and those after him are under my banner."

The virtues associated with places and times are due to the acts of worship specified by Almighty Allah. In of themselves these places and times possess no inherent nobility; rather, the nobility which they possess is solely on account of those exclusive preferences associated with them. So consider the virtues that Almighty Allah has made specific for this month and Mondays. Can you not see that the tremendous virtue of fasting on Mondays is because the Holy Prophet ﷺ was born on that day?

When this month enters, on the aforementioned basis it should be honoured, magnified, and shown the utmost reverence that it is deserving of. It should be done in obedience to the Holy Prophet ﷺ, who performed pious deeds and gave charity abundantly during times that had specific virtues. Have you not considered the statement of Ibn ᶜAbbās ؓ, who said, "The Messenger of Allah ﷺ was the most generous of people, and he exhibited the most generosity during the month of *Ramaḍān*"? We should therefore magnify, to the best of our ability, the virtuous times as the Prophet ﷺ did.

Someone might retort, saying: "The acts that the Prophet ﷺ performed in these virtuous times are known, but he did not perform any specific actions in this month (*Rabīᶜ al-Awwal*) as he did in other months." To this, we reply: That is due to what is known from the Prophet's noble care and his desire of ease for his *Umma*, especially in those things that is related to his own person. Case and point is when the Holy Prophet ﷺ declared Medina inviolable as Ibrāhīm ؑ declared Mecca inviolable, he did not set punishment for hunting or cutting branches off trees. This was out of mercy for his *Umma* and is done for the sake of lightening the burden upon them. For the sake of easing the burden upon his *Umma*, the Holy Prophet ﷺ would leave a command that is related to him, even if it was a virtuous one.[1]

---

[1] Ibn al-Ḥājj, *al-Madkhal ilā tanmiya al-aᶜmāl bi taḥsīn al-niyyāt wa al-*

Ibn al-Ḥājj al-Mālikī further writes:

فَإِن قَالَ قَائِلٌ: مَا الْـحِكْمَةُ فِي كَوْنِهِ عَلَيْهِ الصَّلَاةُ وَالسَّلَامُ خُصَّ مَوْلِدُهُ الْكَرِيْمُ بِشَهْرِ رَبِيعِ الْأَوَّلِ وَبِيَوْمِ الْاِثْنَيْنِ مِنْهُ عَلَى الصَّحِيْحِ وَالْـمَشْهُوْرِ عِنْدَ أَكْثَرِ الْعُلَمَاءِ، وَلَـمْ يَكُنْ فِي شَهْرِ رَمَضَانَ الَّذِي أُنْزِلَ فِيهِ الْقُرْآنُ، وَفِيْهِ لَيْلَةُ الْقَدْرِ، وَاخْتُصَّ بِفَضَائِلَ عَدِيْدَةٍ، وَلَا فِي الْأَشْهُرِ الْـحُرُمِ الَّتِي جَعَلَ اللهُ لَـهَا الْـحُرْمَةَ يَوْمَ خَلَقَ السَّمَوَاتِ وَالْأَرْضَ وَلَا فِي لَيْلَةِ النِّصْفِ مِنْ شَعْبَانَ، وَلَا فِي يَوْمِ الْـجُمُعَةِ وَلَا فِي لَيْلَتِهَا؟

فَالْـجَوَابُ مِنْ أَرْبَعَةِ أَوْجُهٍ:

اَلْوَجْهُ الْأَوَّلُ: مَا وَرَدَ فِي الْـحَدِيْثِ مِنْ أَنَّ اللهَ خَلَقَ الشَّجَرَ يَوْمَ الْاِثْنَيْنِ. وَفِي ذَلِكَ تَنْبِيْهٌ عَظِيْمٌ وَهُوَ أَنَّ خَلْقَ الْأَقْوَاتِ وَالْأَرْزَاقِ وَالْفَوَاكِهِ وَالْـخَيْرَاتِ الَّتِي يَتَغَذَّى بِهَا بَنُو آدَمَ وَيَحْيَوْنَ، وَيَتَدَاوَوْنَ وَتَنْشَرِحُ صُدُوْرُهُمْ لِرُؤْيَتِهَا وَتَطِيْبُ بِهَا نُفُوْسُهُمْ وَتَسْكُنُ بِهَا خَوَاطِرُهُمْ عِنْدَ رُؤْيَتِهَا لِاطْمِئْنَانِ نُفُوْسِهِمْ بِتَحْصِيْلِ مَا يُبْقِي حَيَاتَهُمْ عَلَى مَا جَرَتْ بِهِ الْعَادَةُ مِنْ حِكْمَةِ الْـحَكِيْمِ سُبْحَانَهُ وَتَعَالَى فَوُجُوْدُهُ ﷺ فِي هَذَا الشَّهْرِ فِي هَذَا الْيَوْمِ قُرَّةُ عَيْنٍ بِسَبَبِ مَا وُجِدَ مِنَ الْـخَيْرِ الْعَظِيْمِ وَالْبَرَكَةِ الشَّامِلَةِ لِأُمَّتِهِ صَلَوَاتُ اللهُ عَلَيْهِ وَسَلَامُهُ.

اَلْوَجْهُ الثَّانِي: أَنَّ ظُهُوْرَهُ عَلَيْهِ الصَّلَاةُ وَالسَّلَامُ فِي شَهْرِ رَبِيْعٍ فِيْهِ إِشَارَةٌ ظَاهِرَةٌ لِـمَنْ تَفَطَّنَ إِلَيْهَا بِالنِّسْبَةِ إِلَى اشْتِقَاقِ لَفْظَةِ رَبِيْعٍ إِذْ أَنَّ فِيْهِ تَفَاؤُلاً حَسَنًا بِبِشَارَتِهِ لِأُمَّتِهِ عَلَيْهِ الصَّلَاةُ وَالسَّلَامُ وَالتَّفَاؤُلُ لَهُ أَصْلٌ أَشَارَ إِلَيْهِ

---

tanbīh ʿalā kathīr min al-bidʿ al-muḥdatha wa al-ʿawāʾid al-muntaḥala, 2:2–4; al-Suyūṭī, *Ḥusn al-maqṣid fī ʿamal al-mawlid*, p.57–59; al-Suyūṭī, *al-Ḥāwī li al-fatāwā*, p.203–204; and al-Ṣāliḥī, *Subul al-hudā wa al-rashād fī sīra Khayr al-ʿibād*, 1:371–372.

عَلَيْهِ الصَّلَاةُ وَالسَّلَامُ. وَقَدْ قَالَ الشَّيْخُ الْإِمَامُ أَبُو عَبْدِ الرَّحْمنِ الصَّقَلِّيُّ:
لِكُلِّ إِنْسَانٍ مِنَ اسْمِهِ نَصِيبٌ.

اَلْوَجْهُ الثَّالِثُ: أَنْ فَصْلَ الرَّبِيعِ أَعْدَلُ الْفُصُوْلِ وَأَحْسَنُهَا.

اَلْوَجْهُ الرَّابِعُ: أَنَّهُ قَدْ شَاءَ الْحَكِيْمُ سُبْحَانَهُ وَتَعَالَى أَنَّهُ عَلَيْهِ الصَّلَاةُ وَالسَّلَامُ تَتَشَرَّفُ بِهِ الْأَزْمِنَةُ وَالْأَمَاكِنُ لَا هُوَ يَتَشَرَّفُ بِهَا بَلْ يُحْصَلُ لِلزَّمَانِ وَالْمَكَانِ الَّذِي يُبَاشِرُهُ عَلَيْهِ الصَّلَاةُ وَالسَّلَامُ الْفَضِيلَةُ الْعُظْمَى وَالْمَزِيَّةُ عَلَى مَا سِوَاهُ مِنْ جِنْسِهِ إِلَّا مَا اسْتُثْنِيَ مِنْ ذَلِكَ لِأَجْلِ زِيَادَةِ الْأَعْمَالِ فِيْهَا وَغَيْرِ ذَلِكَ. فَلَوْ وُلِدَ ﷺ فِي الْأَوْقَاتِ الْمُتَقَدِّمِ ذِكْرُهَا لَكَانَ ظَاهِرُهُ يُوْهِمُ أَنَّهُ يَتَشَرَّفُ بِهَا.

One might ask what is the wisdom behind the Prophet's noble birth taking place in the month of *Rabīʿ al-Awwal* on a Monday (the popular opinion amongst majority of the scholars), and not, say, in the month of *Ramaḍān*, the month in which the Qurʾān was revealed and in which the Night of Destiny (*Layla al-Qadr*) appears, or in the sacred months, the sanctity of which has been established by Allah, or on the 15th night of *Shaʿbān*, or on a Friday or its night?

There are four angels to this reply:

Firstly, it is narrated in a hadith that Allah, the Most High, created the trees on a Monday. This contains a great indication, for it shows that Monday is the day in which sustenance, provision, fruits, and other types of goodness have been created. These are the things by which the children of Ādam live and enjoy pleasure. The blessed birth of the beloved Prophet on this day of the month is the coolness of the eyes, and due to his blessed birth, the *Umma* was bestowed abundance of goodness and the greatest blessing.

Secondly, if we consider its etymology, the word

'*Rabī*ᶜ' is a subtle indication and a good omen. Abū ᶜAbd al-Raḥmān al-Ṣaqlī said, 'Every person acquires some portion from his name.' The good omen of this month is that the *Umma* of the beloved Prophet ﷺ was given the glad tiding of his auspicious arrival.

Thirdly, the Spring (*al-Rabī*ᶜ) is the most balanced of the seasons and the best of them, and the Prophet's Sacred Law (Sharia) is the most just and balanced of laws.

Fourthly, Almighty Allah wanted to honour the time in which the most exalted Prophet ﷺ was born; for if the Prophet ﷺ was born in the aforementioned times, then one might mistakenly suppose that he was honoured by being born in that time.[1]

6.11 Imam Shams al-Dīn al-Dhahabī (673–748 AH)

Imam Shams al-Dīn Abū ᶜAbd Allāh Muhammad b. Aḥmad b. ᶜUthmān al-Dhahabī (1274–1348 CE) is hailed as one of the greatest historians and hadith scholars of the Muslim world. He contributed immensely to the fields of hadith principles and biographical evaluation (*ᶜilm al-rijāl*) by compiling a number of works, such as *Tajrīd al-uṣūl fī aḥādīth al-Rasūl*, *Mīzān al-iᶜtidāl fī naqd al-rijāl*, *al-Mushtaba fī asmā' al-rijāl*, and *Ṭabaqāt al-ḥuffāẓ*, etc. *Tārīkh al-Islām wa wafiyāt al-mashāhīr wa al-aᶜlām* is one of his popular compendiums on history. In the science of biographical evaluation (*ᶜilm al-rijāl*), his book *Siyar aᶜlām al-nubalā'* is an excellent work in which the author discusses the biographical circumstances of hadith narrators; this book enjoys a distinguished position within academic circles.

Imam al-Dhahabī narrates a detailed praise of the brother-in-law of Ṣalāḥ al-Dīn al-Ayyūbī (Saladin), Sultan Muẓaffar al-Dīn Abū Saᶜīd al-Kawkabrī (d. 630 AH), who was the king of Irbil.

---

[1] Ibn al-Ḥājj, *al-Madkhal ilā tanmiya al-aᶜmāl bi taḥsīn al-niyyāt wa al-tanbīh ᶜalā kathīr min al-bidᶜ al-muḥdatha wa al-ᶜawā'id al-muntaḥala*, 2:26–29; al-Suyūṭī, *Ḥusn al-maqṣid fī ᶜamal al-mawlid*, p.67–68; al-Suyūṭī, *al-Ḥāwī li al-fatāwā*, p.207; and al-Nabhānī, *Ḥujja Allāh ᶜalā al-ᶜālimīn fī muᶜjazāt Sayyid al-mursalīn*, p.238.

Abū Saʿīd al-Kawkabrī was an extremely generous and hospitable person who established four hospitals for the terminally sick and blind, which he would visit on Mondays and Thursdays. He also erected homes for widows, orphans and children who had no guardian, and he would routinely visit the sick. He established separate institutes for *Ḥanafī* and *Shāfiʿī* students and lodges for the Sufis. Imam al-Dhahabī writes that this king was Sunni in creed, and he was good-hearted and pious. He relates this in detail in both *Siyar aʿlām al-nubalāʾ* and *Tārīkh al-Islām wa wafiyāt al-mashāhīr wa al-aʿlām*.

Imam al-Dhahabī has the following to say about the king and his celebration of *Mawlid al-Nabī* ﷺ:

وَأَمَّا احْتِفَالُهُ بِالْمَوْلِدِ فَيَقْصُرُ التَّعْبِيْرُ عَنْهُ؛ كَانَ الْخَلْقُ يَقْصِدُوْنَهُ مَنَ الْعِرَاقِ وَالْجَزِيْرَةِ... وَيُخْرِجُ مِنَ الْبَقَرِ وَالإِبِلِ وَالْغَنَمِ شَيئًا كَثِيْراً فَتُنْحَرُ وَتُطْبَخُ الْأَلْوَانُ، وَيَعْمَلُ عِدَّةَ خِلَعٍ لِلصُّوْفِيَّةِ، وَيَتَكَلَّمُ الْوُعَّاظُ فِي الْمِيْدَانِ، فَيُنْفِقُ أَمْوَالاً جَزِيْلَةً. وَقَدْ جَمَعَ لَهُ ابْنُ دِحْيَةَ «كِتَابَ الْمَوْلِدِ» فَأَعْطَاهُ أَلْفَ دِيْنَارٍ. وَكَانَ مُتَوَاضِعًا، خَيْراً، سُنِّيّاً، يُحِبُّ الْفُقَهَاءَ وَالْمُحَدِّثِيْنَ... وَقَالَ سِبْطُ الْجَوْزِيُّ: كَانَ مُظَفَّرُ الدِّيْنِ يُنْفِقُ فِي السَّنَةِ عَلَى الْمَوْلِدِ ثَلَاث مِائَةِ أَلْفِ دِيْنَارٍ، وَعَلَى الْخَانَقَاهِ مِائَتَيْ أَلْفِ دِيْنَار... وَقَالَ: قَالَ مَنْ حَضَرَ الْمَوْلِدَ مَرَّةً عُدِّدَتْ عَلَى سِمَاطِهِ مِائَةُ فَرَسٍ قَشْلَمِيْشٍ، وَخَمْسَةُ آلَافِ رَأْسٍ شَوِيٍّ، وَ عَشَرَةُ آلَافِ دَجَّاجَةٍ، مِائَةُ أَلْفِ زُبْدِيَّةٍ، وَ ثَلَاثِيْنَ أَلْفَ صِحْنِ حَلْوَاءَ.

Words cannot describe his commemoration of the *mawlid*! People from Iraq and the Arabian Peninsula would undertake journeys to attend (his celebration)... He would sacrifice a large number of cows, camels, and sheep, and cook a variety of foods. He would honor the Sufis with many robes of distinction. Sermonisers would be allowed to address the audience in the main square, and the king would spend enormous sums of money. Ibn Diḥya wrote a book on the prophetic birth, to which the king awarded him one thousand dinars. King Muẓaffar was a humble and good Sunni who loved the poor and the hadith scholars. Sibṭ al-Jawzī said, "King Muẓaffar's yearly expenditure for the *mawlid* would amount to three hundred thousand dinars; and he would spend two hundred thousand dinars for the Sufi lodges [*khānqāh*]... It was mentioned by one of the participants in al-Muẓaffar's *mawlid* celebration that the royal table-spread was laid out with one hundred earthen tumblers, five thousand goat heads, ten thousand chickens, one hundred thousand plates of dried fruits, and thirty thousand plates of sweets..."[1]

6.12 Imam Kamāl al-Dīn al-Adfawī (685–748 AH)

Imam Kamāl al-Dīn Abū al-Faḍl Jaʿfar b. Thaʿlab b. Jaʿfar al-Adfawī (1286–1347 CE) writes in *al-Ṭāliʿ al-saʿīd al-jāmiʿ li-asmāʾ nujabāʾ al-ṣaʿīd*:

حَكَى لَنَا صَاحِبُنَا الْعَدْلُ نَاصِرُ الدِّيْنِ مَحْمُوْدُ بْنُ الْعِمَادِ أَنَّ أَبَا الطَّيِّبِ مُحَمَّدَ بْنَ إِبْرَاهِيْمَ السَّبْتِيَّ الْمَالِكِيَّ نَزِيْلَ قَوْصٍ، أَحَدَ الْعُلَمَاءِ الْعَامِلِيْنَ، كَانَ يَجُوْزُ بِالْمَكْتَبِ فِي الْيَوْمِ الَّذِي وُلِدَ فِيْهِ النَّبِيُّ ﷺ، فَيَقُوْلُ: يَا فَقِيْهُ! هَذَا يَوْمُ سُرُوْرٍ، اصْرِفِ الصِّبْيَانَ، فَيَصْرِفُنَا.

وَهَذَا مِنْهُ دَلِيْلٌ عَلَى تَقْرِيْرِهِ وَعَدَمِ إِنْكَارِهِ، وَهَذَا الرَّجُلُ كَانَ فَقِيْهاً مَالِكِيًّا مُتَفَنِّناً فِي عُلُومٍ، مُتَوَرِّعاً، أَخَذَ عَنْهُ أَبُوْ حَيَّانَ وَغَيْرُهُ، مَاتَ سَنَةَ خَمْسٍ وَتِسْعِيْنَ وَسِتِّمِائَةٍ.

Our reliable friend Nāṣir al-Dīn Maḥmūd b. al-ʿImād related to us that Abū al-Ṭayyab Muhammad b. Ibrāhīm

[1] Al-Dhahabī, *Siyar aʿlām al-nubalāʾ*, 16:274–275; al-Dhahabī, *Tārīkh al-Islām wa wafayāt al-mashāhīr wa al-aʿlām* (621–630 AH), 45:402–405.

al-Sabtī al-Mālikī, resident of Fūṣ and one of the pious scholars, used to pass by the local primary school [maktab] and say, 'O scholar! Today is a day of delight; let the children out.' And so he would be let out."

This is a proof from him that he accepted it (the *mawlid* celebration) and did not censure it—and he was a Mālikī jurist skilled in the various sciences and was scrupulous. Abū Ḥayyān and others studied under him and he passed away in the year 695 AH.[1]

6.13 Taqī al-Dīn Abū al-Ḥasan al-Subkī (683–756 AH)

Shaykh Ismāʿīl Ḥaqqī (1063–1137 AH) said the following about Taqī al-Dīn Abū al-Ḥasan ʿAlī b. ʿAbd al-Kāfī al-Subkī (1284–1355 CE):

وَقَدِ اجْتَمَعَ عِنْدَ الْإِمَامِ تَقِيِّ الدِّيْنِ السُّبْكِيِّ جَمْعٌ كَثِيْرٌ مِنْ عُلَمَاءِ عَصْرِهِ، فَأَنْشَدَ مُنْشِدٌ قَوْلَ الصَّرْصَرِيِّ فِي مَدْحِهِ:

قَلِيْلٌ لِمَدْحِ الْمُصْطَفَى الْخَطُّ بِالذَّهَبِ
عَلَى وَرَقٍ مِنْ خَطٍّ أَحْسَنَ مِنْ كُتُبِ
وَإِنْ تَنْهَضِ الْأَشْرَافُ عِنْدَ سَمَاعِهِ
قِيَامًا صُفُوْفًا أَوْ جِثِيًّا عَلَى الرُّكَبِ

A large cohort of learned men who were contemporaries of Taqī al-Dīn al-Subkī would gather under him. A reciter would recite the eulogy of the Prophet ﷺ composed by al-Ṣarṣarī al-Ḥanbalī:

---

[1] Al-Suyūṭī, *Ḥusn al-maqṣid fī ʿamal al-mawlid*, p.66–67; al-Suyūṭī, *al-Ḥāwī li al-fatāwā*, p.206; al-Nabhānī, *Ḥujja Allāh ʿalā al-ʿālimīn fī muʿjazāt Sayyid al-mursalīn*, p.238.

Insufficient, for the praise of al-Muṣṭafā,
is gold penned on paper, in the most beautiful calligraphy.
And the nobles salute him when they hear of him
Standing in rows or crawling on their knees.[1]

6.14 ʿIMĀD AL-DĪN B. KATHĪR (701–774 AH)

Al-Ḥāfiẓ ʿImād al-Dīn Abū al-Fidāʾ Ismāʿīl b. Kathīr (1301–1373 CE) is a renowned exegete, hadith scholar, historian and jurist. His work, *Tafsīr al-Qurʾān al-ʿaẓīm*, is an authority in the field of exegesis. In his work, *Jāmiʿ al-masānīd wa al-sunan*, he transcribes a vast amount of hadiths. His book *al-Bidāya wa al-nihāya* is a famous and magnificent work in the field of history. In this book, he has recorded in detail the *mawlid* celebrations of the king of Irbil, Abū Saʿīd Muẓaffar al-Dīn. Besides this, Ibn Kathīr has composed a pamphlet, entitled *Dhikr mawlid Rasūl Allāh* ﷺ *wa raḍāʿihī*. He writes:

أَوَّلُ مَا أَرْضَعَتْهُ ثُوَيْبَةُ مَوْلَاةُ عَمِّهِ أَبِي لَـهَبٍ، وَكَانَتْ قَدْ بَشَّرَتْ عَمَّهُ بِمِيْلَادِهِ فَأَعْتَقَهَا عِنْدَ ذَلِكَ، وَلِـهَذَا لَـمَّـا رَآهُ أَخُوْهُ الْعَبَّاسُ بْنُ عَبْدِ الْـمُطَّلِبِ بَعْدَ مَا مَاتَ، وَرَآهُ فِي شَرِّ حَالَةٍ، فَقَالَ لَهُ: مَا لَقِيْتَ؟ فَقَالَ: لَـمْ أَلْقَ بَعْدَكُمْ خَيْراً، غَيْرَ أَنِّي سُقِيْتُ فِي هَذِهِ - وَأَشَارَ إِلَى النُّقْرَةِ الَّتِي فِي الْإِبْهَامِ - بِعَتَاقَتِي ثُوَيْبَةَ.

وَأَصْلُ الْـحَدِيْثِ فِي الصَّحِيْحَيْنِ.

فَلَمَّـا كَانَتْ مَوْلَاتُهُ قَدْ سَقَتِ النَّبِيَّ ﷺ، مِنْ لَبَنِهَا عَادَ نَفْعُ ذَلِكَ عَلَى عَمِّهِ أَبِي لَـهَبٍ، فَسُقِيَ بِسَبَبِ ذَلِكَ، مَعَ أَنَّهُ الَّذِي أَنْزَلَ اللهُ فِي ذَمِّهِ سُوْرَةً فِي الْقُرْآنِ تَامَّةً.

---

[1] Ismāʿīl Ḥaqqī, *Tafsīr rūḥ al-bayān*, 9:56; and al-Ḥalabī in *Insān al-ʿuyūn fī sīra al-Amīn al-Maʾmūn*, 1:84.

The first lady to nurse the Prophet ﷺ was Thuwayba, the free-slave of Abū Lahab (the Prophet's uncle). She is the one who brought the glad tidings of his birth to him and he subsequently emancipated her out of happiness. His brother, ʿAbbās b. ʿAbd al-Muṭṭalib, saw him (in a dream) after his death in a dire state, he asked, 'What has become of you?' And Abū Lahab replied, 'I am in the hellfire. However, my punishment is lightened every Monday evening and so I am able to drink water from these finger tips (and he pointed to the tips of his index and middle finger)—and this is because I freed Thuwayba when she brought me the good news of the Prophet's birth.'

The source of this hadith is in the *Ṣaḥīḥayn*.

So, because his freed slave girl (Thuwayba) had given her milk to the Prophet ﷺ, the benefit of that was returned to his uncle Abū Lahab; and so he was quenched because of it, despite the fact that a complete chapter of the Qurʾān was revealed in his condemnation.[1]

6.14.1 The Celebration of *Mawlid al-Nabī* ﷺ held by Abū Saʿīd al-Muẓaffar (Saladin's brother in-law)

King Abū Saʿīd al-Muẓaffar (d. 630 AH) was the brother in-law of the conquering hero, Sultan Ṣalāḥ al-Dīn al-Ayyūbī (532–589 AH/1138–1193 CE); the blood sister of the Sultan, Rabīʿa Khātūn, was wedded to him. The Sultan had great love for the king. These two individuals would mutually serve Islam with their heart and soul. The king was known to be highly virtuous, pious, and generous. Seeing the lofty religious and spiritual state of the king in addition to his services to Islam, the Sultan married his sister to him.

After describing Abū Saʿīd al-Muẓaffar in this manner, via the words of Ṣalāḥ al-Dīn, Ibn Kathīr goes on to further illustrate the fine qualities of this man in a paragraph, depicting his biography and shedding light upon his good-heartedness, piety, and nature. He writes a lengthy description about his celebration of *Mawlid al-*

---

[1] Ibn Kathīr, *Dhikr mawlid Rasūl Allāh ﷺ wa raḍāʿihī*, p.28–29.

Nabī ﷺ. In it, he portrays his endeavours and enthusiasm, showing the extents of the happiness and joy expressed on this blessed occasion. Ibn Kathīr writes:

اَلْـمَلِكُ الْـمُظَفَّرُ أَبُوْ سَعِيْدٍ كَوْكَبْرِيُّ بْنُ زَيْنِ الدِّيْنِ عَلِيُّ بْنُ تُبْكتَكِيْنَ أَحَدُ الْأَجْوَادِ وَالسَّادَاتِ الْكُبَرَاءِ وَالْـمُلُوْكِ الْأَمْجَادِ، لَهُ آثَارٌ حَسَنَةٌ وَقَدْ عُمِّرَ الْجَامِعُ الْـمُظَفَّرِيُّ بِسَفْحِ قَاسِيُوْنَ، وَكَانَ قَدْ هَمَّ بِسِيَاقَةِ الْـمَاءِ إِلَيْهِ مِنْ مَاءِ بَرْزَةَ فَمَنَعَهُ الْـمُعَظَّمُ مِنْ ذَلِكَ، وَاعْتَلَّ بِأَنَّهُ قَدْ يَمُرُّ عَلَى مَقَابِرِ الْـمسْلِمِيْنَ بِالسُّفُوْحِ، وَكَانَ يَعْمَلُ الْـمَوْلِدَ الشَّرِيْفَ فِي رَبِيْعِ الْأَوَّلِ وَيَحْتَفِلُ بِهِ احْتِفَالاً هَائِلاً، وَكَانَ مَعَ ذَلِكَ شَهْماً شُجَاعاً فَاتِكاً بَطَلاً عَاقِلاً عَالِماً عَادِلاً رَحِمَهُ اللهُ وَأَكْرَمَ مَثْوَاهُ. وَقَدْ صَنَّفَ الشَّيْخُ أَبُو الْـخَطَّابِ بْنُ دِحْيَةَ لَهُ مُجَلَّداً فِي الْـمَوْلِدِ النَّبَوِيِّ سَمَّاهُ «التَّنْوِيْرُ فِي مَوْلِدِ الْبَشِيْرِ النَّذِيْرِ» فَأَجَازَهُ عَلَى ذَلِكَ بِأَلْفِ دِيْنارٍ، وَقَدْ طَالَتْ مُدَّتُهُ فِي الْـمُلْكِ فِي زَمَانِ الدَّوْلَةِ الصَّلَاحِيَّةِ، وَقَدْ كَانَ مُحَاصِراً عَكَّا وَإِلَى هَذِهِ السَّنَةِ مَحْمُوْدُ السِّيْرَةِ وَالسَّرِيْرَةِ. قَالَ السِّبْطُ: حَكَى بَعْضُ مَنْ حَضَرَ سِمَاطَ الْـمُظَفَّرِ فِي بَعْضِ الْـمَوَالِدِ كَانَ يُمَدُّ فِي ذَلِكَ السِّمَاطِ خَمْسَةُ آلَافِ رَأْسٍ مَشْوِيٍّ. وَعَشْرَةُ آلَافِ دَجَّاجَةٍ، وَمِائَةُ أَلْفِ زُبْدِيَّةٍ، وَثَلَاثِيْنَ أَلْفَ صِحْنِ حَلْوَى.

King Muẓaffar: He is Abū Saʿīd Kawkabrī b. Zayn al-ʿĀbidīn ʿAlī b. Baktagīn, one of the generous and senior liege lords and noble kings. He left behind good works and constructed the al-Muẓaffarī Congregational Mosque at the top of Mount Qāsyūn. At one point, he considered drawing water from Barza and piping it to the mosque, but al-Muʿaẓẓam prevented him because it might have passed through the graveyards of the Muslims located atop the mountain.

He used to organise the noble *mawlid* celebration in the month of *Rabīʿ al-Awwal* and participate in it with great festivity. He was a pure-hearted, courageous, intelligent, and educated man. May Allah have mercy upon him and grant him an honorable abode in the Hereafter.

Shaykh Abū al-Khaṭṭāb b. Diḥya wrote a book for him that was used in the celebration of the Prophet's birth ﷺ. It was called *al-Tanwīr fī mawlid al-Bashīr al-Nadhīr* (Illumination on the birth of the Bearer of Glad Tidings and Warner). Al-Muẓaffar awarded Ibn Diḥya one thousand dinars for this book. He remained in power during the Ṣalāḥiya state and was under siege in Akka until his death [in 630 AH] during the crusader's siege of Akka, and this book remained with him throughout. He was a man of praiseworthy character and piety.

Said Sibṭ Ibn al-Jawzī: "It was mentioned by one of the participants in al-Muẓaffar's *mawlid* celebration that the royal table-spread was laid out with five thousand goat heads, ten thousand chickens, one hundred thousand clay containers of milk, and thirty thousand plates of sweets.[1]

Now, ponder over the following statement of Ibn Kathīr:

وَكَانَ يَحْضُرُ عِنْدَهُ فِي الْـمَوْلِدِ أَعْيَانُ الْعُلَمَـاءِ وَالصُّوْفِيَّةِ فَيَخْلَعُ عَلَيْهِمْ وَيُطْلِقُ لَـهُمْ وَيَعْمَلُ لِلصُّوْفِيَّةِ سَمَـاعًا مِنَ الظُّهْرِ إِلَى الْعَصْرِ، وَيَرْقُصُ بِنَفْسِهِ مَعَهُمْ، وَكَانَتْ لَهُ دَارُ ضِيَافَةٍ لِلْوَافِدِيْنَ مِنْ أَيِّ جِهَةٍ عَلَى أَيِّ صِفَةٍ. وَكَانَتْ صَدَقَاتُهُ فِي جَمِيْعِ الْقُرَبِ وَالطَّاعَاتِ عَلَى الْـحَرَمَيْنِ وَغَيْرِهِمَا، وَيَتَفَكُّ مِنَ الْفَرَنْجِ فِي كُلِّ سَنَةٍ خَلْقًا مِنَ الْأَسَارَى، حَتَّى قِيْلَ إِنَّ جُمْلَةً مَنِ اسْتَفَكَّهُ مِنْ أَيْدِيْهِمْ سِتُّوْنَ أَلْفَ أَسِيْرٍ، قَالَتْ زَوْجَتُهُ رَبِيْعَةُ خَاتُوْنُ بِنْتُ

[1] Ibn Kathīr, *al-Bidāya wa al-nihāya*, 9:18; Muḥibī, *Khulāṣa al-athar fī aʿyān al-qarn al-ḥādī ʿashar*, 3:233; al-Suyūṭī, *Ḥusn al-maqṣid fī ʿamal al-mawlid*, p.42–44; al-Suyūṭī, *al-Ḥāwī li al-fatāwā*, p.200; Aḥmad b. Zaynī al-Daḥlān, *al-Sīra al-Nabawiyya*, 1:53–54.

أَيُّوْبَ - وَكَانَ قَدْ زَوَّجَهُ إِيَّاهَا أَخُوْهَا صَلَاحُ الدِّيْنِ، لِـمَـا كَانَ مَعَهُ عَلَى عَكَّا - قَالَتْ: كَانَ قَمِيْصُهُ لَا يُسَاوِي خَمْسَةَ دَرَاهِمَ فَعَاتَبْتُهُ بِذَلِكَ، فَقَالَ: لُبْسِي ثَوْبًا بِخَمْسَةٍ وَأَتَصَدَّقُ بِالْبَاقِي خَيْرٌ مِنْ أَنْ أَلْبِسَ ثَوْبًا مُثْمَنًا وَأَدَعُ الْفَقِيْرَ الْـمِسْكِيْنَ، وَكَانَ يَصْرِفُ عَلَى الْـمَوْلِدِ فِي كُلِّ سَنَةٍ ثَلَاثَمِـائَةِ أَلْفِ دِيْنَارٍ، وَعَلَى دَارِ الضِّيَافَةِ فِي كُلِّ سَنَةٍ مِائَةَ أَلْفِ دِيْنَارٍ. وَعَلَى الْـحَرَمَيْنِ وَالْـمِيَاهِ بِدَرْبِ الْـحِجَازِ ثَلَاثِيْنَ أَلْفَ دِيْنَارٍ سِوَى صَدَقَاتِ السِّرِّ، رَحِمَهُ اللهُ تَعَالَى، وَكَانَتْ وَفَاتُهُ بِقَلْعَةِ إِرْبِلَ، وَأَوْصَى أَنْ يُحْمَلَ إِلَى مَكَّةَ فَلَمْ يَتَّفِقْ فَدُفِنَ بِمَشْهَدِ عَلِيٍّ.

The eminent scholars and Sufis used to attend the *mawlid*, and King al-Muẓaffar would honour them with robes of distinction and royal favour. He would have the Sufis convene a gathering of spiritual singing (*samāʿ*) from the time of the Afternoon Prayer until the Dawn Prayer, and he would also dance (by circumambulation [*yarquṣ*]) along with them. He also had a guesthouse for the visiting delegations, and people would come there from all regions and walks of life. His charity would go to good deeds and acts of obedience; thus, he would spend on the charities of the two Sacred Sanctuaries and other sites, and he would free a large number of Frankish prisoners each year. In fact, it is said that he freed over sixty thousand prisoners in total.

His wife, Rabīʿa Khātūn bint Ayyūb (whose brother, Ṣalāḥ al-Dīn al-Ayyūbī, married her to him when the two were together in Akka), said, "His over garment was worth no more than five dirhams. When I criticised him for his choice of clothing, he said to me, 'That I spend five (*dirhams*) on a garment and give the rest away in charity is more beloved to me than wearing an expensive garment and neglecting the poor and indignant.'" His yearly expenditure for the *mawlid* would amount to three hundred thousand dinars, and he would also spend two

> hundred thousand dinars yearly for the upkeep of the guesthouse. He would also spend thirty thousand dinars yearly for the upkeep of the two Sacred Sanctuaries [Mecca and Medina] and the watering stations situated around the Hejaz region. None of these expenditures, we should note, included al-Muẓaffar's secret charity. He died at the citadel of Irbil and ordered that his body be brought to Mecca for burial; however, that was not possible, so he was buried at Mashad ʿAlī.[1]

Three hundred thousand dinars (300,000) were spent by the king for the *mawlid* celebration. Clearly, Ibn Kathīr approved of this huge spending, as he did not utter a single word in criticism of it. Bear in mind that one dinar was approximately equal to two British pounds; in light of this, the actual figure spent on celebrating *Mawlid al-Nabī* ﷺ totalled six hundred thousand pounds (£600,000). Additionally, we are speaking of the value of six hundred thousand pounds some 800 years ago. If we were to compare this amount to today's standards, then it could be said that in those days, one dinar was worth at least the value of a quarter of an ounce of gold—this is equal to four thousand Pakistani rupees (Rs 4,000) in our time. Likewise, one dinar would equal forty British pounds (£40) today. So if forty pounds is multiplied by three hundred thousand pounds, it equals twelve million pounds (£12,000,000). Again, this is but an estimate.

6.15 BURHĀN AL-DĪN B. JAMĀʿA (725–790 AH)

Burhān al-Dīn Abū Isḥāq Ibrāhīm b. ʿAbd al-Raḥīm b. Ibrāhīm b. Jamāʿa al-Shāfiʿī (1325–1388 CE) was a famous judge and exegete of the Holy Qurʾān. He composed a commentary of the Holy Qurʾān, amounting to ten volumes. Regarding his stance on *mawlid*, Mullā ʿAlī al-Qārī (d. 1014 AH) in *al-Mawrid al-rawī fī mawlid al-nabawī wa nasabihi al-ṭāhir* documents:

---

[1] Ibn Kathīr, *al-Bidāya wa al-nihāya*, 9:18; al-Suyūṭī, *Ḥusn al-maqṣid fī ʿamal al-mawlid*, p.44; al-Suyūṭī, *al-Ḥāwī li al-fatāwā*, p.200; al-Ṣāliḥī, *Subul al-hudā wa al-rashād fī sīra Khayr al-ʿibād*, 1:362–363; and al-Nabhānī, *Ḥujja Allāh ʿalā al-ʿālimīn fī muʿjazāt Sayyid al-mursalīn*, p.236.

فَقَدِ اتَّصَلَ بِنَا أَنَّ الزَّاهِدَ الْقُدْوَةَ الْـمُعَمَّرَ أَبَا إِسْحَاقَ إِبْرَاهِيْمَ بْنَ عَبْدِ الرَّحِيْمِ بْنِ إِبْرَاهِيْمَ جَمَاعَةً لِـمَـا كَانَ بِالْـمَدِيْنَةِ النَّبَوِيَّةِ - عَلَى سَاكِنِهَا أَفْضَلُ الصَّلَاةِ وَأَكْمَلُ التَّحِيَّةِ - كَانَ يَعْمَلُ طَعَاماً فِي الْـمَوْلِدِ النَّبَوِيِّ، وَيُطْعِمُ النَّاسَ، وَيَقُوْلُ: لَوْ تَمَكَّنْتُ عَمِلْتُ بِطُولِ الشَّهْرِ كُلَّ يَوْمٍ مَوْلِداً.

It has reached us that when the worldly-abstinent (*zuhd*) and devout exemplar, Abū Isḥāq Ibrāhīm b. ʿAbd al-Raḥīm b. Ibrāhīm b. Jamāʿa, was in the city of the Prophet—may the excellent salutations and perfect salam be upon its resident—he would prepare food for the *mawlid* celebration and proclaim, "If only I were able to, I would hold a *mawlid* celebration every day of the month."[1]

6.16 Zayn al-Dīn b. Rajab al-Ḥanbalī (736–795 AH)

Zayn al-Dīn ʿAbd al-Raḥmān b. Aḥmad b. Rajab al-Ḥanbalī (–1336 1393 CE) is a renowned jurist of the Ḥanbalī school and a researcher who wrote numerous works. In his book, *Laṭāʾif al-maʿārif fī-mā li-mawāsim al-ʿām min al-waẓāʾif*, he has written about Islamic months, their virtues and the good deeds and supplications that should be performed in them. He has penned three chapters about the month of *Rabīʿ al-Awwal*; two are related to details regarding the blessed birth of the Holy Prophet ﷺ and the inauguration of prophethood, whereas the third chapter touches upon his physical demise. In the chapter on *Rabīʿ al-Awwal*, the author has gathered several hadiths on the events that occurred in this month, initiating it with traditions concerning *Mawlid al-Nabī* ﷺ. He states:

خَرَّجَ الْإِمَامُ أَحْمَدُ مِنْ حَدِيْثِ الْعِرْبَاضِ بْنِ سَارِيَةَ قَالَ: قَالَ رَسُولُ اللهِ ﷺ: «إِنِّي عَبْدُ اللهِ لَـخَاتَمُ النَّبِيِّيْنَ وَإِنَّ آدَمَ عَلَيْهِ السَّلَامُ لَـمُنْجَدِلٌ فِي طِينَتِهِ،

[1] Mullā ʿAlī al-Qārī, *al-Mawrid al-rawī fī mawlid al-nabawī wa nasabihi al-ṭāhir*, p.17.

وَسَأُنَبِّئُكُمْ بِأَوَّلِ ذَلِكَ دَعْوَةُ أَبِي إِبْرَاهِيمَ وَبِشَارَةُ عِيسَى بِي، وَرُؤْيَا أُمِّي الَّتِي رَأَتْ وَكَذَلِكَ أُمَّهَاتُ النَّبِيِّينَ تَرَيْنَ.»

> Aḥmad b. Ḥanbal has referenced the narration of ʿIrbāḍ b. Sāriya al-Sulamī ﷺ, who narrates that the Prophet ﷺ said, 'Verily, I was predetermined as the seal of prophethood on the sacred tablet whilst Ādam was yet being moulded from clay. I shall inform you the meaning of this: I am the answer to the supplication of my forefather Ibrāhīm,[1] the fulfilment of the glad-tidings that ʿĪsā gave to his community,[2] and the realisation of the vision of my noble mother. She witnessed that such radiance emitted from her blessed body that illuminated even the palaces of Syria. The mothers of prophets did indeed observe such dreams.[3]

After this, the author mentions several hadiths regarding this issue[4] by which it is apparent that reporting the marvels that transpired in *Rabīʿ al-Awwal* at the time of the Holy Prophet's birth ﷺ are acceptable, honourable, and excellent matters.

6.17 Walī al-Dīn Abū Zurʿa al-ʿIrāqī (762–826 AH)

Walī al-Dīn Abū Zurʿa Aḥmad b. ʿAbd al-Raḥīm b. Ḥusayn al-ʿIrāqī (1361–1423 CE) is a well-known scholar of hadith and jurisprudence. He was once asked whether celebrating *Mawlid al-*

---

1 Qur'ān 2:129.

2 Qur'ān 6:61.

3 Aḥmad b. Ḥanbal in *al-Musnad*, 4:127–128 §17,190–17,191 & 17,203; Ibn Ḥibbān in *al-Ṣaḥīḥ*, 14:312, §6,404; al-Ḥakim in *al-Mustadrak*, 2:656 §4174; al-Ṭabarānī in *al-Muʿjam al-kabīr*, 18:253 §631; al-Ṭabarānī in *Musnad al-shāmiyyīn*, 2:340 §1455; Ibn Saʿd in *al-Ṭabaqāt al-kubrā*, 1:149; al-Haythamī in *Mawārid al-ẓamʾān ilā zawāʾid Ibn Ḥibbān*, p.512 §2093; al-Haythamī in *Majmaʿ al-zawāʾid wa manbaʿ al-fawāʾid*, 8:223; al-ʿAsqalānī in *Fatḥ al-Bārī*, 6:583; and Ibn Kathīr in *al-Bidāya wa al-nihāya*, 2:321.

4 Ibn Rajab al-Ḥanbalī, *Laṭāʾif al-maʿārif fīmā li-mawāsim al-ʿām min al-waẓāʾif*, p.158–216.

Nabī ﷺ was recommended or reprehensible, or whether there was any other existing ruling that could be observed in relation to this act. He replied:

إِطْعَامُ الطَّعَامِ مُسْتَحَبٌّ فِي كُلِّ وَقْتٍ، فَكَيْفَ إِذَا انْضَمَّ لِذَلِكَ السُّرُوْرُ بِظُهُوْرِ نُوْرِ النُّبُوَّةِ فِي هَذَا الشَّهْرِ الشَّرِيْفِ، وَلَا نَعْلَمُ ذَلِكَ مِنَ السَّلَفِ، وَلَا يَلْزَمُ مِنْ كَوْنِهِ بِدْعَةً كَوْنُهُ مَكْرُوْهاً، فَكَمْ مِنْ بِدْعَةٍ مُسْتَحَبَّةٍ بَلْ وَاجِبَةٍ.

It is always recommended to feed others, so if it also includes displays of happiness with the light of prophethood during this noble month (of *Rabīʿ al-Awwal*), then it will be more blessed. We are not aware of this being practiced by the early forebears; but the fact that it is an innovation does not necessitate that it is detested, for how many innovations are recommended or even obligatory![1]

6.18 Shams al-Dīn Muḥammad al-Dimashqī (777–842 AH)

Shams al-Dīn Muhammad b. Nāṣir al-Dīn al-Dimashqī writes in his book, *Mawlid al-ṣādī fī mawlid al-Hādī*:

وَقَدْ صَحَّ أَنَّ أَبَا لَهَبٍ يُخَفَّفُ عَنْهُ عَذَابُ النَّارِ فِي مِثْلِ يَوْمِ الْاِثْنَيْنِ، لِإِعْتَاقِهِ ثُوَيْبَةَ سُرُوْراً بِمِيْلَادِ النَّبِيِّ ﷺ.

It is authentically reported that Abū Lahab will receive a lightened punishment on Mondays due to him having set Thuwayba free because of his delight at the Prophet's birth ﷺ...

إِذَا كَانَ هَذَا كَافِرًا جَآءَ ذَمُّهُ

وَتَبَّتْ يَدَاهُ فِي الْجَحِيْمِ مُخَلَّدَا

[1] ʿAlī b. Ibrāhīm, *Tashnīf al-ādhān bi-asrār al-ādhān*, p.136.

أَتَى أَنَّهُ فِي يَوْمِ الْاِثْنَيْنِ دَائِمًا
يُخَفَّفُ عَنْهُ لِلسُّرُوْرِ بِأَحْمَدَا
فَمَا الظَّنُّ بِالْعَبْدِ الَّذِي طُوْلَ عُمْرِهِ
بِأَحْمَدَ مَسْرُوْراً وَمَاتَ مُوَحِّدَا

If this disbeliever who was condemned
And whose hands were bound forever in the Fire
Mentioned that every Monday
His punishment was lightened due to his delight in Aḥmad
So what say you of the servant
Who is delighted his entire life with Aḥmad
And died with belief in divine oneness?[1]

6.19 IBN ḤAJAR AL-ᶜASQALĀNĪ (773–852 AH)

The commentator of *Ṣaḥīḥ al-Bukhārī*, Shihāb al-Dīn Abū al-Faḍl Aḥmad b. ᶜAlī b. Ḥajar al-ᶜAsqalānī (1372–1449 CE) has categorically proven the legality of celebrating *Mawlid al-Nabī* ﷺ. He has provided an evidence on the permissibility of commemorating the day in which the Prophet ﷺ was born. Imam Jalāl al-Dīn al-Suyūṭī (849–911 AH), transmitting Ibn Ḥajar's proof on this issue, writes:

وَقَدْ سُئِلَ شَيْخُ الْإِسْلَامِ حَافِظُ الْعَصْرِ أَبُوْ الْفَضْلِ ابْنُ حَجَرٍ عَنْ عَمَلِ الْمَوْلِدِ، فَأَجَابَ بِمَا نَصُّهُ: قَالَ:

وَقَدْ ظَهَرَ لِي تَخْرِيْجُهَا عَلَى أَصْلٍ ثَابِتٍ، وَهُوَ مَا ثَبَتَ فِي الصَّحِيحَيْنِ مِنْ: أَنَّ النَّبِيَّ ﷺ قَدِمَ الْمَدِيْنَةَ، فَوَجَدَ الْيَهُوْدَ يَصُوْمُوْنَ يَوْمَ عَاشُوْرَاءَ،

[1] Al-Suyūṭī, *Ḥusn al-maqṣid fī ᶜamal al-mawlid*, p.66; al-Suyūṭī, *al-Ḥāwī li al-fatāwā*, p.206; al-Ṣāliḥī, *Subul al-hudā wa al-rashād fī sīra Khayr al-ᶜibād*, 1:367; Aḥmad b. Zaynī al-Daḥlān, *al-Sīra al-Nabawiyya*, 1:54; and al-Nabhānī, *Ḥujja Allāh ᶜalā al-ᶜālimīn fī muᶜjazāt Sayyid al-mursalīn*, p.238.

فَسَأَلَـهُمْ، فَقَالُوْا: هُوَ يَوْمٌ أَغْرَقَ اللهُ فِيْهِ فِرْعَوْنَ، وَنَجَّى مُوْسَى، فَنَحْنُ نَصُوْمُهُ شُكْرًا لله تَعَالَـى.

فَيُسْتَفَادُ مِنْهُ فِعْلُ الشُّكْرِ لله تَعَالَى عَلَى مَا مَنَّ بِهِ فِي يَوْمٍ مُعَيَّنٍ مِنْ إِسْدَاءِ نِعْمَةٍ، أَوْ دَفْعِ نِقْمَةٍ، وَيُعَادُ ذَلِكَ فِي نَظِيْرِ ذَلِكَ الْيَوْمِ مِنْ كُلِّ سَنَةٍ.

وَالشُّكْرُ لله تَعَالَـى يَحْصُلُ بِأَنْوَاعِ الْعِبَادَاتِ كَالسُّجُوْدِ وَالصِّيَامِ وَالصَّدَقَةِ وَالتِّلَاوَةِ، وَأَيُّ نِعْمَةٍ أَعْظَمُ مِنْ النِّعْمَةِ بِبُرُوْزِ هَذَا النَّبِيِّ ﷺ الَّذِي هُوَ نَبِيُّ الرَّحْمَةِ فِي ذَلِكَ الْيَوْمِ.

وَعَلَى هَذَا فَيَنْبَغِي أَنْ يُتَحَرَّى الْيَوْمَ بِعَيْنِهِ، حَتَّى يُطَابِقَ قِصَّةَ مُوْسَى عليه السلام فِي يَوْمِ عَاشُوْرَاءَ.

وَمَنْ لَـمْ يُلَاحِظْ ذَلِكَ لَا يُبَالِـي بِعَمَلِ الْـمَوْلِدِ فِي أَيِّ يَوْمٍ فِي الشَّهْرِ، بَلْ تَوَسَّعَ قَوْمٌ حَتَّى نَقَلُوْهُ إِلَـى يَوْمٍ مِنَ السَّنَةِ. وَفِيْهِ مَا فِيْهِ. فَهَذَا مَا يَتَعَلَّقُ بِأَصْلِ عَمَلِ الْـمَوْلِدِ.

وَأَمَّا مَا يُعْمَلُ فِيْهِ فَيَنْبَغِي أَنْ يُقْتَصَرَ فِيْهِ عَلَى مَا يُفْهَمُ الشُّكْرُ لله تَعَالَى مِنْ نَحْوِ مَا تَقَدَّمَ ذِكْرُهُ مِنَ التِّلَاوَةِ، وَالْإِطْعَامِ، وَالصَّدَقَةِ، وَإِنْشَادِ شَيْءٍ مِنَ الْـمَدَائِحِ النَّبَوِيَّةِ وَالزُّهْدِيَّةِ الْـمُحَرِّكَةِ لِلْقُلُوْبِ إِلَى فِعْلِ الْـخَيْرَاتِ وَالْعَمَلِ لِلْآخِرَةِ.

The hadith master and Shaykh al-Islām of his era, Abū al-Faḍl Ibn Ḥajar al-ʿAsqalānī was asked about the celebration of the *mawlid*. He replied:

There has occurred to me a legal text from which we may infer a basis for the *mawlid*. It is the hadith located in the two rigorously authentic collections of al-Bukhārī and Muslim. In the hadith, it states that the Prophet ﷺ came to Medina and found the Jews fasting on the day of *ʿĀshūrāʾ*.

When he asked them concerning this, they replied, "It is the day on which Allah drowned Pharaoh and saved Mūsā, so we fast this day out of gratitude to Allah Most High." This indicates the validity of giving thanks to Allah, the Most High, for the blessings He bestowed on a particular day in providing a benefit or averting a harm, and repeating that show of thanks each year.

Giving thanks to Allah, the Most High can be shown by many acts of worship, such as prostration, fasting, charity, or reciting [the Qur'ān]. And what bounty is greater than the blessing of the birth of this Prophet ﷺ—the Prophet of mercy—on this day?

On the basis of this, it is important that endeavours are made on this particular day so that Mūsā's episode accords with the day of *ʿĀshūrāʾ*.

However, if one does not act upon this, then there is no harm in celebrating the *mawlid* on any day throughout the month. In fact, some people have left this matter completely open in terms of it being commemorated on any specific day of the year. This is what can be said about the basis of *mawlid*.

As for what is practised in the *mawlid*, it is important that it is confined to those deeds which are understood as acts of showing gratitude to Almighty Allah ﷻ, such as the deeds which have been mentioned earlier, like reciting the Qur'ān, showing hospitality, giving charity, reciting poetry in praise of the Holy Prophet ﷺ or poetry which inclines peoples' hearts towards goodness and reminds them of the Hereafter, and so forth.[1]

[1] Al-Suyūṭī, *Ḥusn al-maqṣid fī ʿamal al-mawlid*, p.63–64; al-Suyūṭī, *al-Ḥāwī li al-fatāwā*, p.205–206; al-Ṣāliḥī, *Subul al-hudā wa al-rashād fī sīra Khayr al-ʿibād*, 1:366; al-Zurqānī, *Sharḥ al-mawāhib al-ladunya bi al-minaḥ al-Muḥammadiyya*, 1:263; Aḥmad b. Zaynī al-Daḥlān, *al-Sīra al-Nabawiyya*, 1:54; and al-Nabhānī, *Ḥujja Allāh ʿalā al-ʿālimīn fī muʿjazāt Sayyid al-mursalīn*, p.237.

6.20 Imam Shams al-Dīn al-Sakhāwī (831–902 AH)

Imam Shams al-Dīn Muhammad b. ʿAbd al-Raḥmān al-Sakhāwī (1428–1497 CE) issued a *fatwā* concerning the celebration of *Mawlid al-Nabī* ﷺ:

وَإِنَّمَا حَدَثَ بَعْدَهَا بِالْمَقَاصِدِ الْحَسَنَةِ، وَالنِّيَّةِ الَّتِي لِلْإِخْلَاصِ
شَامِلَةٌ، ثُمَّ لَا زَالَ أَهْلُ الْإِسْلَامِ فِي سَائِرِ الْأَقْطَارِ وَالْمُدُنِ الْعِظَامِ يَحْتَفِلُوْنَ
فِي شَهْرِ مَوْلِدِهِ ﷺ وَشَرَفٍ وَكَرَمٍ بِعَمَلِ الْوَلَائِمِ الْبَدِيْعَةِ، وَالْمَطَاعِمِ
الْمُشْتَمِلَةِ عَلَى الْأُمُوْرِ الْبَهِيَّةِ وَالْبَدِيْعَةِ، وَيَتَصَدَّقُوْنَ فِي لَيَالِيْهِ بِأَنْوَاعِ
الصَّدَقَاتِ، وَيُظْهِرُوْنَ الْمَسَرَّاتِ وَيَزِيْدُوْنَ فِي الْمَبَرَّاتِ، بَلْ يَعْتَنُوْنَ
بِقَرَابَةِ مَوْلِدِهِ الْكَرِيْمِ، وَيَظْهَرُ عَلَيْهِمْ مِنْ بَرَكَاتِهِ كُلُّ فَضْلٍ عَظِيْمٍ عَمِيْمٍ،
بِحَيْثُ كَانَ مِمَّا جُرِّبَ كَمَا قَالَ الْإِمَامُ شَمْسُ الدِّيْنِ بْنُ الْجَزَرِيِّ
الْمُقْرِيُّ، أَنَّهُ أَمَانٌ تَامٌّ فِي ذَلِكَ الْعَامِ وَبُشْرَى تُعَجِّلُ بِنَيْلِ مَا يَنْبَغِي وَيُرَامُ.

The basis for the noble *mawlid* celebration was not transmitted from any of the righteous forebears of the first three virtuous generations; it was started after their time with pious motives and good and sincere intentions. The people of Islam throughout the lands and major metropolises continue to celebrate it during the month of the Prophet's birth—may Allah send salutations and prayers upon him and grant him honour and exaltation—by arranging elaborate meals and gatherings. During its nights, they engage in various forms of charitable giving and display happiness and increase in good acts. Indeed, they take advantage of the closeness of the Prophet's birthplace ﷺ and every great bounty manifests upon them due to its blessings—and that is tried and true, as Imam Shams al-Dīn al-Jazarī the reciter said: 'It is a source of security for the entire year and an early glad tiding for every good thing that is sought after.'[1]

6.21 Imam Jalāl al-Dīn al-Suyūṭī (849–911 AH)

Imam Jalāl al-Dīn ʿAbd al-Raḥmān b. Abī Bakr al-Suyūṭī (1445–1505 CE) is acknowledged as amongst those great writers and researchers who have expressed their views on the topic of *Mawlid al-Nabī* ﷺ in great detail. In this regard, we shall refer to his work, *Ḥusn al-maqṣid fī ʿamal al-mawlid*. This is an extract from another of his major works, *al-Ḥāwī li al-fatāwā*. The respected writer has presented references from the Qurʾān and hadith in addition to the intellectual arguments in favour of *Mawlid al-Nabī* ﷺ, as well as covering the religious, historical, juristic and legal aspects in much detail. In doing so, he cites the opinions of numerous other scholars.

The following are some significant passages from this book:

١. إِنَّ أَصْلَ عَمَلِ الْمَوْلِدِ الَّذِي هُوَ اجْتِمَاعُ النَّاسِ، وَقِرَاءَةُ مَا تَيَسَّرَ مِنَ الْقُرْآنِ، وَرِوَايَةُ الْأَخْبَارِ الْوَارِدَةِ فِي مَبْدَأِ (أَمْرِ) النَّبِيِّ ﷺ، وَمَا وَقَعَ فِي مَوْلِدِهِ مِنَ الْآيَاتِ، ثُمَّ يُمَدُّ لَهُمْ سِمَاطاً يَأْكُلُوْنَهُ، وَيَنْصَرِفُوْنَ مِنْ غَيْرِ زِيَادَةٍ عَلَى ذَلِكَ مِنَ الْبِدَعِ (الْحَسَنَةِ) الَّتِي يُثَابُ عَلَيْهَا صَاحِبُهَا؛ لِمَا فِيْهِ مِنْ تَعْظِيْمِ قَدرِ النَّبِيِّ ﷺ، وَإِظْهَارِ الْفَرَحِ وَالْاِسْتِبْشَارِ بِمَوْلِدِهِ (ﷺ) الشَّرِيْفِ.

1. The celebration of the *mawlid* entails gathering with the people, reading a portion of the Qurʾān, citing the

---

[1] Mullā ʿAlī al-Qārī, *al-Mawrid al-rawī fī mawlid al-nabawī wa nasabihi al-ṭāhir*, p.12–13; al-Ṣāliḥī, *Subul al-hudā wa al-rashād fī sīra Khayr al-ʿibād*, 1:362; al-Ḥalabī in *Insān al-ʿuyūn fī sīra al-Amīn al-Maʾmūn*, 1:84; Ismāʿīl Ḥaqqī, *Tafsīr rūḥ al-bayān*, 9:56–57; Aḥmad b. Zaynī al-Daḥlān, *al-Sīra al-Nabawiyya*, 1:53; and al-Nabhānī, *Ḥujja Allāh ʿalā al-ʿālimīn fī muʿjazāt Sayyid al-mursalīn*, p.233.

narrations about the prophetic precursors to the Prophet's mission and the wondrous signs that took place during his birth, and then eating a bit of food and leaving. As I see it, this practice is a good innovation that merits reward. That is because it is an exaltation of the Prophet's rank ﷺ and a display of delight and happiness with his noble birth.[1]

٢.   إِنَّ وِلَادَتَهُ ﷺ أَعْظَمُ النِّعَمِ عَلَيْنَا، وَوَفَاتَهُ أَعْظَمُ الْـمَصَائِبِ لَنَا، وَالشَّرِيْعَةُ حَثَّتْ عَلَى إِظْهَارِ شُكْرِ النِّعَمِ وَالصَّبْرِ وَالسُّكُوْنِ وَالْكَتْمِ عِنْدَ الْـمَصَائِبِ، وَقَدْ أَمَرَ الشَّرْعُ بِالْعَقِيْقَةِ عِنْدَ الْوِلَادَةِ وَهِيَ إِظْهَارُ شُكْرٍ وَفَرَحٍ بِالْـمَوْلُوْدِ، وَلَـمْ يَأْمُرْ عِنْدَ الْـمَوْتِ بِذَبْحٍ وَلَا بِغَيْرِهِ. بَلْ نُهِيَ عَنِ النِّيَاحَةِ وَإِظْهَارِ الْـجَزَعِ، فَدَلَّتْ قَوَاعِدُ الشَّرِيْعَةِ عَلَى أَنَّهُ يَحْسُنُ فِي هَذَا الشَّهْرِ إِظْهَارُ الْفَرَحِ بِوِلَادَتِهِ ﷺ دُوْنَ إِظْهَارِ الْـحُزْنِ فِيْهِ بِوَفَاتِهِ.

2. Certainly, the Prophet's birth ﷺ is the greatest bounty upon us, and his passing is the worst calamity to afflict us. The Sacred Law (Sharia) encourages us to be thankful for bounties and to observe patience, resignation, and tranquility with calamities. The Law Giver has commanded us to perform the *ʿaqīqa* ceremony when a child is born, and that is in order to show gratitude and happiness for the newborn child, but he has not ordered us to sacrifice an animal or do anything of that nature when a child dies. In fact, he has forbidden the act of wailing and showing displeasure (with the divine decree). Therefore, the principles of the Sacred Law indicate that in this month, it is praiseworthy to express happiness with

[1] Al-Suyūṭī, *Ḥusn al-maqṣid fī ʿamal al-mawlid*, p.41; al-Suyūṭī, *al-Ḥāwī li al-fatāwā*, p.199; al-Ṣāliḥī, *Subul al-hudā wa al-rashād fī sīra Khayr al-ʿibād*, 1:367; and al-Nabhānī, *Ḥujja Allāh ʿalā al-ʿālimīn fī muʿjazāt Sayyid al-mursalīn*, p.236.

the Prophet's birth ﷺ, and it has not indicated that it is praiseworthy to express sadness with his passing ﷺ.[1]

٣. وَظَهَرَ لِي تَخْرِيجُهُ عَلَى أَصْلٍ آخَرَ، وَهُوَ مَا أَخْرَجَهُ الْبَيْهَقِيُّ، عَنْ أَنَسٍ ﷺ أَنَّ النَّبِيَّ ﷺ عَقَّ عَنْ نَفْسِهِ بَعْدَ النُّبُوَّةِ. مَعَ أَنَّهُ قَدْ وَرَدَ أَنَّ جَدَّهُ عَبْدَ الْمُطَّلِبِ عَقَّ عَنْهُ فِي سَابِعِ وِلَادَتِهِ، وَالْعَقِيقَةُ لَا تُعَادُ مَرَّةً ثَانِيَةً، فَيُحْمَلُ ذَلِكَ عَلَى أَنَّ الَّذِي فَعَلَهُ النَّبِيُّ ﷺ إِظْهَارًا لِلشُّكْرِ عَلَى إِيجَادِ اللهِ تَعَالَى إِيَّاهُ، رَحْمَةً لِلْعَالَمِينَ وَتَشْرِيفًا لِأُمَّتِهِ، كَمَا كَانَ يُصَلِّي عَلَى نَفْسِهِ، لِذَلِكَ فَيُسْتَحَبُّ لَنَا أَيْضًا إِظْهَارُ الشُّكْرِ بِمَوْلِدِهِ بِاجْتِمَاعِ الْإِخْوَانِ، وَإِطْعَامِ الطَّعَامِ، وَنَحْوِ ذَلِكَ مِنْ وُجُوهِ الْقُرُبَاتِ، وَإِظْهَارِ الْمَسَرَّاتِ.

3. I say: There has occurred to me another legal text from which we may infer a basis for the *mawlid*. It is the narration of al-Bayhaqī, from Anas ﷺ, who reported that the Prophet ﷺ performed the ʿ*aqīqa* ceremony for himself after his (declaration of) Prophethood. His grandfather, ʿAbd al-Muṭṭalib, performed the Prophet's ʿ*aqīqa* rites on the seventh day after his birth, but the ʿ*aqīqa* is not repeated a second time, so it can be understood from this that the Prophet ﷺ performed his own ʿ*aqīqa* to display gratitude for Allah creating him as a mercy unto the worlds and to honour his *Umma*. Therefore, it is also recommended for us to display gratitude for his birth by gathering with the brethren, feeding others, and other forms of good deeds and displays of happiness.[2]

---

[1] Al-Suyūṭī, *Ḥusn al-maqṣid fī ʿamal al-mawlid*, p.54–55; and al-Suyūṭī, *al-Ḥāwī li al-fatāwā*, p.203.

[2] Al-Suyūṭī, *Ḥusn al-maqṣid fī ʿamal al-mawlid*, p.64–65; al-Suyūṭī, *al-Ḥāwī li al-fatāwā*, p.206; al-Ṣāliḥī, *Subul al-hudā wa al-rashād fī sīra Khayr al-ʿibād*, 1:367; al-Zurqānī, *Sharḥ al-mawāhib al-ladunya bi al-minaḥ al-Muḥammadiyya*, 1:263–264; and al-Nabhānī, *Ḥujja Allāh ʿalā al-ʿālimīn fī muʿjazāt Sayyid al-mursalīn*, p.237.

6.22 SHIHĀB AL-DĪN ABŪ AL-ʿABBĀS AL-QASṬALLĀNĪ (851–923 AH)

Shihāb al-Dīn Abū al-ʿAbbās Aḥmad b. Abī Bakr al-Qasṭallānī (1448–1517 CE), the author of *Irshād al-ṣārī li- sharḥ Ṣaḥīḥ al-Bukhārī*, wrote in regards to the *mawlid*:

وَقَدْ رُؤِيَ أَبُوْلَـهَبٍ بَعْدَ مَوْتِهِ فِي النَّوْمِ، فَقِيْلَ لَهُ: مَا حَالُكَ؟ فَقَالَ: فِي النَّارِ، إِلَّا أَنَّهُ خُفِّفَ عَنِّي كُلَّ لَيْلَةِ اثْنَيْنِ، وَأَمُصُّ مِنْ بَيْنِ أُصْبُعَيْ هَاتَيْنِ مَاءً - وَأَشَارَ بِرَأْسِ أُصْبُعِهِ - وَأَنَّ ذَلِكَ بِإِعْتَاقِي لِثُوَيْبَةَ عِنْدَمَا بَشَّرَتْنِي بِوِلَادَةِ النَّبِيِّ ﷺ وَبِإِرْضَاعِهَا لَهُ.

قَالَ ابْنُ الْـجَوْزِيِّ: فَإِذَا كَانَ هَذَا أَبُوْلَـهَبٍ الْكَافِرُ الَّذِي نَزَلَ الْقُرآنُ بِذَمِّهِ جُوْزِيَ فِي النَّارِ بِفَرَحِهِ لَيْلَةَ مَوْلِدِ النَّبِيِّ ﷺ بِهِ، فَمَـا حَالُ الْـمُسْلِمِ الْـمُوَحِّدِ مِنْ أُمَّتِهِ يَسُرُّ بِمَوْلِدِهِ، وَيَبْذُلُ مَا تَصِلُ إِلَيْهِ قُدْرَتُهُ فِي مَحَبَّتِهِ ﷺ؟ لَعَمْرِي! إِنَّمَـا يَكُوْنُ جَزَاؤُهُ مِنَ اللهِ الْكَرِيْمِ أَنْ يُدْخِلَهُ بِفَضْلِهِ الْعَمِيْمِ جَنَّاتِ النَّعِيْمِ.

وَلَا زَالَ أَهْلُ الْإِسْلَامِ يَحْتَفِلُوْنَ بِشَهْرِ مَوْلِدِهِ، وَيَعْمَلُوْنَ الْوَلَائِمَ، وَيَتَصَدَّقُوْنَ فِي لَيَالِيْهِ بِأَنْوَاعِ الصَّدَقَاتِ، وَيُظْهِرُوْنَ السُّرُوْرَ وَيَزِيْدُوْنَ فِي الْـمَبَرَّاتِ. وَيَعْتَنُوْنَ بِقِرَاءَةِ مَوْلِدِهِ الْكَرِيْمِ، وَيَظْهَرُ عَلَيْهِمْ مِنْ بَرَكَاتِهِ كُلُّ فَضْلٍ عَظِيْمٍ.

وَمِـمَّـا جُرِّبَ مِنْ خَوَاصِّهِ أَنَّهُ أَمَانٌ فِي ذَلِكَ الْعَامِ، وَبُشْرَى عَاجِلَةٌ بِنَيْلِ الْبُغْيَةِ وَالْـمَرَامِ، فَرَحِمَ اللهُ امْرَءًا اتَّخَذَ لَيَالِـي شَهْرِ مَوْلِدِهِ الْـمُبَارَكِ أَعْيَادًا، لِيَكُوْنَ أَشَدَّ عِلَّةً عَلَى مَنْ فِي قَلْبِهِ مَرَضٌ وَأَعْيَا دَاءٍ.

Abū Lahab was seen in a dream after his death. He was asked, 'What has become of you?' Abū Lahab replied, 'I am in the hellfire. However, my punishment is lightened every Monday evening and so I am able to drink water from these finger tips (and he pointed to the tips of his index and middle finger)—and this is because I freed Thuwayba when she brought me the good news of the Prophet's birth and thus she was able to nurse him.'

Ibn al-Jazarī said: "If this is Abū Lahab, the disbeliever whom the Qurʾān condemned, and yet he is rewarded in the Fire because of the delight he felt on the night of the Prophet's birth ﷺ, what say you about the Muslim believer in divine oneness who is of the Prophet's *Umma* and who feels happiness during the occasion of his blessed birth and spends what he can in celebration of his love for him ﷺ? Certainly his reward from Allah the Most Generous is that He bestows upon him of His vast bounty and allows him to enter the Paradise of Delight!"

The adherents to Islam continue to celebrate it during the month of the Holy Prophet's birth—may Almighty Allah send salutations and prayers upon him and grant him honour and exaltation—by arranging elaborate meals and gatherings. During its nights, they engage in various forms of charitable giving and display happiness and increase in good acts. They show eagerness in reciting the accounts of the Prophet's noble birth, and every great bounty is evident upon them due to its blessings.

One of the unique qualities of the *mawlid* celebration that has been experienced is that it is a source of security for the entire year and an early glad tiding for every good thing that is sought after. May Almighty Allah have mercy upon the person who takes the nights of the Prophet's birth as an annual celebration with the intention of it acting as the strongest cure to the sickness that ails his heart.[1]

---

[1] Al-Qasṭallānī, *al-Mawāhib al-ladunya bi al-minaḥ al-Muḥammadiyya,* 1:147–

The above quote from Imam al-Qasṭallānī clearly proves that it has always been the habit of the pious predecessors to rejoice throughout the month of *Rabīᶜ al-Awwal* by holding gatherings, donating generously, increasing one's good deeds. It has been an intermediary by which they attain Almighty Allah's mercy, grace, and blessings.

6.23 Naṣīr al-Dīn b. al-Ṭabbākh

Shaykh Naṣīr al-Dīn b. al-Ṭabbākh states:

لَيْسَ هَذَا مِنَ السُّنَنِ، وَلَكِنْ إِذَا أُنْفِقَ فِي هَذَا الْيَوْمِ وَأُظْهِرَ السُّرُوْرُ فَرَحاً بِدُخُوْلِ النَّبِيِّ ﷺ فِي الْوُجُوْدِ وَاتُّخِذَ السَّمَاعُ الْخَالِي عَنِ اجْتِمَاعِ الْمُرْدَانِ وَإِنْشَادِ مَا يُثِيْرُ نَارَ الشَّهْوَةِ مِنَ الْعِشْقِيَّاتِ وَالْمُشَوِّقَاتِ لِلشَّهَوَاتِ الدُّنْيَوِيَّةِ كَالْقَدِّ والْخَدِّ وَالْعَيْنِ وَالْحَاجِبِ، وَإِنْشَادُ مَا يُشَوِّقُ إِلَى الآخِرَةِ وَيُزَهِّدُ فِي الدُّنْيَا فَهَذَا اجْتِمَاعٌ حَسَنٌ يُثَابُ قَاصِدُ ذَلِكَ وَفَاعِلُهُ عَلَيْهِ، إِلَّا أَنَّ سُؤَالَ النَّاسِ مَا فِي أَيْدَيْهِمْ بِذَلِكَ فَقَطْ بِدُوْنِ ضَرُوْرَةٍ وَحَاجَةٍ سُؤَالٌ مَكْرُوْهٌ، وَاجْتِمَاعُ الصُّلَحَاءِ فَقَطْ لِيَأْكُلُوْا ذَلِكَ الطَّعَامَ وَيَذْكُرُوْا اللهَ تَعَالَى وَيُصَلُّوْا عَلَى رَسُوْلِ اللهِ ﷺ يُضَاعِفُ لَهُمُ الْقُرُبَاتِ وَالْمَثُوْبَاتِ.

This is not from the Sunna practices; however, if someone spends of his money on this day and displays happiness and delight on account of the Prophet ﷺ entering this world, and if he does not listen to gatherings (*samāᶜ*) that are about worldly desires and lusts... but instead listens to those that are reminders for the Hereafter and encourage

---

148; al-Zurqānī, *Sharḥ al-mawāhib al-ladunya bi al-minaḥ al-Muḥammadiyya*, 1:260–263; and al-Nabhānī, *Ḥujja Allāh ᶜalā al-ᶜālimīn fī muᶜjazāt Sayyid al-mursalīn*, p.233–234.

piety and abstinence from the world—in this case, the gathering is good, and the one who attends it and has a good intention will be rewarded. The only point that bears mentioning is that it is abominable (*makrūh*) to ask people for help without necessity or need. For them, to simply invite the righteous for a feast and to then remember Allah Most High and send salutation and greetings upon the Messenger of Allah ﷺ will multiply their rewards.[1]

6.24 Jamāl al-Dīn b. ʿAbd al-Raḥmān al-Kattānī

Jamāl al-Dīn b. ʿAbd al-Raḥmān b. ʿAbd al-Mālik al-Kattānī writes:

مَوْلِدُ رَسُوْلِ اللهِ ﷺ مُبَجَّلٌ مُكَرَّمٌ، قُدِّسَ يَوْمُ وِلَادَتِهِ وَشُرِّفَ وَعُظِّمَ وَكَانَ وُجُوْدُهُ ﷺ مَبْدَأَ سَبَبِ النَّجَاةِ لِمَنِ اتَّبَعَهُ وَتَقْلِيْلِ حَظِّ جَهَنَّمَ لِمَنْ أُعِدَّ لَهَا لِفَرَحِهِ بِوِلَادَتِهِ ﷺ وَتَمَّتْ بَرَكَاتُهُ عَلَى مَنِ اهْتَدَى بِهِ، فَشَابَهَ هَذَا الْيَوْمُ يَوْمَ الْجُمُعَةِ مِنْ حَيْثُ أَنَّ يَوْمَ الْجُمُعَةِ لَا تُسَعَّرُ فِيْهِ جَهَنَّمُ، هَكَذَا وَرَدَ عَنْهُ ﷺ فَمِنَ الْمُنَاسِبِ إِظْهَارُ السُّرُوْرِ وَإِنْفَاقُ الْمَيْسُوْرِ وَإِجَابَةُ مَنْ دَعَاهُ رَبُّ الْوَلِيْمَةِ لِلْحُضُوْرِ.

The commemoration of the birth of Allah's Messenger ﷺ is honoured and magnified and is a means of revering and honouring the day of his blessed birth. His existence was the means of salvation for those who follow him and the means of diminishing the denizens of Hell (for those who display happiness with his blessed birth). It is for this reason that it is appropriate to openly display happiness and spend wealth (on that day) ﷺ, and his blessings are complete for those who follow his guidance. This day resembles Friday in that the Hellfire is not stoked on Friday—as was reported from the Prophet ﷺ—and so for

[1] Ibid., 1:364.

that reason, one should display delight and spend of what he can and respond to those who invite him as he would respond to a wedding banquet (*walīma*).[1]

6.25 Imam Yūsuf b. ʿAlī b. Zarīq al-Shāmī

Ibn Ẓufar reports that Yūsuf b. ʿAlī b. Zarīq al-Shāmī (who was Levantine by origin and was born in the city of *Ḥajjār* in Egypt) would hold gatherings of *Mawlid al-Nabī* ﷺ at his home, and he said:

رَأَيْتُ النَّبِيَّ ﷺ فِي الْـمَنَامِ مُنْذُ عِشْرِيْنَ سَنَةً، وَكَانَ لِي أَخٌ فِي اللهِ تَعَالَى يُقَالُ لَهُ: اَلشَّيْخُ أَبُوْ بَكْرٍ الْـحَجَّارُ، فَرَأَيْتُ كَأَنَّنِي وَأَبَا بَكْرٍ هَذَا بَيْنَ يَدَيْ النَّبِيِّ ﷺ جَالِسَيْنِ، فَأَمْسَكَ أَبُوْ بَكْرٍ لِـحْيَةَ نَفْسِهِ وَفَرَّقَهَا نِصْفَيْنِ، وَذَكَرَ لِلنَّبِيِّ ﷺ كَلاماً لَـمْ أَفْهَمْهُ. فَقَالَ النَّبِيُّ ﷺ مُجِيْباً لَهُ: لَوْلَا هَذَا لَكَانَتْ هَذِهِ فِي النَّارِ. وَدَارَ إِلَيَّ، وَقَالَ: لَأَضْرِبَنَّكَ. وَكَانَ بِيَدِهِ قَضِيْبٌ، فَقُلْتُ: لِأَيِّ شَيْءٍ يَا رَسُوْلَ اللهِ؟ فَقَالَ: حَتَّى لَا تُبْطِلَ الْـمَوْلِدَ وَلَا السُّنَنَ.

قَالَ يُوْسُفُ: فَعَمِلْتُهُ مُنْذُ عِشْرِيْنَ سَنَةً إِلَى الآنِ.

قَالَ: وَسَمِعْتُ يُوْسُفَ الْـمَذْكُوْرَ، يَقُوْلُ: سَمِعْتُ أَخِي أَبَا بَكْرٍ الْـحَجَّارَ يَقُوْلُ: سَمِعْتُ مَنْصُوْرًا النَّشَّارَ يَقُوْلُ: رَأَيْتُ النَّبِيَّ ﷺ فِي الْـمَنَامِ يَقُوْلُ لِـي: قُلْ لَهُ: لَا يُبْطِلُهُ. يَعْنِي الْـمَوْلِدَ مَا عَلَيْكَ مِـمَّنْ أَكَلَ وَمِـمَّنْ لَـمْ يَأْكُلْ. قَالَ: وَسَمِعْتُ شَيْخَنَا أَبَا عَبْدِ اللهِ بْنَ أَبِـي مُحَمَّدٍ النُّعْمَـانَ يَقُوْلُ: سَمِعْتُ الشَّيْخَ أَبَا مُوْسَى الزَّرْهُوْنِـيَّ يَقُوْلُ: رَأَيْتُ النَّبِيَّ ﷺ فِي النَّوْمِ فَذَكَرْتُ لَهُ مَا يَقُوْلُهُ الْفُقَهَاءُ فِي عَمَلِ الْوَلَائِمِ فِي الْـمَوْلِدِ. فَقَالَ ﷺ: مَنْ فَرِحَ بِنَا فَرِحْنَا بِهِ.

[1] Ibid.

Once while I was in his home, I heard Yūsuf b. ʿAlī b. Zarīq, of Levantine origin and Cairene by birth, al-Ḥajjār, author of a work on the *mawlid* say, "I beheld the Prophet ﷺ in a dream twenty years ago. At the time, I had a brother whom I loved for Allah's sake and he was called Shaykh Abū Bakr al-Ḥajjār. In my dream, it was as if he and I were sitting in front of the Prophet ﷺ. My friend Abū Bakr grasped his beard and divided it into two halves, uttering incomprehensible words to the Prophet ﷺ. Then the Prophet ﷺ responded to him, saying, 'Were it not for this, it would be in the Hellfire.' Then the Prophet ﷺ turned to me and said, 'I shall certainly strike you'—and he was carrying a stick in his hand. I said, 'Why, O Messenger of Allah?' He replied, 'So the *mawlid* and the Sunna are not stopped.' That is why I have convened *mawlid* celebrations for twenty years until now."

I also heard Shaykh Yūsuf say, "I heard my brother, Abū Bakr al-Ḥajjār, say, 'I heard Manṣūr al-Nashhār say, "I beheld the Prophet ﷺ in a dream and he said to me, 'Tell him that he must not let it stop (i.e., the *mawlid* celebration); it is not your concern whether someone eats or doesn't eat.'"'" I also heard my Shaykh, Abū ʿAbd Allāh b. Abī Muhammad al-Nuʿmān, say, "I heard Shaykh Abū Mūsā al-Zarhūnī say, 'I beheld the Prophet ﷺ in a dream and mentioned to him the words of the jurists regarding the practice of holding banquets in celebration of the *mawlid*. He said to me, "He who is delighted by us, we will be delighted with him."'"[1]

6.26 MUHAMMAD B. YŪSUF AL-ṢĀLIḤĪ AL-SHĀMĪ (D. 942 AH)

Abū ʿAbd Allāh Muhammad b. Yūsuf b. ʿAlī b. Yūsuf al-Ṣāliḥī al-Shāmī (d. 1536 CE) is the author of the wonderful and renowned biography of the Prophet ﷺ, *Subul al-hudā wa al-rishād fī sīra Khayr*

[1] Ibid, 1:363.

al-ʿibād ﷺ. In the very first volume, he devotes an entire chapter to the topic of *Mawlid al-Nabī* ﷺ. He transmits the statement of scholars on this issue and their manner of commemorating it. This book has been quoted extensively within this chapter.

6.27 Ibn al-Ḥajar al-Haytamī al-Makkī (909–973 AH)

Aḥmad b. Muhammad b. ʿAlī b. Ḥajar al-Haythamī al-Makkī (1503–1566 CE) was asked whether the gatherings of *mawlid* and *dhikr* were Sunna or *bidʿa*. The imam replied:

الْـمَوَالِدُ وَالْأَذْكَارُ الَّتِي تُفْعَلُ عِنْدَنَا أَكْثَرُهَا مُشْتَمِلٌ عَلَى خَيْرٍ، كَصَدَقَةٍ، وَذِكْرٍ، وَصَلَاةٍ وَسَلَامٍ عَلَى رَسُوْلِ اللهِ ﷺ وَمَدْحِهِ.

> Most of the *mawlid* celebrations and accompanying forms of remembrance that take place here are comprised of noble deeds like charity, remembrance, and prayers and salutations upon the Messenger of Allah ﷺ.[1]

Ibn Ḥajar al-Haythamī al-Makkī wrote a treatise on the *mawlid* entitled '*Mawlid al-Nabī* ﷺ', in which he remarks:

أَوَّلُ مَنْ أَرْضَعَتْهُ ثُوَيْبَةُ مَوْلَاةُ عَمِّهِ أَبِي لَـهَبٍ، أَعْتَقَهَا لَـمَّا بَشَّرَتْهُ بِوِلَادَتِهِ فَخَفَّفَ اللهُ عَنْهُ مِنْ عَذَابِهِ كُلَّ لَيْلَةِ اثْنَيْنِ جَزَاءً لِفَرَحِهِ فِيْهَا بِمَوْلِدِهِ ﷺ.

> The first lady to nurse the Prophet ﷺ was Thuwayba, who was the freed slave-girl of his uncle Abū Lahab. Abū Lahab freed her when she informed him of the Prophet's birth. Subsequently, Allah ﷻ reduced his punishment every Monday night as a recompense for his display of happiness upon the Prophet's birthday.[2]

---

1 Al-Haythamī, *al-Fatāwā al-ḥadīthiyya*, p.202.

2 Al-Haythamī, *Mawlid al-Nabī* ﷺ, p.27.

6.28 MUHAMMAD B. JĀR ALLĀH B. ẒAHĪRA AL-ḤANAFĪ (D. 986 AH)

Jamāl al-Dīn Muhammad Jār Allāh b. Muhammad Nūr al-Dīn b. Ẓahīra al-Qurashī al-Ḥanafī (d. 1587 AH) in his work, *al-Jāmiᶜ al-laṭīf fī faḍl Makka wa ahlihā wa bināʾ al-bayt al-sharīf*, described the custom of the inhabitants of Mecca in celebrating the *mawlid*. He states:

وَجَرَتِ الْعَادَةُ بِمَكَّةَ لَيْلَةَ الثَّانِي عَشَرَ مِنْ رَبِيْعِ الْأَوَّلِ فِي كُلِّ عَامٍ أَنَّ قَاضِيَ مَكَّةَ الشَّافِعِيَّ يَتَهَيَّأُ لِزِيَارَةِ هَذَا الْـمَحَلِّ الشَّرِيْفِ بَعْدَ صَلَاةِ الْـمَغْرِبِ فِي جَمْعٍ عَظِيْمٍ، مِنْهُمُ الثَّلَاثَةُ الْقُضَاةُ وَأَكْثَرُ الْأَعْيَانِ مِنَ الْفُقَهَاءِ وَالْفُضَلَاءِ، وَذَوِي الْبُيُوْتِ بِفَوَانِيْسَ كَثِيْرَةٍ وَشُمُوْعٍ عَظِيْمَةٍ وَزِحَامٍ عَظِيْمٍ. وَيُدْعَى فِيْهِ لِلسُّلْطَانِ وَلِأَمِيْرِ مَكَّةَ، وَلِلْقَاضِي الشَّافِعِيِّ بَعْدَ تَقَدُّمِ خُطْبَةٍ مُنَاسِبَةٍ لِلْمَقَامِ، ثُمَّ يَعُوْدُ مِنْهُ إِلَـى الْـمَسْجِدِ الْـحَرَامِ قُبَيْلَ الْعِشَاءِ، وَيَجْلِسُ خَلْفَ مَقَامِ الْـخَلِيْلِ عليه السلام بِإِزَاءِ قُبَّةِ الْفَرَاشِيْنِ، وَيَدْعُو الدَّاعِي لِـمَنْ ذُكِرَ آنِفًا بِحُضُوْرِ الْقُضَاةِ وَأَكْثَرِ الْفُقَهَاءِ. ثُمَّ يُصَلُّوْنَ الْعِشَاءَ وَيَنْصَرِفُوْنَ، وَلَـمْ أَقِفْ عَلَى أَوَّلِ مَنْ سَنَّ ذَلِكَ، سَأَلْتُ مُؤَرِّخِي الْعَصْرِ فَلَمْ أَجِدْ عِنْدَهُمْ عِلْمًـا بِذَالِكَ.

One of the customs of Mecca is that each year, on the night of the 12th of *Rabīᶜ al-Awwal*, the *Shāfiᶜī* judge of Mecca prepares to visit this noble site (the Prophet's birthplace ﷺ) after the *maghrib* prayer with an enormous assembly, including the other three judges (of the Ḥanafī, Mālikī, and Ḥanbalī school) and most of the notable jurists, people of virtue, and noble households with many chandeliers, enormous candles and crowds. In this gathering, the people pray for the Sultan and then the Emir of Mecca, and the *Shāfiᶜī* judge deliver sermons that are appropriate for the occasion, and then they return to the Sacred Mosque before the *ᶜishā* prayer. There, they sit behind the prayer-station of Ibrāhīm ﷺ in front of the *Qibla al-Farānish*. The announcer we just mentioned then calls for the presence of the judges and most of the jurists, and then they pray the *ᶜishā* prayer and depart. I have been unable to discover the first person to inaugurate this practice, and when I asked the historians of the time, I did not find an answer.[1]

6.29 Quṭb al-Dīn al-Ḥanafī (d. 988 AH)

Quṭb al-Dīn al-Ḥanafī has written in some detail about the practice of the inhabitants of Mecca in his book, *Kitāb al-iᶜlām bi-aᶜlām bayt Allāh al-ḥarām fi tārīkh Makka al-musharrafa*. He explains that the residents of Mecca have been celebrating *Mawlid al-Nabī* ﷺ for centuries:

يُزَارُ مَوْلِدُ النَّبِيِّ ﷺ الْـمَكَانِـيُّ فِـي اللَّيْلَةِ الثَّانِيَةِ عَشَرَ مِنْ شَهْرِ رَبِيْعِ الْأَوَّلِ فِـي كُلِّ عَامٍ، فَيَجْتَمِعُ الْفُقَهَاءُ وَالْأَعْيَانُ عَلَى نِظَامِ الْـمَسْجِدِ الْـحَرَامِ وَالْقُضَاةُ الْأَرْبَعَةُ بِمَكَّةَ الْـمُشَرَّفَةِ بَعْدَ صَلَاةِ الْـمَغْرِبِ بِالشُّمُوْعِ الْكَثِيْرَةِ وَالْـمُفَرَّغَاتِ وَالْفَوَانِيْسِ وَالْـمَشَاعِلِ وَجَمِيْعِ الْـمَشَائِخِ مَعَ طَوَائِفِهِمْ بِالْأَعْلَامِ الْكَثِيْرَةِ وَيَخْرُجُوْنَ مِنَ الْـمَسْجِدِ إِلَـى سُوْقِ اللَّيْلِ وَيَمْشُوْنَ فِيْهِ إِلَـى مَحَلِّ الْـمَوْلِدِ الشَّرِيْفِ بِازْدِحَامٍ وَيَخْطُبُ فِيْهِ شَخْصٌ وَيَدْعُوْ لِلسَّلْطَنَةِ الشَّرِيْفَةِ، ثُمَّ يَعُوْدُوْنَ إِلَـى الْـمَسْجِدِ الْـحَرَامِ وَيَجْلِسُوْنَ صُفُوْفًا فِـي وَسَطِ الْـمَسْجِدِ مِنْ جِهَةِ الْبَابِ الشَّرِيْفِ خَلْفَ مَقَامِ الشَّافِعِيَّةِ وَيَقِفُ رَئِيْسُ زَمْزَمَ بَيْنَ يَدَيْ نَاظِرِ الْـحَرَمِ الشَّرِيْفِ وَالْقُضَاةِ وَيَدْعُوْ لِلسُّلْطَانِ وَيُلْبِسُهُ النَّاظِرُ خِلْعَةً وَيُلْبِسُ شَيْخَ الْفِرَاشِيْنَ خِلْعَةً. ثُمَّ يُؤَذِّنُ

[1] Ibn Ẓahīra, *al-Jāmiᶜ al-laṭīf fī faḍl Makka wa ahlihā wa bināʾ al-bayt al-sharīf*, p.201–202.

لِلْعِشَاءِ وَيُصَلِّي النَّاسُ عَلَى عَادَتِهِمْ، ثُمَّ يَمْشِي الْفُقَهَاءُ مَعَ نَاظِرِ الْحَرَمِ إِلَى الْبَابِ الَّذِي يُخْرَجُ مِنْهُ مِنَ الْمَسْجِدِ، ثُمَّ يَتَفَرَّقُوْنَ. وَهَذِهِ مِنْ أَعْظَمِ مَوَاكِبِ نَاظِرِ الْحَرَمِ الشَّرِيْفِ بِمَكَّةَ الْمُشَرَّفَةِ وَيَأْتِي النَّاسُ مِنَ الْبَدْوِ وَالْحَضَرِ وَأَهْلِ جَدَّةَ، وَسُكَّانِ الْأَوْدِيَةِ فِي تِلْكَ اللَّيْلَةِ وَيَفْرَحُوْنَ بِهَا.

During the night of the 12th of *Rabīᶜ al-Awwal* each year, the site of the Prophet's birth is visited, and the jurists, the notables in charge of the Sacred Mosque (*al-Ḥaram*), and the four judges of Mecca all assemble after the *maghrib* prayer, carrying large numbers of candles, chandelier and torches, and all of the sheikhs with their retinues and announcers come. They leave the Mosque and head to *Sūq al-Layl*, where they then walk to the noble birthplace that is crowded with people. A person amongst them will deliver a sermon and pray for the noble sultanate, and then they will return to the Sacred Mosque where they sit in rows in the middle of the Mosque, facing *al-Bāb al-Sharīf*. The judges then call for the Sultan and a caretaker... and clothe him with a piece [of the *Kiswa*], and then the *ādhān* is called and the people pray the *ᶜishā* prayer as they normally do. After the prayer, the jurists walk with the caretaker of the Mosque and exit from his door and go their separate ways. This is one of the greatest honours for the caretakers of the Noble Sanctuary of Mecca. People from the remote country side and the cities and from Jeddah and the valleys all assemble on this night and take delight in it.[1]

6.30 THE RESEARCH OF MULLĀ ᶜALĪ AL-QĀRĪ (D. 1014 AH)

The renowned Ḥanafī hadith scholar and jurist, author of

---

[1] Quṭb al-Dīn al-Ḥanafī, *Kitāb al-iᶜlām bi-aᶜlām bayt Allāh al-ḥarām fi tārīkh Makka al-musharrafa*, p.355–356.

masterpieces of the likes of *Sharḥ al-Shifā* and *Mirqāt al-mafātīḥ sharḥ Mishkāt al-maṣābīḥ*, Mullā ʿAlī b. Sulṭān al-Harawī al-Qārī (d. 1606 CE) has also compiled a noteworthy thesis on *Mawlid al-Nabī* ﷺ, called *al-Mawlid al-rawī fī mawlid al-nabawī wa nasabihi al-ṭāhir*. He discusses the validity of commemorating the *mawlid* and elaborates the history of this function in the Arab and non-Arab world. Mullā ʿAlī al-Qārī writes:

وَفِي قَوْلِهِ تَعَالَى: ﴿لَقَدْ جَآءَكُمْ رَسُولٌ﴾ إِشْعَارٌ بِذَلِكَ وَإِيْمَاءٌ إِلَى تَعْظِيْمِ وَقْتِ مَجِيْئِهِ إِلَى هُنَالِكَ. قَالَ: وَعَلَى هَذَا فَيَنْبَغِي أَنْ يُقْتَصَرَ فِيْهِ عَلَى مَا يُفْهَمُ الشُّكْرُ لله تَعَالَى مِنْ نَحْوِ مَا ذُكِرَ، وَأَمَّا مَا يَتَّبِعُهُ مِنَ السَّمَاعِ وَاللَّهْوِ وَغَيْرِهِمَا فَيَنْبَغِي أَنْ يُقَالَ مَا كَانَ مِنْ ذَلِكَ مُبَاحًا بِحَيْثُ يُعِيْنُ عَلَى السُّرُوْرِ بِذَلِكَ الْيَوْمِ فَلَا بَأْسَ بِإِلْحَاقِهِ، وَمَا كَانَ حَرَامًا أَوْ مَكْرُوْهًا فَيُمْنَعُ. وَكَذَا مَا كَانَ فِيْهِ خِلَافٌ، بَلْ نُحْسِنُ فِي أَيَّامِ الشَّهْرِ كُلِّهَا وَ لَيَالِيْهِ يَعْنِي كَمَا جَاءَ عَنِ ابْنِ جَمَاعَةَ تَمَنِّيْهِ فَقَدِ اتَّصَلَ بِنَا أَنَّ الزَّاهِدَ الْقُدْوَةَ الْمُعَمَّرَ أَبَا إِسْحَاقَ إِبْرَاهِيْمَ بْنَ عَبْدِ الرَّحِيْمِ بْنِ إِبْرَاهِيْمَ بْنِ جَمَاعَةَ لَمَّا كَانَ بِالْمَدِيْنَةِ النَّبَوِيَّةِ عَلَى سَاكِنِهَا أَفْضَلُ الصَّلَاةِ وَأَكْمَلُ التَّحِيَّةِ كَانَ يَعْمَلُ طَعَامًا فِي الْمَوْلِدِ النَّبَوِيِّ وَيُطْعِمُ النَّاسَ وَيَقُوْلُ: لَوْ تَمَكَّنْتُ عَمِلْتُ بِطُوْلِ الشَّهْرِ كُلَّ يَوْمٍ مَوْلِدًا.

قُلْتُ: وَأَنَا لَمَّا عَجَزْتُ عَنِ الضِّيَافَةِ الصُّوْرِيَّةِ كَتَبْتُ هَذِهِ الْأَوْرَاقَ لِتَصِيْرَ ضِيَافَةً مَعْنَوِيَّةً نُوْرِيَّةً مُسْتَمِرَّةً عَلَى صَفَحَاتِ الدَّهْرِ غَيْرَ مُخْتَصَّةٍ بِالسَّنَةِ وَالشَّهْرِ، وَسَمَّيْتُهُ: بِالْمَوْرِدِ الرَّوِيِّ فِي مَوْلِدِ النَّبِيِّ ﷺ.

The verse, ﴾*Certainly, there has come to you a (magnificent) Messenger*﴿,[1] alludes to this and indicates

[1] Qurʾān, 9:128.

that the time of his appearance should be celebrated with reverence. Ibn al-Ḥajar continued: "As for what is done in the *mawlid*, it should be confined to what expresses gratitude to Allah Most High, such as the aforementioned practices such as reciting the Qurʾān, feeding others, giving charity, and singing something of the odes that praise the Prophet ﷺ and encourage renunciation [*zuhd*], and songs that move the heart and encourage it to do good deeds and work for the Hereafter. As for what is added to this, such as singing and amusement and the like, what should be said concerning it is that the permissible therein that displays joy over the day is of no harm if joined with it, while the unlawful, disliked, or offensive [*khilāf al-awlā*] is forbidden [*yumnaʿ*]."

Now, this also applies to areas wherein there are differences of opinion [*khilāf*]. Indeed, we should be committed to doing deeds of excellence every day and night of the month, as was reported from the Ibn Jamāʿa, who hoped to do that. It has reached us that when the ascetic and devout exemplar, Abū Isḥāq Ibrāhīm b. ʿAbd al-Raḥīm b. Ibrāhīm b. Jamāʿa, was in the city of the Prophet—may the greatest salutation and perfect blessings be upon its resident—he would prepare food for the *mawlid* celebration and proclaim, "If only I was able, I would hold a *mawlid* celebration every day of the month." I say: So since I am unable to host people for the *mawlid* celebration physically, I have written these pages in order that they may host people metaphorically and with light for all times to come—without restriction to a particular year or month. I have named this work *al-Mawlid al-rawī fī mawlid al-Nabī*.[1]

Mullā ʿAlī al-Qārī also writes:

[1] Mullā ʿAlī al-Qārī, *al-Mawrid al-rawī fī mawlid al-nabawī wa nasabihi al-ṭāhir*, p.17.

وَقَدْ رُؤِيَ أَبُوْلَـهَبٍ بَعْدَ مَوْتِهِ فِـي النَّوْمِ، فَقِيْلَ لَهُ: مَا حَالُكَ؟ فَقَالَ: فِـي النَّارِ، إِلَّا أَنَّهُ خُفِّفَ عَنِّي كُلَّ لَيْلَةِ اثْنَتَيْنِ، فَأَمُصُّ مِنْ بَيْنِ أُصْبُعَيْ هَاتَيْنِ مَاءً - وَأَشَارَ إِلَـى رَأْسِ أَصَابِعِهِ - وَإِنَّ ذَلِكَ بِإِعْتَاقِي لِثُوَيْبَةَ عِنْدَ مَا بَشَّرَتْنِي بِوِلَادَةِ النَّبِيِّ ﷺ وَبِإِرْضَاعِهَا لَهُ.

قَالَ ابْنُ الْـجَوْزِيِّ: فَإِذَا كَانَ هَذَا أَبُوْلَـهَبٍ الْكَافِرُ الَّذِي نَزَلَ الْقُرْآنُ بِذَمِّهِ جُوْزِيَ فِـي النَّارِ بِفَرَحِهِ لَيْلَةَ مَوْلِدِ النَّبِيِّ ﷺ، فَمَـا حَالُ الْـمُسْلِمِ الْـمُوَحِّدِ مِنْ أُمَّتِهِ يَسُرُّ بِمَوْلِدِهِ، وَيَبْذُلُ مَا تَصِلُ إِلَيْهِ قُدْرَتُهُ فِـي مَحَبَّتِهِ ﷺ؟ لِعَمْرِي! إِنَّمَـا يَكُوْنُ جَزَاؤُهُ مِنَ اللهِ الْكَرِيْمِ أَنْ يُدْخِلَهُ بِفَضْلِهِ الْعَمِيْمِ جَنَّاتِ النَّعِيْمِ.

Abū Lahab was seen in a dream after his death. He was asked, 'What has become of you?' Abū Lahab replied, 'I am in the hellfire. However, my punishment is lightened every Monday evening and so I am able to drink water from these finger tips (and he pointed to the tips of his index and middle finger)—and this is because I freed Thuwayba when she brought me the good news of the Prophet's birth and thus she was able to nurse him.'

Ibn al-Jazarī said: "If this is Abū Lahab, the disbeliever whom the Qur'ān condemned, and yet he is rewarded in the Fire because of the delight he felt on the night of the Prophet's birth ﷺ, what would be the status of a Muslim (who believes in Divine oneness) who is of the Prophet's *Umma* and who feels happiness during the occasion of his blessed birth and spends what he can in celebration of his immense love for him ﷺ? Certainly his reward from Allah Most Generous is that He bestows upon him of His vast bounty and allows him to enter the Paradise of Delight!"[1]

---

[1] Ibid., p.42–43.

6.31 MUJADDID ALF THĀNĪ (971–1034 AH)

Shaykh Aḥmad Sirhindī Mujaddid Alf Thānī (1564–1624 CE) writes in his *Maktūbāt*:

نفس قرآن خواندن بصوتِ حسن و در قصائد نعت و منقبت خواندن چه مضائقه است؟ ممنوع تحریف و تغییر حروفِ قرآن است. والتزام رعاية مقامات نغمه و تردید صوت بآن، به طریق الحان با تصفیق مناسب آن که در شعر نیز غیر مباح است. اگر به نهجي خوانند که تحریفِ کلمات قرآني نشود.... چه مانع است؟

What impediment is there to reciting the Qurʾān in a melodious voice, singing *qaṣāʾid* and eulogies? The only prohibited thing is to alter, distort, or over-stretch the words of the Qurʾān; such acts are impermissible in poetry too. If the Qurʾān and poetry are recited in the correct manner and do not contain any of the aforementioned prohibitions, why should there be any antagonism to it?'[1]

6.32 IMAM ʿALĪ B. IBRĀHĪM AL-ḤALABĪ (975–1044 AH)

Imam Nūr al-Dīn ʿAlī b. Ibrāhīm b. Aḥmad b. ʿAlī b. ʿUmar b. Burhān al-Dīn al-Ḥalabī al-Qāhirī al-Shāfiʿī is an extremely competent scholar and widely accepted authority amongst the scholars. He was granted the title *al-Imām al-Kabīr* and *ʿAllāma al-Zamān*, owing to his vast knowledge. He was matchless amongst his contemporaries. He is the author and commentator of numerous authentic books. He composed a wonderful work on the Prophet's biography, called *Insān al-ʿuyūn fī sīra al-Amīn al-Maʾmūn*, popularly referred to as *al-Sīra al-Ḥalabiyya*. After presenting evidence for the celebration of *Mawlid al-Nabī* ﷺ, he proves its permissibility and states that it is recommended. He writes:

---

[1] Mujaddid Alf Thānī, *Maktūbāt*, *Daftar Sawm*, *Maktūb*, no.: 72.

وَالْـحَاصِلُ أَنَّ الْبِدْعَةَ الْـحَسَنَةَ مُتَّفَقٌ عَلَى نَدْبِهَا، وَعَمَلُ الْـمَوْلِدِ وَاجْتِمَـاعُ النَّاسِ لَهُ كَذَلِكَ أَيْ بِدْعَةٌ حَسَنَةٌ.

The gist of the discussion is that there is consensus on the recommendation of the good innovation (*bidʿa ḥasana*). The practice of *mawlid* and gathering people for it is a good innovation (*bidʿa ḥasana*).'[1]

6.33 Shaykh ʿAbd al-Ḥaqq Muḥaddith al-Dihlawī (958–1052 AH)

The gnostic, the exemplar of the hadith scholars, Shaykh ʿAbd al-Ḥaqq Muḥaddith al-Dihlawī (1551–1642 CE) in his book, *Mā thabata min al-Sunna fī ayyām al-sana*, has documented in some detail the virtues and merits of every month and certain special days and nights in the year; he has included the types of worship that should be offered on each particular occasion. Under the month of *Rabīʿ al-Awwal*, he establishes the permissibility of *Mawlid al-Nabī* ﷺ and proves its superiority over *Layla al-Qadr*.

He writes:

وَقَدْ رُؤِيَ أَبُوْلَـهَبٍ بَعْدَ مَوْتِهِ فِي النَّوْمِ، فَقِيْلَ لَهُ: مَا حَالُكَ؟ قَالَ: فِـي النَّارِ، إِلَّا أَنَّهُ خُفِّفَ كُلَّ لَيْلَةِ اثْنَتَيْنِ، وَأَمُصُّ مِنْ بَيْنِ أُصْبُعَي هَاتَيْنِ مَاءً - وَأَشَارَ إِلَى رَأسِ إِصْبَعَيْهِ - وَإِنَّ ذَلِكَ بِإِعْتَاقِي لِثُوَيْبَةَ عِنْدَ مَا بَشَّرَتْنِي بِوِلَادَةِ النَّبِيِّ ﷺ وَبِإِرْضَاعِهَا لَهُ.

قَالَ ابْنُ الْـجَوْزِيِّ: فَإِذَا كَانَ أَبُوْلَـهَبٍ الْكَافِرُ الَّذِي نَزَلَ الْقُرْآنُ بِذَمِّهِ جُوْزِيَ فِـي النَّارِ بِفَرَحِهِ لَيْلَةَ مَوْلِدِ النَّبِيِّ ﷺ، فَمَـا حَالُ الْـمُسْلِمِ مِنْ أُمَّتِهِ يَسُرُّ بِمَوْلِدِهِ، وَيَبْذُلُ مَا تَصِلُ إِلَيْهِ قُدْرَتُهُ فِـي مَحَبَّتِهِ ﷺ؟ لَعَمْرِي! إِنَّمَـا كَانَ جَزَاؤُهُ مِنَ اللهِ الْكَرِيْمِ أَنْ يُدْخِلَهُ بِفَضْلِهِ جَنَّاتِ النَّعِيْمِ.

[1] Al-Ḥalabī, *Insān al-ʿuyūn fī sīra al-Amīn al-Maʾmūn*, 1:84.

وَلَا يَزَالُ أَهْلُ الْإِسْلَامِ يَحْتَفِلُوْنَ بِشَهْرِ مَوْلِدِهِ ﷺ وَيَعْمَلُوْنَ الْوَلَائِمَ وَيَتَصَدَّقُوْنَ فِـي لَيَالِيْهِ بِأَنْوَاعِ الصَّدَقَاتِ وَيُظْهِرُوْنَ السُّرُوْرَ وَيَزِيْدُوْنَ فِـي الْـمَبَرَّاتِ وَيَعْتَنُوْنَ بِقِرَاءَةِ مَوْلِدِهِ الْكَرِيْمِ وَيَظْهَرُ عَلَيْهِمْ مِنْ مَكَانِهِ كُلُّ فَضْلٍ عَمِيْمٍ.

وَمِـمَّـا جُرِّبَ مِنْ خَوَاصِّهِ أَنَّهُ أَمَانٌ فِـي ذَلِكَ الْعَامِ وَبُشْرَى عَاجِلٌ بِنَيْلِ الْبُغْيَةِ وَالْـمَرَامِ، فَرَحِمَ اللهُ امْرَأً اتَّخَذَ لَيَالِـي شَهْرِ مَوْلِدِهِ الْـمُبَارَكِ أَعْيَاداً لِيَكُوْنَ أَشَدَّ غَلَبَةً عَلَى مَنْ فِـي قَلْبِهِ مَرَضٌ وَعِنَادٌ.

Abū Lahab was seen in a dream after his death. He was asked, ‘What has become of you?’ Abū Lahab replied, ‘I am in the hellfire. However, my punishment is lightened every Monday evening and so I am able to drink water from these finger tips (and he pointed to the tips of his index and middle finger)—and this is because I freed Thuwayba when she brought me the good news of the Prophet’s birth and thus she was able to nurse him.’

Ibn al-Jazarī said: “If this is Abū Lahab, the disbeliever whom the Qur᾽ān condemned, and yet he is rewarded in the Fire because of the delight he felt on the night of the Prophet’s birth ﷺ, what would be the status of a Muslim (believes in divine oneness) who is of the Prophet’s *Umma* and who feels happiness during the occasion of his blessed birth and spends what he can in celebration of his immense love for him ﷺ? Certainly his reward from Allah the Most Generous is that He bestows upon him of His vast bounty and allows him to enter the Paradise of Delight!”

The adherents to Islam continue to celebrate it during the month of the Prophet’s birth—may Almighty Allah send salutations and blessings upon him and grant him honour and exaltation—by arranging elaborate meals and gatherings. During its nights, they engage in various forms of charitable giving and display happiness and increase in good acts. They show eagerness in reciting

> the accounts of the Prophet's noble birth and every great bounty manifests upon them due to its blessings.
>
> One of the unique qualities of the *mawlid* celebration that has been experienced is that it is a source of security for the entire year and an early glad tiding for every good thing that is sought after. May Almighty Allah have mercy upon the person who takes the nights of the Prophet's birth as an annual celebration with the intention of it acting as the strongest cure to the sickness that ails his heart.[1]

Shaykh ʿAbd al-Ḥaqq Muḥaddith al-Dihlawī has mentioned the above account and further elaborates upon the virtue of celebrating *Mawlid al-Nabī* ﷺ in his book on *sīra*, written in the Persian language, called *Madārij al-Nubuwwa* (2:18–19). From this, it is clear how great a deed celebrating *mawlid* is according to him.

6.34 Imam Muhammad al-Zurqānī (1055–1122 AH)

Imam Abū ʿAbd Allāh Muhammad b. ʿAbd al-Bāqī b. Yūsuf al-Mālikī al-Zurqānī (1645–1710 CE), in his commentary of the famous book on *sīra*, *al-Mawāhib al-laduniyya bi al-minaḥ al-Muḥammadiyya*, writes:

> اسْتَمَرَّ أَهْلُ الْإِسْلَامِ بَعْدَ الْقُرُوْنِ الثَّلَاثَةِ الَّتِي شَهِدَ الْمُصْطَفَى ﷺ بِخَيْرِيَّتِهَا، فَهُوَ بِدْعَةٌ. وَفِي أَنَّهَا حَسَنَةٌ، قَالَ السُّيُوْطِيُّ: وَهُوَ مُقْتَضَى كَلَامِ ابْنِ الْحَاجِّ فِي مَدْخَلِهِ فَإِنَّهُ إِنَّمَا ذَمَّ مَا احْتَوَى عَلَيْهِ مِنَ الْمُحَرَّمَاتِ مَعَ تَصْرِيْحِهِ قَبْلُ بِأَنَّهُ يَنْبَغِي تَخْصِيْصُ هَذَا الشَّهْرِ بِزِيَادَةِ فِعْلِ الْبِرِّ وَكَثْرَةِ الصَّدَقَاتِ وَالْخَيْرَاتِ وَغَيْرِ ذَلِكَ مِنْ وُجُوْهِ الْقُرُبَاتِ. وَهَذَا هُوَ عَمَلُ الْمَوْلِدِ مُسْتَحْسَنٌ وَالْحَافِظُ أَبُو الْخَطَّابِ بْنُ دِحْيَةَ أَلَّفَ فِي ذَالِكَ «التَّنْوِيْرَ فِي مَوْلِدِ الْبَشِيْرِ النَّذِيْرِ» فَأَجَازَهُ الْمَلِكُ الْمُظَفَّرُ صَاحِبُ إِرْبِلَ

[1] ʿAbd al-Ḥaqq, *Mā thabata min al-sunna fī ayyām al-sana*, p.60.

بِأَلْفِ دِيْنَارٍ، وَاخْتَارَهُ أَبُو الطَّيِّبِ السَّبْتِيُّ نَزِيْلُ قَوْصٍ وَهَؤُلَاءِ مِنْ أَجِلَّةِ الْـمَـالِكِيَّةِ أَوْ مَذْمُوْمَةٌ وَعَلَيْهِ التَّاجُ الْفَاكِهَانِـيُّ وَتَكَفَّلَ السُّيُوْطِيُّ، لِرَدِّ مَا اسْتَنَدَ إِلَيْهِ حَرْفاً حَرْفاً وَالْأَوَّلُ أَظْهَرُ، لِـمَـا اشْتَمَلَ عَلَيْهِ مِنَ الْـخَيْرِ الْكَثِيْرِ.

يَحْتَفِلُوْنَ: يَهْتَمُّوْنَ بِشَهْرِ مَوْلِدِهِ عَلَيْهِ الصَّلَوةُ وَالسَّلَامُ وَيَعْمَلُوْنَ الْوَلَائِمَ وَيَتَصَدَّقُوْنَ فِـي لَيَالِيْهِ بِأَنْوَاعِ الصَّدَقَاتِ وَيُظْهِرُوْنَ السُّرُوْرَ بِهِ، وَيَزِيْدُوْنَ فِـي الْـمَبَرَّاتِ وَيَعْتَنُوْنَ بِقِرَاءَةِ قِصَّةِ مَوْلِدِهِ الْكَرِيْمِ وَيَظْهَرُ عَلَيْهِمْ مِنْ بَرَكَاتِهِ كُلُّ فَضْلٍ عَمِيْمٍ.

It (the *mawlid*) was not celebrated by the people of Islam from the first three generations whose goodness was attested to by the Chosen One (al-Muṣṭafā) ﷺ, so in that sense it is an innovation. This innovation, however, is considered good, as al-Suyūṭī said, "The takeaway from Ibn al-Ḥājj's words is that he does not outright condemn the *mawlid* celebration, rather he condemns the unlawful and evil things that take place in it. In the first part of his discussion, he clearly states that this month (*Rabīʿ al-Awwal*) should be specified with extra acts of piety, goodness, charity, and other acts that draw one near (to Allah). This, in essence, is the content of the *mawlid* celebration that we have deemed good."

Al-Ḥāfiẓ Abū al-Khaṭṭāb b. Diḥya (also supported it, and) wrote a book on the *mawlid* called *al-Tanwīr fī mawlid al-Bashīr al-Nadhīr*, and King Muẓaffar of Irbil awarded him one thousand dinars. The *mawlid* was also supported by Abū al-Ṭayyab al-Sabtī, resident of Qawṣ. Now, these scholars were all Mālikīs and they supported it; however, there are others, such as al-Tāj al-Fākahānī, who said it an innovation, and Imam al-Suyūṭī took it upon himself to refute al-Fākahānī letter by letter.

The first opinion is the most apparent, since it includes many types of goodness. The people celebrate it (taking great concern) during the month of the Prophet's birth ﷺ by arranging elaborate meals and gatherings. During its nights, they engage in various forms of charitable giving and display happiness (with him ﷺ) and increase in good acts. They show eagerness in reciting the accounts (the stories) of the Prophet's noble birth and every great bounty manifests upon them due to its blessings.[1]

6.35 Shāh ʿAbd al-Raḥīm al-Dihlawī (1054–1131 AH)

The father of Quṭb al-Dīn Aḥmad Shāh Walī Allāh Muḥaddith al-Dihlawī (1114–1174 AH), Shāh ʿAbd al-Raḥīm al-Dihlawī states:

كُنْتُ أَصْنَعُ فِي أَيَّامِ الْمَوْلِدِ طَعَاماً صِلَةً بِالنَّبِيِّ ﷺ، فَلَمْ يُفْتَحْ لِي سَنَةً مِنَ السِّنِيْنِ شَيْءٌ أَصْنَعُ بِهِ طَعَاماً، فَلَمْ أَجِدْ إِلَّا حُمُّصًا مَقْلِيًّا فَقَسَمْتُهُ بَيْنَ النَّاسِ، فَرَأَيْتُهُ ﷺ وَبَيْنَ يَدَيْهِ هَذَا الْحُمُّصُ مُتَبَهِّجاً بَشَّاشاً.

> Each year I would serve food during the *mawlid* celebration and donate its reward to the Prophet ﷺ. One year, however, I did not have much food to prepare; the only food I had was boiled chickpeas. I took those boiled chickpeas and distributed them amongst the people, and soon, I beheld the Prophet ﷺ in the dream standing before me with the chickpeas, happy and smiling.[2]

Shāh Walī Allāh Muḥaddith al-Dihlawī is a scholar who is highly respected and accepted as an authority amongst all schools of thoughts in the Indian Subcontinent. Shāh Walī Allāh mentions his father's practice and the subsequent dream; by doing so, it acts as an evidence for the permissibility of celebrating *Mawlid al-Nabī* ﷺ.

[1] Al-Zurqānī, *Sharḥ al-mawāhib al-ladunya bi al-minaḥ al-Muḥammadiyya*, 1:261–262.

[2] Shāh Walī Allāh, *al-Durr al-thamīn fī mubashirāt al-Nabī al-Amīn*, p.40.

6.36 SHAYKH ISMĀᶜĪL AL-ḤAQQĪ (1063–1137 AH)

Shaykh Ismāᶜīl al-Ḥaqqī al-Barūsawī (1724–1652 CE) writes in *Tafsīr rūḥ al-bayān*:

وَمِنْ تَعْظِيْمِهِ عَمَلُ الْـمَوْلِدِ إِذَا لَـمْ يَكُنْ فِيْهِ مُنْكَرٌ. قَالَ الْإِمَامُ السُّيُوْطِيُّ قُدِّسَ سِرُّهُ: يَسْتَحِبُّ لَنَا إِظْهَارُ الشُّكْرِ لِـمَوْلِدِهِ.

> To celebrate his birth is to venerate him, so long as there are no wrong actions involved. Imam al-Suyūṭī said, 'It is highly recommended that we display gratitude on the Prophet's birthday.'[1]

6.37 SHĀH WALĪ ALLĀH MUḤADDITH AL-DIHLAWĪ (1114–1174 AH)

Quṭb al-Dīn Aḥmad Shāh Walī Allāh Muḥaddith al-Dihlawī (1703–1762 CE), treading in the footsteps of his father and the pious predecessors and lovers of the Prophet ﷺ, used to partake in the gatherings of *Mawlid al-Nabī* ﷺ. Describing his stay in Mecca, he says:

وَكُنْتُ قَبْلَ ذَلِكَ بِمَكَّةَ الْـمُعَظَّمَةِ فِـي مَوْلِدِ النَّبِيِّ ﷺ فِـي يَوْمِ وِلَادَتِهِ، وَالنَّاسُ يُصَلُّوْنَ عَلَى النَّبِيِّ ﷺ وَيَذْكُرُوْنَ إِرْهَاصَاتِهِ الَّتِي ظَهَرَتْ فِـي وِلَادَتِهِ وَمُشَاهَدَاتِهِ قَبْلَ بِعْثَتِهِ، فَرَأَيْتُ أَنْوَاراً سَطَعَتْ دُفْعَةً وَاحِدَةً لَا أَقُوْلُ إِنِّـي أَدْرَكْتُهَا بِبَصَرِ الْـجَسَدِ، وَلَا أَقُوْلُ أَدْرَكْتُهَا بِبَصَرِ الرُّوْحِ فَقَطْ، وَاللهُ أَعْلَمُ كَيْفَ كَانَ الْأَمْرُ بَيْنَ هَذَا وَذَلِكَ، فَتَأَمَّلْتُ تِلْكَ الْأَنْوَارَ فَوَجَدْتُهَا مِنْ قِبَلِ الْـمَلَائِكَةِ الْـمُوَكَّلِيْنَ بِأَمْثَالِ هَذِهِ الْـمَشَاهِدِ وَبِأَمْثَالِ هَذِهِ الْـمَجَالِسِ، وَرَأَيْتُ يُخَالِطُهُ أَنْوَارُ الْـمَلَائِكَةِ أَنْوَارَ الرَّحْمَةِ.

---

[1] Ismāᶜīl al-Ḥaqqī, *Tafsīr rūḥ al-bayān*, 9:56.

> Before that, I was in Mecca, the Revered, during a *mawlid* celebration on the day of the Prophet's birth ﷺ. The people were sending salutations upon the Messenger of Allah ﷺ and mentioning the precursors to prophecy (*irhāṣ*) that were manifested upon him when he was born and the events that took place before he was charged with the prophetic mission. During that gathering, I beheld resplendent lights that dawned in one single burst. I do not say I beheld them with my physical eye, nor do I say that I beheld them with my soul alone—Allah knows best how it was between the two. I contemplated deeply on these lights and found that they were from the angels put in charge over these events and gatherings. I saw the angelic lights were descending along with the lights of Divine mercy.[1]

The fact that a prominent figure such as Shāh Walī Allāh Muḥaddith al-Dihlawī attended *mawlid* gatherings in Mecca is evidence for its permissibility. Moreover, this is clear proof that the inhabitants of Mecca used to partake in the *mawlid*. Even if today the *mawlid* is not celebrated officially, this does not mean in any way that gatherings of *Mawlid al-Nabī* ﷺ are not held in Mecca by lovers and devotees of the Prophet ﷺ. The passionate people there are still celebrating the *mawlid*.

6.38 Shāh ᶜAbd al-ᶜAzīz Muḥaddith al-Dihlawī (1159–1239 AH)

The illuminating star of the Walī Allāh family, Shāh ᶜAbd al-ᶜAzīz Muḥaddith al-Dihlawī (1745–1822 CE), writes in his *Fatāwā*:

وَبَرَكَةُ رَبِيْعِ الْأَوَّلِ بِمَوْلِدِ النَّبِيِّ ﷺ فِيْهِ ابْتِدَاءٌ وَبِنَشْرِ بَرَكَاتِهِ ﷺ عَلَى الْأُمَّةِ حَسَبَ مَا يَبْلُغُ عَلَيْهِ مِنْ هَدَايَا الصَّلَوةِ وَالْإِطْعَامَاتِ مَعاً.

[1] Shāh Walī Allāh, *Fuyūḍ al-Ḥaramayn*, p.80–81.

The blessings of *Rabīᶜ al-Awwal* are due to the birthday of the esteemed Prophet ﷺ therein. The amount of blessing that will be showered upon the *Umma* shall be in accordance with the level of salutations and peace conferred upon him, as well as the quantity of food distributed.[1]

6.39 ᶜAbd Allāh b. Muhammad b. ᶜAbd al-Wahhāb al-Najdī (1165–1242 AH)

ᶜAbd Allāh b. Muhammad is the son of Muhammad b. ᶜAbd al-Wahhāb al-Najdī (1115–1206 AH/ 1703–1791 CE), the founder of the Salafi movement. ᶜAbd Allāh b. Muhammad has authored a commentary on his father's book, *Mukhtaṣar sīra al-Rasūl*. In this commentary, he writes:

وَأَرْضَعَتْهُ ﷺ ثُوَيْبَةُ عَتِيْقَةُ أَبِـي لَـهَبٍ، أَعْتَقَهَا حِيْنَ بَشَّرَتْهُ بِوِلَادَتِهِ ﷺ. وَقَدْ رُؤِيَ أَبُوْلَـهَبٍ بَعْدَ مَوْتِهِ فِي النَّوْمِ، فَقِيْلَ لَهُ: مَا حَالُكَ؟ فَقَالَ: فِـي النَّارِ، إِلَّا أَنَّهُ خُفِّفَ عَنِّي كُلَّ اثْنَيْنِ، وَأَمُصُّ مِنْ بَيْنِ أُصْبُعَي هَاتَيْنِ مَاءً - وَأَشَارَ بِرَأْسِ أُصْبُعِهِ - وَإِنَّ ذَلِكَ بِإِعْتَاقِي لِثُوَيْبَةَ عِنْدَمَا بَشَّرَتْنِي بِوِلَادَةِ النَّبِيِّ ﷺ وَبِإِرْضَاعِهَا لَهُ.

قَالَ ابْنُ الْـجَوْزِيِّ: فَإِذَا كَانَ هَذَا أَبُوْلَـهَبٍ الْكَافِرُ الَّذِي نَزَلَ الْقُرْآنَ بِذَمِّهِ جُوْزِيَ بِفَرَحِهِ لَيْلَةَ مَوْلِدِ النَّبِيِّ ﷺ بِهِ، فَمَـا حَالُ الْـمُسْلِمِ الْـمُوَحِّدِ مِنْ أُمَّتِهِ يَسُرُّ بِمَوْلِدِهِ.

Thuwayba, the freed slave of Abū Lahab, nursed the Prophet ﷺ. Abū Lahab freed her when she gave him glad tidings of the Prophet's birth. He was seen in a dream after his death. He was asked, 'What has become of you?' Abū Lahab replied, 'I am in the hellfire. However, my

---

[1] ᶜAbd al-ᶜAzīz Muḥaddith al-Dihlawī, *Fatāwā*, 1:163.

punishment is lightened every Monday evening and so I am able to drink water from these finger tips (and he pointed to the tips of his index and middle finger)—and this is because I freed Thuwayba when she brought me the good news of the Prophet's birth and thus she was able to nurse him.'

If this is Abū Lahab, the disbeliever whom the Qurʾān condemned, and yet he is rewarded in the Fire because of the delight he felt on the night of the Prophet's birth ﷺ, what would be the status of a Muslim (who believes in Divine oneness) who is of the Prophet's *Umma* and who feels happiness during the occasion of his blessed birth?

6.40 Shāh Aḥmad Saʿīd Mujaddidī al-Dihlawī (d. 1277 AH)

Shāh Aḥmad Saʿīd Mujaddidī al-Dihlawī (d. 1860 CE) is a renowned intellectual and spiritual personality of the Indian Subcontinent. He passed away in Medina and was buried besides ʿUthmān b. ʿAffān ﷺ. He composed a treatise by the name of *Ithbāt al-mawlid wa al-qiyām*, in which he writes:

أَيُّهَا الْعُلَمَاءُ السَّائِلُوْنَ عَنْ دَلَائِلِ الْمَوْلِدِ الشَّرِيْفِ لِنَبِيِّنَا وَسَيِّدِنَا ﷺ! فَاعْلَمُوْا أَنَّ مَحْفَلَ الْمَوْلِدِ الشَّرِيْفِ يَشْتَمِلُ عَلَى ذِكْرِ الْآيَاتِ وَالْأَحَادِيْثِ الصِّحَاحِ الدَّالَّةِ عَلَى جَلَالَةِ قَدْرِهِ وَأَحْوَالِ وِلَادَتِهِ وَمِعْرَاجِهِ وَمُعْجِزَاتِهِ وَوَفَاتِهِ ﷺ. كُلَّمَا ذَكَرَهُ الذَّاكِرُوْنَ وَكُلَّمَا غَفَلَ عَنْ ذِكْرِهِ الْغَافِلُوْنَ. فَإِنْكَارُكُمْ مَبْنِيٌّ عَلَى عَدَمِ اسْتِمَاعِهِ.

O you scholars who eagerly demand evidences in support of the *mawlid* of our Master and Prophet ﷺ! Know that these gatherings of *mawlid* consist of recitation of those Qurʾānic verses and sound hadiths that speak of his excellent dignity, the incidents surrounding his birth, his Heavenly Ascension, miracles and passing away from

> this world. Only those who are mindful make mention of his remembrance, whilst those who are heedless are unmindful of it. Thus your rejection is based on your own neglect.

6.41 MUFTĪ MUHAMMAD ᶜINĀYAT AḤMAD AL-KĀKAWRAWĪ (1228–1279 AH)

Muftī Muhammad ᶜInāyat Aḥmad al-Kākūrawī (1813–1863 CE), author of works such as *ᶜIlm al-farāʾiḍ*, *ᶜIlm al-ṣīgha*, and *Naqsha mawāqiʿ al-nujūm*, writes in *Tawārīkh Ḥabīb Ilāh yaᶜnī sīrat Sayyid al-Mursalīn*—the first book on the Prophet's biography written in the Urdu language:

> Monday 12th of *Rabīᶜ al-Awwal*, on account of the Prophet's birth, was granted distinction and honour. It is the custom of the two Sacred Sanctuaries and the majority of the Islamic world in the month of *Rabīᶜ al-Awwal* that Muslims gather together for the recitation of the *mawlūd*; they invoke abundant salutations and blessings upon the Prophet ﷺ, invite people for food, and distribute sweets. This deed is surely worthy of abundant blessings and is an effective means of increasing one's love for the Prophet ﷺ. On the 12th of *Rabīᶜ al-Awwal*, a blessed gathering is held at the Prophet's Mosque in the city of Medina, whilst in Mecca it takes place at the birthplace of the Prophet ﷺ.'[1]

Muftī al-Kākūrawī also narrates the incident relating to Shāh Muḥaddith al-Dihlawī, the mention of which can be found in the preceding pages. After narrating this incident, he remarks:

> The Muslims should organise and partake in the gatherings of *Mawlid al-Nabī* ﷺ out of their love for the Prophet ﷺ. However, the condition is that one's intention should be sincere, and free from ostentation. Furthermore, the anecdotes related should be authentic, and the Prophetic miracles should be related from reliable sources, since

[1] Al-Kākūrawī, *Tawārīkh Ḥabīb Ilāh yaᶜnī sīrat Sayyid al-Mursalīn*, p.14–15.

> most people are content to attend these types of functions merely to hear poetry or unreliable traditions. The scholars have also maintained that the Prophet's passing away should not be mentioned in these gatherings as these are events of high spirits; recollections of melancholy are inappropriate within such gatherings. The topic of the Prophet's passing away is never brought up in the two Sacred Mosques.[1]

Muftī al-Kākūrawī cites the incident related to Abū Lahab:

> ʿAbbās reports that he saw Abū Lahab in a dream after his death, and asked, 'What has become of you?' Abū Lahab replied, 'I am in the hellfire. However, my punishment is lightened every Monday evening and so I am able to drink water from between my index and middle finger, and this is because I freed Thuwayba when she brought me the good news of the Prophet's birth. I get to drink water, and so my punishment is lightened for me.
>
> After mentioning this incident, the hadith scholars conclude that if this is Abū Lahab, the disbeliever whom the Qurʾān condemned, who is rewarded in the Fire because of the delight he felt on the night of the Prophet's birth ﷺ, what would be the status of a Muslim (who believes in Divine oneness) who is of the Prophet's *Umma* and who feels happiness during the occasion of his blessed birth?

6.42 Aḥmad ʿAlī Sahāranpūrī (d. 1297 ah)

Aḥmad ʿAlī Muḥaddith Sahāranpūrī Deobandī, regarding a query on commemorating *Mawlid al-Nabī* ﷺ, states:

إِنَّ ذِكْرَ الْوِلَادَةِ الشَّرِيْفَةِ لِسَيِّدِنَا رَسُوْلِ اللهِ ﷺ بِرِوَايَاتٍ صَحِيْحَةٍ فِي أَوْقَاتٍ خَالِيَةٍ عَنْ وَظَائِفِ الْعِبَادَاتِ الْوَاجِبَاتِ وَبِكَيْفِيَّاتٍ لَمْ

[1] Ibid., p.15.

تَكُنْ مُخَالِفَةً عَنْ طَرِيْقَةِ الصَّحَابَةِ وَأَهْلِ الْقُرُوْنِ الثَّلَاثَةِ الْـمَشْهُوْدِ لَـهَا بِالْـخَيْرِ، وَبِالْإِعْتِقَادَاتِ الَّتِي مُوْهِمَةٌ بِالشِّرْكِ وَالْبِدْعَةِ وَبِالْآدَابِ الَّتِي لَـمْ تَكُنْ مُخَالِفَةً عَنْ سِيْرَةِ الصَّحَابَةِ الَّتِي هِيَ مِصْدَاقُ قَوْلِهِ: مَا أَنَا عَلَيْهِ وَأَصْحَابِـي وَفِـي مَجَالِسَ خَالِيَةٍ عَنِ الْـمُنْكَرَاتِ الشَّرْعِيَّةِ مُوْجِبٌ لِلْخَيْرِ وَالْبَرَكَةِ بِشَرْطِ أَنْ يَكُوْنَ مَقْرُوْنًا بِصِدْقِ النِّيَّةِ وَالْإِخْلَاصِ وَاعْتِقَادِ كَوْنِهِ دَاخِلاً فِي جُمْلَةِ الْأَذْكَارِ الْـحَسَنَةِ الْـمَنْدُوْبَةِ غَيْرِ مُقَيَّدٍ بِوَقْتٍ مِنَ الْأَوْقَاتِ. فَإِذَا كَانَ كَذٰلِكَ لَا نَعْلَمُ أَحَدًا مِنَ الْـمُسْلِمِيْنَ أَنْ يَحْكُمَ عَلَيْهِ بِكَوْنِهِ غَيْرَ مَشْرُوْعٍ أَوْ بِدْعَةً.

Indeed, remembering the noble birth of Allah's Messenger ﷺ from authentic sources, at times free from the duties of obligatory worship, in a manner that does not contravene the practices of the Companions and the first three generation whose piety was attested to, with creed that is pure from the suspicion of *shirk* and *bidʿa*, with etiquettes that do not contradict the Companion's example which is testimony to the Prophet's statement, 'The path I am on and my Companions', in gatherings free from what the Sharia forbids, is a blessed and good practice on the condition that it is executed with pure intentions, utmost sincerity, and the belief that it is one of the several forms of recommended *dhikr*, unrestricted to any specific time. If this is the case, then we are unaware of a single Muslim who would rule it to be against the Sharia or an innovation.'[1]

6.43 SAYYID AḤMAD B. ZAYNĪ AL-DAḤLĀN (1233–1304 AH)

Sayyid Aḥmad b. Zaynī al-Daḥlān al-Ḥasanī al-Hāshimī al-Qurashī was born in Mecca. In this very city, he was a *muftī* and ranked highly amongst his contemporaries. He has written on almost every

[1] Sahāranpūrī, *al-Muhannad ʿalā al-mufannad*, p.61–62.

subject and has authored more than 35 books and epistles. In his book *al-Sīra al-Nabawiyya* (1:53–54), he compiled the statements of several notable scholars, proving that even a non-Muslim is not deprived of benefit and reward by celebrating the Prophet's birthday. So what then will be the reward of a Muslim who dies a monotheist? The legitimate pleas and heartfelt aspirations of such an individual will be swiftly answered by Almighty Allah.

6.44 ʿAbd al-Ḥayy Lakhnawī (1264–1304 AH)

Abū al-Ḥasanāt Muhammad ʿAbd al-Ḥayy Farangī Maḥallī Lakhnawī (1848–1886 CE), regarding the *mawlid*, writes the following:

> Therefore, if a disbeliever like Abū Lahab, on account of his happiness on the Prophet's birth, can have his punishment lightened, then what about the Muslim who expresses happiness on his birth and spends what he can of his wealth in his love—will he not receive any reward? This is what Ibn al-Jawzī (510–579 AH) and ʿAbd al-Ḥaqq Muḥaddith al-Dihlawī (958–1052 AH) have written.[1]

As far as specifying a date and time for celebrating *mawlid* is concerned, he writes:

> Whenever this auspicious gathering is held, it is a source of reward. The people from the two Sacred Sanctuaries, as well as Basra, Syria and Yemen, express happiness when the new moon heralding *Rabīʿ al-Awwal* appears—they hold gatherings consisting of Qurʾānic recitation and *samāʿ*. Aside from *Rabīʿ al-Awwal*, in other months there are gatherings of *mawlid* in these countries. Therefore, one must not believe that reward for commemorating the *mawlid* is received only in the month of *Rabīʿ al-Awwal* alone.[2]

---

[1] ʿAbd al-Ḥayy al-Lakhnawī, *Majmūʿa Fatāwā*, 2:282.

[2] Ibid., 2:283.

6.45 Nawāb Siddīq Ḥasan Khān Bhopālī (d. 1307 AH)

The famous Salafi scholar, Nawāb Ṣiddīq Ḥasan Khān Bhopālī, writes:

> If a person cannot do the *dhikr* of the Holy Prophet ﷺ on a daily basis, what harm is there then in specifying a time to remember him on a weekly or monthly basis, by dedicating a certain day to commemorate his biography, birth, demise and struggles? Thus, do not let the days of *Rabīᶜ al-Awwal* pass by without fruition—recite those traditions and narrations which are proven to be authentic.[1]

Further on, he writes:

> The one who hears the narrations of the Prophet's birth and does not rejoice and thank Almighty Allah ﷻ for this blessing, he is not a Muslim.[2]

6.46 Ḥājī Imdād Allāh Muhājir al-Makkī (1233–1317 AH)

The great scholar of the Indian Subcontinent, particularly of those associated with the Deobandi seminary, Ḥājī Imdād Allāh Muhājir al-Makkī (1817–1899 CE) migrated from India to settle in Mecca, where he began teaching. He passed away in this city and was buried in *Janna al-Muᶜallā*.[3] Ḥājī Imdād Allāh Muhājir al-Makkī would accept devotees from all four prominent *Sufi* orders: the founder of Dār al-ᶜUlūm Deoband, Muhammad Qāsim al-Nānotwī (1248–1297 AH/ 1833–1880 CE), and the institute's principal, Rashīd Aḥmad Gangohī (1244–1323 AH/ 1829–1905 CE), were amongst his disciples; Pīr Mehr ᶜAlī Shāh al-Golarwī (1275–1356 AH/ 1859–1937 CE), Ashraf ᶜAlī Thānwī (1280–1362 AH/ 1863–1943 CE), Maḥmūd al-Ḥasan Deobandī (d. 1339 AH/ 1920 CE) and several other leading intellectuals

---

[1] Bhopālī, *al-Shamāma al-ᶜanbariyya min mawlid Khayr al-bariyya*, p.5.

[2] Ibid., p.12.

[3] The author was privileged to visit his resting place during his childhood, in the year 1963. At that time, his burial place consisted of a single room.

and spiritual masters were amongst his spiritual successors.

In *Shamā'im Imdādiyya* (p. 47 and 50), in reply to the question, 'What is your opinion in relation to celebrating the *mawlid*?', he writes:

> All the inhabitants of the two Sacred Sanctuaries commemorate the *mawlid*, and this suffices for us as proof of its validity. How could the remembrance of the Prophet ﷺ ever be considered blameworthy? However, those excesses that people have invented should not be practiced—I will not say anything regarding the *qiyām*; indeed, I experience something unique in it.[1]

He adds:

> Our scholars tend to quarrel a great deal on the topic of *mawlid*, but I am inclined towards those in support of it. If there is evidence for its validity, why then is there all this animosity? For us, following the inhabitants of the two Sacred Sanctuaries suffices. However, one should not imagine during the *qiyām* that the birth is occurring at that moment; but, there is no problem in believing that the Prophet ﷺ could potentially grace the gathering with his blessed presence. The reason being is that the material realm is confined by time and space, whereas the spiritual realm is not. Thus, to imagine that the blessed Prophet ﷺ may arrive in the gathering is not far-fetched.'[2]

From the above mentioned passage of Ḥājī Imdād Allāh Muhājir al-Makkī, it is absolutely evident that there was not an opposing opinion on commemorating the *mawlid* amongst the inhabitants of Mecca and Medina—they all unanimously agreed upon its validity and celebrated it. This is as much of authority for us as it is proof

---

[1] Imdād Allāh, *Shamā'im imdādiyya*, p.47. Mawlānā Ashraf ʿAlī Thānwī has recorded this passage in his book, *Imdād al-mushtāq ilā Ashraf al-akhlāq* (p. 52–53).

[2] Imdād Allāh, *Shamā'im imdādiyya*, p.50. Mawlānā Ashraf ʿAlī Thānwī has recorded this passage in his book, *Imdād al-mushtāq ilā ashraf al-akhlāq* (p. 58).

for those who object to it.

Ḥājī Imdād Allāh Muhājir al-Makkī answered seven questions relating to beliefs which have been documented in his book, *Fayṣala haft masʾala*[1]. One of the queries was about his position on *Mawlid al-Nabī* ﷺ, to which he replied:

> The habit of this humble servant is to participate in the *mawlid*—in fact, for the sake of attaining blessings, I hold annual celebrations. I experience a particular ecstatic state during the *qiyām* in such gatherings.'[2]

In another place, he writes:

> This leaves the question on the issue of whether the Prophet ﷺ graces the gatherings of *mawlid* with his illuminating presence—it is very disproportionate to charge this belief with *shirk* and *bidʿa*. This is possible and it can be proven both rationally and from revealed sources; in fact, at times this actually does take place. Doubting as to how the Prophet ﷺ can be informed of such congregations and how he can possibly arrive at such destinations is a futile doubt. This doubt is nothing in front of the extent of the Prophet's knowledge and spiritual abilities, as established from the authentic traditions and the spiritual unveilings of the saints.[3]

Those people who charge the gatherings of *mawlid* with *bidʿa*

---

[1] Some Deobandi scholars claim that the book, *Fayṣala haft masʾala* is not the work of Ḥājī Imdād Allāh Muhājir al-Makkī whereas Mawlānā Ashraf ʿAlī Thānwī himself states that it is actually the work of Ḥājī Imdād Allāh, in his book, *Ashraf al-sawāniḥ* (3:355–356). Mawlānā Rashīd Aḥmad al-Gangūhī writes in *Fatāwā Rashīdiyya* (p.130–131) that Ḥājī Imdād Allāh dictated this treatise and then proofread it; hence whatever is stated therein is certainly the stance of Ḥājī Imdād Allāh. Furthermore, Deobandi publishers have released *Kulliyāt Imdādiyya*, a collection of ten papers by Ḥājī Imdād Allāh, amongst which *Fayṣala haft masʾala* is included: Kutub Khāna Ashrafiyya and Rāshid Company (Deoband, India); and Idāra Islāmiyāt (Lahore, Pakistan), have published this collection.

[2] Imdād Allāh, *Fayṣala haft masʾala*, p.7.

[3] Ibid., p.6.

and claim that it contradicts the Sharia ought to at least read and reflect upon these comments written by their very own teacher and *shaykh*.

6.47 NAWĀB WAḤĪD AL-ZAMĀN (D. 1338 AH)

The famous Salafi scholar, Nawāb Waḥīd al-Zamān (d. 1920 CE), states the following about the *mawlid*:

> وَكَذَلِكَ مَنْ يَزْجُرُ النَّاسَ بِالْعُنْفِ وَالتَّشَدُّدِ عَلَى سَمَاعِ الْغِنَاءِ أَوِ الْمَزَامِيْرِ أَوْ عَقْدِ مَجْلِسٍ لِلْمِيْلَادِ أَوْ قِرَاءَةِ الْفَاتِحَةِ الْمَرْسُوْمَةِ وَيُفَسِّقُهُمْ أَوْ يُكَفِّرُهُمْ عَلَى هَذَا.
>
> Likewise, to fiercely and sternly rebuke those who hold the gatherings (*samāʾ*) of *mawlid* with flutes and *nashīds*, or to condemn and excommunicate those who make *Fātiḥa* as immoral is a transgression in itself (i.e., the act of making *takfīr* of them).[1]

6.48 YŪSUF B. ISMĀʿĪL AL-NABHĀNĪ (1265–1350 AH)

The celebrated hadith scholar and exemplar of the Arab world, Yūsuf b. Ismāʿīl b. Yūsuf al-Nabhānī in his book *Ḥujja Allāh ʿalā al-ʿālimīn fī muʿjazāt Sayyid al-Mursalīn* ﷺ has dedicated a chapter on the *mawlid* with the heading: *Ijtimāʿ al-nās li-qirāʾa qiṣṣa Mawlid al-Nabī* ﷺ [Gathering people for the recitation of the Prophet's birth]. In this chapter, he quotes the verdicts of numerous scholars on the *mawlid* and concludes that the establishment of the *mawlid* is a sound and desirable act.

In another of his works, *al-Anwār al-Muḥammadiyya min al-mawāhib al-laduniyya*, al-Nabhānī writes:

> وَلَيْلَةُ مَوْلِدِهِ ﷺ أَفْضَلُ مِنْ لَيْلَةِ الْقَدْرِ. وَوُلِدَ ﷺ فِي مَكَّةَ فِي الدَّارِ الَّتِي كَانَتْ لِمُحَمَّدِ بْنِ يُوْسُفَ. وَأَرْضَعَتْهُ ﷺ ثُوَيْبَةُ عَتِيْقَةُ أَبِي لَهَبٍ،

---

[1] Waḥīd al-Zamān, *Hadya al-mahdī min al-fiqh al-Muḥammadi*, p.118–119.

أَعْتَقَهَا حِيْنَ بَشَّرَتْهُ بِوِلَادَتِهِ عَلَيْهِ الصَّلَاةُ وَالسَّلَامُ.

وَقَدْ رُؤِيَ أَبُوْلَـهَبٍ بَعْدَ مَوْتِهِ فِي النَّوْمِ، فَقِيْلَ لَهُ: مَا حَالُكَ؟ فَقَالَ: فِي النَّارِ، إِلَّا أَنَّهُ خُفِّفَ عَنِّي فِي كُلِّ لَيْلَةِ اثْنَيْنِ، وَأَمُصُّ مِنْ بَيْنَ أَصْبعَيْ هَاتَيْنِ مَاءً - وَأَشَارَ بِرَأْسِ إِصْبَعِهِ - وَإِنْ ذَلِكَ بِإِعْتَاقِي لِثُوَيْبَةَ عِنْدَمَا بَشَّرَتْنِي بِوِلَادَةِ النَّبِيِّ ﷺ وَبِإِرْضَاعِهَا لَهُ.

قَالَ ابْنُ الْـجَزَرِي: فَإِذَا كَانَ هَذَا أَبُوْلَـهَبٍ الْكَافِرُ الَّذِي نَزَلَ الْقُرآنُ بِذَمِّهِ جُوْزِيَ فِي النَّارِ بِفَرَحِهِ لَيْلَةَ مَوْلِدِ النَّبِيِّ ﷺ بِهِ، فَمَـا حَالُ الْـمُسْلِمِ الْـمُوَحِّدِ مِنْ أُمَّتِهِ يَسُرُّ بِمَوْلِدِهِ، وَيَبْذُلُ مَا تَصِلُ إِلَيْهِ قُدْرَتُهُ فِي مَحَبَّتِهِ ﷺ؟ لَعُمْرِي! إِنَّمَـا يَكُوْنُ جَزَاؤُهُ مِنَ اللهِ الْكَرِيْمِ أَنْ يَدْخُلَهُ بِفَضْلِهِ الْعَمِيْمِ جَنَّاتِ النَّعِيْمِ.

وَلَا زَالَ أَهْلُ الإِسْلَامِ يَحْتَفِلُوْنَ بِشَهْرِ مَوْلِدِهِ، وَيَعْمَلُوْنَ الْوَلَائِمَ، وَيَتَصَدَّقُوْنَ فِي لَيَالِيْهِ بِأَنْوَاعِ الصَّدَقَاتِ، وَيُظْهِرُوْنَ السُّرُوْرَ وَيَزِيْدُوْنَ فِي الْـمُبَرَّاتِ. وَيَعْتَنُوْنَ بِقِرَاءَةِ مَوْلِدِهِ الْكَرِيْمِ، وَيَظْهَرُ عَلَيْهِمْ مِنْ بَرَكَاتِهِ كُلُّ فَضْلٍ عَظِيْمٍ.

وَمِمَّا جَرَّبَ مِنْ خَوَاصِّهِ أَنَّهُ أَمَانٌ فِي ذَالِكَ الْعَامِّ، وَبُشْرَى عَاجِلَةٌ بِنَيْلِ الْبُغْيَةِ وَالْـمَرَامِ، فَرَحِمَ اللهُ امْرءًا اتَّخَذَ لَيَالِي شَهْرِ مَوْلِدِهِ الْـمُبَارَكِ أَعْيَادًا.

The night of his birth is superior to the Night of Destiny. He was born in Mecca in the house which belongs to Muhammad b. Yūsuf. Thuwayba, the freed slave girl of Abū Lahab, nursed him—he freed her when she gave him glad-tidings of the Prophet's birth ﷺ.

Abū Lahab was seen in a dream after his death. He was asked, 'What has become of you?' Abū Lahab replied, 'I am in the hellfire. However, my punishment is lightened every Monday evening and so I am able to drink water from these finger tips (and he pointed to the tips of his index and middle finger)—and this is because I freed Thuwayba when she brought me the good news of the Prophet's birth and thus she was able to nurse him.'

Ibn al-Jazarī said: "If this is Abū Lahab, the disbeliever whom the Qur'ān condemned, and yet he is rewarded in the Fire because of the delight he felt on the night of the Prophet's birth ﷺ, what would be the status of a Muslim (who believes in Divine oneness) who is of the Prophet's *Umma* and who feels happiness during the occasion of his blessed birth and spends what he can in celebration of his love for him ﷺ? Certainly his reward from Allah Most Generous is that He bestows upon him of His vast bounty and allows him to enter the Paradise of Delight!"

The adherents to Islam continue to celebrate it during the month of the Prophet's birth—may Almighty Allah send salutations and prayers upon him and grant him honour and exaltation—by arranging elaborate meals and gatherings. During its nights, they engage in various forms of charitable giving and display happiness and increase in good acts. They show eagerness in reciting the accounts of the Prophet's noble birth and every great bounty manifests upon them due to its blessings.

One of the unique qualities of the *mawlid* celebration that has been experienced is that it is a source of security for the entire year and an early glad tiding for every good thing that is sought after. May Almighty Allah have mercy upon the person who takes the nights of the Prophet's birth as an annual celebration.[1]

6.49 Dr. Muhammad Iqbāl (1294–1357 AH)

The poet of the east, Dr. Muhammad Iqbāl, (1877–1938 CE) once said:

[1] Al-Nabhānī, *al-Anwār al-Muḥammadiyya min al-mawāhib al-ladunya*, p.28–29.

In sum, amongst those holy days which are sacred for Muslims is the day of *Mawlid al-Nabī* ﷺ. I believe it is fundamental for the intellectual and emotional nurturing of man that he constantly observes and refreshes his memory of any article that benefits his spiritual wellbeing. Hence, for Muslims it is essential that they retain information about the perfect example set by the Holy Prophet ﷺ in order to rejuvenate the zeal to emulate him and to act righteously. There are three methods in which this zeal can be maintained:

The first method is to constantly invoke peace and blessings upon the Holy Prophet ﷺ; this is an elementary aspect of the daily life of a believer—he always allocates time for this. I have been informed that in the Arab world, when two people become aggressive with one another in the marketplace and a third individual begins invoking peace and blessings loudly on the Holy Prophet ﷺ, the two assailants calm down immediately; the opponents instantly draw back their fists. This is the impact of prophetic salutations: the remembrance of whoever it is recited for should impact one's heart.

The first method is at the individual level. The second method is congregation, i.e., the public should be congregated and someone who is fully aware of the Prophet's biography should narrate events from there in order for the community to be motivated to passionately follow in his footsteps. This is the objective of our assembly here today.

The third method, albeit a challenging one, nevertheless has to be mentioned. It is that the remembrance of the Holy Prophet ﷺ be done so frequently and in such a manner that the hearts of people are automatically drawn towards the various aspects of his prophecy. In other words, the zeal and enthusiasm created by the holy presence of the Prophet ﷺ some thirteen centuries ago can be revived today in the spirits of the people.[1]

---

[1] Ghulām Dastagīr Rashīd, *Āthār-e-Iqbāl*, p.306–307.

6.50 Ashraf ʿAlī Thānwī (1280–1362 AH)

Ashraf ʿAlī Thānwī (1863–1943 CE) is a famous graduate of Dār al-ʿUlūm Deoband, who took *bayʿa* at the hands of Ḥājī Imdād Allāh Muhājir al-Makkī Chishtī. His work on *sīra*, *Nashr al-ṭīb fī dhikr al-Nabī al-Ḥabīb* ﷺ, is overflowing with love and devotion for the beloved Prophet ﷺ. In the opening chapter of this publication, he mentions the celebrated hadith of Jābir on the light (*nūr*) of the Holy Prophet ﷺ. Thereafter, he relates similar traditions of this type. Likewise, a collection of his lectures on *Mawlid al-Nabī* ﷺ have been published. In one of his gatherings, he declares:

> It has been my habit for some years now, during the blessed time which is referred to as *Rabīʿ al-Awwal*, the virtues of which were described by the lover of the Prophet ﷺ, Mullā ʿAlī al-Qārī:
>
> لِـهَذَا الشَّهْرِ فِـي الْإِسْلَامِ فَضْلٌ
>
> مَنْقَبَتُهُ تَفُوْقُ عَلَى الشُّهُوْرِ
>
> رَبِيْعٌ فِـي رَبِيْعٍ فِـي رَبِيْعِ
>
> وَنُوْرٌ فَوْقَ نُوْرٍ فَوْقَ نُوْرِ
>
> *This month in Islam holds distinction,*
> *Its prestige is superior to other months.*
> *Spring in a spring in a spring,*
> *Light upon light upon light!*
>
> Therefore, whenever this blessed month arrives, I would narrate those distinct qualities of the Holy Prophet ﷺ, which are specifically related to his birth. I would relate them briefly, not seeing it as an obligation as there are some differences in the opinions of the scholars on that (i.e., confining it to a specific time). So, without seeing it as an obligation, I would do this for two reasons:

> The first reason being that the very remembrance of the Holy Prophet ﷺ per se is obedience and is a means of acquiring blessing.
>
> And secondly, so that the public may be made aware that we people, who prohibit the gatherings of *mawlid*, do not prohibit the gatherings on account of the remembrance, as we consider the remembrance as obedience, but solely on the account of the wrong elements that have become associated with it. Otherwise, we fully endorse the remembrance of the Holy Prophet ﷺ, which is our goal.
>
> These were the apparent reasons. The fact is that my heart yearns to remember the Holy Prophet ﷺ more during those days in comparison to other days. It is very natural that the heart is inclined towards something during the time in which the actual event occurred. When the mind is routinely prone towards it, what impairment is there if the tongue subsequently begins to narrate this matter? This is completely to be expected.[1]

In another place in the same speech, he says:

> My tendency to pay tribute to the distinctive attributes of the Holy Prophet ﷺ in *Rabīʿ al-Awwal* was something of my constant practice and not something I did as an obligation (i.e., specifically at that time). Therefore, for some years, I spoke of the merits of the Holy Prophet ﷺ routinely, in numerous speeches the names of which rhyme and have the same syllable at the end: *al-nūr*, *al-ẓuhūr*, *al-surūr*, *al-shadhūr*, *al-ḥabūr*. Later on, due to some natural obstacles, there was some gap in the routine for a while. Perhaps one reason was that the people would imagine that this practice is an obligation although this is opposed to the routine. The biggest reason of the routine was that my remembrance of the merits or virtues of the Holy Prophet was more enhanced in those days than other

---

[1] Ashraf ʿAlī Thānwī, *Khuṭabāt Mīlād al-Nabī* ﷺ, p.190.

> days instead of the requirement of Sharia or the belief.[1]

Commentating on the words, *faḍl* and *raḥma*, he says:

> In this verse, when looking at its context, we can see that it refers to the Qur'ān. However, if we were to take it as a general meaning, then the Qur'ān should be taken as one of the objects—which is more appropriate. That is, *faḍl* and *raḥma* should refer to the Holy Prophet's blessed arrival. According to this understanding, all the blessings, whether they are worldly or religious, the Qur'ān including, are contained within this. This is because the Prophet's blessed being is the source of all other blessings, and the essence of all bounty and mercy. Thus, this is the most comprehensive explanation; and on the basis of this exegesis, the summary of this verse is that whether it be the existence of the Prophet's light (*nūr*) or his physical birth, one should express their happiness, as he is the means of all blessing. (Apart from other general blessing,) the most superior blessing is faith (*īmān*), which quite obviously was brought to us by the Prophet ﷺ. In conclusion, taking all the information into account, *faḍl* and *raḥma* are the Prophet's auspicious being. Thus, one can never do enough to express one's happiness and joy upon the existence of his blessed person.[2]

These statements by Ashraf ʿAlī Thānwī clearly demonstrate that his belief was certainly not against the *mawlid per se*; rather, he was not in favour of confining it to a specific time. In his view, commemorating the *mawlid* in every form was legitimate and commendable.

6.51 Muftī Rashīd Aḥmad Ludhyānwī (b. 1341 AH)

Muftī Rashīd Aḥmad Ludhyānwī (b. 1922 CE) states:

---

[1] Ibid., p.198–199.

[2] Ibid., p.64–65.

> If a condemned disbeliever like Abū Lahab has his punishment lightened on account of the happiness he expressed on the Prophet's birth, then what about the Muslim who expresses happiness and expends of what he can of his wealth out of his love—will he not attain any reward?[1]

6.52 MUFTĪ MUHAMMAD MAẒHAR ALLĀH AL-DIHLAWĪ

Muftī Muhammad Maẓhar Allāh al-Dihlawī writes:

> Holding gatherings of *mawlid*, on the condition that it is based on sound traditions and processions on the 12th of *Rabīᶜ al-Awwal*, on the condition that it is done without committing any prohibited action, are both lawful. To suggest otherwise would require valid evidence from the Sharia—may I ask what proof the critics have against it? To argue that the Companions did not celebrate the *mawlid* or organise processions in this fashion cannot be used as evidence, because non-performance of a permissible act is not an evidence of impermissibility.[2]

6.53 THE RESEARCH OF SHAYKH MUHAMMAD RIḌĀ AL-MIṢRĪ

Taking a historic perspective, the eminent historian, Shaykh Muhammad Riḍā al-Miṣrī, has accumulated the scholars' verdicts on the issue of *mawlid* in his renowned book, *Muhammad Rasūl Allāh* ﷺ. He has authored three pages regarding the gatherings of *mawlid* the world over. These pages have been translated below:

> Imam Abū Shāma, the Shaykh of Imam al-Nawawī, said, "One of the best things that have been inaugurated in our time is the celebration that takes place on the day corresponding to the anniversary of the esteemed Prophet's birth ﷺ. On that day, charity is gathered, good acts are performed, and fine raiments and happiness are displayed. Such actions, beyond being acts of kindness to

---

[1] Ludhyānwī, *Aḥsan al-fatāwā*, 1:347–348.

[2] *Fatāwā Maẓharī*, p.435–436.

the indigent, also indicate that the people have feelings of immense love, esteem, and exaltation for the Prophet ﷺ in their hearts, as well as gratitude to Allah for having blessed them by creating His beloved Messenger whom He sent as a Mercy unto the Worlds ﷺ."

Imam al-Sakhāwī states, "The basis for the noble *mawlid* celebration was transmitted after the righteous forebears of the first three virtuous generations. Thereafter, the people of Islam throughout the lands and major metropolises continue to celebrate the *mawlid*. During its nights, they engage in various forms of charitable giving and pay attention to the recitation of his birth. And every great bounty manifests upon them due to its blessings."

Ibn al-Jawzī states, "One of the unique qualities (of the *mawlid* celebration) is that it is a source of security for the entire year and an early glad tiding for every good thing that is sought after. The first person to inaugurate the *mawlid* was King Muẓaffar Abū Saʿīd, the ruler of Irbil. Ḥāfiẓ Abū Diḥya wrote a book (used in the celebration) that he called *al-Tanwīr fī mawlid al-Bashīr al-Nadhīr* (Illumination on the birth of the Bearer of Glad Tidings and Warner), and al-Muẓaffar awarded him one thousand dinars for it. King Muẓaffar organised the *Mawlid* celebration in the month of *Rabīʿ al-Awwal* and participated in it with great festivity. He was a pure-hearted, courageous, intelligent, and just man. Some say that he would spend 300,000 dinars for the *mawlid* celebration.

"The king of *Tilimsān*, Sultān Abū Ḥamw Mūsā, was also accustomed to commemorating the *mawlid* with a grand celebration, just as was done by the kings of Morocco and Andalusia in his time and before him. Al-Ḥāfiẓ Sayyidī Abū ʿAbd Allāh al-Tunsī al-Tilimsānī recounted his celebration in his book, *Rāḥ al-arwāḥ fī-mā qālahū al-Mawlā Abū Ḥamw min al-shiʿr wa qīla fīhi min al-amdāḥ* [Tranquillity for the souls in the poetry of

Abū Ḥamw and what was said of it of exaltation].

"He writes that the king of *Tilimsān*, Sultān Abū Ḥamw Mūsā, used to hold an open conference on the night of the Holy Prophet's birth in which a large cohort of people, noble men and commoners, would gather. A stage with lavish rugs and exquisite sheets embroidered with flowers were laid out; large cushions with golden pillowcases were set out for the comfort of the participants; tall lamps like tall pillars were ignited; huge banquets were feasted upon; fire pans were kindled with incense—it seemed as if it was melting gold; every type of delicious dish was presented to the attendees in such a decorative manner as though they were bouquets of fresh flowers. The colourful dishes stirred up the appetite of onlookers; their eyes glowed with delight upon the very sight of the edibles; the most beautiful fragrances emanated and perfumed the gathering. Guests were seated according to rank as deemed appropriate for the function.

At the conclusion of the function, attendees were treated to eulogies that paid tribute to the grandeur of the Holy Prophet ﷺ. Sermons were delivered that enjoined good, forbade evil and encouraged repentance. These eloquent words were delightful to the ears and were infused in to the hearts of the listeners..."

In this age of ours, Muslims all over the Islamic world celebrate the Prophet's birthday. In Egypt, there are public readings of his birth, and charity is donated to the poor and needy. In Cairo, after midday, there is a stream of people which passes by the head governorate's office and directs itself towards the Abbasiya Square, striding past the streets in police-protected areas. This procession passes through Ghouria, Ashraqiya, Quella market and el-Hosayneya; it halts at el-Abaseya. Whilst travelling through these areas, crowds join, and thus, the size of the procession increases significantly. The police stand at the forefront of the procession whilst soldiers stand on either side. This day is a national holiday in Egypt; thus, tents are erected for the ministers. The ruling king or his representative also attends and is saluted by the army before entering the marquee.

Thereafter, leaders of all the Sufi orders raise their respective flags and exalt the Holy Prophet ﷺ by delivering sermons on the *mawlid*. On the conclusion of the event, the ruling leader awards the speakers with a royal robe. Sweets and drinks are distributed amongst the attendees. The royal delegation departs to the sound of roaring cannons.

In the evening, lights are placed on the tents, displaying a wonderful sight. In the morning, every office is closed due to the national holiday. The biography of the Holy Prophet ﷺ is narrated in the vicinity of al-Husseini mosque in the presence of the head governor of Egypt. Nowadays, many innovations have been eradicated, thanks to the efforts of the scholars and authorities.

This is the account of the *mawlid*. Along with this, we continuously request that the ruling elite vehemently condemn everything which opposes the religion, such as sin and futile talk, as it portrays a negative image of Islam and stains the noble aims of the *mawlid* of Allah's Messenger.[1]

6.54 THE UNANIMOUS OPINION OF THE SCHOLARS OF DEOBAND

The scholars of Mecca and Medina questioned the scholars of Deoband on 26 issues relating to creed and disputed matters. Khalīl Aḥmad Sahāranpūrī (1269–1346 AH), in 1325 AH, gave a written reply in the form of a book called, *al-Muhannad ʿalā al-mufannad*. 24 prominent Deobandi scholars approved these answers, including: Maḥmūd al-Ḥasan Deobandī (d. 1339 AH), Aḥmad Ḥasan Amrūhī (d. 1330 AH), the grand mufti of Dār al-

1 Muhammad Riḍā, *Muhammad Rasūl Allāh* ﷺ, p.26–28.

ᶜUlūm Deoband, Muftī ᶜAzīz al-Raḥmān (d. 1347 AH), Ashraf ᶜAlī Thānwī (d. 1362 AH), and ᶜĀshiq Ilāhī Mirathī, amongst others. These 24 scholars unambiguously endorsed this text, stating that it was in accordance to their creed and the creed of their predecessors.

In this book, question 21 is about the *mawlid*. They were asked:

أَتَقُوْلُوْنَ إِنَّ ذِكْرَ وِلَادَتِهِ ﷺ مُسْتَقْبَحٌ شَرْعًا مِنَ الْبِدْعَاتِ السَّيِّئَةِ الْـمُحَرَّمَةِ أَمْ غَيْرِ ذَلِكَ؟

> Do you maintain that relating the Prophet's birth is a blameworthy innovation and prohibited according to the Sharia, or not?

The Deobandi scholars unanimously replied:

حَاشَا أَنْ يَقُوْلَ أَحَدٌ مِنَ الْـمُسْلِمِيْنَ فَضْلاً أَنْ نَقُوْلَ نَحْنُ أَنَّ ذِكْرَ وِلَادَتِهِ الشَّرِيْفَةِ عَلَيْهِ الصَّلَاةُ وَالسَّلَامُ، بَلْ وَذِكْرُ غُبَارِ نِعَالِهِ وَبَوْلِ حِمَارِهِ ﷺ مُسْتَقْبَحٌ مِنَ الْبِدْعَاتِ السَّيِّئَةِ الْـمُحَرَّمَةِ. فَالْأَحْوَالُ الَّتِي لَـهَا أَدْنَى تَعَلُّقٍ بِرَسُوْلِ اللهِ ﷺ ذِكْرَهَا مِنْ أَحَبِّ الْـمَنْدُوْبَاتِ وَأَعْلَى الْـمُسْتَحَبَّاتِ عِنْدَنَا سَوَاءٌ، كَانَ ذِكْرُ وِلَادَتِهِ الشَّرِيْفَةِ أَوْ ذِكْرُ بَوْلِهِ وَبَرَازِهِ وَقِيَامِهِ وَقُعُوْدِهِ وَنَوْمِهِ وَنَبْهَتِهِ، كَمَا هُوَ مُصَرَّحٌ فِي رِسَالَتِنَا الْـمُسَمَّاةِ بِالْبَرَاهِيْنِ الْقَاطِعَةِ فِي مَوَاضِعَ شَتَّى مِنْهَا.

> Far be it that any Muslim should say, let alone ourselves, that relating the Prophet's blessed birth, rather mentioning the dust of his blessed sandals or the urine of his donkey, is a reprehensible innovation. The recollection of anything which has the slightest connection to the Prophet ﷺ is, according to us, amongst the most beloved deeds and the highest commendable action, regardless of whether it be the remembrance of his birth, or the mention of his

> blessed excretion, his standing and sitting, or his state of sleep and wakefulness—as is clearly stated in several passages in our treatise entitled, *al-Barāhīn al-qāṭiʿa*.[1]

Despite the availability of such literature, it is indeed regretful that there is so much unfamiliarity with regards to Islamic history. Preachers in England, America, Europe and the Arab world are misguiding the younger generation through their speeches by alleging that there is no basis for the *mawlid*—according to them, it is a blameworthy innovation which takes place only in the Indian Subcontinent. If this statement is to be believed, then every distinguished Muslim scholar throughout history, such as those cited in this book, would be deemed heretics and innovators; their followers would also have to be declared as deviators. None in the history of Islam would consequently be saved from this grave accusation and finger pointing.

6.55 The History of *Mawlid* Celebrations in the Muslim World

When the month of *Rabīʿ al-Awwal* draws near, Muslims all over the world, with fervour and enthusiasm, begin to make preparations for the *mawlid*. In each Muslim country, in accordance to their respective custom and tradition, this month is commemorated ardently. It should be borne in mind that the Prophet's birthday was not only celebrated by the Muslims of the contemporary age, but it has always been recognised as a significant day in the near and distant past and has been commemorated accordingly.

Ibn al-Jawzī (510–579 AH/ 1116–1201 CE) states:

لَا زَالَ أَهْلُ الْحَرَمَيْنِ الشَّرِيْفَيْنِ وَمِصْرَ وَالْيَمَنِ وَالشَّامِ وَسَائِرُ بِلَادِ الْعَرَبِ مِنَ الْمَشْرِقِ وَالْمَغْرِبِ يَحْتَفِلُوْنَ بِمَجْلِسِ مَوْلِدِ النَّبِيِّ ﷺ، وَيَفْرَحُوْنَ بِقُدُوْمِ هِلَالِ شَهْرِ رَبِيْعِ الْأَوَّلِ وَيَهْتَمُّوْنَ اهْتِمَامًا بَلِيْغًا عَلَى

[1] Sahāranpūrī, *al-Muhannad ʿalā al-mufannad*, p.60–61.

السَّمَـاعِ وَالْقِرَاءَةِ لِـمَوْلِدِ النَّبِيِّ ﷺ، وَيَنَالُوْنَ بِذَلِكَ أَجْرًا جَزِيْلاً وَفَوْزًا عَظِيْمًـا.

The people from the two Sacred Sanctuaries, as well as Egypt, Yemen, the Levant, and the other Arab lands from east to west, continue to celebrate the birth of the Prophet ﷺ and express happiness when the new moon heralding *Rabīʿ al-Awwal* appears. They go to great lengths in singing religious odes and reciting the birth of the Prophet ﷺ, and in all of this they shall obtain a bountiful reward and mighty triumph.[1]

Imam al-Sakhāwī (831–902 AH/ 1428–1497 CE), Imam al-Qasṭallānī (851–923 AH/ 1448–1517 CE), Shaykh ʿAbd al-Ḥaqq Muḥaddith al-Dihlawī (958–1052 AH/ 1551–1642 CE), and Imam Yūsuf b. Ismāʿīl al-Nabhānī (1265–1350 AH) state:

وَإِنَّمَـا حَدَثَ بَعْدَهَا بِالْـمَقَاصِدِ الْـحَسَنَةِ، وَالنِّيَّةِ الَّتِي لِلْإِخْلَاصِ شَامِلَةٌ، ثُمَّ لَا زَالَ أَهْلُ الْإِسْلَامِ فِي سَائِرِ الْأَقْطَارِ وَالْـمُدُنِ الْعِظَامِ يَحْتَفِلُوْنَ فِي شَهْرِ مَوْلِدِهِ ﷺ وَشَرُفَ وَكَرُمَ بِعَمَلِ الْوَلَائِمِ الْبَدِيْعَةِ، وَالْـمَطَاعِمِ الْـمُشْتَمِلَةِ عَلَى الْأُمُوْرِ الْبَهِيَّةِ وَالْبَدِيْعَةِ، وَيَتَصَدَّقُوْنَ فِي لَيَالِيْهِ بِأَنْوَاعِ الصَّدَقَاتِ، وَيُظْهِرُوْنَ الْـمَسَرَّاتِ وَيَزِيْدُوْنَ فِي الْـمُبَرَّاتِ، بَلْ يَعْتَنُوْنَ بِقِرَابَةِ مَوْلِدِهِ الْكَرِيْمِ، وَيُظْهِرُ عَلَيْهِمْ مِنْ بَرَكَاتِهِ كُلُّ فَضْلٍ عَظِيْمٍ عَمِيْمٍ.

It was only introduced after their time with pious motives and good and sincere intentions. The people of Islam throughout the lands and major metropolises continue to celebrate it during the month of the Prophet's birth—may Almighty Allah send salutations upon him and grant him honour and exaltation—by arranging elaborate meals and gatherings. During its nights, they engage in various forms of charitable giving and display happiness and

[1] Ibn al-Jawzī, *Bayān al-Mīlād al-Nabawī*, p.58.

increase in good acts. Indeed, they take advantage of the closeness of the Prophet's birthplace ﷺ and every great bounty manifests upon them due to its blessings.[1]

Muftī Muhammad ʿInāyat Aḥmad al-Kākūrawī (1228–1279 AH/ 1813–1863 CE) writes:

> It is the custom of the two Sacred Sanctuaries and the majority of the Islamic world in the month of *Rabīʿ al-Awwal* that Muslims gather together for the recitation of the *mawlūd*; they invoke abundant salutations and blessings upon the Prophet ﷺ, invite people for food, and distribute sweets. This deed is surely worthy of abundant blessings and is an effective means of increasing one's love for the Prophet ﷺ. On the 12th of *Rabīʿ al-Awwal*, a blessed gathering is held at the Prophet's Mosque in the city of Medina, whilst in Mecca it takes place at the birthplace of the Holy Prophet ﷺ.'[2]

Having presented some general references about the locations where *Mawlid al-Nabī* ﷺ is celebrated, we shall now proceed to show how the *mawlid* was celebrated in each part of the Muslim world:

6.55.1 THE CELEBRATION OF *MAWLID AL-NABĪ* ﷺ IN MECCA

Imam al-Sakhāwī (831–902 AH/ 1428–1497 CE) writes:

---

[1] Mullā ʿAlī al-Qārī, *al-Mawrid al-rawī fī mawlid al-Nabawī wa nasabihi al-ṭāhir*, p.12–13; al-Qasṭallānī, *al-Mawāhib al-ladunya bi al-minaḥ al-Muḥammadiyya,* 1:148; al-Ṣāliḥī, *Subul al-hudā wa al-rashād fī sīra Khayr al-ʿibād*, 1:362; al-Ḥalabī, *Insān al-ʿuyūn fī sīra al-Amīn al-Maʾmūn*, 1:84; ʿAbd al-Ḥaqq, *Mā thabata min al-sunna fī ayyām al-sana*, p.60; al-Zurqānī, *Sharḥ al-mawāhib al-ladunya bi al-minaḥ al-Muḥammadiyya*, 1:261–262; Ismāʿīl Ḥaqqī, *Tafsīr rūḥ al-bayān*, 9:57; Aḥmad b. Zaynī al-Daḥlān, *al-Sīra al-Nabawiyya*, 1:53; al-Nabhānī, *Ḥujja Allāh ʿalā al-ʿālimīn fī muʿjazāt Sayyid al-mursalīn*, p.233–234; and al-Nabhānī, *al-Anwār al-Muḥammadiyya min al-mawāhib al-ladunya*, p.29.

[2] Al-Kākūrawī, *Tawārīkh Ḥabīb Ilāh yaʿnī sīrat Sayyid al-Mursalīn*, p.14–15.

وَأَمَّا أَهْلُ مَكَّةَ مَعْدِنُ الْـخَيْرِ وَالْبَرَكَةِ فَيَتَوَجَّهُوْنَ إِلَى الْـمَكَانِ الْـمُتَوَاتِرِ بَيْنَ النَّاسِ أَنَّهُ مَحَلُّ مَوْلِدِهِ، وَهُوَ فِـي «سُوْقِ اللَّيْلِ» رَجَاءَ بُلُوْغِ كُلٍّ مِنْهُمْ بِذَالِكَ الْـمَقْصِدِ، وَيَزِيْدُ اهْتِمَـامُهُمْ بِهِ عَلَى يَوْمِ الْعِيْدِ حَتَّى قَلَّ أَنْ يَتَخَلَّفَ عَنْهُ أَحَدٌ مِنْ صَالِحٍ وَطَالِحٍ، وَمُقِلٍّ وَسَعِيْدٍ سِيَّمَـا «الشَّرِيْفُ صَاحِبُ الْـحِجَازِ» بِدُوْنِ تَوَارٍ وَحِجَازٍ. وَجُوْدُ قَاضِيْهَا وَعَالِـمِهَا الْبُرْهَانِـيِّ الشَّافِعِيِّ إِطْعَامَ غَالِبِ الْوَارِدِيْنَ وَكَثِيْرٍ مِنَ الْقَاطِنِيْنَ الْـمُشَاهِدِيْنَ فَاخِرَ الْأَطْعِمَةِ وَالْـحَلْوَى، وَيُمَدُّ لِلْجَمْهُوْرِ فِـي مَنْزِلِهِ صَبِيْحَتَهَا سِمَـاطاً جَامِعاً رَجَاءً لِكَشْفِ الْبَلْوَى، وَتَبِعَهُ وَلَدُهُ الْـجَمَـالِـيُّ فِـي ذَلِكَ لِلْقَاطِنِ وَالسَّالِكِ.

During the *mawlid* celebration, the inhabitants of Mecca, the treasure-store of goodness and blessings, proceed in mass to *Sūq al-Layl*, which is the site most considered to be the location of the most gracious Prophet's birth ﷺ. They head to this site in hopes of obtaining their objectives. Their celebrations on this day exceed their celebrations on the day of *ʿīd*, and few are wont to miss it, whether they are righteous or not righteous, mindful or negligent. This is especially true for the Sharif of the Hejaz; however, these days he visits the site at other times. The munificence of Mecca's judge and scholar, al-Burhānī al-Shāfiʿī, includes feeding the visitors, residents, and attendees with the most exquisite foods and sweets in hopes of having afflictions removed. Al-Burhānī's son, al-Jamālī, dutifully followed in his father's footsteps and gives to the residents and travelers.[1]

---

1 Mullā ʿAlī al-Qārī, *al-Mawrid al-rawī fī mawlid al-Nabawī wa nasabihi al-ṭāhir*, p.15.

Mullā ʿAlī al-Qārī (d. 1014 AH/ 1606 CE), reflecting on this, writes:

قُلْتُ: أَمَّا الآنَ فَمَـا بَقِيَ مِنْ تِلْكَ الْأَطْعِمَةِ إِلَّا الدُّخَانُ، وَلَا يَظْهَرُ مِـمَّـا ذُكِرَ إِلَّا بِرِيْحِ الرَّيْحَانِ، فَالْـحَالُ كَمَـا قَالَ:

أَمَّا الْـخِيَامُ فَإِنَّهَا كَخِيَامِهِمْ

وَأَرَى نِسَاءَ الْـحَيِّ غَيْرَ نِسَائِهِمْ

I say: As for today, only the smoke from the cooking fire remains and none of what we mentioned is seen, except as a lingering fragrance of flowers. The situation is as some say:

Their tents are like their tents;
But I see that the women are not their women.[1]

Muhammad Jār Allāh b. Ẓahīra al-Ḥanafī (d. 986 AH/ 1587 CE), describing the commemoration of *Mawlid al-Nabī* ﷺ in Mecca, writes:

وَجَرَتِ الْعَادَةُ بِمَكَّةَ لَيْلَةَ الثَّانِي عَشَرَ مِنْ رَبِيْعِ الْأَوَّلِ فِي كُلِّ عَامٍ أَنَّ قَاضِيَ مَكَّةَ الشَّافِعِيَّ يَتَهَيَّأُ لِزِيَارَةِ هَذَا الْـمَحَلِّ الشَّرِيْفِ بَعْدَ صَلَاةِ الْـمَغْرِبِ فِي جَمْعٍ عَظِيْمٍ، مِنْهُمُ الثَّلَاثَةُ الْقُضَاةُ وَأَكْثَرُ الْأَعْيَانِ مِنَ الْفُقَهَاءِ وَالْفُضَلَاءِ، وَذَوِي الْبُيُوْتِ بِفَوَانِيْسَ كَثِيْرَةٍ وَشُمُوْعٍ عَظِيْمَةٍ وَزِحَامٍ عَظِيْمٍ. وَيُدْعَى فِيْهِ لِلسُّلْطَانِ وَلِأَمِيْرِ مَكَّةَ، وَلِلْقَاضِي الشَّافِعِيِّ بَعْدَ تَقَدُّمِ خُطْبَةٍ مُنَاسِبَةٍ لِلْمَقَامِ، ثُمَّ يَعُوْدُ مِنْهُ إِلَـى الْـمَسْجِدِ الْـحَرَامِ قُبَيْلَ الْعِشَاءِ، وَيَجْلِسُ خَلْفَ مَقَامِ الْـخَلِيْلِ عليه السلام بِإِزَاءِ قُبَّةِ الْفَرَاشِيْنَ، وَيَدْعُو الدَّاعِي لِـمَنْ ذُكِرَ

[1] Ibid.

آنِفًا بِحُضُوْرِ الْقُضَاةِ وَأَكْثَرِ الْفُقَهَاءِ. ثُمَّ يُصَلُّوْنَ الْعِشَاءَ وَيَنْصَرِفُوْنَ، وَلَمْ أَقِفْ عَلَى أَوَّلِ مَنْ سَنَّ ذَلِكَ، سَأَلْتُ مُؤَرِّخِي الْعَصْرِ فَلَمْ أَجِدْ عِنْدَهُمْ عِلْمًا بِذَالِكَ.

One of the customs of Mecca is that each year, on the night of the 12th of *Rabīʿ al-Awwal*, the *Shāfiʿī* judge of Mecca prepares to visit this noble site (the Prophet's birthplace ﷺ) after the *maghrib* prayer with an enormous assembly, including the other three judges (of the Ḥanafī, Mālikī, and Ḥanbalī school) and most of the notable jurists, people of virtue, and noble households, with many chandeliers, enormous candles, and crowds. In this gathering, the people pray for the Sultan and then the Emir of Mecca, and the *Shāfiʿī* judge deliver sermons that are appropriate for the occasion, and then they return to the Sacred Mosque before the *ʿīsha* prayer. There, they sit behind the prayer-station of Ibrāhīm ﷺ in front of the *Qibla al-Farānish*. The announcer we just mentioned then calls for the presence of the judges and most of the jurists, and then they pray the *ʿīshāʾ* prayer and depart. I have been unable to discover the first person to inaugurate this practice, and when I asked the historians of the time, I did not find an answer.[1]

Quṭb al-Dīn al-Ḥanafī has written in some detail about the practice of the inhabitants of Mecca in his book, *Kitāb al-iʿlām bi-aʿlām bayt Allāh al-ḥarām fi tārīkh Makka al-musharrafa*. He explains that the residents of Mecca have been celebrating *Mawlid al-Nabī* ﷺ for centuries:

يُزَارُ مَوْلِدُ النَّبِيِّ ﷺ الْمَكَانِيُّ فِي اللَّيْلَةِ الثَّانِيَةِ عَشَرَ مِنْ شَهْرِ رَبِيْعِ الْأَوَّلِ فِي كُلِّ عَامٍ، فَيَجْتَمِعُ الْفُقَهَاءُ وَالْأَعْيَانُ عَلَى نِظَامِ الْمَسْجِدِ الْحَرَامِ

---

[1] Ibn Ẓahīra, *al-Jāmiʿ al-laṭīf fī faḍl Makka wa ahlihā wa bināʾ al-bayt al-sharīf*, p.201–202.

وَالْقُضَاةُ الْأَرْبَعَةُ بِمَكَّةَ الْـمُشَرَّفَةِ بَعْدَ صَلَاةِ الْـمَغْرِبِ بِالشُّمُوْعِ الْكَثِيْرَةِ وَالْـمُفَرَّغَاتِ وَالْفَوَانِيْسِ وَالْـمَشَاغِلِ وَجَمِيْعِ الْـمَشَائِخِ مَعَ طَوَائِفِهِمْ بِالْأَعْلَامِ الْكَثِيْرَةِ وَيَخْرُجُوْنَ مِنَ الْـمَسْجِدِ إِلَـى سُوْقِ اللَّيْلِ وَيَمْشُوْنَ فِيْهِ إِلَـى مَحَلِّ الْـمَوْلِدِ الشَّرِيْفِ بِازْدِحَامٍ وَيَخْطُبُ فِيْهِ شَخْصٌ وَيَدْعُوْ لِلسَّلْطَنَةِ الشَّرِيْفَةِ، ثُمَّ يَعُوْدُوْنَ إِلَـى الْـمَسْجِدِ الْـحَرَامِ وَيَجْلِسُوْنَ صُفُوْفًا فِـي وَسَطِ الْـمَسْجِدِ مِنْ جِهَةِ الْبَابِ الشَّرِيْفِ خَلْفَ مَقَامِ الشَّافِعِيَّةِ وَيَقِفُ رَئِيْسُ زَمْزَمَ بَيْنَ يَدَيْ نَاظِرِ الْـحَرَمِ الشَّرِيْفِ وَالْقُضَاةِ وَيَدْعُوْ لِلسُّلْطَانِ وَيُلْبِسُهُ النَّاظِرُ خِلْعَةً وَيُلْبِسُ شَيْخَ الْفَرَاشِيْنِ خِلْعَةً. ثُمَّ يُؤَذِّنُ لِلْعِشَاءِ وَيُصَلِّي النَّاسُ عَلَى عَادَتِهِمْ، ثُمَّ يَمْشِي الْفُقَهَاءُ مَعَ نَاظِرِ الْـحَرَمِ إِلَـى الْبَابِ الَّذِي يَخْرُجُ مِنْهُ مِنَ الْـمَسْجِدِ، ثُمَّ يَتَفَرَّقُوْنَ. وَهَذِهِ مِنْ أَعْظَمِ مَوَاكِبِ نَاظِرِ الْـحَرَمِ الشَّرِيْفِ بِمَكَّةَ الْـمُشَرَّفَةِ وَيَأْتِـي النَّاسُ مِنَ الْبَدْوِ وَالْـحَضَرِ وَأَهْلِ جَدَّةَ، وَسُكَّانِ الْأَوْدِيَةِ فِـي تِلْكَ اللَّيْلَةِ وَيَفْرَحُوْنَ بِهَا.

During the night of the 12th of *Rabīʿ al-Awwal* each year, the site of the Prophet's birth is visited, and the jurists, the notables in charge of the Sacred Mosque (*al-Ḥaram*), and the four judges of Mecca all assemble after the *maghrib* prayer, carrying large numbers of candles, chandeliers, and torches, and all of the sheikhs with their retinues and announcers come. They leave the Mosque and head to *Sūq al-Layl*, where they then walk to the noble birthplace that is crowded with people. A person amongst them will deliver a sermon and pray for the noble sultanate, and then they will return to the Sacred Mosque where they sit in rows in the middle of the Mosque, facing *al-Bāb al-Sharīf*. The judges then call for the Sultan and a caretaker... and cloths him with a piece [of the *Kiswa*], and then the ādhān is called and the people pray the *ʿīsha* prayer as they normally do. After the prayer, the jurists walk with the caretaker of the Mosque and exit from his door and go their separate ways. This is one of the greatest honours for the caretaker of the Noble Sanctuary of Mecca. People from the remote country side and the cities and the people of Jeddah and the valleys all assemble on this night and take delight in it.[1]

Shāh Walī Allāh Muḥaddith al-Dihlawī (1114–1174 AH/ 1703–1762 CE), describing his visit of Mecca, states:

وَكُنْتُ قَبْلَ ذَلِكَ بِمَكَّةَ الْـمُعَظَّمَةِ فِي مَوْلِدِ النَّبِيِّ ﷺ فِي يَوْمِ وِلَادَتِهِ، وَالنَّاسُ يُصَلُّوْنَ عَلَى النَّبِيِّ ﷺ وَيَذْكُرُوْنَ إِرْهَاصَاتِهِ الَّتِي ظَهَرَتْ فِي وِلَادَتِهِ وَمُشَاهَدَاتِهِ قَبْلَ بِعْثَتِهِ، فَرَأَيْتُ أَنْوَاراً سَطَعَتْ دُفْعَةً وَاحِدَةً لَا أَقُوْلُ إِنِّي أَدْرَكْتُهَا بِبَصَرِ الْـجَسَدِ، وَلَا أَقُوْلُ أَدْرَكْتُهَا بِبَصَرِ الرُّوْحِ فَقَطْ، وَاللهُ أَعْلَمُ كَيْفَ كَانَ الْأَمْرُ بَيْنَ هَذَا وَذَلِكَ، فَتَأَمَّلْتُ تِلْكَ الْأَنْوَارَ فَوَجَدْتُهَا مِنْ قِبَلِ الْـمَلَائِكَةِ الْـمُوَكَّلِيْنَ بِأَمْثَالِ هَذِهِ الْـمَشَاهِدِ وَبِأَمْثَالِ هَذِهِ الْـمَجَالِسِ، وَرَأَيْتُ يُخَالِطُهُ أَنْوَارُ الْـمَلَائِكَةِ أَنْوَارَ الرَّحْمَةِ.

Before that, I was in Mecca, the Revered, during a *mawlid* celebration on the day of the Prophet's birth ﷺ. The people were sending salutations upon the Messenger of Allah ﷺ and mentioning the precursors to prophecy (*irhāṣ*) that manifested upon him when he was born and the events that took place before he was charged with the prophetic mission. During that gathering, I beheld resplendent lights that dawned in one single burst. I do not say I beheld them with my physical eye, nor do I say that I beheld them with my soul alone—Allah knows best how it was between the two. I contemplated deeply on these lights and found that they were from the angels put in charge over these events

[1] Quṭb al-Dīn al-Ḥanafī, *Kitāb al-iʿlām bi-aʿlām bayt Allāh al-ḥarām fi tārīkh Makka al-musharrafa*, p.355–356.

and gatherings. I saw the angelic lights were descending along with the lights of Divine mercy.[1]

6.55.1.1 Eyewitness Accounts of the *Mawlid* in Mecca

1. On the occasion of the most exalted Prophet's birthday, there is a great celebration in Mecca; it is referred to as *ʿĪd Mawlid al-Nabī* ﷺ. During this period, sweets are sold in dozens. In the Sacred Mosque, a stage is set up behind the Ḥanafī prayer area. The Sharīf of Hejaz, with his commanders and staff, attended the function, donned in colourful attire. They visit the Prophet's birthplace to briefly recite some odes in his praise. There are two files of people holding lanterns between the Sacred Mosque and the Prophet's birthplace; there is so much light that the shops and homes en-route are illuminated. The blessed birthplace appears to be an emblem of light on this occasion. On the way to this sacred place, visitors graciously sing odes in melodious voices.

After the *ʿīshāʾ* prayer, on the 11th of *Rabīʿ al-Awwal*, a grand conference takes place in the vicinity of the Sacred Mosque. Until 2 AM, eulogies about the Holy Prophet's birth are recited. On the night of his birth, several clusters of people set out to the birthplace and recite odes therein. From the *maghrib* prayer on the 11th of *Rabīʿ al-Awwal* until the *ʿasr* prayer of the 12th, Turkish cannons are fired from the Ajyad fortress 21 times following the completion of each prayer between this period. The inhabitants of Mecca rejoice to the highest degree during these days, singing odes in his praise and holding many gatherings in his honour.[2]

2. On the 11th of *Rabīʿ al-Awwal*, as soon as the call to prayer was made for the *ʿasr* prayer, the sound of roaring cannons was heard throughout Mecca. The residents congratulated each other on the arrival of *Mawlid al-Nabī* ﷺ. The Sharīf, Ḥussayn, offered the *maghrib* prayer in a huge gathering at the Ḥanafī prayer area. After the prayer ended, the chief judge presented his best wishes

---

[1] Shāh Walī Allāh, *Fuyūḍ al-Ḥaramayn*, p.80–81.

[2] *Ṭarīqat Magazine*, Lahore.

to the Sharīf on the advent of the Prophet's birthday. Thereafter, all the ministers and members of the Sultanate collectively set out for the Prophet's birthplace. This splendid crowd made its way towards it in a very dignified and disciplined fashion. From the royal palace to the blessed location, there are two files of people accompanied with lighting. As for the sacred birthplace itself, its light radiated so brightly and magnificently that it seemed like it was a heavenly garden.

Upon reaching the sacred site, an assembly of visitors stand there with utmost courtesy, listening devotedly to the Prophet's life-story which is recited by someone in a very effective manner. Whilst listening to the reciter, there was total silence. The fact that they were in such a consecrated place did not admit them to utter a single word—all were lost in the magic of the moment of this historical occurrence.

Soon afterwards, the deputy foreign minister, Shaykh Fuwād, delivered a powerful speech that shed light upon the life of that inspiring and most influential personality in the history of mankind, who was the centre of focus for all in attendance. Finally, the eloquent speaker recited a poem that deeply shook the audience. When the programme ended, each individual roamed around the area where the Prophet's birth took place, after which they returned to the Sacred Mosque to perform the *ʿīshāʾ* prayer. After performing the prayer, they gathered in a section of the mosque to hear the annual sermon on *mawlid*. Here too, the lecturer delivered a most expressive, fluent and articulate speech about the morality and commendations of the most benevolent Prophet ﷺ.

All government departments, offices, and schools were closed on the 12th of *Rabīʿ al-Awwal* on account of this auspicious occasion. This is a general description of this wonderful day. I pray that Almighty Allah enables me to witness such a marvellous day again in my lifetime. *Āmīn.*[1]

---

[1] Extract from *al-Qibla Newspaper*, Mecca; and *Ṭarīqat Magazine*, Lahore. N.B. These accounts were taken from an edition of *Imroz Magazine* (dated 21-10-1988 CE). The author is grateful to Saeed Badr for kind permission to reproduce this narration.

این دعا از من و از جمله جهان آمین باد

(O my Lord), may my supplication be granted from me and from the whole world.

The aforementioned account reminds us of the not too distant past when the *mawlid* was celebrated with fervour and devotion in Mecca. Such magnificent preparations were undertaken, and they have been preserved through eye-witness accounts. Alas, how unfortunate it is that this very nation in our time is in argument about the permissibility of this blessed day.

6.55.2 The Celebration of *Mawlid al-Nabī* ﷺ in Medina

وَلِأَهْلِ الْمَدِيْنَةِ - كَثَّرَهُمُ اللهُ تَعَالَى - بِهِ احْتِفَالٌ وَعَلَى فِعْلِهِ إِقْبَالٌ وَكَانَ لِلْمَلِكِ الْمُظَفَّرِ صَاحِبِ «إِرْبَلَ» بِذَلِكَ فِيْهَا أَتَمُّ الْعِنَايَةِ وَاهْتِمَامًا بِشَأْنِهِ جَاوَزَ الْغَايَةَ، فَأَثْنَى عَلَيْهِ بِهِ الْعَلَّامَةُ أَبُوْ شَامَةَ أَحَدُ شُيُوْخِ النَّوَوِيِّ السَّابِقُ فِي الْإِسْتِقَامَةِ فِي كِتَابِهِ «الْبَاعِثِ عَلَى الْبِدَعِ وَالْحَوَادِثِ». وَقَالَ مِثْلَ هَذَا الْحَسَنُ: يُنْدَبُ إِلَيْهِ وَيُشْكَرُ فَاعِلُهُ وَيُثْنَى عَلَيْهِ. زَادَ ابْنُ الْجَزَرِيِّ: وَلَوْ لَمْ يَكُنْ فِي ذَلِكَ إِلَّا إِرْغَامُ الشَّيْطَانِ وَسُرُوْرُ أَهْلِ الْإِيْمَانِ.

قَالَ يَعْنِي الْجَزَرِيَّ: وَإِذَا كَانَ أَهْلُ الصَّلِيْبِ اتَّخَذُوْا لَيْلَةَ مَوْلِدِ نَبِيِّهِمْ عِيْداً أَكْبَرَ فَأَهْلُ الْإِسْلَامِ أَوْلَى بِالتَّكْرِيْمِ وَأَجْدَرُ.

The inhabitants of Medina—may Allah the Most High increase them—celebrate the *mawlid* with great fervour. Al-Mālik al-Muẓaffar, may Almighty Allah have mercy upon him, used to go to great lengths in his celebration and preparations for it. The erudite Abū Shāma, one of al-Nawawī's teachers known for his upright rectitude, praised al-Muẓaffar for this in his book *al-Bāʿith ʿalā*

> *al-bidʿa wa al-ḥawādith* and said: "Actions like this are good and recommended, and the one who performs them should be praised and lauded. Ibn al-Jazarī added, 'Even if it only enrages Satan and brings delight to the people of faith.' Al-Jazarī also said, 'If the people of the cross [i.e., the Christians] took the birth night of their Prophet as a major celebration, the Muslims have even more right to honor [the Prophet ﷺ] by expressing their immense happiness and joy on his blessed birth.'[1]

Mullā ʿAlī al-Qārī (d. 1014 AH/ 1606 CE), regarding the custom of Imam Burhān al-Dīn b. al-Jamāʿa al-Shāfiʿī (725–790 AH/ 1325–1388 CE), states:

> فَقَدِ اتَّصَلَ بِنَا أَنَّ الزَّاهِدَ الْقُدْوَةَ الْـمُعَمَّرَ أَبَا إِسْحَاقَ إِبرَاهِيْمَ بْنَ عَبْدِ الرَّحِيْمِ بْنِ إِبْرَاهِيْمَ بْنِ جَمَاعَةَ لَـمَّـا كَانَ بِالْـمَدِيْنَةِ النَّبَوِيَّةِ عَلَى سَاكِنِهَا أَفْضَلُ الصَّلَاةِ وَأَكْمَلُ التَّحِيَّةِ كَانَ يَعْمَلُ طَعَامًا فِي الْـمَوْلِدِ النَّبَوِيِّ وَيُطْعِمُ النَّاسَ وَيَقُوْلُ: لَوْ تَـمَكَّنْتُ عَمِلْتُ بِطُوْلِ الشَّهْرِ كُلَّ يَوْمٍ مَوْلِدًا.
>
> It has reached us that when the worldly-abstinent and devout exemplar, Abū Isḥāq Ibrāhīm b. ʿAbd al-Raḥīm b. Ibrāhīm b. Jamāʿa, was in the city of the Prophet—may the excellent salutation and perfect blessings be upon its resident—he would prepare food for the *mawlid* celebration and proclaim, "If only I was able to, I would hold a *mawlid* celebration every day of the month."[2]

6.55.3 THE CELEBRATION OF *MAWLID AL-NABĪ* ﷺ IN EGYPT AND THE LEVANT

> فَأَكْثَرُهُمْ بِذَلِكَ عِنَايَةً أَهْلُ مِصْرَ وَالشَّامِ، وَلِسُلْطَانِ مِصْرَ فِي تِلْكَ اللَّيْلَةِ مِنَ

---

[1] Mullā ʿAlī al-Qārī, *al-Mawrid al-rawī fī mawlid al-nabawī wa nasabihi al-ṭāhir*, p.15–16.

[2] Ibid., p.17.

الْعَامِ أَعْظَمُ مَقَامٍ، قَالَ: وَلَقَدْ حَضَرْتُ فِي سَنَةِ خَمْسٍ وَثَمَانِيْنَ وَسَبْعِمِائَةٍ لَيْلَةَ الْمَوْلِدِ عِنْدَ الْمَلِكِ الظَّاهِرِ بَرْقُوْق بِقَلْعَةِ الْجَبَلِ الْعَلِيَّةِ. فَرَأَيْتُ مَا هَالَنِي وَسَرَّنِي وَمَا سَاءَنِي، وَحَرَّرْتُ مَا أَنْفَقَ فِي تِلْكَ اللَّيْلَةِ عَلَى الْقُرَّاءِ وَالْحَاضِرِيْنَ مِنَ الْوُعَّاظِ وَالْمُنْشِدِيْنَ وَغَيْرِهِمْ مِنَ الْأَتْبَاعِ وَالْغِلْمَانِ وَالْخُدَّامِ الْمُتَرَدِّدِيْنَ بِنَحْوِ عَشْرَةِ آلَافِ مِثْقَالٍ مِنَ الذَّهَبِ مَا بَيْنَ خِلَعٍ وَمَطْعُوْمٍ وَمَشْرُوْبٍ وَمَشْمُوْمٍ وَشُمُوْعٍ وَغَيْرِهَا مَا يَسْتَقِيْمُ بِهِ الضُّلُوْعُ. وَعَدَدْتُ فِي ذَلِكَ خَمْساً وَعِشْرِيْنَ مِنَ الْقُرَّاءِ الصَّيِّتِيْنَ الْمَرْجُوِّ كَوْنُهُمْ مُثْبِتِيْنَ، وَلَا يَزَالُ وَاحِدٌ مِنْهُمْ إِلَّا بِنَحْوِ عِشْرِيْنَ خِلْعَةً مِنَ السُّلْطَانِ وَمِنَ الْأُمَرَاءِ الْأَعْيَانِ.

قَالَ السَّخَاوِيُّ: قُلْتُ: وَلَمْ يَزَلْ مُلُوْكُ مِصْرَ خُدَّامَ الْحَرَمَيْنِ الشَّرِيْفَيْنِ مِمَّنْ وَفَّقَهُمُ اللهُ لِهَدْمِ كَثِيْرٍ مِنَ الْمَنَاكِيْرِ وَالشَّيْنِ، وَنَظَرُوْا فِي أَمْرِ الرَّعِيَّةِ كَالْوَالِدِ لِوَلَدِهِ، وِ شَهَرُوْا أَنْفُسَهُمْ بِالْعَدْلِ، فَأَسْعَفَهُمُ اللهُ بِجُنْدِهِ وَمَدَدِهِ.

The inhabitants of Egypt and the Levant are the keenest of people (when it comes to the celebration of the *mawlid*). The Sultan of Egypt convenes on that night one of the greatest gatherings. I once attended the *mawlid* celebration there in the year 785 AH in the fortress of *al-Jabal al-ʿAliya* in the company of al-Malik al-Muẓaffar Barqūq—may Almighty Allah have mercy upon him. In that celebration, I beheld what gladdened me the most and nothing was disliked by me, too. I calculated what he [al-Malik al-Muẓaffar] spent that night upon the reciters and those in attendance amongst the orators, singers, young children and servants, etc., and I estimated it at ten thousand *mithqāl*s [450 kg] of gold spent on things like royal garments, food, drinks, scents, candles, and other forms of sustenance. On that night I also counted

25 melodious reciters—and it is hoped that they will stay that way. Not a single reciter amongst them was left to receive around 20 royal garments from the Sultan and other leaders.

The rulers of Egypt and the servants of the two Sacred Sanctuaries were among those people whom Almighty Allah bestowed the grace to abolish many evils and iniquities. They have looked after the citizenry like a father looks after his child, and they are renowned for their justice. May Almighty Allah grant them His Divine help.[1]

Ḥujja al-Dīn Imam Abū ʿAbd Allāh Muhammad b. ʿAbd Allāh b. Ẓufar al-Makkī (497–565 AH/1104–1170 CE) narrates that it is mentioned in *al-Durr al-muntaẓim*:

وَقَدْ عَمِلَ الْـمُحِبُّوْنَ لِلنَّبِيِّ ﷺ فَرَحاً بِمَوْلِدِهِ الْوَلَائِمَ، فَمِنْ ذٰلِكَ مَا عَمِلَهُ بِالْقَاهِرَةِ الْـمُعِزِّيَّةِ مِنَ الْوَلَائِمِ الْكِبَارِ الشَّيْخُ أَبُو الْـحَسَنِ الْـمَعْرُوْفُ بِابْنِ قُفْلٍ قَدَّسَ اللهُ تَعَالَى سِرَّهُ، شَيْخُ شَيْخِنَا أَبِي عَبْدِ اللهِ مُحَمَّدِ بْنِ النُّعْمَانِ، وَعَمِلَ ذٰلِكَ قَبْلُ جَمَالُ الدِّيْنِ الْعَجَمِيُّ الْـهَمَذَانِيُّ. وَمِـمَّنْ عَمِلَ ذٰلِكَ عَلٰى قَدْرِ وُسْعِهِ يُوْسُفُ الْـحَجَّارُ بِمِصْرَ، وَقَدْ رَأَى النَّبِيَّ ﷺ وَهُوَ يُحَرِّضُ يُوْسُفَ الْـمَذْكُوْرَ عَلٰى عَمَلِ ذٰلِكَ.

Out of their delight for his birth, those who love the Prophet ﷺ have organised banquets to celebrate it. One of them, in Cairo the Honoured, is an incredible banquet organised by Shaykh Abū al-Ḥasan, known as Ibn Quful—may Allah the Most High sanctify his secret. He is the teacher of our teacher, Abū ʿAbd Allāh Muhammad b. al-Nuʿmān. Before him, the *mawlid* celebration was organised by Jamāl al-Dīn al-ʿAjamī al-Hamadhānī. Others, such as Yūsuf al-Ḥajjār in Egypt, have strove to

[1] Ibid., p.13.

their utmost in organising them, and in fact he beheld the Prophet ﷺ (in a dream) encouraging him to continue.[1]

6.55.4 The Celebration of *Mawlid al-Nabī* ﷺ in Qaws

Imam Kamāl al-Dīn al-Adfuwī (685–748 AH/ 1286–1347 CE) writes in *al-Ṭāliʿ al-saʿīd al-jāmiʿ li-asmāʾ nujabāʾ al-ṣaʿīd*:

حَكَى لَنَا صَاحِبُنَا الْعَدْلُ نَاصِرُ الدِّيْنِ مَحْمُوْدُ بْنُ الْعِمَـادِ أَنَّ أَبَا الطَّيِّبِ مُحَمَّدَ بْنَ إِبْرَاهِيْمَ السَّبْتِيَّ الْـمَـالِكِيَّ نَزِيْلَ قَوْصٍ، أَحَدَ الْعُلَمَـاءِ الْعَامِلِيْنَ، كَانَ يَجُوْزُ بِالْـمَكْتَبِ فِي الْيَوْمِ الَّذِي وُلِدَ فِيْهِ النَّبِيُّ ﷺ، فَيَقُوْلُ: يَا فَقِيْهُ! هَذَا يَوْمُ سُرُوْرٍ، اصْرِفِ الصِّبْيَانَ. فَيَصْرِفُنَا.

وَهَذَا مِنْهُ دَلِيْلٌ عَلَى تَقْرِيْرِهِ وَعَدَمِ إِنْكَارِهِ، وَهَذَا الرَّجُلُ كَانَ فَقِيْهاً مَالِكِيًّا مُتَفَنِّناً فِـي عُلُوْمٍ، مُتَوَرِّعاً، أَخَذَ عَنْهُ أَبُوْ حَيَّانَ وَغَيْرُهُ، مَاتَ سَنَةَ خَمْسٍ وَتِسْعِيْنَ وَسِتِّمِـائَةٍ.

Our reliable friend Nāṣir al-Dīn Maḥmūd b. al-ʿImād related to us that Abū al-Ṭayyab Muhammad b. Ibrāhīm al-Sabtī al-Mālikī, resident of *Fūṣ* and one of the pious scholars, used to pass by the local primary school [*maktab*] and say, 'O scholar! Today is a day of delight; let the children out.' And so he would be let out."

This is a proof from him that he accepted it [the *mawlid* celebration] and he is an authority on the absence of its refusal—and he was a *Mālikī* jurist skilled in the various sciences and was scrupulous. Abū Ḥayyān and others studied under him, and he passed away in the year 695 AH.[2]

---

[1] Al-Ṣāliḥī, *Subul al-hudā wa al-rashād fī sīra Khayr al-ʿibād*, 1:363.

[2] Al-Suyūṭī, *Ḥusn al-maqṣid fī ʿamal al-mawlid*, p.66–67; al-Suyūṭī, *al-Ḥāwī li al-fatāwā*, p.206; al-Nabhānī, *Ḥujja Allāh ʿalā al-ʿālimīn fī muʿjazāt Sayyid al-mursalīn*, p.238.

6.55.5 THE CELEBRATION OF *MAWLID AL-NABĪ* ﷺ IN ANDALUSIA AND ROME

وَأَمَّا مُلُوْكُ الْأَنْدَلُسِ وَالْغَرْبِ فَلَهُمْ فِيْهِ لَيْلَةٌ تَسِيْرُ بِهَا الرُّكْبَانُ يَجْتَمِعُ فِيْهَا أَئِمَّةُ الْعُلَمَـاءِ الْأَعْلَامِ، فَمَنْ يَلِيْهِمْ مِنْ كُلِّ مَكَانٍ وَعَلُّوْا بَيْنَ أَهْلِ الْكُفْرِ كَلِمَةَ الْإِيْمَـانِ، وَأَظُنُّ أَهْلَ الرُّوْمِ لَا يَتَخَلَّفُوْنَ عَنْ ذَلِكَ، اقْتِفَاءً بِغَيْرِهِمْ مِنَ الْـمُلُوْكِ فِيْمَـا هُنَالِكَ.

The rulers of Andalusia and the Maghreb have a night in which the leading scholars and others assemble *en masse* from every locale, and even the non-believers attend. I believe that the Romans also do not want to miss that gathering, since they want to emulate the other kings in their region.[1]

6.55.6 THE CELEBRATION OF *MAWLID AL-NABĪ* ﷺ IN THE INDIAN SUBCONTINENT

وَبِلَادُ الْـهِنْدِ تَزِيْدُ عَلَى غَيْرِهَا بِكَثِيْرٍ كَمَـا أَعْلَمَنِيْهِ بَعْضُ أُوْلِي النَّقْدِ وَالتَّحْرِيْرِ. وَأَمَّا الْعَجَمُ فَمِنْ حَيْثُ دَخَلَ هَذَا الشَّهْرُ الْـمُعَظَّمُ وَالزَّمَانُ الْـمُكَرَّمُ لِأَهْلِهَا مَجَالِسُ فِخَامٌ مِنْ أَنْوَاعِ الطَّعَامِ لِلْقُرَّاءِ الْكِرَامِ وَلِلْفُقَرَاءِ مَنَ الْـخَاصِّ وَالْعَامِّ، وَقِرَاءَاتُ الْـخَتَمَـاتِ وَالتِّلَاوَاتِ الْـمُتَوَالِيَاتِ وَالْإِنْشَادَاتِ الْـمُتَعَالِيَاتِ، وَأَنْوَاعِ السُّرُوْرِ وَأَصْنَافِ الْـحُبُوْرِ حَتَّى بَعْضُ الْعَجَائِزِ - مِنْ غَزْلِـهِنَّ وَنَسْجِهِنَّ - يَجْمَعْنَ مَا يَقُمْنَ بِجَمْعِهِ الْأَكَابِرُ وَالْأَعْيَانُ وَبِضِيَافَتِهِنَّ مَا يَقْدِرُوْنَ عَلَيْهِ فِـي ذَلِكَ الزَّمَانِ. وَمِنْ تَعْظِيْمِ مَشَايِخِهِمْ وَعُلَمَـائِهِمْ هَذَا الْـمَوْلِدِ الْـمُعَظَّمِ وَالْـمَجْلِسِ الْـمُكَرَّمِ أَنَّهُ لَا

[1] Mullā ʿAlī al-Qārī, *al-Mawrid al-rawī fī mawlid al-nabawī wa nasabihi al-ṭāhir*, p.14.

يَأْبَاهُ أَحَدٌ فِي حُضُوْرِهِ، رَجَاءَ إِدْارَكِ نُوْرِهِ وَسُرُوْرِهِ.

وَقَدْ وَقَعَ لِشَيْخِ مَشَايْـخِنَا مَوْلَانَا زَيْنُ الدِّيْنِ مَحْمُوْدُ الْـهَمْدَانِـيُّ النَّقْشَبَنْدِيُّ – قَدَّسَ اللهُ سِرَّهُ الْعَلِيَّ – أَنَّهُ أَرَادَ سُلْطَانُ الزَّمَانِ وَخَاقَانُ الدَّوْرَانِ هُمَايُون بَادْشَاه تَغَمَّدَهُ اللهُ وَأَحْسَنَ مَثْوَاهُ أَنْ يَجْتَمِعَ بِهِ وَيَحْصُلَ لَهُ الْـمَدَدُ وَالْـمَدَدُ بِسَبَبِهِ فَأَبَاهُ الشَّيْخُ، وَامْتَنَعَ أَيْضًا أَنْ يَأْتِيَهُ السُّلْطَانُ اسْتِغْنَاءً بِفَضْلِ الرَّحْمٰنِ فَأَلَحَّ السُّلْطَانُ عَلَى وَزِيْرِهِ بِيْرَم خَان بِأَنَّهُ لَا بُدَّ مِنْ تَدْبِيْرٍ لِلْاِجْتِمَـاعِ فِـي الْـمَكَانِ، وَلَوْ فِـي قَلِيْلٍ مِنَ الزَّمَانِ. فَسَمِعَ الْوَزِيْرُ أَنَّ الشَّيْخَ لَا يَحْضُرُ فِي دَعْوَةٍ مِنْ هَنَاءٍ وَعَزَاءٍ إِلَّا فِـي مَوْلِدِ النَّبِيِّ ﷺ تَعْظِيْمًـا لِذَلِكَ الْـمَقَامِ. فَأَنْهَى إِلَى السُّلْطَانِ، فَأَمَرَهُ بِتَهْيِئَةِ أَسْبَابِهِ الْـمُلُوْكَانِيَّةِ فِـي أَنْوَاعِ الْأَطْعِمَةِ وَالْأَشْرِبَةِ وَمِـمَّـا يُتَمَّمُ بِهِ وَيُبْخَرُ فِـي الْـمَجَالِسِ الْعِلْمِيَّةِ. وَنَادَى الْأَكَابِرَ وَالْأَهَالِـي.

وَحَضَرَ الشَّيْخُ مَعَ بَعْضِ الْـمَوَالِـي فَأَخَذَ السُّلْطَانُ الْإِبْرِيْقَ بِيَدِ الْأَدَبِ وَمُعَاوَنَةِ التَّوْفِيْقِ، وَالْوَزِيْرُ أَخَذَ الطَّشْتَ مِنْ تَحْتِ أَمْرِهِ رَجَاءَ لُطْفِهِ وَنَظَرِهِ وَغَسَلَا يَدَا الشَّيْخِ الْـمُكَرَّمِ، وَحَصَلَ لَـهُمَـا بِبَرَكَةِ تَوَاضُعِهَا لله وَلِرَسُوْلِهِ ﷺ الْـمَقَامُ الْـمُعَظَّمُ وَالْـجَاهُ الْـمُفَخَّمُ.

Some of the verifying scholars have informed me that the celebrations in India surpass those of other lands. As for the non-Arabs, when this esteemed and honored month begins, the non-Arabs (*ʿajam*) convene huge gatherings with varieties of food that are given to the noble reciters and the poor amongst the commoners and elite. During these celebrations, they complete many recitals of the Qurʾān and engage in continual reading and singing of *nashīds*. These celebrations are full of delight and goodness, and even the elderly women spend their money that they earned (by knitting and spinning the yarn) to the best of their abilities on the feast for the noble men and guides. Their shaykhs and scholars are so keen to celebrate this honoured *mawlid* and noble gathering that no one fails to attend it, in hopes of receiving its light and felicity.

The Shaykh of our Shaykhs, Zayn al-Dīn Maḥmūd al-Hamadānī al-Naqshabandī—may Allah bless him—mentioned that once, the ruler of his time, Khāqān al-Dawrān Hamābūn Bādshāh—may Almighty Allah grant him a heavenly abode—wanted the Shaykh to visit him so he could obtain spiritual assistance, but the Shaykh, sufficing himself with the All-Merciful, turned down the ruler's invitation and refused to let him visit as well. The ruler pleaded with his minister, Bayram Khān, to devise a ruse by which the two could gather in the same place—even if only for a short amount of time. The minister heard that the Shaykh never attended gatherings of happiness or sadness unless the gathering was a celebration of the Prophet's birth ﷺ, and that was due to the Shaykhs reverence for the Prophet's station. When the news of this reached the Sultan, he ordered that the necessary preparations be made, as well as arrangements for various types of food and drink and other items needed for gatherings of sacred knowledge. Then he invited the elite and their families. The Shaykh came with some of his followers, whereupon the Sultan, hoping to gain the Shaykh's gentleness and gaze, humbly took the water-pitcher with his own hands and his minister took the bowl, and they proceeded to wash the Shaykh's noble hands. Due to the blessing of their humbleness for the sake of Almighty Allah and His Messenger ﷺ, the Sultan and his minister gained a tremendous station and noble rank.[1]

[1] Ibid., p.14–5.

From these detailed accounts, we can gather that the Muslims of Mecca, Medina, Egypt, the Levant, Cordoba, and Granada, and even the Muslims of India and other non-Arab countries, were accustomed to commemorating *Mawlid al-Nabī* ﷺ on the 12th of *Rabīᶜ al-Awwal* annually. This is a historical fact, which holds true even till now.

Let it be clear that none of these personalities were '*Barelvis*'. In Mecca, Medina, Egypt and the Levant, there was no such thing as a '*Barelvi*' school of thought. How cruel it is that such individuals, who are clueless about our Islamic heritage, have nothing better to do, except to cause chaos and confusion in the minds of people—they are bent on sowing the seed of doubt in those areas of Islamic teaching which are unanimously agreed upon. They themselves have no grounding in Islamic history owing to which they spread blatant lies, conceal the truth, and present distortions to the public. These pseudo-scholars transmit nothing but ignorance; they have never spared the time to consult those books of the past which have been written on the topic of *Mawlid al-Nabī* ﷺ.

6.56 Significant Literature on the *Mawlid*

From the age of the pious forbearers till the present day, the imams and hadith scholars have, according to their own disposition and temperament, incessantly compiled works on the topic of *Mawlid al-Nabī* ﷺ. Prose and poetry, amounting to thousands, have been compiled on this genre—some of them are concise while others are lengthy.

The majority of imams and hadith scholars have incorporated the subject of the Holy Prophet's birth in their books of hadith, *sīra*, Prophetic virtues, and history. For instance, Imam al-Tirmidhī (210–279 AH) in his *al-Jāmiᶜ al-Ṣaḥīḥ* has placed this topic in the second chapter of *Kitāb al-Manāqib* under the chapter-heading *mā jā'a fī mīlād al-Nabī* ﷺ (What has been narrated concerning the Prophet's birth). Ibn Isḥāq (85–151 AH) in *al-Sīra al-Nabawiyya*, Ibn Ḥishām (d. 213 AH) in his *al-Sīra al-Nabawiyya*, Ibn Saᶜd (168–230 AH) in *al-Ṭabaqāt al-kubrā*, Abū Nuᶜaym (336–430 AH) in *Dalā'il al-Nubuwwa*, al-Bayhaqī (384–458 AH) in *Dalā'il al-*

Nubuwwa wa maʿrifa aḥwāl Ṣāḥib al-Sharīʿa, Abu Saʿd Kharkūshī al-Nīsābūrī (d. 406 AH) in *Kitāb sharaf al-Muṣṭafā*, Ibn al-Athīr (555–630 AH) in *al-Kāmil fī al-tārīkh*, al-Ṭabarī (224–310 AH) in *Tārīkh al-umam wa al-mulūk*, Ibn Kathīr (701–744 AH) in *al-Bidāya wa al-nihāya*, Ibn ʿAsākir (499–571 AH) in *Tārīkh Dimashq al-kabīr*, and in fact all of the renowned and celebrated imams and scholars have penned something or the other on the subject of the Prophet's birth. Furthermore, Imam Muhammad b. Yūsuf al-Ṣāliḥī al-Shāmī (d. 944 AH) has written extensively on it in *Subul al-hudā wa al-rashād fī sīra Khayr al-ʿibād*, having offered an array of intellectual proofs in its support. Imam Abū ʿAbd Allāh b. al-Ḥājj al-Mālikī (d. 737 AH) in *al-Madkhal ilā tanmiya al-aʿmāl bi taḥsīn al-niyyāt wa al-tanbīh ʿalā kathīr min al-bidʿ al-muḥdatha wa al-ʿawāʾid al-muntaḥala* has discussed this topic in detail. Imam al-Zurqānī (1055–1122 AH) in *al-Mawāhib al-laduniyya bi al-minaḥ al-Muḥammadiyya*, Shaykh ʿAbd al-Ḥaqq Muḥaddith al-Dihlawī (958–1052 AH) in *Mā thabata min al-Sunna fī ayyām al-sana*, and Imam Yūsuf b. Ismāʿīl al-Nabhānī (1265–1350 AH) in *Ḥujja Allāh ʿalā al-ʿālimīn fī muʿjizāt Sayyid al-Mursalīn* as well as in *Jawāhir al-biḥār fī faḍāʾil al-Nabī al-Mukhtār* have all covered the subject of *mawlid* in much detail.

The following is a list of some prominent books written on the subject:

6.56.1 Abū al-ʿAbbās Aḥmad al-Iqlīshī (d.550 AH)

Abū al-ʿAbbās Aḥmad b. Maʿd b. ʿĪsā al-Iqlīshī al-Andalūsī (d. 550 AH) composed a book on the *mawlid* with the title *al-Durr al-munaẓẓam fī mawlid al-Nabī al-Aʿẓam* ﷺ. It has ten sections.[1]

6.56.2 Ibn al-Jawzī (510 – 597 AH)

ʿAbd al-Raḥmān b. ʿAlī b. Maḥmūd b. ʿAlī b. ʿAbd Allāh b. Ḥamādī al-Qurashī al-Ḥanbalī is known by the epithet Jamāl al-Dīn. He was born in 510 AH in Baghdad and passed away in the same city in 597 AH.

He commenced his education at an early age and undertook the duty of preaching and missionary work. He excelled in the science of hadith and was famously known as a *ḥāfiẓ* and *muḥaddith*. He

[1] Bāshā Baghdādī, *Īḍāḥ al-maknūn*, p.451.

authored at least 159 books, mainly in the areas of hadith, history, and religious counselling. He authored two volumes on the *mawlid*:

1. *Bayān al-mīlād al-Nabawī*
2. *Mawlid al-ʿurūs*

6.56.3 IBN DIḤYA AL-KALBĪ (544 – 633 AH)

Abū al-Khaṭṭāb ʿUmar b. Ḥasan b. ʿAlī b. Muhammad b. Diḥya al-Kalbī was born in Andalusia. His thirst for knowledge took him as far as the Levant, Iraq, and Central Asia, eventually settling in Egypt. He is a famous hadith scholar, an authentic historian, and an honourable writer. He penned several treatises, leaving behind a legacy of knowledge. His written works include a thesis on the *mawlid*, called *al-Tanwīr fī mawlid al-Bashīr wa al-Nadhīr* ﷺ.

6.56.4. HAFIZ SHAMS AL-DĪN AL-JAZARĪ (D. 660 AH)

Abū al-Khayr Shams al-Dīn Muhammad b. ʿAbd Allāh al-Jazarī al-Shāfiʿī (d.1262 CE) was the foremost Qurʾān reciter and hadith scholar of his age. He wrote a book on the *mawlid* by the title, *ʿUrf al-taʿrīf bi al-mawlid al-sharīf*.

6.56.5 ABŪ BAKR AL-JAZĀʾIRĪ (D. 707 AH)

Shaykh Abū Bakr Muhammad b. ʿAbd Allāh b. Muhammad b. Muhammad b. Aḥmad al-ʿAṭṭār al-Jazāʾirī authored a volume on the *mawlid* called, *al-Mawrid al-ʿadhb al-maʿīn fī mawlid Sayyid al-khalq ajmaʿīn* ﷺ.

6.56.6 IMAM KAMĀL AL-DĪN AL-ADFUWĪ (685–748 AH)

Imam Kamāl al-Dīn Abū al-Faḍl Jaʿfar b. Thaʿlab b. Jaʿfar al-Adfuwī wrote in detail about the *mawlid* festivities of his native Morocco in his book, *al-Ṭāliʿ al-saʿīd al-jāmiʿ li- asmāʾ nujabāʾ al-ṣaʿīd*.

6.56.7 SAʿĪD AL-DĪN AL-KĀZARŪNĪ (D. 758 AH)

Muhammad b. Masʿūd b. Muhammad Saʿīd al-Dīn al-Kāzarūnī wrote a book called *Manāsik al-ḥijz al-muntaqā min siyar mawlid al-Muṣṭafā* ﷺ.

6.56.8 ABŪ SAᶜĪD KHALĪL B. KĪKLADĪ (694 – 761 AH)

Abū Saᶜīd Khalīl b. Kīkladī b. ᶜAbd Allāh al-Aᶜlāᶜī al-Dimashqī al-Shāfiᶜī wrote a book called *al-Durra al-sunniyya fī mawlid Khayr al-bariyya* ﷺ.

6.56.9. IMAM ᶜIMĀD AL-DĪN B. KATHĪR (701 – 774 AH)

The author of *Tafsīr al-Qurʾān al-ᶜaẓīm*, ᶜĪmād al-Dīn Abū al-Fidāʾ Ismāᶜīl b. Kathīr, has also authored a volume on the *mawlid*, called *Dhikr mawlid Rasūl Allāh* ﷺ *wa raḍāᶜihi*.

6.56.10 SULAYMĀN BARSAWĪ AL-ḤANAFĪ

Sulaymān b. ᶜIwad Bāshā b. Maḥmūd Barsawī al-Ḥanafī died around the year 780 AH. He was a notable imam in the era of Sulṭān Bāyazīd ᶜUthmānī. He composed a memoir on the *mawlid* in the Turkish language, called *Wasīla al-najāh*.

6.56.11. IMAM ᶜABD AL-RAḤĪM AL-BARᶜĪ (D. 803 AH)

ᶜAbd al-Raḥīm b. Aḥmad al-Barᶜī al-Yamānī (d. 1400 CE) composed a well-known treatise on the *mawlid* entitled *Mawlid al-Barᶜī*.

6.56.12. HAFIZ ZAYN AL-DĪN AL-ᶜIRĀQĪ (725–808 AH)

Ḥāfiẓ Abū al-Faḍl Zayn al-Dīn ᶜAbd al-Raḥīm b. Ḥusayn b. ᶜAbd al-Raḥmān al-Miṣrī al-ᶜIrāqī was a unique personality of his time, the leader of his era, the saviour of Islam, the possessor of the highest morals, an intellectual, and a great researcher. He mastered the fields of hadith, its chains of narrations, and the accuracy of its reports. Any student with the most rudimentary knowledge of the science of hadith is well aware of his position in this field. This outstanding imam wrote a paper on the *mawlid* called *al-Mawrid al-hanī fī mawlid al-sunnī*.

6.56.13 SULAYMAN BARSŪNĪ

Ḥājī Khalīfa wrote in *Kashf al-ẓunūn ᶜan usāmī al-kutub wa al-funūn* (2:1910) that Sulayman Barsūnī died in 808 AH. He wrote a well organised chronicle on the *mawlid* in the Turkish language, which was read in the *mawlid* assemblies in Rome.

6.56.14. Imam Muhammad b. Yaʿqūb Fayrūzābādī (729–817 AH)

Abū Ṭāhir Muhammad b. Yaʿqūb b. Muhammad b. Ibrāhīm Fayrūzābādī was a great imam. He is the author of eminent works, such as *Tanwīr al-miqbās min tafsīr Ibn al-ʿAbbās*, *al-Ṣalāt wa al-bushr fī al-Salāt ʿalā Khayr al-bashar* and, *al-Qāmūs al-Muḥīt*, an important work on linguistics. On the *mawlid*, he wrote *al-Nafḥa al-ʿanbariyya fī mawlid Khayr al-bariyya* ﷺ.

6.56.15. Imam Shams al-Dīn b. Nāṣir al-Dīn al-Dimashqī (777–842 AH)

Shams al-Dīn Muhammad b. Abī Bakr b. ʿAbd Allāh Qīsī al-Shāfiʿī, more popularly known as Ibn Nāṣir al-Dīn al-Dimashqī, is one of the great imams who authored something on the *mawlid*. He was a first-rate historian, author of numerous books, commentator of several major works, and a great contributor to Islam's intellectual heritage. He was appointed as *Shaykh al-ḥadīth* of *Dār al-Ḥadīth* in Damascus. He compiled many papers on the subject of the *mawlid*. Ḥājī Khalīfa noted three of them in *Kashf al-ẓunūn ʿan usāmī al-kutub wa al-funūn* (2:1910):

1. *Jāmiʿ al-āthār fī mawlid al-Nabī al-Mukhtār* ﷺ
2. *Al-Lafẓ al-rāʾiq fī mawlid Khayr al-khalāʾiq*
3. *Mawrid al-ṣādī fī mawlid al-Hādī* ﷺ

6.56.16 ʿAfīf al-Dīn al-Tabrīzī (d. 855 AH)

ʿAfīf al-Dīn Muhammad b. Sayyid Muhammad b. ʿAbd Allāh al-Ḥusaynī al-Tabrīzī al-Shāfiʿī passed away in Medina in 855 AH. He wrote a commentary on the *Arbaʿīn* of Imam al-Nawawī (631–677 AH) and *al-Shamāʾil al-Muḥammadiyya* of Imam al-Tirmidhī (210–279 AH). He wrote a book called *Mawlid al-Nabī* ﷺ.

6.56.17 Muhammad b. Fakhr al-Dīn (d. 867 AH)

Shams al-Dīn Abū al-Qāsim Muhammad b. Fakhr al-Dīn ʿUthmān Luʾluʾī al-Dimashqī al-Ḥanbalī is famous by the title of al-Luʾluʾ b. al-Fakhr. He wrote *al-Durr al-munaẓẓam fī mawlid al-Nabī al-*

Muʿaẓẓam ﷺ. Afterwards, he composed *al-Lafẓ al-jamīl bi mawlid al-Nabī al-Jalīl* which is a summary of the former work.

6.56.18 Aṣīl al-Dīn al-Harawī (d. 883 AH)

Sayyid Aṣīl al-Dīn ʿAbd Allāh b. ʿAbd al-Raḥmān al-Harawī wrote *Darj al-durar fī mīlād Sayyid al-bashar* ﷺ.

6.56.19. Imam ʿAbd Allāh al-Ḥusaynī al-Shīrāzī (d. 884 AH)

Aṣīl al-Dīn ʿAbd Allāh b. ʿAbd al-Raḥmān Ḥusaynī Shīrāzī wrote *Darj al-durar fī mīlād Sayyid al-bashar* ﷺ, as is mentioned by Ḥājī Khalīfa in his book, *Kashf al-ẓunun* (1:745).

6.56.20 ʿAlāʾ al-Dīn al-Mardāwī (d. 885 AH)

Abū al-Ḥasan ʿAlāʾ al-Dīn ʿAlī b. Sulaymān b. Aḥmad b. Muhammad al-Mardāwī was a great Ḥanbalī jurist who hailed from Damascus. On the topic of *mawlid*, he wrote *al-Manhal al-ʿadhb al-qarīr fī mawlid al-Hādī al-Bashīr al-Nadhīr* ﷺ.

6.56.21 Burhān al-Dīn Abū al-Ṣafāʾ (d.887 AH)

Burhān al-Dīn Abū al-Ṣafāʾ b. Abī al-Wafāʾ compiled the treatise, *Fatḥ Allāh ḥasbī wa kafā fī mawlid al-Muṣṭafā* ﷺ.

6.56.22 Shaykh ʿUmar b. ʿAbd al-Raḥmān Bā ʿAlawī (d. 889 AH)

ʿUmar b. ʿAbd al-Raḥmān b. Muhammad b. ʿAlī b. Muhammad b. Aḥmad Bā ʿAlawī Haḍramī authored the book called *Kitāb mawlid al-Nabī* ﷺ.

6.56.23 Imam Shams al-Dīn al-Sakhāwī (831–902 AH)

Shams al-Dīn Muhammad b. ʿAbd al-Raḥmān b. Muhammad al-Qāharī al-Sakhāwī is recognised as an eminent scholar of Islam. It was once said about him that after al-Dhahabī in the science of hadith, a master of the likes of al-Sakhāwī cannot be found and that hadith expertise ended with him. Al-Shawkānī remarked that if al-Sakhāwī had not written any book except *al-Ḍawʾ al-*

lāmiʿ, then this book alone would be a sufficient testament to his expertise.

On the *mawlid*, al-Sakhāwī composed *al-Fakhr al-ʿalawī fī al-mawlid al-Nabawī*; he refers to this book in *al-Ḍawʾ al-lāmiʿ* (18:8). Apart from this, he has listed the names of scholars who wrote books or articles on the *mawlid* in *al-Ḍawʾ al-lāmiʿ*.[1]

6.56.24 Imam Nūr al-Dīn al-Samhūdī (844–911 AH)

Al-Mawrid al-haniyya fī mawlid Khayr al-bariyya ﷺ is another significant book on the *mawlid* written by Nūr al-Dīn Abū al-Ḥasan ʿAlī b. ʿAbd Allāh b. Aḥmad al-Husaynī al-Shāfiʿī al-Samhūdī. The author is considered a reliable authority who wrote about the history of Medina.

6.56.25 Imam Jalāl al-Dīn al-Suyūṭī (849–911 AH)

The scholarly repute of Imam Jalāl al-Dīn ʿAbd al-Raḥmān b. Abī Bakr al-Suyūṭī is recognised and appreciated by everyone. It is recorded that his written works exceeded 700 titles. In relation to the legality of *mawlid*, his treatise *Ḥusn al-Maqṣid fī ʿamal al-mawlid* is accepted worldwide. It is available in the collection of his *fatwas*, *al-Ḥāwī li al-Fatāwā*.

6.56.26 ʿĀʾishā b. Yūsuf Bāʿūniyya (d. 922 AH)

ʿĀʾishā b. Yūsuf Bāʿūniyya al-Dimashqiyya al-Shāfiʿiyya is a famous *ṣūfī* scholar and researcher with several titles to her name. Her poem, *Mawlūd al-Nabī* ﷺ, is her contribution to the *mawlid* genre.

6.56.27 Abū Bakr b. Muhammad al-Ḥalabī (d. 930 AH)

Abū Bakr b. Muhammad b. Abī Bakr al-Ḥubayshī al-Ḥalabī authored a book called *al-Kawākib al-durriyya fī mawlid Khayr al-bariyya* ﷺ.

6.56.28 Mullā ʿArab al-Wāʿiẓ (d. 938 AH)

Mullā ʿArab al-Wāʿiẓ wrote a book by the title *Mawlid al-Nabī* ﷺ.

---

[1] Ḥājī Khalīfa, *Kashf al-ẓunūn ʿan usāmī al-kutub wa al-funūn*, 2:1910.

6.56.29 Ibn Dībaʿ al-Shaybānī (866–944 AH)

Wajīh al-Dīn ʿAbd al-Raḥmān b. ʿAlī b. Muhammad al-Shaybānī al-Shāfiʿī is better known as Ibn Dībaʿ. He delivered over a hundred lectures on *Ṣaḥīḥ al-Bukhārī*; on one occasion, he completed it in just six days. He has also written on the *mawlid*.

6.56.30 Shaykh ʿAbd al-Karīm al-Adrantawī (d. 965 AH)

ʿAbd al-Karīm al-Adrantawī al-Khalwatī composed a poem on the *mawlid* in the Turkish language.

6.56.31. Imam Ibn Ḥajar al-Haytamī al-Makkī (909–973 AH)

The Imam of the two Sacred Sanctuaries, Abū al-ʿAbbās Aḥmad b. Muhammad b. ʿAlī b. Ḥajar al-Haytamī al-Makkī al-Shāfiʿī, needs no introduction. Works such as *al-Fatāwā al-ḥadīthiyya*, *al-Khayrāt al-ḥisān fī manāqib al-Imām al-Aʿẓam Abī Ḥanīfa al-Nuʿmān*, *al-Ṣawāʿiq al-muḥraqa fī al-radd ʿalā ahl al-bidʿa wa al-zandaqa* and *al-Jawhar al-munaẓẓam fī ziyāra al-qabar al-sharīf al-Nabawī al-Mukarram al-Muʿaẓẓam* are witness to his scholarly calibre. In the science of hadith, he was the outstanding student of Shaykh al-Islam Zakariyyā al-Miṣrī. Ibn Ḥajar al-ʿAsqalānī was his shaykh's shaykh. Mullā ʿAlī al-Qārī and the pride of India, ʿAlāʾ al-Dīn ʿAlī al-Muttaqī al-Hindī, the author of *Kanz al-ʿummāl fī sunan al-aqwāl wa al-afʿāl*, were amongst those who benefitted from his circles of knowledge. He wrote a number of works on the *mawlid*:

1. *Taḥrīr al-kalām fī al-qiyām ʿinda dhikr al-mawlid Sayyid al-anām* ﷺ
2. *Tuḥfa al-akhyār fī mawlid al-Mukhtār* ﷺ
3. *Itmām al-niʿma ʿalā al-ʿālam bi-mawlid Sayyid walad Ādam* ﷺ
4. *Mawlid al-Nabī* ﷺ

Excluding these, he also touched on this topic in some detail in *al-Fatāwā al-ḥadīthiyya*.

6.56.32. IMAM KHAṬĪB AL-SHURBĪNĪ (D. 977 AH)

Shams al-Dīn Muhammad b. Aḥmad al-Khaṭīb al-Shurbīnī authored fifty pages on the *mawlid*.

6.56.33 ABŪ AL-THANĀʾ AḤMAD AL-ḤANAFĪ (D. 1006 CE)

Abū al-Thanāʾ Aḥmad b. Muhammad b. ʿĀrif al-Rūmī al-Ḥanafī wrote a book called *Mawlid al-Nabī* ﷺ.

6.56.34 MULLĀ ʿALĪ AL-QĀRĪ (D. 1014 AH)

The *ḥāfiẓ* of hadith, *mujtahid* of his era, Mulla ʿAlī Qārī b. Sultān b. Muhammad al-Harawī, is amongst those who composed something on the *mawlid*. Al-Shawkānī remarks in *al-Badr al-ṭāliʿ* that the Imam possessed encyclopaedic knowledge of the traditional sciences, photographic memory, and a sharp intellect; he was a hero of the Muslim world. *Al-Mawlid al-rawī fī mawlid al-nabawī wa nasabihi al-ṭāhir* is his contribution to the *mawlid* genre. In it, he collects the accounts of various *mawlid* gatherings around the world.

6.56.35 IMAM ABD AL-RAʾŪF AL-MANĀWĪ (952–1031 AH)

ʿAbd al-Raʾūf b. Tāj al-ʿĀrifīn b. ʿAlī b. Zayn al-ʿĀbidīn al-Manāwī (1545–1621 CE) is the well-known author of *Fayḍ al-qadīr sharḥ al-Jāmiʿ al-ṣaghīr* and *Sharḥ al-Shamāʾil ʿalā jamʿ al-wasāʾil*. He composed a treatise on the *mawlid*, which is popularly referred to as *Mawlid al-Manāwī*.

6.56.36 MUḤY AL-DĪN ʿABD AL-QĀDIR AL-ʿĪDRŪSĪ (987–1038 AH)

Muḥy al-Dīn ʿAbd al-Qādir b. Shaykh b. ʿAbd Allāh al-ʿĪdrūsī is the author of *al-Muntakhab al-muṣaffā fī akhbār mawlid al-Muṣṭafā* ﷺ.

6.56.37 IMAM ʿALĪ ʿALĪ B. IBRĀHĪM AL-ḤALABĪ (975–1044 AH)

Nūr al-Dīn ʿAlī b. Ibrāhīm b. Aḥmad b. ʿAlī al-Ḥalabī al-Qāhirī al-Shāfiʿī is the author of *Insān al-ʿuyūn fī sīra al-Amīn al-Maʾmūn*

ﷺ, the popular work on *sīra*, commonly referred to as *al-Sīra al-Ḥalabiyya. Al-Kawākib al-munīr fī mawlid al-Bashīr al-Nadhīr* ﷺ is a work on the *mawlid* that is attributed to him. In *al-Sīra al-Ḥalabiyya*, he recounts the phenomena that were observed at the time of the Prophet's birth and then goes on to establish the legitimacy of the *mawlid* celebrations.

6.56.38 Imam Muhammad b. ʿAllān al-Ṣiddīqī (996–1057 AH)

Muhammad ʿAli b. Muhammad b. ʿAllān al-Bakrī al-Ṣiddiqī al-ʿAlawī (1588–1647 CE), an eminent exegete and hadith-scholar, composed the book *Mawlid al-ṣafā fī mawlid al-Muṣṭafā* ﷺ.

6.56.39 Shaykh Zayn al-ʿĀbidīn al-Khalīfatī (d. 1130 AH)

Zayn al-ʿĀbidīn Muhammad b. ʿAbd Allāh ʿAbbāsī was a famed orator who hailed from Medina. He was famously known as al-Khalīfatī. On the *mawlid*, he wrote *al-Jāmiʿ al-ẓāhir al-munīr fī dhikr mawlid al-Bashīr al-Nadhīr* ﷺ.

6.56.40 Imam ʿAbd al-Ghanī al-Nābalusī (d. 1143 AH)

ʿAbd al-Ghanī al-Nābalusī was a noteworthy imam who published a concise and succinct work named *al-Mawlid al-Nabawī*.

6.56.41 Shaykh Jamāl al-Dīn b. ʿAqīla al-Makkī al-Ẓāhir (d. 1130 AH)

Jamāl al-Dīn Abū ʿAbd Allāh Muhammad b. Aḥmad b. Saʿīd b. Masʿūd al-Makkī al-Ẓāhir also wrote a book called *Mawlid al-Nabī* ﷺ.

6.56.42 Sulaymān al-Naḥīfī al-Rūmī (d. 1151 AH)

Sulaymān b. ʿAbd al-Raḥmān b. Ṣāliḥ al-Naḥīfī al-Rūmī translated the *Mathnawī* of Jalāl al-Dīn al-Rūmī (604–672 AH) to the Turkish language—in the same language, he also composed a poem on the *mawlid*.

6.56.43 Yūsuf Zādah al-Rūmī (1085–1167 AH)

ʿAbd Allāh Ḥilmī b. Muhammad b. Yūsuf b. ʿAbd al-Mannān al-Rūmī al-Ḥanafī al-Muqrī, popularly referred to as Yūsuf Zādah, Shaykh al-Qurrāʾ, was a renowned expert of hadith. He wrote *al-Iʾtilāf fī wujūd al-ikhtilāf fī al-qirāʾa*, which discusses the various methods of reciting the Qurʾān. Regarding the *mawlid*, he compiled a book by the name, *al-Kalām al-sanī al-muṣaffā fī mawlid al-Muṣṭafā* ﷺ.

6.56.44 Ḥasan b. ʿAlī al-Madābaghī (d. 1170 AH)

Ḥasan b. ʿAlī b. Aḥmad b. ʿAbd Allāh al-Manṭāwī, better known as al-Madābaghī in his day, passed away in Egypt in 1170 CE. *Risāla fī al-mawlid al-Nabawī* was authored by him.

6.56.45 ʿAbd Allāh al-Kāshgharī (d. 1174 AH)

ʿAbd Allāh b. Muhammad al-Kāshghirī al-Bindāʾī al-Naqshbandī al-Zāhidī used to lecture in the city of Constantinople, where he also taught the philosophy of the Naqshbandi Sufi-order. He also wrote a book called *Mawlid al-Nabī* ﷺ.

6.56.46 Aḥmad b. ʿUthmān al-Ḥanafī (1100–1174 AH)

Aḥmad b. ʿUthmān Diyār Bakrī Āmadī al-Ḥanafī authored a book called *Mawlid al-Nabī* ﷺ.

6.56.47 ʿAbd al-Karīm al-Barzanjī (d. 1177 AH)

Sayyid Jaʿfar b. Ḥasan b. ʿAbd al-Karīm al-Barzanjī al-Shāfiʿī was the grand mufti and eminent hadith-scholar from Medina. The author of *Tāj al-ʿurūs min jawāhir al-qāmūs* (a popular book on the Arabic language), Sayyid Murtaḍā al-Zabīdī (1145–1205 AH) met the imam and attended his seminars at the Prophet's Mosque. He authored a renowned book on the *mawlid* called *ʿIqd al-jawhar fī mawlid al-Nabī al-azhar* ﷺ, popularly known as *Mawlūd al-Barzanjī*. The universal acceptance and popularity of this book can be surmised by the fact that thousands of Arabs and non-

Arabs memorise it and recite it in their gatherings. Its account of the Prophet's birth comprises a summarisation of the *sīra* of the esteemed Messenger ﷺ; it mentions his prophecy, migration, mannerisms, and expeditions, until his passing away. In the opening lines, he writes:

أَبْتَدِئُ الْإِمْلَاءَ بِاسْمِ الذَّاتِ الْعَلِيَّةِ، مُسْتَدِرًّا فَيْضَ الْبَرَكَاتِ عَلَى مَا أَنَالَهُ وَأَوْلَاهُ.

> I commence this dictation with the name of the Highest Being, seeking thereby the emanation of blessings in what He has caused me to attain.

Shaykh Abū ʿAbd Allāh Muhammad b. Aḥmad ʿAlīsh (d. 1299 AH) wrote a very beneficial and comprehensive commentary on this book by the name *al-Qawl al-munjī ʿalā mawlid al-Barzanjī*, which has been published repeatedly in Egypt. His grandson, the knowledgeable jurist and historian, Sayyid Jaʿfar b. Ismāʿīl b. Zayn al-ʿĀbidīn al-Barzanjī (d. 1317 AH), who was the Muftī of Medina, published this commentary in the form of 198 couplets. Its initiating verse is:

بَدَأْتُ بِاسْمِ الذَّاتِ عَالِيَةِ الشَّأْنِ

بِهَا مُسْتَدِرًّا فَيْضَ جُوْدٍ وَإِحْسَانِ

I commence with the name of the Being
whose status is Most High,
Seeking thereby the emanation of munificence and
benevolence

This poem is called *al-Kawkab al-anwār ʿalā ʿaqd al-jawhar fī mawlid al-Nabī al-azhar* ﷺ.

6.56.48 SAYYID MUHAMMAD B. ḤUSAYN AL-ḤANAFĪ AL-JAʿFARĪ (1149–1186 AH)

Sayyid Muhammad b. Ḥusayn al-Madanī al-ʿAlawī al-Ḥanafī al-Jaʿfarī authored many books on the biographies of the righteous guided caliphs and the Prophet's pure progeny. Amongst them are: *al-Fatḥ wa al-bushrā fī manāqib Sayyida Fāṭima al-Zahrāʾ* ؓ, *Qurrat al-ʿayn fī baʿḍ manāqib Sayyidinā al-Ḥusayn* ؓ, *Manāqib al-khulafāʾ al-arbaʿa* ؓ, *al-Mawāhib al-ʿazār fī manāqib Sayyidinā ʿAlī al-karār* ؓ. On the Prophet's birth, he has written the book *Mawlid al-Nabī* ﷺ.

6.56.49 MUHAMMAD B. AḤMAD AL-ʿADAWĪ (D. 1201 AH)

Aḥmad b. Muhammad b. Aḥmad al-ʿAdawī al-Mālikī al-Miṣrī is known by the title 'Dardīr'. His concise contribution to the discussion on *Mawlid al-Nabī* ﷺ was published in Egypt with the title *Mawlid al-Dardīr*. Owing to his intellectual competence, this book used to be studied by the professors and students of al-Azhar University. Shaykh al-Azhar Ibrāhīm b. Muhammad b. Aḥmad al-Bayjūrī (1198–1277 AH) authored a very beneficial annotation to this book.

6.56.50 ASHRAF ZĀDAH AL-BARSAWĪ (D. 1202 AH)

ʿAbd al-Qādir Najīb al-Dīn b. Shaykh ʿIzz al-Dīn Aḥmad, commonly known as Ashraf Zādah al-Barsawī al-Ḥanafī, was a Turkish poet. He wrote a book on *taṣawwuf* named *Sirr al-dawrān fī al-taṣawwuf*. He also composed something on the *mawlid* in his native language.

6.56.51 MUHAMMAD SHĀKIR ʿAQQĀD AL-SĀLIMĪ (D. 1202 AH)

Muhammad Shākir b. ʿAlī b. Ḥasan ʿAqqād al-Sālimī is the author of *Tadhkira ahl al-khayr fī al-mawlid al-Nabawī*.

6.56.52 ʿABD AL-RAḤMĀN B. MUHAMMAD AL-MUQRĪ (D. 1210 AH)

ʿAbd al-Raḥmān b. Muhammad al-Naḥrāwī al-Miṣrī al-Muqrī wrote a commentary on the *Risāla fī al-mawlid al-Nabawī* of Ḥasan b. ʿAlī al-Madābighī (d. 1170 AH), called *Ḥāshiyya ʿalā mawlid al-*

Nabī ﷺ *li al-Madābighī.*

6.56.53 Salāmī al-Azmīrī (d. 1228 AH)

Muṣṭafā b. Ismāᶜīl Sharḥī al-Azmīrī Salāmī penned an account of the *mawlid* in the Turkish language.

6.56.54 Muhammad b. ᶜAlī al-Shanwānī (d. 1233 AH)

Muhammad b. ᶜAlī al-Miṣrī al-Azharī al-Shāfiᶜī al-Shanwānī wrote *al-Jawāhir al-sunniyya fī mawlid Khayr al-bariyya* ﷺ, a discourse on the *mawlid.*

6.56.55 ᶜAbd Allāh al-Suwaydān (d. 1234 AH)

ᶜAbd Allāh b. ᶜAlī b. ᶜAbd al-Raḥmān al-Damlījī al-Ḍarīr al-Miṣrī al-Shādhilī, popularly known as al-Suwaydān, penned a thesis called *Maṭāliᶜ al-anwār fī mawlid al-Nabī al-mukhtār* ﷺ.

6.56.56 Ibn Ṣalāḥ al-Amīr

Sayyid ᶜAlī b. Ibrāhīm b. Muhammad b. Ismāᶜīl b. Ṣalāḥ al-Amīr al-Ṣanᶜānī was born in 1171 AH and died around the year 1236 AH. *Taʾnīs arbāb al-ṣafā fī mawlid al-Muṣṭafā* ﷺ is his account of the *mawlid.*

6.56.57 Muhammad al-Maghribī (d. 1240 AH)

Imam Muhammad al-Maghribī, a celebrated researcher, *Sufi* and saint, authored *al-Mawlid al-Nabawī* on the Prophet's birth. He quotes numerous narrations of hadith scholars and the sayings of prominent Sufis on the issue.

6.56.58 Shaykh Ibrāhīm b. Muhammad al-Bājūrī (d. 1276 AH)

Ibrāhīm b. Muhammad al-Bājūrī al-Shāfiᶜī al-Miṣrī is the author of *Tuḥfa al-bashar ᶜalā mawlid Ibn Ḥajar.*

6.56.59 Shāh Aḥmad Saᶜīd Mujaddidī al-Dihlawī (d. 1277 AH)

Shāh Aḥmad Saʿīd Mujaddidī al-Dihlawī (d. 1860 CE) is an illustrious academic and spiritual master who hailed from the Indian Subcontinent. In relation to the *mawlid*, he is the author of *Ithbāt al-mawlid wa al-qiyām*.

6.56.60 Sayyid Aḥmad al-Marzūqī

Sayyid Abū al-Fawz Aḥmad b. Muhammad b. Ramaḍān al-Makkī al-Mālikī al-Marzūqī was a teacher in the Sacred Mosque at Mecca. In 1281 AH, he wrote *Bulūgh al-marām li-bayān alfāẓ mawlid Sayyid al-anām fī sharḥ mawlid Aḥmad al-Bukhārī*. Apart from this, he penned an account of the *mawlid* in *ʿAqīda al-ʿawām*. A commentary of the latter book was also written by him under the title, *Taḥṣīl nayl al-marām*.

6.56.61 Shaykh Muhammad Maẓhar b. Aḥmad Saʿīd. 1301 AH)

Muhammad Maẓhar b. Aḥmad Saʿīd (d. 1884 CE) wrote a chronicle on the *mawlid* titled *al-Risāla al-Saʿīdiyya*.

6.56.62 ʿAbd al-Hādī al-Abyārī (d. 1305 AH)

ʿAbd al-Hādī al-Abyārī al-Miṣrī wrote a concise summary on the *mawlid*.

6.56.63 ʿAbd al-Fattāḥ b. ʿAbd al-Qādir al-Dimashqī (1250–1305 AH)

ʿAbd al-Fattāḥ b. ʿAbd al-Qādir b. Ṣāliḥ al-Dimashqī al-Shāfiʿī compiled a work on the *mawlid* under the heading *Surūr al-abrār fī mawlid al-Nabī al-Mukhtār* ﷺ.

6.56.64 Nawāb Ṣiddīq Ḥasan Khān Bhopālī (d. 1307 AH)

Nawāb Ṣiddīq Ḥasan Khān Bhopālī is a renowned *Salafi* scholar. He wrote a book on the *mawlid* called *al-Shamāma al-ʿAnbariyya min mawlid Khayr al-bariyya* ﷺ.

6.56.65 Ibrāhīm al-Ṭarābulusī al-Ḥanafī (d.

1308 AH)

Ibrāhīm b. Sayyid ʿAlī al-Ṭarābulusī al-Ḥanafī wrote a poetical account of the *mawlid* called *Manẓūma fī mawlid al-Nabī* ﷺ.

6.56.66 HIBAT ALLĀH MUHAMMAD B. ʿABD AL-QĀDIR AL-DIMASHQĪ (D.1311 AH)

Hibat Allāh Abū al-Farḥ Muhammad b. ʿAbd al-Qādir b. Muhammad Ṣāliḥ al-Dimashqī al-Shāfiʿī wrote an epistle called *Mawlid al-Nabī* ﷺ.

6.56.67 ABŪ ʿABD AL-MUʿṬĪ MUHAMMAD NUWAYR AL-JĀWĪ (D. 1315 AH)

Abū ʿAbd al-Muʿṭī Muhammad Nuwayr b. ʿUmar b. ʿArabī b. ʿAlī al-Nawawī al-Jāwī is the author of *Bughya al-ʿawām fī sharḥ mawlid Sayyid al-anām* ﷺ.

6.56.68 MUFTĪ ADRANA MUHAMMAD AL-FAWZĪ AL-RŪMĪ (D.1318 AH)

Muftī Adrana Muhammad al-Fawzī b. ʿAbd Allāh al-Rūmī composed the work *Ithbāt al-muḥsināt fī tilāwa mawlid Sayyid al-sādāt.*

6.56.69 SAYYID AḤMAD B. ʿABD AL-GHANĪ AL-DIMASHQĪ (D. 1320 AH)

Sayyid Aḥmad b. ʿAbd al-Ghanī b. ʿUmar ʿĀbidīn al-Dimashqī was a distinguished Ḥanafī jurist, researcher, and nephew of the author of *Radd al-muḥtār ʿalā durr al-mukhtār ʿalā tanwīr al-abṣār*, Muhammad b. Muhammad Amīn b. ʿĀbidīn al-Shāmī al-Dimashqī (1198–1252 AH). He penned a voluminous commentary on the *mawlid* of Ibn Ḥajar al-Haytamī al-Makkī (909–973 AH), called *Nathr al-durar ʿalā mawlid Ibn Ḥajar*.

6.56.70. IMAM AḤMAD RIḌĀ KHĀN (1272–1340 AH)

Aḥmad Riḍā b. Naqī ʿAlī Khān al-Qādirī (1856–1921 CE) wrote the following two works on the *mawlid*:

1. *Nuṭq al-hilāl bi arkh wilādat al-Ḥabīb wa al-wiṣāl*
2. *Iqāma al-qiyāma ʿalā ṭāʿin al-qiyām li-Nabī tihāma*

6.56.71 Muhammad b. Jaʿfar al-Kittānī (d.1345 AH)

The Gnostic Sayyid Sharīf Muhammad b. Jaʿfar al-Kattānī was a prominent and reliable hadith scholar. His treatise on the *mawlid*, *al-Yumn wa al-isʿād bi mawlid Khayr al-ʿibād* ﷺ, consists of sixty pages of classical and contemporary verdicts on the *mawlid*.

6.56.72 Imam Yūsuf b. Ismāʿīl al-Nabhānī (1265–1350 AH)

Imam Yūsuf b. Ismāʿīl al-Nabhānī is a famous personality and hadith expert who emerged from the Arab world. His poem, *Jawāhir al-naẓm al-badīʿ fī mawlid al-Shafīʿ* ﷺ, is his contribution to the genre.

6.56.73 Mawlānā Ashraf ʿAlī Thānwī (1280–1362 AH)

Ashraf ʿAlī Thānwī (1863–1943 CE) is a famous Deobandi scholar. His work on *sīra*, *Nashr al-ṭīb fī dhikr al-Nabī al-Ḥabīb* ﷺ, commences with a discourse on the creation of the Prophet's *nūr* as well as a detailed account of the miracles that were witnessed at the time of his birth. He also compiled *Ṭarīqa mawlūd*.

6.56.74 Shaykh Maḥmūd ʿAṭṭār al-Dimashqī (1284–1362 AH)

Maḥmūd b. Muhammad Rashīd ʿAṭṭār al-Ḥanafī was a well renowned hadith scholar from Damascus. He sought knowledge from the leading scholars of his day; even till today, the Damascene scholars are considered as his students or his students' students. The shaykh wrote a paper on the *mawlid* called *Istiḥbāb al-qiyām ʿinda dhikr wilādatihi ʿalayhi al-ṣalāt wa al-salām*.

6.56.75 Muhammad Zāhid al-Kawtharī (1296–1371 AH)

The celebrated Arab scholar and *mujaddid* of Islam, Muhammad

Zāhid al-Kawtharī, has authored several papers on the *mawlid.*

6.56.76 ʿABD ALLĀH B. MUHAMMAD AL-HIRARĪ (D. 1389 AH)

ʿAbd Allāh b. Muhammad Shībī ʿAbdarī al-Hirarī al-Ḥabashī (d. 1969 CE) composed two volumes on the *mawlid*:
1. *Kitāb al-mawlid al-Nabawī*
2. *Al-Rawāʾiḥ al-zakīya fī mawlid Khayr al-barīya* ﷺ

6.56.77. SHAYKH MUHAMMAD RASHĪD RIḌĀ AL-MIṢRĪ

Muhammad Rashīd Riḍā al-Miṣrī, the eminent historian, researcher, hadith-scholar and exegete, published a title on the *mawlid* called *Dhikr al-mawlid wa khulāṣa al-sīra al-Nabawiyya wa ḥaqīqa al-daʿwa al-Islāmiyya.*

6.56.78. SHAYKH MUHAMMAD B. ʿALAWĪ AL-MĀLIKĪ AL-MAKKĪ (D.1425 AH)

The late Muhammad b. ʿAlawī al-Mālikī al-Makkī (d. 2004 CE), the illustrious personality and hadith expert of Mecca, published booklets on the *mawlid* in which he summarised the views of three of the most competent scholars of Islam:
1. Ibn Kathīr: *Dhikr mawlid Rasūl Allāh wa raḍāʿihi.*
2. Mullā ʿAlī al-Qārī: *al-Mawlid al-rawī fī mawlid al-nabawī wa nasabihi al-ṭāhir* (Shaykh ʿAlawī al-Mālikī has reviewed this publication).
3. Ibn Ḥajar al-Haytamī al-Makki: *Mawlid al-Nabī* ﷺ.

He has also written a paper on the *mawlid* by the title of *Ḥawl al-iḥtifāl bi dhikr al-mawlid al-Nabawī al-sharīf.* Furthermore, he has collected the sayings and edicts of the great scholars regarding its validity; its title is *al-Iʿlām bi fatāwā aʾimma al-Islām ḥawla mawlidihī ʿalayhi al-ṣalāt wa al-salām.*

6.56.79 SHAYKH ʿABD AL-ʿAZĪZ B. MUHAMMAD

ʿAbd al-ʿAzīz b. Muhammad was a first rate researcher. He was the president of 'The Committee for the Promotion of Virtue and the Prevention of Vice'. He authored the book *Biʿtha al-Muṣṭafā fī mawlid al-Muṣṭafā* ﷺ.

6.56.80 Sayyid Māḍī Abū al-ʿAzāʾim

He is the author of *Bashāʾir al-akhyār fī mawlid al-Mukhtār*. In this book, he cites the narrations concerning the Prophet's creation being of *nūr*. He relates the accounts of his childhood, prophecy, and his supremacy over other Prophets. He also gives evidence in support of commemorating the *mawlid*.

6.56.81 Sayyid Muhammad ʿUthmān al-Mīrghanī

He authored a treatise called *al-Asrār al-Rabbāniyya al-maʿrūf bi mawlid al-Nabī* ﷺ. In this treatise, the Prophet's lineage, birth and different facets of his blessed life are discussed.

6.56.82 Muhammad b. Muhammad al-Manḍūrī al-Shāfiʿī al-Khayyāt

He wrote a commentary on the *mawlid* of Ibn Ḥajar al-Haythamī called *Iqtināṣ al-shawārid min mawārid al-mawārid*.

83. Aḥmad b. Qāsim al-Mālikī al-Bukhārī al-Ḥarīrī: *Mawlid al-Nabī* ﷺ.
84. Abū al-Ḥasan al-Bakrī: *al-Anwār fī mawlid al-Nabī Muhammad* ﷺ.
85. Ibrāhīm al-Abyārī: *Mawlid Rasūl Allāh* ﷺ.
86. Ṣalāḥ al-Dīn al-Huwwārī: *al-Mawlid al-Nabawī al-Sharīf*.
87. Abū Muhammad Veltori: *Ibtighāʾ al-wuṣūl li ḥubb Allāh bi madḥ al-Rasūl* ﷺ.
88. Zayn al-Dīn Makhdūm al-Fanānī: *al-Bunyān al-marṣūṣ fī sharḥ al-mawlid al-manqūṣ*.
89. ʿAbd Allāh ʿAfīfī: *al-Mawlid al-Nabawī al-Mukhtār* ﷺ.
90. ʿAbd Allāh Ḥimsī al-Shādhilī: *Mawlid al-Nabī* ﷺ.
91. Shaykh Khālid b. Wālidī: *Mawlid al-Nabī* ﷺ.
92. Shaykh Muhammad Wafā al-Ṣiyādī: *Mawlid al-Nabī* ﷺ.
93. Shaykh Maḥmūd Maḥfūẓ al-Dimashqī al-Shāfiʿī: *Mawlid al-Nabī* ﷺ.
94. Shaykh ʿAbd Allāh b. Muhammad al-Manāwī al-Shādhilī:

Mawlid al-jalīl ḥusn al-shakl al-jamīl.

95. Hafiz ʿAbd al-Raḥmān b. ʿAlī al-Shaybānī: *Mawlid al-Nabī* ﷺ.

96. Sayyid ʿAbd al-Qādir al-Iskandarānī: *al-Ḥaqāʾiq fī qirāʾa mawlid al-Nabī* ﷺ.

97. Muhammad b. Muhammad al-Dimyāṭī: *Mawlid al-ʿazb.*

98. Shaykh Muhammad Hāshim al-Rifāʿī: *Mawlid al-Nabī* ﷺ.

99. Shaykh Muhammad Hishām Kabbānī: *al-Mawlid fī al-Islām bayna al-bidʿa wa al-īmān.*

100. Saʿīd b. Masʿūd b. Muhammad al-Kāzrūnī: *Taʿrīb al-muttaqā fī siyar mawlid al-Nabī al-Muṣṭafā* ﷺ.

101. Shaykh Muhammad Nūrī b. ʿUmar b. ʿArabī b. ʿAlī al-Nawawī al-Shāfiʿī: *al-Ibrīz al-dānī fī mawlid Sayyidinā Muhammad al-ʿAdnānī* ﷺ.

102. Shaykh Muhammad Nūrī b. ʿUmar b. ʿArabī b. ʿAlī al-Nawawī al-Shāfiʿī: *Bughya al-ʿawwām fī sharḥ mawlid Sayyid al-anām* ﷺ.

103. Zayn al-ʿĀbidīn Muhammad al-ʿAbbāsī: *al-Jamʿ al-ẓāhir al-munīr fī dhikr mawlid al-Bashīr al-Nadhīr* ﷺ.

104. Abū Shākir ʿAbd Allāh al-Shalabī: *al-Durr al-munaẓẓam sharḥ al-kanz al-muṭalsam fī mawlid al-Nabī al-Muʿaẓẓam* ﷺ.

105. Sayf al-Dīn Abū Jaʿfar ʿUmar b. Ayyūb b. ʿUmar b. al-Ḥumayrī al-Turkumānī al-Dimashqī al-Ḥanafī: *al-Durr al-naẓīm fī mawlid al-Nabī al-Karīm* ﷺ.

106. Abū Hāshim Muhammad Sharīf al-Nūrī: *Iḥrāz al-maziya fī mawlid al-Nabī Khayr al-bariya* ﷺ.

107. Badr al-Dīn Yūsuf al-Maghribī: *Fatḥ al-qadīr fī sharḥ mawlid al-Dardīr.*

108. Abū al-Futūḥ al-Ḥalabī: *al-Fawāʾid al-bahiyya fī mawlid Khayr al-bariyya* ﷺ.

109. Suwaydān ʿAbd Allāh b. ʿAlī b. al-Dimlījī al-Miṣrī: *Maṭāliʿ al-anwār fī mawlid al-Nabī al-Mukhtār* ﷺ.

110. Ibn ʿAllān Muhammad ʿAlī al-Ṣiddīqī al-Makkī: *Mawrid al-ṣafā fī mawlid al-Muṣṭafā* ﷺ.

111. Sayyid Muhammad b. Khalīl al-Ṭarābulusī, also known as al-Qāqūwjī: *Mawlid al-Nabī* ﷺ.

112. Shaykh Abū ʿAbd Allāh Muhammad b. Aḥmad b. Muhammad al-ʿAṭṭār al-Jazāʾirī: *al-Mawrid al-ʿadhb al-mubīn fī mawlid Sayyid al-khalq ajmaʿīn* ﷺ.

113. Abū al-Ḥasan Aḥmad b. ʿAbd Allāh al-Bakrī: *Kitāb al-anwār wa miftāḥ al-surūr wa al-afkār fī mawlid Muhammad* ﷺ.
114. Aḥmad b. ʿAlī b. Saʿīd: *Ẓill al-ghamāma fī mawlid Sayyid yihāma* ﷺ.
115. Ibn al-Shaykh Āq Shams al-Dīn Ḥamd Allāh: *al-Mawlid al-jismānī wa al-mawrid al-ruḥānī* ﷺ.
116. Muhammad b. Ḥasan b. Muhammad b. Aḥmād b. Jamāl al-Dīn al-Khalwatī al-Samnūdī: *al-Durr al-thamīn fī mawlid Sayyid al-awwalīn wa al-ākhirīn* ﷺ.[1]

In the pages above, 125 published works which have been written on the subject of the most compassionate Prophet's blessed birth, authored by a sum of 116 renowned scholars and authorities, have been mentioned. Conversely, the reality is that the number of works written on the incidents surrounding the Holy Prophet's birth and memoirs of the *mawlid* celebration and its merits are far greater in number than what has been cited here. Numerous more titles can be widely and effortlessly found in languages such as Urdu, Punjabi, Sindhi, Balochi, Pashto, Saraiki, Hindi, Persian, and English—in fact, titles can be found in every language in places where there is a community of Muslims.

We can conclude from these details that to commemorate the most gracious Prophet's birthday, to relate the incidents which took place during his blessed birth, to mention accounts from his biography, and to recite odes in his praise are not actions which have been instigated by the Muslims of the contemporary age, or of the not-so-distant past by a certain group of people belonging to a particular part of the world; rather, it has been practiced by Muslims all over, continuously without interruption.

---

[1] The following references were also referred to whilst compiling this list of books written on the *mawlid*:

Ibn Nadīm, *Kitāb al-Fihrist*; Ḥājī Khalīfa, *Kashf al-ẓunūn ʿan usāmī al-kutub wa al-funūn*; Bābānī, *Hadya al-ʿĀrifīn*; Edward Van Dyck, *Iktifāʾ al-qanūʿ bimā huwa maṭbūʿ*; al-Khawārizmī, *Mafātīḥ al-ʿulūm*; Bāshā al-Baghdādī, *Īḍāḥ al-maknūn*; ʿAbd al-Ḥayy al-Kittānī, *Fahras al-fahāris wa al-athbāt wa muʿjam al-maʿājim wa al-mashīkhāt wa al-musalsalāt*; Ilyān Sarkīs, *Muʿjam al-maṭbūʿāt al-ʿarabiyya wa al-muʿarraba*; al-Qanūjī, *Abjad al-ʿulūm al-washī al-marqūm fī bayān aḥwāl al-ʿulūm*; and al-Kittānī, *al-Risāla al-mustaṭrifa li bayān mashūr kutub al-sunna al-musharrafa*.

Mawlid al-Nabī ﷺ has always served as a means by which the Muslims become culturally aware of their identity—through its celebration they revive their faith. If, God-forbid, the *mawlid* is a reprehensible innovation, as some people allege, then logically speaking, why would so many high ranking imams and proficient scholars fall prey to partaking in this so called heterodoxy, or even produce literature in favour of it?

Those people who oppose this blessed endeavour by speaking against it do so on the basis of their own preconceived notions, caused by their own personal predilections. It is most unfortunate indeed that these people distance others from the most generous Prophet ﷺ, thereby belittling the importance of one's emotional attachment with his person. In their false obsession with *tawḥīd*, they obstruct others from acquiring blessings and bounties from the Holy Prophet ﷺ; turning people away from the Prophets and Messengers عليهم السلام has been the hallmark of Satan in every age. All incorrect practices performed during the *mawlid* celebration by certain unlearned individuals should definitely be eradicated. However, the *mawlid* as a celebration should not be dismissed altogether or declared impermissible; and most certainly its practitioner should not be abused with derogatory terms such as *shirk* and *bidʿa*.

Chapter 7

Why the First Generation of Muslims did not Celebrate the *Mawlid*

To express happiness and joy on the birthday of the Beloved of Allah ﷺ, and to organise events in commemoration of it, is the greatest honour for a believer. But unfortunately, there are some individuals who still consider and declare the *mawlid* as an act in contradiction to the Sharia. To support this belief of theirs, they argue that the *mawlid* celebration did not take place during the age of the noble Companions; rather, it came into existence many generations later. What is to follow is an enquiry into why the noble Companions, after the demise of the most esteemed Prophet ﷺ, did not take *Mawlid al-Nabī* ﷺ as an act of celebration. Its reason will be explained taking into account the circumstances of that period.

7.1 The Prophet's Passing Away was Extremely Painful for the Companions ﵃

The blessed birth of the Mercy of all the worlds, the Holy Prophet ﷺ, is more significant for the Muslims than all the joy and happiness in the world. For the first generation of Muslims in general and the blessed Companions in particular, what could be more important than the Prophet's arrival into this temporal realm? Who could appreciate more this greatest favour ﷺ, if not the noble Companions? The Muslims of today are incapable of even perceiving the immeasurable joy and delight the companions felt.

If after the Prophet's passing away, the Companions did not commemorate the *mawlid* with fervour and zeal, there was an earnest reason behind it. It is common knowledge that the date of his birth is also the date of his passing away. Whenever the 12th of *Rabīʿ al-Awwal* arrived, the companions, who were heartbroken upon his physical demise, were reminded of his passing away and subsequently, the feelings of grief and sadness overcame any feelings of joy and happiness. The blessed Companions were reminded of the time they spent with the Holy Prophet ﷺ and were then also reminded of his departure, which as a result led to mixed emotions of joy and sorrow. Therefore, the companions did not celebrate the *mawlid*; rather, they expressed feelings of gloom and despair at his passing away.

7.1.1 Human Nature Does Not Allow One to Openly Express Joy During Times of Sadness

Daily experience tells us that whenever someone dies, there is a feeling of grief. If in any bereaved household a wedding has been prearranged, the marriage ceremony will almost certainly be cancelled. And if the wedding cannot be postponed, then the service is likely to be performed in the simplest manner possible as a mark of respect for the deceased.

If in the same household, five or ten years later, a wedding is held, it will be observed that the wedding is celebrated with great fanfare in accordance with prevailing customs and culture. Nobody will accuse the family of disrespecting the death of their relative by celebrating the wedding lavishly. This is because naturally after sorrow, feelings of sadness and despair become dominant over the human psyche; and as time passes, the effects of the pain slowly wear off, and the incident, however tragic, becomes a thing of the past.

7.2 The Immense Grief was an Impediment to the Expression of Joy amongst the First Generation

Subject to human nature, the grief of losing the Beloved ﷺ weighed heavily upon the noble companions. Due to the concurrence of the date in which the beloved Prophet ﷺ was born and had passed away, the feelings of sorrow felt by the Companions in comparison to joy were greater. The Companions were a living example of selflessness and sacrifice. They would happily sacrifice their lives upon the furrowing of the brow of the Prophet ﷺ. Their intense love for the Prophet ﷺ was the foremost measure of faith amongst them.

Nothing was more painful for the Companions than the passing away of their Beloved ﷺ. The news of his demise left them utterly distraught; it must have felt as if their entire world had been turned upside down. It is almost impossible to imagine how these devoted servants dealt with the news of their beloved Prophet ﷺ passing away. The Companions did not like, not even for a moment, to be separated from the Prophet ﷺ. When the Prophet ﷺ left this temporal world, even the lion-hearted Companion, ʿUmar ؓ, was unable to control his emotions; one can hardly imagine how the rest of the Companions reacted.

For the Companions and the Blessed Household of the Holy Prophet ﷺ, this news was traumatic, as it meant that their Beloved had now departed—this was far too much for them to bear. Their reaction was a natural response since they had sacrificed their homeland, family and possessions, and in fact everything, to be with the Holy Prophet ﷺ. Therefore, the thought of no longer having the Beloved ﷺ besides them had never crossed their minds; it was absolutely inconceivable to them. A glimpse of the emotional response of some of the Companions to the news of the Prophet's passing away will be discussed in the sections below:

7.2.1 SEPARATION FROM THE PROPHET ﷺ: THE CAUSE OF ABŪ BAKR'S DEATH

After the esteemed Prophet's passing away, the leader of the lovers, Abū Bakr al-Ṣiddīq ؓ, was overcome with immense grief. His constantly remembering of the Holy Prophet ﷺ eventually became the cause of his death. ʿAbd Allāh b. ʿUmar ؓ narrates:

كَانَ سَبَبُ مَوْتِ أَبِيْ بَكْرٍ مَوْتَ رَسُوْلِ اللهِ ﷺ مَا زَالَ جِسْمُهُ يَجْرِيْ حَتَّى مَاتَ.

The cause of Abū Bakr's death was the (grief he felt at the) Prophet's passing away. His body would not cease to become emaciated until ultimately it led to his death.[1]

[1] Narrated by al-Ḥākim in *al-Mustadrak*, 3:63–64 §4410; Ibn al-Jawzī in *Ṣafwa al-ṣafwa*, 1:263; and al-Suyūṭī in *Musnad Abī Bakr al-Ṣiddīq*, p.198 §631.

Ziyād b. Ḥanẓala narrates:

كَانَ سَبَبُ مَوْتِ أَبِيْ بَكْرٍ الْكَمَدَ عَلَى رَسُوْلِ اللهِ ﷺ.

The cause of Abū Bakr's death was his bereavement for the Prophet ﷺ.[1]

7.2.2 ʿUmar's Reaction to the Prophet's Demise

The news of the Prophet's demise came as a great shock to a vigorous, valiant and bold character, such as ʿUmar b. al-Khaṭṭāb رضي الله عنه. He was unable to control his emotions and in his extreme grief, he announced, 'If anyone says that the Prophet ﷺ has passed away, I will cut his head off.'[2] His reaction has been recorded in the books of biography and history:

إِنَّ رِجَالاً مِّنَ الْـمُنَافِقِيْنَ يَزْعَمُوْنَ: أَنَّ رَسُوْلَ اللهِ ﷺ قَدْ تُوُفِّيَ، وَإِنَّ رَسُوْلَ اللهِ ﷺ مَا مَاتَ، وَلَكِنَّهُ ذَهَبَ إِلَى رَبِّهِ كَمَـا ذَهَبَ مُوْسَى بْنُ عِمْرَانَ، فَقَدْ غَابَ عَنْ قَوْمِهِ أَرْبَعِيْنَ لَيْلَةً، ثُمَّ رَجَعَ إِلَيْهِمْ بَعْدَ أَنْ قِيْلَ: مَاتَ، وَوَاللهِ! لَيَرْجِعَنَّ رَسُوْلُ اللهِ ﷺ كَمَـا رَجَعَ مُوْسَى، فَلْيَقْطَعَنَّ أَيْدِيَ رِجَالٍ وَّأَرْجُلَهُمْ زَعَمُوْا: أَنَّ رَسُوْلَ اللهِ ﷺ مَاتَ.

The hypocrites assume that the Prophet ﷺ has passed away, but the Prophet has not died; rather, he has gone to his Lord like the way Prophet Mūsā b. ʿImrān عليه السلام went to his Lord. He was absent from his people for forty nights, and when he returned, the news of his death had already spread. By Allah, the Prophet ﷺ will certainly return like Prophet Mūsā. Then the Prophet will surely severe the hands and feet of those that even entertained the idea of his death.[3]

---

[1] Al-Suyūṭī, *Musnad Abī Bakr al-Ṣiddīq*, p.198 §632.

[2] Al-Ṭabarī, *Tārīkh al-umam wa al-mulūk*, 2:233.

[3] Narrated by Ibn Isḥāq in *al-Sīra al-Nabawiyya*, p.713; Aḥmad b. Ḥanbal

Although one can say that ʿUmar's reaction was very intense, one cannot say that it was unnatural. When one's dearest beloved passes away, anyone can be overcome with great grief and thus react in a similar fashion.

During his tenure, ʿUmar ﵁ used to spend his nights strolling through the streets of Medina to make sure that the citizenry of his caliphate were comfortable. ʿUmar ﵁ would do this out of the deep sense of self-accountability that he was responsible for their wellbeing on the Day of Judgment. Zayd b. Aslam relates: One night when ʿUmar ﵁ went out in order to check the health of his nation, he saw a house in which a lamp was burning. There was an old woman spinning wool: she was lost in the remembrance of the Prophet ﷺ, reciting the following verses:

عَلَى مُحَمَّدٍ صَلَاةُ الْأَبْرَارِ
صَلَّى عَلَيْكَ الْمُصْطَفُوْنَ الْأَخْيَارْ
قَدْ كُنْتَ قَوَّاماً بَكِيَّ الْأَسْحَارْ
يَا لَيْتَ شِعْرِيْ وَالْمَنَايَا أَطْوَارْ
هَلْ تَجْمَعُنِيْ وَحَبِيْبِي الدَّارْ

Upon Muhammad ﷺ, the blessings of the righteous
The elect and chosen invoke blessings upon you
You were vigilant in worship, weeping late at night
Alas! When death gives us different forms,
Will it join me to my beloved in the Abode?[1]

---

in *al-Musnad*, 3:196 §13,051; Ibn Ḥibbān in *al-Ṣaḥīḥ*, 14:588 §6620; Ibn Hishām in *al-Sīra al-Nabawiyya*, p.1134; Ibn Saʿd in *al-Ṭabaqāt al-kubrā*, 2:270; Ibn Athīr in *al-Kāmil fī al-tārīkh*, 2:187; al-Suhaylī in *al-Rawḍ al-unuf fī tafsīr al-sīrā al-Nabawiyya li-Ibn Hishām*, 4:443; and al-Suyūṭī in *al-Durr al-manthūr fī al-tafsīr bi al-maʾthūr*, 2:377.

[1] Ibn al-Mubārak, *al-Zuhd*, p.362–363 §1024; Qāḍī ʿIyāḍ, *al-Shifāʾ bi taʿrīf ḥuqūq al-Muṣṭafā*, 2:569; and Mullā ʿAlī al-Qārī, *Sharḥ al-shifāʾ*, 2:42–43.

Upon hearing these verses, the brave ʿUmar ﷺ was also reduced to tears, and the memories of the Prophet ﷺ came flooding back. *Amīr al-muʾminīn fī al-ḥadīth*, ʿAbd Allāh b. al-Mubārak (118–181 AH), who was the student of al-Imām al-Aʿẓam Abū Ḥanīfa (80–150 AH) and the teacher of Imam al-Bukhārī (194–256 AH), narrates:

فَجَلَسَ عُمَرُ يَبْكِي فَمَا زَالَ يَبْكِي حَتَّى قَرَعَ الْبَابَ عَلَيْهَا، فَقَالَتْ: مَنْ هَذَا؟ قَالَ: عُمَرُ بْنُ الْخَطَّابِ. فَقَالَتْ: مَا لِي وَلِعُمَرَ؟ وَمَا يَأْتِي بِعُمَرَ هَذِهِ السَّاعَةَ؟ فَقَالَ: اِفْتَحِيْ، رَحِمَكِ اللهُ، وَلَا بَأْسَ عَلَيْكِ، فَفَتَحَتْ لَهُ، فَدَخَلَ. وَقَالَ: رُدِّي عَلَيَّ الْكَلِمَاتِ الَّتِي قُلْتِ آنِفًا، فَرَدَّتْهُ عَلَيْهِ، فَلَمَّا بَلَغَتْ آخِرَهُ، قَالَ: أَسْأَلُكِ أَنْ تُدْخِلَنِي مَعَكُمَا. قَالَتْ: وَعُمَرُ، فَاغْفِرْ لَهُ يَا غَفَّارُ. فَرَضِيَ عُمَرُ وَرَجَعَ.

(Upon hearing this,) ʿUmar sat and cried and continued crying until eventually he knocked on the old woman's door. The woman asked, 'Who is it?' And he replied, 'It is ʿUmar b. al-Khaṭṭāb.' The woman asked, 'What is the matter with me with ʿUmar? What brings him at this hour?' He replied, 'May Allah have mercy upon you. Please open the door. There is nothing to be worried about.' So the woman permitted him to enter. ʿUmar entered her house and said, 'Those verses of poetry you just recited—please repeat them for me.' The old woman repeated the verses, and when she reached to the end of it, ʿUmar requested, 'I beg you, include me with the two of you.' The woman prayed, 'And ʿUmar (too). Forgive him, O the Most-Forgiving!' Thus ʿUmar was pleased and returned (to his home).[1]

According to the statement of Qāḍī Sulaymān Manṣūrpūrī,

[1] Ibn al-Mubārak, *al-Zuhd*, p.362–363 §1024; and Khifājī, *Nasīm al-riyāḍ fī sharḥ shifāʾ al-Qāḍī ʿIyāḍ*, 4:428–429.

ʿUmar b. al-Khaṭṭāb ﷺ became bedridden[1] after this incident, and for several days, the Companions ﷺ would visit him to inquire about his health.

7.2.3 THE GRIEF OF FĀṬIMA AL-ZAHRĀʾ ﷺ

The leader of the women of Paradise, Sayyida Fāṭima al-Zahrāʾ ﷺ, had the everlasting honoured position of being the Prophet's beloved daughter. She loved the Prophet ﷺ immensely, and the Prophet ﷺ declared her as 'a part of him'.[2] History has recorded the untold grief and feelings of despair experienced by Sayyida Fāṭima upon the Prophet's passing.

Sayyida Fāṭima al-Zahrāʾ ﷺ was the first from the blessed household to depart from this life after the esteemed Prophet ﷺ had passed away—as foretold by him. Concerning this there are varying reports: some historians allege that she passed away eight months after the esteemed Prophet ﷺ passed away; others say that it was one hundred days; and there are others who have stated that it was seventy days. The most accurate opinion is six months. She was 29 years of age when she breathed her last on the 3rd of *Ramaḍān* 11 AH.[3] The cause of her death at such a young age is that she could not bear the feelings of loss and despair: Sayyida

---

[1] Manṣūrpūrī, *Raḥmatan liʾl-ʿĀlamīn*, 2:343.

[2] Miswar b. Makharama reports that the Prophet ﷺ said:

«فَاطِمَةُ بَضْعَةٌ مِنِّي.»

Faṭima is a part of me.

Narrated by al-Bukhārī in *al-Ṣaḥīḥ*: *Kitāb al-Manāqib* [The Book of Exemplary Virtues], chapter: 'The virtues of the Prophet's relatives', 3:1361 §3510; al-Bukhārī in *al-Ṣaḥīḥ*: *Kitāb al-manāqib* [The Book of Exemplary Virtues], chapter: 'The exemplary virtue of Faṭima', 3:1347 §3556; and Muslim in *al-Ṣaḥīḥ*: *Kitāb Faḍāʾil al-Ṣaḥāba* [The Book of the Companions' Exemplary Virtues], chapter: 'The Prophet's daughter, Faṭima', 4:1903 §2449.

[3] Narrated by al-Ḥakim in *al-Mustadrak*, 3:176 §4761; Muḥibb al-Ṭabarī in *Dhakhāʾir al-ʿuqbā fī manāqib dhawī al-qurbā*, p.101; Ibn al-Jawzī in *Ṣafwa al-ṣafwa*, 2:8–9; and Ibn Athīr in *Asad al-ghāba fī maʿrifa al-Ṣaḥāba*, 7:221.

Fāṭima ﵂ always remained in a state of sorrow and was known not to have ever laughed after the Prophet ﷺ passed away.[1]

In the *Ṣaḥīḥ* of Imam al-Bukhārī (194–256 AH), Anas ﵁ narrates that Sayyida Fāṭima ﵂, at the loss of her father, struggled with so much grief that she used to cry:

يَا أَبَتَاهُ! أَجَابَ رَبًّا دَعَاهُ

يَا أَبَتَاهُ! مَنْ جَنَّةُ الْفِرْدَوْسِ مَأْوَاهُ

يَا أَبَتَاهُ! إِلَى جِبْرِيْلَ نَنْعَاهُ

O father, you accepted the order of your Lord (by returning to Him)!
O father, you are residing in the highest level of Paradise!
O father, I am expressing my grief for Archangel Jibrāʾīl to hear![2]

In the *Sunan* of Ibn Mājah (209–273 AH), it is recorded that Sayyida Fāṭima ﵂ recited the following verses:

وَا أَبَتَاهُ! إِلَى جِبْرِيْلَ أَنْعَاهُ

وَا أَبَتَاهُ! مِنْ رَبِّهِ مَا أَدْنَاهُ

وَا أَبَتَاهُ! جَنَّةُ الْفِرْدَوْسِ مَأْوَاهُ

وَا أَبَتَاهُ! أَجَابَ رَبًّا دَعَاهُ

---

[1] Dūlābī, *al-Dhuriyya al-ṭāhira*, p.111, §212; Muḥibb al-Ṭabarī, *Dhakhāʾir al-ʿuqbā fī manāqib dhawī al-qurbā*, p.103; Ibn Athīr, *Asad al-ghāba fī maʿrifa al-Ṣaḥāba*, 7:221; and Ibn Rajab al-Ḥanbalī, *Laṭāʾif al-maʿārif fīmā li-mawāsim al-ʿām min al-waẓāʾif*, p.214.

[2] Narrated by al-Bukhārī in *al-Ṣaḥīḥ*: *Kitāb al-Maghāzī* [The Book of Expedition], chapter: 'The Prophet's final illness and his passing away', 4:1619 §4193; Aḥmad b. Ḥanbal in *al-Musnad*, 3:197 §13,054; al-Dārimī in *al-Sunan*, 1:41 §88; al-Ṭabarānī in *al-Muʿjam al-kabīr*, 22:416 §1029; and Ibn Kathīr in *al-Bidāya wa al-nihāya*, 4:254.

O father, I am expressing my grief for Archangel Jibrāʾīl to hear!
O father, you are in the close proximity of your Lord!
O father, you are residing in the highest level of Paradise!
O father, you accepted the order of your Lord (by returning to Him)![1]

In the *Ṣaḥīḥ* of Imam al-Bukhārī, it states that when the noble Companions ﷺ had returned from the funeral preparations of the beloved Prophet ﷺ, Sayyida Fāṭima ﷺ, in a state of utter despair, addressed them saying:

يَا أَنَسُ، أَطَابَتْ أَنْفُسُكُمْ أَنْ تَحْثُوا عَلَى رَسُولِ اللهِ ﷺ التُّرَابَ.

O Anas! How could you endure to bury Allah's Messenger ﷺ by placing dust over him?[2]

Imam Aḥmad b. Ḥanbal (164–241 AH) relates in his *Musnad* that Sayyida Fāṭima ﷺ said to Anas ﷺ:

يَا أَنَسُ، أَطَابَتْ أَنْفُسُكُمْ أَنْ دَفَنْتُمْ رَسُولَ اللهِ ﷺ فِي التُّرَابِ وَرَجَعْتُمْ.

O Anas! How could you endure to bury Allah's Messenger ﷺ in the earth whilst you yourselves return?[3]

---

[1] Narrated by Ibn Mājah in *al-Sunan*: *Kitāb al-Janāʾiz* [The Book of Funeral Prayer], chapter: 'Mention of the Prophet's passing away and burial', 2:103 §1630; al-Nasāʾī in *al-Sunan*: *Kitāb al-Janāʾiz* [The Book of Funeral Prayer], chapter: 'Weeping upon the deceased,' 4:12 §1844; Ibn Ḥibbān in *al-Ṣaḥīḥ*, 14:591–592 §6622; al-Ḥakim in *al-Mustadrak*, 1:537 §1408; Ibid., 3:61 §4396; Ibn Saʿd in *al-Ṭabaqāt al-kubrā*, 2:311; al-Dhahabī in *Tārīkh al-Islām wa wafayāt al-mashāhīr wa al-aʿlām* (*al-Sīra al-Nabawiyya*), 1:562.

[2] Narrated by al-Bukhārī in *al-Ṣaḥīḥ*: *Kitāb al-Maghāzī* [The Book of Expedition], chapter: 'The Prophet's final illness and his passing away', 4:1619 §4193; Abū Yaʿlā in *al-Musnad*, 1:402 §1364; ʿAbd b. Ḥamīd in *al-Musnad*, 1:402 §1364; al-Ḥakim in *al-Mustadrak*, 1:537 §1408; al-Ṭabarānī in *al-Muʿjam al-kabīr*, 22:416 §1029; and al-Bayhaqī in *al-Sunan al-kubrā*, 3:409 §6519.

[3] Narrated by Aḥmad b. Ḥanbal in *al-Musnad*, 3:204 §13,139; Ibn Kathīr in *al-Bidāya wa al-nihāya*, 4:254; and al-Ḥalabī in *Insān al-ʿuyūn fī sīra*

Imam al-Ṭabarānī (260–360 AH) records in *al-Muʿjam al-kabīr*:

فَلَمَّا انْصَرَفَ النَّاسُ قَالَتْ فَاطِمَةُ لِعَلِيٍّ ﵇: يَا أَبَا الْحَسَنِ! دَفَنْتُمْ رَسُولَ اللهِ ﷺ؟ قَالَ: نَعَمْ. قَالَتْ فَاطِمَةُ ﵍: كَيْفَ طَابَتْ أَنْفُسُكُمْ أَنْ تَحْثُوا التُّرَابَ عَلَى رَسُولِ اللهِ ﷺ؟ أَمَا كَانَ فِي صُدُورِكُمْ لِرَسُولِ اللهِ ﷺ الرَّحْمَةُ؟ أَمَا كَانَ مُعَلِّمَ الْخَيْرِ؟ قَالَ: بَلَى، يَا فَاطِمَةُ! وَلَكِنْ أَمَرَ اللهُ الَّذِي لَا مَرَدَّ لَهُ. فَجَعَلَتْ تَبْكِي وَتَنْدُبُ، وَهِيَ تَقُولُ: يَا أَبَتَاهُ! الْآنَ انْقَطَعَ جِبْرِيلُ ﵇، وَكَانَ جِبْرِيلُ يَأْتِينَا بِالْوَحْيِ مِنَ السَّمَاءِ.

> When the Companions returned from burying the Prophet ﷺ, Sayyida Fāṭima ﵍ addressing ʿAlī b. Abī Ṭālib ﵁ said, 'O Abū al-Ḥasan! Have you buried Allah's Messenger ﷺ?' He replied, 'Yes.' She said, 'How could you endure to bury Allah's Messenger ﷺ by placing dust over him? Was there not any mercy in your hearts for him? Was he not a teacher of benevolence?' ʿAlī b. Abī Ṭālib replied, 'Of course, O Fāṭima! But no one can postpone Almighty Allah's command.' Hearing this, Sayyida Fāṭima ﵍ started weeping profusely, saying, 'O father! Now the period of Jibrāʾīl's visits is at an end; Jibrāʾīl used to bring Allah's revelation from the heavens.'[1]

After the Holy Prophet's passing, the noble Companions remained in a constant state of grief, and many of them were seen never to smile again. Regarding Sayyida Fāṭima ﵍, Abū Jaʿfar says:

---

al-Amīn al-Maʾmūn, 3:493. Ḥammād narrates that when Thābit al-Bunānī, the renowned Successor who was the student of Anas, reported this tradition, 'he would weep until his ribs would come out of its place.' Narrated by Ibn al-Jawzī in *al-Wafāʾ bi aḥwāl al-Muṣṭafā*, p.803.

[1] Narrated by al-Ṭabarānī in *al-Muʿjam al-kabīr*, 3:64 §2676; and Abū Nuʿaym in *Ḥilya al-awliyāʾ wa ṭabaqāt al-aṣfiyāʾ*, 4:79.

مَا رَأَيْتُ فَاطِمَةَ ﵂ ضَاحِكَةً بَعْدَ رَسُوْلِ اللهِ ﷺ.

I never saw Sayyida Fāṭima laugh after the Prophet's passing away.[1]

It is narrated from ʿAlī b. Abī Ṭālib ﵁ that when Sayyida Fāṭima ﵂ used to visit the blessed grave of the Prophet ﷺ, she used to take a handful of its soil and place it over her eyes. Then she would weep and say:

أَخَذَتْ قَبْضَةً مِّنْ تُرَابِ الْقَبْرِ، فَوَضَعَتْهُ عَلَى عَيْنَيْهَا، فَبَكَتْ وَأَنْشَأَتْ تَقُوْلُ:

مَاذَا عَلَى مَنْ شَمَّ تُرْبَةَ أَحْمَدَ

أَنْ لَّا يَشُمَّ مَدَى الزَّمَانِ غَوَالِيَا

صُبَّتْ عَلَيَّ مَصَائِبُ لَوْ أَنَّهَا

صُبَّتْ عَلَى الْأَيَّامِ صِرْنَ لَيَالِيَا

Whoever has smelt the sweet smell of the soil of your grave
has no need for any other fragrance for the rest of his life.
If the amount of troubles I have had to deal with since you passed away were given to the days instead, then those days would surely turn into nights (due to the excessive suffering).[2]

During these sorrowful times, when Sayyida Fāṭima ﵂ was close to passing away, she welcomed it willingly because the death from this finite realm meant that she would meet Almighty Allah and be united with her beloved father ﷺ. The imams and hadith-scholars have documented this:

عَنْ أُمِّ سَلَمَةَ ﵂ قَالَتِ: اشْتَكَتْ فَاطِمَةُ شَكْوَاهَا الَّتِي قُبِضَتْ فِيْهَا،

[1] Ibn al-Jawzī, *al-Wafāʾ bi aḥwāl al-Muṣṭafā*, p.803.

[2] Al-Dhahabī, *Siyar aʿlām al-nubalāʾ*, 2:134; and Ibn Qudāma, *al-Mughnī*, 2:213.

فَكُنْتُ أُمَرِّضُهَا، فَأَصْبَحَتْ يَوْمًا كَأَمْثَلِ مَا رَأَيْتُهَا فِي شَكْوَاهَا تِلْكَ، قَالَتْ: وَخَرَجَ عَلِيٌّ لِبَعْضِ حَاجَتِهِ فَقَالَتْ: يَا أُمَّهْ، اسْكُبِي لِي غُسْلًا. فَسَكَبْتُ لَهَا غُسْلًا، فَاغْتَسَلَتْ كَأَحْسَنِ مَا رَأَيْتُهَا تَغْتَسِلُ. ثُمَّ قَالَتْ: يَا أُمَّهْ، أَعْطِينِي ثِيَابِيَ الْجُدُدَ. فَأَعْطَيْتُهَا فَلَبِسَتْهَا، ثُمَّ قَالَتْ: يَا أُمَّهْ، قَدِّمِي لِي فِرَاشِي وَسَطَ الْبَيْتِ. فَفَعَلْتُ وَاضْطَجَعَتْ وَاسْتَقْبَلَتِ الْقِبْلَةَ وَجَعَلَتْ يَدَهَا تَحْتَ خَدِّهَا، ثُمَّ قَالَتْ: يَا أُمَّهْ، إِنِّي مَقْبُوضَةٌ الْآنَ. وَقَدْ تَطَهَّرْتُ فَلَا يَكْشِفُنِي أَحَدٌ فَقُبِضَتْ مَكَانَهَا، قَالَتْ: فَجَاءَ عَلِيٌّ فَأَخْبَرْتُهُ.

> Umm Salama narrates, "When Sayyida Fāṭima was in the last stage of her illness, I used to take care of her. One morning she got up feeling better than any other time throughout that illness. ʿAlī had left (that day) for some duty of his. Sayyida Fāṭima said, "Dear mother! Prepare for me some water so that I may have a bath." So I prepared some water and she bathed herself thoroughly. Then she said, "Dear mother! Give me some new clothes." So I gave it to her and she wore it on. Then she said, "Dear mother! Prepare for me bedding in the middle of the house." And I did so, and then she laid on the ground facing the *qibla* with her hand placed below her cheek. Then she said, "Dear mother! I am to be taken away now and I have been purified. Let nobody uncover me." Then she breathed her last in that place and later ʿAlī came and so I informed him of it."[1]

Biographers and historians have asserted that Sayyida Fāṭima passed away between the *maghrib* and *ʿishāʾ* prayers. In accordance

[1] Narrated by Aḥmad b. Ḥanbal in *al-Musnad*, 6:461–462 §27,656; Aḥmad b. Ḥanbal in *Faḍāʾil al-Ṣaḥāba*, 2:629 & 725 §1074 & 1243; al-Dūlābī in *al-Dhurriyya al-ṭāhira*, p.113; al-Haythamī in *Majmaʿ al-zawāʾid wa manbaʿ al-fawāʾid*, 9:211; al-Zaylaʿī in *Naṣb al-rāya li-aḥādīth al-hidāya*, 2:250; Muḥibb al-Ṭabarī in *Dhakhāʾir al-ʿuqbā fī manāqib dhawī al-qurbā*, p.103; and Ibn Athīr in *Asad al-ghāba fī maʿrifa al-Ṣaḥāba*, 7:221.

to her instructions, she was buried at night and ʿAlī b. Abī Ṭālib, ʿAbbās and Faḍl b. ʿAbbās ؓ were the ones to lower her body into her grave. This is the manner in which she went to meet her beloved father ﷺ.[1]

When such is the grief of being separated from Allah's Messenger ﷺ, not forgetting that the day of his birth was also the day of his passing, how could the Companions ؓ possibly bear to commemorate his birth?

7.2.4 THE GRIEF OF ANAS B. MĀLIK ؓ

Anas b. Mālik ؓ served the Holy Prophet ﷺ for a period of ten years. During this time, the beautiful character of Allah's Messenger ﷺ left such an indelible impression on his person that he was constantly in a state of grief owing to his loss; the Prophet's passing away was for him a devastating catastrophe. He would crave for a moment with his Beloved ﷺ, and it was hard to endure his separation. He would constantly weep in the remembrance of this exalted personage. To bring peace to his ailing heart, he would behold the beloved Prophet's blessed possessions and remember him in gatherings; he would yearn for him and make others yearn for him too.

On one occasion, he described the physical appearance of the Mercy of all the Worlds, the Holy Prophet ﷺ. Recounting his beauty, he narrates:

وَلَا مَسِسْتُ خَزَّةً وَلَا حَرِيرَةً أَلْيَنَ مِنْ كَفِّ رَسُولِ اللهِ ﷺ، وَلَا شَمِمْتُ مِسْكَةً وَلَا عَبِيرَةً أَطْيَبَ رَائِحَةً مِنْ رَائِحَةِ رَسُولِ اللهِ ﷺ.

I have not touched silk softer than the palms of Allah's

---

[1] Narrated by al-Ḥakim in *al-Mustadrak*, 3:177–178 §4763–4765; Ibn Abī Shayba in al-*Muṣannaf*, 3:31 §11,826; Ibid., 7:25 §33,938; al-Bayhaqī in *al-Sunan al-kubrā*, 4:31; Muḥibb al-Ṭabarī in *al-Riyāḍ al-naḍra fī manāqib al-ʿashra*, 1:175–176; Muḥibb al-Ṭabarī in *Dhakhāʾir al-ʿuqbā fī manāqib dhawī al-qurbā*, p.104; al-Shaybānī in *al-Āḥād wa al-mathānī*, 5:355 §2,937; Ibn Saʿd in *al-Ṭabaqāt al-kubrā*, 8:29; Ibn al-Jawzī in *Ṣafwa al-ṣafwa*, 2:8; and Ibn Athīr in *Asad al-ghāba fī maʿrifa al-Ṣaḥāba*, 7:221.

> Messenger ﷺ. I have not smelt a fragrance nor a scent more pleasant than the scent of Allah's Messenger ﷺ.[1]

Anas used to see the Holy Prophet ﷺ often in his dreams. Muthannā b. Saʿīd narrates that he heard Anas ؓ say:

> مَا مِنْ لَيْلَةٍ إِلاَّ وَأَنَا أَرَى فِيْهَا حَبِيبِي، ثُمَّ يَبْكِي.
>
> There is not a night except that I see my Beloved ﷺ. Thereafter, he wept profusely.[2]

Anas, whilst describing the Holy Prophet's entry into Medina and his passing, said:

> لَـمَّـا كَانَ الْيَوْمُ الَّذِي دَخَلَ فِيهِ رَسُولُ الله ﷺ الْـمَدِينَةَ، أَضَاءَ مِنْهَا كُلُّ شَيْءٍ، فَلَـمَّـا كَانَ الْيَوْمُ الَّذِي مَاتَ فِيهِ أَظْلَمَ مِنْهَا كُلُّ شَيْءٍ.
>
> Everything became illuminated the day in which the Prophet ﷺ entered Medina. And the day in which the Prophet passed away, everything became darkened (for me).[3]

---

[1] Narrated by al-Bukhārī in *al-Ṣaḥīḥ*: *Kitāb al-Ṣawm* [The Book of Fasting], chapter: 'What has been mentioned of the Prophet's fasting and breaking fast', 2:696 §1872; Muslim in *al-Ṣaḥīḥ*: *Kitāb al-Faḍāʾil* [The Book of Exemplary Virtues], chapter: 'The Prophet's beautiful scent, his soft touch, and the blessings (*tabarruk*) obtained from the passing of his hands', 4:1814 §2330; al-Dārimī in *al-Sunan*, *al-Muqaddama*, chapter: 'The Prophet's beauty', 1:45 §61; Ibn Ḥibbān in *al-Ṣaḥīḥ*, 14:211 §6303; and Aḥmad b. Ḥanbal in *al-Musnad*, 3:107.

[2] Ibn Saʿd, *al-Ṭabaqāt al-kubrā*, 7:20; and al-Dhahabī, *Siyar aʿlām al-nubalāʾ*, 3:403.

[3] Narrated by Tirmidhī in *al-Jāmiʿ al-Ṣaḥīḥ*: *Kitāb al-Manāqib* [The Book of Exemplary Virtues], chapter: 'The Prophet's exemplary virtue', 6:13 §3618; Ibn Mājah in *al-Sunan*: *Kitāb al-Janāʾiz* [The Book of Funeral Prayer], chapter: 'Mention of the Prophet's passing away and burial', 1:522 §1631; Aḥmad b. Ḥanbal in *al-Musnad*, 3:268 §13,857; Ibn Ḥibbān in *al-Ṣaḥīḥ*, 14:601 §6634; Abū Yaʿlā in *al-Musnad*, 6:51 & 110 §3296 & 3378; and al-Maqdisī in *al-Aḥādīth al-mukhtāra*, 4:418–419 §1592–1593.

Anas felt that a shadow was cast over them due to the lack of the physical presence of the Beloved Prophet ﷺ.

Ibrāhīm al-Bayjūrī explains this statement of Anas in the following manner:

اِسْتَنَارَ مِنَ الْمَدِيْنَةِ الشَّرِيْفَةِ كُلُّ شَيْءٍ نُوْراً حِسِّيًّا وَمَعْنَوِيًّا، لِأَنَّهُ ﷺ نُوْرُ الْأَنْوَارِ وَالسِّرَاجُ الْوَهَّاجُ وَنُوْرُ الْهِدَايَةِ الْعَامَّةِ وَرَفْعُ الظُّلْمَةِ التَّامَّةِ، وَقَوْلُهُ: أَظْلَمَ مِنْهَا كُلُّ شَيْءٍ؛ أَيْ لِفَقْدِ النُّوْرِ وَالسِّرَاجِ مِنْهَا فَذَهَبَ ذَلِكَ النُّوْرُ بِمَوْتِهِ.

> Everything in Medina was illuminated with a perceivable and metaphorical light. This is because his sacred person is the fountainhead of all the lights, a shining lamp; he is the light of guidance for all and an eradicator of all oppression. His statement, 'everything became darkened', refers to the absence of his light and his illumination, as it went away with his passing.[1]

7.2.5 The Grief of Bilāl b. Rabāḥ ؓ

The devout lover of the Prophet ﷺ, Sayyidinā Bilāl ؓ, could not cope with the feelings of grief and despair of being separated from his Beloved. Unable to cope with his feelings, he migrated from Medina to abide in Aleppo, Syria. In Medina, he would constantly be reminded of the memories he shared with the Holy Prophet ﷺ. He could not bear to live in that city, now that the Holy Prophet ﷺ was no longer physically present.

The commentator of *Ṣaḥīḥ al-Bukhārī*, al-Kirmānī (717–786 AH), records that when the Holy Prophet ﷺ passed away, Bilāl ؓ due to a heavy heart, decided to leave Medina. When Abū Bakr al-Ṣiddīq ؓ was informed of this decision, he tried to persuade Bilāl not to leave, asking him to continue giving the call to prayer in the Prophet's Mosque. Bilāl ؓ said in reply:

---

[1] Al-Bayjūrī, *al-Mawāhib al-ladunya ʿalā al-shamāʾil al-Muḥammadiyya*, p.287.

إِنِّي لَا أُرِيْدُ الْـمَـدِيْنَةَ بِدُوْنِ رَسُوْلِ اللهِ ﷺ وَلَا أَتَحَمَّلُ مَقَامَ رَسُوْلِ اللهِ ﷺ خَالِياً عَنْهُ.

I do not want a Medina void of Allah's Messenger. I cannot bear the Prophet's place empty of him.[1]

In *Ṣaḥīḥ al-Bukhārī*, his response is recorded as thus:

يَا أَبَا بَكْرٍ، إِنْ كُنْتَ إِنَّمَـا اشْتَرَيْتَنِي لِنَفْسِكَ فَأَمْسِكْنِي، وَإِنْ كُنْتَ إِنَّمَـا اشْتَرَيْتَنِي لِلّٰهِ فَدَعْنِي.

O Abū Bakr! If you bought me only for yourself, then stop me; and if you freed me only for the sake of Allah, then leave me.[2]

Mūsā b. Muhammad b. Ḥārith al-Taymī narrates from his father:

لَـمَّـا تُوُفِّيَ رَسُوْلُ اللهِ ﷺ أَذَّنَ بِلَالٌ وَرَسُوْلُ اللهِ ﷺ لَـمْ يُقْبَرْ، فَكَانَ إِذَا قَالَ: أَشْهَدُ أَنَّ مُحَمَّداً رَسُوْلُ اللهِ انْتَحَبَ النَّاسُ فِي الْـمَسْجِدِ. قَالَ: فَلَـمَّـا دُفِنَ رَسُوْلُ اللهِ ﷺ قَالَ لَهُ أَبُوْبَكْرٍ: أَذِّنْ، فَقَالَ: إِنْ كُنْتَ إِنَّمَـا أَعْتَقْتَنِي لِأَنْ أَكُوْنَ مَعَكَ فَسَبِيْلُ ذٰلِكَ، وَإِنْ كُنْتَ أَعْتَقْتَنِي لِلّٰهِ فَخَلِّنِيْ وَمَنْ أَعْتَقْتَنِي لَهُ، فَقَالَ: مَا أَعْتَقْتُكَ إِلَّا لِلّٰهِ. قَالَ فَإِنِّي لَا أُؤَذِّنُ لِأَحَدٍ بَعْدَ رَسُوْلِ اللهِ ﷺ.

When the Prophet ﷺ had passed away, Bilāl made the call

[1] Kirmānī, *al-Kawākib al-darārī fī sharḥ al-Ṣaḥīḥ al-Bukhārī*, 15:24.

[2] Narrated by al-Bukhārī in *al-Ṣaḥīḥ*: *Kitāb Faḍāʾil al-Ṣaḥāba* [The Book of the Companions' Exemplary Virtues], chapter: 'The exemplary virtue of Bilāl b. Rabāḥ', 3:1371 §3545; Ibn Abī Shayba in al-*Muṣannaf*, 6:396 §32,336; al-Ṭabarānī in *al-Muʿjam al-kabīr*, 1:337 §1010; Ibn Saʿd, *al-Ṭabaqāt al-kubrā*, 3:238; al-Maqrīzī, *Imtāʿ al-asmāʿ bi mā li-Nabī min al-aḥwāl wa al-amwāl wa al-ḥafda wa al-matāʿ*, 10:132–133; Muḥibb al-Ṭabarī in *al-Riyāḍ al-naḍra fī manāqib al-ʿashra*, 2:24; and al-Ḥalabī in *Insān al-ʿuyūn fī sīra al-Amīn al-Maʾmūn*, 1:481.

to prayer whilst the Prophet ﷺ had not yet been buried. When he proclaimed, 'I testify that Muhammad is Allah's Messenger,' the people present in the mosque began to cry uncontrollably. When the Prophet ﷺ had been buried, Abū Bakr requested that Bilāl make the call to prayer. Bilāl said in reply, 'If you freed me only for yourself, then I will do as you ask; but if you freed me for the sake of Allah, then leave me and the one for whom you freed me.' Abū Bakr replied, 'I freed you only for the sake of Allah.' Bilāl then said, 'I will not make the call to prayer for anyone other than the Messenger of Allah ﷺ.'[1]

After mentioning a complete chain of narration for this incident, the well renowned author of *al-Qāmūs al-muḥīṭ*, Yaʿqūb Fayrūzābādī (817–729 AH), writes:

كَذَا ذَكَرَهُ ابْنُ عَسَاكِرَ فِيْ تَرْجَمَةِ بِلَالٍ ﵁، وَذَكَرَهُ أَيْضاً فِيْ تَرْجَمَةِ إِبْرَاهِيْمَ بْنِ مُحَمَّدِ بْنِ سُلَيْمَانَ بِسَنَدٍ آخَرَ إِلَى مُحَمَّدِ بْنِ الْفَيْضِ، فَذَكَرَهُ سِوَاء، وَابْنُ الْفَيْضِ رَوَى عَنْ خَلَائِقَ، وَرَوَى عَنْهُ جَمَاعَةٌ، مِنْهُمْ: أَبُوْ أَحْمَدَ بْنُ عَدِيٍّ وَأَبُوْ أَحْمَدَ الْحَاكِمُ، وَأَبُوْبَكْرٍ ابْنُ الْمُقْرِيِّ فِيْ مُعْجَمِهِ وَآخَرُوْنَ.

Ibn ʿAsākir has recorded this incident under the introduction to Bilāl. Ibrāhīm b. Muhammad b. Sulaymān has also recorded this with a different chain of narration ending with (the famous hadith scholar) Muhammad b. al-Fayḍ. Ibn al-Fayḍ took it from many narrators, and many narrators took it from him: Abū Aḥmad b. ʿAdī, Abū Aḥmad al-Ḥākim, Abū Bakr b. al-Maqrī in his *Muʿjam*, and others were amongst them.[2]

---

[1] Narrated by al-Bayhaqī in *al-Sunan al-kubrā*, 1:419 §1828; Ibn Saʿd, *al-Ṭabaqāt al-kubrā*, 3:236–237; al-Azdī in *al-Jāmiʿ*, 11:234; Abū Nuʿaym in *Ḥilya al-awliyāʾ wa ṭabaqāt al-aṣfiyāʾ*, 1:150–151; Ibn al-Jawzī in *Ṣafwa al-ṣafwa*, 1:439; and Ibn ʿAsākir in *Tārīkh Dimashq al-kabīr*, 10:361.

[2] Fayrūzābādī, *al-Ṣalāt wa al-bishr fī al-Salāt ʿalā Khayr al-bashar*, p.187–188.

Bilāl left for Syria and stayed there for six months before the Prophet ﷺ appeared in his dream and said:

مَا هَذِهِ الْـجَفْوَةُ، يَا بِلَالُ! أَمَا آنَ لَكَ أَنْ تَزُوْرَنِيْ؟

> O Bilāl! What type of loyalty is this? Will you not come to visit me?

As soon as Bilāl awoke, he mounted his camel saying, 'I am at your service, my master, O Messenger ﷺ of Allah!', and set out for Medina. Upon entering Medina, Bilāl desperately searched for the Prophet ﷺ everywhere from the Mosque to his private residence, but eventually went to the blessed grave and rested his head upon it, saddened at not being able to locate the Messenger of Allah ﷺ. He began crying and saying, 'O Messenger of Allah! You ordered me to visit you and your servant has travelled from Aleppo to see you.' Saying this, he fell unconscious beside the Prophet's grave and remained there for a long period of time.

After waking up, he found that the news of his arrival had spread like wildfire throughout Medina. Everybody in the blessed city began requesting Bilāl to make the call to prayer as he had done in the time of the Prophet ﷺ. Bilāl refused, saying, 'Forgive me, but I can no longer make the call, as when I used to deliver the words, 'I testify that Muhammad is the Messenger of Allah ﷺ,' I would look at the blessed face of the Prophet ﷺ and I would derive immense pleasure from it. If I was to recite it now, who will I look to?' The Companions decided it would be better if they asked the grandsons of the Prophet ﷺ to intercede on their behalf, because if they were to forward a request, then Bilāl would not decline it. As a result, Imam Ḥusayn took his hand and said:

يَا بِلَالُ! نَشْتَهِيْ نَسْمَعُ أَذَانَكَ الَّذِي كُنْتَ تُؤَذِّنُ بِهِ لِرَسُوْلِ اللهِ ﷺ فِي الْـمَسْجِدِ.

> O Bilāl! We desire to hear the call to prayer from you which you used to make for the Messenger of Allah (our grandfather) ﷺ in the Mosque.

Bilāl, unable to refuse any longer, made the call to prayer in the very spot he was accustomed to during the Prophet's time. This state of affair was recorded in the books of *sīra*:

> فَلَمَّـا أَنْ قَالَ: اَللهُ أَكْبَرُ، اللهُ أَكْبَرُ، ارْتَجَّتِ الْـمَدِيْنَةُ، فَلَمَّـا أَنْ قَالَ: أَشْهَدُ أَنْ لَّا إِلَهَ إِلَّا اللهُ، ازْدَادَ رَجَّتُهَا، فَلَمَّـا قَالَ: أَشْهَدُ أَنَّ مُحَمَّداً رَسُوْلُ اللهِ، خَرَجَتِ الْعَوَاتِقُ مِنْ خُدُوْرِهِنَّ، وَقَالُوْا: بُعِثَ رَسُوْلُ اللهِ ﷺ فَمَـا رُئِيَ يَوْمٌ أَكْثَرَ بَاكِياً وَلَا بَاكِيَةً بِالْـمَدِيْنَةِ بَعْدَ رَسُوْلِ اللهِ ﷺ مِنْ ذَلِكَ الْيَوْمِ.
>
> So when he proclaimed, 'Allah is the greatest; Allah is the Greatest', there was an echo in Medina, and his emotions were enhanced as he was proclaiming. When he proclaimed, 'I testify that there is no deity worthy of worship, except Allah,' the echo intensified. When he proclaimed, 'I testify that Muhammad ﷺ is the Messenger of Allah', even the veiled womenfolk came out of their homes, and it was such an astonishing and touching scene of lamenting. The people began to say, 'Allah's Messenger ﷺ has arrived'. On this day, the men and women cried more than they had ever cried since Allah's Prophet ﷺ passed away.[1]

---

[1] Narrated by Subkī in *Shifāʾ al-siqām fī ziyāra Khayr al-ānām*, pp.39–40; Ibn ʿAsākir in *Tārīkh Dimashq al-kabīr*, 7:97; al-Dhahabī in *Tārīkh al-Islām wa wafayāt al-mashāhīr wa al-aʿlām*, 3:204–205; al-Dhahabī in *Siyar aʿlām al-nubalāʾ*, 1:358; Fayrūzābādī in *al-Ṣalāt wa al-bishr fī al-Salāt ʿalā Khayr al-bashar*, p.187; al-Haythamī in *al-Jawhar al-munaẓẓam fī ziyāra al-qabr al-sharīf al-Nabawī al-Mukarram al-Muʿaẓẓam*, p.27 states that this incident is reported with a good chain of narration; al-Sakhāwī in *al-Tuḥfa al-laṭīfa fī tārīkh al-Madīna al-sharīfa*, p.221; al-Ṣāliḥī al-Shāmī, *Subul al-hudā wa al-rashād fī sīra Khayr al-ʿibād*, 12:359; and al-Ḥalabī in *Insān al-ʿuyūn fī sīra al-Amīn al-Maʾmūn*, 2:308–309.

Iqbāl, declaring Bilāl's call to prayer as the anthem of love, states:

اذاں ازل سے ترے عشق کا ترانہ بنی

نماز اُس کے نظارے کا اِک بہانہ بنی

The call, since eternity, has been an anthem of love
The prayer became an excuse to see you.[1]

7.2.6 THE GRIEF OF ʿABD ALLĀH B. ʿUMAR

In the books of hadith and biography, it relates:

مَا ذَكَرَ ابْنُ عُمَرَ رَسُولَ اللهِ ﷺ إِلَّا بَكَى، وَلَا مَرَّ عَلَى رَبْعِهِمْ إِلَّا غَمَّضَ عَيْنَيْهِ.

Ibn ʿUmar never mentioned Allah's Messenger ﷺ except that he wept. And whenever he passed by any of the Prophet's residence, he used to close his eyes (due to the feelings of immense sadness).[2]

7.2.7 THE GRIEF OF ʿABD ALLĀH B. ZAYD AND THE LOSS OF HIS EYESIGHT

It is reported regarding ʿAbd Allāh b. Zayd that when his son gave him the news of the Prophet's passing away, he was working in the fields. Upon hearing the news, he became distraught and was so agonised by it that he immediately raised his hands in supplication and prayed:

اَللَّهُمَّ! أَذْهِبْ بَصَرِي حَتَّى لَا أَدْرِي بَعْدَ حَبِيبِي مُحَمَّدٍ أَحَداً.

---

[1] Iqbāl, *Kulliyāt: Bāng-e-darā*, p.81.
[2] Narrated by al-Bayhaqī in *al-Madkhal ilā ʾal-sunan al-kubrā*, 1:148 §113; al-ʿAsqalānī in *al-Iṣāba fī tamyīz al-Ṣaḥāba*, 4:187; and Dhahabī in *Tadhkira al-ḥuffāẓ*, 1:38.

> O Allah! Take away my eyesight so that I may come to know no one except my Beloved Muhammad ﷺ.[1]

The Companion's supplication was immediately granted by Allah and subsequently his eyesight was taken away.

Qāsim b. Muhammad states:

> إِنَّ رَجُلاً مِّنْ أَصْحَابِ مُحَمَّدٍ ذَهَبَ بَصَرُهُ فَعَادُوْهُ.
>
> One of the Prophet's Companions lost his eyesight so the Companions went to console him.

When the noble Companions ﷺ began offering their condolences, the Companion ﷺ said:

> كُنتُ أُرِيْدُهُمَا لِأَنْظُرَ إِلَى النَّبِيِّ ﷺ، فَأَمَّا إِذَا قُبِضَ النَّبِيُّ ﷺ، فَوَاللهِ، مَا يَسُرُّنِي أَنَّ مَا بِهِمَا بِظَبْيٍ مِنْ ظِبَاءِ تَبَالَةَ.
>
> I only loved those eyes of mine because I was able to see the Messenger of Allah ﷺ with them, but now that he has passed away, if I was given the eyes of a deer, even then I would feel no joy whatsoever.[2]

7.2.8 More Narrations on the Companions' Grief

Al-Ālūsī records that when the blessed Companions ﷺ felt the absence of the Prophet ﷺ, they would set out in search of some of his relics:

> فَجَاءَ إِلَى مَيْمُوْنَةَ ﷺ، فَأَخْرَجَتْ لَهُ مِرْآتَهُ، فَنَظَرَ فِيْهَا، فَرَأَى صُوْرَةَ رَسُوْلِ اللهِ ﷺ وَلَمْ يَرَ صُوْرَةَ نَفْسِهِ.

[1] Al-Qasṭallānī, *al-Mawāhib al-ladunya bi al-minaḥ al-Muḥammadiyya*, 3:279; and al-Zurqānī, *Sharḥ al-mawāhib al-ladunya bi al-minaḥ al-Muḥammadiyya*, 9:84–85.

[2] Al-Bukhārī, *al-Adab al-Mufrad*, 1:188 §533.

So he came to Maymūna and she took out for him the Prophet's mirror. He looked into it and he beheld the Prophet's reflection; he did not see his own reflection.[1]

It is reported regarding Qatāda:

أَنَّهُ كَانَ إِذَا سَمِعَ الْـحَدِيْثَ أَخَذَهُ الْعَوِيْلُ وَالزَّوِيْلُ.

Whenever he heard a hadith, his state would change and he would weep bitterly.[2]

In one narration, it states:

أَنَّ امْرَأَةً قَالَتْ لِعَائِشَةَ: اِكْشِفِي لِي قَبْرَ رَسُوْلِ اللهِ ﷺ، فَكَشَفَتْهُ لَـهَا، فَبَكَتْ حَتَّى مَاتَتْ.

A woman said to ʿĀʾisha ﵂, 'Uncover for me the grave of Allah's Messenger ﷺ'. ʿĀʾisha uncovered it for her. The woman cried so much that she died.[3]

Iqbāl, explaining this grief, writes:

وقتِ قلب و جگر گردد نبی

آز خدا محبوب تر گردد نبی

The person of the Holy Prophet causes the heart's strength to intensify even beyond his love for God.[4]

---

[1] Al-Ālūsī, *Rūḥ al-maʿānī fī Tafsīr al-Qurʾān al-ʿaẓīm wa al-Sabʿ al-Mathānī*, 22:39.

[2] Qāḍī ʿIyāḍ, *al-Shifāʾ bi taʿrīf ḥuqūq al-Muṣṭafā*, 2:598.

[3] Qāḍī ʿIyāḍ, *al-Shifāʾ bi taʿrīf ḥuqūq al-Muṣṭafā*, 2:570; Ibn al-Jawzī in *Ṣafwa al-ṣafwa*, 2:204 §203; and Mullā ʿAlī al-Qārī, *Sharḥ al-Shifāʾ*, 2:44.

[4] Iqbāl, *Kulliyāt: Asrār wa ramūz*, p.113.

سوزِ صديق و علي آز حق طلب

ذرهٔ عشق نبي آز حق طلب

So desire the Prophet's love possessed by Abū Bakr al-Ṣiddīq and ʿAlī b. Abī Ṭālib. Then implore the Lord for a portion of the Prophet's love.[1]

Al-Qāḍī ʿIyāḍ (476–544 AH) writes:

لَقَدْ كَانَ عَبْدُ الرَّحْمَنِ بْنُ الْقَاسِمِ يَذْكُرُ النَّبِيَّ ﷺ فَيَنْظُرُ إِلَى لَوْنِهِ كَأَنَّهُ نَزَفَ مِنْهُ الدَّمُ، وَقَدْ جَفَّ لِسَانُهُ فِي فَمِهِ هَيْبَةً لِرَسُوْلِ اللهِ ﷺ.

Whenever (the great-grandson of Abū Bakr al-Ṣiddīq) ʿAbd al-Raḥmān b. al-Qāsim would remember the Holy Prophet ﷺ, the colour of his face would change as though the blood was drained out; his tongue would become dry in awe of the Holy Prophet ﷺ.[2]

7.2.9 The Grief of the Animals that Served the Prophet ﷺ

The Companions were not the only ones who were overcome with sadness on the Prophet's passing away; even the animals were unable to bear the grief of separation. Mentioning this state of affair, Shaykh ʿAbd al-Ḥaqq Muḥaddith al-Dihlawī writes:

وناقهٔ آنحضرت علف نميخورد وآب نمي نوشيد تاآنكه مُرد. از جمله آياتي كه ظاهر شد بعد از موتِ آنحضرت آن حماری كه آنحضرت گاهي بران سوار ميشد چندان حزن كرد كه خود را در چاهي انداخت.

[1] Iqbāl, *Kulliyāt: Piyām-e-mashriq*, p.203.

[2] Qāḍī ʿIyāḍ, *al-Shifāʾ bi taʿrīf ḥuqūq al-Muṣṭafā*, 2:36.

> The Prophet's she-camel did not eat or drink anything until she died. One of the peculiar occurrences which took place after his passing away was that the donkey upon which the Prophet ﷺ used to ride on was so overwhelmed with grief that one night it jumped straight into a well, killing itself as it no longer had the will to live.[1]

7.3 Joy and Sorrow were Equally Felt in the Month of *Rabīᶜ al-Awwal*

Whenever the Companions ﷺ witnessed the month of *Rabīᶜ al-Awwal*, the feelings of joy they felt on the Holy Prophet's birth was ultimately overshadowed by feelings of grief and sorrow. This is why it was not possible for the Companions to commemorate the *mawlid* with much joy and jubilation. This condition continued through the age of the Successors and their students (*taba tābiᶜīn*). Even though the Successors (*tābiᶜīn*) did not witness or experience the esteemed Prophet's company, they were very much aware of the memories and recollections the Companions had had of the esteemed Prophet ﷺ; these were later transmitted to their students and the generations to come.

7.4 As Time Passed, Joy Prevailed Over Grief

After the age of the Successors had passed, those who came later did not experience the Holy Prophet's Companionship, nor did they experience the grief that was felt with the Holy Prophet's passing away. Due to the passing of time, joy slowly began to prevail over grief. The *Umma*, in relation to this great blessing, began to disremember its feelings of grief and remorse: certainty was achieved in that the Holy Prophet's life and death were both a source of blessing for the *Umma*. The esteemed Prophet's life in the *barzakh* was a concept which brought them comfort and tranquillity.

---

[1] ᶜAbd al-Ḥaqq Muḥaddith al-Dihlawī, *Madārij al-Nabuwwa*, 2:444; and al-Ḥalabī, *Insān al-ᶜuyūn fī sīra al-Amīn al-Maʾmūn*, 3:433.

7.5 THE PROPHET'S BIRTH AND HIS PASSING AWAY ARE BOTH A MERCY

For the *Umma*, the Holy Prophet's birth and his passing away are both a source of mercy. ʿAbd Allāh b. Masʿūd relates that the Prophet ﷺ said:

«حَيَاتِي خَيْرٌ لَكُمْ تُحَدِّثُوْنَ وَنُحَدِّثُ لَكُمْ، وَوَفَاتِي خَيْرٌ لَكُمْ، تُعْرَضُ عَلَيَّ أَعْمَالُكُمْ، فَمَا رَأَيْتُ مِنْ خَيْرٍ حَمِدْتُ اللهَ عَلَيْهِ، وَمَا رَأَيْتُ مِنْ شَرٍّ اِسْتَغْفَرْتُ اللهَ لَكُمْ.»

> My life is good for you because you get new matters (regarding the religion) and we bring new matters for you. And my demise is good for you because your actions are presented to me: if I see your good deed, I praise Allah for it; and if I see bad, I ask Allah that He forgives you.[1]

---

[1] Narrated by al-Bazzār in *al-Baḥr al-Zukhār* (*al-Musnad*) 5:308–309 §1925; Ibn Abī Usāma in *Musnad al-Ḥārith*, 2:884 §953 narrates this with an authentic chain of transmission; Ḥākīm Tirmidhī in *Nawādir al-uṣūl fī aḥādīth al-Rasūl*, 4:176; al-Daylamī in *al-Firdaws bi maʾthūr al-Khiṭāb*, 1:183 §686 narrates this from Abū Hurayra; Qāḍī ʿIyāḍ, *al-Shifāʾ bi taʿrīf ḥuqūq al-Muṣṭafā*, 1:19; al-Haythamī in *Majmaʿ al-zawāʾid wa manbaʿ al-fawāʾid*, 9:24 narrates that the one reported by al-Bazzār and all his narrators are authentic; Ibn Kathīr, *al-Bidāya wa al-nihāya*, 4:257; and Zayn al-Dīn Abū al-Faḍl al-ʿIrāqī in *Ṭarḥ al-tathrīb fī sharḥ al-taqrīb*, 3:297 has declared this narration authentic.

With some different wordings, this narration is also reported by Anas b. Mālik:

Reported by al-Daylamī in *al-Firdaws bi-maʾthūr al-khiṭāb*, 2:137–138 §2701; and al-ʿAjlūnī in *Kashf al-khafāʾ wa muzīl al-ilbās*, 1:442 §1178.

Bakr b. ʿAbd Allāh al-Muznī reports this narration through a *mursal* chain:

Reported by Ibn Saʿd in *al-Ṭabaqāt al-kubrā*, 2:194; Ibn Isḥāq in *Faḍl al-ṣalāt ʿalā al-Nabī*, 1:38–39 §25–26; al-Subkī in *Shifāʾ al-siqām fī ziyāra Khayr al-ānām*, p.34; Aḥmad b. ʿAbd al-Hādī in *al-Ṣārim al-munkī fī al-radd ʿalā al-Subkī*, p.266–267 narrates this with an authentic chain of narration and Bakr is a reliable narrator; Muḥaddith Ibn al-Jawzī in *al-Wafāʾ bi-aḥwāl al-Muṣṭafā*, p.826 §1564–1565 narrates this from both Anas b. Mālik and

This hadith clearly points out the fact that the esteemed Prophet's demise is as much a mercy for the *Umma* as his physical presence is for the whole world.

7.6 THE PROPHET'S PASSING AWAY IS A SOURCE OF INTERCESSION FOR HIS COMMUNITY

Abū Mūsā al-Ashʿarī ﷺ relates that the Prophet ﷺ, regarding his physical demise, said:

«إِنَّ اللهَ عَزَّ وَجَلَّ إِذَا أَرَادَ رَحْمَةَ أُمَّةٍ مِنْ عِبَادِهِ قَبَضَ نَبِيَّهَا قَبْلَهَا، فَجَعَلَهُ لَهَا فَرَطًا وَسَلَفًا بَيْنَ يَدَيْهَا؛ وَإِذَا أَرَادَ هَلَكَةَ أُمَّةٍ عَذَّبَهَا وَنَبِيُّهَا حَيٌّ، فَأَهْلَكَهَا وَهُوَ يَنْظُرُ، فَأَقَرَّ عَيْنَهُ بِهَلَكَتِهَا حِينَ كَذَّبُوهُ وَعَصَوْا أَمْرَهُ.»

When Allah intends a mercy for a Community, He takes the Prophet before it. He makes him a source of intercession for his people. And whenever He intends to punish a nation, He torments that nation with severe punishments and then destroys those inhabitants within the lifetime of that Prophet; as a result, the Prophet of that nation is comforted with this as they were the ones who rejected him and disobeyed his commandments.[1]

Bakr b. ʿAbd Allāh; al-Suyūṭī in *Kifāyat al-ṭālib al-labīb fī khaṣāʾiṣ al-Ḥabīb* ﷺ, 2:491 and *Manāhil al-ṣafā fī takhrīj aḥādīth al-shifāʾ*, p.3, writes that Ibn Abī Usāma in his *al-Musnad* reports it from Bakr b. ʿAbd Allāh and al-Bazzār in his *al-Musnad* reports it from ʿAbd Allāh b. Masʿūd with an authentic chain of narration; this is also supported by ʿAllāma Khifājī and Mullā ʿAlī al-Qārī report this in the commentaries of *al-Shifāʾ bi taʿrīf ḥuqūq al-Muṣṭafā*, *Nasīm al-riyāḍ*, 1:102, and *Sharḥ al-Shifāʾ*, 1:45, respectively; and al-ʿAjlūnī in *Kashf al-khafāʾ wa muzīl al-ilbās*, 1:442 §1178.

[1] Reported by Muslim in *al-Ṣaḥīḥ*: *Kitāb al-Faḍāʾil* [The Book of Exemplary Virtues], chapter: 'When Allah intends a mercy for a community, He takes the Prophet before it', 4:1791–1792 §2288; Ibn Ḥibbān in *al-Ṣaḥīḥ*, 15:22 §6647; al-Bazzār in *al-Baḥr al-zukhār (al-Musnad)*, 8:154 §3177; al-Ṭabarānī in *al-Muʿjam al-awsaṭ*, 4:315 §4306; and Ibn ʿAsākir in *Tārīkh Dimashq al-kabīr*, 13:11–12.

Mullā ʿAlī al-Qārī (d. 1014 ah), explaining what the word '*faraṭ*' means, writes:

أَصْلُ الْفَرَطِ هُوَ الَّذِي يَتَقَدَّمُ الْوَارِدِيْنَ لِيُهَيِّئَ لَـهُمْ مَا يَحْتَاجُوْنَ إِلَيْهِ عِنْدَ نُزُوْلِـهُمْ فِي مَنَازِلِـهِمْ، ثُمَّ اسْتُعْمِلَ لِلشَّفِيْعِ فِيْمَنْ خَلْفَهُ.

> *Faraṭ* in its original usage refers to the one who precedes others so that he may prepare for them what they need when they stop off at a place. Then this word came to be used for the one who intercedes on behalf of others who have not yet come after him.[1]

How great a blessing it is that Almighty Allah, prior to a person entering the afterlife, has called His Beloved Prophet ﷺ to Himself so that he can be a source of intercession for his community members. This is why the Prophet ﷺ declared his passing away a mercy. Therefore, it is established beyond doubt that both the Prophet's physical presence and his passing away are a source of mercy and blessing. His coming is the greatest blessing for his community and through its means we attained the second blessing (of his intercession).

7.7 To be Grateful for a Blessing is Allah's Decree

In the chapters that have preceded us, we have explained that it is Almighty Allah's decree that we express joy and happiness for a blessing and that we are grateful for it. On the contrary, Almighty Allah has not decreed that we express sorrow on any previous grievous occurrence; doing so would be an expression of ungratefulness towards Almighty Allah's blessings. This is why Almighty Allah declared:

﴿وَلَئِن كَفَرْتُمْ إِنَّ عَذَابِي لَشَدِيدٌ﴾

If you are thankful, I shall certainly increase (My blessings

---

[1] Mullā ʿAlī al-Qārī, *Sharḥ al-Shifāʾ*, 1:45.

> *on) you, and if you are ungrateful, then My torment is surely severe.*[1]

Sorrow is expressed when a blessing has ceased and when that blessing no longer benefits anybody, e.g. if somebody gives birth to a son but then that son dies, one can express grief and mourn on this occasion. However, the thankful servants of Almighty Allah will not complain to their Lord regarding their loss, because they do not complain about the loss of family and wealth as these trials come in one's life. And Almighty Allah always replaces one blessing with another if the first blessing is taken away. Therefore, expressing grief and mourning on the Holy Prophet's passing away is not appropriate for us because we still benefit from his blessings.

7.8 We Are in Receipt of His Blessings, so Why the Sorrow?

If the Prophet's blessings were no longer descending upon us or our connection with the Holy Prophet ﷺ had been broken, then it would be reasonable for us to express grief. But even today the Holy Prophet ﷺ is aware of the state of his community, and he supports and assists it in its each and every step. In the 1400 years that have passed since his demise, there has not been a decrease in his blessings; there has not been a decrease in his favours, guidance, and miracles. When his elegant beauty, esteemed station, the seal of prophethood, his grace and attention have remained unaffected, then why is there any need of grief or sorrow? Allah ﷻ states:

﴿كُلُّ نَفْسٍ ذَآئِقَةُ ٱلْمَوْتِ﴾

> *Every soul is to taste death and then to Us you will be returned.*[2]

The Prophet ﷺ, without doubt, had also tasted this transition from one life to the next, which was in reality the beginning of his

---

[1] Qur'ān 7:14.

[2] Qur'ān 21:35 and 29:57.

real and permanent life. When there is an immense difference in the life Hereafter of a believer and a disbeliever, then what similarity could there possibly be with the Prophet's afterlife and the afterlife of an ordinary individual? The Prophet ﷺ passed away from the eyes of the common person, but those closest to him, the chosen ones amongst the pious believers, are still able to perceive him in their conscious state. Imam Jalāl al-Dīn al-Suyūṭī (849–911 AH) was one of those elected servants of Allah, who was privileged to see the Holy Prophet ﷺ with his own eyes roughly 75 times throughout his life.[1]

Dear reader! Do you visit the sacred tomb of the Prophet ﷺ in Medina in the same manner that you visit other graves? The sacred tomb of the Holy Prophet ﷺ is that place in which the likes of Junayd al-Baghdādī and Bā-Yazīd al-Bustāmī used to breathe quietly in awe and respect. One is required to respect that place as one would if the beloved Prophet ﷺ was physically present there today. We are unfortunate in this day and age that we as a whole are unaware of the reality of the Prophet's esteemed stature, or the sanctity of those places associated with him: we in reality are walking talking corpses that are void of life, whilst those special servants of Almighty Allah, who are in their graves, are the ones that are truly alive.

The Holy Prophet ﷺ is not only alive today, he listens to our salutations and even responds to them.[2] We, however, are unable to hear his reply as our ears and eyes are blocked from perceiving

---

1 Al-Shaʿrānī, *al-Mīzān al-kubrā*, 1:44.

2 Reported by Abū Dāwūd in *al-Sunan*: *Kitāb al-Manāsik* [The Book of Pilgrimage rites], chapter: 'Visiting the graves', 2:175 §2041; Aḥmad b. Ḥanbal in *al-Musnad*, 2:527; al-Ṭabarānī in *al-Muʿjam al-awsaṭ*, 4:84 §3116; al-Bayhaqī in *al-Sunan al-kubrā*, 5:245; al-Bayhaqī in *Shuʿab al-Īmān*, 2:217 §1581; Abū Nuʿaym in *Ḥilya al-awliyāʾ wa ṭabaqāt al-aṣfiyāʾ*, 6:349; Mundhirī in *al-Targhīb wa al-tarhīb min al-ḥadīth al-sharīf*, 2:362 §2573; al-Haythamī in *Majmaʿ al-zawāʾid wa manbaʿ al-fawāʾid*, 10:162; al-Maqrīzī in *Imtāʿ al-asmāʿ bi mā li Nabī min al-aḥwāl wa al-amwāl wa al-ḥafada wa al-matāʿ*, 11:59; Ibn al-Qayyim in *Jalāʾ al-afhām fī al-ṣalā wa al-salām ʿalā Khayr al-anām*, p.19 §20; and al-Sakhāwī in *al-Qawl al-badīʿ fī al-ṣalā ʿalā al-Ḥabīb al-Shafīʿ*, p.156.

this reality (as opposed to the pious slaves of Almighty Allah). Therefore, as a Muslim community of believers, we are obliged to express our joy, as there are no grounds for the expression of grief and sorrow.

7.9 The Prophet's Prophecy is Established till the Day of Judgment

The statement, 'there is no god but Allah; Muhammad ﷺ is Allah's Messenger', is indicative of this reality that just as the Prophet's prophecy was true in his physical life, it still holds true till the Day of Judgment. No one can claim that 'Muhammad *was* Allah's Messenger'; if anyone does make such a statement, then that person has not yet entered the fold of Islam, because it is a condition that one believes in the permanence of the Prophet's prophecy till the Day of Judgment. This is a fundamental requirement of faith.

Likewise, the Prophet ﷺ is *khātim al-nabiyyīn*, the seal of prophecy. All previous Prophets came and went; their prophecy came to an end with the arrival of the next Prophet. But the Holy Prophet ﷺ is Almighty Allah's last and final Messenger; there will be no new prophet who will come after him to terminate his prophecy. Therefore, it is compulsory to believe that the Holy Prophet ﷺ is our Prophet ﷺ, just as he was the Companions' Prophet; and that he will also be the Prophet ﷺ for all forthcoming generations until the Day of Judgment.

The only difference, if there is any, is that for 63 years, the noble Companions were able to see him with their physical eyes, whereas now, only a select few are fortunate enough to perceive him every so often in their dreams or state of wakefulness. The Holy Prophet ﷺ shows his mercy to his loyal servants even today in that he guides them, he allows them to see him in their visions, and when they are about to depart this world, he also arrives to welcome their souls.

7.10 Expressing Joy is not an Innovation: it is Human Nature

Expressing joy and happiness on receiving a blessing is a

fundamental part of human nature. In the pages that have preceded us, we have mentioned the example of a funeral and the feeling of despair felt by the family. We said that if in that very household there was to be a wedding within a short time of the funeral, the wedding ceremony would most certainly be cancelled. Even if the marriage is not postponed, the service is performed in the simplest manner possible as a mark of respect for the deceased. If in the same household, five or ten years later, a wedding is held, then it is performed according to all the rituals and customs with utmost delight. This does not mean that the family has completely forgotten the deceased or has gotten over their grief. Put simply, it is part of human nature that for a certain period, the feelings of devastation and grief take hold, but as time passes, people are able to control themselves, and one is able to overcome the grief of past events, however tragic.

The great scholars of Islam have clarified that commemorating the Holy Prophet's birth is the essence of the Sharia and a fundamental requirement of human nature, whilst expressing grief upon the Holy Prophet's passing is against the Sharia and contrary to Islam's immutable principles. Imam al-Suyūṭī (849–911 AH), concerning this principle, states:

إِنَّ وِلَادَتَهُ ﷺ أَعْظَمُ النِّعَمِ عَلَيْنَا، وَوَفَاتَهُ أَعْظَمُ الْمَصَائِبِ لَنَا، وَالشَّرِيْعَةُ حَثَّتْ عَلَى إِظْهَارِ شُكْرِ النِّعَمِ وَالصَّبْرِ وَالسُّكُوْنِ وَالْكَتْمِ عِنْدَ الْمَصَائِبِ، وَقَدْ أَمَرَ الشَّرْعُ بِالْعَقِيْقَةِ عِنْدَ الْوِلَادَةِ وَهِيَ إِظْهَارُ شُكْرٍ وَفَرَحٍ بِالْمَوْلُوْدِ، وَلَمْ يَأْمُرْ عِنْدَ الْمَوْتِ بِذِبْحٍ وَّلَا بِغَيْرِهِ. بَلْ نَهَى عَنِ النِّيَاحَةِ وَإِظْهَارِ الْجَزَعِ، فَدَلَّتْ قَوَاعِدُ الشَّرِيْعَةِ عَلَى أَنَّهُ يَحْسُنُ فِي هَذَا الشَّهْرِ إِظْهَارُ الْفَرَحِ بِوِلَادَتِهِ ﷺ دُوْنَ إِظْهَارِ الْحُزْنِ فِيْهِ بِوَفَاتِهِ.

Certainly, the Prophet's birth ﷺ is the greatest bounty upon us, and his passing is the worst calamity to afflict us. The Sacred Law encourages us to be thankful for bounties and to observe patience, resignation, and tranquility with

> calamities. The Law Giver has commanded us to perform the ᶜ*aqīqa* ceremony when a child is born, and that is in order to show gratitude and happiness for the newborn child, but he has not ordered us to sacrifice an animal or do anything of that nature when a child dies. In fact, he has forbidden the act of wailing and showing displeasure (with the divine decree). Therefore, the principles of Sacred Law indicate that in this month, it is praiseworthy to express happiness with the Prophet's blessed birth ﷺ, and it has not indicated that it is praiseworthy to express sadness with his passing ﷺ.[1]

The Holy Prophet's passing away dictates that the Muslims should never forget about it as his bounties of prophethood will remain till the Last Day. The Holy Prophet's life in the *barzakh* (Intermediate Realm) is superior to his physical life on earth. Concerning this, Mullā ᶜAlī al-Qārī states:

لَيْسَ هُنَاكَ مَوْتٌ وَلَا فَوْتٌ بَلِ انْتِقَالٌ مِنْ حَالٍ إِلَى حَالٍ وَارْتِحَالٌ مِّنْ دَارٍ إِلَى دَارٍ.

> There is no death or passing away, but a transfer from one state to another, from one abode to the next.[2]

It has already been explained previously why the first generation of Muslims did not celebrate the *mawlid*; this being due to the fact that they had lived with the Holy Prophet ﷺ. As a result, whenever the 12th of *Rabīᶜ al-Awwal* came, the Companions were reminded of his life amongst them and were simultaneously reminded of his passing away, which as a result led to mixed emotions of joy and sadness with the overwhelming feeling of grief prevailing. Centuries later, these feelings subsided and were replaced by the feelings of delight at the Holy Prophet's blessed birth, and thus, in line with human nature, the commemoration of *Mawlid al-Nabī*

---

[1] Al-Suyūṭī, *al-Ḥāwī li al-fatāwā*, p.203; and al-Suyūṭī, *Ḥusn al-maqṣid fī ᶜamal al-mawlid*, p.54–55.

[2] Mullā ᶜAlī al-Qārī, *Sharḥ al-Shifā*ʾ, 1:45.

ﷺ was initiated—and this practice has continued till the present day. Regarding this, Muftī Muhammad Maẓhar Allāh al-Dihlawī writes:

> Holding gatherings of *mawlid*, on the condition that it is based on sound traditions, and processions on the 12th of *Rabīᶜ al-Awwal*, on the condition that it is done without committing any prohibited action, are both lawful. To suggest otherwise would require valid evidence from the Sharia—may I ask what proof the critics have against it? To argue that the Companions did not celebrate the *mawlid* or organise processions in this fashion cannot be used as evidence against it, because non-performance of a permissible act is not an evidence of impermissibility.[1]

The first book to be written on the Holy Prophet's biography in the Urdu language was written by Muftī Muhammad ᶜInāyat Aḥmad Kākūrawī (1228–1279 AH). He writes that the *mawlid* is organised so that happiness can be expressed on the Prophet's birth and that expressing sorrow on this occasion is intolerable. He writes:

> The Muslims should organise and partake in the gatherings of *Mawlid al-Nabī* ﷺ out of their love for the Holy Prophet ﷺ. However, the condition is that one's intention should be sincere and free from ostentation. Furthermore, the anecdotes related should be authentic, and the Prophetic miracles should be related from reliable sources, since most people are content to attend these types of functions merely to hear poetry or fictitious traditions. The scholars have also maintained that the Holy Prophet's passing away should not be mentioned in these gatherings, as these are events of high spirits—recollections of sadness are inappropriate within such gatherings. The topic of the Prophet's passing away is never brought up in the two Sacred Mosques.[2]

---

[1] Maẓhar Allāh al-Dihlawī, *Fatāwā Maẓharī*, pp. 435–436.

[2] Al-Kākūrawī, *Tawārīkh Ḥabīb Ilāh yaᶜnī sīrat Sayyid al-Mursalīn*, p.15.

Consequently, commemorating the *mawlid* is not an innovation; rather, it is human nature per se. It is not wrong to say that the gatherings of *Mawlid al-Nabī* ﷺ have become an intrinsic part of Islamic culture.

7.11 It was not the Culture of the First Generation to Celebrate Events

Celebrating the *mawlid* is a cultural expression of one's emotional attachment to the Holy Prophet ﷺ. If we take a brief analysis of Islamic history from the first generation till the present, in each age there would be different ways in which the different branches of human society would express their feelings of joy and happiness as well as grief and sorrow. In this regards, some examples of events which have changed the course of history will be mentioned:

7.11.1 The Migration to Medina

It is recorded in the books of history that when the people of Medina became acquainted with the Holy Prophet's resolve to emigrate to Medina, they would travel three kilometres south of Medina to a place called '*Ḥarra*' each morning after the *fajr* prayer, waiting there to receive him, even though the temperature was soaring. When the heat intensified and there was no shade left, only then did they return to their homes with heavy hearts. ʿAbd al-Raḥmān b. ʿUwaym b. Sāʿida, regarding the inhabitants of Medina, states:

لَـمَّـا سَمِعْنَا بِمَخْرَجِ رَسُوْلِ اللهِ ﷺ مِنْ مَكَّةَ، وَتَوَكَّفْنَا قُدُوْمَهُ، كُنَّا نَخْرُجُ إِذَا صَلَّيْنَا الصُّبْحَ، إِلَى ظَاهِرِ حَرَّتِنَا، نَنْتَظِرُ رَسُوْلَ اللهِ ﷺ، فَوَاللهِ! مَا نَبْرَحُ حَتَّى تَغْلِبَنَا الشَّمْسُ عَلَى الظِّلَالِ، فَإِذَا لَـمْ نَجِدْ ظِلاًّ دَخَلْنَا، وَذَلِكَ فِي أَيَّامٍ حَارَّةٍ.

When we heard that the Prophet ﷺ left Mecca, we began anticipating his arrival. When we performed the *fajr* prayer, we used to set out to the open space of *Ḥarra*,

> waiting for Allah's Messenger ﷺ. By Allah, we used to wait there until there was no longer any shade from the sun. If we did not find any shade, we would return home—and that was in the days of intense heat.[1]

When the Holy Prophet ﷺ arrived in Medina, the inhabitants of the city were overjoyed and elated. They expressed so much delight upon the arrival of the Holy Prophet ﷺ that everyone came out of the city to welcome the Messenger of Allah ﷺ. The children of Medina played the tambourine and sang welcoming songs of joy and pleasure; they all raised slogans of salutations as they formed a procession, marching with the Holy Prophet ﷺ till they reached the house of Abū Ayyūb al-Anṣārī ﷺ—the Prophet's place of residence.

The migration to Medina was a unique event in the history of Islam. This migration laid the foundation for the establishment of an Islamic state that ultimately led to the dominance of Islam over the Arabian Peninsula. The day of his arrival into Medina was therefore a day of great significance and joy. Nevertheless, the people of Medina did not celebrate this day as this was not part of their culture or tradition. However, on the occasion of the Holy Prophet's arrival, the inhabitants of Medina organised an astounding reception for the very esteemed Prophet ﷺ; from this at least, it can be deduced that expressing happiness and joy on a significant occasion and commemorating it with elaborate celebrations is both a permissible and intrinsic part of human nature. This issue is related to man's natural instinct and his emotions—there is nothing in this which negates the Sharia. Therefore, throwing allegations of *bidʿa* at it and making it grounds for its rejection is indicative of an illness related to the state of one's heart and is not a religious justification.

---

[1] Reported by Ibn Hishām in *al-Sīra al-Nabawiyya*, p.423; al-Ṭabarī in *Tārīkh al-umam wa al-mulūk*, 1:571; al-Dhahabī in *Tārīkh al-Islām wa wafayāt al-mashāhīr wa al-aʿlām* (*al-Sīra al-Nabawiyya*), 1:331; Ibn Kathīr in *al-Bidāya wa al-nihāya*, 3:196; and al-Khazāʿī in *Takhrīj al-dalālāt al-samʿiyya ʿalā mā kāna fī ʿahd Rasūl Allāh min al-ḥarf*, p.446.

7.11.2 The Constitution of Medina

After entering Medina, the Holy Prophet ﷺ, in consultation with the Medinan Helpers and Meccan Immigrants, drew up a contract with the Jewish tribes of Medina. This historic treaty is remembered as the Pact of Medina. On this day, the first Islamic state was established and the Holy Prophet ﷺ became the first constitutional head of state. For the Muslims, this occasion was truly worthy of celebration, yet the people of Medina did not commemorate this day as it was simply not part of their culture to do so.

7.11.3 The Day of *Badr*

After the migration, the most joyous day for the Muslims was the Day of *Badr*, when truth overcame falsehood in a decisive victory. This day was a source of inspiration for the Muslims, as the victory came as a sign from Almighty Allah; it was so significant that the Qur'ān referred to it as *Yawm al-Furqān* (The Day of Decision).[1] Though the anniversary of this day came year after year, the Companions did not make any effort in commemorating it, as such a thing was not part of their culture.

7.11.4 The Conquest of Mecca

Likewise, after the emigration to Medina, the day in which the Conquest of Mecca took place was also significant; this was the day when Islam became the most powerful force in the whole of Arabia. The Holy Prophet ﷺ entered Mecca as a victor with an army of 10,000 men. This was the same city from where the Holy Prophet ﷺ and his Companions emigrated to Medina, due to the cruelty and enmity of the disbelievers. The Qur'ān has referred to this glorious day as *al-Fatḥ al-Mubīn* (The Clear Victory).[2] Which day can be more joyous than this day? Yet, the first generation of Muslims did not celebrate it as it was not part of their culture or tradition.

---

[1] Qur'ān, 8:41.

[2] Qur'ān, 48:1.

7.11.5 The Night of Destiny: The Night of the Qur'ān's Descent

The 27th night of the month of *Ramaḍān* is that blessed night in which the Qur'ān was first revealed. On this auspicious night, Almighty Allah gifted us with the greatest gift, the most esteemed Prophet ﷺ, who became a means of our guidance till the Day of Judgment. But even this night was not a cause for annual celebration, as this was not the custom of that age.

7.11.6 New Requirements for a New Age

If we take a close look at the world today, we will realise that we do not just celebrate significant days related to our culture and civilisation, but, according to the requirements of the modern age, there are many new celebrations which have been introduced which we celebrate on a national basis.

The whole sum of this discussion is that it was not the tradition of the first generation of Muslims to celebrate important days of religious and national significance. Historic moments such as the Day of the Qur'ān's descent, the Day of *Badr*, and the Conquest of Mecca were not celebrated by the Companions as it was simply not their custom. Irrespective of this fact, this does not diminish in anyway the importance of marking significant days in the history of Islam.

Today, Pakistan, like many other Muslim majority countries around the world, celebrates its Independence Day with growing confidence and grandeur, as is the custom of other nations in the 21st century—it has now become an intrinsic part of modern culture and identity. Similarly, Saudi Arabia and several other Arab countries rejoice on the days their leaders ascended to the throne when their kingdoms became established. They celebrate that day, referring to it as '*al-ʿīd al-waṭanī*' (National Day of Festivity). In the same way, each country and nation celebrates their respective days differently according to their own customs and ideological makeup, thereby transmitting their national identity to the coming generations.

In light of these changes, the *mawlid* has now become more

important than ever, and anyone with sound intellect and reason would not deny this fact. The *mawlid* is the easiest method of lighting the flame of love and passion for our beloved Prophet ﷺ in our hearts and the hearts of our future generations, and it is a means by which that broken link with our beloved Prophet ﷺ can be recovered.

Chapter 8

The Formative Constituents of *Mawlid al-Nabī* ﷺ

THROUGHOUT THE YEAR, THERE ARE VARIOUS GATHERINGS IN which the beautiful descriptions of the most exalted Prophet ﷺ are mentioned, and yet as soon as the month of *Rabīʿ al-Awwal* arrives, happiness and joy reaches its climax. In every street and almost every home in the Muslim world, and even those places where there are pockets of Muslims living in non-Muslim lands, gatherings of *mawlid* are held wherein people congregate simply to express their adoration and reverence for the beloved Prophet ﷺ. Others express their joy differently by distributing sweets, decorating their homes, and holding processions in the streets. In the *mawlid* gatherings, people raise tributes and slogans expressing their immense love for the Holy Prophet ﷺ; poets recite hymns and odes in his honour; and attendees recite the Qurʾān melodiously, and scholars are called from afar to deliver speeches that inspire true love for the Beloved ﷺ. In short, everyone is motivated in expressing their intense love and devotion for the most compassionate Prophet ﷺ.

On the occasion of *Mawlid al-Nabī* ﷺ, what are the methods of expressing our joy and happiness on the most esteemed Prophet's blessed birth? When celebrating, what are the practices of the devout lovers? What are the ingredients which constitute the *mawlid* celebration? In this chapter, we will answer all of these questions and explore each issue in light of the Qurʾān and Sunna in order to determine which elements within the *mawlid* are permissible, and which, if any, are impermissible. One can determine whether an act is permissible and deserving of reward by analysing each single feature of that affair—this is the issue that will be dealt with in this chapter.

The faith enlightening and exhilarating activities of the formative constituents of *Mawlid al-Nabī* ﷺ are listed below:

1. Holding gatherings and congregations

2. Relating the Prophet's ﷺ biography and virtues
3. Reciting odes and poems in praise of the Prophet ﷺ
4. Sending salutations and invoking peace on the Prophet ﷺ
5. *Qiyām* (ritual standing)
6. Arranging lighting
7. Distributing food
8. *Mawlid* processions

In the following sections, each of the above mentioned constituents will be explained exclusively in detail.

Section 1

Holding Gatherings and Congregations

Special gatherings are organised in order for the participants to remember the most esteemed Prophet ﷺ. In these gatherings odes and hymns are recited in praise of the Prophet ﷺ, and peace and blessings are invoked upon his blessed person. People attend these gatherings with great reverence and enthusiasm. They illuminate their minds and souls with glorified descriptions of the beloved of Almighty Allah. Such assemblies of *Mawlid al-Nabī* ﷺ were also organised by the beloved Prophet himself. There are many hadiths to substantiate this, and some are mentioned below:

8.1 The Prophet ﷺ Making Mention of his Creation which Took Place before his Birth

Abū Hurayra ؓ narrates that the Companions asked the Prophet ﷺ:

يَا رَسُولَ اللهِ، مَتَى وَجَبَتْ لَكَ النُّبُوَّةُ؟

O Messenger of Allah, when was prophethood bestowed upon you?

This was an unusual enquiry, because who amongst the noble companions did not know that the Holy Prophet ﷺ declared his prophethood at the age of 40? Hence, it is evident that the noble Companions were not asking about the moment the Prophet ﷺ received prophecy, but they were asking about the inception of his spiritual existence when Almighty Allah bestowed on him the cloak of prophecy. Thus, the Holy Prophet ﷺ replied:

«آدَمُ بَيْنَ الرُّوحِ وَالْجَسَدِ.»

> (I was a prophet, when the creation of) Ādam was between the spirit and the body.[1]

The meaning of this hadith is that the Holy Prophet ﷺ was bestowed prophecy at the time when Ādam's creation had not been completed yet. In this way, the beloved Prophet ﷺ explained his creation prior to his birth to the noble Companions.

8.2 THE PROPHET ﷺ ORGANISED A GATHERING FOR THE MENTION OF HIS BIRTH

Besides the Friday sermons, it was the Holy Prophet's practice to organise gatherings in which he discussed religious, moral, spiritual, educational, theological, political, social, cultural, legal, organisational and administrative issues with the noble Companions ﷺ. Apart from this, he would organise gatherings in which he would mention the excellence of his lineage and matchless nobility, and the incidents surrounding his blessed birth. Below, some narrations are mentioned, which quite clearly substantiate this point:

1. Muṭṭalib b. Abī Wadāʿa ﷺ narrates:

جَاءَ الْعَبَّاسُ إِلَى رَسُولِ اللهِ ﷺ فَكَأَنَّهُ سَمِعَ شَيْئًا، فَقَامَ النَّبِيُّ ﷺ عَلَى الْمِنْبَرِ، فَقَالَ: «مَنْ أَنَا؟» فَقَالُوا: أَنْتَ رَسُولُ اللهِ عَلَيْكَ السَّلَامُ! قَالَ: «أَنَا مُحَمَّدُ بْنُ عَبْدِ اللهِ بْنِ عَبْدِ الْمُطَّلِبِ، إِنَّ اللهَ خَلَقَ الْخَلْقَ فَجَعَلَنِي فِي خَيْرِهِمْ فِرْقَةً، ثُمَّ جَعَلَهُمْ فِرْقَتَيْنِ فَجَعَلَنِي فِي خَيْرِهِمْ فِرْقَةً، ثُمَّ جَعَلَهُمْ

---

[1] Narrated by al-Tirmidhī in *al-Jāmiʿ al-Ṣaḥīḥ*: *Kitāb al-Manāqib* [The Book of Virtuous Merits], chapter: 'The excellent merits of the Prophet', 5:585 §3609; Ibn Mustafāḍ in *Kitāb al-qadr*, p.27 §14 has stated that the narrators are reliable; Tamām Rāzī in *Kitāb al-fawāʾid*, 1:241 §581; Ibn Ḥibbān in *Kitāb al-thiqāt*, 1:47; Lālakāʾī in *Iʿtiqād Ahl al-Sunna*, 1:422 §1403; al-Ḥākim in *al-Mustadrak*, 2:665 §4210; al-Bayhaqī in *Dalāʾil al-Nubuwwa wa maʿrifa aḥwāl Ṣāḥib al-Sharīʿa* ﷺ, 2:130; al-Suyūṭī in *al-Durr al-manthūr fī al-tafsīr bi al-Maʾthūr*, 6:569; and Nāṣir al-Dīn Albānī in *Ṣaḥīḥ al-ṣīra al-Nabawiyya*, p.54 §53 has declared this hadith authentic.

قَبَائِلَ فَجَعَلَنِي فِي خَيْرِهِمْ قَبِيلَةً، ثُمَّ جَعَلَهُمْ بُيُوتًا فَجَعَلَنِي فِي خَيْرِهِمْ بَيْتًا وَخَيْرِهِمْ نَسَبًا.»

> Al-ᶜAbbās came to Allah's Messenger ﷺ, for he seemed to have heard something (indecent from the unbelievers and was in a rage and wanted to tell the Holy Prophet, or the Holy Prophet was already aware of it due to his prophetic knowledge) so the Prophet ﷺ stood on the pulpit and said: 'Who am I?' They said: 'You are Allah's Messenger. Peace be upon you!' He said: 'I am Muhammad, the son of ᶜAbd Allāh b. ᶜAbd al-Muṭṭalib. Allah created the creatures, so He put me among the best of them (the human beings). Then He divided them into two segments (the Arabs and the non-Arabs) and He put me among the best of them (the Arabs). Then he made them tribes and He put me among the best of them (the tribe of Quraysh). Then He made them households and He put me among the best of them as a household (Banū Hāshim), and the best of them in lineage. (So I am the most exalted of the entire creation, my lineage, my tribe, my household, and personal glory.)'[1]

In this narration, there are several noteworthy points:

i. Whenever the Holy Prophet ﷺ wished to make a critical point that he wished to emphasise to the Muslims, he would ascend to the pulpit and deliver his sermon. Otherwise, if the issue at hand was not of critical importance, then he would just inform those who were nearby as opposed to ascending the pulpit and delivering

---

[1] Narrated by al-Tirmidhī in *al-Jāmiᶜ al-Ṣaḥīḥ*: *Kitāb al-Daᶜwāt* [The Book of Supplications], 5:543 §3532; al-Tirmidhī in *al-Jāmiᶜ al-Ṣaḥīḥ*: *Kitāb al-Manāqib* [The Book of Excellent Merits], chapter: 'The Prophet's excellent merits', 5:584 §3608 narrates the words 'best of them in person' in the place of the words 'best of them in lineage'; Aḥmad b. Ḥanbal in *al-Musnad*, 1:210 §1788 has added the words, 'I am the best of you in household and the best of you in person'; Ibid., 4:165; al-Haythamī in *Majmaᶜ al-zawāʾid wa manbaᶜ al-fawāʾid*, 8:216; and al-Bayhaqī in *Dalāʾil al-Nubuwwa wa maᶜrifa aḥwāl Ṣāḥib al-Sharīᶜa* ﷺ, 1:169.

a sermon. In the narration above, the Holy Prophet ﷺ ascends to the pulpit; hence, this is an indication that the issue at hand was of critical importance.

ii. The most revered Prophet ﷺ asked the Companions, 'Who am I?' They all replied, 'You are Allah's Messenger. Peace be upon you!' Although the reply of the Companions was based on truth, it was not the expected answer, as on this occasion the required answer was different. When he did not receive the answer that he was seeking, he himself replied: 'I am Muhammad, the son of ᶜAbd Allāh b. ᶜAbd al-Muṭṭalib.' This is a clear indication that he wanted to inform the noble Companions about the excellence of his sublimely noble lineage and blessed birth. This is a topic related directly to the subject of *Mawlid al-Nabī* ﷺ. Although the noble Companions were already aware of these facts, this statement with so much emphasis indicates that he wished to make his *mawlid* as one of his Sunnas.

iii. In the above mentioned hadith, he did not inform the noble Companions of any commandment of Almighty Allah or any topic on deeds and morality; rather, he told them about his blessed birth, and the superiority of his lineage. This is from the acts of *Mawlid al-Nabī*.

iv. The Holy Prophet ﷺ did not make mention of his *mawlid* on an individual level privately, but he held a congregation comprising the noble Companions, which is indicative that special arrangements were made for this gathering.

In the books of hadith, biography and Prophetic virtues and merits, authored by great scholars like Imam al-Bukhārī (194-256 AH), Imam Muslim (206-261 AH), Imam al-Tirmidhī (210-279 AH), al-Qāḍī ᶜIyāḍ (476-544 AH), al-Qasṭallānī (851-923 AH) and al-Nabhānī (1265-1350 AH), there are numerous narrations that have no relation to matters of the religion;, rather, they are concerned with the Prophet's birth, nobility, lineage, and his excellent virtues and merits.

2. ᶜAbbās b. ᶜAbd al-Muṭṭalib رضي الله عنه narrates:

قُلْتُ: يَا رَسُولَ اللهِ، إِنَّ قُرَيْشًا جَلَسُوا فَتَذَاكَرُوا أَحْسَابَهُمْ بَيْنَهُمْ، فَجَعَلُوا

مِثْلَكَ مِثْلَ نَخْلَةٍ فِي كَبْوَةٍ مِنَ الْأَرْضِ، فَقَالَ النَّبِيُّ ﷺ: «إِنَّ اللهَ خَلَقَ الْـخَلْقَ فَجَعَلَنِي مِنْ خَيْرِهِمْ مِنْ خَيْرِ فِرَقِهِمْ وَخَيْرِ الْفَرِيقَيْنِ، ثُمَّ تَخَيَّرَ الْقَبَائِلَ فَجَعَلَنِي مِنْ خَيْرِ قَبِيلَةٍ، ثُمَّ تَخَيَّرَ الْبُيُوتَ فَجَعَلَنِي مِنْ خَيْرِ بُيُوتِهِمْ، فَأَنَا خَيْرُهُمْ نَفْسًا وَخَيْرُهُمْ بَيْتًا.»

I said: 'O Messenger of Allah, the Quraysh whilst mentioning their lineage said that your example is that of a date-palm tree on a mound (hillock).' Hearing this, he replied: 'Allah created His creation and He made me amongst the best of them, from the best of their groups and the better of the two groups. Then he made them tribes and He put me among the best of them (the tribe of Quraysh). Then He made them households and He put me among the best of them as a household (Banū Hāshim). So I am the most exalted of the entire creation in person and household.'[1]

3. Wāthila b. Asqaᶜ ﷺ narrates that the Prophet ﷺ said:

«إِنَّ اللهَ اصْطَفَى مِنْ وَلَدِ إِبْرَاهِيمَ إِسْمَعِيلَ، وَاصْطَفَى مِنْ وَلَدِ إِسْمَعِيلَ بَنِي كِنَانَةَ، وَاصْطَفَى مِنْ بَنِي كِنَانَةَ قُرَيْشًا، وَاصْطَفَى مِنْ قُرَيْشٍ بَنِي هَاشِمٍ، وَاصْطَفَانِي مِنْ بَنِي هَاشِمٍ.»

Allah ﷻ has chosen Ismāᶜīl from the children of Ibrāhīm. He has chosen the tribe of Kināna from the offspring of Ismāᶜīl. He has chosen Quraysh from Kināna. He has chosen Banū Hāshim from Quraysh, and He has chosen me from Banū Hāshim.[2]

---

[1] Narrated by al-Tirmidhī in *al-Jāmiᶜ al-Ṣaḥīḥ*: *Kitāb al-Manāqib* [The Book of Virtuous Merits], chapter: 'The excellent merit of the Prophet', 5:584 §3607; Aḥmad b. Ḥanbal in *Faḍāʾil al-Ṣaḥāba*, 2:937 §1803; and Abū Yaᶜlā in *al-Musnad*, 4:140 §1316.

[2] Narrated by al-Tirmidhī in *al-Jāmiᶜ al-Ṣaḥīḥ*: *Kitāb al-Manāqib* [The Book of Virtuous Merits], chapter: 'The excellent merit of the Prophet', 5:583

In this hadith, the most exalted Prophet ﷺ has mentioned his ancestry. He also used the word *iṣṭafā* (to choose) since his honorific title is *al-Muṣṭafā*—the Chosen One. This title can also be attributed to the whole of his lineage.

8.3 Organising Special Gatherings for the Mention of Virtues and Excellence

Apart from his *mawlid*, the most gracious Prophet ﷺ organised gatherings for the mention of his virtues and excellence.

1. ʿAbbās narrates:

جَلَسَ نَاسٌ مِنْ أَصْحَابِ رَسُولِ اللهِ ﷺ يَنْتَظِرُونَهُ، قَالَ: فَخَرَجَ حَتَّى إِذَا دَنَا مِنْهُمْ سَمِعَهُمْ يَتَذَاكَرُونَ فَسَمِعَ حَدِيثَهُمْ. فَقَالَ بَعْضُهُمْ عَجَبًا: إِنَّ اللهَ عَزَّ وَجَلَّ اتَّخَذَ مِنْ خَلْقِهِ خَلِيلًا اتَّخَذَ إِبْرَاهِيمَ خَلِيلًا. وَقَالَ آخَرُ: مَاذَا بِأَعْجَبَ مِنْ كَلَامِ مُوسَى كَلَّمَهُ تَكْلِيمًا! وَقَالَ آخَرُ: فَعِيسَى كَلِمَةُ اللهِ وَرُوحُهُ. وَقَالَ آخَرُ: آدَمُ اصْطَفَاهُ اللهُ فَخَرَجَ عَلَيْهِمْ فَسَلَّمَ. وَقَالَ: «قَدْ سَمِعْتُ كَلَامَكُمْ وَعَجَبَكُمْ، إِنَّ إِبْرَاهِيمَ خَلِيلُ اللهِ وَهُوَ كَذَلِكَ، وَمُوسَى نَجِيُّ اللهِ وَهُوَ كَذَلِكَ، وَعِيسَى رُوحُ اللهِ وَكَلِمَتُهُ وَهُوَ كَذَلِكَ، وَآدَمُ اصْطَفَاهُ اللهُ وَهُوَ كَذَلِكَ، أَلَا! وَأَنَا حَبِيبُ اللهِ وَلَا فَخْرَ، وَأَنَا حَامِلُ لِوَاءِ الْحَمْدِ يَوْمَ الْقِيَامَةِ وَلَا فَخْرَ، وَأَنَا أَوَّلُ شَافِعٍ وَأَوَّلُ مُشَفَّعٍ يَوْمَ الْقِيَامَةِ وَلَا فَخْرَ، وَأَنَا أَوَّلُ مَنْ يُحَرِّكُ حِلَقَ الْـجَنَّةِ فَيَفْتَحُ اللهُ لِي فَيُدْخِلُنِيهَا، وَمَعِي فُقَرَاءُ الْـمُؤْمِنِينَ وَلَا فَخْرَ، وَأَنَا أَكْرَمُ الْأَوَّلِينَ وَالْآخِرِينَ وَلَا فَخْرَ.»

---

§3605; Muslim in *al-Ṣaḥīḥ*: *Kitāb al-Faḍāʾil* [The Book of Excellent Merits], chapter: 'The excellent merit of the Prophet's lineage and the stone reciting salutations upon him before his prophecy' 4:1782 §2276; Aḥmad b. Ḥanbal in *al-Musnad*, 4:107; Ibn Abī Shayba in *al-Muṣannaf*, 6:317 §31,731; Abū Yaʿlā in *al-Musnad*, 13:469 & 472 §7485 & 7487; al-Ṭabarānī in *al-Muʿjam al-kabīr*, 22:66 §161; al-Bayhaqī in *al-Sunan al-kubrā* in 6:365 §12,852; and al-Bayhaqī in *Shuʿab al-īmān*, 2:139 §1391.

Some Companions of Allah's Messenger ﷺ were sitting and waiting for him. Meanwhile, he came outside. When he drew near to them, he heard them making some conversation. One of them said: 'How amazing it is that Allah chose a sincere bosom friend from among His creatures! He chose Ibrāhīm as a sincere friend!' Another said: 'What is more amazing than the discourse of Mūsā?! Almighty Allah spoke to Him directly!' Another said: "ʿĪsā is the Word of Allah and His Spirit!' Another said: 'Ādam was chosen by Allah!' Allah's Messenger then approached them, greeted them with the salutation of peace, and said: 'I heard your discourse and your amazement that Ibrāhīm is Allah's Sincere Friend [Khalīl Allāh], and that is how he is, and that Mūsā is Allah's Confidant [Najiyy Allāh], for that is how he is, and that ʿĪsā is Allah's Spirit and His Word [Rūḥ Allāh wa Kalimatuh], for that is how he is, and that Ādam was chosen by Allah, for that is how he is (the exalted one)! Listen! I am indeed the Beloved of Allah [Ḥabīb Allāh] and that is no boast! I am the bearer of the banner of praise on the Day of Resurrection, and that is no boast, and I am the first intercessor and the first whose intercession is accepted on the Day of Resurrection and that is no boast! I am the first one to knock the chain of Paradise, for Allah will open the gate for me, then He will cause me to enter it, accompanied by the poor, ascetic and the destitute and the devout believers, and that is no boast! I am the most revered and honoured of the first and the last (in the sight of Allah), and that is no boast!'[1]

2. ʿUqba b. ʿĀmir ؓ narrates:

---

[1] Narrated by al-Tirmidhī in *al-Jāmiʿ al-Ṣaḥīḥ: Kitāb al-Manāqib* [The Book of Virtuous Merits], chapter: 'The excellent merit of the Prophet', 2:202 §3616; al-Dārimī in *al-Sunan*, 1:39 §47; al-Baghawī in *Sharḥ al-Sunna*, 13:198 & 204 §3617 & 3625; al-Rāzī in *Mafātīḥ al-ghayb (al-Tafsīr al-kabīr)*, 6:167; Ibn Kathīr in *Tafsīr al-Qurʾān al-ʿaẓīm*, 1:560; and al-Suyūṭī in *al-Durr al-manthūr fī al-tafsīr bi al-maʾthūr*, 2:705.

أَنَّ النَّبِيَّ ﷺ خَرَجَ يَوْمًا، فَصَلَّى عَلَى أَهْلِ أُحُدٍ صَلَاتَهُ عَلَى الْـمَيِّتِ، ثُمَّ انْصَرَفَ إِلَى الْـمِنْبَرِ، فَقَالَ: «إِنِّي فَرَطٌ لَكُمْ وَأَنَا شَهِيدٌ عَلَيْكُمْ. وَإِنِّي وَاللهِ، لَأَنْظُرُ إِلَى حَوْضِي الْآنَ، وَإِنِّـي أُعْطِيتُ مَفَاتِيحَ خَزَائِنِ الْأَرْضِ أَوْ مَفَاتِيحَ الْأَرْضِ؛ وَإِنِّـي وَاللهِ، مَا أَخَافُ عَلَيْكُمْ أَنْ تُشْرِكُوا بَعْدِي، وَلَكِنْ أَخَافُ عَلَيْكُمْ أَنْ تَنَافَسُوا فِيهَا.»

One day Allah's Messenger ﷺ visited the ground of Uḥud and prayed as if he was praying the funeral prayer over the martyrs of Uḥud, (after eight years). Then he mounted the pulpit and said: 'I am your forerunner in front of you, and I am a witness over you (aware of your accounts). By Allah! I am watching the Basin [*al-Ḥawḍ*] and I am looking towards it from this station of mine and I have been bestowed the keys of all the treasure of the earth. By Allah! I have not been afraid that you might become polytheists, but I am afraid that you might get involved in the worldly lust.' That was the last time I had the (eye-cooling and heart-soothing) sight of Allah's Messenger ﷺ.[1]

From the words, 'then he mounted the pulpit', a question arises: are there pulpits in the graveyard? Pulpits are made so that one may deliver sermons in a mosque; however, there was no mosque at Uḥud: there were only the graves of the martyrs. There was only one pulpit at that time, and that was in the mosque of the

[1] Narrated by al-Bukhārī in *al-Ṣaḥīḥ*: *Kitāb al-Janāʾiz* [The Book of the Funeral Ceremonies], chapter: 'The ritual prayer over the martyr, 1:451 §1279; al-Bukhārī in *al-Ṣaḥīḥ*: *Kitāb al-Manāqib* [The Book of Virtuous Merits], chapter: 'Signs of prophecy', 3:1317 §1401; al-Bukhārī in *al-Ṣaḥīḥ*: *Kitāb al-Maghāzī* [The Book of Military Expeditions], chapter: 'Uḥud loves us', 4:1498 §3857; al-Bukhārī in *al-Ṣaḥīḥ*: *Kitāb al-Riqāq* [The Book of Softening the Heart], chapter: 'Being wary of worldly attraction and competing one another for it', 5:2361 §6062; al-Bukhārī in *al-Ṣaḥīḥ*: *Kitāb al-Ḥawḍ* [The Book of the Basin], chapter: 'The Basin', 5:2408 §6218; Muslim in *al-Ṣaḥīḥ*: *Kitāb al-Faḍāʾil* [The Book of Excellent Merits], chapter: 'Affirming the Basin', 4:1795 §2296; Aḥmad b. Ḥanbal in *al-Musnad*, 4:149 & 153; Ibn Ḥibbān in *al-Ṣaḥīḥ*, 7:473 §3168; and Ibid., 8:18 §3224.

Holy Prophet ﷺ in Medina. It may seem on the face of it this incident did not occur: but the reality is that a pulpit was brought to the graveyard of Uḥud, indicating that either the Holy Prophet ﷺ ordered it or the noble Companions brought it with them when they came. However, the point of interest here is not 'what', but 'why'. By bringing the pulpit to Uḥud, we can see that special arrangements were made for the gathering in which the most benevolent Prophet's virtues and excellence were mentioned—a gathering which was conducted by the most compassionate Prophet ﷺ himself. As a means of 'proclaiming the blessing', the Holy Prophet ﷺ informed the noble Companions of his virtues and excellence, which is what this hadith comprises; and consequently, this hadith is clear evidence on holding gatherings of *Mawlid al-Nabī* ﷺ.

The above mentioned hadiths establish the fact that to organise gatherings for the Holy Prophet's virtues and excellence is in accordance to the Sunna of the Holy Prophet ﷺ. Organising *mawlid* gatherings is a means by which this Sunna can be fulfilled. In our age of transgression, holding such gatherings is of paramount significance; in fact, it is of more importance today than ever before so that the heart of each and every individual of this community is enlightened with deep love and affection for Allah's Messenger ﷺ and is inclined to follow his perfect example.

Section 2

Relating the Prophet's Biography and Virtues

In the auspicious gatherings of *Mawlid al-Nabī* ﷺ, there occurs remembrance of the Prophetic biography and virtues. This Prophetic remembrance is described below in five aspects.

8.4 Mentioning the Rulings of the Sharia

In the *mawlid* gatherings, matters pertaining to the ritual prayer, fasting, alms-due, Pilgrimage, and other rulings of the Sharia are mentioned. The Prophet's teaching and instructions, which are related to the fundamentals of the Sharia and upon which the pillars of *īmān* and *Islam* are established, are discussed. Rather than the issues related to jurisprudence and other branches of the Sharia, the attendees are educated regarding how they can perfect their worship so that it attains acceptance and how they can attain the pleasure of Almighty Allah. They are told how our obedience and love of Allah's Messenger ﷺ can open up the doors to success, and how it helps us to strengthen our faith. Other similar matters are mentioned so that, in light of the perfect Prophetic character, one can implant the essence of servitude within one's behaviour and that one makes a resolution to change his life for the better.

8.5 Mentioning the Prophetic Natural Talent and Conduct

The second method used in the gatherings of *Mawlid al-Nabī* ﷺ is to make mention of the Prophet's *khaṣāʾil* (i.e., his beautiful conduct and noble character), as evident in his excellent example. Its purpose is to inspire those listening to change their lives at a personal, communal, and national level by adopting his Sunna in every aspect of their lives. This is the second subject discussed by the scholars. Although the original purpose of these gatherings is to express joy at the birth of the Holy Prophet ﷺ, the scholars also use this opportunity to give discourses from the Qurʾān and hadith, and they also address moral, spiritual, and educational issues in their sermons.

8.6 MENTIONING THE PROPHET'S PHYSICAL TRAITS

In the recounting of the description of prophethood, the excellent abilities and virtues of the Holy Prophet ﷺ are mentioned. His elegant, glorified, and exquisite beauty is also described. The description of the most gracious and perfect beauty of the Holy Prophet ﷺ has been disclosed in a splendid and endearing manner in the Qurʾān, hadith and by the Companions. The beautiful and heart touching descriptions about the glowing face and dark, fragrant tresses of the most gracious Prophet ﷺ bring intense pleasure to the listener. He was the embodiment of the most elegant beauty, and it was impossible to assess the extent of the exalted rank of his glorified appearance. The noble Companions used to experience a state of ecstasy by looking at the beauty of the most elegant Prophet ﷺ, and they felt humility when describing him. The truth is that it is beyond our scope to describe the perfection of the divinely bestowed beauty of the beloved Prophet ﷺ. Even the Arabs, who were famed for the eloquence and mastery of their linguistic skills, were unable to describe him as he deserved to be portrayed.

The whole month of *Rabīʿ al-awwal* is spent earnestly attempting to describe the matchless beauty of the most gracious Prophet ﷺ. Some spend their time making mention of his blessed fragrant tresses and glowing face. Some praise the gracious gaze of his sacred eyes, some send salutations to the beauty of his blessed ears and its unparalleled hearing, and others send salutations to his delicate lips, which were like heavenly petals of a flower. Some speak about the miracles performed by his blessed hands. Some sing the melody of his sacred mouth and the blessings of his saliva. The description of these exclusive qualities of the Holy Prophet ﷺ brings the state of ecstasy and the distribution of the Prophetic blessings from his court. These are the states of gathering that bring the illumination of the faith in one's heart and soul. These are the supplies for the Hereafter, indispensable for a believer's eternal journey. The whole month of *Rabīʿ al-Awwal* is spent earnestly attempting to describe the Prophet ﷺ.

8.7 Mentioning the Prophet's Excellent Virtues and Exceptionality

Another method is to mention the Prophet's excellent virtues and exceptionality (*faḍāʾil wa khaṣāʾiṣ*). These are his exclusive and virtuous attributes and excellences that distinguish him from other prophets and the rest of mankind. He is the perfect sum of all of the commendable and miraculous qualities contained in all the other prophets. Allah bestowed His Beloved Prophet ﷺ nobility and superiority over all others; He bestowed him the leadership of the first and last and of all the people of all ages that preceded or followed him. Almighty Allah bestowed him special proximity and invited him to draw near to His presence on the night of the Heavenly Ascension, permitting him to behold His sanctified vision.

In the Holy Qurʾān, it states that obedience to the Holy Prophet ﷺ is obedience to Almighty Allah[1]; the pleasure of the Prophet ﷺ is the pleasure of Almighty Allah[2]; pledging allegiance to the Holy Prophet ﷺ is pledging allegiance to Almighty Allah[3]; the Holy Prophet's action is Almighty Allah's action[4]; the Holy Prophet's utterance is Almighty Allah's revelation[5]; disobedience to the Holy Prophet ﷺ is disobedience to Almighty Allah[6]; opposition to the Holy Prophet ﷺ is opposition to Almighty Allah[7]; and the Holy Prophet's bestowal is the bestowal of Almighty Allah[8]. In addition to this, the Holy Prophet ﷺ is given unlimited and unprecedented virtues and merits in his worldly life and the life Hereafter.

Discourses on the Holy Prophet's elegant beauty and conduct

---

1 Qurʾān 4:80.

2 Qurʾān 9:62.

3 Qurʾān 48:10.

4 Qurʾān 8:17.

5 Qurʾān 53:3-4.

6 Qurʾān 4:14.

7 Qurʾān 9:63.

8 Qurʾān 9:59 & 74.

do take place indeed, but alongside these descriptions, there are numerous other virtues that enlighten the heart of a believer with deep love and passion for the most esteemed Prophet ﷺ. Some hadiths that mention these excellent virtues and exceptionality are referenced below:

1. Anas b. Mālik relates that the Prophet ﷺ said:

«أَنَا أَوَّلُـهُمْ خُرُوْجاً، وَأَنَا قَائِدُهُمْ إِذَا وَفَدُوْا وَأَنَا خَطِيْبُهُمْ إِذَا أَنْصَتُوْا، وَأَنَا مُشَفِّعُهُمْ إِذَا حَبَسُوْا، وَأَنَا مُبَشِّرُهُمْ إِذَا أَيِسُوْا. الْكَرَامَةُ وَالْـمَفَاتِيْحُ يَوْمَئِذٍ بِيَدِي، وَأَنَا أَكْرَمُ وَلَدِ آدَمَ عَلَى رَبِّي، يَطُوْفُ عَلَيَّ أَلْفُ خَادِمٍ كَأَنَّهُمْ بَيْضٌ مَّكْنُوْنٌ أَوْ لُؤْلُؤٌ مَّنْثُوْرٌ.»

> I am the first of them to come forth (from the enlightened grave). I will be their leader when they will go in congregation. I will be their spokesman when they will be quiet. I will be their intercessor when they will be checked, and I will be their bringer of glad tidings when they are in despair. Nobility and the keys of Paradise will be in my hands on that Day, for I am the noblest of the children of Ādam in the sight of my Lord. A thousand servants will circle round me (that Day) as if they are concealed eggs (hidden beauty) or scattered pearls.[1]

This hadith makes mention of the Prophet's status and his position on the Day of Judgment, and this too is related to the

---

[1] Narrated by al-Dārimī in *al-Sunan*, 1:39 §48; al-Tirmidhī in *al-Jāmiʿ al-Ṣaḥīḥ*: *Kitāb Tafsīr al-Qurʾān* [Interpretation of the Qurʾān], chapter: 'From *Sūra Banī Isrāʾīl*', 5:308 §3148; al-Tirmidhī in *al-Jāmiʿ al-Ṣaḥīḥ*: *Kitāb al-Manāqib* [The Book of Virtuous Merits], chapter: 'The excellent merit of the Prophet', 5:585 §3610; Abū Yaʿlā in *al-Muʿjam*, p.147 §160; Qazwīnī in *al-Tadwīn fī akhbār Qazwīn*, 1:234-235; al-Daylamī in *al-Firdaws bi maʾthūr al-Khiṭāb*, 1:47 §117; al-Baghawī in *Sharḥ al-Sunna*, 13:203 §3624; Ibn Abī Ḥātim al-Rāzī in *Tafsīr al-Qurʾān al-ʿaẓīm*, 10:3212 §18,189; al-Bayhaqī in *Dalāʾil al-Nubuwwa wa maʿrifa aḥwāl Ṣāḥib al-Sharīʿa* ﷺ, 5:484; Abū Naʿīm in *Dalāʾil al-Nabuwwa*, 1:64-65 §24; al-Baghawī in *Muʿālim al-tanzīl*, 3:131; and al-Suyūṭī in *al-Durr al-manthūr fī al-tafsīr bi al-maʾthūr*, 8:376.

subject of *Mawlid al-Nabī* ﷺ.

2. Abū Saᶜīd al-Khudrī relates that the Prophet ﷺ said:

«أَنَا سَيِّدُ وَلَدِ آدَمَ يَوْمَ الْقِيَامَةِ وَلَا فَخْرَ، وَبِيَدِي لِوَاءُ الْحَمْدِ وَلَا فَخْرَ، وَمَا مِنْ نَبِيٍّ يَوْمَئِذٍ آدَمَ فَمَنْ سِوَاهُ إِلَّا تَحْتَ لِوَائِي، وَأَنَا أَوَّلُ مَنْ تَنْشَقُّ عَنْهُ الْأَرْضُ وَلَا فَخْرَ.»

I will be the leader of the children of Ādam on the Day of Resurrection and that is no boast. The banner of praise will be in my hand and that is no boast. Ādam and all other Prophets will be under my banner (and that is no boast). I will be the first for whom the earth will split and that is no boast.[1]

3. Abū Hurayra narrates that the Prophet ﷺ said:

«أَنَا أَوَّلُ مَنْ تَنْشَقُّ عَنْهُ الْأَرْضُ، فَأُكْسَى حُلَّةً مِنْ حُلَلِ الْجَنَّةِ، ثُمَّ أَقُومُ عَنْ يَمِينِ الْعَرْشِ، لَيْسَ أَحَدٌ مِنَ الْخَلَائِقِ يَقُومُ ذَلِكَ الْمَقَامَ غَيْرِي.»

I will be the first for whom the earth will split. I will be clothed with a dressing of Paradise. Then, I will stand to the right of the ᶜ*Arsh* where none amongst creation will stand except me.[2]

These hadiths have been referenced here to show that no aspect of the Sharia (such as *ḥalāl* and *ḥarām*), propagation of the

---

[1] Narrated by al-Tirmidhī in *al-Jāmiᶜ al-Ṣaḥīḥ*: *Kitāb al-Manāqib* [The Book of Virtuous Merits], chapter: 'The excellent merit of the Prophet', 5:587 §3615; Muslim in *al-Ṣaḥīḥ*: *Kitāb al-Faḍā'il* [The Book of Excellent Merits], chapter: 'Superiority of our Prophet over the entire creation', 4:1782 §2278; Ibn Ḥibbān in *al-Ṣaḥīḥ*, 14:398 §6478; Aḥmad b. Ḥanbal in *al-Musnad*, 1:281; Ibid., 3:2; Abū Yaᶜlā in *al-Musnad*, 13:480 §7493; and al-Maqdasī in *al-Aḥādīth al-mukhtāra*, 9:455 §428.

[2] Narrated by al-Tirmidhī in *al-Jāmiᶜ al-Ṣaḥīḥ*: *Kitāb al-Manāqib* [The Book of Virtuous Merits], chapter: 'The excellent merit of the Prophet', 5:585 §3611; and Ibn Kathīr in *al-Bidāya wa al-nihāya*, 10:263.

teachings of Islam, or the Holy Prophet's biography and mighty character have been mentioned here. Rather, the ongoing theme that has been the subject of discussion is the Holy Prophet's virtues and exceptionality and his esteemed rank amongst the children of Ādam. In the books of excellent virtues and merits (*faḍāʾil wa manāqib*), this is the theme which is contained, and this essentially is the subject matter of *Mawlid al-Nabī* ﷺ.

8.8 Mentioning the Accounts of His Blessed Birth and the Spiritual Signs and Sublimity that Took Place

The fifth method is to mention the accounts of the Holy Prophet's blessed birth and the spiritual signs and sublimity that became evident. This is one of the special features of the *mawlid* gatherings. The miracles surrounding his blessed birth, the Holy Prophet's blessed childhood, and his youth are discussed in detail; the accounts of his life are mentioned from his blessed birth up to the moment of the announcement of his prophecy. The spectacular signs that were shown at the time of his blessed birth in Mecca and the different parts of the world are all described.

There are discourses on the prophecies and glad tidings that have been recorded in previous scriptures brought by other prophets regarding his arrival. Every prophet, from Ādam to ʿĪsā ﷺ, has mentioned the imminent arrival of Almighty Allah's Final Messenger. And all of this comprises the subject matter of *Mawlid al-Nabī* ﷺ. Likewise, the participants are informed of the Prophet's passage through the pure loins of his ancestors as a light till he manifested himself in the womb of Sayyida Āmina and that he was born into this world as an orphan. They are informed that the Holy Prophet ﷺ was sent as a bounty and a great favour for mankind.

The mention of the most esteemed Prophet's birth and childhood, which he spent under the loving attention of Sayyida Āmina and Sayyida Ḥalīma Saʿdiya, tugs at the strings of the hearts and souls of the participants. The most esteemed Prophet's miracles are described.The scenes of ecstasy (*wajd*) can only be imagined and observed—no one has the power to speak and write about them.

The *mawlid* gatherings are the most effective methods of rekindling the flame of faith in the heart of a believer. It is a source of strength, which, according to Iqbāl is the power of immense love by which the radiance of the name 'Muhammad ﷺ' illuminates the horizons. This is the very aim and objective of *Mawlid al-Nabī* ﷺ. Iqbāl says:

قوت عشق سے ہر پست کو بالا کر دے

دہر میں اسمِ محمد ﷺ سے اُجالا کر دے

With the strength of love turn every loss into success;
And light up the world with the name of Muhammad.[1]

[1] Iqbāl, *Kulliyāt: Bāng-e-darā*, 1:207/207.

Section 3

Reciting Odes and Poems in Praise of the Prophet ﷺ

AN IMPORTANT CONSTITUENT OF THE *MAWLID* IS THE RECITATION of odes and poems in praise of the most esteemed Prophet ﷺ. By composing and reciting poetry in his honour, the Muslims are able to express the intense love and affection they feel for their beloved Prophet ﷺ. Poetic praise of the Holy Prophet ﷺ is not a new act; rather, it is established from the Qur᾽ān and hadiths. In this chapter, some evidences for this are cited below:

8.9 Poetic Praise of the Prophet ﷺ in the Qur᾽ān

Throughout the Qur᾽ān, there are numerous places where Almighty Allah has praised His Beloved Prophet ﷺ, yet He never addresses him directly by name. Instead, Almighty Allah refers to him as 'O mantled' or 'O enwrapped', and in another verse as *Yā-Sīn*. In other verses of the Qur᾽ān, Almighty Allah swears an oath by the illuminating countenance of His Beloved, saying, 'By the morning bright'; and when He says 'By the sprawling murky night', He swears an oath on the Prophet's beautiful dark black locks (of hair). The Qur᾽ān in its totality is a eulogy in praise of the Prophet ﷺ. Below are some verses which illustrate this point:

1. The broadening of his chest, the removal of his grief, and his exalted remembrance are mentioned in the following way:

﴿أَلَمۡ نَشۡرَحۡ لَكَ صَدۡرَكَ ۝١ وَوَضَعۡنَا عَنكَ وِزۡرَكَ ۝٢ ٱلَّذِيٓ أَنقَضَ ظَهۡرَكَ ۝٣ وَرَفَعۡنَا لَكَ ذِكۡرَكَ ۝٤﴾

Have We not broadened your breast for you (for the light of knowledge, wisdom and spiritual gnosis)? And We have taken off the load (of grief of the Umma *[Community]) from you, (The load) which was growing heavier on your (holy) back. And We exalted for you your remembrance (by annexing it to Ours everywhere in the world and in the Hereafter).*[1]

2. Almighty Allah and His angels are constantly sending their salutations upon the Prophet ﷺ:

﴿إِنَّ ٱللَّهَ وَمَلَـٰٓئِكَتَهُۥ يُصَلُّونَ عَلَى ٱلنَّبِيِّ ۚ يَـٰٓأَيُّهَا ٱلَّذِينَ ءَامَنُوا۟ صَلُّوا۟ عَلَيْهِ وَسَلِّمُوا۟ تَسْلِيمًا﴾

Surely, Allah and (all) His angels send blessings and greetings on the Holy Prophet ﷺ. *O believers! Invoke blessings on him and salute him with a worthy salutation of peace abundantly (and fervently).*[2]

3. Regarding paying respect at his court, Almighty Allah says:

﴿وَمَآ أَرْسَلْنَا مِن رَّسُولٍ إِلَّا لِيُطَاعَ بِإِذْنِ ٱللَّهِ ۚ وَلَوْ أَنَّهُمْ إِذ ظَّلَمُوٓا۟ أَنفُسَهُمْ جَآءُوكَ فَٱسْتَغْفَرُوا۟ ٱللَّهَ وَٱسْتَغْفَرَ لَهُمُ ٱلرَّسُولُ لَوَجَدُوا۟ ٱللَّهَ تَوَّابًا رَّحِيمًا﴾

And We have not sent any Messenger but that he must be obeyed by the command of Allah. And, (O Beloved,) if they, having wronged their souls, had come to you imploring the forgiveness of Allah, and the Messenger ﷺ *had also asked forgiveness for them, then (owing to this mediation and intercession) they would certainly have found Allah Most Relenting, Ever-Merciful.*[3]

4. Obedience to the Holy Prophet ﷺ is obedience to Almighty Allah:

﴿مَّن يُطِعِ ٱلرَّسُولَ فَقَدْ أَطَاعَ ٱللَّهَ ۖ وَمَن تَوَلَّىٰ فَمَآ أَرْسَلْنَـٰكَ عَلَيْهِمْ حَفِيظًا﴾

---

1 Qurʾān 94:1-4.

2 Qurʾān 33:56.

3 Qurʾān 4:64.

Whoever obeys the Messenger ﷺ *obeys (but) Allah indeed, but he who turns away—We have not sent you to watch over them.*[1]

5. His name is mentioned in the Torah and Gospel:

﴿ٱلَّذِينَ يَتَّبِعُونَ ٱلرَّسُولَ ٱلنَّبِيَّ ٱلْأُمِّيَّ ٱلَّذِى يَجِدُونَهُۥ مَكْتُوبًا عِندَهُمْ فِى
ٱلتَّوْرَىٰةِ وَٱلْإِنجِيلِ يَأْمُرُهُم بِٱلْمَعْرُوفِ وَيَنْهَىٰهُمْ عَنِ ٱلْمُنكَرِ وَيُحِلُّ لَهُمُ
ٱلطَّيِّبَٰتِ وَيُحَرِّمُ عَلَيْهِمُ ٱلْخَبَٰٓئِثَ وَيَضَعُ عَنْهُمْ إِصْرَهُمْ وَٱلْأَغْلَٰلَ ٱلَّتِى
كَانَتْ عَلَيْهِمْ ۚ فَٱلَّذِينَ ءَامَنُوا۟ بِهِۦ وَعَزَّرُوهُ وَنَصَرُوهُ وَٱتَّبَعُوا۟ ٱلنُّورَ ٱلَّذِىٓ
أُنزِلَ مَعَهُۥٓ ۙ أُو۟لَٰٓئِكَ هُمُ ٱلْمُفْلِحُونَ﴾

(They are the people) who follow the Messenger, the Prophet (titled as) al-Ummī *(who imparts to the people from Allah the news of the unseen and knowledge and secrets of socio-economic disciplines of life without himself being taught by any human in the world); whose (eminent attributes and exquisite powers) these people find written in the Torah and the* Injīl *(Gospel); who enjoins on them virtues and forbids them vices, declares wholesome things lawful and impure ones unlawful for them and removes from them their heavy burdens and yokes (i.e., shackles) weighing upon them (due to their acts of disobedience and blesses them with freedom). So those who will believe in this (most exalted Messenger* ﷺ*) and venerate and revere him and serve and support him (in his* Dīn *[Religion]) and follow this light (the Qurʾān) that has been sent down with him, it is they who will flourish and prosper.*[2]

6. Explaining the universality of his prophethood:

---

[1] Qurʾān 4:80.

[2] Qurʾān 7:157.

﴿قُلْ يَٰٓأَيُّهَا ٱلنَّاسُ إِنِّى رَسُولُ ٱللَّهِ إِلَيْكُمْ جَمِيعًا ٱلَّذِى لَهُۥ مُلْكُ ٱلسَّمَٰوَٰتِ وَٱلْأَرْضِ﴾

Say: O humankind! I have (come) to all of you (as) the Messenger of Allah to Whom belongs the kingdom of the heavens and the earth.[1]

7. Almighty Allah attributes to Himself the Holy Prophet's act of casting pebbles at the disbelievers on the Day of Badr:

﴿وَمَا رَمَيْتَ إِذْ رَمَيْتَ وَلَٰكِنَّ ٱللَّهَ رَمَىٰ﴾

And (O Glorious Beloved,) when you smote (them with pebbles), it was not you who smote them, but Allah.[2]

8. The Holy Prophet ﷺ being clement and merciful to his Community is mentioned:

﴿لَقَدْ جَآءَكُمْ رَسُولٌ مِّنْ أَنفُسِكُمْ عَزِيزٌ عَلَيْهِ مَا عَنِتُّمْ حَرِيصٌ عَلَيْكُم بِٱلْمُؤْمِنِينَ رَءُوفٌ رَّحِيمٌ﴾

Surely, a (Glorious) Messenger from amongst yourselves has come to you. Your suffering and distress (becomes) grievously heavy on him (blessings and peace be upon him). (O mankind,) he is ardently desirous of your (betterment and guidance. And) he is most (deeply) clement and merciful to the believers.[3]

9. Almighty Allah swears an oath by his blessed age:

﴿لَعَمْرُكَ إِنَّهُمْ لَفِى سَكْرَتِهِمْ يَعْمَهُونَ﴾

(O Glorious Beloved!) By your (sacred) life, surely these

[1] Qur'ān 7:158.

[2] Qur'ān 8:17.

[3] Qur'ān 9:128.

people (too) are wandering astray, possessed by their lust (like the people of Lūṭ [Lot]).[1]

10. Almighty Allah did not like to see the beloved Prophet ﷺ in a state of difficulty, so He said:

﴿طه ﴿١﴾ مَآ أَنزَلۡنَا عَلَيۡكَ ٱلۡقُرۡءَانَ لِتَشۡقَىٰٓ ﴿٢﴾﴾

Ṭā-Ḥā (Only Allah and the Messenger ﷺ know the real meaning). (O My Esteemed Beloved!) We have not revealed the Qurʾān to you that you land in distress.[2]

11. The Holy Prophet ﷺ is a mercy for all the worlds:

﴿وَمَآ أَرۡسَلۡنَٰكَ إِلَّا رَحۡمَةٗ لِّلۡعَٰلَمِينَ﴾

And, (O Esteemed Messenger,) We have not sent you but as a mercy for all the worlds.[3]

12. Whilst teaching the Muslims about the etiquettes of the court of the Holy Prophet ﷺ, Almighty Allah says:

﴿لَّا تَجۡعَلُواْ دُعَآءَ ٱلرَّسُولِ بَيۡنَكُمۡ كَدُعَآءِ بَعۡضِكُم بَعۡضٗاۚ قَدۡ يَعۡلَمُ ٱللَّهُ
ٱلَّذِينَ يَتَسَلَّلُونَ مِنكُمۡ لِوَاذٗاۚ فَلۡيَحۡذَرِ ٱلَّذِينَ يُخَالِفُونَ عَنۡ أَمۡرِهِۦٓ أَن
تُصِيبَهُمۡ فِتۡنَةٌ أَوۡ يُصِيبَهُمۡ عَذَابٌ أَلِيمٌ﴾

(O Muslims!) Do not regard the calling of the Prophet amongst you like your calling of one another. (When calling the Holy Prophet is not like your mutual calling amongst you, then how can the Holy Personality of the Prophet be like yours?) Surely, Allah knows those from amongst you (well) who slip away quietly (from the presence of the Holy Prophet ﷺ) under the shelter of

---

1 Qurʾān 15:72.

2 Qurʾān 20:1-2.

3 Qurʾān 21:107.

one another. So let those who go against the Messenger's command (of veneration and devotion) feel afraid lest some trial should overtake them (here in the world) or a painful torment seize them in the Hereafter.[1]

13. Almighty Allah states that the Holy Prophet ﷺ is closer to the believers than their own souls:

﴿ٱلنَّبِيُّ أَوْلَىٰ بِٱلْمُؤْمِنِينَ مِنْ أَنفُسِهِمْ ۖ وَأَزْوَٰجُهُۥٓ أُمَّهَـٰتُهُمْ﴾

This (Esteemed) Prophet is nearer to and has a greater claim on the believers than their own souls and his (pure) wives are their mothers.[2]

14. Almighty Allah made him a witness, a bearer of glad tidings, a warner, an inviter towards Almighty Allah, and a bright Sun. He says:

﴿يَـٰٓأَيُّهَا ٱلنَّبِيُّ إِنَّآ أَرْسَلْنَـٰكَ شَـٰهِدًا وَمُبَشِّرًا وَنَذِيرًا ۝٤٥ وَدَاعِيًا إِلَى ٱللَّهِ
بِإِذْنِهِۦ وَسِرَاجًا مُّنِيرًا ۝٤٦﴾

O (Esteemed) Prophet! Surely, We have sent you as a Witness (to the truth and the creation), a Bearer of glad tidings (of the beauty of the Hereafter) and a Warner (of the torment in the Hereafter) And (as) an Inviter towards Allah by His command and as a Sun spreading Light.[3]

15. The Holy Prophet's unrivalled, unparalleled qualities are mentioned in another place:

﴿إِنَّآ أَرْسَلْنَـٰكَ شَـٰهِدًا وَمُبَشِّرًا وَنَذِيرًا ۝٨ لِّتُؤْمِنُوا۟ بِٱللَّهِ وَرَسُولِهِۦ وَتُعَزِّرُوهُ
وَتُوَقِّرُوهُ ۚ وَتُسَبِّحُوهُ بُكْرَةً وَأَصِيلًا ۝٩﴾

---

[1] Qur'ān 24:63.

[2] Qur'ān 33:6.

[3] Qur'ān 33:45-46.

Indeed, We have sent you as an eyewitness (of the actions and the state of affairs of the Umma *[Community] to bear testimony on the Day of Reckoning) and as a Bearer of good news and as a Warner, So that, (O people,) you may believe in Allah and His Messenger* ﷺ *and may help his (*Dīn *[Religion]), and revere and venerate him heart and soul, and (with that) glorify Allah morning and evening.*[1]

16. Almighty Allah praises the Holy Prophet ﷺ, saying:

﴿يسٓ ۝١ وَٱلْقُرْءَانِ ٱلْحَكِيمِ ۝٢ إِنَّكَ لَمِنَ ٱلْمُرْسَلِينَ ۝٣﴾

Yā-Sīn. *(Only Allah and the Messenger* ﷺ *know the real meaning.) By the Qur'ān, full of wisdom, You are indeed one of the Messengers.*[2]

17. To pledge allegiance to the Holy Prophet ﷺ is to pledge allegiance to Almighty Allah:

﴿إِنَّ ٱلَّذِينَ يُبَايِعُونَكَ إِنَّمَا يُبَايِعُونَ ٱللَّهَ يَدُ ٱللَّهِ فَوْقَ أَيْدِيهِمْ ۚ فَمَن نَّكَثَ فَإِنَّمَا يَنكُثُ عَلَىٰ نَفْسِهِۦ ۖ وَمَنْ أَوْفَىٰ بِمَا عَـٰهَدَ عَلَيْهُ ٱللَّهَ فَسَيُؤْتِيهِ أَجْرًا عَظِيمًا﴾

(O Beloved!) Indeed, those who pledge allegiance to you in fact pledge allegiance to Allah alone. Allah's hand is over their hands (in the form of your hand). Then whoever breaks his pledge breaks it only to his own harm. But he who fulfils what he has promised to Allah, He will bless him with immense reward.[3]

18. Almighty Allah forbade anyone from raising their voice above the Holy Prophet's voice or calling him in the same manner they

[1] Qur'ān 48:8-9.

[2] Qur'ān 36:1-3.

[3] Qur'ān 48:10.

call others, warning that this could destroy all their good deeds:

﴿يَـٰٓأَيُّهَا ٱلَّذِينَ ءَامَنُوا۟ لَا تَرْفَعُوٓا۟ أَصْوَٰتَكُمْ فَوْقَ صَوْتِ ٱلنَّبِىِّ وَلَا تَجْهَرُوا۟ لَهُۥ بِٱلْقَوْلِ كَجَهْرِ بَعْضِكُمْ لِبَعْضٍ أَن تَحْبَطَ أَعْمَـٰلُكُمْ وَأَنتُمْ لَا تَشْعُرُونَ﴾

O believers! Do not raise your voices above the voice of the Prophet ﷺ, and (also) do not speak to him so loud as you are loud when you speak to one another (lest) all your actions should come to nothing (including your faith), and you are not even aware (that your faith and all pious works have been wrecked).[1]

19. Keeping one's voice low in the presence of the Holy Prophet ﷺ is declared a criterion of piety:

﴿إِنَّ ٱلَّذِينَ يَغُضُّونَ أَصْوَٰتَهُمْ عِندَ رَسُولِ ٱللَّهِ أُو۟لَـٰٓئِكَ ٱلَّذِينَ ٱمْتَحَنَ ٱللَّهُ قُلُوبَهُمْ لِلتَّقْوَىٰ ۚ لَهُم مَّغْفِرَةٌ وَأَجْرٌ عَظِيمٌ﴾

Assuredly, those who keep their voices low in the presence of Allah's Messenger (out of profound veneration and submissiveness), it is they whose hearts Allah has chosen for God-wariness and permeated with sincerity. For them alone is forgiveness and an immense reward.[2]

20. The Heavenly Night of Ascension is described as thus:

﴿سُبْحَـٰنَ ٱلَّذِىٓ أَسْرَىٰ بِعَبْدِهِۦ لَيْلًا مِّنَ ٱلْمَسْجِدِ ٱلْحَرَامِ إِلَى ٱلْمَسْجِدِ ٱلْأَقْصَا ٱلَّذِى بَـٰرَكْنَا حَوْلَهُۥ لِنُرِيَهُۥ مِنْ ءَايَـٰتِنَآ ۚ إِنَّهُۥ هُوَ ٱلسَّمِيعُ ٱلْبَصِيرُ﴾

Holy (i.e., free of any imperfection, weakness and insufficiency) is He Who took His (most beloved and

[1] Qur'ān 49:2.

[2] Qur'ān 49:3.

intimate) Servant in a small portion of a night from the Sacred Mosque to the al-Aqsa Mosque, whose surroundings We have blessed, in order that We might show him (the Perfect Servant) Our signs. Surely, He is the One Who is All-Hearing, All-Seeing.[1]

21. *Sūra al-Najm* describes the accounts of the Heavenly Night of Ascension in detail:

﴿وَٱلنَّجْمِ إِذَا هَوَىٰ ﴿١﴾ مَا ضَلَّ صَاحِبُكُمْ وَمَا غَوَىٰ ﴿٢﴾ وَمَا يَنطِقُ عَنِ
ٱلْهَوَىٰٓ ﴿٣﴾ إِنْ هُوَ إِلَّا وَحْىٌ يُوحَىٰ ﴿٤﴾ عَلَّمَهُۥ شَدِيدُ ٱلْقُوَىٰ ﴿٥﴾ ذُو مِرَّةٍ
فَٱسْتَوَىٰ ﴿٦﴾ وَهُوَ بِٱلْأُفُقِ ٱلْأَعْلَىٰ ﴿٧﴾ ثُمَّ دَنَا فَتَدَلَّىٰ ﴿٨﴾ فَكَانَ قَابَ قَوْسَيْنِ
أَوْ أَدْنَىٰ ﴿٩﴾ فَأَوْحَىٰٓ إِلَىٰ عَبْدِهِۦ مَآ أَوْحَىٰ ﴿١٠﴾ مَا كَذَبَ ٱلْفُؤَادُ مَا رَأَىٰٓ ﴿١١﴾
أَفَتُمَٰرُونَهُۥ عَلَىٰ مَا يَرَىٰ ﴿١٢﴾ وَلَقَدْ رَءَاهُ نَزْلَةً أُخْرَىٰ ﴿١٣﴾ عِندَ سِدْرَةِ
ٱلْمُنتَهَىٰ ﴿١٤﴾ عِندَهَا جَنَّةُ ٱلْمَأْوَىٰٓ ﴿١٥﴾ إِذْ يَغْشَى ٱلسِّدْرَةَ مَا يَغْشَىٰ ﴿١٦﴾ مَا زَاغَ
ٱلْبَصَرُ وَمَا طَغَىٰ ﴿١٧﴾ لَقَدْ رَأَىٰ مِنْ ءَايَٰتِ رَبِّهِ ٱلْكُبْرَىٰٓ ﴿١٨﴾﴾

By the bright star (Muhammad ﷺ) when (he ascended during the Ascension Night in the twinkling of an eye and) descended. He who bestowed on you his companionship (i.e., the Messenger, who made you his companions by blessing you with his companionship,) has never lost his way, nor has he (ever) strayed from the right path. And he does not speak out of his (own) desire. His speech is nothing but Revelation, which is sent to him. (The Lord) of Mighty Powers (directly) conferred on him (perfect) knowledge, He Who is absolute beauty. Then He (the Effulgence of Beauty) decided to unveil (Himself). And he (Muhammad ﷺ) was on the uppermost horizon (of the realm of creation during the Ascension Night i.e., on the apex of the created cosmos). Then He (the Lord

[1] Qur'ān 17:1.

of Honour) drew closer (to His Beloved Muhammad ﷺ) and then drew even closer. Then a distance measuring only two bow-lengths was left (between Allah Unveiled and His Esteemed Beloved), or even less than that (in extreme nearness). So (on that station of nearness) He (Allah) revealed to His (Beloved) servant whatever He revealed. (His) heart did not take it contrary to what (his) eyes beheld. Do you argue with him about what he saw? And assuredly, he saw Him (Allah Unveiled) the second time (again and you argue only about seeing Him once). At the farthest Lote-Tree? Sidrat al-Muntahā, Adjacent to that is the Eternal Paradise? Janna al-Maʾwā, When theophanies (i.e., effulgent disclosures) of the divine light wrapped up al-Sidra (the Lote-Tree at the Far End), covering it expansively. His eye neither inclined aside nor overstepped the limit; (it gazed in ecstasy at Whom it was to gaze). Surely, he saw the greatest signs of His Lord (during the Ascension Night).[1]

22. Almighty Allah describes him as an exalted character:

﴿وَإِنَّكَ لَعَلَىٰ خُلُقٍ عَظِيمٍ﴾

And assuredly, you are placed high on the Most Glorious and Exalted (seat of) character (i.e., adorned with the Qurʾānic morality and endowed with the character traits of Allah).[2]

23. Almighty Allah swore an oath by the city of the Holy Prophet ﷺ (Mecca) saying:

﴿لَآ أُقْسِمُ بِهَٰذَا ٱلْبَلَدِ ۝١ وَأَنتَ حِلٌّۢ بِهَٰذَا ٱلْبَلَدِ ۝٢ وَوَالِدٍ وَمَا وَلَدَ ۝٣﴾

I swear by this city (Mecca), (O My Esteemed Beloved,) because you are residing in it. (O My Esteemed Beloved!)

---

[1] Qurʾān 53:1-18.

[2] Qurʾān 68:4.

by (your) father (Ādam or Ibrāhīm [Abraham]) and by those who are born.[1]

24. Almighty Allah swore an oath by his glowing face and fragrant tresses, saying:

﴿وَٱلضُّحَىٰ ١ وَٱلَّيۡلِ إِذَا سَجَىٰ ٢ مَا وَدَّعَكَ رَبُّكَ وَمَا قَلَىٰ ٣ وَلَلۡأٓخِرَةُ
خَيۡرٞ لَّكَ مِنَ ٱلۡأُولَىٰ ٤ وَلَسَوۡفَ يُعۡطِيكَ رَبُّكَ فَتَرۡضَىٰٓ ٥ أَلَمۡ يَجِدۡكَ يَتِيمٗا
فَـَٔاوَىٰ ٦ وَوَجَدَكَ ضَآلّٗا فَهَدَىٰ ٧ وَوَجَدَكَ عَآئِلٗا فَأَغۡنَىٰ ٨ فَأَمَّا ٱلۡيَتِيمَ
فَلَا تَقۡهَرۡ ٩ وَأَمَّا ٱلسَّآئِلَ فَلَا تَنۡهَرۡ ١٠ وَأَمَّا بِنِعۡمَةِ رَبِّكَ فَحَدِّثۡ ١١﴾

By the growing morning bright (when the sun gains height and spreads its radiance), Or: (O My Esteemed Beloved,) I swear by (your holy face glowing like) the growing morning bright, (the radiant face, whose effulgence has illumined the dark souls,) Or: By (the growing sunshine of your Messengership rising like) the morning bright (whose radiance has replaced the darkness of ignorance with the enlightenment of guidance,) And by the night when it covers up, Or: (O My Esteemed Beloved,) I swear by (your fragrant tresses spread like) the sprawling murky night (over your effulgent face and shoulders,) Or: By (the veil of your essence that is keeping under layered covers your real nucleus of radiance like) the dark night when it envelops, (Ever since He has chosen you,) your Lord has not forsaken you. Nor is He displeased (ever since He has taken you as His Beloved). Indeed, every following hour is a better (source of eminence and exaltation) for you than the preceding one. And soon your Lord shall bestow upon you (so much) that you will be well-pleased. (O Beloved!) Did He not find you an orphan, and then provided you (a dignifying and graceful) abode? Or: Did He not find you (compassionate) and provided (in

[1] Qurʾān 90:1-3.

> *your person) a shelter for orphans? And He found you engrossed and lost in His love and then made you achieve the coveted objective. Or: And He found in you (a leader) for a straying people so He provided them guidance (through you). And He found you seeking (closeness with your Lord), and (then blessed you with the pleasure of His sight and) freed you of every need (forever). Or: And He found you compassionate and benevolent, then (through you) made the destitute non-liable. So, never should you be strict with any orphan, Nor reproach any beggar (seeking help at your door), And proclaim (well) the bounties of your Lord.*[1]

25. Regarding the innumerable bounties that the Holy Prophet ﷺ has received, Almighty Allah says:

﴿إِنَّآ أَعۡطَيۡنَٰكَ ٱلۡكَوۡثَرَ ۝١ فَصَلِّ لِرَبِّكَ وَٱنۡحَرۡ ۝٢ إِنَّ شَانِئَكَ هُوَ ٱلۡأَبۡتَرُ ۝٣﴾

> *Indeed, We have bestowed on you an infinite abundance (every kind of superiority, bliss and bounty). So pray to your Lord and offer sacrifice (a token of gratitude). Indeed, your enemy will remain childless and his race will be cut off.*[2]

The above-mentioned verses clearly demonstrate how the excellence, superiority, greatness and most exalted rank of the Holy Prophet ﷺ was illuminated by Allah—this is the reason why odes and poems are recited in his honour. Consequently, anyone who denies the permissibility of reciting poetry in praise of the Holy Prophet ﷺ is in reality opposing these verses of the Qur'ān.

8.10 The Prophet ﷺ Himself Listened to Odes in

---

[1] Qur'ān 93:1-11.

[2] Qur'ān 108:1-3.

HIS HONOUR

The Holy Prophet ﷺ himself used to hold the gatherings of poetry which were recited in praise of him: he used to order Ḥassān b. Thābit to recite the poetry which he had composed in his honour. Apart from Ḥassān, many others from the noble Companions were excellent enough to recite poetic praise in front of the Holy Prophet ﷺ. A few examples are mentioned below:

8.10.1 LISTENING TO POETIC PRAISE FROM ḤASSĀN B. THĀBIT ؓ

1. Mother of the believers, Sayyida ʿĀʾisha al-Ṣiddīqa ؓ narrates:

كَانَ رَسُوْلُ اللهِ ﷺ يَضَعُ لِـحَسَّانَ مِنْبَراً فِي الْـمَسْجِدِ يَقُوْمُ عَلَيْهِ قَائِماً يُفَاخِرُ عَنْ رَسُوْلِ اللهِ ﷺ أَوْ قَالَتْ: يُنَافِحُ عَنْ رَسُوْلِ اللهِ ﷺ .

> Allah's Messenger used to install a pulpit for Ḥassān in the mosque, on which he would stand to eulogise and hymn on behalf of Allah's Messenger, defending him against the unbelievers.

The word '*kāna*' in the hadith illustrates that this event occurred on a recurring basis, i.e., it was a habitual practice. The Holy Prophet ﷺ repeatedly called Ḥassān to the mosque and used to bring him a pulpit in order to recite his eulogies in his honour and to refute the disbelievers' allegations. Sayyida ʿĀʾisha also states that whenever Ḥassān recited his poems, the Holy Prophet ﷺ would become very happy and say:

«إِنَّ اللهَ يُؤَيِّدُ حَسَّانَ بِرُوحِ الْقُدُسِ، مَا يُفَاخِرُ أَوْ يُنَافِحُ عَنْ رَسُولِ اللهِ ﷺ».

> Allah's Messenger would say: 'Surely, Allah will support Ḥassān with the Holy Spirit, as long as he glorifies and defends Allah's Messenger.'[1]

---

[1] Narrated by al-Tirmidhī in *al-Jāmiʿ al-Ṣaḥīḥ*: *Kitāb al-Adab* [The Book of Proper Conduct], chapter: 'What has come to us about the recitation

2. Mother of the believers, Sayyida ʿĀʾisha al-Ṣiddīqa also narrates that the Holy Prophet ﷺ said to Ḥassān:

«إِنَّ رُوْحَ الْقُدُسِ لَا يَزَالُ يُؤَيِّدُكَ مَا نَافَحْتَ عَنِ اللهِ وَرَسُوْلِهِ. ... هَجَاهُمْ حَسَّانُ فَشَفَى وَاشْتَفَى.»

The Holy Spirit will not cease to support you, as long as you defend Allah and His Messenger... Ḥassān has ridiculed the unbelievers and this way he consoled (the Muslims) and has restored himself to calmness.

Ḥassān read the following lines of poetry:

هَجَوْتَ مُحَمَّدًا فَأَجَبْتُ عَنْهُ
وَعِنْدَ اللهِ فِي ذَاكَ الْجَزَاءُ
هَجَوْتَ مُحَمَّدًا بَرًّا حَنِيفًا
رَسُولَ اللهِ شِيمَتُهُ الْوَفَاءُ
فَإِنَّ أَبِي وَوَالِدَهُ وَعِرْضِي
لِعِرْضِ مُحَمَّدٍ مِنْكُمْ وِقَاءُ

You ridiculed Muhammad, so I returned it to you on his behalf and with Allah be the recompense for that.
You ridiculed Muhammad, a righteous devotee, Allah's Messenger, whose nature is fidelity.
So let my father and grandfather and my honour (and everything) be a shield to defend the honour of Muhammad (and his Prophetic glory).[1]

---

of poetry', 5:138 §2846; Aḥmad b. Ḥanbal in *al-Musnad*, 6:72 §24,481; al-Ḥākim in *al-Mustadrak*, 3:554 §6058; and Abū Yaʿlā in *al-Musnad*, 8:189 §4746.

[1] Narrated by Muslim in *al-Ṣaḥīḥ*: *Kitāb al-Faḍāʾil al-Ṣaḥāba* [The Book of the Virtuous Merits of the Companions], chapter: 'The virtuous merits of

3. Ḥassān was convinced by the false allegations of the hypocrites when they accused the Mother of the believers, Sayyida ʿĀʾisha al-Ṣiddīqa, of infidelity; Sayyida ʿĀʾisha, however, forgave him as he was one of those who used to recite poetry in the Prophet's honour. She states, 'He has composed and recited (this eulogy in the glory of the Holy Prophet ﷺ):

$$\text{فَإِنَّ أَبِي وَوَالِدَهُ وَعِرْضِي}$$

$$\text{لِعِرْضِ مُحَمَّدٍ مِنْكُمْ وِقَاءُ}$$

So let my father and grandfather and my honour (and everything) be a shield to defend the honour of Muhammad (and his Prophetic glory).'¹

4. Ḥassān b. Thābit asked Abū Hurayra, 'I implore you by Almighty Allah, have you heard the Prophet say:

$$\text{«يَا حَسَّانُ! أَجِبْ عَنْ رَسُولِ اللهِ ﷺ، اَللَّهُمَّ أَيِّدْهُ بِرُوحِ الْقُدُسِ.»}$$

O Ḥassān! Respond on behalf of Allah's Messenger. O Allah, assist him with the Holy Spirit.'

Abū Hurayra ؓ replied, 'Yes, I have heard the Holy Prophet ﷺ say this.'²

Ḥassān b. Thābit', 4:1936 §2490; al-Bayhaqī in *al-Sunan al-kubrā*, 10:238; al-Ṭabarānī in *al-Muʿjam al-kabīr*, 4:38 §3582; and Ḥassān b. Thābit in *Dīwān*, p.20-21.

¹ Narrated by al-Bukhārī in *al-Ṣaḥīḥ*: *Kitāb al-Maghāzī* [The Book of Military Expedition], chapter: 'The incident of the slander', 4:1518 §3910; Muslim in *al-Ṣaḥīḥ*: *Kitāb al-Tawba* [The Book of Repentance], chapter: 'The incident of the slander and the repentance of the slanderers', 4:2137 §2770; Aḥmad b. Ḥanbal in *al-Musnad*, 6:197; al-Nasāʾī in *al-Sunan al-kubrā*, 5:296 §8931; Abū Yaʿlā in *al-Musnad*, 8:341 §4933; and Ḥassān b. Thābit in *Dīwān*, p.21.

² Narrated by al-Bukhārī in *al-Ṣaḥīḥ*: *Kitāb al-Adab* [The Book of Proper Conduct], chapter: 'Ridiculing the polytheists', 5:2279 §5800; al-Bukhārī in *al-Ṣaḥīḥ*: *Kitāb al-Ṣalā* [The Book of the Ritual Prayer], chapter: 'Poetry

5. Al-Barāʾ b. ʿĀzib narrates that the Prophet ﷺ said the following to Ḥassān:

«اهْجُهُمْ أَوْ قَالَ: هَاجِهِمْ وَجِبْرِيلُ مَعَكَ.»

> (O Ḥassān) scorn the polytheists through satiric poetry and Jibrāʾīl is with you (in the venture).[1]

Almighty Allah alone knows how long Ḥassān used to continue to recite poetry in the Prophet's honour whilst in the Prophet's company.

8.10.2 Listening to Poetic Praise from al-Aswad b. Sarīʿ

Al-Aswad b. Sarīʿ narrates that he asked the Holy Prophet ﷺ:

يَا رَسُوْلَ اللهِ! إِنِّي قَدْ مَدَحْتُ اللهَ بِمَدْحَةٍ وَمَدَحْتُكَ بِأُخْرَى.

> O Messenger of Allah, I have eulogised Allah with a hymn and eulogised you with another.

Upon hearing this, the most exalted Prophet ﷺ said:

---

in the mosque', 1:173 §444; Muslim in *al-Ṣaḥīḥ*: *Kitāb al-Faḍāʾil al-Ṣaḥāba* [The Book of the Virtuous Merits of the Companions], chapter: 'The virtuous merits of Ḥassān b. Thābit', 4:1933 §2485; al-Nasāʾī in *al-Sunan al-kubrā*, 6:51 §10,000; Abū Yaʿlā in *al-Musnad*, 10:411 §6017; al-Bayhaqi in *al-Sunan al-kubrā*, 10:237; and al-Ṭabarānī in *al-Muʿjam al-awsaṭ*, 1:208 §668.

[1] Narrated by al-Bukhārī in *al-Ṣaḥīḥ*: *Kitāb al-Adab* [The Book of Proper Conduct], chapter: 'Ridiculing the polytheists', 5:2279 §5801; al-Bukhārī in *al-Ṣaḥīḥ*: *Kitāb al-Badʾ al-Khalq* [The Book of the Beginning of Creation], chapter: 'Mentioning the angels', 3:1176 §3041; al-Bukhārī in *al-Ṣaḥīḥ*: *Kitāb al-Maghāzī* [The Book of Military Expedition], chapter: 'Prophet's return from the Battle of *Aḥzāb* and his setting out to *Banū Qurayẓa*', 4:1512 §3897; Muslim in *al-Ṣaḥīḥ*: *Kitāb Faḍāʾil al-Ṣaḥāba* [The Book of the Virtuous Merits of the Companions], chapter: 'The virtuous merits of Ḥassān b. Thābit', 4:1933 §2486; Aḥmad b. Ḥanbal in *al-Musnad*, 4:302; al-Ṭayālsī in *al-Musnad*, 1:99 §730; al-Bayhaqi in *al-Sunan al-kubrā*, 10:237; and al-Ṭabarānī in *al-Muʿjam al-kabīr*, 4:41 §3588.

«هَاتِ وَابْدَأْ بِمَدْحَةِ اللهِ عَزَّ وَجَلَّ.»

Bring it! (Recite it to me first) begin with the hymn (in the glory) of Allah.[1]

8.10.3 LISTENING TO POETIC PRAISE FROM ᶜABD ALLĀH B. RAWĀḤA

1. Haytham b. Abī Sanān states: 'Abū Hurayra, whilst mentioning the most exalted Prophet ﷺ in his sermon, said: 'Your brother, ᶜAbd Allāh b. Rawāḥa, does not speak in vain.' Saying this, Abū Hurayra recited some of ᶜAbd Allāh b. Rawāḥa's poetry:

وَفِينَا رَسُولُ اللهِ يَتْلُو كِتَابَهُ
إِذَا انْشَقَّ مَعْرُوفٌ مِنَ الْفَجْرِ سَاطِعُ
أَرَانَا الْهُدَى بَعْدَ الْعَمَى فَقُلُوبُنَا
بِهِ مُوقِنَاتٌ أَنَّ مَا قَالَ وَاقِعُ
يَبِيتُ يُجَافِي جَنْبَهُ عَنْ فِرَاشِهِ
إِذَا اسْتَثْقَلَتْ بِالْمُشْرِكِينَ الْمَضَاجِعُ

Among us is the Messenger of Allah, who recites His Book
as the sun appears shining at daybreak.
He brought guidance after our blindness, and so our hearts
are certain that what he says will take place.
He spends the night, his side shunning his bed, while the
idol worshipper's beds hold them in deepest sleep.[2]

---

[1] Reported by Aḥmad b. Ḥanbal in *al-Musnad*, 4:24 §16,300; Ibn Abī Shayba in *al-Muṣannaf*, 6:180; al-Ṭabarānī in *al-Muᶜjam al-kabīr*, 1:287 §842; and al-Bayhaqī in *Shuᶜab al-īmān*, 4:89 §4365.

[2] Narrated by al-Bukhārī in *al-Ṣaḥīḥ*: *Kitāb al-Tahajjud* [The Book of the Night Vigil Prayer], chapter: 'The excellence of someone who wakes up at night and prays', 1:387 §1104; al-Bukhārī in *al-Ṣaḥīḥ*: *Kitāb al-Adab* [The Book of Proper Conduct], chapter: 'Ridiculing the polytheists',

2. Anas ﷺ related that when the most exalted Prophet ﷺ entered Mecca on the occasion of the Visitation, ʿAbd Allāh b. Rawāḥa was walking ahead of the Holy Prophet ﷺ, reciting the following verses in a raised voice:

خَلُّوا بَنِي الْكُفَّارِ عَنْ سَبِيلِهِ

الْيَوْمَ نَضْرِبُكُمْ عَلَى تَنْزِيلِهِ

ضَرْبًا يُزِيلُ الْـهَامَ عَنْ مَقِيلِهِ

وَيُذْهِلُ الْـخَلِيلَ عَنْ خَلِيلِهِ

Turn away from his path, you children of unbelievers,
For today we shall strike you on his welcome arrival,
With a blow that will knock the heads off the necks,
And cause the sincere friend to forget the sincere bosom friend!

Hearing this ʿUmar said:

يَا ابْنَ رَوَاحَةَ! بَيْنَ يَدَيْ رَسُوْلِ اللهِ ﷺ وَفِي حَرَمِ اللهِ تَقُوْلُ الشِّعْرَ؟

O Ibn Rawāḥa, in front of Allah's Messenger and in Allah's Sanctuary, are you reciting poetry?

The most exalted Prophet ﷺ said in reply to ʿUmar's question:

«خَلِّ عَنْهُ يَا عُمَرُ، فَلَهِيَ أَسْرَعُ فِيهِمْ مِنْ نَضْحِ النَّبْلِ.»

Leave him alone, O ʿUmar, for it strikes them more rapidly than the flight of arrows.[1]

5:2278 §5799; al-Bukhārī in *al-Tārīkh al-kabīr* in 8:212 §2754; al-Bukhārī in *al-Tārīkh al-ṣaghīr*, p.23 §71; Aḥmad b. Ḥanbal in *al-Musnad*, 3:451; al-Bayhaqī in *al-Sunan al-kubrā*, 10:239; and Ibn Kathīr in *al-Bidāya wa al-nihāya*, 3:465.

[1] Narrated by al-Tirmidhī in *al-Jāmiʿ al-Ṣaḥīḥ*: *Kitāb al-Adab* [The Book of

8.10.4 LISTENING TO POETIC PRAISE FROM ʿĀMIR B. AKWAʿ IN AN OPEN GATHERING

Salma b. Akwaʿ narrates: One night we were travelling to Khaybar with Almighty Allah's Messenger ﷺ. Someone from within the travelling party said to my brother, ʿĀmir b. Akwaʿ, 'Recite some of your poetry for us.' He got off his camel and recited the following verses:

اَللّٰهُمَّ! لَوْ لَا أَنْتَ مَا اهْتَدَيْنَا

وَلَا تَصَدَّقْنَا وَلَا صَلَّيْنَا

فَاغْفِرْ فِدَاءً لَكَ مَا أَبْقَيْنَا

وَثَبِّتِ الْأَقْدَامَ إِنْ لَاقَيْنَا

O Allah, were it not for You, we would not have been
guided nor given charity nor prayed!
We are ransom to You so forgive us so long as we are pious,
and make our feet firm when we meet the enemy.

Hearing this, the most exalted Prophet ﷺ said:

«مَنْ هَذَا السَّائِقُ؟»

Who is this driver (reciting for me)?

The Companions replied, 'O Messenger ﷺ of Allah! This is ʿĀmir b. Akwaʿ. The Prophet ﷺ was delighted and made a prayer for him, saying:

Proper Conduct], chapter: 'What has come to us about the recitation of poetry', 5:139 §2847 has declared this hadith as *ḥasan ṣaḥīḥ*; al-Nasāʾī in *al-Sunan*: *Kitāb Manāsik al-Ḥajj* [The Book of Pilgrimage Rites], chapter: 'Reciting poetry in the *ḥaram*', 5:202 §2873; and al-Qurṭubī in *al-Jāmiʿ li-aḥkām al-Qurʾān*, 13:151.

«يَرْحَمُهُ اللهُ.»

> May Allah shower His mercy upon him.[1]

It was the blessed Sunna of the Holy Prophet ﷺ to pray for the ones who recited poetry in his honour and enrich them with his spiritual attention and abundance.

8.10.5 Listening to Poetic Praise from ʿAbbās b. ʿAbd al-Muṭṭalib

Kharīm b. Aws narrates that when the most honoured Prophet ﷺ returned from the battle of Tabūk, he accepted Islam at the hands of the most honoured Prophet ﷺ. At that time, he heard ʿAbbās b. ʿAbd al-Muṭṭalib say: 'O Messenger of Allah! I want to praise you.' Upon hearing this request, the Prophet ﷺ said:

«قُلْ، لَا يَفْضُضِ اللهُ فَاكَ.»

> Proceed. May Allah never destroy the seal of your mouth (i.e., his teeth).

Then ʿAbbās recited the following poetry in the Holy Prophet's honour:

مِنْ قَبْلِهَا طِبْتَ فِي الظِّلَالِ وَفِي
مُسْتَوْدَعٍ حَيْثُ يَخْصَفُ الْوَرَقُ

---

[1] Narrated by al-Bukhārī in *al-Ṣaḥīḥ*: *Kitāb al-Maghāzi* [The Book of Military Expedition], chapter: 'The expedition of Khaybar', 4:1537 §3960; al-Bukhārī in *al-Ṣaḥīḥ*: *Kitāb al-Adab* [The Book of Proper Conduct], chapter: 'What is permitted of poetry', 5:2277 §5796; Muslim in *al-Ṣaḥīḥ*: *Kitāb al-Jihād* [The Book of Martial *Jihād*], chapter: 'The expedition of Khaybar', 3:1428 §1802; Abū ʿAwāna in *al-Musnad*, 4:314 §6830; al-Bayhaqī in *al-Sunan al-kubrā*, 10:227; and al-Ṭabarānī in *al-Muʿjam al-kabīr*, 7:32 §6294.

Before you came to this world, you were excellent
in the shadows and in the repository (in the time of Ādam)
when they covered themselves with leaves.

ثُمَّ هَبَطْتَ الْبِلَادَ لَا بَشَرٌ

أَنْتَ وَلَا مُضْغَةٌ وَلَا عَلَقٌ

Then you fell through the ages, not as a mortal,
nor a lump of flesh, nor as a hanging mass.

بَلْ نُطْفَةٌ تَرْكَبُ السَّفِيْنَ وَقَدْ

أَلْـجَمَ نَسْرًا وَأَهْلَهُ الْغَرَقُ

But as a drop which rode the ark and put the bridle on the idol Nasr whilst its people (the Community of Nūḥ) were drowned.

تُنْقَلُ مِنْ صَالِبٍ إِلَى رَحِمٍ

إِذَا مَضَى عَالَمٌ بَدَا طَبَقٌ

The drop was transferred from pious loin to pious womb.
As the world proceeded, the next era appeared.

حَتَّى احْتَوَى بَيْتُكَ الْـمُهَيْمِنُ

خِنْدِفَ عَلْيَاءَ تَحْتَهَا النُّطُقُ

Then your guardian house contained loftiness from Khindif
underneath which were mountain ranges.

وَأَنْتَ لَـمَّا وُلِدْتَ أَشْرَقَتِ

الْأَرْضُ وَضَاءَتْ بِنُوْرِكَ الْأُفُقُ

When you were born, the earth shone
And the horizon was illuminated by your light.

فَنَحْنُ فِي ذَلِكَ الضِّيَاءِ وَفِي

النُّوْرِ وَسُبُلِ الرَّشَادِ نَخْتَرِقُ

We travel in that illumination
And in the light and the paths of right guidance.[1]

8.10.6 Listening to Poetic Praise from Kaʿb and the Gifting of the Cloak

Muhammad b. Isḥāq narrates: Kaʿb b. Zuhayr b. Abī Salmā arrived in Medina as a fugitive and stayed with a person he knew from the tribe of Juhayna. At the time of the *fajr* prayer, they took him to the Holy Prophet ﷺ. After offering the ritual prayer with the noble Companions, someone informed him that the Holy Prophet ﷺ was sitting over there (in the mosque). So Kaʿb went and sat in front of the Messenger of Allah and put his hands into the blessed hands of the Holy Prophet ﷺ and said, 'O Messenger of Allah, indeed Kaʿb b. Zuhayr has come to you seeking repentance;, if I call him before you, will you forgive him?' The Holy Prophet ﷺ said, 'Yes.' Hearing this, he told the Holy Prophet ﷺ that he was in fact Kaʿb b. Zuhayr. Suddenly, a man from the Anṣār rose up and said, 'O Messenger of Allah, give me permission to cut off the head of this enemy?' The Holy Prophet ﷺ replied, 'Leave him be, no doubt he is seeking forgiveness for his (past) state and has escaped to be here.' Then, he (Kaʿb) recited the poem of *Bānat Suʿād*:

[1] Narrated by al-Ḥākim in *al-Mustadrak*, 3:369-370 §5417; al-Ṭabarānī in *al-Muʿjam al-kabīr*, 4:213 §4167; Ibn al-Jawzī in *Ṣafwa al-ṣafwa*, 1:54; Ibn Athīr in *Asad al-ghāba fī maʿrifa al-Ṣaḥāba*, 2:165-166; al-Haythamī in *Majmaʿ al-zawāʾid wa manbaʿ al-fawāʾid*, 8:218; Aḥmad b. Zaynī al-Daḥlān in *al-Sīra al-Nabawiyya*, 1:46; and al-Nabhānī in *al-Anwār al-Muḥammadiyya min al-mawāhib al-ladunya*, p.25.

بَانَتْ سُعَادُ فَقَلْبِي الْيَوْمَ مَتْبُوْلُ

مُتَيَّمٌ إِثْرَهَا لَـمْ يُفْدَ مَكْبُوْلُ

Suʿād is gone, and today my heart is love-lorn
Enthralled, put in chain, no blood wit coming to unrein.

In this poem, he also recited:

أُنْبِئْتُ أَنَّ رَسُوْلَ اللهِ أَوْعَدَنِي

وَالْعَفْوُ عِنْدَ رَسُوْلِ اللهِ مَأْمُوْلُ

I have been informed a bounty has been placed on me
Clemency from the Messenger of Allah is expected

Then he continued, saying:

إِنَّ الرَّسُوْلَ لَنُوْرٌ يُسْتَضَاءُ بِهِ

وَصَارِمٌ مِنْ سُيُوْفِ اللهِ مَسْلُوْلُ

The Messenger is a light that illuminates
An Indian blade, a sword of Allah, drawn[1]

Ibn Qāniʿ al-Baghdādī (D. 351 AH) narrates that when Kaʿb recited this poem, the most gracious Prophet ﷺ gifted him his cloak:

فَكَسَاهُ النَّبِيُّ ﷺ بُرْدَةً لَهُ، فَاشْتَرَاهَا مُعَاوِيَةُ مِنْ وَلَدِهِ بِمَالٍ، فَهِيَ الْبُرْدَةُ الَّتِي تَلْبَسُهَا الْـخُلَفَاءُ فِي الأَعْيَادِ.

---

[1] Narrated by al-Ḥākim in *al-Mustadrak*, 3:670-673 §6477; al-Ṭabarānī in *al-Muʿjam al-kabīr*, 19:157-159 §403; al-Bayhaqi in *al-Sunan al-kubrā*, 10:243; Ibn Isḥāq in *al-Sīra al-Nabawiyya*, p.591-594; Ibn Hishām in *al-Sīra al-Nabawiyya*, p.1011-1020; al-Haythamī in *Majmaʿ al-zawāʾid wa manbaʿ al-fawāʾid*, 9:393; and Ibn Kathīr in *al-Bidāya wa al-nihāya*, 3:582-588.

> The most honoured Prophet covered him with a cloak of his. Later, Muʿāwiya purchased it from his son for an amount of money. This is the cloak the caliph dons on the days of *ʿīd*.[1]

It is established from this hadith that to listen to a poet and to offer him a gift is a Sunna of the Prophet ﷺ.

8.10.7 Listening to Poetic Praise from Nābigha al-Jaʿdī

It is related from Nābigha al-Jaʿdī that he entered the presence of the most exalted Prophet ﷺ and recited a lengthy poem to him (consisting of 200 verses). Some of its verses are mentioned below:

وَلَا خَيْرَ فِي حِلْمٍ إِذَا لَـمْ يَكُنْ لَهُ

بَوَادِرُ تَحْمِي صَفْوَهُ أَنْ يُكَدَّرَا

وَلَا خَيْرَ فِي جَهْلٍ إِذَا لَـمْ يَكُنْ لَهُ

حَلِيْمٌ إِذَا مَا أَوْرَدَ الْأَمْرَ أَصْدَرَا

There is no benefit of this clemency, if it is not accompanied by the heat of anger, which keeps the purity from becoming muddy.
And in this ignorance there is no good if there is no one who is clement, who is willing to stop any (evil) occurrence.

The most exalted Prophet ﷺ prayed for him, saying:

«لَا يَفْضُضِ اللهُ فَاكَ.»

[1] Narrated by Ibn Qāniʿ in *Muʿjam al-Ṣaḥāba*, 12:4466, §1657; and Ibn al-Jawzī in *al-Wafāʾ bi aḥwāl al-Muṣṭafā*, p.463 §813.

May Allah never destroy the seal of your mouth (i.e., his teeth).

The narrator reports:

وَكَانَ مِنْ أَحْسَنِ النَّاسِ ثَغْراً، وَكَانَ إِذَا سَقَطَتْ لَهُ سِنٌّ نَبَتَتْ.

He had the best set of teeth amongst us. Every time a tooth fell out, another would grow in its place.[1]

In the above narration, Nābigha al-Jaʿdī praised the Holy Prophet ﷺ by employing a metaphor. In the first verse, he describes that the Prophet's 'forbearance and majesty' is the paragon of compassion and mercy. Whereas in the second verse, he speaks of 'the clement one remaining with the ignorant'; in other words, he humbly describes himself as being ignorant and fortunate enough to be in the company of the most compassionate Prophet ﷺ, as the most merciful Prophet ﷺ is the one who will protect him from the afflictions and calamities of life. In this way, he has metaphorically praised the most clement Prophet ﷺ; and in turn, the most benevolent Prophet ﷺ was pleased with his attempt and prayed for him.

8.10.8 The Girls of Medina Recited Poetic Praise with Hand Drums (*Daff*)

When the most gracious Prophet ﷺ emigrated from Mecca to Medina, the girls of Medina, from amongst the *Anṣār*, welcomed the most glorious Prophet ﷺ upon his blessed arrival with hand drums, singing the celebrated lines of poetry related below:

طَلَعَ الْبَدْرُ عَلَيْنَا   مِنْ ثَنِيَّاتِ الْوَدَاعِ

[1] Narrated by Ḥārith in *al-Musnad*, 2:844 §894; al-Haythamī in *Majmaʿ al-zawāʾid wa manbaʿ al-fawāʾid*, 8:126; Ibn Ḥayyān in *Ṭabaqāt al-muḥaddithīn bi Aṣbahān*, 1:274 §11; Ibn ʿAbd al-Barr in *al-Istīʿāb fī maʿrifa al-aṣḥāb*, 4:1516 §2648; Ibn al-Jawzī in *al-Wafāʾ bi aḥwāl al-Muṣṭafā*, p.462-463 §812; Ibn Athīr in *Asad al-ghāba fī maʿrifa al-Ṣaḥāba*, 5:276-278; and al-ʿAsqalānī in *al-Iṣāba fī tamyīz al-Ṣaḥāba*, 6:394 §8645.

وَجَبَ الشُّكْرُ عَلَيْنَا مَا دَعَا لِلّٰهِ دَاعٍ
أَيُّهَا الْـمَبْعُوثُ فِينَا جِئْتَ بِالْأَمْرِ الْمُطَاعِ

O the full white moon rose over us
From the valley of al-Wadāʿ
And we owe it to show gratefulness
Where the call is to Allah
O (beloved) you were raised among us
Came with a command to be obeyed[1]

8.10.9 Imam al-Būṣīrī's Recovery and His Receiving the Prophet's Cloak as a Gift

Imam Sharaf al-Dīn al-Būṣīrī (608-696 AH), the author of *Qaṣīda al-Burda*, is in need of no introduction. In his time, he was a renowned and a very learned scholar, poet, and world renown writer. He was given a great intellect by Almighty Allah, earning him the estimation of the rulers and sultans of his day. One day while walking in the street, he met a righteous man who asked him, 'Būṣīrī, have you ever seen the most exalted Prophet ﷺ in your dream?' Imam Būṣīrī replied in the negative. This meeting struck a chord in the heart of Imam Būṣīrī, and his love and passion for the beloved Prophet ﷺ increased manifold to the point that he was constantly absorbed in his love; during this time, he would recite odes and poems in praise of the beloved Prophet ﷺ.

One day the Imam suffered from a stroke, which left half of

[1] Narrated by Ibn Abī Ḥātim al-Rāzī in *al-Thiqāt*, 1:131; Ibn ʿAbd al-Barr in *al-Tamhīd limā fī al-muwaṭṭā min al-maʿānī wa al-asānīd*, 14:82; Abū ʿUbayd al-Andalusī in *Muʿjam mā istaʿjama min asmāʾ al-bilād wa al-mawāḍ iʿ*, 4:1373; Muḥibb al-Ṭabarī in *al-Riyāḍ al-naḍra fī manāqib al-ʿashra*, 1:480; al-Bayhaqī in *Dalāʾil al-Nubuwwa wa maʿrifa aḥwāl Ṣāḥib al-Sharīʿa* ﷺ, 2:507; Ibn Kathīr in *al-Bidāya wa al-nihāya*, 2:583; Ibid., 3:260; al-ʿAsqalānī in *Fatḥ al-Bārī*, 7:261; Ibid., 8:129; al-Qasṭallānī in *al-Mawāhib al-ladunya bi al-minaḥ al-Muḥammadiyya*, 1:634; al-Zurqānī in *Sharḥ al-mawāhib al-ladunya bi al-minaḥ al-Muḥammadiyya*, 4:100-101; and Aḥmad b. Zaynī al-Daḥlān in *al-Sīra al-Nabawiyya*, 1:323.

his body paralysed. He remained in this state for a long time: all methods of medical treatment proved fruitless. Whilst in this state of ill-health, a thought crossed his mind:, 'Before this illness, I used to write poetry in honour of worldly kings and rulers, so why do I not write a poem in honour of the chief of the created beings, the Holy Prophet ﷺ, and hope for a cure for this untreatable illness?' As a result, he penned a poem. That night when he went to sleep, his fate changed for the better: he was bestowed the dignity of seeing the Holy Prophet ﷺ in his dream. He had the good fortune to recite the poem in its entirety to the most exalted Prophet ﷺ. After listening to it, the Holy Prophet ﷺ was so delighted that he placed his cloak on Imam al-Būṣīrī and passed his healing hand over his paralysed body, and miraculously, his illness and all signs of his ailment disappeared. The next morning when he woke, he left his house and the first person he met was an eminent shaykh by the name of Abū al-Rajāʾ. The shaykh stopped the imam and asked him to recite the poem he had composed in the Prophet's honour. The imam asked, 'Which poem are you referring to?' The shaykh replied, 'The one that commences with the verse:

أَمِنْ تَذَكُّرِ جِيْرَانٍ بِذِي سَلَمِ

مَزَجْتَ دَمْعًا جَرَى مِنْ مُّقْلَةٍ بِدَمِ

Is it from remembering the neighbours of Dhū Salam
That you mingle with blood tears shed from your eyes?'

Astonished with what he heard, the imam exclaimed, 'I have not discussed this poem with anyone, how is that you know about it?' The shaykh replied, 'I swear by Almighty Allah that when you recited this to the Messenger ﷺ of Almighty Allah, I was there listening to it.' It was not long before the eternal fame of this incident spread far and wide, and even till today, this poem is recited by people of all languages and culture, and it is a continuous source of blessings for all.

This ode became renowned with the appellation '*Qaṣīda Burda*' due to the Prophet's granting Imam al-Būṣīrī his own cloak and passing his healing hand over his body curing his illness. It was on account of this connection that this poem was named as such.[1]

8.11 A List of the Noble Companions who Recited Poetry in Honour of the Prophet ﷺ

Many of the greatest Companions were blessed with the honour of reciting poetry in praise of the most glorified Prophet ﷺ. The Imam of the Successors, Muhammad b. Sīrīn (D.110 AH), mentions some of them below:

كَانَ شُعَرَاءُ النَّبِيِّ ﷺ: حَسَّانَ بْنَ ثَابِتٍ، وَكَعْبَ بْنَ مَالِكٍ، وَعَبْدَ اللهِ بْنَ رَوَاحَةَ، فَكَانَ كَعْبُ بْنُ مَالِكٍ يُخَوِّفُهُمُ الْحَرْبَ، وَكَانَ حَسَّانُ يُقْبِلُ عَلَى الْأَنْسَابِ، وَكَانَ عَبْدُ اللهِ بْنُ رَوَاحَةَ يُعَيِّرُهُمْ بِالْكُفْرِ.

The poets of the Prophet ﷺ were: Ḥassān b. Thābit, Kaʿb b. Mālik and ʿAbd Allāh b. Rawāḥa. Kaʿb b. Mālik used to frighten the Prophet's enemies by the mention of war; Ḥassān used to question the disbelievers' lineage; and ʿAbd Allāh b. Rawāḥa used to make them feel embarrassed about their disbelief (by taunting them).[2]

Ibn al-Jawzī (510-597 AH) also mentions a few of them:

وَقَدْ أَنْشَدَهُ جَمَاعَةٌ، مِنْهُمُ الْعَبَّاسُ وَعَبْدُ اللهِ بْنُ رَوَاحَةَ، وَحَسَّانٌ، وَضِمَارٌ، وَأَسَدُ بْنُ زَنِيمٍ، وَعَائِشَةُ، فِي خَلْقٍ كَثِيرٍ قَدْ ذَكَرْتُهُمْ فِي كِتَابِ الْأَشْعَارِ.

There was a large number of people who would recite poetry in praise of him. Amongst them were: ʿAbbās, ʿAbd Allāh b. Rawāḥa, Ḥassān, Ḍimār, Asad b. Zanīm, and Sayyida ʿĀʾisha, and many more who I have mentioned in

---

[1] Kharpūtī, *ʿAṣīda al-shuhda sharḥ qasīda al-burda*, p.3-5.

[2] Ibn Athīr, *Asad al-ghāba fī maʿrifa al-Ṣaḥāba*, 4:461.

the books of poetry.[1]

Listed below are the names of those noble Companions who recited poetry in the Prophet's honour:

1. The Prophet's uncle, ʿAbbās (D. 32 AH)[2]
2. The Prophet's uncle, Hamza (D. 3 AH)[3]
3. The Prophet's uncle, Abū Ṭālib (D. 10 *Nabwī*)[4]
4. Abū Bakr al-Ṣiddīq (D. 13 AH)[5]
5. ʿUmar al-Fārūq (D. 23 AH)[6]
6. ʿUthmān al-Ghanī (D. 35 AH)[7]
7. ʿAlī b. Abī Ṭālib (D. 40 AH)[8]
8. Mother of the believers, ʿĀʾisha al-Ṣiddīqa (D. 58 AH)[9]
9. Sayyida Fāṭima al-Zahrāʾ (D. 11 AH)[10]

---

[1] Ibn al-Jawzī, *al-Wafāʾ bi aḥwāl al-Muṣṭafā*, p.463.

[2] Al-Ḥākim, *al-Mustadrak*, 3:369-370 §5417; al-Ṭabarānī, *al-Muʿjam al-kabīr*, 4:213 §4167; Ibn al-Jawzī, *al-Wafāʾ bi aḥwāl al-Muṣṭafā*, p.463; Ibn al-Jawzī, *Ṣafwa al-ṣafwa*, 1:54; Ibn Athīr, *Asad al-ghāba fī maʿrifa al-Ṣaḥāba*, 2:165-166; al-Haythamī, *Majmaʿ al-zawāʾid wa manbaʿ al-fawāʾid*, 8:218; Aḥmad b. Zaynī al-Daḥlān, *al-Sīra al-Nabawiyya*, 1:46; and al-Nabhānī, *al-Anwār al-Muḥammadiyya min al-mawāhib al-ladunya*, p.25.

[3] Ibn Isḥāq, *al-Sīra al-Nabawiyya*, p.212-213; and Ibn Hishām, *al-Sīra al-Nabawiyya*, p.503-504.

[4] Al-Bukhārī, *al-Ṣaḥīḥ*: *Kitāb al-Istisqāʾ* [The Book of the Prayer for Rain], chapter: 'The people's asking the Imam to pray for rain when they are afflicted with drought', 1:342 §963; Ibn Mājah, *al-Sunan*: *Kitāb iqāma al-ṣalāh wa al-sunna fīhā* [The Book of Establishing the Prayer and the Sunna therein], chapter: 'What has been related concerning the supplication for rain', 1:405 §1272; Aḥmad b. Ḥanbal, *al-Musnad*, 2:93; al-Bayhaqī, *al-Sunan al-kubrā*, 3:352; Ibn Hishām, *al-Sīra al-Nabawiyya*, p.246-253; al-Bayhaqī, *Dalāʾil al-Nubuwwa wa maʿrifa aḥwāl Ṣāḥib al-Sharīʿa* ﷺ, 6:142-143; and Ibn Kathīr, *al-Bidāya wa al-nihāya*, 4:471-472.

[5] Abū Zayd al-Qurashī, *Jamhara ashʿār al-ʿArab*, p.10.

[6] Ibid.

[7] Ibid.

[8] Ibid.

[9] Ibn al-Jawzī, *al-Wafāʾ bi aḥwāl al-Muṣṭafā*, p.463.

[10] Al-Bukhārī, *al-Ṣaḥīḥ*: *Kitāb al-Maghāzi* [The Book of Military Expedition], chapter: 'The Prophet's illness and his passing away', 4:1619

10. Sayyida Ṣafya b. ʿAbd al-Muṭṭalib (D. 20 AH)[1]
11. Sayyida Shīmā b. Ḥalīma Saʿdiyya[2]
12. Abū Sufyān b. al-Ḥārith (the Prophet's cousin)[3]
13. ʿAbd Allāh b. Rawāḥa (D. 8 AH)[4]
14. Kaʿb b. Mālik al-Anṣārī (D. 51 AH)[5]
15. Ḥassān b. Thābit (D. 40 AH)[6]

---

§4193; Ibn Mājah, *al-Sunan*: *Kitāb al-Janāʾiz* [The Book of the Funeral Ceremonies], chapter: 'Mention of the Prophet's passing away and burial', 2:103 §1630; al-Nasāʾī, *al-Sunan*: *Kitāb al-Janāʾiz* [The Book of the Funeral Ceremonies], chapter: 'Weeping over the deceased', 4:12 §1844; Aḥmad b. Ḥanbal, *al-Musnad*, 3:197 §13,054; al-Dārimī, *al-Sunan*, p.56 §88; Ibn Ḥibbān, *al-Ṣaḥīḥ*, 14:591-592 §6622; al-Ḥākim, *al-Mustadrak*, 1:537 §1408; Ibid. 3:61 §4396; al-Ṭabarānī, *al-Muʿjam al-kabīr*, 22:416 §1029; Ibn Saʿd, *al-Ṭabaqāt al-kubrā*, 2:311; al-Dhahabī, *Tārīkh al-Islām wa wafayāt al-mashāhīr wa al-aʿlām* (*al-Sīra al-Nabawiyya*), 1:562; and Ibn Kathīr, *al-Bidāya wa al-nihāya*, 4:254.

[1] Ḥāfiẓ Shams al-Dīn b. Nāṣir al-Dīn al-Dimashqī, *Mawrid al-ṣādī fī mawlid al-Hādī*.

[2] Al-ʿAsqalānī, *al-Iṣāba fī tamyīz al-Ṣaḥāba*, 7:165-166 §11,378.

[3] Ibn ʿAbd al-Barr, *al-Istīʿāb fī maʿrifa al-aṣḥāb*, 4:1675; and Ibn Athīr, *Asad al-ghāba fī maʿrifa al-Ṣaḥāba*, 6:142-143.

[4] Al-Bukhārī, *al-Ṣaḥīḥ*: *Kitāb al-Tahajjud* [The Book of the Night Vigil Prayer], chapter: 'The excellence of someone who wakes up at night and prays', 1:387 §1104; al-Bukhārī, *al-Ṣaḥīḥ*: *Kitāb al-Adab* [The Book of Proper Conduct], chapter: 'Ridiculing the polytheists', 5:2278 §5799; al-Tirmidhī, *al-Jāmiʿ al-Ṣaḥīḥ*: *Kitāb al-Adab* [The Book of Proper Conduct], chapter: 'What has come to us about the recitation of poetry', 5:139 §2847; al-Nasāʾī in *al-Sunan*: *Kitāb Manāsik al-Ḥajj* [The Book of Pilgrimage Rites], chapter: 'Reciting poetry in the *ḥaram*', 5:202 §2873; al-Bukhārī, *al-Tārīkh al-kabīr*, 8:212 §2754; al-Bukhārī, *al-Tārīkh al-ṣaghīr*, p.23 §71; Aḥmad b. Ḥanbal, *al-Musnad*, 3:451; al-Bayhaqī, *al-Sunan al-kubrā*, 10:239; Ibn al-Jawzī, *al-Wafāʾ bi aḥwāl al-Muṣṭafā*, p.463; Ibn Kathīr, *al-Bidāya wa al-nihāya*, 3:465; and al-Qurṭubī, *al-Jāmiʿ li-aḥkām al-Qurʾān*, 13:151.

[5] Ibn Abī ʿĀṣim, *al-Āḥād wa al-mathānī*, p.663 §1171.

[6] Al-Bukhārī, *al-Ṣaḥīḥ*: *Kitāb al-Ṣalā* [The Book of the Ritual Prayer], chapter: 'Poetry in the mosque', 1:173 §442; al-Bukhārī, *al-Ṣaḥīḥ*: *Kitāb al-Badʾ al-Khalq* [The Book of the Beginning of Creation], chapter: 'Mentioning the angels', 3:1176 §3041; al-Bukhārī, *al-Ṣaḥīḥ*: *Kitāb al-Manāqib* [The Book of Virtuous Merits], chapter: 'Whoever wants their lineage not to be insulted', 3:1299 §3338; al-Bukhārī, *al-Ṣaḥīḥ*: *Kitāb al-*

16. Zuhayr b. Ṣurd al-Jathmī[1]
17. ᶜAbbās b. Mirdās al-Sulamī[2]
18. Kaᶜb b. Zuhayr (composer of *Qasīda Bānat Suᶜād*)[3]
19. ᶜAbd Allāh b. al-Zabaᶜrā[4]
20. Abū ᶜIzza al-Khuḥamjī[5]
21. Sayyida Qatīla b. al-Ḥārith al-Qurashiyya[6]
22. Mālik b. Namaṭ al-Hamdānī[7]

Maghāzi [The Book of Military Expedition], chapter: 'Prophet's return from the Battle of *Aḥzāb* and his setting out to *Banī Qurayẓa*', 4:1512 §3897; al-Bukhārī, *al-Ṣaḥīḥ: Kitāb al-Maghāzi* [The Book of Military Expedition], chapter: 'The incident of the slander', 4:1518 §3910; al-Bukhārī, *al-Ṣaḥīḥ: Kitāb al-Adab* [The Book of Proper Conduct], chapter: 'Ridiculing the polytheists', 5:2279 §5800-5801; Muslim, *al-Ṣaḥīḥ: Kitāb al-Faḍā'il al-Ṣaḥāba* [The Book of the Virtuous Merits of the Companions], chapter: 'The virtuous merits of Ḥassān b. Thābit', 4:1933 §2485-2486; Muslim, *al-Ṣaḥīḥ: Kitāb al-Faḍā'il al-Ṣaḥāba* [The Book of the Virtuous Merits of the Companions], chapter: 'The virtuous merits of Ḥassān b. Thābit', 4:1936 §2490; Muslim, *al-Ṣaḥīḥ: Kitāb al-Tawba* [The Book of Repentance], chapter: 'The incident of the slander and the repentance of the slanderers', 4:2137 §2770; and al-Tirmidhī, *al-Jāmiᶜ al-Ṣaḥīḥ: Kitāb al-Adab* [The Book of Proper Conduct], chapter: 'What has come to us about the recitation of poetry', 5:138 §2846.

1 Ibn ᶜAbd al-Barr, *al-Istīᶜāb fī maᶜrifa al-aṣḥāb*, 2:97-98 §723; and Ibn Athīr, *Asad al-ghāba fī maᶜrifa al-Ṣaḥāba*, 2:325 §1769.

2 Ibn Hishām, *al-Sīra al-Nabawiyya*, p.949 & 977; Ibn ᶜAbd al-Barr, *al-Istīᶜāb fī maᶜrifa al-aṣḥāb*, 2:362-364 §1387; and Ibn Kathīr, *al-Bidāya wa al-nihāya*, 3:547-553.

3 Al-Ḥākim, *al-Mustadrak*, 3:670-673 §6477; al-Ṭabarānī, *al-Muᶜjam al-kabīr*, 19:157-159 §403; al-Bayhaqi, *al-Sunan al-kubrā*, 10:243; Ibn Isḥāq, *al-Sīra al-Nabawiyya*, p.591-594; Ibn Hishām, *al-Sīra al-Nabawiyya*, p.1011-1020; al-Haythamī, *Majmaᶜ al-zawā'id wa manbaᶜ al-fawā'id*, 9:393; Ibn al-Jawzī, *al-Wafā' bi aḥwāl al-Muṣṭafā*, p.463 §813; and Ibn Kathīr, *al-Bidāya wa al-nihāya*, 3:582-588.

4 Ibn Isḥāq, *al-Sīra al-Nabawiyya*, p.536; and Ibn Hishām, *al-Sīra al-Nabawiyya*, p.942-943; and Ibn Athīr, *Asad al-ghāba fī maᶜrifa al-Ṣaḥāba*, 3:239-240 §2946.

5 Ibn Hishām, *al-Sīra al-Nabawiyya*, p.555.

6 Ibid. p.635-636.

7 Ibn Hishām, *al-Sīra al-Nabawiyya*, p.1089; and Ibn Athīr, *Asad al-ghāba fī*

23. Anas b. Zanīm (Unās b. Zanīm)[1]
24. Aṣyad b. Salma al-Sulamī[2]
25. Leader of the *Hawāzin*, Mālik b. ʿAwf al-Naṣrī[3]
26. Qays b. Baḥr al-Ashjaʿī[4]
27. ʿAmr b. Subayʿ al-Rahāwī[5]
28. Nābigha al-Jaʿdī (D. 70 AH)[6]
29. Māzin b. al-Ghaḍūba al-Ṭāʾī[7]
30. Al-Aʿshī al-Māzinī[8]
31. Faḍāla al-Laythī[9]
32. ʿAmr b. Sālim al-Khuzaʿī[10]
33. Asyad b. Abī Unās al-Kinānī[11]
34. ʿAmr b. Murra al-Jahnī[12]

---

maʿrifa al-Ṣaḥāba, 5:46-47 §4651.

[1] Ibn Isḥāq, *al-Sīra al-Nabawiyya*, p.539-540; Ibn Hishām, *al-Sīra al-Nabawiyya*, p.947; and Ibn al-Jawzī, *al-Wafāʾ bi aḥwāl al-Muṣṭafā*, p.463.

[2] Ibn Athīr, *Asad al-ghāba fī maʿrifa al-Ṣaḥāba*, 1:253-254 §191; and al-ʿAsqalānī, *al-Iṣāba fī tamyīz al-Ṣaḥāba*, 1:85-86 §211.

[3] Ibn Hishām, *al-Sīra al-Nabawiyya*, p.1002-1003.

[4] Ibn Hishām, *al-Sīra al-Nabawiyya*, p.760-761; and Ibn Athīr, *Asad al-ghāba fī maʿrifa al-Ṣaḥāba*, 4:394 §4327.

[5] Ibn Athīr, *Asad al-ghāba fī maʿrifa al-Ṣaḥāba*, 4:214-215 §3932.

[6] Ibn ʿAbd al-Barr, *al-Istīʿāb fī maʿrifa al-aṣḥāb*, 4:1516 §2648; Ibn al-Jawzī, *al-Wafāʾ bi aḥwāl al-Muṣṭafā*, p.462-463 §812; and Ibn Athīr, *Asad al-ghāba fī maʿrifa al-Ṣaḥāba*, 5:276-278 §5162.

[7] Ibn ʿAbd al-Barr, *al-Istīʿāb fī maʿrifa al-aṣḥāb*, 3:1344; Ibn Athīr, *Asad al-ghāba fī maʿrifa al-Ṣaḥāba*, 5:4 §4553; and al-ʿAsqalānī, *al-Iṣāba fī tamyīz al-Ṣaḥāba*, 5:21-22 §7584.

[8] Ibn Saʿd, *al-Ṭabaqāt al-kubrā*, 7:53; Ibn ʿAbd al-Barr, *al-Istīʿāb fī maʿrifa al-aṣḥāb*, 1:229 §159; and Ibn Athīr, *Asad al-ghāba fī maʿrifa al-Ṣaḥāba*, 1:256-257 §196.

[9] Al-Fākahī, *Akhbār Makka fī qadīm al-dahr wa ḥadīthihī*, 2:222–223; Ibn Athīr, *Asad al-ghāba fī maʿrifa al-Ṣaḥāba*, 4:347 §4233; and al-ʿAsqalānī, *al-Iṣāba fī tamyīz al-Ṣaḥāba*, 4:346 §6999.

[10] Al-Bayhaqi, *al-Sunan al-kubrā*, 9:233; Ibn Hishām, *al-Sīra al-Nabawiyya*, p.923; and Ibn Athīr, *Asad al-ghāba fī maʿrifa al-Ṣaḥāba*, 4:212-213 §3929.

[11] Ibn Athīr, *Asad al-ghāba fī maʿrifa al-Ṣaḥāba*, 1:236 §161.

[12] Ibn Kathīr, *al-Bidāya wa al-nihāya*, 2:288-289 & 327.

35. Qays b. Baḥr al-Ashjaʿī[1]
36. ʿAbd Allāh b. Ḥārith b. Qays[2]
37. ʿUthmān b. Maẓʿūn[3]
38. Abū Aḥmad b. Ḥajash[4]
39. Al-Surāqa b. Mālik b. Jaʿsham[5]
40. Al-Aswad b. Sarīʿ[6]
41. ʿĀmir b. Akwaʿ[7]
42. Umm Maʿbad ʿĀtika b. Khālid al-Khazāʿī[8]
43. The girls of Medina[9]

---

[1] Ibn Hishām, *al-Sīra al-Nabawiyya*, p.761.

[2] Ibn Isḥāq, *al-Sīra al-Nabawiyya*, p.254; and Ibn Hishām, *al-Sīra al-Nabawiyya*, p.293.

[3] Abū Nuʿaym, *Ḥilya al-awliyāʾ wa ṭabaqāt al-aṣfiyāʾ*, 1:104.

[4] Ibn Hishām, *al-Sīra al-Nabawiyya*, p.407-408; and Ibn Kathīr, *al-Bidāya wa al-nihāya*, 2:522.

[5] Al-Suhaylī, *al-Rawḍ al-unuf fī tafsīr al-sīrā al-Nabawiyya li-Ibn Hishām*, 2:322; and Ibn Kathīr, *al-Bidāya wa al-nihāya*, 2:570.

[6] Aḥmad b. Ḥanbal, *al-Musnad*, 4:24 §16,300; Ibn Abī Shayba, *al-Muṣannaf*, 6:180; al-Ṭabarānī, *al-Muʿjam al-kabīr*, 1:287 §842; and al-Bayhaqī, *Shuʿab al-īmān*, 4:89 §4365.

[7] Al-Bukhārī, *al-Ṣaḥīḥ*: *Kitāb al-Maghāzi* [The Book of Military Expedition], chapter: 'The expedition of Khaybar', 4:1537 §3960; al-Bukhārī, *al-Ṣaḥīḥ*: *Kitāb al-Adab* [The Book of Proper Conduct], chapter: 'What is permitted of poetry', 5:2277 §5796; Muslim, *al-Ṣaḥīḥ*: *Kitāb al-Jihād* [The Book of Martial *Jihād*], chapter: 'The expedition of Khaybar', 3:1428 §1802; Abū ʿAwāna, *al-Musnad*, 4:314 §6830; al-Bayhaqi, *al-Sunan al-kubrā*, 10:227; and al-Ṭabarānī, *al-Muʿjam al-kabīr*, 7:32 §6294.

[8] Ibn Saʿd, *al-Ṭabaqāt al-kubrā*, 1:230-231.

[9] Ibn Abī Ḥātim al-Rāzī, *al-Thiqāt*, 1:131; Ibn ʿAbd al-Barr, *al-Tamhīd limā fī al-muwaṭṭā min al-maʿānī wa al-asānīd*, 14:82; Abū ʿUbayd al-Andalusī, *Muʿjam mā istaʿjama min asmāʾ al-bilād wa al-mawāḍiʿ*, 4:1373; Muḥibb al-Ṭabarī, *al-Riyāḍ al-naḍra fī manāqib al-ʿashra*, 1:480; al-Bayhaqī, *Dalāʾil al-Nubuwwa wa maʿrifa aḥwāl Ṣāḥib al-Sharīʿa* ﷺ, 2:507; Ibn Kathīr, *al-Bidāya wa al-nihāya*, 2:583; Ibid., 3:260; al-ʿAsqalānī, *Fatḥ al-Bārī*, 7:261; Ibid., 8:129; al-Qasṭallānī, *al-Mawāhib al-ladunya bi al-minaḥ al-Muḥammadiyya*, 1:634; al-Zurqānī, *Sharḥ al-mawāhib al-ladunya bi al-minaḥ al-Muḥammadiyya*, 4:100-101; and Aḥmad b. Zaynī al-Daḥlān, *al-Sīra al-Nabawiyya*, 1:323.

44. The Ethiopian delegate[1]
45. ʿAmr Jinnī (a *Jinn* Companion of the Holy Prophet ﷺ)[2]

All these noble personalities not only composed poetry, but they also recited it in gatherings designated especially for this purpose. Everywhere today, there are gatherings in which odes and poems are recited in the Prophet's honour of the most dignified Prophet ﷺ. The poems of Ḥassān b. Thābit, as well as other noble Companions, are recited with the intention of attaining blessings.

In conclusion to our discussion, I would say that to compose poetry in honour of the most praised one, the Holy Prophet ﷺ, and to recite eulogy, to listen to it, and to organise special gatherings for this purpose is not only permissible according to the Qurʾān and Sunna, but it is also a desirable command. From the large number of noble Companions who composed and recited poetic praise of the most glorified Prophet ﷺ, one can deduce that this was their practice. When we organise events and gatherings for the very same purpose, we are following the Sunna of these glorious Companions and the Sunna of the great personalities of Islam. This practice continued from the era of the noble companions till our times and it is in fact a sign of true faith.

---

[1] Aḥmad b. Ḥanbal, *al-Musnad*, 3:152; Ibn Ḥibbān, *al-Ṣaḥīḥ*, 13:179 §5870; Maqdisī, *al-Aḥādīth al-mukhtāra*, 5:60 §1681; and al-Haythamī, *Mawārid al-ẓamʾān ilā zawāʾid Ibn Ḥibbān*, p.493 §2012.

[2] Ibn Hishām, *al-Sīra al-Nabawiyya*, p.419; and al-Suhaylī, *al-Rawḍ al-unuf fī tafsīr al-sīrā al-Nabawiyya li-Ibn Hishām*, 2:324.

SECTION 4

SENDING SALUTATIONS AND INVOKING PEACE ON THE PROPHET ﷺ

SENDING GIFTS OF SALUTATIONS UPON THE MOST EXALTED Prophet ﷺ is an integral part of the *mawlid*. It is a unique action that is guaranteed acceptance in the court of Almighty Allah. This action brings one nearer to Almighty Allah and His beloved Prophet ﷺ. It is exceptional because it is actually a Sunna (practice) of Almighty Allah and the angels, as they endlessly convey their salutations upon him. The believers are also enjoined to do the same; in fact, under this command, sending salutations all the time on the Beloved ﷺ is a routine of the Muslims. When the blessed day of the most esteemed Prophet's ﷺ *mawlid* arrives, the noble act of invoking salutations by the lovers of the beloved Prophet ﷺ intensifies, and the melody of salutations echoes everywhere.

8.12 Salutations on the Prophet ﷺ is the Sunna of Almighty Allah and His Decree

Almighty Allah says:

﴿إِنَّ ٱللَّهَ وَمَلَٰٓئِكَتَهُۥ يُصَلُّونَ عَلَى ٱلنَّبِيِّۚ يَٰٓأَيُّهَا ٱلَّذِينَ ءَامَنُواْ صَلُّواْ عَلَيۡهِ
وَسَلِّمُواْ تَسۡلِيمًا﴾

> *Surely, Allah and (all) His angels send blessings and greetings on the Holy Prophet ﷺ. O believers! Invoke blessings on him and salute him with a worthy salutation of peace abundantly (and fervently).*[1]

The Qurʾān's injunction of sending salutations is absolute (*muṭlaq*): it is an act which is not restricted by time or space. It can be performed in any position: one can perform it sitting, standing, or lying down. Similarly, just as it can be recited outside of the

---

[1] Qurʾān 33:56.

gatherings of *Mawlid al-Nabī* ﷺ, it can also be recited within the gatherings. Sending salutations on the Holy Prophet ﷺ in the standing position is more virtuous, as this is the pinnacle of respect and veneration. The word '*taslīma*' quoted in the verse of *sūra al-Aḥzāb* explains the manner of invoking peace and blessings in the court of the Holy Prophet ﷺ. This action is a Sunna of Almighty Allah. Some actions, due to a change in circumstance or culture, may necessitate in some modification, but this is an act of Almighty Allah, so it never alters at any time. The most esteemed rank of this Sunna of Almighty Allah is perpetually and eternally established, and the manner in which these invocations of peace and blessings are sent does not differ slightly. Almighty Allah says:

﴿فَلَن تَجِدَ لِسُنَّتِ ٱللَّهِ تَبۡدِيلًا﴾

And you will not find any amendment in Allah's Sunna.[1]

Almighty Allah has enjoined the believers and emphasised to venerate and honour the most beloved Prophet ﷺ:

﴿لِّتُؤۡمِنُواْ بِٱللَّهِ وَرَسُولِهِۦ وَتُعَزِّرُوهُ وَتُوَقِّرُوهُ﴾

So that, (O people,) you may believe in Allah and His Messenger ﷺ *and may help his (*Dīn *[Religion]), and revere and venerate him heart and soul, and (with that) glorify Allah morning and evening.*[2]

The noble Companions were commanded to lower their voices in the presence of the Messenger of Allah ﷺ:

﴿يَٰٓأَيُّهَا ٱلَّذِينَ ءَامَنُواْ لَا تَرۡفَعُوٓاْ أَصۡوَٰتَكُمۡ فَوۡقَ صَوۡتِ ٱلنَّبِيِّ وَلَا تَجۡهَرُواْ لَهُۥ بِٱلۡقَوۡلِ كَجَهۡرِ بَعۡضِكُمۡ لِبَعۡضٍ أَن تَحۡبَطَ أَعۡمَٰلُكُمۡ وَأَنتُمۡ لَا تَشۡعُرُونَ﴾

---

[1] Qur'ān 35:43.

[2] Qur'ān 48:9.

O believers! Do not raise your voices above the voice of the Prophet ﷺ, and (also) do not speak to him so loud as you are loud when you speak to one another (lest) all your actions should come to nothing (including your faith), and you are not even aware (that your faith and all pious works have been wrecked).[1]

Just as the believers are instructed to venerate and honour the most esteemed Prophet ﷺ, similarly they are also required to exemplify the required etiquette whilst sending salutations upon him.

8.13 THE SIGNIFICANCE OF SENDING SALUTATIONS OF PEACE [*SALĀM*]

In light of the Qurʾān, *salām* has a significant importance. In the Qurʾān, certain incidents have been mentioned in which Almighty Allah sends His salutations of peace upon his favoured servants. The following verses bring home this point:

1. Sending peace on Yaḥyā on the occasion of his birth is mentioned below:

﴿وَسَلَٰمٌ عَلَيْهِ يَوْمَ وُلِدَ وَيَوْمَ يَمُوتُ وَيَوْمَ يُبْعَثُ حَيًّا﴾

And peace be on Yaḥyā (John), the day he was born, the day he dies, and the day he will be raised up alive![2]

2. The following statement is attributed to ʿĪsā (Jesus):

﴿وَٱلسَّلَٰمُ عَلَيَّ يَوْمَ وُلِدتُّ وَيَوْمَ أَمُوتُ وَيَوْمَ أُبْعَثُ حَيًّا﴾

And peace be upon me on the day of my birth, the day of my demise and the day I shall be raised up alive![3]

---

[1] Qurʾān 49:2.

[2] Qurʾān 19:15.

[3] Qurʾān 19:33.

In the verses mentioned above, in view of a prophet's birth, raising, and death, the significance of invoking *salām* on the occasion of the *mawlid* of the most gracious Prophet ﷺ is appraised.
3. As a whole, invocations of peace are sent upon all the prophets and messengers.

﴿وَسَلَٰمٌ عَلَى ٱلْمُرْسَلِينَ﴾

And peace be upon (all) the Messengers.[1]

4. Almighty Allah instructs the Holy Prophet ﷺ to praise Him and to invoke the salutations of peace upon his chosen servants:

﴿قُلِ ٱلْحَمْدُ لِلَّهِ وَسَلَٰمٌ عَلَىٰ عِبَادِهِ ٱلَّذِينَ ٱصْطَفَىٰٓ﴾

Say: All praise be to Allah, and peace be upon His Servants whom He has chosen (and exalted).[2]

The Qur'ān mentions the manner and Sunna routine of the prophets that whenever they meet someone, they greet with the salutations of peace. Below are some examples of this:
5. Almighty Allah states:

﴿وَإِذَا جَآءَكَ ٱلَّذِينَ يُؤْمِنُونَ بِـَٔايَٰتِنَا فَقُلْ سَلَٰمٌ عَلَيْكُمْ﴾

And when those who believe in Our Revelations come to you, then say (affectionately): Peace be upon you![3]

6. Almighty Allah states:

﴿وَلَقَدْ جَآءَتْ رُسُلُنَآ إِبْرَٰهِيمَ بِٱلْبُشْرَىٰ قَالُوا۟ سَلَٰمًا ۖ قَالَ سَلَٰمٌ﴾

And indeed, Our deputed angels came to Ibrāhīm (Abraham), bearing glad tidings. They greeted him,

[1] Qur'ān 37:181.

[2] Qur'ān 27:59.

[3] Qur'ān 6:54.

saying: Peace (be on you), and Ibrāhīm (Abraham) reciprocated: Peace (be on you).[1]

7. Almighty Allah states:

﴿إِذْ دَخَلُواْ عَلَيْهِ فَقَالُواْ سَلَٰمًا قَالَ إِنَّا مِنكُمْ وَجِلُونَ﴾

When they came to Ibrāhīm (Abraham), they greeted (him with): Peace. Ibrāhīm (Abraham) said: We are feeling somewhat afraid of you.[2]

8. Injunctions have been given to greet the believers with peace when entering the home:

﴿يَٰٓأَيُّهَا ٱلَّذِينَ ءَامَنُواْ لَا تَدْخُلُواْ بُيُوتًا غَيْرَ بُيُوتِكُمْ حَتَّىٰ تَسْتَأْنِسُواْ
وَتُسَلِّمُواْ عَلَىٰٓ أَهْلِهَا ۚ ذَٰلِكُمْ خَيْرٌ لَّكُمْ لَعَلَّكُمْ تَذَكَّرُونَ﴾

O believers! Do not enter houses other than your own until you obtain their permission. And greet their residents (immediately after you enter). This (advice) is better for you so that you may contemplate (its rationale).[3]

9. Allah states:

﴿فَإِذَا دَخَلْتُم بُيُوتًا فَسَلِّمُواْ عَلَىٰٓ أَنفُسِكُمْ تَحِيَّةً مِّنْ عِندِ ٱللَّهِ مُبَٰرَكَةً
طَيِّبَةً﴾

Then, when you enter the houses, greet (the members of) your (family) with the greeting of peace and security. (This) is a blissful and pure greeting from Allah.[4]

1 Qur'ān 11:69.

2 Qur'ān 15:52.

3 Qur'ān 24:27.

4 Qur'ān 24:61.

10. On the Night of Power (*Layla al-Qadr*) when Jibrāʾīl and thousands of angels descend to earth, there is peace till dawn. Almighty Allah states:

﴿تَنَزَّلُ ٱلْمَلَٰٓئِكَةُ وَٱلرُّوحُ فِيهَا بِإِذْنِ رَبِّهِم مِّن كُلِّ أَمْرٍ ۝٤ سَلَٰمٌ هِىَ حَتَّىٰ مَطْلَعِ ٱلْفَجْرِ ۝٥﴾

The angels and the Spirit of Peace (Gabriel) descend by their Lord's command during this (night) with decrees concerning all matters (of blessings and bounties). This (night) is (absolute) peace and security till daybreak.[1]

The echoes of peace can be heard in all directions till the dawn.

11. When the believers will reach the plain of gathering (*ḥashr*) on the Day of Judgment, Almighty Allah for the sake of His Prophet ﷺ will receive them with the greeting of peace and they will meet one another with peace. Almighty Allah states:

﴿سَلَٰمٌ قَوْلًا مِّن رَّبٍّ رَّحِيمٍ﴾

Peace (be upon you)! (This) greeting will be conveyed (to them) from the Ever-Merciful Lord.[2]

12. Almighty Allah states:

﴿تَحِيَّتُهُمْ يَوْمَ يَلْقَوْنَهُۥ سَلَٰمٌ﴾

On the Day when they (the believers) will meet Him, their gift (of the meeting/greeting) will be: Peace.[3]

When the chosen ones will be called to meet Almighty Allah and to behold the Divine vision, on that day they will be bestowed the special gift of *salām*, and this *salām* will be a peculiar and rare gift.

---

[1] Qurʾān 97:4-5.

[2] Qurʾān 36:58.

[3] Qurʾān 33:44.

13. Allah, the most high, has placed great emphasis on invoking peace upon His chosen servants. On the Day of Judgment, when the chosen ones will enter Paradise, they will be welcomed by Allah with the greeting of peace. The Qur'ān mentions this in several places:

﴿وَنَادَوْاْ أَصْحَٰبَ ٱلْجَنَّةِ أَن سَلَٰمٌ عَلَيْكُمْ﴾

And they will call out to the people of Paradise: Peace be upon you.[1]

14. Almighty Allah states:

﴿جَنَّٰتُ عَدْنٍ يَدْخُلُونَهَا وَمَن صَلَحَ مِنْ ءَابَآئِهِمْ وَأَزْوَٰجِهِمْ وَذُرِّيَّٰتِهِمْ ۖ وَٱلْمَلَٰٓئِكَةُ يَدْخُلُونَ عَلَيْهِم مِّن كُلِّ بَابٍ ﴿٢٣﴾ سَلَٰمٌ عَلَيْكُم بِمَا صَبَرْتُمْ ۚ فَنِعْمَ عُقْبَى ٱلدَّارِ ﴿٢٤﴾﴾

(There) are evergreen gardens. They will enter them with the pious from amongst their ancestors, their wives and their children. And the angels will come to them through every door (of Paradise). (Greeting, they will say:) Peace be upon you as a reward for your patience! So (see now) what a beautiful home the Hereafter is![2]

15. Almighty Allah states:

﴿ٱلَّذِينَ تَتَوَفَّىٰهُمُ ٱلْمَلَٰٓئِكَةُ طَيِّبِينَ يَقُولُونَ سَلَٰمٌ عَلَيْكُمُ ٱدْخُلُواْ ٱلْجَنَّةَ بِمَا كُنتُمْ تَعْمَلُونَ﴾

The angels take their lives whilst they are pure, clean, pleased and contented (due to obedience and piety. The angels tell them the moment they take their lives:) Peace

---

[1] Qur'ān 7:46.

[2] Qur'ān 13:23-24.

be upon you! Enter Paradise due to (the pious deeds) that you used to do.[1]

16. Almighty Allah states:

﴿فَسَلَٰمٞ لَّكَ مِنۡ أَصۡحَٰبِ ٱلۡيَمِينِ﴾

Then (it will be said to him:) Peace for you from those on the Right Hand! (Or, O Prophet, peace on you from those on the Right Hand!).[2]

The thing that needs explanation and the central point that needs to be emphasised in this discourse is about invoking *salām*. Almighty Allah, Angel Jibrāʾīl and all the other angels continuously invoke peace and blessings, as it is their practice. On the Night of Destiny, the descent of the residents of the heavens, the angels, from the height of the heavens to the earth, is a routine. When the believers enter Paradise, they will be greeted with peace and the chosen pious people will have the chance to meet Almighty Allah, the Most High, who in turn will confer on them the gift of peace. According to the Qurʾān, it is the Sunna of the prophets they would make the following invocation: "*peace be upon me on the day of my birth*". This highlights the importance of sending salutations of peace in the Qurʾān.

8.14 The Perpetual Independent Status of Sending Salutations of Peace

With regards to the implementation of the injunction contained in the following verse of the Qurʾān, there are some misunderstandings and misinterpretations.

Almighty Allah states:

﴿إِنَّ ٱللَّهَ وَمَلَٰٓئِكَتَهُۥ يُصَلُّونَ عَلَى ٱلنَّبِيِّۚ يَٰٓأَيُّهَا ٱلَّذِينَ ءَامَنُواْ صَلُّواْ عَلَيۡهِ وَسَلِّمُواْ تَسۡلِيمًا﴾

[1] Qurʾān 16:32.

[2] Qurʾān 56:91.

> *Surely, Allah and (all) His angels send blessings and greetings on the Holy Prophet ﷺ. O believers! Invoke blessings on him and salute him with a worthy salutation of peace abundantly (and fervently).*[1]

This injunction is directed at the believers. Almighty Allah has distinguished between *ṣalāt* (blessing) and *salām* (peace). Some people object, stating that there is no difference between the two, and that *salām* is included in *ṣalāt*, as in the *Ṣalāt Ibrāhīm*:

اَللّٰهُمَّ صَلِّ عَلٰى مُحَمَّدٍ وَّعَلٰى آلِ مُحَمَّدٍ كَمَا صَلَّيْتَ عَلٰى إِبْرَاهِيْمَ وَعَلٰى آلِ إِبْرَاهِيْمَ إِنَّكَ حَمِيْدٌ مَّجِيْدٌ.

> O Allah! Send blessings upon Muhammad and his family as You sent blessings upon Ibrāhīm and his family. You are, undoubtedly, worthy of (all) praise and hold majesty.

According to these people, *salām* is a portion of *ṣalāt*. For this reason, there is no need to differentiate between the two. This point of view is unsustainable, because *salām*, despite being a portion of *ṣalāt*, nevertheless holds an independent status of its own. Almighty Allah commands us with regards to two things:

1. Invoke blessings on him.
2. And salute him with a worthy salutation of peace abundantly.

Here, Almighty Allah has mentioned both *ṣalāt* and *salām* independently. Therefore, just as the injunctions have come for both separately, executing the expectations are also separate from the other. Hence, both *ṣalāt* (the invocation of blessing) and *salām* (the salutation of peace) will be offered to the most esteemed Prophet ﷺ.

Below are the points that further highlight the significance of reciting the salutations of peace:

---

[1] Qur'ān 33:56.

8.14.1 ACCEPTANCE OF ONE'S PRAISE FOR ALLAH IS THROUGH THE MEANS OF SENDING SALUTATIONS ON THE PROPHET ﷺ

Sending salutations is of such significance that one's acceptance of the praise of Allah, the Most High, is contingent on the salutations of peace one sends. The Qur'ān states:

﴿سُبۡحَٰنَ رَبِّكَ رَبِّ ٱلۡعِزَّةِ عَمَّا يَصِفُونَ ۝١٨٠ وَسَلَٰمٌ عَلَى ٱلۡمُرۡسَلِينَ ۝١٨١ وَٱلۡحَمۡدُ لِلَّهِ رَبِّ ٱلۡعَٰلَمِينَ ۝١٨٢﴾

Holy is your Lord, the Lord of Honour, Transcendent above these (things) which they utter. And peace be upon (all) the Messengers! And all praise be to Allah alone, the Lord of all the worlds.[1]

In this verse, Almighty Allah is directing His speech towards those who are absorbed in His remembrance, announcing that He is transcendent of their praise and remembrance. He is informing them that they can never fulfil the rights of His praise with their tributes. He further states that if they wish that their praise and glorification are to be accepted, then they must send their salutations of peace upon the messengers and prophets. Unless this condition is met, whatever effort they exert will neither be acknowledged nor accepted.

The sending of salutations of peace upon the messengers is the means by which our praise reaches Almighty Allah. The reason for this is that Almighty Allah always accepts the sending of salutations of peace upon His messengers; therefore, by including the salutations of peace with this praise, it is certain that it reaches Him without any hurdles. In other words, Almighty Allah is saying that any glorification which is accompanied with salutations will definitely be accepted.

---

1 Qur'ān 37:180-182.

8.14.2 THE SALUTATIONS OF PEACE IN THE *TASHAHHUD*

In the ritual prayer, the *tashahhud* commences with the praise of Almighty Allah, followed by the sending of peace upon the most exalted Prophet ﷺ. It is then followed by the testimony of faith (*shahāda*), which contains the bearing of witness to the oneness of Almighty Allah and the messengership of the Holy Prophet ﷺ; this is then followed by the *Ṣalāt Ibrāhīm*, ending with a supplication. If we analyse the *tashahhud*, we will find that it is composed of four ingredients:

1. Praise of Almighty Allah: the first part of the *tashahhud* is specified solely for the praise of Allah:

اَلتَّحِيَّاتُ لِلّٰهِ وَالصَّلَوَاتُ وَالطَّيِّبَاتُ.

> All my acts of worship, whether by saying or by acting with limbs or by spending, are only for (the sake of) Almighty Allah.

2. Salutations of peace: the second part is dedicated to sending salutations of peace upon the most exalted Prophet ﷺ:

اَلسَّلَامُ عَلَيْكَ أَيُّهَا النَّبِيُّ وَرَحْمَةُ اللهِ وَبَرَكَاتُهُ.

> O Prophet! May peace be upon you and Allah's mercy and blessings!

In this way, one part is specified solely for Almighty Allah and another for His beloved Prophet ﷺ.

3. The testimony of faith: this third part is for both Almighty Allah and His beloved Prophet ﷺ:

أَشْهَدُ أَنْ لَّا إِلٰـهَ إِلَّا اللهُ وَأَشْهَدُ أَنَّ مُحَمَّدًا عَبْدُهُ وَرَسُوْلُهُ.

> I bear witness that there is no God except Allah and I testify that Muhammad is the Messenger and slave of Allah.

In this testimony, the first half is specified for Almighty Allah and the other half is specified for His beloved Prophet ﷺ.

> I bear witness that there is no God but Allah; and I bear witness that Muhammad is His servant and Messenger.

4. *Ṣalāt Ibrāhīm*: the fourth part is the salutations of peace and blessings, which is purely for Allah's Messenger ﷺ:

اَللّٰهُمَّ صَلِّ عَلَى مُحَمَّدٍ وَّعَلَى آلِ مُحَمَّدٍ كَمَا صَلَّيْتَ عَلَى إِبْرَاهِيْمَ وَعَلَى آلِ إِبْرَاهِيْمَ إِنَّكَ حَمِيْدٌ مَّجِيْدٌ. اَللّٰهُمَّ بَارِكْ عَلَى مُحَمَّدٍ وَّعَلَى آلِ مُحَمَّدٍ كَمَا بَارَكْتَ عَلَى إِبْرَاهِيْمَ وَعَلَى آلِ إِبْرَاهِيْمَ إِنَّكَ حَمِيْدٌ مَّجِيْدٌ.

> O Allah! Send blessings upon Muhammad and his family as You sent blessings upon Ibrāhīm and his family. You are, undoubtedly, worthy of (all) praise and hold majesty. O Allah! Send blessings upon Muhammad and his family as You sent blessings upon Ibrāhīm and his family. You are, undoubtedly, worthy of (all) praise and hold majesty.

In conclusion, one could say that in light of the arrangement of the *tashahhud* which has been placed by Almighty Allah, only one and a half is dedicated to the praise of Almighty Allah whilst two and half is dedicated to Allah's Messenger ﷺ. And when we attach our supplication to this, our prayers and supplication are both accepted. After completing the prayer, the 'exiting from the prayer' (*khurūj ʿan al-ṣalā*) is also contingent on the salutations of peace. The prayer ends with the following greetings:

اَلسَّلَامُ عَلَيْكُمْ وَرَحْمَةُ اللهِ.

> Peace be upon you and may the mercy of Allah be upon you (too).

Apart from the most esteemed Prophet ﷺ, this greeting of peace is also directed to the *awliyā'* (divine friends of Almighty Allah), righteous believers, and the members of this community (*Umma*).

The above discussion has clearly outlined the esteemed status and central importance of sending salutations of peace. How can we possibly avoid the performance of this integral act?

8.14.3 THE PROPHET'S INJUNCTION ON SENDING *SALĀM* AFTER *ṢALĀT*

The Prophet ﷺ has instructed the believers that regardless of where they may be, it is imperative that they send salutations of peace (*salām*) after invoking blessings (*ṣalāt*).

ʿAlī b. Ḥusayn narrates from his grandfather, ʿAlī b. Abī Ṭālib, that the Holy Prophet ﷺ said:

«وَصَلُّوا عَلَيَّ وَسَلِّمُوا حَيْثُمَا كُنْتُمْ، فَسَيَبْلُغُنِي سَلَامُكُمْ وَصَلَاتُكُمْ.»

> Invoke blessings and send salutations of peace upon me, wherever you may be. Your salutations of peace and invocations of blessings will reach me.[1]

In the above hadith, two things are being instructed: invocations of blessings (*ṣalāt*) and salutations of peace (*salām*). If the Holy Prophet ﷺ has made this distinction, then how can we possibly consider them to be one and the same? This is the Prophet's instruction to the believers.

8.15 SALUTATIONS REACHING THE PROPHET ﷺ

The believer's tributes, invoking peace and blessings, reache the chief of the created world, the Holy Prophet ﷺ, in a number of different ways: this is substantiated by many narrations. These narrations are transmitted below:

[1] Narrated by Ibn Isḥāq in *Faḍl al-ṣalā ʿalā al-Nabī*, p.35 §20; Aḥmad b. Ḥanbal in *al-Musnad*, 2:367 §8790; Ibn Abī Shayba in *al-Muṣannaf*, 2:150 §7542; Ibn Kathīr in *Tafsīr al-Qurʾān al-ʿaẓīm*, 3:515 instead of the word '*fa-sa-yablughunī*', transmits the word, '*fa-tablughunī*'; al-ʿAsqalānī in *Lisān al-mīzān*, 2:106 also mentions the word, '*fa-tablughunī*'; and Hindī in *Kanz al-ʿummāl fī sunan al-aqwāl wa al-afʿāl*, 1:498 §2199.

8.15.1 Invocations of Peace and Blessings Reach the Prophet ﷺ Directly

One of the many distinguishing attributes of the chief of the created beings, the Holy Prophet ﷺ, is that regardless of where the believer may be when sending his invocation of peace and blessings, his invocation will always reach the Holy Prophet ﷺ directly. The words, '*tablughunī*', '*fa-tablughunī*', '*yablughunī*', '*fa-sa-yablughunī*' and other such expressions in the hadiths clearly illustrate this. This is because in light of Arabic grammar, the words are in the active voice and not the passive; furthermore, the subject of these verbs is either 'your invocation of blessings' (*ṣalātukum*) or 'your salutations of peace' (*salāmukum*), proving that the invocation themselves reach the Holy Prophet ﷺ.

1. Abū Hurayra narrates that the most exalted Prophet ﷺ said:

«صَلُّوا عَلَيَّ، فَإِنَّ صَلَاتَكُمْ تَبْلُغُنِي حَيْثُ كُنْتُمْ.»

> Invoke blessings upon me. Surely, your invocation reaches me wherever you may be.[1]

2. ʿAlī b. Ḥusayn narrates from his grandfather, ʿAlī b. Abī Ṭālib, that the Holy Prophet ﷺ said:

«فَإِنَّ تَسْلِيْمَكُمْ يَبْلُغُنِي أَيْنَ مَا كُنْتُمْ.»

> Surely, your salutations of peace reach me wherever you may be.[2]

---

[1] Narrated by Abū Dāwūd in *al-Sunan*: *Kitāb al-Manāsik* [The Book of Pilgrimage Rites], chapter: 'Visiting the graves', 2:176 §2042; Aḥmad b. Ḥanbal in *al-Musnad*, 2:367; Ibn Abī Shayba, in *al-Muṣannaf*, 2:150 §7542; al-Ṭabarānī in *al-Muʿjam al-kabīr*, 8:82-83 §8030; al-Bayhaqī in *Shuʿab al-īmān*, 3:491 §4162; al-Maqrīzī in *Imtāʿ al-asmāʿ bi mā li-Nabī min al-aḥwāl wa al-amwāl wa al-ḥafda wa al-Matāʿ*, 11:59 &71; Ibn al-Qayyim in *Jalāʾ al-afhām fī al-ṣalā wa al-salām ʿalā Khayr al-anām*, p.42 §61; Ibn Kathīr in *Tafsīr al-Qurʾān al-ʿaẓīm*, 3:514; and al-ʿAsqalānī in *Fatḥ al-Bārī*, 6:488.

[2] Narrated by Abū Yaʿlā in *al-Musnad*, 1:361 §469; al-Maqdasī in *al-Aḥādīth al-mukhtāra*, 2:49 §428; al-Ḥaythamī in *Majmaʿ al-zawāʾid wa*

3. Ḥasan b. ʿAlī narrates that the Holy Prophet ﷺ said:

«صَلُّوا عَلَيَّ وَسَلِّمُوا، فَإِنَّ صَلَاتَكُمْ وَسَلَامَكُمْ يَبْلُغُنِي أَيْنَ مَا كُنْتُمْ.»

Invoke peace and blessings upon me. Surely, your invocations of peace and blessings reach me wherever you may be.[1]

4. Ḥasan b. Ḥasan b. ʿAlī narrates from his father that the Holy Prophet ﷺ said:

«حَيْثُمَا كُنْتُمْ فَصَلُّوا عَلَيَّ، فَإِنَّ صَلَاتَكُمْ تَبْلُغُنِي.»

Wherever you may be, invoke blessings upon me. For indeed, your invocations reach me.[2]

5. Ḥasan b. Ḥusayn narrates that the Holy Prophet ﷺ said:

«وَصَلُّوْا عَلَيَّ، فَإِنَّ صَلَا تَكُمْ تَبْلُغُنِي حَيْثُمَا كُنْتُمْ.»

Invoke blessings upon me. Surely, your invocations reach me wherever you may be.[3]

---

manbaʿ al-fawāʾid, 4:3; and al-ʿAsqalānī in *Lisān al-mīzān*, 2:106.

[1] Narrated by Abū Yaʿlā in *al-Musnad*, 12:131 §6761; and Ibn al-Qayyim in *Jalāʾ al-afhām fī al-ṣalā wa al-salām ʿalā Khayr al-anām*, p.42 §60.

[2] Narrated by al-Ṭabarānī in *al-Muʿjam al-kabīr*, 3:82 §2729; Aḥmad b. Ḥanbal in *al-Musnad*, 2:367 has narrated it with these words from Abū Hurayra; al-Ṭabarānī in *al-Muʿjam al-awsaṭ*, 1:238 §367 states that the narrator is Ḥusayn b. Ḥasan b. ʿAlī; ʿAbd al-Razzāq in *al-Muṣannaf*, 3:577 §6726 has narrated this with some difference in wordings; Dūlābī in *al-Dhurriya al-ṭāhira*, p.73 §199; Mundhirī in *al-Targhīb wa al-tarhīb min al-ḥadīth al-sharīf*, 2:362 states that Imam al-Ṭabarānī has narrated this in *al-Muʿjam al-kabīr* with a fine (*ḥasan*) chain of narration; al-Ḥaythamī in *Majmaʿ al-zawāʾid wa manbaʿ al-fawāʾid*, 10:162; and Ibn al-Qayyim in *Jalāʾ al-afhām fī al-ṣalā wa al-salām ʿalā Khayr al-anām*, p.42 §61.

[3] Narrated by Ibn Isḥāq in *Faḍl al-ṣalā ʿalā al-Nabī*, p.45 §30; Ibn Abī Shayba, in *al-Muṣannaf*, 2:150 §7543; and ʿAbd al-Razzāq in *al-Muṣannaf*, 3:17 §4839 has narrated this from Ḥasan b. ʿAlī.

8.15.2 The Holy Prophet ﷺ Listens to the Invocations and Salutations Directly

Invoking peace and blessings upon the beloved Prophet ﷺ is such an excellent act (which has also attained acceptance in the divine court), that Almighty Allah Himself partakes in it along with the angels and the worshipful servants. Almighty Allah has blessed the most esteemed Prophet ﷺ with the exclusive ability to directly hear the recitation of these invocations. Abū al-Dardā᾿ narrates that the most esteemed Prophet ﷺ said:

«أَكْثِرُوا الصَّلَاةَ عَلَيَّ يَوْمَ الْجُمُعَةِ، فَإِنَّهُ يَوْمٌ مَشْهُوْدٌ تَشْهَدُهُ الْمَلَائِكَةُ، لَيْسَ مِنْ عَبْدٍ يُصَلِّي عَلَيَّ إِلاَّ بَلَغَنِي صَوْتُهُ حَيْثُ كَانَ.»

> Increase the invocation of blessings upon me on Friday; for it is a day of attestation witnessed by the angels. There is not a worshipful servant who invokes blessings upon me, except that his voice reaches me wherever he may be.

The noble Companions asked the most esteemed Prophet ﷺ, 'Should we continue this action after you pass away?' The Holy Prophet ﷺ replied:

«وَبَعْدَ وَفَاتِي، إِنَّ اللهَ حَرَّمَ عَلَى الْأَرْضِ أَنْ تَأْكُلَ أَجْسَادَ الْأَنْبِيَاءِ.»

> And (even) after my departure from life: Indeed, Allah has declared the bodies of the Prophets forbidden to the earth.[1]

The statement, 'his voice reaches me', indicates that the most

[1] Narrated by Ibn al-Qayyim in *Jalā᾿ al-afhām fī al-ṣalā wa al-salām ʿalā Khayr al-anām*, p.63 §108 states that al-Ṭabarānī has narrated it; al-Ḥaythamī in *al-Durr al-manḍūd fī al-ṣalā wa al-salām ʿalā Ṣāḥib al-maqām al-maḥmūd*, p.155-156; al-Sakhāwī in *al-Qawl al-badīʿ fī al-ṣalā ʿalā al-Ḥabīb al-Shafīʿ*, p.158-159 states that al-Ṭabarānī has narrated it; and al-Nabhānī, *Ḥujja Allāh ʿalā al-ʿālimīn fī muʿjazāt Sayyid al-mursalīn*, p.713.

esteemed Prophet ﷺ does not hear by means of an intermediary, such as an angel, but he actually hears himself. There is no condition of proximity in terms of it being far or near, rather, the most esteemed Prophet ﷺ himself hears the recitation of these invocations. Imam Aḥmad Riḍā Khān (1272-1340 AH) beautifully explains this:

دور و نزدیک کے سننے والے وہ کان

کانِ لعلِ کرامت پہ لاکھوں سلام

Those blessed ears that are able to hear that which is near and afar
May hundreds of thousands of salutations be upon those (ears that are) miraculous jewels.[1]

On one occasion, the most esteemed Prophet ﷺ was asked regarding those who invoked peace and blessings on him, irrespective of distance and even after his passing away and whether these invocations reach him. The Holy Prophet ﷺ replied:

«أَسْمَعُ صَلَاةَ أَهْلِ مَحَبَّتِي وَأَعْرِفُهُمْ.»

I hear the invocations of (blessings recited by) my lovers and I recognise them.[2]

From this it can be understood that the most esteemed Prophet ﷺ not only listens to the invocations of peace and blessings recited by his lovers, but he also recognises them and knows who they are, even if they may be physically distant from him and living in a different age from him (i.e., there are no restrictions of time and space).

---

[1] Aḥmad Riḍā Khān, *Ḥadāʾiq-e-bakhshish*, 2:206.

[2] Narrated by al-Jazūlī in *Dalāʾil al-khayrāt wa shawāriq al-anwār fī dhikr al-ṣalā ʿalā al-Nabī al-Mukhtār*, p.18; and al-Fāsī in *Maṭāliʿ al-masarrāt bi-jalāʾ dalāʾil al-khayrāt wa shawāriq al-anwār fī dhikr al-ṣalā ʿalā al-Nabī al-Mukhtār*, p.81.

8.15.3 The Prophet ﷺ Replies to the Salutations

The most esteemed Prophet ﷺ not only listens to the invocations of peace and blessings recited upon him, but he replies to them too. Abū Hurayra narrates that the most esteemed Prophet ﷺ said:

«مَا مِنْ أَحَدٍ يُسَلِّمُ عَلَيَّ إِلَّا رَدَّ اللهُ عَلَيَّ رُوحِي، حَتَّى أَرُدَّ عَلَيْهِ السَّلَامَ.»

> There is no one who sends salutations of peace upon me except that Almighty Allah returns to me my soul until I return to him his greeting.[1]

It is narrated from Abū Hurayra that the most esteemed Prophet ﷺ said:

«مَا مِنْ مُسْلِمٍ سَلَّمَ عَلَيَّ فِي شَرْقٍ وَّلاَ غَرْبٍ، إِلَّا أَنَا وَمَلَائِكَةُ رَبِّي نَرُدُّ عَلَيْهِ السَّلَامَ.»

> There is not a Muslim in the east or the west who sends salutations of peace upon me except that I and the angels of my Lord return to him his greeting.[2]

8.15.4 The Angels Invoke Peace and Blessings on the Prophet ﷺ

The most eminent status of the most esteemed Prophet ﷺ is that he himself listens to the invocations of peace and blessings recited

---

[1] Narrated by Abū Dāwūd in *al-Sunan*: *Kitāb al-Manāsik* [The Book of Pilgrimage Rites], chapter: 'Visiting the graves', 2:175 §2041; Aḥmad b. Ḥanbal in *al-Musnad*, 2:527; al-Ṭabarānī in *al-Muʿjam al-awsaṭ*, 4:84 §3116; al-Bayhaqī in *al-Sunan al-kubrā*, 5:245; al-Bayhaqī in *Shuʿab al-īmān*, 2:217 §1581; Mundhirī in *al-Targhīb wa al-tarhīb min al-ḥadīth al-sharīf*, 2:362 §2573; and al-Ḥaythamī in *Majmaʿ al-zawāʾid wa manbaʿ al-fawāʾid*, 10:162.

[2] Narrated by Abū Nuʿaym in *Ḥilya al-awliyāʾ wa ṭabaqāt al-aṣfiyāʾ*, 6:349; al-Maqrīzī in *Imtāʿ al-asmāʿ bi mā li-Nabī min al-aḥwāl wa al-amwāl wa al-ḥafda wa al-Matāʿ*, 11:59; Ibn al-Qayyim in *Jalāʾ al-afhām fī al-ṣalā wa al-salām ʿalā Khayr al-anām*, p.19 §20; and al-Sakhāwī in *al-Qawl al-badīʿ fī al-ṣalā ʿalā al-Ḥabīb al-Shafīʿ*, p.156.

by his loyal servants; however, Almighty Allah assigned angels to bring the salutations to His beloved Prophet ﷺ, due to this esteemed reverence.However, Anas b. Mālik narrates that the Holy Prophet ﷺ said:

«مَنْ صَلَّى عَلَيَّ فِي يَوْمِ الْـجُمُعَةِ وَلَيْلَةِ الْـجُمُعَةِ مِائَةَ مَرَّةٍ، قَضَى اللهُ لَهُ مِائَةَ حَاجَةٍ: سَبْعِيْنَ مِنْ حَوَائِجِ الْآخِرَةِ وَثَلَاثِيْنَ مِنْ حَوَائِجِ الدُّنْيَا، ثُمَّ يُوَكِّلُ اللهُ بِذَلِكَ مَلَكًا يُدْخِلُهُ فِي قَبْرِي كَمَا يُدْخَلُ عَلَيْكُمُ الْـهَدَايَا، يُخْبِرُنِي مَنْ صَلَّى عَلَيَّ بِاسْمِهِ وَنَسَبِهِ إِلَى عَشِيْرَتِهِ، فَأُثْبِتُهُ عِنْدِي فِي صَحِيْفَةٍ بَيْضَاءَ.»

Whoever invokes blessings upon me on Friday and its (preceding) night one hundred times, Allah will fulfil for him one hundred of his needs: seventy of his needs in the hereafter, and thirty of his needs in this life. Thereafter, because of it, Allah will appoint an angel, who will present it to me as one presents a gift to you; he will inform me about the invocations along with the reciter's name, lineage, and family. Then, I will record it in a white scroll I have with me.[1]

ʿAbd Allāh b. Masʿūd relates that the Holy Prophet ﷺ said:

«إِنَّ لِلّٰهِ مَلَائِكَةً سَيَّاحِيْنَ فِي الْأَرْضِ يُبَلِّغُونِي مِنْ أُمَّتِي السَّلَامَ.»

There are angels of Allah, who roam through the earth relaying to me the salutations of peace recited by the members of my community.[2]

---

[1] Narrated by al-Bayhaqī in *Shuʿab al-īmān*, 3:111 §3035; Fayrūz Ābādī in *al-Ṣalāt wa al-bishr fī al-ṣalā ʿalā Khayr al-bashr*, p.77; al-Suyūṭī in *al-Durr al-manthūr fī al-tafsīr bi al-maʾthūr*, 5:219; al-Zurqānī in *Sharḥ al-mawāhib al-ladunya bi al-minaḥ al-Muḥammadiyya*, 7:372; and al-Sakhāwī in *al-Qawl al-badīʿ fī al-ṣalā ʿalā al-Ḥabīb al-Shafīʿ*, p.156.

[2] Narrated by al-Nasāʾī in *al-Sunan*: *Kitāb al-Sahw* [The Book of Faith], chapter: 'Invoking peace on the Prophet,' 3:31 §1282; al-Nasāʾī in *ʿAmal al-yawm wa al-layla*, p.167 §66; Aḥmad b. Ḥanbal in *al-Musnad*, 1:387, 441

Abū Umāma narrates that the most esteemed Prophet ﷺ said:

«أَكْثِرُوْا عَلَيَّ مِنَ الصَّلَاةِ فِي كُلِّ يَوْمِ جُمُعَةٍ، فَإِنَّ صَلَاةَ أُمَّتِي تُعْرَضُ عَلَيَّ فِي كُلِّ يَوْمِ جُمُعَةٍ، فَمَنْ كَانَ أَكْثَرَهُمْ عَلَيَّ صَلَاةً كَانَ أَقْرَبَهُمْ مِنِّي مَنْزِلَةً.»

Increase your invocations of blessings upon me on Friday. Surely, the invocations recited by the members of my community are presented to me every Friday. Whoever amongst you recites the most invocations upon me will be the closest to me in rank.[1]

It is evident from these hadiths that irrespective of distance, whether it be far or near, the most exalted Prophet ﷺ listens to the invocations of peace and blessings recited by the loyal members of his community. The angels, only to maintain the etiquettes of his court, relay the invocations. Otherwise, not only does the servant's voice reach him, but the most esteemed Prophet ﷺ honours him by replying to his salutations. Despite such clear and explicit rulings and its many virtues, if someone still raises objections criticising the gatherings of *Mawlid al-Nabī* ﷺ, it is nothing but his misfortue. These antagonists should learn the truth through the evidence of the Qur'ān and Sunna.

In this section, we have only related a small selection of hadiths

& 452; al-Dārimī in *al-Sunan*, 2:409 §2774; Ibn Ḥibbān in *al-Ṣaḥīḥ*, 3:195 §914; al-Bazzār in *al-Baḥr al-zukhār (al-musnad)*, 5:307-308 §1924-1925; Abū Ya'lā in *al-Musnad*, 9:137 §5213; and Ibn Abī Shayba in *al-Muṣannaf*, 2:215 §3116. The narration reported by Ibn Ḥibbān is authentic (*ṣaḥīḥ*) according to the conditions set by Imam Muslim and all of its narrators are reliable. Ḥākim declares this narration to be authentic (*ṣaḥīḥ*) whilst Dhahabī concurs with him. Ibn al-Qayyim declares the chain of narration to be authentic (*ṣaḥīḥ*).

[1] Narrated by al-Bayhaqī in *Shu'ab al-īmān*, 3:110 §3032; al-Bayhaqī in *al-Sunan al-kubrā*, 3:249 §5791; al-Daylamī in *al-Firdaws bi-ma'thūr al-khiṭāb*, 1:81 §250; Mundhirī in *al-Targhīb wa al-tarhīb min al-ḥadīth al-sharīf*, 2:328 §2583; Subkī in *Shifā' al-siqām fī ziyāra Khayr al-anām*, p.136; al-Maqrīzī in *Imtā' al-asmā' bi mā li-Nabī min al-aḥwāl wa al-amwāl wa al-ḥafda wa al-Matā'*, 11:66; Ibn al-Qayyim in *Jalā' al-afhām fī al-ṣalā wa al-salām 'alā Khayr al-anām*, p.40 §56; and 'Aẓīm Ābādī in *Awn al-ma'būd 'alā Sunan Abī Dāwūd*, 4:272.

on the excellent virtues and significance of invoking peace and blessings; otherwise, there is a whole treasure of hadiths available on this topic. The scholars have composed fully fledged books on the subject. For further information, one should consult my book, *al-Badr al-tamām fī al-ṣalā ʿalā Ṣāḥib al-dunuww wa al-maqām*.

Section 5

Qiyām (The Ritual Standing)

In the gatherings of *Mawlid al-Nabī* ﷺ, sending one's salutations on the most praised Prophet ﷺ in the standing position is the hallmark of the lovers; it is a praiseworthy deed. Just as in the most revered Prophet's life, respect and reverence for his person was compulsory upon the believers—the noble Companions were very cautious in maintaining their reverence and respect. Similarly today, the same respect and reverence is compulsary. In the *mawlid* gatherings or in the assemblies of poetical praise, standing whilst sending one's salutations on the most esteemed Prophet ﷺ is a continuation of this show of respect and reverence. The gatherings in which the *qiyām* is performed are certainly blessed by the descent of Divine light and *baraka*. This standing out of respect has been made a source of contention by some: according to them, it is contrary to the Sharia. Hence, in the discourse below, some important points will be highlighted:

8.16 Is the Ritual Standing (*Qiyām*) Exclusive to Allah?

Some people hold the opinion that the *qiyām* (ritual standing) is not permissible for anyone other than Almighty Allah. For them, standing is actually a form of worship, and worship is exclusive to Almighty Allah. Consequently in their worldview, standing for anyone other than Almighty Allah falls within the confines of polytheism (*shirk*). This is why, according to them, it is impermissible to stand in respect for the most gracious Prophet ﷺ in the *mawlid*.

This claim is baseless and mistaken: if standing is a part of worship, then sitting and lying down should also be considered a part of worship, because in the Qurʾān, they have been mentioned in conjunction with standing. Almighty Allah says:

﴿ٱلَّذِينَ يَذْكُرُونَ ٱللَّهَ قِيَـٰمًا وَقُعُودًا وَعَلَىٰ جُنُوبِهِمْ﴾

These are the people who, remembering Allah, remain standing (as the epitome of submissiveness), sitting (as reverence incarnate), and (also keep) changing sides (in discomfort of love).[1]

In the above verse of the Qur'ān, three states have been mentioned in connection to Almighty Allah's worship and remembrance: standing, sitting and lying down. If standing is for Almighty Allah, then for whom is sitting and lying down? According to the above verse, sitting and lying down should also be exclusive to Almighty Allah; if standing for someone other than Almighty Allah is associating partners with Him (*shirk*), then sitting and lying down for anyone else should also be considered *shirk* as they constitute a part of worship—what then is left behind? If such is the case, then the whole system of life will become interrupted, as standing, sitting, and lying down for someone other than Almighty Allah will become polytheism. Therefore, to declare these motions as worship is ridiculous.

Further explanation on the difference between worship (*ʿibāda*) and reverence (*taʿẓīm*) is given below:

8.16.1 The Different Positions of Prayer are not Worship Per Se

One should keep in mind that the prayer positions are not in of themselves acts of worship. Thus they have no connection with *shirk* (associating partners with Almighty Allah). The reason for this is that the crux of worship is one's intention. The Holy Prophet ﷺ said:

«إِنَّمَا الْأَعْمَالُ بِالنِّيَّاتِ.»

Actions are valued according to the intentions.[2]

---

[1] Qur'ān 3:191.

[2] Narrated by al-Bukhārī in *al-Ṣaḥīḥ*: *Kitāb Bad' al-Waḥī* [The Book of the Beginning of Revelation], chapter: 'The beginning of revelation', 1:3 §1; Muslim in *al-Ṣaḥīḥ*: *Kitāb al-Imāra* [The Book of Leadership], chapter: 'Actions are valued according to intentions', 3:1515 §1907.

Any action void of intention is not accepted. Standing has no connection with worship as long as no intention (of worship) is involved. According to the science of Islamic jurisprudence (*fiqh*), placing one hand over the other is neither considered obligatory (*farḍ*) nor mandatory (*wājib*); the *qiyām* is simply to stand in an erect position. Regardless of whether one performs the *qiyām* according to the *Ḥanafī*, *Shāfiʿī*, *Mālikī*, or *Ḥanbalī* school of thought, it will be considered valid in the Sharia. In one school, clasping the hands together is considered a position of prayer whilst in another school, leaving the hands hanging by one's sides is considered a position of prayer; in reality, both are considered positions of prayer as long as one has the intention of worship in mind. One cannot claim, 'my act of *qiyām* is worship, whilst your *qiyām* of reverence is polytheism'. This is because if the intention of worship is not included, how then can it be considered an act of polytheism? If the action is done for the purpose of veneration, then there is no possibility of *shirk* being attributed to it. It is imperative that a distinction is made between actions which are done for the purpose of worship and actions which are done for sake of veneration.

The whole sum of this discussion is that worship is connected to one's intention, not the act of standing per se. *Qiyām* is simply to stand in an erect position; the position of one's hands has nothing to do with it, whether they are clasped or left hanging.

8.16.2 If the Standing Position is Worship, Then What About the Other Positions?

If we closely observe the ritual prayer after the standing, there is the bowing, prostration, and sitting positions—all of which are the integral elements of the prayer. If the standing position is a constituent element of the ritual prayer, then the sitting position is also: if the standing is worship, then the sitting is also worship; and if the standing is exclusively for Almighty Allah, then the sitting is also exclusively for Him. All of these positions are the obligatory parts of the ritual prayer. And the interesting point is that within the *tashahhud*, Almighty Allah has made the sending of salutations on His beloved Prophet ﷺ an intrinsic aspect. If performing these positions for anyone besides Almighty Allah is *shirk*, i.e., associating partners with Him, then we are all guilty of committing it within the ritual prayer (as salutations are recited on the Holy Prophet ﷺ in the sitting position). In reality it is not the case that *shirk* being practiced, because the position of standing and sitting are performed as acts of worship for Almighty Allah, and as acts of veneration for the most esteemed Prophet ﷺ. If during the ritual prayer, invoking peace and blessings upon the most esteemed Prophet ﷺ in the sitting position is not considered worship, how then can it be considered so in the standing position outside of the ritual prayer?

8.16.3 In Which Way is the Ritual Standing Worship?

During the ritual prayer, the hands are folded underneath the navel. Some people believe that standing in this way, as is done in the West to show respect to a dignitary is an act of worship, and hence polytheism (*shirk*). If this is the case, then what about the followers of the *Mālikī* and *Jaʿfarī* schools of thought? In these two schools, the hands are not folded but are left hanging loose on the sides (*irsāl al-yadayn*); if the followers of these two schools of thought stand in front of someone else with their hands hanging loose, will it be considered worship? Obviously not! To make such a statement is only a result of a lack of knowledge.

8.17 The Ritual Standing (*Qiyām*) in Light of the Sunna is Permissible

In the discourses that have preceded us, it has become apparent that standing in-of-itself is not worship. What brings it into the scope of worship is the intention behind it. The ritual standing (*qiyām*) is a permissible act, irrespective if it is performed as an act of reverence or not. We must ask ourselves: is the ritual standing (*qiyām*) established in the Sunna, or is it simply permissible? Below are details which categorically demonstrate through the hadiths that the *qiyām* is an act which is established in the Sunna of the Holy Prophet ﷺ:

8.18 The Classifications of the Ritual Standing (*Qiyām*)

It is proven from the hadiths that to stand for others is established in the Sunna of the Holy Prophet ﷺ. There are different reasons why the *qiyām* is performed. A thorough reading of the hadiths informs us that there are seven situations when a person stands for another person:

1. Standing to welcome someone (*qiyām li al-istiqbāl*)
2. Standing out of love (*qiyām li al-maḥabba*)
3. Standing out of joy (*qiyām li al-farḥa*)
4. Standing out of veneration (*qiyām li al-taʿẓīm*)
5. Standing for human dignity (*qiyām li al-ikrām al-insānī*)
6. Standing for remembrance (*qiyām li al-dhikr*)
7. Standing to invoke peace and blessings (*qiyām li al-ṣalāt wa al-salām*)

This classification has been arranged to facilitate its understanding and to make it more systematic.

8.18.1 Standing to Welcome Someone (*Qiyām li al-Istiqbāl*)

To get up for a special guest or respected leader in order to receive them is called *qiyām al-istiqbāl*, or standing to welcome someone. This has its origins in the Sunna of the Holy Prophet ﷺ.

During the battle of *Aḥzāb*, the tribe of Banū Qurayẓa breached their treaty with the most compassionate Prophet ﷺ; they betrayed the Muslims by aiding the disbelievers. In order to bring them to justice, the most exalted Prophet ﷺ went to them straight after the battle and appointed Saʿd b. Muʿādh, the leader of Aws (an ally tribe of Banū Qurayẓa), as their arbitrator.

Abū Saʿīd al-Khudrī narrates:

فَأَرْسَلَ النَّبِيُّ ﷺ إِلَى سَعْدٍ، فَأَتَى عَلَى حِمَارٍ، فَلَمَّا دَنَا مِنَ الْمَسْجِدِ قَالَ لِلْأَنْصَارِ: «قُومُوا إِلَى سَيِّدِكُمْ أَوْ خَيْرِكُمْ.»

> The Prophet ﷺ called for Saʿd; and he came on a donkey. When he drew near to the mosque, the Prophet ﷺ said to the Anṣār: 'Stand for your master (or the best among you).'[1]

The statement, 'the best among you', clearly indicates that the Prophet's command was for *qiyām li al-istiqbāl*; it can also be interpreted as *qiyām li al-taʿẓīm*. Some people have tried to brush aside this incident, claiming that Saʿd b. Muʿādh was ill and that is why the Holy Prophet ﷺ ordered some people to get up for him in order to help him get off his ride.

If we are to believe this, then why did the Holy Prophet ﷺ not order a few people to help him, as opposed to the whole tribe? The words of the hadith are: 'the Prophet ﷺ said to the Anṣār: 'Stand for your master''. The whole of the tribe, not a few individuals, was ordered to stand, hence the claim that they rose to help him due to his illness is against the text of the hadith. This commandment was on account of Saʿd's mastery over them, and therefore the standing was a means of welcoming him. Moreover, the final statement, 'the best among you', is also indicative of this.

Abū Dāwūd (275-202 AH) has recorded this narration in his *Sunan*, in *Kitāb al-Adab* [The Book of Proper Conduct], under the chapter, 'What has been related concerning the ritual standing (*qiyām*)', where he has recorded similar narrations of people standing for others. Therefore, this objection that it was to assist him to get off his ride is totally without foundation, because if this narration was not about standing for others, the hadith scholars would not have placed this narration in the chapter about the etiquettes of the ritual standing.

---

[1] Narrated by al-Bukhārī in *al-Ṣaḥīḥ*: *Kitāb al-Maghāzī* [The Book of Military Expeditions], chapter: 'The Prophet's return from the battle of *Aḥzāb*,' 4:1511 §3895; al-Bukhārī in *al-Ṣaḥīḥ*: *Kitāb al-Istiʾdhān* [The Book of Asking Permission to Enter], chapter: 'The Prophet's statement: Stand for your master', 5:2310 §5907; Muslim in *al-Ṣaḥīḥ*: *Kitāb al-Jihād* [The Book of Martial *Jihād*], chapter: 'The permissibility of killing someone who breaches the treaty', 3:1388 §1768; and Abū Dāwūd in *al-Sunan*: *Kitāb al-Adab* [The Book of Proper Conduct], chapter: 'What has been related concerning the ritual standing (*qiyām*)', 4:355 §5215.

8.18.2 STANDING OUT OF LOVE (*QIYĀM LI AL-MAḤABBA*)

Standing for someone can also be done out of love. This is known as *qiyām li al-maḥabba* or *qiyām fī al-ḥubb*. A parent's standing or getting up for his child, a teacher for his student, a *shaykh* for his special devotee, or any senior for his junior comes under this category. This type of standing can even be done for a four or five year old child. This particular act of standing is directly established from the practice of the most esteemed Prophet ﷺ. Some narrations on this are mentioned below:

Mother of the believers, ʿĀʾisha al-Ṣadīqa, narrates:

مَا رَأَيْتُ أَحَدًا أَشْبَهَ سَمْتًا وَدَلًّا وَهَدْيًا بِرَسُولِ اللهِ فِي قِيَامِهَا وَقُعُودِهَا مِنْ فَاطِمَةَ بِنْتِ رَسُولِ اللهِ ﷺ، قَالَتْ: وَكَانَتْ إِذَا دَخَلَتْ عَلَى النَّبِيِّ ﷺ قَامَ إِلَيْهَا فَقَبَّلَهَا وَأَجْلَسَهَا فِي مَجْلِسِهِ، وَكَانَ النَّبِيُّ ﷺ إِذَا دَخَلَ عَلَيْهَا قَامَتْ مِنْ مَجْلِسِهَا فَقَبَّلَتْهُ وَأَجْلَسَتْهُ فِي مَجْلِسِهَا.

> I have not seen anyone closer in conduct and manners to the Messenger of Allah ﷺ, in regards to standing and sitting, than Fāṭima, the daughter of the Prophet. Whenever she would enter the Prophet's company, he would stand for her and kiss her on the forehead and seat her in his place; and whenever the Prophet ﷺ would enter her company, she would stand for him and kiss his blessed hand and seat him in her place.[1]

In this hadith, Sayyida Fāṭima's expression of love and reverence for her beloved father, the Holy Prophet ﷺ, and his expression of love and joy for her is self-evident. In this one narration alone,

---

[1] Narrated by Tirmidhī in *al-Jāmiʿ al-Ṣaḥīḥ*: *Kitāb al-manāqib* [The Book of Exemplary Virtues], chapter: 'The exemplary virtue of Fāṭima', 6:175 §3872; Abū Dāwūd in *al-Sunan*: *Kitāb al-Adab* [The Book of Proper Conduct], chapter: 'What has been related concerning the ritual standing (*qiyām*)', 4:355 §5217; al-Nasāʾī in *al-Sunan al-kubrā*, 5:96 §8369; Ibn Ḥibbān in *al-Ṣaḥīḥ*, 15:403 §9953; al-Ḥākim in *al-Mustadrak*, 3:174 §4753; and Ibn Rāhawayh in *al-Musnad*, 1:8 §6.

we can establish the basis for both the *qiyām li al-farḥa wa al-maḥabba* and the *qiyām li al-taʿẓīm*.

In another narration, Anas b. Mālik narrates:

رَأَى النَّبِيُّ ﷺ النِّسَاءَ وَالصِّبْيَانَ مُقْبِلِينَ، قَالَ: حَسِبْتُ أَنَّهُ قَالَ: مِنْ عُرْسٍ فَقَامَ النَّبِيُّ ﷺ مُمْتَنًّا. فَقَالَ: «اللَّهُمَّ أَنْتُمْ مِنْ أَحَبِّ النَّاسِ إِلَيَّ»؛ قَالَهَا ثَلَاثَ مِرَارٍ.

The most esteemed Prophet ﷺ saw the women and children coming—I think Anas said, 'from a wedding'—and the Prophet ﷺ stood up and said, 'O Allah! You are the most beloved people to me!' He said it thrice.[1]

8.18.3 Standing out of Joy (*Qiyām li al-Farḥa*)

This is the standing which is an expression of extreme happiness and joy. When a person is joyed by someone's arrival, he stands up as an expression of his happiness. Some hadiths on this are narrated below:

1. ʿAwn b. Ḥujayfa narrates from his father:

لَمَّا قَدِمَ جَعْفَرٌ مِنْ هِجْرَةِ الْحَبَشَةِ، تَلَقَّاهُ النَّبِيُّ ﷺ، فَعَانَقَهُ وَقَبَّلَ مَا بَيْنَ عَيْنَيْهِ، وَقَالَ: «مَا أَدْرِي بِأَيِّهِمَا أَنَا أَسَرُّ: بِفَتْحِ خَيْبَرَ أَوْ بِقُدُومِ جَعْفَرٍ؟»

When Jaʿfar came (to Medina) from the migration to Abyssinia, the Prophet ﷺ got up to receive him; he

[1] Narrated by al-Bukhārī in *al-Ṣaḥīḥ*: *Kitāb al-faḍāʾil al-ṣaḥāba* [The Book of the Companions' Exemplary Virtues], chapter: 'The Prophet's statement to the Anṣār: 'You are the most beloved people to me', 3:1379 §3574; al-Bukhārī in *al-Ṣaḥīḥ*: *Kitāb al-Nikāḥ* [The Book of Marriage], chapter: 'Women and children going to a wedding', 5:1985 §4558; Muslim in *al-Ṣaḥīḥ*: *Kitāb Faḍāʾil al-Ṣaḥāba* [The Book of the Companions' Exemplary Virtues], chapter: 'The exemplary virtues of the Anṣār', 4:1984 §2508; Aḥmad b. Ḥanbal in *al-Musnad*, 3:175 §12,820; and Ibn Abī Shayba in al-*Muṣannaf*, 6:398 §32,350.

embraced him and kissed him on his forehead, saying, 'I do not know which pleases me most: the conquest of Khaybar or the coming of Jaʿfar?'[1]

2. ʿIkrima left for Yemen on the occasion of the conquest of Mecca, but his wife played a vital role in bringing him back. Thanks to her involvement, ʿIkrima became a Muslim and came into the Holy Prophet's presence. According to the narration:

فَلَمَّا بَلَغَ بَابَ رَسُوْلِ اللهِ ﷺ، اِسْتَبْشَرَ وَوَثَبَ لَهُ رَسُوْلُ اللهِ ﷺ قَائِماً عَلَى رِجْلَيْهِ فَرِحاً بِقُدُومِهِ.

When he reached to the Prophet's court, the Prophet ﷺ was delighted and got up for him, standing on his feet out of happiness for his arrival.[2]

This standing was *qiyām li al-farḥa*, which was on account of Ikrima's (Abū Jahl's son) conversion to Islam. The Holy Prophet ﷺ was so overjoyed by his arrival that he got up to receive him.

3. One day the Holy Prophet ﷺ was in the house of Sayyida ʿĀʾisha when Zayd b. Ḥāritha knocked on the door. Realising who it was, the most esteemed Prophet ﷺ got up for him immediately. This standing was *qiyām li al-farḥa* and *qiyām li al-istiqbāl*. The hadith scholars have recorded this narration in the books of Islamic etiquettes, which is indicative of its permissibility.

Sayyida ʿĀʾisha narrates: when Zayd b. Ḥāritha came to Medina, the most gracious Prophet ﷺ was in my house. He knocked on the door:

فَقَامَ إِلَيْهِ رَسُولُ اللهِ ﷺ عُرْيَانًا يَجُرُّ ثَوْبَهُ وَاللهِ، مَا رَأَيْتُهُ عُرْيَانًا قَبْلَهُ وَلَا بَعْدَهُ، فَاعْتَنَقَهُ وَقَبَّلَهُ.

---

[1] Narrated by al-Ṭabarānī in *al-Muʿjam al-kabīr*, 2:108 §1470; and al-Ṭaḥāwī in *Sharḥ maʿānī al-āthār*, 4:92 §6764.

[2] Narrated by al-Ḥākim, in *al-Mustadrak*, 3:269 §5055; and al-Bayhaqī, in *al-Madkhal ilā al-sunan al-kubrā*, p.398 §710.

> The Prophet ﷺ got up for him with his body uncovered, dragging his cloth. By Allah, I have never seen the Prophet (meeting someone) in his casual clothes before it or after. The Prophet ﷺ embraced him and kissed him (on his forehead).[1]

The Holy Prophet ﷺ, as soon as he heard Zayd's voice, spontaneously got up for him to express his love and joy. In this way, he taught his community the right etiquettes and proper conduct that when a beloved person arrives, one should stand up to receive him. From this, in the realm of showing one's love and happiness, to kiss one's beloved is the next step after the *qiyām li al-istiqbāl* and the *qiyām li al-farḥa*.

8.18.4 STANDING OUT OF VENERATION (*QIYĀM LI AL-TAʿẒĪM*)

This standing is done out of veneration, in which respect and reverence is the intent, such as a believer's standing for his beloved Prophet ﷺ, a child for his father, a devotee for his shaykh, a student for his teacher, and a junior for his senior. This standing is done due to someone's nobility and dignity.

8.18.4.1 THE DIFFERENCE BETWEEN *QIYĀM LI AL-ISTIQBĀL* AND *QIYĀM LI AL-TAʿẒĪM*

The *qiyām li al-istiqbāl* is to instil confidence in the individual arriving and it is not driven by the motivation of showing respect and reverence. A good example of this is when people stand for the entourage, which arrives with the groom at a wedding; one may not even know all of the people arriving, but one still stands to welcome them. People often stand for a new guest they have met, but this standing is in contrast to the standing of a student for

---

[1] Narrated by Tirmidhī in *al-Jāmiʿ al-Ṣaḥīḥ*: *Kitāb al-Istiʾdhān wa al-Ādāb* [The Book of Asking Permission to Enter and Proper Conduct], chapter: 'What has been related concerning embracing and kissing', 4:450 §2732; al-Ṭaḥāwī in *Sharḥ maʿānī al-āthār*, 4:92 §6765; Zaylaʿī in *Naṣb al-rāya li-takhrīj aḥādīth al-hidāya*, 4:256; al-ʿAsqalānī in *Fatḥ al-Bārī*, 11:52; and al-ʿAsqalānī in *al-Iṣāba fī tamyīz al-Ṣaḥāba*, 2:601.

his teacher or a disciple for his shaykh. Similarly, one may stand out of respect and reverence for the recitation of the Qurʾān, the mentioning of the most revered Prophet ﷺ, and veneration of one's spiritual guide.

8.18.4.2 THE COMPANIONS' PRACTICE OF STANDING FOR THE PROPHET ﷺ OUT OF VENERATION

It was the practice of the noble Companions to stand for the most exalted Prophet ﷺ as an act of veneration.

1. Abū Hurayra ؓ narrates:

كَانَ النَّبِيُّ ﷺ يَجْلِسُ مَعَنَا فِي الْـمَجْلِسِ يُحَدِّثُنَا، فَإِذَا قَامَ قُمْنَا قِيَامًا، حَتَّى نَرَاهُ قَدْ دَخَلَ بَعْضَ بُيُوتِ أَزْوَاجِهِ.

> The Messenger of Allah used to sit with us in the mosque and converse with us. When he arose, we stood standing (as an act of veneration), and we would continue to stand until we saw that he entered one of the homes of his wives.[1]

It is apparent from the above hadith that whenever the Prophet ﷺ got up to leave, the noble Companions would stand up for him. The statement, 'when he arose, we stood standing', clearly indicates that the Companions stood up for the most exalted Prophet ﷺ as an act of veneration and did not sit down until the Holy Prophet ﷺ entered one of his homes. This was their daily practice—not a one-off incident.

Even after the most exalted Prophet ﷺ got up to leave, the gathering would still continue. This does not rule out the possibility that when he left, no person would stop him on his way out, asking him for the fulfilment of his needs. In this manner, before the Holy Prophet ﷺ reached his home, some time would have passed. Despite this, the noble Companions would remain standing until the Holy

---

[1] Narrated by Abū Dāwūd in *al-Sunan*: *Kitāb al-Adab* [The Book of Proper Conduct], chapter: 'Forbearance and the Prophet's character', 4:247 §4775; al-Bayhaqī in *Shuʿab al-īmān*, 6:467 §8930; al-Bayḥaqī, in *al-Madkhal ilā al-sunan al-kubrā*, p.401 §717; and al-ʿAsqalānī in *Fatḥ al-Bārī*, 11:52.

Prophet ﷺ had finally entered his sacred home; they did not leave the Holy Prophet and go to their homes. From this, it is clear that this standing was out of veneration for the Holy Prophet ﷺ.

2. Sayyida Fāṭima used to stand for the Holy Prophet ﷺ out of respect and reverence, as mentioned by Sayyida ʿĀʾisha:

> وَكَانَ النَّبِيُّ ﷺ إِذَا دَخَلَ عَلَيْهَا قَامَتْ مِنْ مَجْلِسِهَا، فَقَبَّلَتْهُ وَأَجْلَسَتْهُ فِي مَجْلِسِهَا.
>
> Whenever the Prophet ﷺ would enter her company, she would stand from her place and then kiss him and seat him in her place.[1]

3. ʿAmar b. Sāʾib narrates that the following hadith was narrated to him:

> أَنَّ رَسُولَ اللهِ ﷺ كَانَ جَالِسًا فَأَقْبَلَ أَبُوهُ مِنَ الرَّضَاعَةِ، فَوَضَعَ لَهُ بَعْضَ ثَوْبِهِ فَقَعَدَ عَلَيْهِ، ثُمَّ أَقْبَلَتْ أُمُّهُ مِنَ الرَّضَاعَةِ فَوَضَعَ لَهَا شِقَّ ثَوْبِهِ مِنْ جَانِبِهِ الْآخَرِ، فَجَلَسَتْ عَلَيْهِ ثُمَّ أَقْبَلَ أَخُوهُ مِنَ الرَّضَاعَةِ، فَقَامَ لَهُ رَسُولُ اللهِ ﷺ فَأَجْلَسَهُ بَيْنَ يَدَيْهِ.
>
> One day when Allah's Messenger ﷺ was sitting, his foster-father arrived so the Prophet ﷺ spread out his cloak for him. Later his foster-mother arrived so he spread out the other half of the cloak and seated her upon it. Then his foster-brother arrived, so he stood up and seated him in front of him.[2]

---

[1] Narrated by Tirmidhī in *al-Jāmiʿ al-Ṣaḥīḥ*: *Kitāb al-manāqib* [The Book of Exemplary Virtues], chapter: 'The exemplary virtue of Fāṭima', 6:175 §3872; Abū Dāwūd in *al-Sunan*: *Kitāb al-Adab* [The Book of Proper Conduct], chapter: 'What has been related concerning the ritual standing (*qiyām*)', 4:355 §5217; al-Nasāʾī in *al-Sunan al-kubrā*, 5:96 §8369; Ibn Ḥibbān in *al-Ṣaḥīḥ*, 15:403 §9953; al-Ḥākim in *al-Mustadrak*, 3:174 §4753; and Ibn Rāhawayh in *al-Musnad*, 1:8 §6.

[2] Narrated by Abū Dāwūd in *al-Sunan*: *Kitāb al-Adab* [The Book of Proper

From the above hadith, the *qiyām li al-taᶜẓīm* is established from the practice of the Holy Prophet ﷺ.

4. It is narrated from Umm Faḍl:

أَتَى النَّبِيُّ ﷺ فَلَمَّا رَآهُ، قَامَ إِلَيْهِ وَقَبَّلَ مَا بَيْنَ عَيْنَيْهِ، ثُمَّ أَقْعَدَهُ عَنْ يَمِيْنِهِ.

> ᶜAbbās came and when the Prophet ﷺ saw him, he stood up for him and kissed him on his forehead, and then he sat him on his right side.[1]

8.18.4.3 THE RITUAL PRAYER IS FOR ALLAH; THE *IQĀMA* IS FOR THE PROPHET ﷺ

According to the majority of Muslims, the Sunna method is to stand for the congregational prayer at the moment when the words '*ḥayya ᶜalā al-ṣalā*' and '*qad qāmat al-ṣalā*' are recited. However, very few people know how this begun and what the motivation was behind it. This standing which takes place when the *iqāma* is recited is in reality an act of veneration for the Holy Prophet ﷺ. It was the Companions' habit that when the *iqāma* was recited and they saw the Holy Prophet ﷺ coming out for the prayer, they would stand in respect for him.

In this way, this standing was not for the *iqāma* but was for the most exalted Prophet ﷺ as an act of veneration in order to make others aware that the Holy Prophet ﷺ had entered the mosque. On this basis, it can be said that the noble Companions' ritual prayer was for Almighty Allah and the *iqāma* was for the most exalted Prophet ﷺ. This is an extremely important point which will be elucidated below:

In our age today, the timings of the prayer are determined

Conduct], chapter: 'Good treatments to parents', 4:337 §5145; Qazwīnī in *al-Tadwīn fī akhbār Qazwīn*, 2:455; and al-ᶜAsqalānī in *Fatḥ al-Bārī*, 11:52.

[1] Narrated by al-Ṭabarānī in *al-Muᶜjam al-awsaṭ*, 10:116 §9246; al-Ṭabarānī in *al-Muᶜjam al-kabīr*, 10:235 §10,580; al-Haythamī in *Majmaᶜ al-zawāʾid wa manbaᶜ al-fawāʾid*, 9:275; and Khaṭīb al-Baghdādī in *Tārīkh Baghdād*, 1:63.

by hours and minutes. The call to prayer (*ādhān*) is called at its appointed time, followed by the *iqāma*. The question that arises here is: in the Holy Prophet's life, how was the ritual prayer established? The answer to this question is that the noble Companions, after listening to the call to prayer for the obligatory prayers, would came to the mosque and offer sunna prayers and then sit in the rows in anticipation of the most esteemed Prophet ﷺ. The time of their ritual prayer was the only moment when the most exalted Prophet ﷺ entered the mosque: until the most esteemed Prophet ﷺ made his appearance, they would remain seated. This was the formula adopted by the Companions.

The Prophet's *muʾadhdhin*, Bilāl b. Rabāḥ, after making the call to prayer, would wait in the corner standing, keeping his gaze fixed towards the Prophet's sacred chambers eagerly, anticipating his arrival. The noble Companions likewise were also eager in anticipation, waiting for the Holy Prophet ﷺ to lead them. Bilāl رضي الله عنه would patiently wait for the sound of the curtain receding; as soon as he heard the curtain move, he would step into the first row and loudly proclaim, 'Allah is the greatest; Allah is the greatest'. From this, the noble Companions would know that the Holy Prophet arrived and thus would stand in their rows with utmost respect and reverence. This was the *qiyām li al-taʿẓīm*, which in the form of the Sunna became one of the signs of Islam.

1. Jābir b. Samura رضي الله عنه narrates:

كَانَ بِلَالٌ يُؤَذِّنُ إِذَا دَحَضَتْ فَلَا يُقِيمُ حَتَّى يَخْرُجَ النَّبِيُّ ﷺ فَإِذَا خَرَجَ أَقَامَ الصَّلَاةَ حِينَ يَرَاهُ.

> Bilāl used to make the call to prayer. He would not recite the *iqāma* until the Prophet ﷺ came out. When he came out, Bilāl would recite the *iqāma* when he saw him.[1]

[1] Narrated by Muslim in *al-Ṣaḥīḥ*: *Kitāb al-Ṣalā* [The Book of the Ritual Prayer], chapter: 'When should people stand for the ritual prayer?', 1:423 §606; al-Tirmidhī in *al-Jāmiʿ al-Ṣaḥīḥ*: *Kitāb al-Ṣalā* [The Book of the Ritual Prayer], chapter: 'What has been related concerning the leader is more worthy of leading the ritual prayer', 1:391 §202; Aḥmad b. Ḥanbal in

Sayyidinā Bilāl would not go to call the most exalted Prophet ﷺ for the ritual prayer. The purpose of the *iqāma* was to inform the noble Companions that the most exalted Prophet ﷺ had come out, and thus they should stand up out of veneration for him. Even today, the standing during the *iqāma* is a means of following this Sunna of the noble Companions; this is the *qiyām li al-istiqbāl* and *qiyām li al-taʿẓīm*.

Bilāl's standing was for the commencement of the *iqāma*, whilst the Companions' standing was for the most exalted Prophet ﷺ. Qāḍī ʿIyāḍ (476-544 AH),) commenting on this hadith, has also mentioned these two classifications. Summarising the differences between them, he states:

بِأَنَّ بِلَالاً رضي الله عنه كَانَ يُرَاقِبُ خُرُوْجَ رَسُوْلِ اللهِ ﷺ مِنْ حَيْثُ لَا يَرَاهُ غَيْرُهُ أَوْ إِلَّا الْقَلِيْلَ، فَلِأَوَّلِ خُرُوْجِهِ أَقَامَ هُوَ: ثُمَّ لَا يَقُوْمُ النَّاسُ حَتَّى يَظْهَرَ لِلنَّاسِ وَيَرَوْهُ، ثُمَّ لَا يَقُوْمُ مَقَامَهُ حَتَّى يَعْدِلُوا صُفُوفَهُمْ.

> Bilāl would wait in anticipation for the Prophet ﷺ in a place where no one could see him, or except a few. At the first instance of the Prophet's entrance, he would recite the *iqāma*; and no one would stand till the Prophet ﷺ became evident to them and they saw him. The Holy Prophet ﷺ would not stand in his place until they straightened their rows.[1]

Qāḍī ʿIyāḍ further states:

وَفِيْهِ أَنَّ الْقِيَامَ لِلصَّلَاةِ لَا يَلْتَزَمُ بِالْإِقَامَةِ أَوْ قَوْلِهِ: قَدْ قَامَتِ الصَّلَاةُ أَوْ حَيَّ عَلَى الْفَلَاحِ، عَلَى مَا نَذْكُرُهُ مِنَ اخْتِلَافِ الْعُلَمَاءِ، وَإِنَّمَا يَلْزَمُ بِخُرُوْجِ الْإِمَامِ.

---

al-Musnad, 5:104 §21,039; and Abū ʿAwāna in *al-Musnad*, 1:372 §1350.

[1] Qāḍī ʿIyāḍ, *Ikmāl al-muʿallim bi fawāʾid Muslim*, 2:556-557.

> It can be established from it that the standing for the ritual prayer is not necessitated by the *iqāma* or by the statement, '*qad qāmat al-ṣalā*', or '*ḥayya ʿalā al-falāḥ*', as we have mentioned in the difference amongst the scholars. It is only necessitated by the arrival of the imam.[1]

Imam Badr al-Dīn al-ʿAynī concerning this states:

وَجْهُ الْـجَمْع بَيْنَهُمَـا أَنَّ بِلَالاً كَانَ يُرَاقِبُ خُرُوْجَ النَّبِيِّ ﷺ مِنْ حَيْثُ لَا يَرَاهُ غَيْرُهُ أَوْ إِلَّا الْقَلِيْلُ، فَعِنْدَ أَوَّلِ خُرُوْجِهِ يُقِيْمُ وَلَا يَقُوْمُ النَّاسُ حَتَّى يَرَوْهُ، ثُمَّ لَا يَقُوْمُ مَقَامَهُ حَتَّى يُعَدِّلَ الصُّفُوفَ.

> The way to reconcile between the two is that Bilāl would wait in anticipation for the Prophet ﷺ in a place where no one could see him, or except a few. At the first instance of the Prophet's entrance, he would recite the *iqāma*, and no one would stand till they saw the Prophet ﷺ. The Prophet ﷺ would not stand in his place until the rows are straightened.[2]

This was the means for Bilāl to fulfil the desire of his consumed love for the most exalted Prophet ﷺ that he should be the first one to behold him. He wanted his eyes to be the first among the others to be placed on the beauty of his Beloved ﷺ. It is as though the proclamation of 'Allah is the greatest, Allah is the greatest' is an announcement that the Beloved ﷺ has arrived, and the noble Companions, after hearing this, would get up to receive him. This was their consistent practice.

And sometimes it just so happened that the most exalted Prophet ﷺ would come out of his blessed home to fulfil some of his needs, and the noble Companions, assuming that the most esteemed Prophet ﷺ has come out to lead them in prayer, would get up, forming their rows. When this happened several times, the Holy

---

[1] Ibid., 2:556.

[2] ʿAynī, *ʿUmda al-qarī sharḥ ṣaḥīḥ al-Bukhārī*, 5:154.

Prophet ﷺ instructed them to form the rows only when he arrived at his place of prayer. In this way, this commandment became the basis for the congregation to stand at the time when the words '*ḥayya ʿalā al-ṣalā*' or '*qad qāmat al-ṣalā*' are recited.

2. Abū Salama b. ʿAbd al-Raḥmān b. ʿAwf states that he heard Abū Hurayra narrate:

أُقِيمَتِ الصَّلَاةُ فَقُمْنَا فَعَدَّلْنَا الصُّفُوفَ قَبْلَ أَنْ يَخْرُجَ إِلَيْنَا رَسُولُ اللهِ ﷺ فَأَتَى رَسُولُ اللهِ ﷺ حَتَّى إِذَا قَامَ فِي مُصَلَّاهُ قَبْلَ أَنْ يُكَبِّرَ ذَكَرَ فَانْصَرَفَ وَقَالَ لَنَا: «مَكَانَكُمْ» فَلَمْ نَزَلْ قِيَامًا نَنْتَظِرُهُ حَتَّى خَرَجَ إِلَيْنَا.

> The *iqāma* for the ritual prayer had been recited, so we straightened our rows before the Messenger of Allah ﷺ came out to us. Allah's Messenger ﷺ came and stood in his place of prayer and just before making the *takbīr* (i.e., commencing the ritual prayer), he remembered (something) and so he went back. He said to us, 'Stay in your places.' So we remained standing, waiting for him, until he came out to us (again).[1]

Thereafter, it became the noble Companions' routine that they would stand for the most exalted Prophet ﷺ upon seeing him, irrespective of whether he came out of his blessed homes or anywhere else. Their act of standing was for veneration. This position is established in the following hadiths:

3. Abū Qatāda narrates that the Prophet ﷺ said:

«إِذَا أُقِيمَتِ الصَّلَاةُ فَلَا تَقُومُوا حَتَّى تَرَوْنِي.»

> When the *iqāma* is recited, do not stand until you see me.[2]

---

[1] Narrated by Muslim in *al-Ṣaḥīḥ*: *Kitāb al-Ṣalā* [The Book of the Ritual Prayer], chapter: 'When should people stand for the ritual prayer?', 1:422 §605; and al-Bayhaqī in *al-Sunan al-kubrā*, 2:398 §3874.

[2] Narrated by al-Bukhārī in *al-Ṣaḥīḥ*: *Kitāb al-Ādhān* [The Book of the

This hadith, which is recorded in *Ṣaḥīḥ al-Bukhārī*, *Ṣaḥīḥ Muslim* and *Jāmiᶜ al-Tirmidhī*, contains the second instruction the Holy Prophet ﷺ gave to his noble Companions, thus resulting in a change in their habit. According to the hadith scholars, one should get up as soon as the *takbīr* is heard.

Imam al-Bukhārī records this hadith in *Kitāb al-Ādhān* [The Book of the Call to Prayer], chapter: 'At the time of reciting the *iqāma* when the imam is seen, when should the people stand?'; Imam Muslim records it in *Kitāb al-Masājid wa Mawāḍiᶜ al-Ṣalā* [The Book of the Mosques and the Ritual Prayer], chapter: 'When should people stand for the prayer?'; and Imam al-Tirmidhī records it in *Kitāb al-Jumuᶜa* [The Book of the Friday Prayer], chapter: 'The reprehensibility for people to wait for the imam whilst they are standing at the start of the prayer'.

The subject of these chapters has been made clear by the imams that the hadiths contained within them are related to standing. Their intention is that they wish to inform people about the time when they should stand before the ritual prayer when the imam is absent or present. They have clarified that one should stand during the recitation of the *iqāma* when they see the imam, as the noble Companions would stand when they saw the most exalted Prophet ﷺ, who was their imam and the imam of all the prophets.

The Prophet's order, 'when the *iqāma* is recited, do not stand until you see me', is worth pondering over. If the intention was not to show respect and reverence to the Holy Prophet, then the Holy Prophet ﷺ would not have ordered them to stand up when they saw him arriving. Rather, he would have ordered them to stand when they heard the *takbīr* of the *iqāma*. It has now been conclusively established that this standing was specific for the Holy Prophet ﷺ and not for the ritual prayer as such, as it was the *qiyām lī al-*

Call to Prayer], chapter: 'At the time of reciting the *iqāma* when the imam is seen, when should the people stand?', 1:228 §611; Muslim in *al-Ṣaḥīḥ*: *Kitāb al-Masājid wa Mawāḍi al-Ṣalā* [The Book of the Mosques and the Ritual Prayer], chapter: 'When should people stand for the prayer?', 1:422 §604; and al-Tirmidhī in *al-Jāmiᶜ al-Ṣaḥīḥ*: *Kitāb al-Jumuᶜa* [The Book of the Friday Prayer], chapter: 'The reprehensibility for people to wait for the imam whilst they are standing at the start of the prayer', 2:287 §592.

istiqbāl and *qiyām lī al-taʿẓīm*.

4. This hadith has been narrated by Imam al-Bukhārī through a different chain of narration through Abū Qatāda, and it was stated that the Prophet ﷺ said:

«إِذَا أُقِيمَتِ الصَّلَاةُ فَلَا تَقُومُوا حَتَّى تَرَوْنِي، وَعَلَيْكُمْ بِالسَّكِينَةِ.»

> When the *iqāma* is recited, do not stand until you see me—calmness is obligated on you (i.e., do not behave hastily for *qiyām*).[1]

This hadith makes it crystal clear that the noble Companions were ordered that they should not stand up during the *iqāma* until they saw the most exalted Prophet ﷺ. This proves that the standing at the time of the *takbīr taḥrīma* is for Almighty Allah and the standing during the *iqāma* is for the most exalted Prophet ﷺ. Almighty Allah has specified the ritual prayer for Himself and the *iqāma* for the most esteemed Prophet ﷺ. Therefore, when the time for the ritual prayer comes, the first standing which takes place is for the Holy Prophet ﷺ, whilst the second one is for Almighty Allah.

5. Isḥāq narrates these additional words from Muʿammar and Shaybān:

«حَتَّى تَرَوْنِي قَدْ خَرَجْتُ.»

> Until you see me that I have come out (for the ritual prayer).[2]

---

[1] Narrated by al-Bukhārī in *al-Ṣaḥīḥ*: *Kitāb al-Ādhān* [The Book of the Call to Prayer], chapter: 'Not to proceed to the prayer hastily and to stand with calmness and dignity ', 1:228 §612; and Ibn Ḥibbān in *al-Ṣaḥīḥ*, 5:51 §1755.

[2] Narrated by Muslim in *al-Ṣaḥīḥ*: *Kitāb al-Ādhān* [The Book of the Call to Prayer], chapter: 'When should people stand for the ritual prayer?', 1:422 §602; al-Tirmidhī, *al-Jāmiʿ al-Ṣaḥīḥ*: *Kitāb al-Jumuʿa* [The Book of the Friday Prayer], chapter: 'The reprehensibility for people to wait for the imam whilst they are standing at the start of the prayer', 2:487 §592; Abū Dāwūd in *al-Sunan*: *Kitāb al-Ṣalā* [The Book of the Ritual Prayer], chapter:

People study *Ṣaḥīḥ Muslim*, but they fail to notice the point the imam is trying to make. The following wordings of *Ṣaḥīḥ Muslim* and the statements of the Companions will make this clear as daylight. This hadith is imbued with the consumed love and reverence for the most exalted Prophet ﷺ. Abū Hurayra narrates:

إِنَّ الصَّلَاةَ كَانَتْ تُقَامُ لِرَسُوْلِ اللهِ ﷺ.

> Surely, the (*qiyām* of the) ritual prayer used to be held for the Prophet ﷺ.

Further, he elaborates that this *iqāma* is only for the sake of the Prophet ﷺ. The reason for this is explained below:

فَيَأْخُذُ النَّاسُ مَصَافَّهُمْ قَبْلَ أَنْ يَقُومَ النَّبِيُّ ﷺ مَقَامَهُ.

> The people would take to their rows before the Prophet ﷺ stood in his place of prayer.[1]

This hadith makes it clear that the *iqāma* was recited so that people would straighten their rows and stand up before the Holy Prophet ﷺ took his place to lead the ritual prayer. Abū Hurayra did not say that the people would straighten their rows for the ritual prayer, rather they would straighten their rows and stand up out of veneration before the Prophet ﷺ took his place. This narration further clarifies that this standing was specific for the Holy Prophet ﷺ and not for the ritual prayer as such, as it was the *qiyām lī al-istiqbāl* and *qiyām lī al-taʿẓīm*.

'The *iqāma* is recited for the ritual prayer and the imam has not yet come, he should be waited for seated', 1:148 §540; Abū ʿAwāna in *al-Musnad*, 2:28; ʿAbd b. Ḥamīd in *al-Musnad*, 1:95 §189; and al-Bayhaqī in *al-Sunan al-kubrā*, 2:20 §2120.

[1] Narrated by Muslim in *al-Ṣaḥīḥ*: *Kitāb al-Ṣalā* [The Book of the Ritual Prayer], chapter: 'When should people stand for the ritual prayer?', 1:423 §605; and Abū Dāwūd in *al-Sunan*: *Kitāb al-Ṣalā* [The Book of the Ritual Prayer], chapter: 'The *iqāma* is recited for the ritual prayer and the imam has not yet come, he should be waited for seated', 1:148 §541.

8.18.5 STANDING FOR HUMAN DIGNITY (*QIYĀM LI AL-IKRĀM AL-INSĀNĪ*)

Honouring a deceased person falls within the ambit of *ikrām li al-insān*. This is established in the Sunna of the Prophet ﷺ. It was the Prophet's practice to stand for a funeral procession as it passed by as a show of respect—this was his practice even if the deceased was not a Muslim. This gesture of respect was on account of a human being.

1. ᶜĀmir b. Rabīᶜa narrates that the Prophet ﷺ said:

«إِذَا رَأَيْتُمُ الْجَنَازَةَ فَقُومُوا حَتَّى تُخَلِّفَكُمْ.»

> If you see the funeral procession, stand (in respect) until it passes you.[1]

2. In another narration, ᶜĀmir b. Rabīᶜa narrates:

«إِذَا رَأَيْتُمُ الْجَنَازَةَ فَقُومُوا لَهَا حَتَّى تُخَلِّفَكُمْ أَوْ تُوضَعَ.»

> If you see the funeral procession, stand for it until it passes you or it is laid to rest.[2]

This command of the Prophet ﷺ is for the dignity of a human body.

3. On this topic of human dignity, Imam al-Bukhārī (194-256

---

[1] Narrated by al-Bukhārī in *al-Ṣaḥīḥ*: *Kitāb al-Janāʾiz* [The Book of Funeral Ceremonies], chapter: 'Standing for the funeral', 1:440 §1245; al-Nasāʾī in *al-Sunan al-kubrā*, 1:625 §2042; Ibn Ḥibbān in *al-Ṣaḥīḥ*, 7:323 §3051; and al-Bayhaqī in *al-Sunan al-kubrā*, 4:25 §6660.

[2] Narrated by Muslim in *al-Ṣaḥīḥ*: *Kitāb al-Janāʾiz* [The Book of Funeral Ceremonies], chapter: 'Standing for the funeral', 2:659 §958; al-Tirmidhī in *al-Jāmiᶜ al-Ṣaḥīḥ*: *Kitāb al-Janāʾiz* [The Book of Funeral Ceremonies], chapter: 'What has been related concerning standing for the funeral', 3:360 §1042; Abū Dāwūd in *al-Sunan*: *Kitāb al-Janāʾiz* [The Book of Funeral Ceremonies], chapter: 'Standing for the funeral', 3:203 §3172; Ibn Mājah in *al-Sunan*: *Kitāb al-Janāʾiz* [The Book of Funeral Ceremonies], chapter: 'What has been related concerning standing for the funeral', 1:492 §1542; and al-Ḥākim in *al-Mustadrak*, 3:404 §5537.

AH) in his *Ṣaḥīḥ* has narrated a hadith regarding a Jew under the chapter-heading, '*man qāma li-janāza yahūdī*' [Whoever stands for the funeral of a Jew] in *Kitāb al-Janāʾiz* [The Book of Funeral Ceremonies]. Jābir b. ʿAbd Allāh narrates:

مَرَّتْ بِنَا جَنَازَةٌ، فَقَامَ لَـهَا النَّبِيُّ ﷺ وَقُمْنَا لَهُ.

A funeral procession passed by, and the Prophet ﷺ stood up for it and we stood up for him.

One should take note of the noble Companions' etiquettes and good conduct here: they did not remain seated, but upon seeing the most exalted Prophet ﷺ standing, they immediately without delay, got up to stand for him. But they asked the Holy Prophet ﷺ what they felt:

يَارَسُوْلَ اللهِ! إِنَّهَا جَنَازَةُ يَهُودِيٍّ؟

O Messenger of Allah! It is a funeral of a Jew.

Listening to what they had to say, the Prophet ﷺ said:

«إِذَا رَأَيْتُمُ الْـجَنَازَةَ فَقُومُوا.»

If you see the funeral procession, stand.[1]

Irrespective of the funeral being of a Jew or a Muslim, whenever a funeral procession passes by, one should stand up for it out of respect. This standing is on account of dignity of a deceased body. There is no difference in humanity between a Jew and a Muslim: both are human beings. Therefore, for the respect of humanity, the dead bodies of both deserve respect.

---

[1] Narrated by al-Bukhārī in *al-Ṣaḥīḥ*: *Kitāb al-Janāʾiz* [The Book of Funeral Ceremonies], chapter: 'Standing for the funeral', 1:441 §1249; Aḥmad b. Ḥanbal in *al-Musnad*, 3:354; al-Ṭaḥāwī in *Sharḥ maʿānī al-āthār*: *Kitāb al-Janāʾiz* [The Book of Funeral Ceremonies], chapter: 'If a funeral procession passes by a people: should they stand for it or not?', 2:14 §2717; and al-Bayhaqī in *al-Sunan al-kubrā*, 4:26.

Imam al-Bukhārī[1] (194-256 AH), Imam Muslim[2] (206-261 AH), Imam Aḥmad b. Ḥanbal[3] (164-241 AH), Imam al-Nasāʾī[4] (215-303 AH),) and Imam al-Ṭaḥāwī[5] (229-321 AH) have all related similar hadiths on this subject.

The lesson that can be derived from these hadiths is that the most exalted Prophet ﷺ, through his example, is teaching his community that one should stand for the funeral procession as a gesture of respect. Those who completely object to the ritual standing (*qiyām*) unfortunately have no connection with the Sunna whatsoever, as it is has been established that the Holy Prophet ﷺ would perform the ritual standing (*qiyām*) in circumstances other than the prayer. The most compassionate Prophet ﷺ set such high standards of good morals that if a person sees a funeral, irrespective of whether it is a funeral of a Muslim or a non-Muslim, one should stand as a gesture of respect. This standing was on account of human dignity, as a means of respecting the humanity of the deceased; and doing such a thing is established in the Prophet's teachings.

If a deceased body is deserving respect and it is the Sunna of the Prophet ﷺ, then how can standing for the most exalted Prophet ﷺ at the time of sending one's salutations on him, reciting poetical praise in his honour, and expressing one's love for him be declared an impermissible act in the Sharia?

---

1 Al-Bukhārī in *al-Ṣaḥīḥ*: *Kitāb al-Janāʾiz* [The Book of Funeral Ceremonies], chapter: 'Standing for the funeral of a Jew', 1:441 §1250.

2 Muslim in *al-Ṣaḥīḥ*: *Kitāb al-Janāʾiz* [The Book of Funeral Ceremonies], chapter: 'Standing for the funeral', 2:661 §961.

3 Aḥmad b. Ḥanbal, *al-Musnad*, 6:6.

4 Al-Nasāʾ in *al-Ṣaḥīḥ*: *Kitāb al-Janāʾiz* [The Book of Funeral Ceremonies], chapter: 'Standing for the funeral of a polytheist', 4:45 §1921; and al-Nasāʾī, *al-Sunan al-kubrā*, 1:626 §2048.

5 Al-Ṭaḥāwī in *Sharḥ maʿānī al-āthār*: *Kitāb al-Janāʾiz* [The Book of Funeral Ceremonies], chapter: 'If a funeral procession passes by a people: should they stand for it or not?', 2:13 §2714.

8.18.6 Standing for Remembrance (*Qiyām li al-Dhikr*)

One of the forms of the ritual standing (*qiyām*) is the standing for remembrance (*qiyām li al-dhikr*). What this entails is the act of standing for some religious or spiritual purpose or for the purpose of promulgating the teachings of the religion. Examples of this include a teacher's standing to teach a lesson, a preacher's standing on the pulpit to deliver a sermon, or a reciter's standing for the recitation of the Qur'ān. Almighty Allah says:

﴿ٱلَّذِينَ يَذْكُرُونَ ٱللَّهَ قِيَـٰمًا وَقُعُودًا وَعَلَىٰ جُنُوبِهِمْ﴾

These are the people who, remembering Allah, remain standing (as the epitome of submissiveness), sitting (as reverence incarnate), and (also keep) changing sides (in discomfort of love).[1]

Salutation of peace is the remembrance of Allah's Beloved ﷺ, and Almighty Allah has declared the Prophet's remembrance His own.[2] This is similar to Almighty Allah decreeing obedience to the Holy Prophet ﷺ as an act of obedience to Him[3]; disobedience to the Holy Prophet ﷺ as an act of disobedience to Him[4]; the Prophet's pleasure as His own pleasure[5]; the Prophet's performance as His own performance[6]; offence to the Holy Prophet ﷺ as an offence to Almighty Allah[7]; and defiance to the Holy Prophet ﷺ as an act of defiance to Almighty Allah[8].

---

[1] Qur'ān 3:191.

[2] Qur'ān 94:4; and Ibn Ḥibbān, *al-Ṣaḥīḥ*, 8:175 §3382.

[3] Qur'ān 4:80.

[4] Qur'ān 4:14; 33:36 & 72:23.

[5] Qur'ān 9:62.

[6] Qur'ān 8:17.

[7] Qur'ān 33:57.

[8] Qur'ān 4:14.

8.18.6.1 The Prophet's Remembrance is Allah's Remembrance

Due to the Holy Prophet's esteemed morality, intense humility and perfect servitude, the Creator of the Universe, Almighty Allah, has declared the Prophet's remembrance as more exalted than anything else in creation.

Almighty Allah says:

﴿وَرَفَعْنَا لَكَ ذِكْرَكَ﴾

And We exalted for you your remembrance (by annexing it to Ours everywhere in the world and in the Hereafter).[1]

Concerning this declaration, the following hadith narrated by Abū Saʿīd al-Khudrī explains this verse beautifully:

أَنَّ رَسُوْلَ اللهِ ﷺ قَالَ: «أَتَانِي جِبْرِيْلُ، فَقَالَ: إِنَّ رَبِّي وَرَبُّكَ يَقُوْلُ لَكَ: كَيْفَ رَفَعْتُ ذِكْرَكَ؟ قَالَ: اللهُ أَعْلَمُ. قَالَ: إِذَا ذُكِرْتُ ذُكِرْتَ مَعِي.»

Allah's Messenger said, 'Jibrāʾīl came to me and said, 'Indeed, my Lord and your Lord has asked you, 'How have I raised your remembrance?'' The Prophet replied, 'Allah knows best.' Allah said, 'If I am remembered, you are remembered with Me.''[2]

In light of this hadith *qudsī*, it is necessary to bring together the remembrance of Almighty Allah and the remembrance of the

[1] Qurʾān 94:4.

[2] Narrated by Ibn Ḥibbān in *al-Ṣaḥīḥ*, 8:175 §3382; Abū Yaʿlā in *al-Musnad*, 2:522 §1380; Khilāl in *al-Sunna*, 1:262 §318, has declared this chain of narration as fine (*ḥasan*); al-Daylamī in *al-Firdaws bi-maʾthūr al-khiṭāb*, 4:405 §7176; al-Ḥaythamī in *Mawārid al-ẓamʾān ilā zawāʾid Ibn Ḥibbān*, p.439 §1772; Ibn Abī Ḥātim al-Rāzī in *Tafsīr al-Qurʾān al-ʿaẓīm*, 10:3445 §19,393; al-ʿAsqalānī in *Fatḥ al-Bārī*, 8:712; Ibn Kathīr in *Tafsīr al-Qurʾān al-ʿaẓīm*, 4:524; and al-Suyūṭī in *al-Durr al-manthūr fī al-tafsīr bi al-maʾthūr*, 8:549.

Holy Prophet ﷺ. The Prophet's remembrance is not something other than Allah's remembrance. In any other scenario, there is no other means of receiving such acceptance in the most exalted court of Almighty Allah. This is because Almighty Allah has made the remembrance of His beloved Prophet ﷺ His remembrance, and hence it is acceptable to remember them together. Remembering Almighty Allah in the standing position is permissible, and therefore remembering the Holy Prophet ﷺ whilst invoking peace and blessings in the standing position is also permissible.

8.18.7 Standing to Invoke Peace and Blessings (*Qiyām li al-Ṣalāt wa al-Salām*)

Amongst the various forms of the ritual standing is the standing to invoke peace and blessings on the Prophet (*qiyām li al-ṣalāt wa al-salām*). In this standing, invocations of peace and blessings are sent on the Prophet's person with utmost repect and reverence. This standing comprises various other types of *qiyām*, such as: *qiyām li al-maḥabba*, *qiyām li al-farḥa*, *qiyām li al-taʿẓīm*, and *qiyām li al-dhikr*.

When we take the issue of standing for invoking peace and blessings, as is practiced in the *mawlid* gatherings, all the discussions on the matter of standing and not standing are irrelevant, as they have no connection with the blessed birth of the chief of the created beings as the standing described here is not the standing to welcome someone (*qiyām li al-istiqbāl*). Hence, from the outset, we consider it absurd to debate whether the *qiyām* should be for *istiqbāl* or not, as this standing is essentially for *taʿẓīm* (respect) which is prompted by *farḥa* (happiness) and *maḥabba* (love). These forms of *qiyām* are established in the Sunna of the Holy Prophet ﷺ, and thus there is no opportunity to oppose or differ on this. Making the *qiyām* in the *mawlid* a source of contention is simply invalid.

Offering invocations of peace and blessings in the Prophet's most exalted court in the standing position is the Sunna of Prophet Mūsā.

1. Anas b. Mālik narrates the following account of the Heavenly Ascension. Regarding the most exalted Heavenly Ascension, the Prophet ﷺ said:

«مَرَرْتُ عَلَى مُوسَى وَهُوَ يُصَلِّي فِي قَبْرِهِ.»

> I passed by Mūsā whilst he was reciting *ṣalāt* in his tomb![1]

2. In a different chain of transmission, Anas b. Mālik narrates that the most exalted Prophet ﷺ said:

«مَرَرْتُ عَلَى مُوسَى لَيْلَةَ أُسْرِيَ بِـي عِنْدَ الْكَثِيبِ الْأَحْمَرِ وَهُوَ قَائِمٌ يُصَلِّي فِي قَبْرِهِ.»

> On the night when I was transported on the Heavenly Ascension, I passed by Mūsā at the red sandbank and (saw that) Mūsā was busy reciting *ṣalāt* in his tomb![2]

Mūsā was invoking blessings (*ṣalāt*) on the Prophet ﷺ. For further clarification, a discourse on the word *ṣalāt* will be discussed below:

---

[1] Narrated by Muslim in *al-Ṣaḥīḥ*: *Kitāb al-Faḍāʾil* [The Book of the Virtuous Merits], chapter: 'The virtuous merits of Mūsā', 4:1845 §2375; al-Nasāʾī in *al-Sunan*: *Kitāb Qiyām al-Layl wa Taṭṭawaᶜ al-Nahar* [The Book of Night Vigil and Supererogatory Prayers in the Day], chapter: 'Mentioning the prayer of Allah's Prophet, Mūsā', 3:151 §1637; al-Nasāʾī in *al-Sunan al-kubrā*, 1:419 §1329; Aḥmad b. Ḥanbal in *al-Musnad*, 3:120; Ibn Ḥibbān in *al-Ṣaḥīḥ*, 1:241 §49; and Abū Yaᶜlā in *al-Musnad*, 7:127 §4085.

[2] Narrated by Muslim in *al-Ṣaḥīḥ*: *Kitāb al-Faḍāʾil* [The Book of the Virtuous Merits], chapter: 'The virtuous merits of Mūsā', 4:1845 §2375; Aḥmad b. Ḥanbal in *al-Musnad*, 3:148; al-Bayhaqī in *Dalāʾil al-Nubuwwa wa maᶜrifa aḥwāl Ṣāḥib al-Sharīᶜa* ﷺ, 2:387; Subkī in *Shifāʾ al-siqām fī ziyāra Khayr al-ānām*, p.137; al-Maqrīzī in *Imtāᶜ al-asmāᶜ bi mā li Nabī min al-aḥwāl wa al-amwāl wa al-ḥafada wa al-matāᶜ*, 8:250; Ibid., 10:304; al-Suyūṭī in *al-Ḥāwī li al-fatāwā*, p.668; and al-Sakhāwī in *al-Qawl al-badīᶜ fī al-ṣalā ᶜalā al-Ḥabīb al-Shafīᶜ*, p.168.

8.18.7.1 The Meaning of *Ṣalāt*: Invocation of Peace and Blessings

Generally, this hadith is translated in the following way that when the master of the created beings, the Holy Prophet ﷺ, passed by Mūsā on the night of the Heavenly Ascension, Mūsā was offering the ritual prayer in his grave.

The interpretation which the author has drawn and inferred that Mūsā was in fact invoking peace and blessings on the Prophet ﷺ, does not contradict the apparent wordings of the hadith. Mūsā along with the rest of the prophets, had gathered to welcome and receive the most exalted Prophet ﷺ at *Masjid al-Aqṣā*. All were aware that the most esteemed Prophet ﷺ had already started his Night Journey, that he would lead them in prayer at *Masjid al-Aqṣā*, and that this would occur prior to the remainder of his Heavenly Ascension. The most exalted Prophet ﷺ was scheduled to meet Mūsā in the heavens, and Mūsā was destined to pray behind him in Jerusalem.

Additionally, this journey was not made by means of any worldly transport, rather it was made by riding on the *Burrāq*, whose speed was such that the human mind simply cannot fathom. The *Burrāq* would cover far greater distances in a moment than the speed of light. Bearing all these facts in minds, how could it be that Mūsā was offering supererogatory cycles of ritual prayer when the Holy Prophet ﷺ passed by his tomb? If the ritual prayer in question was obligatory, then this would be understandable; but there is no obligatory prayer after one's death in the life of *barzakh*. If any such acts of worship are offered by prophets and saints, it would fall under the category of the supererogatory ritual prayers.

The important point to bear in mind is that Mūsā was well aware that the most exalted Prophet ﷺ was about to pass by him on his Journey of Ascension from *Masjid al-Ḥarām*. Therefore, it is not correct to suggest that Mūsā was offering supererogatory ritual prayers whilst the most exalted Prophet ﷺ passed by his tomb. Thus, the interpretation of the above hadith is that Mūsā was standing in his grave and invoking peace and blessings upon the Holy Prophet ﷺ. This conclusion is not contrary to the apparent text of the hadith since all the prophets were aware that the most exalted Prophet ﷺ will be the prayer-leader and that Mūsā would be praying behind the Prophet ﷺ at *Masjid al-Aqṣā*. Hence, it is unreasonable to suggest that he would offer supererogatory ritual prayers when he was well aware of his appointed meeting with the Prophet ﷺ.

8.18.7.2 THE LITERAL MEANING OF THE WORD *ṢALĀT*

The correct meaning of the word '*ṣalāt*' in the statement, 'he was reciting *ṣalāt* in his tomb,' is not the ritual prayer, but invoking peace and blessings. The word '*ṣalāt*' is not only used for the ritual prayer, but it is also used for showering mercy, praising someone, and sending salutations.

Imam al-Murtaḍā al-Zabīdī concerning the meaning of the word '*ṣalāt*', writes:

وَقَالَ ابْنُ الأَعْرَابِيّ: اَلصَّلَاةُ مِنَ اللهِ الرَّحْمَةُ، وَمِنْهُ ﴿هُوَ ٱلَّذِى يُصَلِّى عَلَيْكُمْ﴾ أَيْ يَرْحَمُ.

Ibn al-Aʿrābī said: *al-ṣalāt* from Allah ﷻ means showering mercy. For example, the verse, ﴾*He is the One who sends ṣalāt upon you*﴿,[1] means that He showers mercy upon you.[2]

Ibn Manẓūr (630-711 AH), regarding the verse, ﴾*It is they upon whom are bestowed successive blessings and mercy from their Lord*﴿'[3] states that it means:

فَمَعْنَى الصَّلَوَاتِ هَهُنَا الثَّنَاءُ عَلَيْهِم مِّنَ اللهِ تَعَالَى.

The meaning of *ṣalawāt* here is Allah's praise for them.[4]

---

[1] Qurʾān 33:43.

[2] Al-Zubaydī, *Tāj al-ʿurūs min jawāhir al-qamūs*, 19:607.

[3] Qurʾān 2:157.

[4] Ibn Manẓūr, *Lisān al-ʿArab*, 14:465.

8.18.7.3 Applying the Literal Meaning of *Ṣalāt*

The application of the word, '*ṣalāt*', can be found in the following verses and hadiths:

1. Almighty Allah states:

﴿إِنَّ ٱللَّهَ وَمَلَٰٓئِكَتَهُۥ يُصَلُّونَ عَلَى ٱلنَّبِيِّۚ يَٰٓأَيُّهَا ٱلَّذِينَ ءَامَنُواْ صَلُّواْ عَلَيۡهِ وَسَلِّمُواْ تَسۡلِيمًا﴾

Surely, Allah and (all) His angels send blessings and greetings on the Holy Prophet ﷺ. O believers! Invoke blessings on him and salute him with a worthy salutation of peace abundantly (and fervently).[1]

2. In another verse, Almighty Allah states:

﴿هُوَ ٱلَّذِي يُصَلِّي عَلَيۡكُمۡ وَمَلَٰٓئِكَتُهُۥ لِيُخۡرِجَكُم مِّنَ ٱلظُّلُمَٰتِ إِلَى ٱلنُّورِ﴾

He is the One Who sends peace and blessings on you and His angels as well, so that He may take you out of the layers of darkness into the light.[2]

3. In the hadiths, this word has been used abundantly in the meaning of invoking peace and blessings. For example, ʿAbd Allāh b. Masʿūd narrates that the Holy Prophet ﷺ said:

«مَنْ صَلَّى عَلَيَّ صَلَاةً صَلَّى اللهُ عَلَيْهِ بِهَا عَشْرًا وَكَتَبَ لَهُ بِهَا عَشْرَ حَسَنَاتٍ.»

Whoever invokes blessings upon me once, Allah will invoke blessings on him in exchange of it ten times, and ten good deeds will be written for him.[3]

---

[1] Qurʾān 33:56.

[2] Qurʾān 33:43.

[3] Narrated by al-Tirmidhī in *al-Jāmiʿ al-Ṣaḥīḥ*: *Kitāb al-Ṣalā* [The Book of the Ritual Prayer], chapter: 'What has been related concerning the

From this explanation, it is known from the above hadith that the word '*ṣalāt*' means 'invoking peace and blessings upon the Prophet ﷺ'. Therefore, when Mūsā stood reciting *ṣalāt*, he was in fact sending his salutations to welcome the most exalted Prophet ﷺ.

Imam al-Shaʿrānī (898-973 AH) writes about the Heavenly Ascent in *al-Yawāqīt wa al-jawāhir fī bayān ʿaqāʾid al-akābir*:

> When the Prophet ﷺ (during the Heavenly Ascension) passed *Sidra al-muntahā,* he left the *Burrāq* behind and then ascended through the *rafraf* to the station interpreted as ﴿*Thumma danā fa tadallā*﴾. He was then admitted and exalted in the court of Almighty Allah at the station described as ﴿*danā fa tadallā*﴾. At this place, apart from Almighty Allah and His Beloved, no one else was present there. Almighty Allah spoke to His beloved and proclaimed:
>
> «يَا مُحَمَّدُ! قِفْ، إِنَّ رَبَّكَ يُصَلِّي.»
>
> O Muhammad! Stop. Your Lord showers His mercy upon you.[1]

It is clear from the circumstances of the night of the Heavenly Ascension that the *ṣalāt* which Almighty Allah was sending on His beloved Prophet ﷺ was the same *ṣalāt* which was being offered by the glorious Prophet Mūsā. That night, Mūsā was not performing supererogatory ritual prayers, but in light of the above, he was sending his salutations of peace and blessings upon the Holy Prophet ﷺ; this blessing was for congratulation, respect, and reverence.

Thus to reiterate, the meaning of *ṣalāt* should not be confined to the ritual prayer. Rather, it should be understood as an act of invoking peace and blessings on the most respectful Prophet ﷺ; this was the act which Mūsā was performing when described in the hadith as 'reciting *ṣalāt* standing'. This information was conveyed

---

excellence of *ṣalāt* upon the Prophet ﷺ', 2:354 §484.

[1] Al-Shaʿrānī, *al-Yawāqīt wa al-jawāhir fī bayān ʿaqāʾid al-akābir*, 2:367.

to us by the most rightful Prophet ﷺ, who states that he saw Mūsā in the state of performing the *ṣalāt*. In other words, Mūsā was standing in his grave, invoking peace and blessings on the Holy Prophet ﷺ.

One may accept any of the two interpretations. But why did the Holy Prophet ﷺ feel the need to mention this incident in the first place? If Mūsā was performing the ritual prayer, then this was a matter between him and Almighty Allah. Every Prophet performs the supererogatory ritual prayer in their illuminated tombs; this is not an unusual thing. But this still begs the question: what was the point that the most venerable Prophet ﷺ was trying to make in the Journey of Ascension? The most esteemed Prophet ﷺ wanted his *Umma* (community) to know that Mūsā was his devoted lover, and that he offered his respects to him when the most exalted Prophet ﷺ passed by on the night of the Heavenly Ascension. In this manner, the Holy Prophet ﷺ was teaching his community the proper etiquettes of sending salutations upon him.

4. Within *Ṣaḥīḥ Muslim* in *Kitāb al-Īmān* [The Book of Faith], chapter: 'Mentioning of the Messiah, the son of Mary, and the Antichrist', a similar hadith on this subject has also been mentioned. Imam al-Sakhāwī (831-902 AH) in *al-Qawl al-badīʿ fī al-ṣalā ʿalā al-Ḥabīb al-Shafīʿ* has also mentioned this hadith concerning Mūsā within the subject of invoking peace and blessings on the Prophet ﷺ:

Abū Hurayra narrates that the most exalted Prophet ﷺ said:

«قَدْ رَأَيتُنِي فِي جَمَاعَةٍ مِنَ الْأَنْبِيَاءِ، فَإِذَا مُوْسَى قَائِمٌ يُصَلِّي، فَإِذَا رَجُلٌ ضَرْبٌ جَعْدٌ كَأَنَّهُ مِنْ رِجَالِ شَنُوءَةَ.»

I saw myself in the company of the prophets. There was Mūsā standing reciting *ṣalāt*. He was a tall, slim man with curly hair, as though he was from amongst the tribesmen of *Shanūʾa*.

«وَإِذَا عِيسَى ابنُ مَرْيَمَ عليه السلام قَائِمٌ يُصَلِّي، أَقْرَبُ النَّاسِ بِهِ شَبَهاً عُرْوَةُ بْنُ مَسْعُودٍ الثَّقَفِيُّ.»

> Then I saw ʿĪsā b. Maryam standing reciting *ṣalāt*. The person resembling him the most is ʿUrwa b. Masʿūd al-Thaqafī.
>
> «وَإِذَا إِبْرَاهِيمَ عَلَيْهِ السَّلَامُ قَائِمٌ يُصَلِّي، أَشْبَهُ النَّاسِ بِهِ صَاحِبُكُمْ يَعْنِي نَفْسَهُ، فَحَانَتِ الصَّلَاةُ فَأَمَمْتُهُمْ.»
>
> Then I saw Ibrāhīm standing reciting *ṣalāt*. The person resembling him the most is your master (i.e. the Prophet ﷺ). Then the time for prayer came, so I lead them in congregation.[1]

This narration explains that on the night of the Heavenly Ascension, all the prophets were standing and reciting their salutations of peace and blessings upon the most esteemed Prophet ﷺ. Once this reception took place, the most exalted Prophet ﷺ led them all in prayer.

8.18.8 STANDING DURING THE *MAWLID* IS NOT HELD TO RECEIVE THE PROPHET ﷺ

On the subject of *qiyām*, we would like to clarify why we perform it and for whom it is done. It is of utmost importance to remove a misconception here that, God-forbid, we do not perform the *qiyām* because we believe that the Prophet's birth is taking place at that time, or that the Holy Prophet ﷺ is entering the gathering at that very moment, and thus we are standing to welcome him. Such an understanding can never be the faith of a Muslim; this is not the 'standing to welcome someone' (*qiyām li al-istiqbāl*). Also, this *qiyām* is not for anyone who participates in the *mawlid* gathering.

---

[1] Narrated by Muslim in *al-Ṣaḥīḥ*: *Kitāb al-Īmān* [The Book of Faith], chapter: 'Mentioning of the Messiah, the son of Mary, and the Antichrist', 1:157 §172; Khaṭīb Tabrīzī in *Mishkāt al-maṣābīḥ: Kitāb Aḥwāl al-Qiyāma wa Badʾ al-Khalq*, 3:379 §5866; al-Bayhaqī in *Dalāʾil al-Nubuwwa wa maʿrifa aḥwāl Ṣāḥib al-Sharīʿa* ﷺ, 2:387; Subkī in *Shifāʾ al-siqām fī ziyāra Khayr al-anām*, p.135 & 138; al-Maqrīzī in *Imtāʿ al-asmāʿ bi mā li Nabī min al-aḥwāl wa al-amwāl wa al-ḥafada wa al-matāʿ*, 8:249; and al-Sakhāwī in *al-Qawl al-badīʿ fī al-ṣalā ʿalā al-Ḥabīb al-Shafīʿ*, p.168.

It is not farfetched that the Holy Prophet ﷺ may come to the gatherings of *Mawlid al-Nabī* ﷺ spiritually. From a spiritual perspective, such a thing is possible. If the Holy Prophet ﷺ wishes, he may go wherever he wants. This is not the case physically, because his blessed body is in a state of rest in his illuminated sacred tomb in Medina. But like the angels and spirits, he can go wherever he wants on a spiritual basis. As has been the case with many *awliyāʿ* (divine friends of Almighty Allah), if someone sees him in a dream or has a vision while being awake, without doubt that person has been blessed in seeing him. Even though it looks like the Holy Prophet ﷺ is being seen physically, in reality it is his spirit appearing in the image of his body (*al-rūḥ al-tamthīl* or *al-rūḥ al-mutamaththila*). An example of this is when Angel Jibrāʾīl or the Angel of Death are witnessed in human form. On this note, there are some examples of this in the Qurʾān and hadith:

In the Qurʾān, it states that Angel Jibrāʾīl came to Sayyida Maryam in the form of a man:

﴿فَأَرْسَلْنَآ إِلَيْهَا رُوحَنَا فَتَمَثَّلَ لَهَا بَشَرًا سَوِيًّا﴾

Then We sent towards her Our Spirit (the angel, Gabriel), who appeared before her in complete form of a human being.[1]

The understanding of '*basharan sawiyyan*' is that Jibrāʾīl came to Sayyida Maryam in the form of a living human being. According to the narrations, Jibrāʾīl came to the Holy Prophet ﷺ in the form of a man.[2]

The true orthodox belief is that the blessed body of the Mercy

---

[1] Qurʾān 19:17.

[2] Narrated by al-Bukhārī in *al-Ṣaḥīḥ*: *Kitāb al-Īmān* [The Book of Faith], chapter: 'Jibrāʾīl's questioning the Prophet concerning *Īmān*, *Islam* and *Iḥsān*', 1:27 §50; al-Bukhārī in *al-Ṣaḥīḥ*: *Kitāb al-Tafsīr al-Qurʾān* [The Book of Exegesis of Qurʾān], chapter: 'His statement: with Allah is the knowledge of the hour', 4:1793 §4499; and Muslim in *al-Ṣaḥīḥ*: *Kitāb al-Īmān* [The Book of Faith], chapter: 'Concerning *Īmān*, *Islam* and *Iḥsān*', 1:37 &39 §8–9.

for the worlds, Prophet Muhammad ﷺ, is resting in his holy shrine, but his sanctified soul is able to appear at any place, any time. It is utmost disrespect to slander the Holy Prophet to say that he cannot go wherever he wishes with his spirit, although he has been bestowed this divinely power to go anywhere spiritually, like the angels. When the spirit appears looking like the body, it is interpreted as *tamaththul al-rūḥ* or *tajassud al-rūḥ*. This is the case when Almighty Allah mentions the account of Jibrāʾīl when he appeared before Sayyida Maryam ﷺ.

Even though the Holy Prophet ﷺ has the capacity to appear spiritually in a physical form, it has never been the faith of any Muslim amongst the *Ahl al-Sunna* to believe that the Holy Prophet ﷺ actually arrives at the gatherings of *mawlid* with his physical body, and because of this, they do not stand up for the purpose of welcoming him (*qiyām li al-istiqbāl*). If anyone says such a thing, it is a false accusation that has nothing to do with reality.

The participants of the *mawlid* stand whilst invoking peace and blessings on the Holy Prophet ﷺ only as a symbol of respect. This standing is not because the most exalted Prophet ﷺ, God forbid, is being born at that moment—only a foolish and an unsound individual would make such a statement. The *qiyām* during the *mawlid* gatherings is only a gesture of respect in honour of that memory. Undoubtedly, the blessed birth of the most exalted Prophet ﷺ carries so much dignity and sublimity that having its remembrance is even more virtuous. This veneration expects that we should offer our salutation of peace on the person and attributes of the Merciful Prophet ﷺ standing.

8.18.9 THE RITUAL STANDING FOR *THE MAWLID* IN ESSENCE IS FOR HAPPINESS AND JOY

Mentioning the Prophet's birth is an expectation of our love, desire and attachment to the most exalted Prophet ﷺ. Whenever the month of his blessed birth draws near, it is essential that we thank Almighty Allah for showering on us the greatest blessing and the greatest benevolence. With the emergence of the Holy Prophet ﷺ, the light of truth, certainty, and guidance spread everywhere, and the darkness of *shirk* (polytheism) vanished.

Through the means of His Beloved Messenger ﷺ, Almighty Allah made the darkness that had enveloped the entire human race to fade away. Amidst the shadows of misguidance and error, the divine light appeared and the radiance of the rays of divine light caused a new dawn to brighten the horizon. Therefore, during the *mawlid* it is binding upon us to express unlimited gratitude to Almighty Allah for this unparalleled grace. This month, and particularly his noble day of birth, is of special blessing and mercy.

The jewel of creation, the Holy Prophet ﷺ, graced this finite world with limitless treasures of happiness and joy that spread throughout the heavens and the earth. To perform the *qiyām* whilst recollecting this event in a state where one is completely absorbed in the love of his beloved is a sign of sound faith.

All the aforementioned hadiths support the concept of the ritual standing (*qiyām*). Similarly, arrays of narration are available in the hadith books regarding the practice of eulogising him through odes and poems. This act is in fact a Sunna that the vast majority of imams and hadith scholars throughout history have maintained by recording these hadiths and voicing their own opinions in favour of it as well.

Concluding this chapter on *qiyām*, we can say that standing is absolutely permissible and legitimate for people according to their status. A student respectfully stands for his teacher, a host for his guest, a disciple out of love for his spiritual guide, and a child out of courtesy for his parents. Not only is *qiyām* valid in all these scenarios, but love and devotion dictate that it is obligatory to do so. There is no trace of anything prohibited within the *qiyām* in these cases when it is done with the intention of love and respect. Therefore, to even bring up the question about the validity of standing out of love and respect for the Holy Prophet ﷺ is simply baseless. This act is irrefutable as the most exalted Prophet ﷺ has a far greater right to be loved and respected than any parent, teacher, or spiritual guide. When we stand during *mawlid* gatherings, it is due to respect, caused by our love and happiness.

8.18.10 PROHIBITION OF *QIYĀM*: ITS CAUSES

As far as the prohibition of *qiyām* is concerned, it is confined to circumstances, such as when a conceited individual desires that others should rise in honour of him whenever he enters a gathering. This is the type of *qiyām* that the Prophet ﷺ warned his noble Companions against, as is narrated by Imam al-Bukhārī (194-256 AH), Imam al-Tirmidhī (210-279 AH),) and Imam Abū Dāwūd (202-275 AH). It is a condemnation of letting one's ego desire that others should stand for him when he joins their assembly.[1] Thus, humbleness and humility are recommended in relation to the qiyām. If people are waiting for someone, then it is recommended for them to stand for respect as it is an expectation of veneration. If someone desires that other people stand for him, then it is an act of condemnation since this leads to pride and ostentation. Hence, it should be made clear that qiyām is performed owing to good moral character and a part of Islamic teachings so that the people develop humbleness and humility. On the other hand, if a person enters a gathering and nobody stands up for him, he ought not to become angry and disappointed since he should be well aware that such a desire is contrary to Islamic morals and etiquettes.

---

[1] Muʿāwiya narrates that the Prophet ﷺ said:

عَنْ مُعَاوِيَةَ ﷺ قَالَ: قَالَ رَسُوْلُ اللهِ ﷺ: «مَنْ سَرَّهُ أَنْ يَتَمَثَّلَ لَهُ الرِّجَالُ قِيَامًا فَلْيَتَبَوَّأْ مَقْعَدَهُ مِنَ النَّارِ.»

Whoever is pleased that people should stand for him let him make his abode in the Hellfire.

Narrated by al-Tirmidhī in *al-Jāmiʿ al-Ṣaḥīḥ*: *Kitāb al-Ādāb* [The Book of Proper Conduct], chapter: 'Blameworthiness of a someone standing for another person', 5:90 §2755; Abū Dāwūd in *al-Sunan*: *Kitāb al-Adab* [The Book of Proper Conduct], chapter: 'A person standing for another person', 4:358 §5229; al-Bukhārī in *al-Adab al-mufrad*, p.339 §977; Aḥmad b. Ḥanbal in *al-Musnad*, 4:93 & 100; al-Ṭabarānī in *al-Muʿjam al-awsaṭ*, 4:282 §4208; and al-Ṭabarānī in *al-Muʿjam al-kabīr*, 19:351 §819.

Section 6

Arranging Lighting

IN THE CELEBRATION OF *MAWLID AL-NABĪ* ﷺ, GATHERINGS of remembrance and sessions of poetical praise are held with utmost respect and reverence. Arranging lighting on the night of his birth is another faith-enlightening aspect of the *mawlid*. Decorative lightings, consisting of a variety of colours, are hung up on buildings and around the streets of the city. The most exalted Prophet ﷺ took mankind out from the depths of darkness into the light of knowledge and guidance: his holy person is the perfect manifestation of the divine light. This is the reason why the anniversary of his blessed arrival is marked by a marvellous display of decorative lighting.

A question may come to one's mind: are there any such examples or precedents amongst the earlier generations of Muslims for this practice? As a matter of fact, according to the reliable reports, this itself is a Sunna of Almighty Allah. The mother of ʿUthmān b. Abī al-ʿĀṣ, Fāṭima b. ʿAbd Allāh al-Thaqfiyya mentions that she was with Sayyida ʿĀmina ﵂ at the time of the Prophet's blessed birth. She narrates:

فَلَمَّا وَلَدَتْهُ خَرَجَ مِنْهَا نُوْرٌ أَضَاءَ لَهُ الْبَيْتُ الَّذِي نَحْنُ فِيْهِ وَالدَّارُ، فَمَا شَيْءٌ أَنْظُرُ إِلَيْهِ إِلاَّ نُوْرٌ.

When she gave birth, a light emitted from her, illuminating for him the house in which we were in and its enclosure, so that there was not a thing except that I saw light.[1]

[1] Narrated by al-Ṭabarānī in *al-Muʿjam al-kabīr*, 25:147 & 186, §355 & 457; al-Shaybānī in *al-Āḥād wa al-Mathānī*, p.631 §1094; al-Māwardī in *Aʿlām al-Nabuwwa*, p. 247; al-Ṭabarī in *Ṭārīkh al-umam wa al-mulūk*, 1:454; al-Bayhaqī in *Dalāʾil al-Nubuwwa wa maʿrifa aḥwāl Ṣāḥib al-Sharīʿa* ﷺ, 1:111; Abū Nuʿaym in *Dalāʾil al-Nabuwwa*, p.135 §76; Ibn al-Jawzī in *al-Munṭaẓẓam fī ṭarīkh al-umam wa al-mulūk*, 2:247; Ibn ʿAsākir in *Tārīkh*

Sayyida ʿĀmina ﵂ herself narrates something similar:

إِنِّى رَأَيْتُ حِيْنَ وَلَدْتُهُ أَنَّهُ خَرَجَ مِنِّي نُوْرٌ أَضَاءَتْ مِنْهُ قُصُوْرُ بُصْرَى مِنْ أَرْضِ الشَّامِ.

When I gave birth to him, I witnessed light emanating from me which illuminated the palaces of Bosra in Syria.[1]

8.19 The Stars Descended Like Fireworks

When people celebrate they make special arrangements for decorative lighting, fireworks, and candles in accordance to their capacity. They illuminate their houses, towns, and markets with these lights. However, when the Creator of the Worlds, Almighty Allah, wished to enlighten the blessed birth of His Beloved ﷺ, He not only illuminated the east and west but included the world of the heavens by drawing the illuminated stars closer to the earth.

ʿUthmān b. Abī al-ʿĀṣ narrates that his mother, Fāṭima b. ʿAbd

Dimashq al-kabīr, 3:79 & in *al-Sīra al-Nabawiyya*, 3:46; Ibn Kathīr in *al-Bidāya wa al-nihāya*, 2:264; al-Haythamī in *Majmaʿ al-zawāʾid wa manbaʿ al-fawāʾid*, 8:220; Ibn Rajab al-Ḥanbalī in *Laṭāʾif al-maʿārif fīmā li-mawāsim al-ʿām min al-waẓāʾif*, p. 173; and al-ʿAsqalānī in *Fatḥ al-Bārī*, 6:583.

[1] Narrated by al-Ṭabarānī in *al-Muʿjam al-kabīr*, 24:214, §545; Ibn Ḥibbān in *al-Ṣaḥīḥ*, 14:313 §6404; ʿAbd al-Razzāq in *al-Muṣannaf*, 5:318; al-Dārimī in *al-Sunan*, 1:20 §13; al-Shaybānī in *al-Āḥād wa al-Mathānī*, 3:56 §1369; Ibid., 4:397 §2446; al-Ḥākim in *al-Mustadrak*, 2:673 §4230; al-Ḥaythamī states in *Majmaʿ al-zawāʾid* (8:222) that Imam Aḥmad and al-Ṭabarānī narrate this tradition, and the one narrated by Imam Aḥmad has a fine (*ḥasan*) chain of transmission; al-Ḥaythamī in *Mawārid al-ẓamʾān ilā zawāʾid Ibn Ḥibbān*, 512 §2093; Ibn Saʿd in *al-Ṭabaqāt al-kubrā*, 1:102; Ibn Isḥāq in *al-Sīra al-Nabawiyya*, 1:97 & 103; Ibn Hishām in *al-Sīra al-Nabawiyya*, 160; al-Ṭabarī in *Tārīkh al-umam wa al-mulūk*, 1:455; Ibn ʿAsākir in *Tārīkh Dimashq al-kabīr*, 1:171–2; Ibn ʿAsākir in *Tārīkh Dimashq al-kabīr*, 3:466 & in *al-Sīra al-Nabawiyya*, 3:46; Ibn Kathīr in *al-Bidāya wa al-nihāya*, 2:275; al-Suyūṭī in *Kifāyat al-ṭālib al-labīb fī khaṣāʾiṣ al-ḥabīb* ﷺ, 1:78; al-Ḥalabī in *Insān al-ʿuyūn fī sīra al-Amīn al-Maʾmūn*, 1:83; and Aḥmad b. Zaynī al-Daḥlān, *al-Sīra al-Nabawiyya*, 1:46.

Allāh al-Thaqfiyya, said:

حَضَرْتُ وِلَادَةَ رَسُوْلِ اللهِ ﷺ فَرَأَيْتُ الْبَيْتَ حِيْنَ وَضَعَ قَدِ امْتَلَأَ نُوراً، وَرَأَيْتُ النُّجُوْمَ تَدْنُو حَتَّى ظَنَنْتُ أَنَّهَا سَتَقَعُ عَلَيَّ.

> When the birth of Allah's Messenger ﷺ was approaching, at that time, I looked at the Sacred House and saw it illuminated; I saw the stars drawing near to the extent that I felt that they would fall on me.[1]

8.20 CANDLE LIGHTING IN MECCA ON THE OCCASION OF THE PROPHET'S BIRTH

Mecca, the revered, is a truly blessed city in that it is home to the sacred House of Almighty Allah and also the birthplace of the Final Messenger ﷺ. This is why Almighty Allah swears an oath by this city. For the Meccans, to be its inhabitant is a great honour. It was a practice of its people that on the occasion of the Prophet's blessed birth, they would hold celebrations and make special arrangements for lighting. The imams have made mention of this in their books. A sample of this will be given below:

Imam Muhammad Jār Allāh b. Ẓahīra al-Ḥanafī (D. 986 AH) describes the *mawlid* celebrations of the inhabitants of Mecca below:

وَجَرَتِ الْعَادَةُ بِمَكَّةَ لَيْلَةَ الثَّانِي عَشَرَ مِنْ رَبِيْعِ الْأَوَّلِ فِي كُلِّ عَامٍ أَنَّ قَاضِيَ

[1] Narrated by al-Suhaylī, *al-Rawḍ al-unuf fī tafsīr al-sīrā al-Nabawiyya li-Ibn Hishām*, 1:278-279; Ibn Athīr in *al-Kāmil fī al-tārīkh*, 1:459; al-Ṭabarī in *Tārīkh al-umam wa al-mulūk*, 1:454; Abū Nuʿaym in *Dalāʾil al-Nabuwwa*, p.135 §76; al-Bayhaqī in *Dalāʾil al-Nabuwwa wa maʿrifa aḥwāl Ṣāḥib al-Sharīʿa* ﷺ, 1:111; Ibn al-Jawzī in *al-Muntaẓam fī tārīkh al-mulūk wa al-umam*, 2:247; Ibn Rajab al-Ḥanbalī in *Laṭāʾif al-maʿārif fīmā li-mawāsim al-ʿām min al-waẓāʾif*, p.173; al-Suyūṭī in *Kifāyat al-ṭālib al-labīb fī khaṣāʾiṣ al-ḥabīb* ﷺ, 1:40; al-Ḥalabī in *Insān al-ʿuyūn fī sīra al-Amīn al-Maʾmūn*, 1:94; and al-Nabhānī, *al-Anwār al-Muḥammadiyya min al-mawāhib al-ladunya*, p.25.

مَكَّةَ الشَّافِعِيَّ يَتَهَيَّأُ لِزِيَارَةِ هَذَا الْـمَحَلِّ الشَّرِيْفِ بَعْدَ صَلَاةِ الْـمَغْرِبِ فِي جَمْعٍ عَظِيْمٍ، مِنْهُمُ الثَّلَاثَةُ الْقُضَاةُ وَأَكْثَرُ الْأَعْيَانِ مِنَ الْفُقَهَاءِ وَالْفُضَلَاءِ، وَذَوِي الْبُيُوْتِ بِفَوَانِيْسَ كَثِيْرَةٍ وَشُمُوْعٍ عَظِيْمَةٍ وَزِحَامٍ عَظِيْمٍ. وَيُدْعَى فِيْهِ لِلسُّلْطَانِ وَلِأَمِيْرِ مَكَّةَ، وَلِلْقَاضِي الشَّافِعِيِّ بَعْدَ تَقَدُّمِ خُطْبَةٍ مُنَاسِبَةٍ لِلْمَقَامِ، ثُمَّ يَعُوْدُ مِنْهُ إِلَى الْـمَسْجِدِ الْـحَرَامِ قُبَيْلَ الْعِشَاءِ، وَيَجْلِسُ خَلْفَ مَقَامِ الْـخَلِيْلِ ﷺ بِإِزَاءِ قُبَّةِ الْفَرَاشِيْنِ، وَيَدْعُو الدَّاعِي لِـمَنْ ذُكِرَ آنِفًا بِحُضُوْرِ الْقُضَاةِ وَأَكْثَرِ الْفُقَهَاءِ. ثُمَّ يُصَلُّوْنَ الْعِشَاءَ وَيَنْصَرِفُوْنَ، وَلَـمْ أَقِفْ عَلَى أَوَّلِ مَنْ سَنَّ ذَلِكَ، سَأَلْتُ مُؤَرِّخِي الْعَصْرِ فَلَمْ أَجِدْ عِنْدَهُمْ عِلْمًـا بِذَالِكَ.

One of the customs of Mecca is that each year, on the night of the 12th of *Rabīʿ al-Awwal*, the *Shāfiʿī* judge of Mecca prepares to visit this noble site (the Prophet's birthplace ﷺ) after the Maghrib prayer with an enormous assembly, including the other three judges (of the Ḥanafī, Mālikī, and Ḥanbalī school) and most of the notable jurists, people of virtue, and noble households, with many chandelier carriers, enormous lamps, and candles. In this gathering, the people pray for the Sultan and then the Emir of Mecca, and the *Shāfiʿī* judge deliver sermons that are appropriate for the occasion, and then they return to the Sacred Mosque before the *ʿīsha* prayer. There, they sit behind the prayer-station of Ibrāhīm ﷺ in front of the *Qibla al-Farānish.* The announcer we just mentioned then calls for the presence of the judges and most of the jurists, and then they pray the *ʿīsha* prayer and depart. I have been unable to discover the first person to inaugurate this practice, and when I asked the historians of the time I did not find an answer.[1]

---

[1] Ibn Ẓahīra, *al-Jāmiʿ al-laṭīf fī faḍl Makka wa ahlihā wa bināʾ al-bayt al-*

ʿAllāma Quṭb al-Dīn al-Ḥanafī has written in some detail about the practice of the inhabitants of Mecca in his book, *Kitāb al-iʿlām bi-aʿlām bayt Allāh al-ḥarām fi tārīkh Makka al-musharrafa*. He writes:

يُزَارُ مَوْلِدُ النَّبِيِّ ﷺ الْمَكَانِيُّ فِي اللَّيْلَةِ الثَّانِيَةِ عَشَرَ مِنْ شَهْرِ رَبِيْعٍ الْأَوَّلِ فِي كُلِّ عَامٍ، فَيَجْتَمِعُ الْفُقَهَاءُ وَالْأَعْيَانُ عَلَى نِظَامِ الْمَسْجِدِ الْحَرَامِ وَالْقُضَاةُ الْأَرْبَعَةُ بِمَكَّةَ الْمُشَرَّفَةِ بَعْدَ صَلَاةِ الْمَغْرِبِ بِالشُّمُوْعِ الْكَثِيْرَةِ وَالْمُفَرَّغَاتِ وَالْفَوَانِيْسِ وَالْمَشَاعِلِ وَجَمِيْعِ الْمَشَائِخِ مَعَ طَوَائِفِهِمْ بِالْأَعْلَامِ الْكَثِيْرَةِ وَيَخْرُجُوْنَ مِنَ الْمَسْجِدِ إِلَى سُوْقِ اللَّيْلِ وَيَمْشُوْنَ فِيْهِ إِلَى مَحَلِّ الْمَوْلِدِ الشَّرِيْفِ بِازْدِحَامٍ وَيَخْطُبُ فِيْهِ شَخْصٌ وَيَدْعُوْ لِلسَّلْطَنَةِ الشَّرِيْفَةِ، ثُمَّ يَعُوْدُوْنَ إِلَى الْمَسْجِدِ الْحَرَامِ وَيَجْلِسُوْنَ صُفُوْفًا فِي وَسَطِ الْمَسْجِدِ مِنْ جِهَةِ الْبَابِ الشَّرِيْفِ خَلْفَ مَقَامِ الشَّافِعِيَّةِ وَيَقِفُ رَئِيْسُ زَمْزَمَ بَيْنَ يَدَيْ نَاظِرِ الْحَرَمِ الشَّرِيْفِ وَالْقُضَاةِ وَيَدْعُوْ لِلسُّلْطَانِ وَيُلْبِسُهُ النَّاظِرُ خِلْعَةً وَيُلْبِسُ شَيْخَ الْفَرَاشِيْنَ خِلْعَةً. ثُمَّ يُؤَذِّنُ لِلْعِشَاءِ وَيُصَلِّي النَّاسُ عَلَى عَادَتِهِمْ، ثُمَّ يَمْشِي الْفُقَهَاءُ مَعَ نَاظِرِ الْحَرَمِ إِلَى الْبَابِ الَّذِي يَخْرُجُ مِنْهُ مِنَ الْمَسْجِدِ، ثُمَّ يَتَفَرَّقُوْنَ. وَهَذِهِ مِنْ أَعْظَمِ مَوَاكِبِ نَاظِرِ الْحَرَمِ الشَّرِيْفِ بِمَكَّةَ الْمُشَرَّفَةِ وَيَأْتِي النَّاسُ مِنَ الْبَدْوِ وَالْحَضَرِ وَأَهْلِ جُدَّةَ، وَسُكَّانِ الْأَوْدِيَةِ فِي تِلْكَ اللَّيْلَةِ وَيَفْرَحُوْنَ بِهَا.

During the night of the 12th of *Rabīʿ al-Awwal* each year, the site of the Prophet's birth is visited, and the jurists, the notables in charge of the Sacred Mosque (*al-Ḥaram*), and the four judges of Mecca all assemble after the Maghrib prayer, carrying large numbers of candles, chandeliers, sweets, and torches, scents, and all of the

sharīf, p.201-202.

> shaykhs with their retinues and announcers come. They leave the Mosque and head to *Sūq al-Layl*, where they then walk to the noble birthplace that is crowded with people. A person among them will deliver a sermon and pray for the noble sultanate, and then they will return to the Sacred Mosque where they sit in rows in the middle of the Mosque, facing *al-Bāb al-Sharīf.* The judges then call for the Sultan and a caretaker... and cloths him with a piece [of the *Kiswa*], and then the *ādhān* is called and the people pray the *ʿīsha* prayer as they normally do. After the prayer, the jurists walk with the caretaker of the Mosque and exit from his door and go their separate ways. This is one of the greatest honours for the caretaker of the Noble Sanctuary of Mecca. People from the remote country side and the cities, from the people of Jeddah and the valleys, all assemble on this night and take delight in it.[1]

From this discourse, it is established that to make arrangements for lighting on an occasion of happiness is a Sunna of Almighty Allah—and what celebration could be more significant than the blessed birth of the most esteemed Prophet ﷺ? Therefore, instead of getting into argument, we should follow the Sunna of Almighty Allah and celebrate the *Mawlid al-Nabī* ﷺ like it was celebrated in Mecca by arranging lighting on this special day.

---

[1] Quṭb al-Dīn al-Ḥanafī, *Kitāb al-iʿlām bi-aʿlām bayt Allāh al-ḥarām fi tārīkh Makka al-musharrafa*, p.355-356.

Section 7
Distributing Food

There are provisions of food and drink for every person who attends the gathering of *Mawlid al-Nabī* ﷺ. A good variety of food and sweets are prepared and generously distributed. Feeding others is a permissible act in the Sharia, and it is held dear in the sight of Almighty Allah and His Messenger ﷺ. A lot of emphasis has been placed on it in the Qur'ān and hadith.

8.21 The Excellent Virtue of Feeding Others in the Qur'ān

1. Feeding others has been described by Almighty Allah in the Qur'ān as an attributive quality of a believer:

﴿وَيُطْعِمُونَ ٱلطَّعَامَ عَلَىٰ حُبِّهِۦ مِسْكِينًا وَيَتِيمًا وَأَسِيرًا ۝٨ إِنَّمَا نُطْعِمُكُمْ لِوَجْهِ ٱللَّهِ لَا نُرِيدُ مِنكُمْ جَزَآءً وَلَا شُكُورًا ۝٩﴾

And they give (their own) food, in deep love of Allah, to the needy, the orphan and prisoner (out of sacrifice, despite their own desire and need for it). We are feeding you only to please Allah. We do not seek any recompense from you nor (wish for) any thanks.[1]

2. One of the rites of Pilgrimage is to sacrifice an animal. Almighty Allah has ordained that the meat of these slaughtered animals is to be consumed by the one executing the sacrifice and should also be dispensed amongst the destitute:

﴿فَكُلُوا۟ مِنْهَا وَأَطْعِمُوا۟ ٱلْبَآئِسَ ٱلْفَقِيرَ﴾

---

[1] Qur'ān 76:8-9.

Then eat of them yourselves and feed the distressed and the needy.[1]

3. In another verse, Almighty Allah says:

﴿فَكُلُواْ مِنۡهَا وَأَطۡعِمُواْ ٱلۡقَانِعَ وَٱلۡمُعۡتَرَّ﴾

Eat of it and (also) feed those who are sitting contented as well as the (needy) who beg.[2]

4. The most benevolent Prophet ﷺ was accustomed to inviting his noble Companions to partake in a meal together, as per the verse of the Qur'ān:

﴿يَـٰٓأَيُّهَا ٱلَّذِينَ ءَامَنُواْ لَا تَدۡخُلُواْ بُيُوتَ ٱلنَّبِيِّ إِلَّآ أَن يُؤۡذَنَ لَكُمۡ إِلَىٰ طَعَامٍ غَيۡرَ نَـٰظِرِينَ إِنَىٰهُ وَلَـٰكِنۡ إِذَا دُعِيتُمۡ فَٱدۡخُلُواْ فَإِذَا طَعِمۡتُمۡ فَٱنتَشِرُواْ وَلَا مُسۡتَـٔۡنِسِينَ لِحَدِيثٍ﴾

O believers! Do not enter the houses of the Holy Prophet (blessings and peace be upon him) unless permission is granted to you for a meal. Nor (reach so early as to) wait for the cooking of the meal. But when you are invited then enter (at that time). Then, when you have eaten the meal, (get up from there and) disperse without delay, and do not linger on in eagerness for talk.[3]

It is clear from these verses that to invite others for a meal and to feed one's friends and the needy and destitute is the exact Sunna of the Holy Prophet ﷺ and the commandment of Almighty Allah.

---

[1] Qur'ān 22:28.

[2] Qur'ān 22:36.

[3] Qur'ān 33:53.

8.22 ENCOURAGEMENT OF FEEDING OTHERS IN THE HADITH

On many occasions, the most gracious Prophet ﷺ stressed the importance of feeding the needy and destitute as well as one's relatives. Below are some narrations which highlight this:

1. ʿAbd Allāh b. ʿAmr narrates that the most exalted Prophet ﷺ was asked, 'Which Islam is the best?' He replied:

«تُطْعِمُ الطَّعَامَ وَتَقْرَأُ السَّلَامَ عَلَى مَنْ عَرَفْتَ وَمَنْ لَمْ تَعْرِفْ.»

> To feed others and to spread the greeting of peace to those you know and those you do not know.[1]

2. ʿAbd Allāh b. Salām narrates that when the most esteemed Prophet ﷺ entered Medina, the first words he heard him say was:

«يَا أَيُّهَا النَّاسُ، أَفْشُوا السَّلَامَ وَأَطْعِمُوا الطَّعَامَ وَصَلُّوا وَالنَّاسُ نِيَامٌ.»

> O people! Spread the greetings of peace, feed others, and offer your ritual prayer when others are asleep, you shall enter Paradise in peace.[2]

---

[1] Narrated by al-Bukhārī in *al-Ṣaḥīḥ*: *Kitāb al-Īmān* [The Book of Faith], chapter: 'Feeding others is Islam', 1:13 §12; al-Bukhārī in *al-Ṣaḥīḥ*: *Kitāb al-Īmān* [The Book of Faith], chapter: 'Spreading the greeting of peace', 1:19 §28; al-Bukhārī in *al-Ṣaḥīḥ*: *Kitāb al-Istiʾdhān* [The Book of Asking Permission to Enter], chapter: 'Greeting those one knows and those one does not know', 5:2302 §5882; Muslim in *al-Ṣaḥīḥ*: *Kitāb al-Īmān* [The Book of Faith], chapter: 'Ranking in faith', 1:65 §39; Abū Dāwūd in *al-Sunan*: *Kitāb al-Adab* [The Book of Proper Conduct], chapter: 'Spreading the greeting of peace', 4:350 §5194; al-Nasāʾī in *al-Sunan*: *Kitāb al-Īmān* [The Book of Faith], chapter: 'Which Islam is the best', 8:107 §5000; and Ibn Mājah in *al-Sunan*: *Kitāb al-Aṭʿima* [The Book of Foodstuff], chapter: 'Feeding others', 2:1083 §3253.

[2] Narrated by Tirmidhī in *al-Jāmiʿ al-Ṣaḥīḥ*: *Kitāb Ṣifa al-Qiyāma wa al-Raqāʾiq wa al-Warʿ* [The Book of the Description of Judgement Day, Softening the Heart, and Scrupulousness], 4:652 §2485; Ibn Mājah in *al-Sunan*: *Kitāb Iqāma al-Ṣalāh wa Sunna Fīhā* [The Book of Establishing the Prayer and the Sunna therein], chapter: 'Night vigil', 1:423 §1334;

3. ᶜAbd Allāh b. ᶜAmr reports that the most exalted Prophet ﷺ said:

«اعْبُدُوا الرَّحْمَنَ وَأَطْعِمُوا الطَّعَامَ وَأَفْشُوا السَّلَامَ تَدْخُلُوا الْـجَنَّةَ بِسَلَامٍ.»

Worship the Most Merciful Almighty Allah, feed others, and spread the greetings of peace, you shall enter Paradise in peace.[1]

4. ᶜUmar reprimanded Ṣuhayb for excessively feeding people, declaring it to be a waste. Justifying his habit, Ṣuhayb responded with the words of the most benevolent Prophet ﷺ:

«خِيَارُكُمْ مَنْ أَطْعَمَ الطَّعَامَ وَرَدَّ السَّلَامَ.»

The best amongst you is the one who feeds others and who replies to the greeting of peace.[2]

5. ᶜAbd Allāh b. ᶜAmr b. al-ᶜĀṣ reports that the most compassionate Prophet ﷺ said:

«مَنْ أَطْعَمَ أَخَاهُ خُبْزاً حَتَّى يُشْبِعَهُ، وَسَقَاهُ مَاءً حَتَّى يَرْوِيَهُ، بَعَّدَهُ اللهُ عَنِ النَّارِ سَبْعَ خَنَادِقَ بُعْدَ مَا بَيْنَ خَنْدَقَيْنِ مَسِيْرَةُ خَمْسِ مِـائَةِ سَنَةٍ.»

Whoever feeds his brother bread until he is satisfied and gives him to drink until he is quenched, Allah will

---

Ibn Mājah in *al-Sunan*: *Kitāb al-Aṭᶜima* [The Book of Foodstuff], chapter: 'Feeding others', 2:1083 §3251; Aḥmad b. Ḥanbal in *al-Musnad*, 5:451 §23,835; and al-Dārimī in *al-Sunan*, 4:405 §1460.

[1] Narrated by Tirmidhī in *al-Jāmiᶜ al-Ṣaḥīḥ*: *Kitāb al-Aṭᶜima* [The Book of Foodstuff], chapter: 'What has been related concerning the virtue of feeding others', 4:2870 §1855; Aḥmad b. Ḥanbal in *al-Musnad*, 2:170 §6587; al-Dārimī in *al-Sunan*, 2:148 §2081; al-Bazzār in *al-Baḥr al-zukhār* (*al-musnad*), 6:383 §2402; and al-Bukhārī in *al-Adab al-Mufrad*, 1:340 §981.

[2] Narrated by Aḥmad b. Ḥanbal in *al-Musnad*, 6:16 §23,971 & 23,974; al-Ṭaḥāwī in *Sharḥ maᶜānī al-āthār*, 4:166-167 §7105; al-Ḥākim in *al-Mustadrak*, 4:310 §7739; and al-Bayhaqī in *Shuᶜab al-īmān*, 6:478 §8973.

distance him from the Fire of Hell by seven trenches—the distance of one trench to the other will be 500 years.[1]

From these *aḥādīth*, it can be deduced that feeding others without discrimination is an act of highest virtue. It is a means of distancing oneself from the Fire of Hell and making one's final abode the gardens of Paradise. Therefore, if on an ordinary day one can receive so much reward, what about the day in which the best of creation, chief of the created beings and the saviour of mankind, the Holy Prophet ﷺ, came to this world? How much more rewardable will it be to feed others on that blessed day?

[1] Narrated by al-Ḥākim in *al-Mustadrak*, 4:144 §7172; al-Ṭabarānī in *al-Muʿjam al-awsaṭ*, 6:320 §6518; al-Bayhaqī in *Shuʿab al-īmān*, 3:218 §3368; al-Daylamī in *al-Firdaws bi-maʾthūr al-khiṭāb*, 3:576 §5807; Mundhirī in *al-Targhīb wa al-tarhīb min al-ḥadīth al-sharīf*, 2:36 §1403; and al-Haythamī in *Majmaʿ al-zawāʾid wa manbaʿ al-fawāʾid*, 3:130.

Section 8

Mawlid Processions

HOLDING PROCESSIONS ON THE OCCASION OF *MAWLID AL-Nabī* ﷺ has become a necessary part of the celebrations of that day. This act of devotion is a Sunna of the noble Companions. In the Prophet's era, processions were held in which the noble Companions were active participants. Below are some hadiths which illustrate this:

The Holy Prophet's migration to Medina has been recollected in the major books of hadith and *sīra* in the following manner:

> During the days in which the arrival of the Holy Prophet ﷺ to Medina was imminent, the elderly and youth, and every man and woman, would march daily towards Qubā', a few miles outside the city, eagerly anticipating the arrival of their beloved Messenger ﷺ. One day, after a long journey when the magnificent Holy Prophet ﷺ arrived, the jubilation of the people knew no bounds. Every individual, without exception, left his home to march in the streets and alleyways of Medina.

According to the words of the hadith:

فَصَعِدَ الرِّجَالُ وَالنِّسَاءُ فَوْقَ الْبُيُوتِ، وَتَفَرَّقَ الْغِلْمَانُ وَالْخَدَمُ فِي الطُّرُقِ يُنَادُونَ: يَا مُحَمَّدُ، يَا رَسُولَ اللهِ.

> Men and women climbed on the top of houses. Children and servants ran in the streets, proclaiming: 'O Muhammad! O Messenger of Allah!'[1]

[1] Narrated by Muslim in *al-Ṣaḥīḥ*: *Kitāb al-Zuhd wa al-Raqā'iq* [The Book of Abstinence and Softening of the Heart], chapter: 'Concerning the incident of the migration', 4:2311 §2009; Ibn Ḥibbān in *al-Ṣaḥīḥ*, 15:289 §68,970; Abū Yaʿlā in *al-Musnad*, 1:107 §116; and al-Marwazī in *Musnad*

Seeing the Prophet's ride, a state of tremendous joy overcame the inhabitant of Medina. According to Imam al-Rūyānī, the citizens were holding a celebratory procession and were proclaiming this tribute:

جَاءَ مُحَمَّدٌ رَسُوْلُ اللهِ ﷺ.

Muhammad ﷺ, the Messenger of Allah, has arrived![1]

The innocent girls from the tribes of Aws and Khazraj were beating hand drums, welcoming their dear guest and singing:

طَلَعَ الْبَدْرُ عَلَيْنَا   مِنْ ثَنِيَّاتِ الْوَدَاعِ

وَجَبَ الشُّكْرُ عَلَيْنَا   مَا دَعَا لِلّٰهِ دَاعِ

أَيُّهَا الْمَبْعُوْثُ فِيْنَا   جِئْتَ بِالْأَمْرِ الْمُطَاعِ

O the full white moon rose over us
From the valley of al-Wadāʿ
And we owe it to show gratefulness
Where the call is to Allah
O (beloved) you were raised among us
And came with a word to be obeyed[2]

Abī Bakr, p.129 §65.

[1] Narrated by Rūyānī in *Musnad al-Ṣaḥāba*, 1:138 §329.

[2] Narrated by Ibn Abī Ḥātim al-Rāzī in *al-Thiqāt*, 1:131; Ibn ʿAbd al-Barr in *al-Tamhīd limā fī al-muwaṭṭā min al-maʿānī wa al-asānīd*, 14:82; Abū ʿUbayd al-Andalusī in *Muʿjam mā istaʿjama min asmāʾ al-bilād wa al-mawāḍ iʿ*, 4:1373; Muḥibb al-Ṭabarī in *al-Riyāḍ al-naḍra fī manāqib al-ʿashra*, 1:480; al-Bayhaqī in *Dalāʾil al-Nubuwwa wa maʿrifa aḥwāl Ṣāḥib al-Sharīʿa* ﷺ, 2:507; Ibn Kathīr in *al-Bidāya wa al-nihāya*, 2:583; Ibid., 3:260; al-ʿAsqalānī in *Fatḥ al-Bārī*, 7:261; Ibid., 8:129; al-Qasṭallānī in *al-Mawāhib al-ladunya bi al-minaḥ al-Muḥammadiyya*, 1:634; al-Zurqānī in *Sharḥ al-mawāhib al-ladunya bi al-minaḥ al-Muḥammadiyya*, 4:100-101; and Aḥmad b. Zaynī al-Daḥlān in *al-Sīra al-Nabawiyya*, 1:323.

In the pages that have preceded us on the formative constituents of *Mawlid al-Nabī* ﷺ, it is clear that to celebrate the Holy Prophet's birthday in the above mentioned manner is totally permissible. This has been the mode of celebration for Muslims over the centuries. There is not a single action mentioned here that does not find its origin in the era of Allah's Messenger ﷺ and his Companions or finds itself in contention with the Qur'ān and Sunna. In the way that these formative constituents are legitimate and agreed upon individually, they are similarly aggregated together as an act of *Mawlid al-Nabī* ﷺ and they attain the position of permissibility in the Sharia.

In making provisions for the *mawlid*, any preparation or arrangement which is made to facilitate the act of expressing happiness is absolutely permissible according to the Sharia. Similarly, the gathering of *Mawlid al-Nabī* ﷺ spiritually is a praiseworthy and acceptable act. Arguing about the legality of this blessed act is to be detached from reality: it is nothing but narrow-mindedness, ignorance and obstinacy.

Chapter 9

Various Aspects of *Mawlid al-Nabī* ﷺ: A Brief Overview

CATERING FOR THE NEEDS OF HUMAN BEINGS, ALMIGHT ALLAH has provided the means by which man's bodily and materialistic needs can be fulfilled. On the other hand, for the continuity of the eternal life, He has gratified them with such righteousness and guidance that they may meet the moral and spiritual expectations properly.

This enlightened caravan of spiritual guidance and righteousness began with the creation of the father of mankind, Ādam ﷺ, followed by a succession of prophets and messengers who rescued the lost human generations by bringing them back to the path of guidance. Yet the dark clutches of misguidance and ignorance eventually left such a negative impact on man that a point in time came in the history wherein no civilisation and politeness was left. Many became victims to the barbarity of injustice, tyranny, and oppression. When the pitch-dark night of human history reached its zenith, then in accordance with the divine decree, a new dawn arose, the eternal brightness of which dispelled the effects of this murky night till the end of time. The breezes of Hejaz echoed with the cries of monotheism. The valley of Mecca became the stage of the birth of that innocent, chaste personality whose emergence had been eagerly anticipated by the heavens and earth—and even time itself from the beginning of creation.

The matchless character of the blessed Prophet ﷺ, the chief of the created beings, had breathed life into lifeless bodies that forever changed the course of history; a new chapter of human dignity was opened. With the emergence of this most benevolent and sacred personality and all his heart attracting charm and grace, the beauty of the worlds itself bowed its head in awe of his magnificence. The poet was left without choice but to exclaim:

ز فرق تا به قدم هر کجا که مي نگرم

کرشمه دامنِ دل مي کشد که جا این جاست

Wherever I glance at him from head to toe;
The elegance of his beauty captivates all my heart.

The most magnificent Prophet's birth marked the dawn of a new era, and though more than fourteen centuries have passed, the appearance of this most exalted personality on the scene of this universe is celebrated even till today. Muslims all over the globe are jubilant, and the greater majority commemorate this blessed day by expressing their heart felt emotions in the month of *Rabīʿ al-Awwal* even after this extensive passage of time.

In this chapter, we shall briefly explore the various aspects of *Mawlid al-Nabī* ﷺ so that no feature of its analysis is omitted:

1. Sharia aspect
2. Historical aspect
3. Cultural aspect
4. Instructional aspect
5. *Daʿwa* aspect
6. Motivational aspect
7. Spiritual aspect

9.1 Sharia Aspect

Throughout this book, we have extensively dealt with the Sharia aspect of celebrating *Mawlid al-Nabī* ﷺ. Thus, here we shall suffice on highlighting a few points:

9.1.1 Remembrance of Allah's Favours

Almighty Allah in the Qurʾān states:

﴿وَلَقَدْ أَرْسَلْنَا مُوسَىٰ بِـَٔايَـٰتِنَآ أَنْ أَخْرِجْ قَوْمَكَ مِنَ ٱلظُّلُمَـٰتِ إِلَى ٱلنُّورِ
وَذَكِّرْهُم بِأَيَّىٰمِ ٱللَّهِ ۚ إِنَّ فِى ذَٰلِكَ لَـَٔايَـٰتٍ لِّكُلِّ صَبَّارٍ شَكُورٍ﴾

And indeed, We sent Mūsā with Our signs: (O Mūsā), bring your people out of the darkness to the light, and remind them of the Days of Allah (which had come upon them and their preceding generations). Surely, there are signs in it for those who are highly steadfast (and) deeply grateful.[1]

Commenting on this verse, Ubayy b. Kaᶜb ؓ reports that he heard the most exalted Prophet ﷺ say:

«إِنَّهُ بَيْنَا مُوْسَى عليه السلام فِي قَوْمِهِ يُذَكِّرُهُمْ بِأَيَّامِ اللهِ، وَأَيَّامُ اللهِ بَلَاؤُهُ وَنَعْمَاؤُهُ.»

Mūsā ؑ would remind his nation of the days of Allah. The days of Allah are His trials and tribulations, and His blessings.[2]

Under the verse ﴾*wa dhakkirhum bi ayyām Allāh*﴿, the exegetes have transmitted the explanation of Ibn ᶜAbbās, stating:

بِنِعَمِ اللهِ عَلَيْهِمْ.

(It is) by Allah granting blessings upon them.[3]

Mujāhid, the famous successor and student of Ibn ᶜAbbās, explains this verse as thus:

بِالنِّعَمِ الَّتِي أَنْعَمَ بِهَا عَلَيْهِمْ: أَنْجَاهُمْ مِنْ آلِ فِرْعَوْنَ وَفَلَقَ لَهُمُ الْبَحْرَ وَظَلَّلَ عَلَيْهِمُ الْغَمَامَ وَأَنْزَلَ عَلَيْهِمُ الْمَنَّ وَالسَّلْوَى.

It is the blessings which He bestowed upon them, (such as:) Allah delivering them from Pharaoh; the parting of the sea; their being shaded by clouds (in the intense heat); and Allah sending them *manna* and quails.[4]

---

1 Qurʾān 14:5.

2 Al-Qurṭubī, *al-Jāmiᶜ li-aḥkām al-Qurʾān*, 9:342.

3 Al-Qurṭubī, *al-Jāmiᶜ li-aḥkām al-Qurʾān*, 9:341; al-Suyūṭī, *al-Durr al-manthūr fī al-tafsīr bi al-maʾthūr*, 5:6; and al-Shawkānī, *Fatḥ al-Qadīr*, 3:95.

4 Al-Ṭabarī, *Jāmiᶜ al-bayān fī tafsīr al-Qurʾān*, 13:184; and al-Suyūṭī, *al-Durr al-manthūr fī al-tafsīr bi al-maʾthūr*, 5:6.

The objective of this verse's revelation was to show that the Children of Israel would recount the blessings bestowed upon them by Almighty Allah so that the generations to come would also recount these blessing and know the significance of these days, such as Allah's delivering them from Pharaoh's despotism by drowning him, providing them with shade in the unbearable heat of the desert, and providing them with heavenly food in the form of *manna* and quails. Hence, Almighty Allah was enjoining them to annually remember these times of prosperity in which they were to revive the memory of His divine grace and subsequently show thanks to Him for His bounties.

9.1.2 Commemorating the Day of the Table-Spread's Descent as an ʿĪd

The Qurʾān affirms:

﴿قَالَ عِيسَى ٱبْنُ مَرْيَمَ ٱللَّهُمَّ رَبَّنَآ أَنزِلْ عَلَيْنَا مَآئِدَةً مِّنَ ٱلسَّمَآءِ تَكُونُ لَنَا عِيدًا لِّأَوَّلِنَا وَءَاخِرِنَا وَءَايَةً مِّنكَ ۖ وَٱرْزُقْنَا وَأَنتَ خَيْرُ ٱلرَّٰزِقِينَ﴾

ʿĪsā, the son of Maryam said: O Allah, our Lord, send down to us from heaven the table spread (with bounties) so that (the day of its descent) becomes (ʿīd) *a festival day for us, and for our predecessors (as well as our) successors, and that (the table-spread) comes as a sign from You, and provide us with sustenance—You are the best Sustainer.*[1]

Ibn Jarīr al-Ṭabarī, commentating on this verse in *Jāmiʿ al-bayān fī tafsīr al-Qurʾān*, states that the soundest narration is that the supplication in this verse means that the day of the table-spread's descent should be taken as an *ʿīd*, as a day in which prayers are offered as an expression of gratitude and commemorated in the

---

[1] Qurʾān 5:114.

same manner people commemorate their festivals of *ᶜīd*.[1]

This explanation of al-Ṭabarī highlights the fact that ᶜĪsā ﷺ wanted to make the day in which the table-spread descended an annual date of thanksgiving and prayer. From this, it is also quite clear that to honour the day in which Almighty Allah bestows a particular blessing upon mankind by expressing gratitude, performing acts of worship, and commemorating it as an *ᶜīd* is the practice of pious and righteous individuals.

Keeping this in mind, the day in which the last and final Messenger ﷺ arrived to this fleeting abode is certainly an *ᶜīd* since it was the time in which the ultimate mercy and favour of Almighty Allah descended on us. This day, therefore, has a greater right to be considered an *ᶜīd*; it is a time of showing gratitude and worshipping Almighty Allah. Undoubtedly, this is a commendable act in the sight of Almighty Allah that has been consistently the habit of His chosen servants.

9.2 HISTORICAL ASPECT

At the governmental level, *Mawlid al-Nabī* ﷺ has been celebrated by the political leaders of Islam. The outstanding name in this regard is Abū Saᶜīd al-Muẓaffar (D. 630 AH), who was the brother in-law of Sultan Salāḥ al-Dīn al-Ayyūbī (589–532 AH). Abū al-Khaṭṭāb b. Diḥya al-Kalbī (633–544 AH) has documented this in some detail in *al-Tanwīr fī mawlid al-Bashīr al-Nadhīr* ﷺ. Abū Muẓaffar Yūsuf (D. 654 AH)—better known as Sibṭ al-Jawzī—related the intricate details of the king's *mawlid* festivities in *Mirʾāt al-zamān fī tārīkh al-aᶜyān*[2].

From a historical perspective, it can be observed that the order to express gratitude is not confined to the *Umma* of Prophet Muhammad ﷺ but to all previous communities as well. The Children of Israel are given the same command in the Qurʾān:

---

[1] Al-Ṭabarī, *Jāmiᶜ al-bayān fī tafsīr al-Qurʾān*, 7:177.

[2] Please refer to chapter six of this book: The position of the hadith scholars and imams on celebrating *Mawlid al-Nabī* ﷺ.

﴿يَٰبَنِيٓ إِسۡرَٰٓءِيلَ ٱذۡكُرُواْ نِعۡمَتِيَ ٱلَّتِيٓ أَنۡعَمۡتُ عَلَيۡكُمۡ وَأَنِّي فَضَّلۡتُكُمۡ عَلَى ٱلۡعَٰلَمِينَ﴾

O Children of Yaʿqūb! Recall those favours that I bestowed upon you, and that I exalted you above all the people (of your age).[1]

In a similar vein, the supplication of ʿĪsā is further supporting of this fact that preceding communities were ordered to express gratitude to Almighty Allah in this manner.

The Qurʾān also describes the glad tidings given to Zakariyyā ﷺ about the future birth of his son, Yaḥyā ﷺ:

﴿يَٰزَكَرِيَّآ إِنَّا نُبَشِّرُكَ بِغُلَٰمٍ ٱسۡمُهُۥ يَحۡيَىٰ لَمۡ نَجۡعَل لَّهُۥ مِن قَبۡلُ سَمِيّٗا﴾

(Allah said:) 'O Zakariyyā, indeed We give you the good news of a son whose name shall be Yaḥyā. We have not given this name to anyone before him.'[2]

The birth of ʿĪsā ﷺ has been mentioned in the Qurʾān as thus:

﴿إِذۡ قَالَتِ ٱلۡمَلَٰٓئِكَةُ يَٰمَرۡيَمُ إِنَّ ٱللَّهَ يُبَشِّرُكِ بِكَلِمَةٖ مِّنۡهُ ٱسۡمُهُ ٱلۡمَسِيحُ عِيسَى ٱبۡنُ مَرۡيَمَ وَجِيهٗا فِي ٱلدُّنۡيَا وَٱلۡأٓخِرَةِ وَمِنَ ٱلۡمُقَرَّبِينَ﴾

When the angels said: 'O Maryam, surely, Allah gives you glad tidings of a (particular) Word from Him named the Messiah, ʿĪsā, the son of Maryam, who would be eminent and exalted, (both) in this world and in the Hereafter, and would be of those who are exceptionally intimate servants of Allah blessed with His nearness.[3]

Through the lens of history, if we analyse the lifestyle of nations past and present, it will be an irrefutable fact that in each age, the

---

1 Qurʾān 2:47.

2 Qurʾān 19:7.

3 Qurʾān 3:45.

days which hold significance in the public memory are celebrated with much display. Even in our time, momentous occasions are marked annually by countries all over the world. Take Pakistan as an example: each year, the 23rd of March, 14th of August, 9th of November, and 25th of December are commemorated as Pakistan Resolution Day, Independence Day, Iqbal Day, and Quaid-e-Azam Day, respectively. In a similar fashion, Arab countries and all other countries of the world commemorate such events. In the Arab world, the accession to the throne by a monarch is celebrated as *al-ʿīd al-waṭanī* (a national day of celebration).

The day of the most exalted Prophet's birth is also one of those events which have been commemorated throughout history as an *ʿīd*. Unlike other celebrations, it is based on authentic sources, such as the Qurʾān and Sunna. The reason for objections by certain people is due to their specific antagonism to the *mawlid*; otherwise, there are no grounds for objection. The most exalted Prophet ﷺ brought a revolution which changed the course of history—this feat can never be repeated again. His successors followed in his footsteps by acting upon his exalted and eternal teachings, thereby creating beacons of light in civilisation, enriching the coming generations culturally and ethically; history itself is proud of this extraordinary accomplishment. Such a massive achievement can never be matched again till the end of time. Therefore, it is paramount for the Muslim community that they do not lag behind any other nation, by celebrating the most exalted Prophet's birth, which served as the catalyst for this unrivalled progress. They should commemorate his birth with such splendour that echoes the sentiments of Iqbāl when he said:

قوتِ عشق سے ہر پست کو بالا کر دے

دہر میں اسمِ محمد سے اُجالا کر دے

Surmount every obstacle with the might of love;
Illuminate the age with Muhammad's name.[1]

---

[1] Iqbāl, *Kulliyāt: Bāl-e-Jibrīl*, p.207.

9.3 Cultural Aspect

From ancient time till the present, the approach of various sectors of human society (on an individual and communal level) and the method of displaying emotions of happiness and sadness have been constantly evolving. Each nation has its own culture by which it is identified: in times of happiness, every community commemorates its celebrations in accordance to its own traditions, notwithstanding that these cultures and customs change over the passage of time.

Muslims are no exception to this rule. The believers of the first Islamic century were fairly simple people who were modest in their expressions of joy; but as time passed, these methods were moulded with the constant flux of culture and norms. The people of the first few centuries were more reserved in their mode of merriment, but this had transformed to a more widespread and vocal style in the modern era. Changes in lifestyle, the population boom, the central influence of electronic media, advancements in technology, and the overall general prosperity are amongst the factors that have contributed to this variation, resulting in the *mawlid* to be celebrated at a larger, more magnificent scale.

An example of a predominant celebration held annually is the 'Basant' festival which is widespread in Pakistan during the spring season. It is commemorated on a national scale and is planned most thoroughly weeks in advance, with laws pertaining to its existence in the High Court and Supreme Court. Hundreds of thousands of rupees are exhausted on the purchase of kites, fireworks, lamps, and varieties of food. People annually travel to Lahore from all corners of the globe just to partake in this extravagance. During this festive occasion, it is difficult to find a place on a plane or train due to the number of participants who attend this function. Whatever outcome there is to be found from Basant is overshadowed by the immoral acts that are part and parcel of it. Several people meet their death by falling in the rush of the crowd; hundreds of thousands of rupees are wasted; there is no concept of segregation between the sexes which results in much immorality and sin taking place. Yet despite all these depressing effects, this festival is considered part and parcel of the tradition of this country—*innā lillāhi wa innā ilayhi rājiʿūn*!

A second example of today's culture can be discovered in the newspapers through their press releases and broadcasts on the first of January. The dawn of the new year is celebrated with great pomp and show, such that it invites Allah's wrath and punishment.

A third example is that of Valentine's Day, which the print and electronic media label as the 'Day of Love,' with the resulting consequence being that the youth are encouraged to imitate Western culture, thereby contravening the Islamic principles of chastity and modesty. The lesson of immorality is openly conveyed to youngsters, who are invited to mixed gatherings with no separation between the genders. What steps is the government of Pakistan taking to prevent such decadence from taking place?

In these miserable circumstances, the importance of organising functions for the celebration of *Mawlid al-Nabī* ﷺ, whereby participants leave with knowledge and spiritual guidance, is more dire than ever. Through the divine blessings that shower upon such gatherings, we may be able to forever rid our societies of the harmful aspects of carnivals such as Basant, New Year's Day, and Valentine's Day. The sad matter is that the public is being deprived of true Islamic teachings with the resultant void being filled by the likes of the above. Therefore it is incumbent upon us to wisely and prudently spread Islamic education amongst the masses according to the needs of the time.

If we study Islamic history, we will conclude that the flight to Medina, the constitution of Medina, the battle of Badr, the conquest of Mecca, and the day of the revelation of the Qurʾān all played a significant role in that age. Each of these episodes significantly altered the course of history and the surrounding environment, but the first generation of Muslims did not commemorate those occurrences. The reason is simple: it frankly was not an aspect of their culture and norm to do so. However, in this day and age, such norms have transformed considerably. Resultantly, not only do we commemorate the aforementioned incidents with great zeal, but we do so in harmony with the common trends of the age; moreover, we should also add to this list the many other historical events, such as Pakistan Day, Independence Day, Defence Day, the Day of the Founder of Pakistan, International Worker's Day, International Women's Day, etc.

During the caliphate of the Ottoman Empire, cannons would be fired 21 times on the most exalted Prophet's birthday. In Mecca, Medina, Yemen, and the Levant, the *mawlid* was likewise celebrated with huge grandeur and zest, as has been clarified in previous chapters. In the present day, the accession to the throne of a king in the Arab world is commemorated not only in that year, but annually thereafter, with the ruler being showered with gifts; cannons roaring in his honour, and sweets distributed amongst the participants with an overall atmosphere of festivity disseminating everywhere. The Western World celebrates Christmas on the 25th of December, although the preparations are undertaken months beforehand. Shops, houses, and marketplaces are decorated to reflect the proximity of this day as an air of festivity resides throughout America and Europe from September till December. If this is the level of celebration displayed at the birth of ʿIsā (Jesus), what should be done for the birthday of the Prophet ﷺ, for whose sake ʿIsā (Jesus) and other Prophets received their prophecy, and who was the fulfilment of Ibrāhīm's supplication? To what extent should the Muslims rejoice upon his birth?

Today, the circumstances of life have changed drastically to the extent that celebrating Independence Day and other events like it have become an inseparable part of our lifestyle and culture. Knowing this, how could we then turn a blind eye to celebrating the *mawlid*, which is a magnificent symbol of the tradition of Islam? The love of the most exalted Prophet ﷺ is the very essence of faith. Along with adhering to his supreme example and teachings, the *mawlid* is the best occasion to manifest one's feelings of adoration for him. It is a grave injustice and very regretful that the Muslim leaders of today celebrate their accession to the throne with unparalleled pomp whilst nobody batters an eyelid or accuses them of *bidʿa* and *shirk*. Yet when the *mawlid* of the chief ﷺ of the created beings is celebrated in a similar fashion, then certain tongues become busy in issuing edicts against it whilst pens are restless in decreeing it to be a form of heterodoxy and polytheism!

9.4 INSTRUCTIONAL ASPECT

It is more imperative than ever, in the current climate, to instil the love of the most exalted Prophet ﷺ in our children so that every corner of their hearts resonates with unlimited adoration for the Prophet ﷺ. Our children should develop an unbreakable bond with him. What can be a better way of achieving this than the gatherings of *Mawlid al-Nabī* ﷺ, which serve as a means of making this link ever more unshakeable? In this regard, we shall present a hadith which actually instructs this:

أَدِّبُوْا أَوْلَادَكُمْ عَلَى ثَلَاثِ خِصَالٍ: حُبِّ نَبِيِّكُمْ، وَحُبِّ أَهْلِ بَيْتِهِ، وَقِرَاءَةِ الْقُرْآنِ.

> Instruct your children in three things: love of your Prophet ﷺ, love of his family, and the recitation of the Qurʾān.[1]

Undoubtedly, one of the most effective methods of fulfilling the requirements of this prophetic tradition is to encourage children from an early age to partake in the *mawlid* gatherings. They should be gently pushed towards such congregations wherein aspects of the prophetic biography and poems eulogising him are recited. Functions should be organised for the realisation of this very purpose in order that young children develop a firm intellectual and emotional attachment to their beloved Messenger ﷺ. When the Communist Revolution took place in China, the audio cassettes of talks by Mao Zedong (1893–1976 CE) were placed in the ears of children almost as soon as they were born; this exploit continued for several years. Likewise, during the Russian Revolution, the

[1] Al-Suyūṭī, *al-Jāmiʿ al-ṣaghīr fī aḥādīth al-Bashīr al-Nadhīr*, 1:25 §311; and al-Hindī, *Kanz al-ʿummāl fī sunan al-aqwāl wa al-afʿāl*, 16:456 §45409.

youths were showered with stories about the achievements of Lenin (1870–1924 CE). In the Iranian Revolution, children were routinely made to hear the speeches of Khomeini (1902–1989 CE). The objective behind these moves was obviously to create an atmosphere in which the mind of the child would become accustomed to constantly hearing a particular philosophy until it became firmly settled in the mind.

9.4.1 The Fundamental Responsibility of Parents

As Muslims and as guardians, it is our fundamental duty to bequeath the fortune of the true faith for the generations to come. Looking back just a few years, we would realise that our own parents made great sacrifices for us to receive the invaluable asset of faith and love of the Prophet ﷺ. Now it is our duty to pass on this inheritance to our own offspring so that this message may continue to reach succeeding generations in the future. In this manner, one candle continues to light the next. If we fail to execute this task properly, then we shall undeniably be interrogated about our heedlessness on the Day of Judgment.

9.4.2 Food for Thought

If we reflect a little on our lives, it is commonly observed that most of us have received wealth, property, and businesses from our parents for our comfort and convenience. Subsequently, we are relentlessly striving day and night to bequeath as much of this world for our children before we depart. How unfortunate it is that we were also recipients of the principle of faith and love of the Prophet ﷺ but are making minimal effort to pass this on to our children. If the same practice is imitated by our children, then what would be the implications for our grandchildren? Would they be left with anything at all from the priceless treasure of faith?

9.4.3 A Strategy for Safeguarding Faith

The pathetic state of the Muslim world is dismaying in the least. The dark forces of secularism and disbelief are falling all over themselves to snatch away the fortune of faith from our youngsters.

In such times, it is more essential than ever to accustom ourselves and our children to the biography and guidance of the most exalted Prophet ﷺ. We ought to be striving as hard as we can, with all means at our disposal, to illuminate our hearts and the hearts of our offspring with love for the beloved Prophet ﷺ in order to keep this light aflame for succeeding generations to benefit from.

This effort nonetheless is taking place throughout the year in the form of promulgating the Prophet's teachings, and establishing study circles about the message of the Qurʾān and Sunna. However, in the month of *Rabīʿ al-Awwal,* these efforts should be stepped up even further in order to strongly communicate the Prophet's high esteem: in this blessed month, there should be mention of his elegant beauty, fragrant curly tresses, the winding streets of Medina, and the serenity of the green dome. These descriptions captivate the hearts and souls of the listeners. The marvels witnessed by Āmina ﵂ at the time of his birth and Ḥalīma ﵂ during his innocent childhood should also be mentioned. In short, the entire month should be devoted to infusing in the hearts the immense love for the Prophet ﷺ, with stories of his noble birth and the amazing anecdotes of his youth being reminisced.

Therefore, what should be more effective than to take full advantage of this golden opportunity to persuade our children to partake in the *mawlid* gatherings and expectantly increase their love and affection for the Holy Prophet ﷺ? Hopefully this way, the hearts and souls of our youth would become connected to the personality of the most exalted Prophet ﷺ on an intellectual and spiritual basis.

9.5 Daʿwa Aspect

Amongst the different aspects of *Mawlid al-Nabī* ﷺ, the *daʿwa* aspect of the *mawlid* holds great significance. When the month of *Rabīʿ al-Awwal* approaches, such functions are held to which the adherents of various schools of thought are invited. The *mawlid* gatherings are arranged in the mosques and events are organised at the governmental and non-government levels wherein the Prophet's biography and character are related abundantly. Odes and poetry in tribute to him are sung. Examples of his morals and educational aspects of his praised conduct and beautiful disposition are taught in detail, and much emphasis is laid on the importance of obeying and imitating the Holy Prophet ﷺ. All this serves to boost the feelings of love, brotherhood and unity amongst the audience.

It is an unquestionable fact that the *mawlid* gatherings are an excellent and productive means of inviting people to Almighty Allah and propagating the truth. Such a golden opportunity must not be allowed to pass by unproductively. It is imperative that scholars and missionaries take advantage of using this opportunity to drift peoples' attention towards the prophetic morals and etiquettes, aspects of his biography, worships and dealings. In this blessed month, the aim should be to awaken the passions in citizens for their beloved Prophet ﷺ, and doing so in *Rabīʿ al-Awwal* is more effective in comparison to other months. Focus should be placed on those particular aspects of his life, virtues and mannerisms that lead to increased admiration and appreciation for him amongst the attendees, who can take these lessons and apply them in their own lives upon returning home.

It was the custom of the inhabitants of Mecca to visit the Prophet's birthplace during the *mawlid*; they would hold functions there and deliver talks on the Prophet's biography. Quṭb al-Dīn al-Ḥanafī relates an eyewitness account of this:

وَيَخْرُجُوْنَ مِنَ الْـمَسْجِدِ إِلَى سُوْقِ اللَّيْلِ وَيَمْشُوْنَ فِيْهِ إِلَى مَحَلِّ الْـمَوْلِدِ الشَّرِيْفِ بِازْدِحَامٍ وَيَخْطُبُ فِيْهِ شَخْصٌ.

> They leave the Mosque and head to *Sūq al-Layl*, where they then walk to the noble birthplace that is crowded with people. A learned person amongst them will deliver a sermon.[1]

9.6 Motivational Aspect

There are two facets to everything:

---

[1] Quṭb al-Dīn al-Ḥanafī, *Kitāb al-iʿlām bi-aʿlām bayt Allāh al-ḥarām fī tārīkh Makka al-musharrafa*, p.355–356.

(i) The external facet
(ii) The internal facet

The external facet of a thing is that facet which can be viewed easily with the naked eye, whereas the internal facet is concealed and cannot be seen. It is commonly experienced that the more hidden and concealed a thing is, the more valuable it becomes. To use a common day example, if you were to have two apples (one is a common apple, and the other is an apple from a special variety), the first one would not emit a special fragrance or taste, whilst the second type would provide a beautiful taste, smell and smooth texture that can be enjoyed and experienced for quite some time. Generally speaking, both look similar and are of the same genus, yet there is a difference in the quality of taste, texture, and the aroma it emits. Whatever is apparent in its shape and size is not as valuable as those features that are hidden from the gaze, such as taste, sweetness, and odour, etc. In other words, the inner qualities are more valued than the outer qualities.

9.6.1 THE EXTERNAL AND INTERNAL FACETS OF DEEDS

Concerning the righteous and pious deeds which are performed according to the regulations dictated by Islam, the most exalted Prophet ﷺ said:

«إِنَّمَا الْأَعْمَالُ بِالنِّيَّاتِ.»

Actions are valued according to the intentions.[1]

[1] Narrated by al-Bukhārī in *al-Ṣaḥīḥ*: *Kitāb Badʾ al-Waḥī* [The Book of the Beginning of Revelation], chapter: 'The beginning of revelation', 1:3 §1; Muslim in *al-Ṣaḥīḥ*: *Kitāb al-Imāra* [The Book of Leadership], chapter: 'Actions are valued according to intentions', 3:1515 §1907; al-Tirmidhī in *al-Jāmiʿ al-Ṣaḥīḥ*: *Kitāb Faḍāʾil al-Jihād* [The Book of the Merits of *Jihād*], chapter: 'What has been related concerning the one who fights out of ostentation and for the world', 4:179 §1647; Abū Dāwūd in *al-Sunan*: *Kitāb al-Ṭalāq* [The Book of Divorce], chapter: 'What is meant by divorce and intention', 2:262 §2201; al-Nasāʾī in *al-Sunan*: *Kitāb al-Ṭahāra* [The Book of Purification], chapter: 'Making intention for the minor ritual ablution', 1:58 §75; and Ibn Mājah in *al-Sunan*: *Kitāb al-Zuhd* [The Book of Austerity], chapter: 'Intention', 2:1413 §4227.

As a manner of worship, Almighty Allah has ordered the establishment of the ritual prayer, which consists of standing, bowing, prostrating, and sitting; it includes glorifications and the recitation of verses from the Qur'ān, yet the basis of its acceptance or rejection in the divine court is a criterion hidden deep in the heart and mind. If the intention is for other than Almighty Allah's pleasure alone, even if such prayers amount to their thousands, they would not be accepted by Almighty Allah. According to Iqbāl:

جو میں سر بسجدہ ہوا کبھی تو، زمیں سے آنے لگی صدا

ترا دل تو ہے صنم آشنا، تجھے کیا ملے گا نماز میں

When I prostrate, a voice comes from the ground; Your heart is ostentatious; what are you then expecting from the prayer?[1]
Though the mosque was built overnight by the believers; Our heart, being an old sinner for years, devout could not be.[2]

From this, it can be deduced that pretension, fakery, and false modesty results in rejection, since sincere intention is the prerequisite for the acceptance of our deeds. Intentions are hidden and cannot be seen; they have no external form. Through sincerity, even two cycles of supererogatory prayers are more valuable than a hundred thousand cycles offered with the wrong objective in mind. True intention and sincerity in our actions can only be realised once we wholeheartedly immerse ourselves into the ambit of true faith, with a heart full of conviction, brimming with genuine love and yearning for the most compassionate Prophet ﷺ. Like our good deeds, this connection also has two facets: the internal facet and the external facet.

---

[1] Iqbāl, *Kulliyāt: Bāng-e-darā*, p.281.

[2] Iqbāl, *Kulliyāt: Bāng-e-darā*, p.291.

9.6.2 THE ESSENCE OF GOOD DEEDS IS LOVE FOR THE PROPHET ﷺ

All acts of worship of Almighty Allah, which we perform in obedience to the Holy Prophet ﷺ in imitation of his precedent, are the external facets of our deeds. These evident endeavours are merely the establishment and implementation of good actions, yet the subtle trait that actually leads them to be acknowledged in the divine court is the true love of the beloved Prophet ﷺ. Anas narrates that Allah's Messenger ﷺ said:

«لَا يُؤْمِنُ أَحَدُكُمْ حَتَّى أَكُونَ أَحَبَّ إِلَيْهِ مِنْ وَالِدِهِ وَوَلَدِهِ وَالنَّاسِ أَجْمَعِينَ.»

None of you will truly believe until I am dearer to him than his offspring and his father, and the people altogether.[1]

Abū Hurayra ؓ reports that the most exalted Prophet ﷺ said:

«فَوَالَّذِي نَفْسِي بِيَدِهِ لَا يُؤْمِنُ أَحَدُكُمْ حَتَّى أَكُونَ أَحَبَّ إِلَيْهِ مِنْ وَالِدِهِ وَوَلَدِهِ.»

'I swear by Him in whose hand lies my soul! None of you truly believes until I am more beloved to him than his parents and children.'[2]

---

[1] Narrated by al-Bukhārī in *al-Ṣaḥīḥ*: *Kitāb al-Īmān* [The Book of Faith], chapter: 'Loving the Prophet is faith', 1:14 §15; Muslim in *al-Ṣaḥīḥ*: *Kitāb al-Imāra* [The Book of Faith], chapter: 'Necessity of loving the Messenger', 1:67 §44; al-Nasāʾī in *al-Sunan*: *Kitāb al-Īmān* [The Book of Faith], chapter: 'The token of faith', 8:114–115 §5013–5014; and Ibn Mājah in *al-Sunan*: *al-Muqaddama* [Prolegomena], chapter: 'Faith', 1:26 §67.

[2] Narrated by al-Bukhārī in *al-Ṣaḥīḥ*: *Kitāb al-Īmān* [The Book of Faith], chapter: 'Loving the Prophet is faith', 1:14 §14; and al-Nasāʾī in *al-Sunan*: *Kitāb al-Īmān* [The Book of Faith], chapter: 'The token of faith', 8:114 §5015.

These narrations unambiguously inform us that the essence of good deeds is the true love of the beloved Prophet ﷺ. If this quality is absent, then these supposedly pious deeds would be fruitless and will come to nothing; these deeds in Almighty Allah's sight will be completely worthless and empty. In this context, the *mawlid* is a key method of reviving this indispensable love, since the eulogies which are recited on this occasion and the speeches that are delivered aim to rekindle the dim light of the love in our hearts for our beloved Messenger ﷺ. These functions, therefore, are a means of rekindling the flames of love, making our hearts shine with the radiance of his proximity. On this, Iqbāl says:

در دلِ مسلم مقامِ مصطفيَ است

آبروي ما ز نامِ مصطفيَ است

Love of the Prophet dwells in the heart of a believer;
Our pride and honour originates from his name.[1]

In other words, only by having the true love for the Holy Prophet ﷺ can our actions be accepted by Almighty Allah; otherwise, they would be nothing except a set of rituals. The first three generations of Muslims lived in an age where love for the Holy Prophet ﷺ was the reality. And unlike our age, there was no need for them to put measures in place for the preservation of their faith: their firm conviction and authentic love is recorded and testified to by all the books of hadith. The biographers of the Holy Prophet ﷺ remarked that the sincere love that these three generations possessed for the Holy Prophet ﷺ was so rich and profuse that were it to be divided amongst all creation, it would be more than sufficient for them until the Day of Judgment.

Coming back to ourselves in this present age of decline, our faith has become weak and thus susceptible to a constant onslaught of vicious attacks from satanic forces. The most assured way of keeping our frail and fragile faith intact is to instil true love of the

---

[1] Iqbāl, *Kulliyāt: Asrār wa rumūz*, p.38.

most exalted Prophet ﷺ in our hearts and to transfer this love to forthcoming generations. This effort should continue throughout the year and be increased manifold in the month of *Rabīʿ al-Awwal*. If this is done effectively, the Prophet's esteem and adoration will be firmly imprinted onto our hearts like the way inscription is carved on a rock.

9.7 SPIRITUAL ASPECT

Listening to the miraculous accounts of *Mawlid al-Nabī* ﷺ is a means of flowering one's spirituality. These gatherings are a source of spiritual strength. Every possible avenue should be exhausted to enhance one's connection with the most benevolent Prophet ﷺ whilst beseeching him as an intercessor for the elimination of hardships. If we submit to the claims of those who object to the *mawlid*, we will certainly be deprived of these potential benefits. Therefore, it is necessary that one should remain in a clean and pure state whilst participating in such auspicious gatherings. One should bear in mind that every effort made towards its organisation, the charity donated, and sacrifices rendered are done purely for the pleasure of Almighty Allah and His beloved Prophet ﷺ.

The hadiths inform us that our salutations are presented to him and that our deeds are presented too. When the chief of the created beings, the Holy Prophet ﷺ, receives news of our good deeds, he is pleased, and when we commit an error, he asks Almighty Allah's forgiveness for us.[1] We should always bear in mind that everything we do during the *mawlid* is also presented in the court of the most exalted Prophet ﷺ. If all the elements of this function are sincere and legitimate, it shall serve as a means of attaining the Prophet's

---

[1] Narrated by al-Bazzār in *al-Baḥr al-Zukhār* (*al-Musnad*) 5:308–309 §1925; Ibn Abī Usāma in *Musnad al-Ḥārith*, 2:884 §953 narrates this with an authentic chain of transmission; Ḥakīm Tirmidhī in *Nawādir al-uṣūl fī aḥādīth al-Rasūl*, 4:176; al-Daylamī in *al-Firdaws bi maʾthūr al-Khiṭāb*, 1:183 §686; Qāḍī ʿIyāḍ, *al-Shifāʾ bi taʿrīf ḥuqūq al-Muṣṭafā*, 1:19; al-Haythamī in *Majmaʿ al-zawāʾid wa manbaʿ al-fawāʾid*, 9:24 narrates that the one reported by al-Bazzār and all his narrators are authentic; Ibn Kathīr, *al-Bidāya wa al-nihāya*, 4:257; and Zayn al-Dīn Abū al-Faḍl al-ʿIrāqī in *Ṭarḥ al-tathrīb fī sharḥ al-taqrīb*, 3:297 has declared this narration authentic.

pleasure; and Almighty Allah, for the sake of His Beloved ﷺ, will bless it with His seal of approval.

On the subject of sincerity, the account written by Shāh Walī Allāh Muḥaddith al-Dihlawī (1114–1174 AH) about his father, Shāh ᶜAbd al-Raḥīm (1054–1131 AH), is a shining example for us to take heed from. The former writes that his father would annually cater for guests on the occasion of the *mawlid*. It so happened that during one particular year, he had nothing to offer due to difficulty in his financial situation. So, he served boiled chickpeas. That night, the Holy Prophet ﷺ appeared to him in his dream with a plate of the same food in front of him, and on the humble but sincere gesture of his servant, he showed his delight and expressed happiness.[1]

When commemorating the *mawlid*, we should take heed from such accounts, keeping a close eye on our sincere intentions and refraining from any action that would potentially displease the chief of the created beings, the Holy Prophet ﷺ.

1 Shāh Walī Allāh, *Durr al-thamīn fī mubashirāt al-Nabī al-Amīn*, p.40.

CHAPTER 10

IS CELEBRATING *MAWLID AL-NABĪ* ﷺ A *BIDʿA*?

AFTER EXAMINING THE PERSPECTIVE OF THE SHARIA ON *MAWLID al-Nabī* ﷺ along with its merits and rewards, what is to follow now in connection with this topic on hand is a discourse on the concept of innovation (*bidʿa*) and its various aspects. A particular emphasis will be placed on abolishing the misconceived notion that every new practice which did not exist in the epoch of Allah's Messenger ﷺ or the noble Companions is rejected and declared impermissible, simply on the basis of it being a new thing irrespective of its soundness. This self-concocted notion on the concept of innovation (*bidʿa*) in Islam shall be clarified in light of the unambiguous and explicit evidences from the Qurʾān and hadith. It should be understood that *Mawlid al-Nabī* ﷺ is a permissible practice which has its legitimacy in the Sharia.

10.1 The Literal Meaning of *Bidʿa*

'*Bidʿa*' is a derivative of the root word '*badaʿa*', which literally means 'to initiate or create some new thing without a precedent'.

According to Ibn Manẓūr (630–711 AH):

أَبْدَعْتَ الشَّيْءَ: اِخْتَرَعْتَهُ لَا عَلَى مِثَالٍ.

> You created a thing; i.e., You invented it without a (prior) example.[1]

Ḥāfiẓ Ibn Ḥajar al-ʿAsqalānī (773–852 AH) describes *bidʿa* as:

اَلْبِدْعَةُ أَصْلُهَا مَا أُحْدِثَ عَلَى غَيْرِ مِثَالٍ سَابِقٍ.

[1] Ibn Manẓūr, *Lisān al-ʿArab*, 8:6.

> *Bidʿa* in its original usage refers to what is originated without a former example.[1]

10.1.1 Confirmation of its Meaning from the Qurʾān

In several passages of the Qurʾān, various derivatives of the word *bidʿa* have appeared and the meaning conveyed in them is in line with the aforementioned definitions. Only two verses will be mentioned here:

1. Almighty Allah has referred to himself as *al-Badīʿ* (the Originator) because He created the heavens and the earth without a prior example:

﴿بَدِيعُ ٱلسَّمَٰوَٰتِ وَٱلْأَرْضِ ۖ وَإِذَا قَضَىٰٓ أَمْرًا فَإِنَّمَا يَقُولُ لَهُۥ كُن فَيَكُونُ﴾

> *He is the One Who has originated the heavens and the earth, and when He wills to (originate) a thing, He only says to it: 'Be,' and it becomes.*[2]

2. In the another place, He states:

﴿بَدِيعُ ٱلسَّمَٰوَٰتِ وَٱلْأَرْضِ﴾

> *He is the One Who is the Originator of the heavens and the earth.*[3]

From these two verses, what is apparent is that the creation of the heavens and the earth is described as an innovation (*bidʿa*), as Almighty Allah is the one who brought them into existence from non-existence—hence His name, the Originator.

---

[1] Al-ʿAsqalānī, *Fatḥ al-Bārī*, 4:253; and al-Shawkānī, *Nayl al-awṭār sharḥ muntaqā al-akhbār*, 3:63.

[2] Qurʾān 2:117.

[3] Qurʾān 6:101.

10.2 The Technical Meaning of *Bidʿa*

According to the people of knowledge, innovation (*bidʿa*) is defined in the following way:

1. According to Imam al-Nawawī (631–677 AH):

اَلْبِدْعَةُ هِيَ إِحْدَاثُ مَا لَمْ يَكُنْ فِي عَهْدِ رَسُوْلِ اللهِ ﷺ.

Innovation is to invent something which did not exist in the epoch of Allah's Messenger ﷺ.[1]

2. According to Ibn Rajab al-Ḥanbalī (736–795 AH):

اَلْمُرَادُ بِالْبِدْعَةِ مَا أُحْدِثَ مِمَّا لَا أَصْلَ لَهُ فِي الشَّرِيْعَةِ يَدُلُّ عَلَيْهِ، وَأَمَّا مَا كَانَ لَهُ أَصْلٌ مِنَ الشَّرْعِ يَدُلُّ عَلَيْهِ فَلَيْسَ بِبِدْعَةٍ شَرْعاً، وَإِنْ كَانَ بِدْعَةً لُغَةً.

What is meant by innovation is the invented matter that has no basis which can be referred to in the Sharia. As for that which does have a base which can be referred to in the Sharia, legally it is not an innovation, though literally speaking it may be.[2]

Ḥāfiẓ Ibn Ḥajar al-ʿAsqalānī (773–852 AH), explaining the difference between the praiseworthy innovation (*bidʿa ḥasana*) and the blameworthy innovation (*bidʿa sayyiʾa*), states:

وَالتَّحْقِيْقُ أَنَّهَا إِنْ كَانَتْ مِمَّا تَنْدَرِجُ تَحْتَ مُسْتَحْسَنٍ فِي الشَّرْعِ فَهِيَ حَسَنَةٌ، وَإِنْ كَانَتْ مِمَّا تَنْدَرِجُ تَحْتَ مُسْتَقْبَحٍ فِي الشَّرْعِ فَهِيَ مُسْتَقْبَحَةٌ.

The fact of the matter is that whatever can be classified under the commendable matters in the Sharia is

---

[1] Al-Nawawī, *Tahdhīb al-asmāʾ wa al-lughāt*, 3:22.

[2] Ibn Rajab, *Jāmiʿ al-ʿulūm wa al-ḥikam fī sharḥ khamsīn ḥadīthan min jawāmiʿ al-kalam*, p.252; ʿAẓīm Ābādī, *ʿAwn al-maʿbūd sharḥ sunan Abī Dāwūd*, 12:235; and Mubārak Pūrī, *Tuḥfa al-aḥwadhī sharḥ jāmiʿ al-Tirmidhī*, 7:366.

> praiseworthy, whilst whatever is classified under the disliked matters in the Sharia is reprehensible.[1]

The above definitions make it clear that every new matter is not automatically prohibited (*ḥarām*) solely on the grounds that it is a new matter. Rather, its legality or illegality is to be judged by whether it contains features that are deemed recommended by the Sharia, and thus it would be classified as a praiseworthy innovation (*bidʿa ḥasana*); or whether it contains features that are disapproved by the Sharia, and thus it would be classified as a blameworthy innovation (*bidʿa sayyiʾa*).

From these preliminary remarks, it can be concluded that the celebration of *Mawlid al-Nabī* ﷺ did not exist amongst the pious predecessors in the form that it is exists today; nonetheless, it still is a lawful practice which is commendable and permitted by the Sharia. This is because its integral constituents, such as the recitation of the Qurʾān, the remembrance of Almighty Allah, the odes recited in praise of the Holy Prophet ﷺ, the charitable assistance of the poor and destitute, and the generous provision of sustenance are all acts which the Sharia has legislated. The only difference between the previous eras and our age was that previous generations would express gratitude to Almighty Allah on the day when a great blessing was bestowed upon them in line with their norms and customs. In the current age, like the way that every facet of life has changed significantly, the celebration of *Mawlid al-Nabī* ﷺ has in the same way evolved in its style of celebration. To examine this further, more clarification has been given below:

10.3 Is Every Aspect of Local Culture *Bidʿa*?

In our everyday lives, we have become accustomed in justifying our each and every action from the Qurʾān and Sunna. Everything is declared an innovation (*bidʿa*). The *mawlid* procession and many other positive aspects, which have become part and parcel of our culture, are criticised as innovations by the people who object to it. There are certain things which are religious in nature and thus

---

1 Al-ʿAsqalānī, *Fatḥ al-Bārī*, 4:253; and al-Shawkānī, *Nayl al-awṭār sharḥ muntaqā al-akhbār*, 3:63.

require explanation or evidence in light of the Qurʾān and Sunna, as it falls within the ambit of legal rulings. An enquiry should be made to find out the legal status of an action and whether it is established from the Sharia or not; if it can be established, then it constitutes a legal ruling, but if it cannot be established, then there is no legal judgement concerning it. If there is no legal judgement concerning it, it can be divided into the following types:

Firstly, it can be that certain actions are related to a particular culture or local tradition. They may not necessarily be directly linked to religious matters since they are simply a facet of the norms, culture, or habits of a specific locality.

Secondly, it may be that certain actions are undertaken in line with the particular needs of the time, according to the changing situation. This is reflective of social trends and collective preferences.

And thirdly, it may be that the traditional and cultural requirements of a certain locality make certain things necessary.

10.3.1 The Cultural Norms of the Companions ﵃

The cultural life of the noble Companions ﵃ was relatively simple. If we analyse their era from a cultural and historical point of view, it would be discovered that their mosques and houses were very plain and uncomplicated in their design: the trunk of palm trees were used to build their houses, whilst the *Kaʿba* was assembled from stone. Had they wished, they could surely have built the Holy Prophet's Mosque with strong material, but their culture and customs were simple and were very close to nature. This was also reflected in their choices and manners of food and clothing. In short, civilisation was undemanding, and hence, every angle of their lives, such as their eating, drinking, and merriment, mirrored this simplicity. Therefore, their manner in commemorating the Holy Prophet's birth was also the reflection of their unique culture.

10.3.2 The Cultural Demonstrations of *Mawlid al-Nabī* ﷺ

In Pakistan, on Pakistan Day and Quaid-e-Azam Day, processions are held. This is the local convention of Pakistani citizens; it is not a legal issue, but a cultural one. Expressing joy and happiness on *Mawlid al-Nabī* ﷺ is established from the Qur'ān and Sunna and its expectation is that a believer's heart be overwhelmed with jubilation. However, there are various cultural demonstrations of this happiness that can be changed over time as it is related to one's culture.

10.3.2.1 The *Mawlid* Processions Belong to Culture

If Pakistan Day can be celebrated annually as a legitimate cultural expression, how then can the day of the Holy Prophet's blessed birth, which is the most important day in history, not be celebrated? If it is deemed acceptable to have a full military parade on Pakistan's Independence Day, why cannot the same be done on the day of *Mawlid al-Nabī* ﷺ? Similarly, on other occasions, decorations are put up and lightings are arranged, so why not on the *mawlid*? If a nation can take pride on its national festivities, why should the *Umma* not express its emotions of pride on the blessed birthday of their Prophet ﷺ, who is a Mercy to the Worlds? Just as the aforementioned cultural demonstrations of happiness do not require evidences, the processions held on the occasion of *Mawlid al-Nabī* ﷺ similarly do not require evidences. When expressing happiness or protesting, we hold parades and processions, which have become part and parcel of our culture and convention. Knowing this, why do we need to demand evidences when someone participates in the *mawlid* processions and invokes blessings and peace upon the beloved Prophet ﷺ?

A question may be posed: why do the Arabs not organise processions to celebrate the *mawlid*? The simple answer is that processions are not as prevalent in their culture as it is in ours. The *mawlid* is celebrated in Arab countries, such as the UAE and Egypt, but holding processions is not their culture. In Pakistan, processions are so widespread and commonplace that even if one's hockey team wins a match, supporters show their jubilation in this manner. The winning team and even the political party that triumphs in an election are accustomed to holding parades in order to give the champions a welcoming reception.

To summarise, any action which has not been outlawed by the Sharia and constitutes a cultural necessity is declared permissible; and if the fundamental purpose of that action is to express happiness on the most exalted Prophet's birth, there should be no reason for raising objections against it.

10.3.2.2 Invoking Blessings on the Prophet ﷺ while Standing Belongs to Culture

The residents of the Indian Subcontinent are accustomed to standing whilst invoking peace and blessings upon the Prophet ﷺ, whilst in the Arab world, the norm is generally to be seated—however, a large group of the inhabitants of Mecca, the sacred, also stand whilst reciting their salutations. After being aware of all this, it is unwarranted to raise objections against this act without a valid reason. There is evidence in Sharia to justify the *qiyām*, and it is also an element of culture. This is done according to one's taste and preference: some people prefer to remain seated whilst invoking blessings on the Prophet ﷺ whereas others like to do so standing.[1]

10.3.2.3 Arranging Decorations on the *Mawlid* Belongs to Culture

The notion of performing righteous deeds was so deeply ingrained in the nature and character of the pious predecessors that they did not require any further stimulus or motivation to perform good deeds—the divine ordinance itself was sufficient. The situation has changed very much in our time. We are very hesitant and stubborn in carrying out virtuous deeds. On account of our stagnant temperament, methods such as lavishly decorating our mosques (even though there are no injunctions in the Qurʾān and hadith that they should be ornamented), allow us to feel enthusiastic about moving ahead with pious deeds. Why has it come to this? The reply is that the apparent and observable reasons become the means of inclinations, as Almighty Allah states:

---

[1] For a detailed discourse on the *qiyām*, please refer to chapter 8: the formative constituents of *Mawlid al-Nabī* ﷺ.

﴿يَٰبَنِيٓ ءَادَمَ خُذُواْ زِينَتَكُمۡ عِندَ كُلِّ مَسۡجِدٖ﴾

O Children of Ādam! Dress up decently every time you offer Prayer.[1]

This aspect in question is not related to the legal rulings of the Sharia, but culture. To beautify the beard, apply antimony (kohl) to the eyes, rub oil on the hair, and to wear elegant clothing are all from the Sunna of the Holy Prophet ﷺ; these are things which bring about outward appeal. The blessed Prophet ﷺ, well aware of the psychological benefits of such beautification, stressed these acts repeatedly. For example, he stated:

«مَنْ أَكَلَ مِنْ هَذِهِ الْبَقْلَةِ فَلَا يَقْرَبَنَّ مَسَاجِدَنَا حَتَّى يَذْهَبَ رِيحُهَا يَعْنِي الثُّومَ.»

Whoever eats of these vegetables (i.e., onions and garlic) should not approach our mosques until the odour disappears (from his mouth).[2]

Is the one who consumes onions and garlic guilty of some major sin for which he should not approach the mosques? Of course not! The most exalted Prophet ﷺ decreed that such an individual ought to refrain from praying in the house of Almighty Allah immediately after consuming these vegetables, since other worshippers would be distracted by the odour that is emitted. All such available hadiths on the issue of bodily beautification and apparent factors that affect the senses indicate that Islam is a religion of wisdom (*ḥikma)* that is concerned with the welfare and wellbeing of people.

After touching upon the fundamentals of *bid*ᶜ*a* and the cultural

---

[1] Qur'ān 7:31.

[2] Narrated by Muslim in *al-Ṣaḥīḥ*: *Kitāb al-Masājid wa Mawāḍi*ᶜ *al-Ṣalā* [The Book of Mosques and the Places of Prayer], chapter: 'Prohibition of eating garlic, onions, or leeks, etc.', 1:394 §561; and Abū Dāwūd in *al-Sunan*: *Kitāb al-Aṭ*ᶜ*ima* [The Book of Foodstuff], chapter: 'On eating garlic', 3:160–161 §3824–3825.

aspects of the *mawlid*, we shall now discuss the true concept of *bidʿa*:

10.4 The True Meaning of *Bidʿa*

The following hadiths shall clarify the true meaning of *bidʿa* and shed light on what exactly constitutes an innovation in the Sharia:

1. Mother of the believers, ʿĀʾisha ؓ narrates:

مَنْ أَحْدَثَ فِي أَمْرِنَا هَذَا مَا لَيْسَ مِنْهُ فَهُوَ رَدٌّ.

> If someone invents in our *Dīn* (Religion) something which does not belong to it, it is rejected.[1]

2. In another narration, she narrates:

مَنْ أَحْدَثَ فِي أَمْرِنَا هَذَا مَا لَيْسَ مِنْهُ فَهُوَ رَدٌّ.

> If someone invents in our *Dīn* (Religion) something which has no root in it, it is rejected.[2]

3. ʿĀʾisha ؓ also narrates:

مَنْ عَمِلَ عَمَلًا لَيْسَ عَلَيْهِ أَمْرُنَا فَهُوَ رَدٌّ.

> If someone performs a practice which is not commanded by us, it is rejected.[3]

---

[1] Narrated by Muslim in *al-Ṣaḥīḥ*: *Kitāb al-Aqḍiya* [The Book of Judgements], chapter: 'The abrogation of false rulings', 3:1343 §1718; Ibn Mājah in *al-Sunan*: al-*Muqaddama* [Prolegomena], chapter: 'Veneration of the speech of Allah's Messenger', 1:7 §14; and Aḥmad b. Ḥanbal in *al-Musnad*, 6:270 §26,372.

[2] Narrated by al-Bukhārī in *al-Ṣaḥīḥ*: *Kitāb al-Ṣulḥ* [The Book of Concord], chapter: 'If they agree on an injustice, the concord is rejected', 2:959 §2550; and Abū Dāwūd in *al-Sunan*: *Kitāb al-Sunna* [The Book of *Sunna*], chapter: 'Concerning the necessity of sticking to the Sunna', 4:200 §4606.

[3] Narrated by Muslim in *al-Ṣaḥīḥ*: *Kitāb al-Aqḍiya* [The Book of Judgement], chapter: 'The abrogation of false rulings', 3:1343 §1718; Aḥmad b. Ḥanbal

10.4.1 Removal of Misconceptions and the Correct Understanding of '*Fa Huwa Radd*'

The words 'invents' (*aḥdatha*), 'which does not belong to it' (*mā laysa minhu*), and 'which has no root in it' (*mā laysa fīhi*) are worthy of attention. In general custom, the word 'invents' (*aḥdatha*) is understood to mean 'introducing a new practice into the religion', whilst the words 'which does not belong to it' (*mā laysa minhu*) further clarify that this refers to innovating something that is not a part of Islam. A question arises that if the word *aḥdatha* implies establishing a new matter, then what was the need of saying *mā laysa minhu* or *mā laysa fīhi*? This is because if that thing was from the religion, i.e., it constituted a part of it, then it cannot be called a new thing (*muḥdatha*), as a new thing is called such when it has no existence in the religion in the first place.

In reply to this question, by reading these hadiths carefully it can be understood that not every new matter is rejected; rather, only those new matters are rejected which are not part of the religion; if that new thing does fall within the scope of the religion, then it is not rejected, but accepted.

To elucidate this further, in the hadith, 'If someone invents in our *Dīn* (Religion) something which does not belong to it/ has no root in it, it is rejected', the statement, 'It is rejected', cannot be applied only on, 'which does not belong to it', nor on the word, 'invents', rather it has to be applied in the situation when both of them come together: i.e., when 'if someone invents' and 'which does not belong to it/ has no root in it' come together, only then that action is rejected, because it is a new action and is without basis in the religion, i.e., devoid of any example or evidence in the Sharia. In order for that new act to be rejected, it must have no connection with any aspect of the religion (i.e., it lacks a single evidence from the Qur'ān and Sunna).

Therefore, in order to declare any new thing an innovation

---

in *al-Musnad*, 6:180 & 256 §25,511 & 26,234; and al-Dārquṭnī in *al-Sunan*, 4:227 §81.

(*bidʿa*) and a misguidance, the following two conditions have to be fulfilled unavoidably:

Firstly, there is no origin for it in the religion, and no such example or evidence for it exists.

Secondly, this new action (*muḥdatha*) does not only contradict or conflict with the religion, but also negates the religion (*Dīn*) or contravenes one of the rulings or Sunna.

In the third hadith mentioned above, 'A practice which is not commanded by us', there is a misinformed opinion that every deed, even if it be a virtuous one, such as conveying reward to the deceased, *Mawlid al-Nabī* ﷺ, and other affairs relating to good conduct and spirituality, is outright rejected and considered an innovation if it is unsupported in the Qurʾān and Sunna. This view stems from pure ignorance and narrow-mindedness. If this meaning was to be taken (that any matter which is not backed by the Qurʾān and Sunna is rejected), then what would be said about all the indifferent (*mubāḥ*) actions of the Sharia—they too will be liable to repudiation.

From the aforementioned hadiths, it is evident that not every new matter is rejected without thought. Rather, only those new matters which have no origin in the Sharia or have no prior example or mention in the Qurʾān or Sunna (either directly or indirectly) and are added at the fundamental level of the religion (like the *ḍurūriyāt al-dīn*[1], the obligatory practices of Islam and the essential beliefs) will be rejected. The Prophet's statements, 'Every innovation is a misguidance' was in reference to such *bidʿa*; innovations of this kind will be classified as an act of transgression (*fitna)* against the *Dīn*.

In light of this discussion, what is apparent is that the *mawlid* contains no such feature that opposes the Qurʾān and Sunna. On the other hand, it consists of many virtuous and commendable deeds which are exactly in accordance with the intended goals of the Sharia.

---

[1] The *ḍurūriyāt al-dīn*, i.e., the necessities of the religion, is a term used for those tenets, the denial of which renders one a disbeliever.

10.5 Inventing Something in the Religion: Its Intended Meaning in the Prophet's Era

In the previous pages, the terms 'innovation' (*bidʿa*) and 'inventing something in the religion' (*iḥdāth fī al-dīn*) have been explained from an intellectual and analogical point of view that any new thing for which evidence exists in the Sharia, legally is not an innovation (*bidʿa*) though linguistically speaking it may be called so. Let us now look into those matters or issues on which the term innovation is applied correctly. A standard needs to be set that we can utilise till the Day of Judgment, by which we can properly determine which of those issues fall within the purview of innovation and which do not. Below, some traditions have been related which serve as litmus tests for this correct application:

1. 'Inventing something in the religion' (*iḥdāth fī al-dīn*) refers to those heresies and apostasy that emerged after the beloved Prophet's passing away during the caliphate of Abū Bakr al-Ṣiddīq ﷺ. ʿAbd Allāh b. Masʿūd ﷺ narrates that the Prophet ﷺ said:

أَنَا فَرَطُكُمْ عَلَى الْـحَوْضِ وَلَيُرْفَعَنَّ مَعِي رِجَالٌ مِنْكُمْ ثُمَّ لَيُخْتَلَجُنَّ دُونِي
فَأَقُولُ: يَا رَبِّ، أَصْحَابِي فَيُقَالُ: إِنَّكَ لَا تَدْرِي مَا أَحْدَثُوا بَعْدَكَ.

> I am your forerunner at the Basin [*al-Ḥawḍ*]. Certain people amongst you will be brought and then will be driven away from me. I will say, 'My Lord! (They are) my Companions.' It will be said, 'You do not know what they invented after you.'[1]

2. Abū al-Dardāʾ ﷺ reports that the Prophet ﷺ said:

قَالَ رَسُوْلُ اللهِ ﷺ: «لَا أُلْفِيَنَّ مَا نُوْزِعْتُ أَحَداً مِنْكُمْ عَلَى الْـحَوْضِ.

[1] Narrated by al-Bukhārī in *al-Ṣaḥīḥ*: *Kitāb al-Riqāq* [The Book of Softening of the Heart], chapter: 'Concerning the Basin [al-*Ḥawḍ*]', 5:2404 §6205; Muslim in *al-Ṣaḥīḥ*: *Kitāb al-Faḍāʾil* [The Book of Virtuous Merits], chapter: 'Affirming the Prophet's Basin [al-*Ḥawḍ*]', 4:1796 §2297; and Aḥmad b. Ḥanbal in *al-Musnad*, 1:439 §4180.

فَأَقُوْلُ: هَذَا مِنْ أَصْحَابِـي. فَيُقَالُ: إِنَّكَ لَا تَدْرِي مَا أَحْدَثُوْا بَعْدَكَ.» قَالَ أَبُو الدَّرْدَاءِ: يَا نَبِيَّ اللهِ! أُدْعُ اللهَ أَنْ لَا يَجْعَلَنِي مِنْهُمْ. قَالَ: «لَسْتَ مِنْهُمْ.»

I do not wish to see any of you approach my Basin [*al-Ḥawḍ*] and then be dragged away from it. I will say, 'These are my Companions.' It will be said, 'You do not know what they invented after you.' Abū al-Dardāʾ said, 'O Prophet of Allah! Please supplicate to Allah that He does not make me from them.' The Prophet ﷺ replied, 'You are not from them.'[1]

The Holy Prophet's reply to Abū al-Dardāʾ that 'you are not from them' is an evident proof that Allah's Messenger ﷺ knew who the mischief-makers were.

3. ʿUmar b. al-Khaṭṭāb ؓ reports that the Prophet ﷺ said:

قَالَ رَسُوْلُ اللهِ ﷺ : «إِنِّـي مُـمْسِكٌ بِحُجَزِكُمْ هَلُمَّ عَنِ النَّارِ، وَأَنْتُمْ تَهَافَتُوْنَ فِيهَا أَوْ تَقَاحَمُوْنَ تَقَاحُمَ الْفَرَاشِ فِي النَّارِ وَالْـجَنَادِبِ يَعْنِي فِي النَّارِ، وَأَنَا مُـمْسِكٌ بِحُجَزِكُمْ، وَأَنَا فَرَطٌ لَكُمْ عَلَى الْـحَوْضِ، فَتَرِدُوْنَ عَلَيَّ مَعاً وَأَشْتَاتاً، فَأَعْرِفُكُمْ بِسِيْمَـاكُمْ، وَأَسْمَـائِكُمْ كَمَـا يَعْرِفُ الرَّجُلُ الْفَرَسَ. وَقَالَ غَيْرُهُ: كَمَـا يَعْرِفُ الرَّجُلُ الْغَرِيْبَةَ مِنَ الْإِبِلِ فِي إِبِلِهِ – فَيُؤْخَذُ بِكُمْ ذَاتَ الشِّمَـالِ، فَأَقُوْلُ: إِلَيَّ يَا رَبِّ! أُمَّتِي أُمَّتِي. فَيَقُوْلُ أَوْ يُقَالُ: يَا مُحَمَّدُ! إِنَّكَ لَا تَدْرِي مَا أَحْدَثُوا بَعْدَكَ، كَانُوْا يَمْشُونَ بَعْدَكَ الْقَهْقَرَى.»

I am indeed holding you back from you casting yourselves into the Fire. However, you are still stumbling into it, (or he said:) you are flocking towards it, like the way moths are attracted to a flame, despite the fact that I am holding

[1] Narrated by al-Ṭabarānī in *al-Muʿjam al-awsaṭ*, 1:125 §397; al-Ṭabarānī in *Musnad al-Shāmiyyin*, 2:311 §1405; Ibn Abī ʿĀṣim in *al-Sunna*, 2:357 §767; al-Daylamī in *al-Firdaws bi-maʾthūr al-khiṭāb*, 1:50 §129; and al-Haythamī in *Majmaʿ al-zawāʾid wa manbaʿ al-fawāʾid*, 9:367 & 10:365.

> you back. I am your forerunner at the Basin [*al-Ḥawḍ*], where you shall be conveyed to me together or scattered. I will recognise you by your names and signs in the way that a man identifies his horse, or like a person recognises his camels. However you shall be dragged away to the left upon which I shall exclaim, 'To me, my Lord! My community! My community!' Allah will reply, or it will be said, 'O Muhammad ﷺ! You do not know what they invented after you. They turned back on their heels (i.e., they became apostates).[1]

On this topic, there are many other hadiths concerning the short time after the Prophet's passing away, in which *iḥdāth* has been mentioned. This *iḥdāth* is in reference to those major transgressions (*fitna*) which sought to bring about fundamental changes within the religion. In the above mentioned hadiths, there is indication to the 'invented matters' (*muḥdathāt al-umūr*) which took the shape of apostasy during the epoch of the rightly guided caliphs. The perpetrators of these innovations were those people who accepted Islam during the life of the Holy Prophet ﷺ but later became apostates, deniers of the alms-due, false claimants of prophethood, and the *khawārij*. There are several hadiths which substantiate this; these are related below:

4. ʿAbd Allāh b. ʿAbbās narrates that the Prophet ﷺ said:

قَالَ رَسُولُ اللهِ ﷺ: «تُحْشَرُونَ حُفَاةً عُرَاةً غُرْلًا ثُمَّ قَرَأَ: ﴿كَمَا بَدَأْنَآ أَوَّلَ خَلْقٍ نُّعِيدُهُۥ وَعْدًا عَلَيْنَآ إِنَّا كُنَّا فَٰعِلِينَ﴾ فَأَوَّلُ مَنْ يُكْسَى إِبْرَاهِيمُ ثُمَّ يُؤْخَذُ بِرِجَالٍ مِنْ أَصْحَابِي ذَاتَ الْيَمِينِ وَذَاتَ الشِّمَالِ فَأَقُولُ: أَصْحَابِي فَيُقَالُ: إِنَّهُمْ لَمْ يَزَالُوا مُرْتَدِّينَ عَلَى أَعْقَابِهِمْ مُنْذُ فَارَقْتَهُمْ فَأَقُولُ كَمَا قَالَ

---

[1] Narrated by al-Bazzār in *al-Baḥr al-zukhār (al-musnad)*, 1:314–315 §204; al-Qaḍāʿī in *Musnad al-Shihāb*, 2:175 §1130; al-Sidūsī in *Musnad ʿUmar b. al-Khaṭṭab*, 1:84; Mundhirī in *al-Targhīb wa al-tarhīb min al-ḥadīth al-sharīf*, 1:318 §1169; and al-Haythamī in *Majmaʿ al-zawāʾid wa manbaʿ al-fawāʾid*, 3:85.

الْعَبْدُ الصَّالِحُ عِيسَى ابْنُ مَرْيَمَ: ﴿وَكُنتُ عَلَيْهِمْ شَهِيدًا مَّا دُمْتُ فِيهِمْ فَلَمَّا تَوَفَّيْتَنِي كُنتَ أَنتَ ٱلرَّقِيبَ عَلَيْهِمْ وَأَنتَ عَلَىٰ كُلِّ شَيْءٍ شَهِيدٌ ۝١١٧ إِن تُعَذِّبْهُمْ فَإِنَّهُمْ عِبَادُكَ وَإِن تَغْفِرْ لَهُمْ فَإِنَّكَ أَنتَ ٱلْعَزِيزُ ٱلْحَكِيمُ﴾»

قَالَ مُحَمَّدُ بْنُ يُوسُفَ الْفَرَبْرِيُّ: ذُكِرَ عَنْ أَبِي عَبْدِ اللهِ عَنْ قَبِيصَةَ قَالَ: هُمُ الْمُرْتَدُّونَ الَّذِينَ ارْتَدُّوا عَلَى عَهْدِ أَبِي بَكْرٍ فَقَاتَلَهُمْ أَبُو بَكْرٍ رضي الله عنه.

You shall indeed be resurrected barefoot and naked. Thereafter, he recited the verse, ﴾*The way We created (the universe) the first time, We shall repeat the same process of creation (after its extinction). We have made it binding upon Us to fulfil this promise. We will do (repeat it)*﴿.[1] The first person to be clothed will be Ibrāhīm. Thereafter, some of my Companions shall be taken from the right and left, upon which I will say, 'My Companions!' It shall be said, 'They turned back on their heels as apostates since you left them.' Then I shall say as the pious slave of Allah, ʿĪsā the son of Maryam, said, ﴾*I said to them nothing except (that) which You ordered me to say: Worship (only) Allah, Who is my Lord and your Lord (too). And I kept a vigilant watch over (their beliefs and actions) so long as I was amongst them. But when You lifted me up, then You alone watched over their affairs), and You are a Witness to everything. If You torment them, they are only Your servants, and if You forgive them, You are indeed Almighty, All-Wise*﴿.[2]

Muhammad b. Yūsuf said: It is mentioned from Abū ʿAbd Allāh from Qubayṣa that 'they are the apostates who left the religion during the caliphate of Abū Bakr, so Abū Bakr fought them.'[3]

---

[1] Qurʾān 21:104.

[2] Qurʾān 5:117–118.

[3] Narrated by al-Bukhārī in *al-Ṣaḥīḥ: Kitāb al-Anbiyā*ʾ [The Book of Prophets], chapter: 'Allah's statement: And recite the account of Maryam

5. Asmā᾽ b. Abī Bakr ؓ reports that the Holy Prophet ﷺ said:

قَالَ النَّبِيُّ ﷺ: «إِنِّي عَلَى الْحَوْضِ حَتَّى أَنْظُرَ مَنْ يَرِدُ عَلَيَّ مِنكُمْ وَسَيُؤْخَذُ نَاسٌ دُونِي فَأَقُولُ: يَا رَبِّ، مِنِّي وَمِنْ أُمَّتِي فَيُقَالُ: هَلْ شَعَرْتَ مَا عَمِلُوا بَعْدَكَ وَاللهِ، مَا بَرِحُوا يَرْجِعُونَ عَلَى أَعْقَابِهِمْ.»

فَكَانَ ابْنُ أَبِي مُلَيْكَةَ يَقُولُ: اللَّهُمَّ إِنَّا نَعُوذُ بِكَ أَنْ نَرْجِعَ عَلَى أَعْقَابِنَا أَوْ نُفْتَنَ عَنْ دِينِنَا.

I will be at the Basin [*al-Ḥawḍ*] until I will be waiting for you to be conveyed to me. Some people will be taken away from me. I will say, 'My Lord! From me and my community' and it will be said, 'Are you aware what they did after you? By Allah, they would not desist from turning on their heels (as apostates).' Ibn Abī Mulayka used to say, 'O Allah! We seek refuge in You from turning on our heels (as apostates) and from being tested in our religion.'[1]

6. Jābir b. ʿAbd Allāh narrates that Allah's Messenger ﷺ said:

قَالَ رَسُولُ اللهِ ﷺ: «أَنَا عَلَى الْحَوْضِ أَنْظُرُ مَنْ يَرِدُ عَلَيَّ قَالَ: فَيُؤْخَذُ نَاسٌ دُونِي فَأَقُولُ: يَا رَبِّ، مِنِّي وَمِنْ أُمَّتِي قَالَ: فَيُقَالُ: وَمَا يُدْرِيكَ مَا عَمِلُوا بَعْدَكَ مَا بَرِحُوا بَعْدَكَ يَرْجِعُونَ عَلَى أَعْقَابِهِمْ.»

---

in the Book when she separated from her family', 3:1271–1272 §3263; al-Bukhārī in *al-Ṣaḥīḥ*: *Kitāb al-Anbiyā᾽* [The Book of Prophets], chapter: 'Allah's statement: And Allah had taken Ibrāhīm for a sincere and intimate friend', 3:1222 §3171; and al-Tirmidhī in *al-Jāmiʿ al-Ṣaḥīḥ*: *Kitāb Ṣifa al-Qiyāma* [The Book of Description of the Day of Resurrection], chapter: 'What has been mentioned concerning the gathering (*ḥashr*)', 4:615 §2423.

[1] Narrated by al-Bukhārī in *al-Ṣaḥīḥ*: *Kitāb al-Riqāq* [The Book of Softening of the Heart], chapter: 'Concerning the *ḥawḍ*', 5:2409 §6220; and Muslim in *al-Ṣaḥīḥ*: *Kitāb al-Faḍā᾽il* [The Book of Virtuous Merits], chapter: 'Affirming the Prophet's water-basin', 4:1794 §2293.

> I will be at the Basin [*al-Ḥawḍ*] waiting for you to be conveyed to me. Some people will be taken away from me. I will say, 'My Lord! From me and my community' and it will be said, 'You do not know what they did after you? They would not desist from turning on their heels (as apostates).'[1]

All of these narrations substantiate our stance that here, the 'invented matters' (*muḥdathāt al-umūr*) refer to apostasy, which took place in the short time after the beloved Prophet's passing away. The following points shall shed more light on this:
7. In the hadith narrated by ʿAbd Allāh b. ʿAbbās, in the latter portion of the hadith, which is *al-marfūʿ al-muttaṣil*[2], the statement 'they turned back on their heels as apostates since you left them' is in reference to those who left the religion after the Holy Prophet passed away. Therefore, the perpetrators of *iḥdāth* (i.e., those who 'invented something') were the apostates.
8. At the conclusion of the hadith narrated by ʿAbd Allāh b. ʿAbbās, Imam al-Bukhārī relates the statement of the hadith scholar, Qubayṣa b. ʿUqba, who, confirming our position, said:

هُمُ الْـمُرْتَدُّوْنَ الَّذِيْنَ ارْتَدُّوْا عَلَى عَهْدِ أَبِي بَكْرٍ، فَقَاتَلَهُمْ أَبُوْ بَكْرٍ ﷺ.

> They are the apostates who left the religion during the caliphate of Abū Bakr, so Abū Bakr fought them.

9. After transmitting the narration of Asmāʾ b. Abī Bakr ﷺ, Imam al-Bukhārī records the supplication of Ibn Abī Mulayka, the successor, who said:

اَللّٰهُمَّ! إِنَّا نَعُوْذُ بِكَ أَنْ نَرْجِعَ عَلَى أَعْقَابِنَا أَوْ نُفْتَنَ عَنْ دِيْنِنَا.

---

[1] Narrated by Aḥmad b. Ḥanbal in *al-Musnad*, 3:384 §15,161; and al-Haythamī in *Majmaʿ al-zawāʾid wa manbaʿ al-fawāʾid*, 10:364.

[2] *Al-marfūʿ al-muttaṣil* is a chain of narration which is attributed to the Prophet ﷺ and is perfectly connected.

> O Allah! We seek refuge in You from turning on our heels (as apostates) and from being tested in our religion.

10. In the aforementioned hadiths, the statement 'By Almighty Allah, they would not desist from turning on their heels (as apostates)' further confirms our stance.
11. In one of the hadiths, Abū al-Dardā' asks, 'O Prophet of Allah! Please supplicate to Almighty Allah that He does not make me from them.' And the Holy Prophet ﷺ in reply to his request said, 'You are not from them.' Imam al-Ṭabarānī, in *Musnad al-Shāmiyyīn* (2:311 §1405) after reporting this hadith writes:

فَمَـاتَ قَبْلَ عُثْمَـانَ بِسَنَتَيْنِ.

> He passed away two years before ʿUthmān.

From this it can be understood that 'inventing something in the religion' (*iḥdāth fī al-dīn*) refers to those transgression of apostasy which took place during the epoch of the rightly guided caliphs.
12. To elucidate this issue further, a significant and pertinent point has been made by Imam al-Ḥākim in his *al-Mustadrak ʿalā al-Ṣaḥīḥayn*. He relates that after the First transgression (*al-fitna al-ūlā*), the eminent successor, Ḥusayn b. Khārija, saw in a dream that Prophet Muhammad ﷺ and Prophet Ibrāhīm ﷺ were having a discussion: Prophet Muhammad ﷺ requested Prophet Ibrāhīm ﷺ to pray for the forgiveness of his community, to which he replied:

إِنَّكَ لَا تَدْرِي مَا أَحْدَثُوْا بَعْدَكَ، أَرَاقُوْا دِمَاءَ هُمْ وَقَتَلُوْا إِمَامَهُمْ.

> Do you not know what they invented after you: they shed the blood (of the Muslims) and killed their leader.[1]

Ibn Ḥajar al-ʿAsqalānī, in *al-Iṣāba fī tamyīz al-Ṣaḥāba* (2:127 §1979) and Ibn ʿAbd al-Barr, in *al-Tamhīd limā fī al-Muwaṭṭā min al-maʿānī wa al-asānīd* (19:222), commented on this narration, stating that *al-fitna al-ūla* was the martyrdom of ʿUthmān and the

[1] Narrated by al-Ḥākim in *al-Mustadrak*, 4:499 §8394.

ensuing transgression which took place after it. From this it can be learnt that those who martyred ʿUthmān where the mischief-makers who were guilty of perpetrating innovation in the religion. These innovators were narrow-minded fanatics, who, after the Battle of *Ṣiffīn*, became known as the Kharijites.

10.6 THE NEW MATTERS (MUḤDATHĀT AL-UMŪR) THAT AROSE IN THE ERA OF THE RIGHTLY GUIDED CALIPHS

Immediately after the Holy Prophet's passing away, during the era of the rightly guided caliphs, many new matters were invented into the religion. The following is a list of those new matters (*muḥdathāt*) which were confirmed as innovation (*bidʿa*) and against which martial *jihad* was declared:

10.6.1 THE TRANSGRESSION OF FALSE ATTRIBUTION OF PROPHETHOOD WAS DECLARED AN INNOVATION

The false claim to prophethood after the Holy Prophet's passing away was declared an innovation (*iḥdāth fī al-dīn*). Aswad b. ʿUnzah al-ʿAnsi, Ṭulayḥa al-Asadī and Musaylama al-Kadhdhāb were such false claimants to prophethood, against whom Abū Bakr al-Ṣiddīq and the Companions waged war.

10.6.2 THE TRANSGRESSION OF APOSTASY WAS DECLARED AN INNOVATION

After the departure of the army of Usāma b. Zayd, yet another ordeal befell the Arabian peninsula in the form of several tribes absconding from the faith and returning to their old, false ways. Consequently, Abū Bakr al-Ṣiddīq declared war against them which lead to their obliteration.[1]

10.6.3 THE TRANSGRESSION OF THE DENIERS OF ALMS-DUE WAS DECLARED AN INNOVATION

Along with turning their backs to Islam, these tribes blatantly refused to pay the alms-due. Abū Bakr declared war against

---

[1] Al-Ṭabarī, *Tārīkh al-umum wa al-mulūk*, 2:254.

them with his famous words:

وَاللهِ، لَأُقَاتِلَنَّ مَنْ فَرَّقَ بَيْنَ الصَّلَاةِ وَالزَّكَاةِ فَإِنَّ الزَّكَاةَ حَقُّ الْمَالِ. وَاللهِ، لَوْ مَنَعُونِي عَنَاقًا كَانُوا يُؤَدُّونَهَا إِلَى رَسُولِ اللهِ ﷺ لَقَاتَلْتُهُمْ عَلَى مَنْعِهَا.

> By Allah! I will fight those who differentiate between the ritual prayer and the alms-due, for indeed the alms-due is the entitlement of the treasury (*bayt al-māl*). By Allah! If they withheld even a young she-goat that they used to pay at the time of Allah's Messenger ﷺ, I would fight them for withholding it.[1]

Thus, Abū Bakr dispatched an army against this rebellion under the command of Khālid b. Walīd.

10.6.4 The Transgression of the *Khawārij* was Declared an Innovation

The Kharijites emerged during the caliphate of Imam ʿAlī al-Murtaḍā. A battle commenced between Imam ʿAlī and Amīr Muʿāwiya for several days at *Ṣiffīn*, in which thousands of noble Companions and successors were martyred. Eventually, both sides decided to appoint two reliable persons as arbitrators who could bring an end to the battle in light of the Qurʾān and Sunna: Abū Mūsā ʿAbd Allāh b. Qays al-Ashʿarī was appointed by Imam ʿAlī, whilst ʿAmr b. al-ʿĀṣ was appointed by Amīr Muʿāwiya. A declaration was signed upon which the conflict ended.

Thereafter, Ashʿath b. Qays took this declaration and read it to all the tribes involved. In the process, he came across Banū Tamīm. ʿUrwa b. Adaya, the brother of Abū Bilāl, was present whilst this

[1] Narrated by al-Bukhārī in *al-Ṣaḥīḥ*: *Kitāb al-Zakā* [The Book of the Alms-due], chapter: 'The obligation of the alms-due', 2:507 §1335; al-Bukhārī in *al-Ṣaḥīḥ*: *Kitāb Istitāba al-Murtadīn* [The Book of Seeking the Repentance of Apostates], chapter: 'Death penalty for the one who denies the obligations', 6:2538 §6526; and Muslim in *al-Ṣaḥīḥ*: *Kitāb al-Īmān* [The Book of Faith], chapter: 'The command to fight people till they profess that there is no god, but Allah; Muhammad is Allah's Messenger', 1:51 §20.

was being read aloud, and he exclaimed:

تُحَكِّمُوْنَ فِي أَمْرِ اللهِ ﷻ الرِّجَالَ؟ لَا حُكْمَ إِلَّا لله.

Do you take men as arbitrators in the matter of Allah? There is no judgment, save God's alone.[1]

After making this statement, he pounced upon the ride of Ashᶜath b. Qays and struck it with his sword. Ashᶜath fell to the ground and a great skirmish was about to ensue amongst the tribe. Imam ᶜAlī, upon returning to *Kūfā*, learnt of this unfortunate incident and said:

اَللهُ أَكْبَرُ! كَلِمَةُ حَقٍّ يُرَادُ بِهَا بَاطِلٌ، إِنْ سَكَتُوا عَمَمْنَاهُمْ، وَإِنْ تَكَلَّمُوا حَجَجْنَاهُمْ، وَإِنْ خَرَجُوْا عَلَيْنَا قَاتَلْنَاهُمْ.

Allah is the greatest! A truthful word, but its intent is mistaken. If they remain quite, we shall prevail over them; if they speak, we will out do them in our evidences; and if they set out against us, we will fight them.[2]

The Kharijites stirred up sentiments against Imam ᶜAlī, asking people to escape to the mountains or migrate to another city whilst denouncing the words of Imam ᶜAlī as a blameworthy innovation. These insurgents, determined in establishing 'God's rule', gathered and settled in *Nahrawān*. At this place, the Kharijites martyred the Companion, ᶜAbd Allāh b. Khabbāb; hearing of this, Imam ᶜAlī said:

دُوْنَكُمُ الْقَوْمَ.

Take these people (i.e., finish them off).

---

[1] Narrated by al-Ṭabarī in *Tārīkh al-umum wa al-mulūk*, 3:104; Ibn Athīr in *al-Kāmil fī al-tārīkh*, 3:196; and Ibn al-Jawzī in *al-Muntaẓam fī tārīkh al-mulūk wa al-umam*, 5:123.

[2] Narrated by al-Ṭabarī in *Tārīkh al-umum wa al-mulūk*, 3:114; and Ibn Athīr in *al-Kāmil fī al-tārīkh*, 3:212–213.

Thus, an army was dispatched by Imam ʿAlī which resulted in a bitter battle. Jundub states:

فَقَتَلْتُ بِكَفِّي هَذِهِ بَعْدَ مَا دَخَلَنِي مَا كَانَ دَخَلَنِي ثَمَانِيَةً قَبْلَ أَنْ أُصَلِّيَ الظُّهْرَ، وَمَا قُتِلَ مِنَّا عَشَرَةٌ وَلَا نَجَا مِنْهُمْ عَشَرَةٌ.

> I killed eight of them with my very hands before I performed the *ẓuhr* ritual prayer. Not even ten of us were killed; nor did ten of them survive.[1]

This is how the Kharijite revolt in the time of Imam ʿAlī come to an end.

These were the tribulations that the most exalted Prophet ﷺ was indicating towards when he spoke to his noble Companions: it is these that were referred to as 'invented matters' (*muḥdathāt al-umūr*) that rose up shortly after the Prophet's ﷺ passing away. Thus, according to the authentic hadiths, these four offshoots (i.e., the false claimants to prophethood, apostates, deniers of the alms-due and the *khawārij*) were the real perpetrations of 'inventing something in the religion' (*iḥdāth fī al-dīn*). Interestingly, the hadiths have exclusively made the word 'invent' (*iḥdāth*) to mean 'apostasy'. Therefore, the misguided innovation (*bidʿa ḍalāla*) leads to the Hellfire and is in reference to those newly invented matters which result in apostasy.

10.6.4.1 In Our Age, What is the Correct Application of Labelling Something an 'Invented Matter' (Muḥdathāt al-Umūr)?

Elucidating what is meant by *bidʿa*, the Prophet ﷺ himself specified its meaning, stating that it referred to 'invented matters' (*muḥdathāt al-umūr*). It refers to such transgressions which alter the fundamental teachings of the religion or result in its denial; such a thing is apostasy in its essence. Therefore, the misguided innovation (*al-bidʿa al-ḍalāla*) does not refer to minor differences

---

[1] Narrated by al-Ṭabarānī in *al-Muʿjam al-awsaṭ*, 4:227 §4051; and al-Haythamī in *Majmaʿ al-zawāʾid wa manbaʿ al-fawāʾid*, 4:227.

of opinion; rather its application is at the level which results in apostasy or forsaking the religion of Islam (*khurūj ʿan al-Islām*). Such a thing presents itself in the *Umma* as a serious cause of divergence (*ikhtilāf kathīr*) resulting in the severing of the Sunna or the affairs of the religion.

Major divergences of this kind are, for example: denying one of the essential themes of creed, such as belief in Almighty Allah, His angels, revealed books, prophecy, the Last Day, destiny and life after death; rejecting one of the five pillars of Islam, such as believing in Almighty Allah and His Messenger ﷺ, the ritual prayer, fasting, the alms-due and Pilgrimage; adding or subtracting from the integrals of Islam; disagreeing with the finality of Prophethood; distorting the Qurʾān (by adding or subtracting from its verses); negating the whole authority of hadith and Sunna; associating oneself to some sect like the *khawārij*; calling for the abrogation of martial *jihad*; permitting usury and the likes of it. Such beliefs will present themselves as transgressions for the *Umma*, and until the Day of Judgment, they will remain in the purview of the misguided innovation (*bidʿa ḍalāla*). The person who holds such a belief will be banished to the Hellfire.

For that reason, *bidʿa* is solely in reference to apostasy and its many manifestations which occurred within the short period after the beloved Prophet's passing away. If such is not the case, then the term *al-bidʿa al-ḍalāla* cannot be applied. Thus, in our time, a set standard should be utilised to outline its correct application. Ancillary issues, which fall within the scope of minor differences, such as the *mawlid*, death-anniversaries, donating reward to the deceased (*īṣāl al-thawāb*) etc., should not be indicted as being *muḥdathāt al-umūr* or *al-bidʿa al-ḍalāla* because such things do not necessitate that a person is an apostate who has forsaken his religion. Rather, such things in their essence are established in the Sharia. *Muḥdathāt al-umūr* refer to those transgressions which cause major divergence within the *Umma*, resulting in the community being severely divided into various factions with wars ensuing and many being killed on account of that transgression.

It is a matter of great shame for those people who declare the *mawlid* or the act of donating reward to the deceased as *muḥdathāt al-umūr* or *al-bidʿa al-ḍalāla*. By declaring such things an innovation, they are negating the Holy Prophet's ﷺ own definition; this audacity with Allah's Messenger ﷺ is tantamount to denial of the authentic hadiths. The reality is that these are commendable matters pertaining to the religion. The jurists have had differences with one another on thousands of issues: they have differed whether something is reprehensible or recommended, and have even differed on the lawfulness or unlawfulness of certain things. These commendable actions (*mustaḥabbāt*) should not be called *bidʿa*, because as per the Holy Prophet's ﷺ definition, such an accusation would make the practice tantamount to apostasy and disbelief; and the injunction concerning such people is that martial *jihad* should be declared upon them—are those who consider the *mawlid* to be *al-bidʿa al-ḍalāla* waging a martial *jihad* against those who commemorate the *Mawlid*?

In the time of the Companions, the compilation of the Qurʾān, congregational offering of the *tarāwīḥ* prayer, and the second *ādhān* for the Friday prayer were all introduced for the benefit of the community. In the same way, the *mawlid* is a means by which broken relations of love can be reconnected with the Messenger ﷺ of Almighty Allah and the desire for the perfect obedience to the most exalted Prophet ﷺ can be revived and strengthened. And likewise, donating rewards to the deceased is a means by which those who have passed away can have their sins forgiven and ranks raised.

10.7 The Concept of Innovation in Light of the Reports of the Companions

In the discourses that have preceded us, whilst explaining the literal meaning of innovation, we have clarified that *bidʿa* literally means a new thing, whilst 'invented matters' (*muḥdathāt al-umūr*) and 'inventing something in the religion' (*iḥdāth fī al-dīn*) refer to apostasy, or transgressions which are at the level of 'forsaking the religion of Islam' (*khurūj ʿan al-Islām*). We will now investigate whether there are examples of this concept of innovation in the report of the noble Companions which can elucidate this matter further. There shall be a brief account of related incidents in connection to Abū Bakr al-Ṣiddīq, ʿUmar, and ʿUthmān ﷺ, as their practice is the most reliable after the Messenger of Allah ﷺ. In order to decimate the transgressions which were to occur after his passing away, the Holy Prophet ﷺ enjoined holding firm onto his Sunna and the Sunna of the rightly guided caliphs who came after him.

10.7.1 The Compilation of the Qurʾān and the Practice of the *Shaykhayn*

After the Holy Prophet's ﷺ passing away, when Abū Bakr settled into the position of caliph, at that time a war was waged at Yamāma against the falsely claimed prophet, Musaylama al-Kadhdhāb, which resulted in the martyrdom of approximately 700 Companions who had committed the Qurʾān to memory. Prior to this in the Holy Prophet's ﷺ lifetime, the Qurʾān had not yet been compiled into a single volume; rather, some of the chapters and verses were written on various materials in isolation to others. ʿUmar felt the need that if this situation of martial *jihad* persisted, one day it may be a real possibility that the protection of the Qurʾān would become difficult. With this fear, ʿUmar proposed to Abū Bakr that the Qurʾān should be compiled together into a single book form. Upon hearing this, Abū Bakr retorted:

كَيْفَ أَفْعَلُ شَيْئًا مَا لَمْ يَفْعَلْهُ رَسُوْلُ اللهِ ﷺ ؟

> How can I do something which the Messenger of Allah ﷺ did not do?

ʿUmar replied, 'O commander of the faithful! It is true that the Holy Prophet ﷺ did not perform this task in his lifetime. However, by Allah, it is good (*huwa wallāhi khayr*). We should not hesitate in its execution.' During this discourse, Abū Bakr's breast was opened by Almighty Allah, and he immediately called for Zayd b. Thābit, who had scribed the revelation in the Prophet's lifetime, to discharge with this duty of compiling this Qurʾān into a single book. He collected the palm leaves, white stone, and other such materials upon which the Qurʾān was written and met with the noble Companions who had committed the Qurʾān to memory in order to undertake this huge assignment. The compiled Qurʾān was passed on from Abū Bakr to ʿUmar and eventually came into the possession of his daughter and the mother of the believers, Sayyida Ḥafṣa. Later, ʿUthmān requested the copy from her and published it anew, distributing it throughout every nook and corner of the Muslim world.[1]

In this way, the first ever praiseworthy innovation (*al-bidʿa al-ḥasana*) to take place was conducted at the blessed hands of Abū Bakr and ʿUmar.

10.7.2 The Initiation of the *Tarāwīḥ* Ritual Prayer in Congregation

As with the compilation of the Qurʾān, this pioneering act was also the idea of ʿUmar. The hadiths mention that the most exalted Prophet performed the *tarāwīḥ* ritual prayer in his whole life in congregation on three nights in the holy month of *Ramaḍān*. Thereafter, fearing that it would become obligatory upon his community, the most compassionate Prophet offered the *tarāwīḥ* ritual prayer in the confines of his blessed home, and the noble Companions followed suit offering their prayers individually. This practice continued for two and a half years during the caliphate of Abū Bakr. When ʿUmar succeeded him, he realised that since everyone was praying on their own accord, potentially this could lead to a decline in motivation, resulting in the prayer becoming abandoned. So he established (i.e. exercised *ijtihād*) and ordered the citizens of Medina to offer the (*tarāwīḥ*) ritual prayer behind Ubayy b. Kaʿb, a prominent *ḥāfiẓ* of the Qurʾān. Seeing the Companions together offering the prayer in congregation, ʿUmar exclaimed:

---

[1] Narrated by al-Bukhārī in *al-Ṣaḥīḥ*: *Kitāb al-Tafsīr* [The Book of Exegeses], chapter: 'Allah's statement: There has certainly come to you a Messenger from amongst yourselves. Grievous to him is what you suffer; [he is] concerned over you', 4:1720 §4402; and al-Tirmidhī in *al-Jāmiʿ al-Ṣaḥīḥ*: *Kitāb al-Tafsīr al-Qurʾān* [The Chapters of the Exegeses of the Qurʾān], chapter: 'From *Sūra al-Tawba*', 5:283 §3103.

$$\text{نِعْمَ الْبِدْعَةُ هَذِهِ وَالَّتِي يَنَامُونَ عَنْهَا أَفْضَلُ مِنَ الَّتِي يَقُومُونَ.}$$

What an excellent innovation this is! Those who sleep through it are superior to the ones who are offering it.[1]

Clarifying this statement of ʿUmar, the eminent successor ʿAbd al-Raḥmān b. ʿAbd al-Qārī states:

$$\text{يُرِيدُ آخِرَ اللَّيْلِ، وَكَانَ النَّاسُ يَقُومُونَ أَوَّلَهُ.}$$

He meant the latter portion of the night as people used to offer the night vigil in the earlier part of the night.[2]

In this narration, ʿUmar, by his statement, 'what an excellent innovation this is', establishes that not every *bidʿa* is a misguidance; in fact, there are many other innovations which are praiseworthy. This division of praiseworthy and blameworthy innovation is based on the above hadith. It is not solely a reasoned division, as it is based on the statement of ʿUmar.

---

[1] Narrated by al-Bukhārī in *al-Ṣaḥīḥ*: *Kitāb Ṣalā al-Tarāwīḥ* [The Book of the *Tarāwīḥ* Prayer], chapter: 'The excellence of the one who performs the night-vigil in *Ramaḍān*', 2:707 §1906; Mālik in *al-Muwaṭṭa*, 1:114 §250; and al-Bayhaqī in *al-Sunan al-kubrā*, 2:493 §4379.

[2] A question springs to mind that if the latter part of the night is more rewarded in terms of worship, why then did ʿUmar initiate the prayer during the earlier part of the night? Ḥāfiẓ Ibn Ḥajr al-ʿAsqalānī (773–852 AH) in *Fatḥ al-Bārī*, 4:253, explains this saying:

$$\text{هَذَا تَصْرِيحٌ مِنْهُ بِأَنَّ الصَّلَاةَ فِي آخِرِ اللَّيْلِ أَفْضَلُ مِنْ أَوَّلِهِ، لَكِنْ لَيْسَ فِيهِ أَنَّ الصَّلَاةَ فِي قِيَامِ اللَّيْلِ فُرَادَى أَفْضَلُ مِنَ التَّجْمِيعِ.}$$

This is an evident statement from him that the ritual prayer is superior in the latter portion of the night as opposed to the former portion; however, there is nothing in it which indicates that the night vigil is superior to be offered individually as opposed to in congregation.

Therefore, it is clear that although it is certainly a commendable act to perform the night vigil in the latter portion of the night (whilst others are asleep); to perform the *tarāwīḥ* ritual prayer in congregation still holds greater merit, notwithstanding.

10.7.3 The Second *Ādhān* before the Friday Congregational Prayer

Prior to the sermon, the second *ādhān* for the Friday congregational prayer was introduced during the caliphate of ʿUthmān b. ʿAffān ﷺ. Imam al-Bukhārī (194–256 AH) writes:

أَنَّ التَّأْذِينَ الثَّانِيَ يَوْمَ الْـجُمُعَةِ أَمَرَ بِهِ عُثْمَـانُ بْنُ عَفَّانَ ﷺ حِينَ كَثُرَ أَهْلُ الْـمَسْجِدِ.

> The second call to prayer on Friday was ordered by ʿUthmān when the congregation size increased.[1]

In like fashion, just as the pious predecessors on the occasion of the Qurʾān's compilation questioned that such a precedent was not left by the Messenger ﷺ of Allah, in our time today there are people who question the *mawlid* and other such virtuous deeds, demanding why the pious predecessors did not perform such acts. And just like the way the breasts of the noble Companions opened, resulting in them accepting these new matters, in the same way we have adopted the celebration of *Mawlid al-Nabī* ﷺ as a righteous deed and as a cause of blessings.

10.8 The Concept of Innovation and Some Contemporary Examples

In this regard, below are some contemporary examples:

10.8.1 The Establishment of an Islamic State

The Sharia has dictated that Muslims should have governance. However, how this comes about, which system of governance it will be, its institutions, and the division of power are details for which the Sharia has given no explicit injunctions. Every Muslim

[1] Narrated by al-Bukhārī in *al-Ṣaḥīḥ*: *Kitāb al-Jumʿa* [The Book of the Friday Congregational Prayer], chapter: 'Sitting on the pulpit when the call to prayer it made', 1:310 §873.

state, according to its discretion, implemented what it felt was necessary.

10.8.2 The Construction of Mosques

In the early days of Islam, to erect solid and firm buildings was somewhat frowned upon; thus, according to the spirit of the Sharia it was considered impermissible to build mosques in such fashion. Thereafter, a time came when the Islamic empire extended from east to west. Consequently, the culture, tradition, and way of living of the people evolved simultaneously. Individuals began erecting magnificent and imposing buildings for themselves. In the glorious days of the Umayyad and Abbasid dynasties, extraordinary palaces were built. Hence, the religious scholars, adapting to the new trends, not only declared the building of ornate mosques to be permissible, but considered it essential in maintaining the glory of Islam.

If changes have taken place in the way mosques were built, its benefit can be fathomed today easily. At that time, homes would be built from simple material, so when they constructed their mosques, they would do so from the same material which their own homes would be built. This was not a matter of shame. But as people began to fashion their buildings with solid material, it made sense that mosques should also be built with similar material in order to maintain their appeal amongst people; thus, religious edicts were issued for its permissibility.

From this it is clear that if one attempts to understand Islam in a literalist manner, then the result will be misguidance—*illā mā shāʾ Allāh*. But if we reflect deeply on the true spirit of the religion and its wisdoms, then and only then would the true understanding of the religion be appreciated.

10.8.3 Translating and Interpreting the Qurʾān

In order to impart the teachings of the Qurʾān to the masses, it was necessary to translate and interpret this sacred text into the various languages of the world. Yet the literalists, who have a narrow understanding of the religion and are ossified in their ultra-conservative approach, even denounced this new initiative as illegitimate. Thus, when Shāh Walī Allāh Muḥaddith al-Dihlawī (1703–1762 CE) for the first time translated the Qur'ān into the Persian language, the clerics of his time opposed him, issuing edicts of *kufr* and *bidʿa* at him—the idea that the Arabic text could be transferred into Farsi (Persian) in their view was tantamount to innovation and disbelief. However, time itself bore testimony that this new action was for the public interest. In the field of propagation, it fulfilled the need of its time, but the clerics were unable to recognise its benefits.

10.9 The Category of Innovation According to the Scholars

Keeping in mind the diversity of the Islamic tradition, the imams and hadith scholars have historically categorised innovation (*bidʿa*) into five kinds. The details of this are as follows:

10.9.1 Imam al-Shāfiʿī (150–204 AH)

The founder of the *Shāfiʿī* school of thought, Imam Muhammad b. Idrīs al-Shāfiʿī, categorises *bidʿa* in the following way:

الْـمُحْدَثَاتُ مِنَ الْأُمُوْرِ ضَرْبَانِ: مَا أُحْدِثَ يُخَالِفُ كِتَاباً أَوْ سُنَّةً أَوْ أَثَرًا أَوْ إِجْمَاعاً فَهَذِهِ الْبِدْعَةُ ضَلَالَةٌ، وَمَا أُحْدِثَ مِنَ الْـخَيْرِ لَا خِلَافَ فِيْهِ لِوَاحِدٍ مِنْ هَذَا، فَهَذِهِ مُحْدَثَةٌ غَيْرُ مَذْمُوْمَةٍ، قَدْ قَالَ عُمَرُ ﷺ فِي قِيَامِ رَمَضَانَ: نِعْمَتِ الْبِدْعَةُ هَذِهِ.

> Newly begun matters are of two kinds: the first is that which contravenes the Qur'ān, the Sunna, the reports of the Companions, or the consensus of the community; this is the misguided innovation (*al-bidʿa al-ḍalāla*). The other is the newly begun matter which is based on good and does not contravene any of these (above mentioned sources of the Sharia); this is the non-blameworthy innovation (*bidʿa ghayr madhmūma*). ʿUmar ﷺ said about the night vigil in

Ramaḍān (i.e., the *tarāwīḥ* ritual prayer), "What an excellent innovation this is."[1]

10.9.2 ʿIzz al-Dīn b. ʿAbd al-Salām (577–660 AH)

ʿIzz al-Dīn b. ʿAbd al-Salām in his book *Qawāʿid al-aḥkām fī maṣāliḥ al-anām* writes:

اَلْبِدْعَةُ فِعْلٌ مَا لَـمْ يَعْهَدْ فِي عَهْدِ النَّبِيِّ ﷺ، وَتَنْقَسِمُ إِلَى خَمْسَةِ أَحْكَامٍ يَعْنِي الْوُجُوْبَ وَالنُّدَبَ ... الخ. وَطَرِيْقُ مَعْرِفَةِ ذَلِكَ أَنْ تُعَرَضَ الْبِدْعَةُ عَلَى قَوَاعِدِ الشَّرْعِ فَأَيُّ حُكْمٍ دَخَلَتْ فِيْهِ فَهِيَ مِنْهُ، فَمِنَ الْبِدَعِ الْوَاجِبَةِ تَعَلُّمُ النَّحْوِ الَّذِي يُفْهَمُ بِهِ الْقُرْآنُ وَالسُّنَّةُ، وَمِنَ الْبِدَعِ الْـمُحَرَّمَةِ مَذْهَبُ نَحْوُ الْقَدَرِيَّةِ، وَمِنَ الْبِدَعِ الْـمَنْدُوبَةِ إِحْدَاثٌ نَحْوُ الْـمَدَارِسِ وَالْاِجْتِمَاعِ لِصَلَاةِ التَّرَاوِيحِ، وَمِنَ الْبِدَعِ الْـمُبَاحَةِ الْـمُصَافَحَةُ بَعْدَ الصَّلَاةِ، وَمِنَ الْبِدَعِ الْـمَكْرُوْهَةِ زَخْرَفَةُ الْـمَساجِدِ وَالْـمَصَاحِفِ أَيْ بِغَيْرِ الذَّهَبِ.

Innovation is a practice which did not exist in the time of the Prophet ﷺ. It is categorised into the five legal rulings, i.e., obligatory, commendable... etc. The way of ascertaining it is to compare the innovation in the light of the principles of the Sharia: whatever category it falls into, that will be its ruling. Thus, from the obligatory innovation (*al-bidʿa al-wājiba*) is to learn syntax, which is a means by which the Qurʾān and Sunna can be understood. From the forbidden innovation (*al-bidʿa al-muḥarrama*) are factions, such as the sect named *Qadriyya*. From the commendable innovation (*al-bidʿa al-mandūba*) are invented matters like schooling and the congregation for the *tarāwīḥ* ritual prayer. From the discretionary (indifferent) innovation (*al-bidʿa al-mubāḥa*) is to shake hands after the prayer. And from the reprehensible

[1] Al-Dhahabī, *Siyar aʿlām al-nubalāʾ*, 10:70; al-Suyūṭī, *al-Ḥāwī li al-fatāwā*, p.202; and al-Suyūṭī, *Ḥusn al-maqṣid fī ʿamal al-mawlid*, p.52–53.

innovation (*al-bidʿa al-makrūha*) is to ornament the mosques and the copies of the Qurʾān (from other than gold).[1]

10.9.3 Mullā ʿAlī al-Qārī al-Ḥanafī (d. 1014 AH)

Mullā ʿAlī al-Qārī al-Ḥanafī, in his commentary of *Mishkāt al-maṣābīḥ*, *Mirqāt al-mafātīḥ*, states:

قَالَ الشَّيْخُ عِزُّ الدِّيْنِ بْنُ عَبْدِ السَّلَامِ فِي آخِرِ كِتَابِ الْقَوَاعِدِ: اَلْبِدْعَةُ: أَمَّا وَاجِبَةٌ كَتَعَلُّمِ النَّحْوِ لِفَهْمِ كَلَامِ اللهِ وَرَسُوْلِهِ وَكَتَدْوِيْنِ أُصُوْلِ الْفِقْهِ وَالْكَلَامِ فِي الْجَرْحِ وَالتَّعْدِيْلِ. وَأَمَّا مُحَرَّمَةٌ كَمَذْهَبِ الْجَبَرِيَّةِ وَالْقَدَرِيَّةِ وَالْمُرْجِئَةِ وَالْمُجَسَّمَةِ. وَالرَّدُّ عَلَى هَؤُلَاءِ مِنَ الْبِدَعِ الْوَاجِبَةِ لِأَنَّ حِفْظَ الشَّرِيعَةِ مِنْ هَذِهِ الْبِدَعِ فَرْضُ كِفَايَةٍ. وَأَمَّا مَنْدُوبَةٌ كَإِحْدَاثِ الرَّبْطِ وَالْمَدَارِسِ وَكُلُّ إِحْسَانٍ لَمْ يَعْهَدْ فِي الصَّدْرِ الْأَوَّلِ وَكَالتَّرَاوِيحِ أَيْ بِالْجَمَاعَةِ الْعَامَّةِ وَالْكَلَامِ فِي دَقَائِقِ الصُّوْفِيَّةِ. وَأَمَّا مَكْرُوهَةٌ كَزَخْرَفَةِ الْمَسَاجِدِ وَتَزْوِيْنِ الْمَصَاحِفِ يَعْنِي عِنْدَ الشَّافِعِيَّةِ، وَأَمَّا عِنْدَ الْحَنَفِيَّةِ فَمُبَاحٌ. وَأَمَّا مُبَاحَةٌ كَالْمُصَافَحَةِ عَقِيْبَ الصُّبْحِ وَالْعَصْرِ أَيْ عِنْدَ الشَّافِعِيَّةِ أَيْضًا وَإِلَّا عِنْدَ الْحَنَفِيَّةِ مَكْرُوهٌ، وَالتَّوَسُّعُ فِي لَذَائِذِ الْمَأْكَلِ وَالْمَشَارِبِ وَالْمَسَاكِنِ وَتوْسِيْعُ الْأَكْمَامِ.

Shaykh ʿIzz al-Dīn b. ʿAbd al-Salām said at the end of his book, *al-Qawāʿid*: Innovation can be obligatory, such as learning syntax (in order to understand the speech of Allah and His Messenger), compiling principles of jurisprudence, and speaking about the reliability of hadith narrators. Forbidden innovation, like creating new sects (such as the *Jabariyya*, *Qadariyya*, *Murjiʾa* and *Mujassama*) refuting them is an obligatory innovation, because protecting the Sharia from these heresies is an

[1] Al-Haythamī, *al-Fatāwā al-ḥadīthiyya*, p.203.

obligation. Commendable innovation includes establishing lodges and schools, every good which was not practiced in the first century, the *tarāwīḥ* ritual prayer in a public congregation, and speaking of the intricacies of Sufism. Reprehensible innovation, which includes, for example, ornamenting the mosques and decorating the copies of the Qurʾān (according to the *Shāfiʿī* school, but according to the *Ḥanafī* school these things are permissible). And discretionary innovation, which includes, for example, shaking hands straight after the *fajr* and *ʿaṣr* prayers (according to the *Shāfiʿī* school, but according to the *Ḥanafī* school it is disliked), consuming an extensive range of delicacies and drinks, living in expansive homes, and wearing shirts with wide sleeves.[1]

10.9.3.1 EVERY INNOVATION IS AN ERROR: THE CORRECT UNDERSTANDING

Mullā ʿAlī al-Qārī, on the correct understanding of 'every innovation is an error' (*kullu bidʿa ḍalāla*), further writes:

أَيْ كُلُّ بِدْعَةٍ سَيِّئَةٍ ضَلَالَةٌ، لِقَوْلِهِ عَلَيْهِ الصَّلَاةُ وَالسَّلَامُ: «مَنْ سَنَّ فِي الْإِسْلَامِ سُنَّةً حَسَنَةً فَلَهُ أَجْرُهَا وَأَجْرُ مَنْ عَمِلَ بِهَا» وَجَمَعَ أَبُوبَكْرٍ وَعُمَرُ الْقُرْآنَ وَكَتَبَهُ زَيْدٌ فِي الْمُصْحَفِ وَجَدَّدَ فِي عَهْدِ عُثْمَانَ ؓ.

That is every 'blameworthy' innovation is an error, because the Prophet ﷺ said, 'If someone introduces a good custom in Islam, he is entitled to its reward and the reward of those who put it into practice after him.' Abū Bakr and ʿUmar compiled the Qurʾān, and Zayd transcribed it into the copies; this effort was renewed in the tenure of ʿUthmān.[2]

---

[1] Mullā ʿAlī al-Qārī, *Mirqāt al-mafātīḥ sharḥ mishkāt al-maṣābīḥ*, 1:216.

[2] Mullā ʿAlī al-Qārī, *Mirqāt al-mafātīḥ sharḥ mishkāt al-maṣābīḥ*, 1:216; and Shabbīr Aḥmad Uthmānī, *Fatḥ al-mulhim bi sharḥ Ṣaḥīḥ Muslim*, 2:406.

Ibn Ḥajar al-Makkī, after categorising innovation into its various kinds, states:

وَفِي الْـحَدِيْثِ: «كُلُّ بِدْعَةٍ ضَلَالَةٌ، وَكُلُّ ضَلَالَةٍ فِي النَّارِ». وَهُوَ مَحْمُوْلٌ عَلَى الْـمُحَرَّمَةِ لَا غَيْرَ.

> The hadith, 'every innovation is an error, and every error is in the Hellfire', is in reference to what is forbidden, nothing else.[1]

From this categorisation of innovation, it can be understood that any innovation which falls under the praiseworthy affairs of the Sharia is a good innovation, whilst those innovations which fall under the blameworthy affairs (i.e., it contravenes the Sharia) are a bad innovation. And anything which does not fall under any of the two is a discretionary innovation.

10.10 The Categories of Innovation

In light of the above definitions of *bidʿa*, the following are the categories of innovation given to us by the imams and hadith scholars.

At the fundamental level, there are two categories of innovation:

1. Praiseworthy innovation (*al-bidʿa al-ḥasana*)
2. Blameworthy innovation (*al-bidʿa al-sayyiʾa*)

These are further divided into subcategories:

10.10.1 The Subcategories of the Praiseworthy Innovation

Praiseworthy innovation (*al-bidʿa al-ḥasana*) is divided into three subcategories:

1. Obligatory innovation (*al-bidʿa al-wājiba*)
2. Commendable innovation (*al-bidʿa al-mustaḥabba/ al-bidʿa al-mustaḥsana*)
3. Discretionary innovation (*al-bidʿa al-mubāḥa*)

[1] Al-Haythamī, *al-Fatāwā al-ḥadīthiyya*, p.203.

10.10.1.1 OBLIGATORY INNOVATION (*AL-BIDʿA AL-WĀJIBA*)

It is a thing which may be an innovation in its appearance, but its existence is necessary like the obligatory (*wājib*) in the *Dīn;* if it is forsaken, there will be an obstacle in the religion. The following are all examples of obligatory innovations (*al-bidʿa al-wājiba*): placing diacritical markings (vowels) on the verses of the Qurʾān, learning and teaching Arabic syntax and morphology as a means of understanding the religion, formulating principles for the exegesis of the Qurʾān and hadith, jurisprudence, teaching other various rational and traditional sciences, establishing institutes for the study of religion, creating curriculums for Islamic scholarship, and introducing nomenclatures within these sciences.

10.10.1.2 COMMENDABLE INNOVATION (*AL-BIDʿA AL-MUSTAḤABBA/ AL-BIDʿA AL-MUSTAḤSANA*)

It is a thing which may be new in its origin and appearance, but the Sharia has not declared it unlawful; it is not necessary like the obligatory (*wājib*), but the Muslims in general consider it to be a praiseworthy thing which they do as a means of gaining reward; the one who does not practice it is not sinful, but the reward is given to the one who practices it. Examples of this subcategory of innovation are: establishing lodges for travellers; building educational centres; instituting good practices which did not exist before; offering the *tarāwīḥ* ritual prayer in a public congregation; holding discourses on the intricacies of *taṣawwuf* and *ṭarīqa*; and celebrating *Mawlid al-Nabī* ﷺ, *ʿurs*, and any other gatherings which people get together for the purpose of gaining reward, so long as there are no sins being committed. ʿAbd Allāh b. Masʿūd narrates:

فَمَا رَآهُ الْمُؤْمِنُ حَسَناً فَهُوَ عِنْدَ اللهِ حَسَنٌ، وَمَا رَآهُ الْمُؤْمِنُونَ قَبِيحاً فَهُوَ عِنْدَ اللهِ قَبِيحٌ.

> Whatever the true believer regards as a good thing is a good thing in the sight of Allah, and whatever the true believers regards as a bad thing is a bad thing in the sight of Allah.[1]

In light of this definition, *Mawlid al-Nabī* ﷺ is a commendable innovation which is practiced by the believers with the intention of receiving reward. According to the statement of ʿAbd Allāh b. Masʿūd, this is accepted by Almighty Allah because the great majority of the believers (*al-sawād al-aʿẓam*) commemorate it.

10.10.1.3 Discretionary Innovation (*al-Bidʿa al-Mubāḥa*)

Any new thing which is not prohibited by the Sharia and is considered lawful by the Muslims and is practiced without any intention of receiving reward is a discretionary innovation. Some examples include shaking hands after the *fajr* and *ʿasr* ritual prayers and consuming appetising delicacies and expensive drinks and beverages.

10.10.2 The Subcategories of the Blameworthy Innovation

Blameworthy innovation (*al-bidʿa al-sayyiʾa*) is divided into two subcategories:

1. Forbidden innovation (*al-bidʿa al-muḥarrama*)
2. Reprehensible innovation (*al-bidʿa al-makrūha*)

10.10.2.1 Forbidden Innovation (*al-Bidʿa al-Muḥarrama*)

Forbidden innovation (*al-bidʿa al-muḥarrama*) is a new thing which

---

[1] Narrated by al-Bazzār in *al-Baḥr al-zukhār* (*al-musnad*), 5:212–213 §1816; al-Ṭayālsī in *al-Musnad*, 1:33 §246; Aḥmad b. Ḥanbal in *al-Musnad*, 1:379 §3600; al-Ḥākim in *al-Mustadrak*, 3:83 §4465; al-Haythamī in *Majmaʿ al-zawāʾid wa manbaʿ al-fawāʾid*, 1:177–178 writes that Imam Aḥmad, al-Bazzār and al-Ṭabarānī have narrated this with a reliable chain of narrators (*wa rijāluhu muwaththiqūn*); and al-ʿAjlūnī in *Kashf al-khafāʾ wa mazīl al-albās*, 2:245 §2214, states that this is a fine narration (*mawqūf ḥasan*).

contravenes the religion or is a cause of discord and dissension, such as the inception of new sect like the *Qadariyya*, *Jabariyya*, *Murjiʾa,* and the *Aḥmadiyya*. To refute these erroneous sects is an obligatory innovation (*al-bidʿa al-wājiba*).

10.10.2.2 Reprehensible Innovation (*al-Bidʿa al-Makrūha*)

This refers to any new thing by which the mandatory recommendation (*al-sunna al-muʾakkada*) or the directory recommendation (*al-sunna ghayr al-muʾakkada*) is omitted. The predecessors used to include ornamenting the mosques without necessity in the subcategory of reprehensible innovation (*al-bidʿa al-makrūha*).

10.10.3 Evidence for the Categorisation of Innovation in Light of the Hadith

To substantiate the concept of innovation given above and its categorisation, the hadith narrated by Jarīr b. ʿAbd Allāh is of paramount significance. The Messenger of Allah ﷺ said:

«مَنْ سَنَّ فِي الْإِسْلَامِ سُنَّةً حَسَنَةً فَلَهُ أَجْرُهَا وَأَجْرُ مَنْ عَمِلَ بِهَا بَعْدَهُ مِنْ غَيْرِ أَنْ يَنْقُصَ مِنْ أُجُورِهِمْ شَيْءٌ وَمَنْ سَنَّ فِي الْإِسْلَامِ سُنَّةً سَيِّئَةً كَانَ عَلَيْهِ وِزْرُهَا وَوِزْرُ مَنْ عَمِلَ بِهَا مِنْ بَعْدِهِ مِنْ غَيْرِ أَنْ يَنْقُصَ مِنْ أَوْزَارِهِمْ شَيْءٌ.»

> If someone introduces a good custom into Islam, he is entitled to its reward and to the reward of those who put it into practice after him, without anything being deducted from their rewards. If someone introduces a bad custom into Islam, he is charged with its sin and the sin of those who put it into practice after him, without anything being deducted from their sins.[1]

[1] Reported by Muslim in *al-Ṣaḥīḥ*: *Kitāb al-Zakā* [The Book of Alms-Due], chapter: 'Urging charitable donation [*ṣadaqa*], even if it is half a date, or a kind word, for it is a shield from the Fire of Hell', 2:704–

In this hadith, the word '*sanna*' linguistically speaking is a synonym of '*abdaʿa*,' which means 'to introduce something'. From this, the concept of the praiseworthy innovation (*al-bidʿa al-ḥasana*) emerges; on the other hand, the statement 'if someone introduces a bad custom into Islam' is an indication towards the blameworthy innovation (*al-bidʿa al-sayyiʾa*). If someone objects, saying that the word Sunna only refers to the Sunna and not *bidʿa*, then what was the purpose of qualifying it with the word, 'good' (*ḥasana*)—can there be a Sunna which is not good? God forbid! Moreover, this objection would have some basis if the verb used was 'whoever practices' (*man ʿamila*) as opposed to 'whoever introduces' (*man sanna*), because can it be possible for a member of the Holy Prophet's community to introduce a new Sunna in Islam? Is it not his duty simply to hear and obey? Thus, it is established here that the word '*sanna*' is not being employed in its popular usage of 'Sunna'; rather, it is being used in its literal meaning, which is 'to introduce a new custom or way'.

The above mentioned categorisation of innovation has been given by the imams of hadith and jurists according to their own particular methodology; for further details, please refer to our book, '*Kitāb al-bidʿa*'.

The summary of the details above is that we should not be caught up in looking at an action and thinking, 'did this exist in the time of the most exalted Prophet ﷺ or not?' Rather, we should consider that maybe this action might be based on a certain norm or convention which may be subject to the requirements of the age; or it may be that there may be some wisdom or benefits which are in the best interest of the public. What is worthy of our consideration is for us to look into the action and consider whether there is a

---

705 §1017; Muslim in *al-Ṣaḥīḥ*: *Kitāb al-ʿilm* [The Book of Knowledge], chapter: 'Someone who establishes a good customary practice or a bad one, and someone who summons to guidance or to error', 4:2059 §1017; al-Nasāʾī in *al-Sunan*: *Kitāb al-Zakā* [The Book of Alms-Due], chapter: 'Encouragement to pay the alms-due', 5:76 §2554; Ibn Mājah in *al-Sunan*: al-*Muqaddama* [Prolegomena], chapter: 'Someone who establishes a good customary practice or a bad one', 1:74 & 75 §203 & 206–207; and Aḥmad b. Ḥanbal in *al-Musnad*, 4:357–359.

basis for it in the Qurʾān and Sunna, i.e., is it directly or indirectly established from these sources or not? Another reason why an action may be blameworthy is if it comes into conflict with an action which may be obligatory, recommended, or commendable. If a new action can be evidently established from the Qurʾān and Sunna, it no longer becomes subject to defamation, objection and error. If it cannot be directly or indirectly established from the Qurʾān and Sunna, but simultaneously it does not contravene these sources either, even then there is no infamy or shame in it, i.e., subjecting it to misguidance and error would be incorrect. It will become impermissible and indicted as a blameworthy innovation only in the situation when the new action contravenes the text of the Qurʾān and Sunna or any established injunction, or it goes against the general constitution of the religion, or it negates the essence of the Sharia.

10.11 *Mawlid al-Nabī* ﷺ has its Basis in the Qurʾān and Hadith

In the previous chapters, from the verses of the Qurʾān and numerous hadiths, the legal status of celebrating *Mawlid al-Nabī* ﷺ and its aims and objectives have been mentioned unequivocally in overwhelming detail. Commemorating the blessed birth of the most exalted Prophet ﷺ in its essence is to express gratitude to Almighty Allah. It is an expression of gratitude for bestowing such a great benevolence on us; displaying happiness is the means of proclaiming the blessing and hence taking it as a festivity (*ʿīd*) is a praiseworthy act which is worthy of being emulated. Expressing happiness on this occasion is not just the practice of Almighty Allah, but it has also been declared the practice of the most exalted Prophet ﷺ and his noble Companions, as established in their reports. Furthermore, the precedent of former communities is also testament to this, as mentioned expressly in the Qurʾān. If anyone still insists on debating its legality, making it a source of contention or maintaining the view that it is impermissible and worthy of condemnation, then such a person is an obstinate individual who is deprived of true knowledge.

10.12 The Majority of the Prophet's Community Cannot Agree upon an Error

The Sharia, concerning many of the dealings, has laid down fundamental concepts and principles; the presentation and details however have been left to the community and its eminent scholars. In the previous pages, we have related the statement of ʿAbd Allāh b. Masʿūd, an eminent Companion. His statement is substantiated by the authentic hadiths whose chain of transmission reaches the Holy Prophet ﷺ (*marfūʿ*). According to these hadiths, the great majority of the community, i.e., *al-sawād al-aʿẓam*, can never be misguided. Instead, those who break away from the majority are the ones who are misguided. Time and again, smaller factions are created, whose creed and worldview differs radically from the majority of the *Umma*. This minority blames the majority of the Muslims to be infidels, polytheists, ignoramuses, and innovators, when in reality they themselves are the ones who are misguided. Hence, at times of dissension and confusion, the believers have been enjoined to hold fast to the overwhelming majority.

Anas b. Mālik reports that the Prophet ﷺ said:

«إِنَّ أُمَّتِي لَا تَجْتَمِعُ عَلَى ضَلَالَةٍ، فَإِذَا رَأَيْتُمُ اخْتِلَافًا فَعَلَيْكُمْ بِالسَّوَادِ الْأَعْظَمِ.»

> My *Umma* (community) will not agree (collectively) upon an error, so if you notice a disagreement, then it is inevitable for you to adhere to the great majority[1] (i.e., collective body).[2]

The most exalted Prophet ﷺ foretold his community about the

[1] Imam Jalāl al-Dīn al-Suyūṭī in his *Ḥāshiya Sunan Ibn Mājah*, p.283, has stated that the '*al-sawād al-aʿẓam*' in this hadith refers to the *Ahl al-Sunna*.

[2] Narrated by Ibn Mājah in *al-Sunan*: *Kitāb al-Fitan* [The Book of Tribulation], chapter: '*al-Sawād al-Aʿẓam*' (The great majority)', 2:1308 §3950; Ibn Abī ʿĀṣim in *al-Sunna*, p.41 §84; al-Ṭabarānī in *al-Muʿjam al-kabīr*, 12:447 §13,623; and al-Daylamī in *al-Firdaws bi-maʾthūr al-khiṭāb*, 1:411 §1662.

ensuing divisions which were going to take place, stating that every faction will go to the Fire of Hell except *al-sawād al-aʿẓam* (the great majority). Abū Umāma relates that the Prophet ﷺ said:

«تَفَرَّقَتْ بَنُوْ إِسْرَائِيْلَ عَلَى إِحْدَى وَسَبْعِيْنَ فِرْقَةً، وَتَفَرَّقَتِ النَّصَارَى عَلَى اثْنَتَيْنِ وَسَبْعِيْنَ فِرْقَةً، وَأُمَّتِي تَزِيْدُ عَلَيْهِمْ فِرْقَةً، كُلُّهَا فِي النَّارِ إِلَّا السَّوَادَ الْأَعْظَمَ.»

The Children of Israel split into 71 groups; the Christians split into 72 groups; and my *Umma* (community) will split into one more group than them—all will go to the Fire of Hell, except the great majority (i.e., collective body).[1]

Highlighting the necessity of keeping with the great majority, Abū Dharr narrates that the Holy Prophet ﷺ said:

«اثْنَانِ خَيْرٌ مِنْ وَاحِدٍ، وَثَلَاثٌ خَيْرٌ مِنَ اثْنَيْنِ، وَأَرْبَعَةٌ خَيْرٌ مِنْ ثَلَاثَةٍ؛ فَعَلَيْكُمْ بِالْجَمَاعَةِ، فَإِنَّ اللهَ عَزَّ وَجَلَّ لَنْ يَجْمَعَ أُمَّتِي إِلَّا عَلَى هُدًى.»

Two are better than one, three are better than two, and four are better than three. You must therefore adhere to the collective body, for Allah will never unite my *Umma* (community) except in agreement upon right guidance.[2]

In the above hadiths, the word *al-jamāʿa* refers to the collective majority of the *Umma*. To elucidate this further, the hadith narrated by ʿAwf b. Mālik expressly mentions that the most esteemed Prophet declared *al-jamāʿa* to be *al-sawād al-aʿẓam* (the great majority):

---

[1] Narrated by al-Ṭabarānī in *al-Muʿjam al-awsaṭ*, 7:176 §7202; Ibn Abī Shayba in *al-Muṣannaf*, 7:554 §37,892; Ḥārith in *al-Musnad*, 2:716 §706; al-Bayhaqi in *al-Sunan al-kubrā*, 8:188; and al-Haythamī in *Majmaʿ al-zawāʾid wa manbaʿ al-fawāʾid*, 7:258.

[2] Narrated by Aḥmad b. Ḥanbal in *al-Musnad*, 5:357–359 §21,331; and al-Haythamī in *Majmaʿ al-zawāʾid wa manbaʿ al-fawāʾid*, 1:177 & 5:218.

«وَالَّذِي نَفْسُ مُحَمَّدٍ بِيَدِهِ! لَتَفْتَرِقَنَّ أُمَّتِي عَلَى ثَلَاثٍ وَسَبْعِينَ فِرْقَةً، وَاحِدَةٌ فِي الْـجَنَّةِ وَثِنْتَانِ وَسَبْعُوْنَ فِي النَّارِ. قِيْلَ: يَا رَسُولَ اللهِ، مَنْ هُمْ؟ قَالَ: الْـجَمَـاعَةُ.»

I swear by Him in whose hands is the life of Muhammad ﷺ. My *Umma* (community) shall certainly split into 73 groups: one will be in Paradise and 72 will be in the Fire of Hell.

يَا رَسُوْلَ اللهِ! مَنْ هُمْ؟

The noble Companions asked, 'O Messenger of Allah! Who are they?'

«الْـجَمَـاعَةُ.»

The Holy Prophet ﷺ replied, 'The collective majority (*al-jamāʿa*).'[1]

In the following hadiths, the intended meaning of the word *al-jamāʿa* as 'the collective majority' has been mentioned expressly. ʿAbd Allāh b. ʿUmar narrates that the most exalted Prophet ﷺ said:

«لَا يَجْمَعُ اللهُ هَذِهِ الْأُمَّةَ عَلَى الضَّلَالَةِ أَبَدًا، يَدُ اللهِ عَلَى الْـجَمَـاعَةِ، فَاتَّبِعُوا السَّوَادَ الْأَعْظَمَ، فَإِنَّهُ مَنْ شَذَّ شُذَّ فِي النَّارِ.»

Allah will not unite this *Umma* (community) in agreement upon an error. Allah's Hand (of Power and Protection) is upon the collective body, so follow the great majority, for the one who breaks away (from the collective body) is cast into the Fire of Hell.[2]

---

[1] Narrated by Ibn Mājah in *al-Sunan*: *Kitāb al-Fitan* [The Book of Troubles], chapter: 'Separation of the Community, 2:1322 §3992; and Lālkāʾī in *Iʿtiqād ahl al-sunna wa al-jamāʿa*, 1:101 §149.

[2] Narrated by al-Ḥākim in *al-Mustadrak*, 1:199–201 §391–397; Ibn Abī

ʿAbd Allāh b. ʿUmar also narrates that the most esteemed Prophet ﷺ said:

> Allah will not unite my *Umma* (community)—or the *Umma* (community) of Muhammad ﷺ—in agreement upon an error. The Hand of (the protection of) Allah is with the collective body and the one who leaves the party deviates towards the Fire of Hell.[1]

This does not mean in any way that the majority are free from tribulation or that no problem whatsoever can arise from the majority. It is a fact that troubles have arisen from the majority, but renewal and restoration in the *Umma* can only be possible when it is according to the Prophetic teachings and when one adheres to the great majority, i.e., *al-sawād al-aʿẓam*. To declare the great majority as deviants and to come out of their fold is actually tantamount to error as well as hypocrisy; and this is what the most compassionate Prophet ﷺ forbade. To commemorate *Mawlid al-Nabī* ﷺ is also amongst those affairs which the great majority of the *Umma* have declared permissible; this is something which they act upon in light of the evidences of the Sharia. If today someone alleges that the great majority of the *Umma* is in error, he has in fact dug a hole for his self, as he is essentially stating that he is misguided and that he has set his path to the Fire of Hell.

10.13 Understanding the True Spirit of the Religion is Essential

It is a sad state of affairs that certain proponents of Islam take minor issues of differences and turn them into a struggle of *īmān* versus *kufr*. Such people overlook the true spirit of Islam. It is for

ʿĀṣim in *Kitāb al-Sunna*, 1:39 §80; Lālkāʾī in *Iʿtiqād ahl al-sunna wa al-jamāʿa*, 1:106 §154; al-Daylamī in *al-Firdaws bi-maʾthūr al-khiṭāb*, 5:258 §8116; and Ḥakīm Tirmidhī in *Nawādir al-uṣūl fī aḥādīth al-Rasūl*, 1:422.

[1] Narrated by al-Tirmidhī in *al-Jāmiʿ al-Ṣaḥīḥ*: *Kitāb al-Fitan* [The Book of Troubles], chapter: 'What has come to us about the necessity of sticking to the congregation', 4:466 §2167; al-Ḥākim in *al-Mustadrak*, 1:200 §394; and Dānī in *al-Sunan al-wārida fī al-fitan*, 3:748 §368.

this reason that the young generations of Muslims, who are never shown the true face of the religion, are becoming ever so distant; instead of developing their understanding, these youths are instead introduced to their religion without knowing its true teaching. As days go past, this gap only seems to widen. Why is this so? Could it be, *illā mā shā' Allāh*, that some personal motive may be involved; or is it simply that some people out of naivety want to make this religion difficult? Whatever it may be, our youth, and particularly the educated class amongst them who are heavily influenced by Western culture, are incessantly drifting away. If we sincerely present the true principles of the Sharia, there is no reason why people, impressed by the beauty of Islam, will not enthusiastically practice the religion.

Some superficial scholars make the celebration of *Mawlid al-Nabī* ﷺ an object of contention, declaring it to be forbidden only because apparently it was not practiced in the early part of Islamic history. With regards to this, the definition of innovation and its legal status, according to the most preeminent scholars, has been clearly discussed in its entirety; and linguistically speaking, the *mawlid* is an innovation, but simply calling it an innovation is not enough to make it a target for criticism and censure—doing so is plain narrow-mindedness and stubbornness. As we have mentioned earlier, the condition of things and its appearance change in every generation in accordance to the requirements of the age. Take the Pilgrimage for example: the way this obligation is fulfilled has evolved over time. Today, people no longer travel by camel or on foot; a distance which once used to take months is now covered in a matter of hours. In the same way, other pillars of Islam are not practiced in the same fashion today. Some modern and contemporary requirements have become integrated, but the essence has not changed.

In light of this, if we take a look at *Mawlid al-Nabī* ﷺ in its current format, we can see that it is absolutely in accordance with the Sunna of the Prophet ﷺ. Just as we, in our celebration of *Mawlid al-Nabī* ﷺ, hold gatherings for the recitation of odes in praise of the most exalted Prophet ﷺ and mention his virtues and exceptionality, which in essence is the very purpose of our gatherings, such gatherings similarly were also held in the Prophet's time where the Holy Prophet ﷺ himself held gatherings of recitation of poetry in his praise.

For detailed information on the concept of innovation in Islam, please refer to our book, '*Kitāb al-bidʿa*'.

Chapter 11

Doctrinal Issues Related to *Mawlid al-Nabī* ﷺ

In the previous chapters, we have presented a plethora of evidence from the Qur'ān and Sunna for the commemoration of *Mawlid al-Nabī* ﷺ, and we have also cited an exhaustive list of renowned imams and hadith scholars who were of the opinion that to commemorate this special occasion is not only permissible, but desirable according to the Sharia and that it results in the attainment of countless mercies and blessings. Every believer must therefore strive with all his strength and valour to make the most out of this unique opportunity. In this concluding chapter, we shall bring this treatise to a close by touching upon those doctrinal issues which are associated with the *mawlid*. By doing so, we hope to totally decimate those objections which the critics lay against this praiseworthy and permissible affair.

11.1 Employing the Term: *Mīlād al-Nabī* ﷺ

Critics of the *mawlid* are very eager to point out that the word '*mīlād*' only seems to be widespread in the Indian Subcontinent whereas in the Arab world, the word '*mawlid*' is prevalent. This is a common misconception. In reality, the Urdu language was formed and adopted by conquering armies and hence consisted of words and phrases from various languages including Arabic and Farsi (Persian). The words *walad*, *wālid*, *wālida*, *mawlūd*, *mīlād* and *mutawallid* are all examples of words borrowed from Arabic. There are many other words and expressions that have been loaned from the Arabic and Persian languages and incorporated into Urdu. In Arabic, the word '*mawlid*' is much more prevalent, but in the books of *sīra*, the term *Mīlād al-Nabī* ﷺ is also used. *Mīlād* is in fact an Arabic word: It has been used by Imam al-Tirmidhī (210–279 AH), al-Ṭabarī (224–310 AH), Ibn Kathīr (701–774 AH), al-Suyūṭī (849–911 AH), and al-ʿAsqalānī (773–852 AH), as well as many other exegetes, hadith scholars, historians and biographers of the Holy Prophet ﷺ.

11.1.1 The Usage of the Word *Mīlād* in the Books of Arabic Linguistics

The following linguists have cited the word '*mīlād*' in their works:
1. Ibn Manẓūr (630–711 AH), ʿAbd al-Qādir al-Rāzī al-Ḥanafī (d. after 660 AH), Murtaḍā al-Zabīdī (1145–1205 AH), and al-Jawharī state:

وَمِيْلَادُ الرَّجُلِ: اسْمُ الْوَقْتِ الَّذِي وُلِدَ فِيْهِ.

> The *mīlād* of a man: it is a noun for the time in which he was born.[1]

2. The famous dictionaries, *al-Muʿjam al-wasīṭ* (2:1056) and *Tāj al-ʿurūs min jawāhir al-qāmūs* (5:327) state:

الْـمِيْلَادُ: وَقْتُ الْوِلَادَةِ.

> *Mīlād* is the time of birth.

11.1.2 The Usage of the Word *Mīlād* in the Books of Hadith and *Sīra*

In the texts of the hadiths and *āthār*, the word '*mīlād*' has been used. Imam al-Tirmidhī (210–279 AH) in *al-Jāmiʿ al-Ṣaḥīḥ*, in the second chapter of *Kitāb al-Manāqib*, has placed a chapter-title called: *bāb mā jāʾa fī mīlād al-Nabī* ﷺ [Chapter: what has been related concerning the Holy Prophet's birth]. Therefore, it is baseless to suggest that the word '*mīlād*' has no origin in the Arabic language. In this narration, it states:

[1] Ibn Manẓūr, *Lisān al-ʿArab*, 3:468; al-Rāzī, *Mukhtār al-ṣiḥāḥ*, p.422; al-Zubaydī, *Tāj al-ʿurūs min jawāhir al-qāmūs*, 5:327; and Jawharī, *al-Ṣiḥāḥ fī al-lugha wa al-ʿulūm*, 2:713.

سَأَلَ عُثْمَانُ بْنُ عَفَّانَ قُبَاثَ بْنَ أَشْيَمَ أَخَا بَنِي يَعْمُرَ بْنِ لَيْثٍ أَأَنْتَ أَكْبَرُ أَمْ رَسُولُ اللهِ ﷺ؟ فَقَالَ: رَسُولُ اللهِ ﷺ أَكْبَرُ مِنِّي وَأَنَا أَقْدَمُ مِنْهُ فِي الْمِيلَادِ.

ʿUthmān b. ʿAffān asked Qubāth b. Ashyam, the brother of Banī Yaʿmur b. Layth, 'Are you older, or the Prophet ﷺ?' Qubāth replied 'The Prophet ﷺ is my elder, but I was born before him.'[1]

The statement of Qubāth b. Ashyam that 'the Prophet ﷺ is my elder, but I was born before him', is a shining example of the most exalted reverence and excellent etiquette with the Messenger of Allah ﷺ.

When the most exalted Prophet ﷺ migrated from Mecca to Medina, he took refuge in cave *Thawr*; at the same time, the polytheists of Mecca were searching to capture him. In the hadiths, it is related:

وَطَلَبَتْ قُرَيْشٌ رَسُوْلَ اللهِ ﷺ أَشَدَّ الطَّلَبِ حَتَّى انْتَهَوْا إِلَى بَابِ الْغَارِ، فَقَالَ بَعْضُهُمْ: إِنَّ عَلَيْهِ الْعَنْكَبُوْتَ قَبْلَ مِيْلَادِ مُحَمَّدٍ ﷺ فَانْصَرَفُوْا.

The *Quraysh* searched intensively for the Messenger of Allah ﷺ until they eventually reached to the mouth of the cave. Some of them (mockingly) said, 'There is a spider-web on it even before the birth of Muhammad ﷺ.' So they went away.[2]

In another narration, it states:

---

[1] Narrated by al-Tirmidhī in *al-Jāmiʿ al-Ṣaḥīḥ*: *Kitāb al-Manāqib* [The Book of Virtuous Merits], chapter: 'What has been related concerning the Prophet's birth', 5:589 §3619; al-Shaybānī in *al-Āḥād wa al-mathānī*, 1:407 §566; al-Ṭabarī in *Tārīkh al-umum wa al-mulūk*, 1:453; al-Bayhaqī in *Dalāʾil al-Nabuwwa wa maʿrifa aḥwāl Ṣāḥib al-Sharīʿa* ﷺ, 1:77; and Ibn Kathīr in *al-Bidāya wa al-nihāya*, 2:216–217.

[2] Narrated by Ibn Saʿd in *al-Ṭabaqāt al-kubrā*, 1:228; and al-Suyūṭī in *Kifāya al-ṭālib al-labīb fī khaṣāʾiṣ al-Ḥabīb* ﷺ, 1:305.

فَلَمَّــا انْتَهَوْا إِلَى فَمِ الْغَارِ، قَالَ قَائِلٌ مِنْهُمْ: ادْخُلُوا الْغَارَ. فَقَالَ أُمَيَّةُ بْنُ خَلْفٍ: وَمَا أَرَى بِكُمْ أَيُّ حَاجَتِكُمْ إِلَى الْغَارِ؟ أَنَّ عَلَيْهِ لَعَنْكَبُوْتًا كَانَ قَبْلَ مِيْلَادِ مُحَمَّدٍ ﷺ.

When the *Quraysh* reached to the mouth of the cave, one of them said, 'Go inside the cave.' Umayya b. Khalaf exclaimed, 'I don't think there is any need of it: there is a spider-web on the mouth of the cave which must have been there before the birth of Muhammad ﷺ!'[1]

Ibn ʿAwn said:

قُتِلَ عَمَّــارٌ، رَحِمَهُ اللهُ، وَهُوَ ابْنُ إِحْدَى وَتِسْعِيْنَ سَنَةً، وَكَانَ أَقْدَمُ فِي الْـمِيْلَادِ مِنْ رَسُوْلِ اللهِ ﷺ.

ʿAmmār—may Allah mercy him—was martyred at the age of 91. His was born before the Messenger of Allah ﷺ.[2]

Ibn Ḥajar al-ʿAsqalānī (773–852 AH), whilst listing the individuals who were named 'Muhammad' in the period of ignorance, wrote about Muhammad b. Muslima:

وَهُوَ غَلَطٌ فَأَنَّهُ وُلِدَ بَعْدَ مِيْلَادِ النَّبِيِّ ﷺ بِمُدَّةٍ، فَفَضُلَ لَهُ خَمْسَةٌ، وَقَدْ خَلَّصَ لَنَا خَمْسَةَ عَشَرَ.

And this is incorrect, since he was born sometime after the birth of the Prophet ﷺ. Hence, five people (who were named Muhammad in the period of ignorance) were

[1] Narrated by al-Ḥalabī in *Insān al-ʿuyūn fī sīra al-Amīn al-Maʾmūn*, 2:209; al-Kalāʿī in *al-Iktifāʾ bi mā taḍmanahu min maghāzī Rasūl Allāh*, 1:339; and al-Suyūṭī in *Kifāya al-ṭālib al-labīb fī khaṣāʾiṣ al-Ḥabīb* ﷺ, 1:306.

[2] Narrated by Ibn Saʿd in *al-Ṭabaqāt al-kubrā*, 3:259; Ibn ʿAsākir in *Tārīkh Dimashq al-kabīr*, 43:471; and Mizzī in *Tahdhīb al-kamāl fī asmāʾ al-rijāl*, 21:224.

before the Prophet ﷺ, and we have concluded that there were 15 people (with that name altogether).[1]

Ibn ʿAbbās narrates:

كَانَ بَيْنَ مُوْسَى بْنِ عِمْرَانَ وَعِيْسَى بْنِ مَرْيَمَ أَلْفُ سَنَةٍ وَتِسْعُمِـائَةِ سَنَةٍ وَلَـمْ تَكُنْ بَيْنَهُمَـا فَتْرَةٌ، وَإِنَّهُ أُرْسِلَ بَيْنَهُمَـا أَلْفُ نَبِيٍّ مِنْ بَنِي إِسْرَائِيْلَ سِوَى مَنْ أُرْسِلَ مِنْ غَيْرِهِمْ، وَكَانَ بَيْنَ مِيْلَادِ عِيْسَى وَالنَّبِيِّ عَلَيْهِ الصَّلَاةُ وَالسَّلَامُ، خَمْسُمِـائَةِ سَنَةٍ وَتِسْعٌ وَّسِتُّوْنَ سَنَةً.

Between Mūsā b. ʿImrān and ʿIsā b. Maryam, there was a period of 1900 years in which there was no *fatra*[2]. During this time, 1000 prophets were sent to the Children of Israel—excluding those who were sent to other communities. The period between the birth of ʿIsā and the Prophet ﷺ was 569 years.[3]

To summarise the above narrations, the point to note here is that several authentic, competent, and renowned hadith scholars have recorded traditions in which the word '*mīlād*' has been mentioned. This word categorically is not an invention of the Indian Subcontinent.

11.1.3 THE USAGE OF THE WORD *MĪLĀD* IN LITERARY WORKS

There have been many great writers and authoritative authors who have composed literary works on the subject of the most exalted Prophet's birth. This has been mentioned in detail in one of the preceding chapters. Some of these authors have used the word

---

[1] Al-ʿAsqalānī, *Fatḥ al-Bārī*, 6:557.

[2] *Fatra* is an interval of time which marks the cessation of prophecy and revelation.

[3] Narrated by Ibn Saʿd in *al-Ṭabaqāt al-kubrā*, 1:53; al-Ṭabarī in *Tārīkh al-umum wa al-mulūk*, 1:495; and al-Qurṭubī in *al-Jāmiʿ li aḥkām al-Qurʾān*, 6:122.

'*mīlād*' in the titles of their books. Ḥājī Khalīfa, in his masterpiece *Kashf al-ẓunūn ᶜan usāmī al-kutub wa al-funūn*, writes about one such book:

«دُرَجُ الدُّرَرِ فِي مِيْلَادِ سَيِّدِ الْبَشَرِ» لِلسَّيِّدِ أَصِيْلِ الدِّيْنِ عَبْدِ اللهِ بْنِ عَبْدِ الرَّحْمَنِ الْحُسَيْنِيِّ الشِّيْرَازِيِّ الْمُتَوَفَّى سَنَةَ ٨٨٤ أَرْبَعٍ وَثَمَانِيْنَ وَثَمَانِ مِائَةٍ.

> *Duraj al-durar fī mīlād Sayyid al-bashar* ﷺ is by al-Sayyid Aṣīl al-Dīn ᶜAbd Allāh b. ᶜAbd al-Raḥmān al-Ḥusaynī al-Shīrāzī (d. 884 AH).[1]

Ibn al-Jawzī (510–579 AH) authored two independent books on the *mawlid*; one of them is called *Bayān al-mīlād al-Nabawī* ﷺ.

From these explanations, every knowledgeable person and opinion giver will know that the word '*mīlād*' is not devised by Indians, but it is an Arabic word which the Arabs have used since time immemorial. If someone still objects to this, then there is certainly something wrong with that individual. There should be no differences in religious terminology between the Muslims of the Arab and non-Arab worlds.

11.2 *Mawlid al-Nabī* ﷺ is an *ᶜĪd* of Happiness: Not an *ᶜĪd* of Sharia

The celebration of *Mawlid al-Nabī* ﷺ is neither an *ᶜīd* of the Sharia, nor do we consider it be so; nonetheless, this day is of greater significance than the Sharia *ᶜīd*. This is because to express happiness is an innate behavior. Hence, it is no exaggeration if it is considered an *ᶜīd* of happiness. *ᶜĪd Mawlid al-Nabī* ﷺ only comes once a year, whilst the gatherings of *mawlid* and the remembrance of the most exalted Prophet ﷺ take place throughout the year without any stipulation of time and space. The word '*ᶜīd*' is ascribed to the actual day on which the most exalted Prophet ﷺ

---

[1] Ḥājī Khalīfa, *Kashf al-ẓunūn ᶜan usāmī al-kutub wa al-funūn*, 1:745.

was born because people use the word *ʿīd* for any day of immense joy and happiness.

Mawlid al-Nabī ﷺ is a day of *ʿīd* in the common usage of the word. It is like when a person, on the occasion that his intimate friend or beloved arrives, exclaims: 'your coming is an *ʿīd* (for me)!' The following Arabic couplets are a true reflection of this meaning:

عِيْدٌ وَعِيْدٌ وَعِيْدٌ صِرْنَ مُجْتَمِعَةً

وَجْهُ الْحَبِيْبِ وَعِيْدُ الْفِطْرِ وَالْجُمُعَةِ

ʿĪd, ʿīd and ʿīd have (all) come together
The beloved's countenance, ʿīd al fiṭr, and Friday

Describing the day of the most exalted Prophet's birth as an *ʿīd* and calling it *ʿīd al-Nabawī* does not negate this fact that in the Sharia, there are only two days of *ʿīd*: *ʿīd al-fiṭr* and *ʿīd al-aḍḥā*. Observed from another angle, however, the *mawlid* is superior to and more blessed than these two celebrations since it was only through the intermediary of the Holy Prophet ﷺ that we became the recipients of the other two blessed days and other great days in Islam. Had it not been for his birth, we would not have been recipients of Islam, prophethood, the Qurʾān, the Heavenly Ascension, the migration, the Divine assistance at *Badr*, or the distinct victory of the conquest of Mecca. All this and much more were bestowed upon us through ther intermediation of the most exalted Prophet ﷺ, born on the 12th of *Rabīʿ al-Awwal*.

The true lovers of the Holy Prophet ﷺ are accustomed to celebrating his person on every significant occasion of happiness, and this delight increases manifold in the month of *Rabīʿ al-Awwal*, reaching its climax on the day in which he ﷺ was born. To seek an explanation as to why we celebrate *mawlid* on the 12th of *Rabīʿ al-Awwal* is completely inappropriate, since this implies that the questioner is demanding an answer as to why we are joyful on the day when the most exalted Prophet ﷺ appeared in this world. It is like asking why we are delightful for the sake of the one who ascended beyond the seven heavens. Is this a question that any Muslim with the slightest faith and love for the Holy Prophet ﷺ could ever ask? It is sufficient to reply to this meaningless inquiry by saying: "I celebrate joy and happiness on the day in which our beloved master ﷺ came to this world and I have deep love for my beloved Prophet ﷺ because I am a *mu'min*." There is no doubt whatsoever that arranging such events, feeding the poor, organising processions, praising the chief of the created beings, the Holy Prophet, and all the other features of this occasion are absolutely lawful and commendable.

It is also a natural instinct that in the month of *Rabīʿ al-Awwal*, the reasons for remembrance of the most glorious Prophet ﷺ are greater in comparison to other times of the year on account of the appropriateness of the occasion—it is a time when people flood to those gatherings in which the Prophet ﷺ is remembered. Common sense is convinced that certain moments, due to some special significance, possess greater nobility and blessings in comparison to others. In this way, the exhilarating remembrances which are induced by these drawing moments have a certain appeal to them which cannot be attained at other times. In this way, people connect the remembrance from the present to the past and to the future together and attain a distinct taste of the remembrance. As the poet describes:

باز گو اَز نجد و اَز یارانِ نجد

تا دَر و دیوار را آري به وجد

Continue to mention the beloved city and its dwellers;
So that its walls and doors manifest through your ecstasy

The *mawlid* gatherings are also a perfect opportunity to invite people to the remembrance of Almighty Allah. In fact, these moments carry the states of complete absorption and ecstasy (in true love) that should not be wasted. It is binding upon the speakers and scholars to take advantage of this golden opportunity to draw participants' attention to matters like the Holy Prophet's

ﷺ biography, morals and etiquettes, and dealings. They should endeavour to encourage attendees to hasten towards benevolent and pious deeds as well as warning them of the miseries and transgressions that have befallen the *Umma* and counsel them about the ways of protecting themselves from the fire. The purpose of the *mawlid* gatherings should not be to show off or to socialise with our acquaintances, but it is necessary that these gatherings should become means of achieving the esteemed aim from these sacred congregations. The participant who does not achieve this religious benefit is deprived of the goodness and blessing of *Mawlid al-Nabī* ﷺ!

11.3 The Hadith-Scholars' Approach in Recounting the Prophet's Merits and the *Mawlid al-Nabī*

It was the approach of Imam Muslim (206–261 AH), Imam al-Tirmidhī (210–279 AH), and other notable hadith scholars that when they used to recount the Holy Prophet's virtues and merits, they would also mention the *mawlid* of the most gracious Prophet ﷺ. Instead of talking about the *sīra* per se, the imams, when discussing the Prophetic exclusive merits and virtues, would also mention the Holy Prophet's blessed birth, the superior lineage, and all such items related to his sacred person.

Both Imam Muslim (206–261 AH) in his *al-Ṣaḥīḥ* in *Kitāb al-Faḍā'il* [The Book of Excellent Merits] and Imam al-Tirmidhī (210–279 AH) in *al-Jāmiʿ al-Ṣaḥīḥ* in *Kitāb al-Manāqib* [The Book of Virtuous Merits] commence their books with the narration of Wāthila b. Asqaʿ, who reports that the Prophet ﷺ said:

«إِنَّ اللهَ اصْطَفَى مِنْ وَلَدِ إِبْرَاهِيمَ إِسْمَاعِيلَ، وَاصْطَفَى مِنْ وَلَدِ إِسْمَعِيلَ بَنِي كِنَانَةَ، وَاصْطَفَى مِنْ بَنِي كِنَانَةَ قُرَيْشًا، وَاصْطَفَى مِنْ قُرَيْشٍ بَنِي هَاشِمٍ، وَاصْطَفَانِي مِنْ بَنِي هَاشِمٍ.»

Allah has chosen Ismāʿīl from the children of Ibrāhīm. He has chosen the tribe of Kināna from the offspring of Ismāʿīl. He has chosen Quraysh from Kināna. He has

> chosen the Banū Hāshim from Quraysh, and He has chosen me from the Banū Hāshim.[1]

In this hadith, the Holy Prophet ﷺ has mentioned his whole ancestry. He also used the word *iṣṭafā* (to choose) since this is his honorific title, *al-Muṣṭafā*—the Chosen One. This title is also attributed to the whole of his lineage.

Imam Muslim (206–261 AH) in his *al-Ṣaḥīḥ* in *Kitāb al-Faḍā'il* [The Book of Excellent Merits] and Imam Tirmidhī (210–279 AH) in *al-Jāmiᶜ al-Ṣaḥīḥ* in *Kitāb al-Manāqib* [The Book of Virtuous Merits] have not commenced their books with the subject of the Prophet's moral excellence or conduct, nor his teachings; rather, the chapter in its entirety is dedicated to *Mawlid al-Nabī* ﷺ. Imam Tirmidhī in the same book, in *bāb faḍl al-Nabī* [Chapter: the Prophet's excellent merits], has also repeated this subject in hadiths no. 2, 3, and 4. The interesting point is that in the fifth hadith, there is mention of the Holy Prophet's creation before his blessed birth when mentioning the creation of Ādam—the moment when man first came into being. This hadith commences in the following way:

Abū Hurayra narrates that the noble Companions asked the most exalted Prophet ﷺ:

يَا رَسُوْلَ اللهِ! مَتَى وَجَبَتْ لَكَ النُّبُوَّةُ؟

> O Messenger of Allah, when was Prophethood made incumbent upon you?

---

[1] Narrated by al-Tirmidhī in *al-Jāmiᶜ al-Ṣaḥīḥ*: *Kitāb al-Manāqib* [The Book of Virtuous Merits], chapter: 'The excellent merits of the Prophet', 5:583 §3605; Muslim in *al-Ṣaḥīḥ*: *Kitāb al-Faḍā'il* [The Book of Excellent Merits], chapter: 'The excellent merit of the Prophet's lineage and the stone reciting salutations upon him before his prophecy' 4:1782 §2276; Aḥmad b. Ḥanbal in *al-Musnad*, 4:107; Ibn Abī Shayba in *al-Muṣannaf*, 6:317 §31,731; Abū Yaᶜlā in *al-Musnad*, 13:469–472 §7485–7487; al-Ṭabarānī in *al-Muᶜjam al-kabīr*, 22:66 §161; al-Bayhaqī in *al-Sunan al-kubrā* in 6:365 §12,852; and al-Bayhaqī in *Shuᶜab al-īmān*, 2:139 §1391.

This was an unusual enquiry, because who amongst the noble Companion did not know that the Holy Prophet ﷺ declared his prophethood at the age of forty when he received revelation in the cave of Ḥirā? They obviously knew this. There was no doubt or misconception about the timing of the announcement of prophecy. So what was the need of asking such a question? Even when the matter was so evident, the Holy Prophet ﷺ did not reply to the noble Companions, asking them why they did not know this, because the noble Companions were well aware of the difference between his raising as a prophet and being bestowed prophecy. This is why, in reply to their question, the most exalted Prophet ﷺ said:

«وَآدَمُ بَيْنَ الرُّوحِ وَالْجَسَدِ.»

> (I was still a prophet) When Ādam was between the spirit and the body.[1]

The meaning of this hadith is that the most exalted Prophet ﷺ was bestowed prophecy at that time when Ādam's spirit and body had not yet been completed together. The reason why we relate this hadith here is that it is not related to the *sīra* per se, but it is in fact related to the *mawlid*. The reason why Imam al-Tirmidhī has mentioned it in *Kitāb al-Manāqib* [The Book of Virtuous Merits] and not in any other book is because it is not related to legal rulings, moral behavior, or etiquettes, etc., but because it is specifically related to the subject of *Mawlid al-Nabī* ﷺ.

---

[1] Narrated by al-Tirmidhī in *al-Jāmiʿ al-Ṣaḥīḥ*: *Kitāb al-Manāqib* [The Book of Virtuous Merits], chapter: 'The excellent merits of the Prophet', 5:585 §3609; Ibn Mustafāḍ in *Kitāb al-qadr*, p. 27 §14 has stated that the narrators are reliable; Tamām Rāzī in *Kitāb al-fawāʾid*, 1:241 §581; Ibn Ḥibbān in *Kitāb al-thiqāt*, 1:47; Lālakāʾī in *Iʿtiqād Ahl al-Sunna*, 1:422 §1403; al-Ḥākim in *al-Mustadrak*, 2:665 §4210; al-Bayhaqī in *Dalāʾil al-Nabuwwa wa maʿrifa aḥwāl Ṣāḥib al-Sharīʿa* ﷺ, 2:130; al-Suyūṭī, *al-Durr al-manthūr fī al-tafsīr bi al-Maʾthūr*, 6:569; and Nāṣir al-Dīn Albānī in *Ṣaḥīḥ al-ṣīra al-Nabawiyya*, p.54 §53 has declared this hadith authentic.

11.3.1 Imam al-Tirmidhī's Approach in Arranging the Chapters of *Kitāb al-Manāqib*

The first chapter of *Kitāb al-Manāqib* of Imam al-Tirmidhī's *al-Jāmiᶜ al-Ṣaḥīḥ* is called *bāb faḍl al-Nabī* ﷺ [Chapter: the Prophet's excellent merits]. The second chapter is called *bāb mā jāʾa fī mīlād al-Nabī* ﷺ [Chapter: what has been related concerning the Prophet's birth].

It is often the case that the Holy Prophet's biography and his raising are discussed after the events of his blessed birth, as chronologically, these occurred later. Can it be possible that the Holy Prophet ﷺ is raised as a Messenger even before his birth? It is a fact that the Prophet's birth took place first, and that the announcement of Prophethood followed much later. Thus, if anyone celebrates the *mawlid*, then he creates a spiritual bond with the esteemed Messenger ﷺ, and owing to which, he is bestowed the spiritual light in his heart. Imam al-Tirmidhī, keeping the Prophet's virtuous merits and excellence in mind, has brought this chapter first. It may be that some people may be unable to comprehend this as they may feel that there is no place for mentioning the Prophetic virtues when the emphasis should be on his conduct and teachings. Those who make such statements should take a close look at Imam al-Tirmidhī's work. Imam Muslim, Imam al-Tirmidhī, and many other imams and hadith scholars have commenced their chapters with the Prophet's virtuous merits followed by a mention of his birth.

After the chapter on the *mīlād*, the third chapter of *Kitāb al-Manāqib* of *al-Jāmiᶜ al-Ṣaḥīḥ* is *bāb mā jāʾa fī badʾ nubuwwa al-Nabī* ﷺ [Chapter: what has been related concerning the commencement of Prophethood]. This is a historical, logical, and rational arrangement which begins with the traditions related to the creation and miraculous birth of the Holy Prophet ﷺ, followed by other events in his life, such as his declaration of prophethood.

The fourth chapter of Imam al-Tirmidhī's work commences with a mention of his raising as a prophet. By arranging the traditions in this fashion, the author is drawing our attention to the fact that the announcement of Prophethood took place at the age of forty whilst the bestowal of Prophethood happened even before Ādam was created. From this, it is evident that there is a big difference between being bestowed prophecy and declaring it. And some people unfortunately, on account of their confusion, are unable to make this distinction and end up entangling the two together.

This arrangement gives us an insight into the creed of Imam al-Tirmidhī and the other hadith scholars of the six authentic books. For example, in the fifth chapter, *bāb fī āyāt ithbāt nubuwwa al-Nabī* ﷺ [Chapter: miracles proving the Prophet's prophecy], Imam al-Tirmidhī commences the chapter with the subject of invoking blessings on the Holy Prophet's person. In this narration, an anecdote is mentioned in which there was a stone in Mecca which used to invoke peace and blessings upon the Holy Prophet ﷺ. Jābir b. Samura ؓ narrates that the most exalted Prophet ﷺ said:

> There is a stone in Mecca which used to recite salutations upon me on the nights I was raised as a Prophet. Indeed, I recognise that stone even now.[1]

Imam ʿAlī narrates:

> كُنْتُ مَعَ النَّبِيِّ ﷺ بِمَكَّةَ فَخَرَجْنَا فِي بَعْضِ نَوَاحِيهَا فَمَا اسْتَقْبَلَهُ جَبَلٌ وَلَا شَجَرٌ إِلَّا وَهُوَ يَقُولُ: السَّلَامُ عَلَيْكَ يَا رَسُولَ اللهِ.
>
> I was with the Prophet ﷺ in Mecca, so we set out in one of its directions, and no mountain and tree on his way came to pass without saying, 'Peace be upon you, O Messenger of Allah!'[2]

---

[1] Narrated by al-Tirmidhī in *al-Jāmiʿ al-Ṣaḥīḥ*: *Kitāb al-Manāqib* [The Book of Virtuous Merits], chapter: 'Miracles proving the Prophet's prophecy', 5:592 §3624; Abū Yaʿlā in *al-Musnad*, 13:459 §7469; al-Ṭabarānī in *al-Muʿjam al-kabīr*, 2:220 §1907; and al-Ṭabarānī in *al-Muʿjam al-awsaṭ*, 2:291 §2012.

[2] Narrated by al-Tirmidhī in *al-Jāmiʿ al-Ṣaḥīḥ*: *Kitāb al-Manāqib* [The Book of Virtuous Merits], chapter: 'Miracles proving the Prophet's prophecy', 5:593 §3626; al-Ḥākim in *al-Mustadrak*, 2:677 §4238; and al-Maqdasī in *al-Aḥādīth al-mukhtāra*, 2:134, §502.

This is the very same salutation which is recited in the gatherings of *Mawlid al-Nabī* ﷺ. Alas! The trees and stones recite salutations on the chief of the created beings, the Holy Prophet ﷺ; but today, certain narrow-minded individuals who make claims to *tawḥīd* are trapped in the motions of declaring even this blessed act a *bidʿa*, even though the authentic books of hadith, such as *Jāmiʿ al-Tirmidhī* and *Ṣaḥīḥ Muslim*, have commenced their books in this way. Imam Muslim and Imam al-Bukhārī were proponents of this belief, as chapters have been devoted for the mention of the Prophet's virtues and merits. Imam al-Tirmidhī has dedicated a chapter for the Holy Prophet's birth and has made mention of the term *Mīlād al-Nabī* ﷺ.

11.4 The Historians' Approach in Recounting the Prophet's Merits and the *Mawlid al-Nabī* ﷺ

Apart from the hadith scholars, the historians and biographers have also followed this approach. Whilst discussing the Prophet's biography, they have placed chapters on the Holy Prophet's blessed birth and pure lineage.

1. Ibn Isḥāq (80–151 AH) composed the foremost book on the Prophet's biography, known as *al-Sīra al-Nabawiyya* ﷺ. He commences this book with the mention of the Holy Prophet's birth and lineage. The following two chapter-titles can be found in this book:

(i) *Dhikr sard al-nasab al-dhakī min Muhammad* ﷺ *ilā Ādam*

(ii) *Mawlid Rasūl Allāh* ﷺ[1]

2. Ibn Hishām (d. 213 AH), in his *al-Sīra al-Nabawiyya* ﷺ, has arranged the chapters on the Prophet's birth and lineage in the following way:

(i) *Dhikr sard al-nasab al-dhakī min Muhammad* ﷺ *ilā Ādam*

(ii) *Wilāda Rasūl Allāh* ﷺ *wa raḍāʿatihi*[2]

3. The famous historian, Ibn Saʿd (168–230 AH) in *al-Ṭabaqāt al-kubrā* (1:20, 25 & 100), begins with chapters mentioning in detail the Prophet's birth and lineage.

---

[1] Ibn Isḥāq, *al-Sīra al-Nabawiyya*, p.17 & 99.

[2] Ibn Hishām, *al-Sīra al-Nabawiyya*, p.23 & 153.

4. Imam Muhammad al-Kharkūshī al-Nīsābūrī (D. 406 AH), in the first volume of *Kitāb sharaf al-Muṣṭafā*, composed several chapters on the *mawlid* under the title: *Jummāᶜ abwāb ẓuhūrihi wa mawlidihi al-sharīf*.

5. Abū Nuᶜaym al-Aṣbahānī (336–430 AH) in *Dalāʾil al-Nubuwwa* (1:14–18) named one of his chapters: *Dhikr faḍīlatihī bi ṭīb mawlidihī wa ḥasabihī wa nasabihī*.

6. The renowned historian and biographer, al-Bayhaqī (384–458 AH), in his masterpiece *Dalāʾil al-nubuwwa wa maᶜrifa aḥwāl Ṣāḥib al-sharīᶜa* ﷺ (1:17), wrote in much detail about the *mawlid* under the heading: *Jummāᶜ abwāb mawlid al-Nabī* ﷺ.

7. Al-Maqrīzī (769–845 AH) wrote several passages about the Prophet's birth in *Imtāᶜ al-asmāᶜ bi mā li al-Nabī min al-aḥwāl wa al-amwāl wa al-ḥafada wa al-matāᶜ*.

8. Al-Qasṭallānī (851–923 AH) wrote a detailed account of the miraculous birth in *al-Mawāhib al-laduniyya bi al-minaḥ al-Muḥammadiyya* under *al-maqṣad al-awwal*.

9. Yūsuf al-Ṣāliḥī al-Shāmī (D. 942 AH) compiled a number of chapters on the *mawlid* in *Subul al-hudā wa al-rashād fī sīra Khayr al-ᶜibād* (1:325–374) in *Jummāᶜ abwāb mawlidihī al-sharīf*.

10. Khalīfa b. Khayyāṭ (160–240 AH) composed a chapter on the *mawlid* in his book, *al-Tārīkh*, called *Mawlid Rasūl Allāh* ﷺ *wa wafātihī*.

11. Al-Ṭabarī (224–310 AH), in *Tārīkh al-umam wa al-mulūk*, penned in considerable detail the pure lineage and birth of the Prophet ﷺ.

12. Ibn ᶜĀsākir (499–571 AH), in *Tārīkh Dimashq al-kabīr* (3:29 & 39), also discusses the Prophet's birth and lineage.

13. Ibn al-Jawzī (510–597 AH) in the first volume of *al-Muntaẓam fī tārīkh al-mulūk wa al-umam* covered the Prophet's birth and ancestry in detail.

14. Ibn al-Athīr al-Jazarī (555–630 AH) in the second volume of *al-Kāmil fī al-tārīkh* touches upon the Prophet's birth and his unadulterated lineage.

15. Al-Dhahabī (673–748 AH) in *Tārīkh al-Islām wa wafiyāt al-mashāhīr wa al-aᶜlām* has written about the *mawlid* under the chapter *Mawliduhū al-mubarāk* in *al-Sīra al-Nabawiyya*.

16. Ibn al-Wardī (d. 749 AH) in the first volume of his book on history, *Tatimma al-mukhtaṣar fī akhbār al-bashar*, compiled a chapter called *Mawlid al-Nabī* ﷺ *wa sharaf nasabihī al-ṭāhir.*
17. Ibn Kathīr (701–774 AH) in *al-Bidāya wa al nihāya*, second volume, penned several chapters on the *mawlid.*
18. Ḥusayn al-Diyārbakrī (d. 966 AH) in *Tārīkh al-khamīs fī aḥwāl anfus nafīs*, at the beginning of the first volume, explicitly mentions the Prophet's birth, as well as the births of other Prophets and Messengers.[1]

From the above references and the tradition of these glorious imams of history and *sira*, it is evident that all of them have mentioned in the commencement of their books the details of the incidents surrounding the Holy Prophet's blessed birth and the purity of his lineage. Apart from these, in virtually all the other books of *sīra* and history, this subject has also been brought under discussion. From this, it can be known that the words *mīlād* and *mawlid* have been used since the early generations; in fact, the eminent scholars have used these words in the titles of the chapters of their book. If anyone after knowing this information still claims that there is no origin for the words *mīlād* and *mawlid*, then it is most unfortunate indeed.

11.5 Demanding Evidences from the Sharia for *Mawlid al-Nabī* ﷺ

The principles which are derived from Divine laws are the basis of every legal action; every action stands firm on the Sunna of the Holy Prophet ﷺ. This is what proves the truthfulness of Islam and distinguishes it from all other religions. In this context, we have already established that celebrating the *mawlid* by expressing one's happiness in the form of an *ʿīd* is proven from the text of the Qurʾān and hadith. However, it is unfortunate that in spite of this, there are certain individuals, who, without any reason, are relentless in issuing fatwas of *bidʿa* and *shirk* at the greater majority of this *Umma*. These narrow minded individuals are obsessed in

[1] For further details on the date of publication, distributors etc., please refer to the bibliography at the end of this book.

demanding evidences for everything from the Qur᾿ān and Sunna: they wrongly assume that there is no basis for such action in the Sharia. Regarding such people, Iqbāl said:

دل بینا بھی کر خدا سے طلب
آنکھ کا نور، دل کا نور نہیں

Supplicate to Allah for a heart that can truly see
For the light of the eyes is not like the light of the heart[1]

Those who demand evidences for the *mawlid*—have they ever thought of doing the same on the many other occasions of happiness? Have these uninformed individuals at the time of expressing happiness ever looked into the matter and seen if there are evidences in the Qur᾿ān and Sunna to support their acts of merriment?

1. Is it not the case that when a couple has a child after a very long time that they distribute sweets and invite people round to celebrate? On this occasion, do they search the books of hadith to see if the noble Companions did the same when any one of them had a son?
2. Each year when the birthdays of children are celebrated and gifts are presented, does it ever cross their mind whether this act of merriment can be proven from the Qur᾿ān or hadith?
3. When it comes to the issue of our son's or daughter's wedding, we prepare months in advance. Invitation cards are designed and circulated, and huge sums of money are spent on the customs and exchange of gifts. A large amount of money is spent on costly wedding outfits and an elaborate *walīma* is arranged wherein family and friends are shown hospitality. Do we ever hesitate for a single moment to think about whether the most exalted Prophet ﷺ or his noble Companions were accustomed to such elaborate display of merriment? Did they also prepare expensive and huge meals? It is ironic that we do not seek out evidences from the Qur᾿ān and

[1] Iqbāl, *Kulliyāt: Bāl-e-Jibrīl*, p.335/43.

Sunna when it comes to our children's weddings, yet we are so bold in demanding evidences when it comes to the birth of our beloved Prophet ﷺ.

4. The 23rd of March is Pakistan Day, when the resolution for independence was passed, resulting in the struggle for freedom and the creation of Pakistan. To celebrate this day, parades are organised and celebrations take place at the governmental level. The 14th of August, the day which marks Pakistan's independence from the British, is also celebrated in a similar fashion. A guard of honour, military parades, and an ostentatious show of aircrafts and tanks are common features on this occasion. To celebrate the 6th of September (Pakistan Defense Day), the army displays its latest armaments in certain parts of the country for the civilian population to see. Even though these celebrations are legitimate, no one seeks to justify them from the Prophet's Sunna.

5. On the birthday of Muhammad Ali Jinnah, the founding father of Pakistan, schools, offices, and other governmental institutions are closed as though it is a day of *ʿīd*. Processions are organised, and speakers and academics are invited from far and wide to honour the efforts of those who struggled to create Pakistan and to recite eulogies in their praise. No evidence is demanded from the sacred texts for these acts, since we seem to take it for granted that the efforts of these national leaders must be remembered; yet on the birthday of the one who was sent as a Mercy to the Worlds, we all of sudden remember that we require 'proof' from the Qurʾān and hadith, and we become adamant in demanding it. Aḥmad Riḍā Khān eloquently sums up this sorry state:

اور تم پر مرے آقا کی عنایت نہ سہی

نجدیو! کلمہ پڑھانے کا بھی احسان گیا

The consideration of my sovereign for you is undeserved
O Najdis! Have you forgotten who taught you your creed?[1]

---

[1] Aḥmad Riḍā Khān, *Ḥadāʾiq-e-bakhshish*, 1:33.

6. When a foreign dignitary arrives, he is greeted with a 21 rifle salute. No evidence from the Qurʾān and hadith is sought for this.
7. When a monarch or head of the state dies, preparations are made for his burial. A funeral procession is organised, rifles are fired, mourning trumpets are played, wreaths are laid, and in short, no cost is spared. Scholars and others alike come to pay their final respects; yet no one has issued a fatwa for its permissibility, nor have examples from the life of the most exalted Prophet ﷺ or his noble Companions been searched to provide a rationale for these actions.

We are not implying here that these preparations are illegitimate, as these are means by which we can acknowledge the efforts of our leaders and display our pride as a nation—such arrangements should be made. Our concern here is, why is it that those who are always demanding evidences for the *mawlid* do not require evidences for such preparations? Why is there such inconsistency in principles? Have they forgotten Almighty Allah's command that the Muslims should rejoice in Allah's *faḍl* and *raḥma*, and that this rejoicing is better than what they amass[1]?

In the whole world, the one who is the most worthy of respect and reverence is the Holy Prophet ﷺ. Loving him is the essence of faith; it is faith per se. Faith is a state of the heart called *ḥāl*. This is an attachment or a connection based on love; it is a flame of love that kindles in the heart. When this love for the beloved Prophet ﷺ takes hold of a *muʾmin*, he celebrates *Mawlid al-Nabī* ﷺ in every moment of his life and decorates his walls and doors. It is imperative for us to know that in the sight of Almighty Allah, the celebration of the blessed birth of His beloved Prophet ﷺ is more virtuous than our half-baked worships.

It is a matter of great regret that those who criticise the *mawlid*, throwing fatwas of *bidʿa* and *shirk* at it, are not once reluctant to spend thousands on their children, but when the month of the Holy Prophet's blessed birth arrives, they are not willing to spend a single penny themselves and also prohibit others too. Let such people be aware that there is no happiness greater than the arrival

---

1 Qurʾān 10:58.

of our beloved Prophet ﷺ; every other happiness is worthless in comparison to rejoicing in him.

11.6 Celebrating *Mawlid al-Nabī* ﷺ is an Act of *Tawḥīd*

It is of paramount importance to realise that celebrating the *mawlid* is in reality an act of *tawḥīd*: it is one of the most significant evidences for Allah's Divine Oneness; because we are openly affirming that the Holy Prophet ﷺ is a worshipful servant of Almighty Allah and His beloved creation. Celebrating someone's birthday is a sign that he is not God, because Almighty Allah does not beget, nor is He begotten.[1] Concerning Prophet Yaḥyā ﷺ, Almighty Allah states:

﴿وَسَلَٰمٌ عَلَيْهِ يَوْمَ وُلِدَ﴾

And peace be on Yaḥyā the day he was born.[2]

Likewise, concerning Prophet ʿĪsā ﷺ, Allah states:

﴿وَٱلسَّلَٰمُ عَلَيَّ يَوْمَ وُلِدتُّ﴾

And peace be upon me on the day of my birth.[3]

This is why by celebrating the *mawlid*, we are making an unambiguous declaration that the Holy Prophet ﷺ is Almighty Allah's creation. There is no creation greater or superior to the most exalted Prophet ﷺ. The gatherings of *Mawlid al-Nabī* ﷺ are an announcement that Almighty Allah is the creator and that the Holy Prophet ﷺ is His creation, that he was born: can there be a greater act of *tawḥīd* than this? Unfortunately, the people of *bidʿa* have even indicted this sincere act of *tawḥīd* as *shirk*, which is totally wrong.

---

[1] Qurʾān 112:3.

[2] Qurʾān 19:15.

[3] Qurʾān 19:33.

11.7 Spending on *Mawlid al-Nabī* ﷺ is not Extravagance

Spending out of happiness on the *mawlid* is not extravagance because it is an act of goodness, and according to the jurists, there is no extravagance in goodness. Below are some verdicts of the scholars, according to whom there is no extravagance in praiseworthy affairs:

1. The son of Ḥasan b. Sahl reports that his father met a man who provided water for people. Ḥasan b. Sahl enquired about his financial state. The man replied that he had fallen on hard times, and he intended to marry off his daughter. Ḥasan b. Sahl was deeply moved by his pitiful state and arranged for this man to be granted a thousand dirhams. However, he was mistakenly bestowed a hundred thousand dirhams. The wife of Ḥasan b. Sahl did not approve of this act of chivalry from her husband's side but was too shy to rebuke him for it. Hence, Ghassān b. ʿIbād, who himself was renowned as a generous gentleman, revoked Ḥasan b. Sahl, exclaiming:

أَيُّهَا الْأَمِيْرُ! إِنَّ اللهَ لَا يُحِبُّ الْمُسْرِفِيْنَ.

> O great leader! Surely Allah does not love those who are profligate (i.e., spendthrift).

Ḥasan b. Sahl responded:

لَيْسَ فِي الْخَيْرِ إِسْرَافٌ.

> There is no extravagance in goodness.

Thereafter, Ḥasan b. Sahl described the miserable plight of the old man and said:

وَاللهِ! لَا رَجَعْتُ عَنْ شَيْءٍ خَطَّتْهُ يَدِيْ.

> I swear by Allah, I shall not take back that which I penned with my own hands.[1]

Thus, the man was made the rightful recipients of those coins.

2. ʿAbd Allāh b. ʿAbbās narrates:

> لَيْسَ فِي الْحَلَالِ إِسْرَافٌ، وَإِنَّمَا السَّرَفُ فِي ارْتِكَابِ الْمَعَاصِي.
>
> There is no extravagance in the lawful. There is only extravagance in acts of disobedience.[2]

3. Sufyān al-Thawrī said:

> اَلْحَلَالُ لَا يَحْتَمِلُ السَّرَفَ.
>
> The *ḥalāl* matters do not carry the possibility of extravagance.[3]

The above verdicts are clearly indicative that no matter how much one spends in charity and good deeds, it will never be counted as extravagance. Therefore, those people who consider the spending on the *mawlid* as wasteful should reform their understanding and not make this good practice a source of blame.

11.8 ARRANGEMENTS FOR THE DISPLAY OF THE MAGNIFICENCE AND GRANDEUR OF ISLAM

Abū Wā'il narrates: I was sitting on a chair besides Shayba near the *Kaʿba* and he said, 'This is where ʿUmar used to sit. I intend to distribute the *Kaʿba*'s treasure.' I said, 'But your two dear

---

[1] Ibn al-Jawzī, *al-Muntaẓam fī tārīkh al-mulūk wa al-umam*, 11:240–241 §1392; Khaṭīb Baghdādī, *Tārīkh Baghdād*, 7:322; and Ibn Jarāda, *Bughya al-ṭalab fī tārīkh Ḥalab*, 5:2386.

[2] Sharbīnī, *Mughnī al-muḥtāj ilā maʿrifa maʿānī alfāẓ al-minhāj*, 1:393; and Damyāṭī, *Iʿāna al-ṭālibīn*, 2:157.

[3] Abū Naʿīm, *Ḥilya al-awliyā' wa ṭabaqāt al-aṣfiyā'*, 6:382; Sharbīnī, *Mughnī al-muḥtāj ilā maʿrifa maʿānī alfāẓ al-minhāj*, 1:393; and Damyāṭī, *Iʿāna al-ṭālibīn*, 2:157.

Companions (the Holy Prophet ﷺ and Abū Bakr) did not do such a thing.' Shayba responded, 'If that is the case, then it is binding upon me to follow in their noble footsteps (i.e. I will not distribute this wealth).'[1]

Ibn Ḥajar al-ʿAsqalānī (773–852 AH) clarifies the reason for not distributing the *Kaʿba*'s treasures:

وَفِي ذَلِكَ تَعْظِيْمُ الْإِسْلَامِ وَتَرْهِيْبُ الْعَدُوِّ.

In that is the honouring of Islam and inspiring awe in the enemies.[2]

He further writes:

وَاسْتَدَلَّ التَّقِيُّ السُّبْكِيُّ بِحَدِيْثِ الْبَابِ عَلَى جَوَازِ تَعْلِيْقِ قَنَادِيْلِ الذَّهَبِ وَالْفِضَّةِ فِـي الْكَعْبَةِ وَمَسْجِدِ الْـمَدِيْنَةِ.

Taqī al-Dīn al-Subkī used this hadith as evidence for the permissibility of hanging gold and silver lamps in the *Kaʿba* and the Prophet's mosque. [3]

In regards to covering the *Kaʿba*, Ibn Ḥajar writes:

أَنَّ تَجْوِيْزَ سِتْرِ الْكَعْبَةِ بِالدِّيْبَاجِ قَامَ الْإِجْمَاعُ عَلَيْهِ.

The permissibility of covering the *Kaʿba* with silk brocade is established through consensus.[4]

---

[1] Narrated by al-Bukhārī in *al-Ṣaḥīḥ*: *Kitāb al-Ḥajj* [The Book of Pilgrimage], chapter: 'Covering the *Kaʿba*', 2:578 §1517; al-Bukhārī in *al-Ṣaḥīḥ*: *Kitāb al-Iʿtiṣām bi al-Kitāb wa al-Sunna* [The Book of Adhering to the Qurʾān and Sunna], chapter: 'Emulating the Sunna of Allah's Messenger', 6:2655 §6847; Aḥmad b. Ḥanbal, *al-Musnad*, 3:410; al-Ṭabarānī, *al-Muʿjam al-kabīr*, 7:300 §7196; and al-Bayhaqī, *al-Sunan al-kubrā*, 5:159 §9511.

[2] Al-ʿAsqalānī, *Fatḥ al-Bārī*, 3:457.

[3] Ibid.

[4] Ibid.

Al-Qāḍī Zayn al-Dīn ʿAbd al-Bāsiṭ was given a royal decree to design the covering of the *Kaʿba*—a task that he undertook with much skill and proficiency. Ibn Ḥajar al-ʿAsqalānī (773–852 AH), commenting on this, states:

بَسَطَ اللهُ لَهُ فِي رِزْقِهِ وَعُمْرِهِ، فَبَالَغَ فِي تَحْسِينِهَا بِحَيْثُ يَعْجِزُ الْوَاصِفُ عَنْ
صِفَةِ حُسْنِهَا، جَزَاهُ اللهُ عَلَى ذَلِكَ أَفْضَلَ الْمُجَازَاةِ.

> May Allah increase him manifold in age and sustenance, for words fail to express its beauty (i.e., in ornamenting the *Kaʿba*)—may Allah give him the best reward.[1]

Thus we can conclude that to inspire awe in the hearts of the enemies of Islam or to display the glory and brilliance of this religion by covering the *Kaʿba* with expensive cloth and decorating the two holy mosques with lamps and chandeliers of gold and silver is absolutely acceptable—if this is the case, how then can it be impermissible on the occasion of the most exalted Prophet's blessed birth to express our earnest emotions by decorating our streets, mosques, and homes? If it was not for the Holy Prophet ﷺ, the whole creation would not have come into existence: he is the heart and soul of creation. We received the *Kaʿba* because of him. If the *Kaʿba* can be ornamented with expensive cloth and golden lamps, then how can one possibly argue that to arrange decorations and lighting on the Holy Prophet's birthday is somehow illicit? To arrange decorations on the occasion of the Holy Prophet's birth is an acceptable and praiseworthy matter.

11.9 The Requirements for Holding Gatherings of *Mawlid al-Nabī* ﷺ

Throughout this book, we have made it clear that to commemorate the birthday of the beloved Messenger ﷺ is a praiseworthy deed which is rewarded. It must however be borne in mind that unless all aspects of the *mawlid* are performed in a sincere and lawful

[1] Ibid., 3:460.

manner, we would be deprived of the prospective blessings of this festivity. One must ensure that the *mawlid* gatherings are executed with pure intentions in an untainted manner, both internally and externally, lest we perform all the supposedly righteous deeds it consists of only to earn the anger and wrath of Almighty Allah and His most revered Messenger ﷺ.

Since *Mawlid al-Nabī* ﷺ, irrespective of whether it is in the form of a gathering or procession, aims to pay rich tribute to the most exalted Prophet ﷺ, it is imperative to maintain the etiquettes and the sanctity as it was maintained in the Holy Prophet's lifetime. Every effort must be made to ensure that that no negative or unlawful action takes place. Alongside this, the arrangement of these sacred gatherings, the provision of food, the distribution of alms, the delivery of lectures and all such operations that are orchestrated with great sacrifice must be exclusively done for the pleasure of Almighty Allah and His beloved Messenger ﷺ. The hadiths inform us that every morning and evening, our salutations, as well as our deeds, are presented in the court of the most exalted Prophet ﷺ; if the Holy Prophet sees anything good, he is pleased, whereas when we perform something bad, he is saddened.[1]

Mawlid al-Nabī ﷺ is no exception. Imagine the sheer joy of the most esteemed Prophet ﷺ if he is informed that his loyal, devoted servants organised an assembly to commemorate his birthday, thanking Almighty Allah for sending him to this world. If it is not done with pure intentions and sincerity, how will Almighty Allah bless it with His Divine excellence? This is something for us to think

---

[1] Narrated by al-Bazzār in *al-Baḥr al-zukhār* (*al-musnad*), 5:308–309 §1925; Ibn Abī Usāma in *Musnad al-Ḥārith*, 2:884 §953 has narrated this with an authentic chain of transmission; Ḥakīm Tirmidhī in *Nawādir al-uṣūl fī aḥādīth al-Rasūl*, 4:176; al-Daylamī in *al-Firdaws bi-maʾthūr al-khiṭāb*, 1:183 §686; Qāḍī ʿIyāḍ in *al-Shifā bi taʿrīf ḥuqūq al-Muṣṭafā*, 1:19; al-Haythamī in *Majmaʿ al-zawāʾid wa manbaʿ al-fawāʾid*, 9:24 narrates that this hadith is narrated by al-Bazzār and all its narrators are authentic; Ibn Kathīr in *al-Bidāya wa al-Nihāya*, 4:257; and Abū al-Faḍl al-ʿIrāqī in *Ṭarḥ al-tathrīb fī sharḥ al-taqrīb*, 3:297 has declared the chain of transmission of this narration authentic.

about. Spending our wealth generously on this occasion does not guarantee acknowledgement from Almighty Allah and His beloved Messenger ﷺ if it is devoid of sincerity and pure intentions. This is why true love and reverence for the most exalted Prophet ﷺ is the foremost prerequisite for the acceptance of our actions.

Besides sincerity, having internal and external purity is also of paramount importance. The Holy Prophet ﷺ himself was extremely meticulous about cleanliness. Just as the maintenance of cleanliness was a concern in his own lifetime, these same values should be reflected in these gatherings in the same way, as they are essentially held in his honour. It may be that the Holy Prophet ﷺ himself may grace these gatherings with his spiritual being. The anecdote which is to follow is reflective of this reality:

The author's father, Dr Farid-ud-Dīn Qadri, mentioned an incident relating to Mawlānā ʿAbd al-Ḥayy Lakhnawī. The latter would smoke tobacco using a *hookah* (water-pipe). It so happened that once after smoking tobacco, he rushed to a *mawlid* gathering, forgetting to rinse his mouth. Whilst sitting in the gathering, the odour from the tobacco could be smelt. Later that night, the Prophet ﷺ appeared in his dream and said, 'O ʿAbd al-Ḥayy! Do you not feel that you attended our gathering whilst your mouth was emitting the odour of tobacco?'

The Holy Prophet's temperament was so pious, pure, and delicate that he used to forbid his noble Companions to approach the mosques if they had just consumed onions and garlic. This was so that their mouths would not emit bad odours, resulting in other worshippers being disturbed.[1]

Likewise, there are many other accounts available in which the Holy Prophet ﷺ in his own physical life, as well after his passing away in the form of legal injunctions and indications, outlawed the use of such items which emit bad odours. Shāh Walī Allāh

---

[1] Narrated by Muslim in *al-Ṣaḥīḥ*: *Kitāb al-Masājid wa Mawāḍiʿ al-Ṣalā* [The Book of Mosques and the Places of Prayer], chapter: 'Prohibition of eating garlic, onions, or leeks, etc.', 1:394 §561; and Abū Dāwūd in *al-Sunan*: *Kitāb al-Aṭʿima* [The Book of Foodstuff], chapter: 'On eating garlic', 3:160–161 §3824–3825.

Muḥaddith al-Dihlawī (1174–1114 AH) in the 28th hadith of his book, *al-Durr al-thamīn fī mubashirāt al-Nabī al-Amīn*, recounts an incident that was transmitted from his father, Shāh ʿAbd al-Raḥīm (1131–1054 AH). He narrates:

Two pious men (one was a scholar and worshipper and the other was only a worshipper) were simultaneously honoured with a vision of the most exalted Prophet ﷺ. However, only the worshipper was granted permission to sit in the sacred presence. This devout worshipper was confused by this and enquired as to why the scholar was deprived of this privilege. He was informed that the scholar would smoke tobacco, which was disliked by the Holy Prophet ﷺ. The next day, the worshipper went to visit the learned individual and found him crying profusely due to his deprivation. When he realised the impediment to this prolific honour was his practice of smoking tobacco, he immediately discarded it and abandoned this harmful habit. The following night, both men again had the wonderful privilege of seeing the Holy Prophet ﷺ in their dreams. This time, not only was the scholarly man bestowed with the vision of the Holy Prophet's company, but he was also seated beside the chief of the created beings, the Holy Prophet ﷺ himself.[1]

11.10 Aspects which Require Reforming

Blessed are the people who organise or participate in the *mawlid* with sincere love and devotion for the most exalted Prophet's birth and consider the celebration of his blessed birth as a part of *Īmān*. This is all well and true, but they still need to consider the prerequisite of this faith in that the fundamental requirements should be fulfilled. Alas! If only these faithful people would also be duly familiar with the teachings and the reverence of the court of the Holy Prophet ﷺ.

In order to benefit from the bounties of these blessed occasions, it is essential that one participates in those gatherings which are free from acts that are incompatible with the Sharia. Regrettably,

[1] Shāh Walī Allāh, *al-Durr al-thamīn fī mubashirāt al-Nabī al-Amīn*, p.43–44.

in the present day and age, some ignorant individuals, unconscious of the etiquettes of reverence and veneration of Almighty Allah's Messenger ﷺ, have contaminated these blessed assemblies with the stains of rebellion and disobedience. Such unruliness is an act of foolishness and disrespect to Allah's Messenger ﷺ. The beating of drums, the playing of obscene music, unrestrained dancing of youth, and unrestricted intermingling between the sexes are to be condemned; such acts negate the very essence of venerating the most esteemed Prophet ﷺ. If this illicit behaviour was to be eradicated, then there would be no justification or excuse for critics to vent their opposition to the *mawlid*.

Therefore it is our fundamental duty to warn those guilty of such disobedience to refrain from spoiling otherwise an otherwise blessed events; otherwise, such sacred and pious events would be reduced to mere rituals with all their blessings divested. We can never become recipients of Divine pleasure and Prophetic favours unless and until we manage the *mawlid* gatherings and processions from sinful practices. If these despicable practices are not eradicated, they would become the cause for Divine anger and chastisement.

It is a sad state of affairs that neither the government nor the authorities make much effort to censure and put an end to these appalling practices. It seems that the silence and passiveness of religious institutions, *illā mā shā' Allāh*, is a result of their greed for personal benefit. Perhaps this is why many turn a blind eye to what should be forcefully and publicly condemned; they may fear that if they strictly stop these practices, people may stop attending such gatherings, and consequently, the wealth and fame they receive for their speeches and sponsors would subsequently be impeded. If material gain is the rationale behind their silence and passiveness, then how miserable is their plight that they would shamelessly take advantage of the Holy Prophet's birthday to satisfy their desires.

The government should not sit idly; it is imperative that it takes effort to ensure that these wrong actions are reformed. Why is it that when the government is opposed, the state apparatus rushes in to brutally and mercilessly put down any resistance, and imprisons those seen as the perpetrators, and yet in the gatherings of the *mawlid* and *ʿurs*, when corrupt individuals utilise these opportunities to openly organise unacceptable music, dance, circuses, and opposition of the pious teachings of the *awliyā* (divine friends of Almighty Allah), they do not take any steps towards reform? The state bears the foremost responsibility for allowing these vices to become widespread as they have refused to make any concerted effort towards policing this type of illicit activity. The authorities should act swiftly to obstruct the future occurrence of such immoral and unacceptable behaviour.

The intent behind the *ʿurs* is for its participants to recite the Qurʾān and to become acquainted with the teachings of the divine friends of Almighty Allah. The *Mawlid al-Nabī* processions are conducted to eulogise the Holy Prophet ﷺ and to relate his exclusive and virtuous attributes and to celebrate his blessed birth according to the *sharia*; but how heart-breaking it is that:

حقیقت خرافات میں کھو گئی

یہ اُمت روایات میں کھو گئی

The reality of the purpose has vanished amidst distortions
This Umma *has become deluded in fabrications*[1]

The symbols of the *Dīn* are being mocked by individuals whilst the government and the thoughtful people are silent.

11.11 THE NECESSITY OF ABSTAINING FROM EXCESSES

The miserable plight of the *Umma* today is that it has split into two extremes: one extreme rebukes the *mawlid* outright as a prohibited innovation, whilst the other extreme, *illā mā shāʾ Allāh*, gains nothing from it except the symptoms of illicit and illegitimate actions, thereby severely tarnishing the image of an otherwise worthy practice. The dire need of the hour is the abandonment of excesses from both sides to be substituted with

---

[1] Iqbal, *Kulliyāt: Bāl-e-Jibrīl*, p.416/124.

balance and moderation. The *Umma* has been alarmingly divided into two under the titles of '*mawlid*' and '*sīra*', with both factions constantly rebuking the other in being unorthodox and ignorant. This is counterproductive and impractical—how could the *sīra* have materialised without the *mawlid*? Likewise, how would the objectives of the *mawlid* be realised without reference to the *sīra*? The *mawlid* and the *sīra* are two sides of the same coin, in that they are both means of remembering, praising, and loving the Messenger of Allah ﷺ. They should be seen therefore as two rays from the same lamp. The *mawlid* should not be rejected outright as a modern creation, nor should it be exploited to transmit fables and dishonest and banned practices.

It would be preferable that participants present themselves at the *mawlid* gatherings in a state of ablution with their hearts brimming with immense love and adoration for Allah's Messenger ﷺ. The *mawlid* should be beautified with accounts from the *sīra*, drawing participants' hearts and minds to the indescribable beauty and endearing character of the most gracious and beloved Prophet ﷺ. The atmosphere should echo with the melodious sound of eulogies that resonate with the emotions of love and passion for his blessed person. This should be the endeavour of every Muslim. This alone is the solution to the dire need of reform and revival that would lead to the ultimate success and salvation of the *Umma*. Otherwise, if Muslim clerics and preachers continue to draw a line between the two realities, i.e., *mawlid* and *sīra*, then how would the masses ever be united and guided towards the right direction?

If these clerics and preachers are sincere in their quest for the protection of the *Dīn* and the reverence and veneration of the Holy Prophet ﷺ, then the responsibility is upon them to wage an intellectual battle against every type of innovation and every unlawful habit and custom. The government is also duty bound to keep an eye on the sanctity of these gatherings in order to uphold the sacredness of these functions by eliminating the immoral components that have crawled into these congregations. The appropriate penalties must be stipulated for anyone who dares to blemish this sacred occasion with inappropriate acts of revelry.

Let us pray that Almighty Allah, for the sake of His beloved Messenger ﷺ, showers His infinite mercy upon us to reform our pitiful plight. May we be bestowed with the descent of Divine benedictions and grace through the celebration of *Mawlid al-Nabī* ﷺ. May we truly implement the lessons of *sīra* into our daily lives whilst simultaneously refraining from every type of vice and depravation—*Āmīn bi-jāhi Sayyid al-mursalīn* ﷺ.

Bibliography

al-Qurʾān

ʿAbbāsī, Zayn al-ʿĀbidīn Muhammad b. ʿAbd Allāh al-Khalīfatī (d. 1130 AH), *al-Jāmiʿ al-ẓāhir al-munīr fī dhikr mawlid al-Bashīr al-Nadhīr* ﷺ. n.d.

ʿAbd Allāh al-Kāshgharī, ʿAbd Allāh b. Muhammad al-Kāshgharī al-Bindāʾī al-Naqshbandī al-Zāhidī (d. 1174 AH), *Mawlid al-Nabī* ﷺ.

ʿAbd Allāh b. Muhammad b. ʿAbd al-Wahhāb (1242–1165 AH), *Mukhtaṣar sīra al-Rasūl* ﷺ, Lahore, Pakistan: al-Maṭbaʿa al-ʿArabiyya, 1399 AH/1979 CE.

ʿAbd al-ʿAzīz b. Muhammad, *Baʿtha al-Muṣṭafā* ﷺ *fī Mawlid al-Muṣṭafā* ﷺ.

Ibn ʿAbd al-Barr, Abū ʿUmar Yūsuf b. ʿAbd Allāh b. Muhammad (463–368 AH/1071–979 CE), *al-Istīʿāb fī Maʿrifa al-Aṣḥāb,* Beirut, Lebanon: Dār al-Jīl, 1412 AH.

—. *al-Istīʿāb fī Maʿrifa al-Aṣḥāb,* Beirut, Lebanon: Dār al-Kutub al-ʿIlmiyya, 1422 AH/2002 CE.

—. *al-Tamhīd li mā fī al-muwaṭṭa min al-maʿānī wa al-asānīd*. Marrakech: Ministry of Religious Affairs, 1387 AH.

ʿAbd al-Ḥaqq Muḥaddith al-Dihlawī, Shaykh (1052–958 AH/–1551 1642 CE), *Ashʿat al-lumʿāt sharḥ mishkāt al-maṣābīḥ*, Sakhar, Pakistan: Maktaba Nūriyya Riḍwiyya, 1976 CE.

—. *Mā thabata min al-Sunna fī ayyām al-sana*, Lahore, Pakistan: Idāra Naʿīmiyya Riḍwiyya & Ḥimāyat Islām Press.

—. *Madārij al-nabuwwa*, Lahore, Pakistan: Nūriyya Riḍwiyya Publishing Company, 1997 CE.

—. *Muqaddima fī uṣūl al-ḥadīth*, Beirut, Lebanon: Dār al-Bashāʾir al-Islāmiyya.

ʿAbd al-Ḥayy al-Kittānī, Ibn ʿAbd al-Kabīr, *Fahras al-fahāris wa al-athbāt wa muʿjam al-maʿājim wa al-mashīkhāt wa al-musalsalāt*, Beirut, Lebanon: Dār al-Gharb al-Islāmī, 1982 CE.

ʿAbd al-Ḥayy, Muhammad Farangī Maḥallī Lakhnawī (1304–1264 AH/1886–1848 CE), *Majmūʿa al-fatāwā*, Karachi, Pakistan: Saʿīd Company.

ᶜAbd b. Ḥumayd, Abū Muhammad b. Naṣr al-Kasī (d. 249 AH/863 CE), *al-Musnad,* Cairo, Egypt: Maktaba al-Sunna, 1408 AH/1988 CE.

Abū ᶜAbd al-Makkī, Jamāl al-Dīn Muhammad b. Aḥmad b. Saᶜīd b. Masᶜūd al-Ẓāhir (d. 1130 AH), *Mawlid al-Nabī* ﷺ.

Abū ᶜAbd al-Muᶜṭī, Muhammad Nuwayr b. ᶜUmar b. ᶜArabī b. ᶜAlī al-Nawawī al-Jāwā (d. 1315 AH), *Bughya al-ᶜawām fī sharḥ mawlid Sayyid al-anām* ﷺ.

ᶜAbd al-Raḥīm al-Barᶜī, Imām ᶜAbd al-Raḥīm b. Aḥmad al-Barᶜī al-Yamānī (d. 803 AH/1400 CE), *Mawlid al-Barᶜī.*

ᶜAbd al-Razzāq, Abū Bakr b. Hammām b. Nāfiᶜ al-Ṣanᶜānī (–126 211 AH/826–744 CE), *al-Muṣannaf,* Beirut, Lebanon: al-Maktab al-Islāmī, 1403 AH.

Ibn ᶜĀbidīn Shāmī, Muhammad (1244–1306 AH) *Radd al-muḥtār ᶜalā al-durr al-mukhtār ᶜalā tanwīr al-abṣār.* Beirut: Dār al-Fikr, 1386 AH.

Abyārī, Ibrāhīm al-, *Mawlid Rasūl Allāh* ﷺ.

al-ᶜAdawī, Aḥmad b. Muhammad b. Aḥmad al-Mālikī al-Miṣrī (d. 1201 AH), *Mawlid al-Dardīr.*

Adfawī, Kamāl al-Dīn Abū al-Faḍl Jaᶜfar b. Thaᶜlab b. Jaᶜfar al- (–685 748 AH/1347–1286 CE), *al-Ṭāliᶜ al-Saᶜīd al-Jāmiᶜ li-Asmāʾ Nujabāʾ al-Ṣaᶜīd.*

ᶜAfīfī, ᶜAbd Allāh, *al-Mawlid al-Nabawī al-Mukhtār* ﷺ.

Aḥmad b. Ḥanbal, Abū ᶜAbd Allāh b. Muhammad (241–164 AH/855–780 CE), *Faḍāʾil al-Ṣaḥāba.* Beruit: Muʾassasa al-Risāla, 1983 CE.

—. *al-Musnad,* Beirut, Lebanon: al-Maktab al-Islāmī, 1408 AH/1988 CE.

—. *al-Musnad,* Riyadh, Saudi Arabia.

—. *al-Musnad,* Beirut, Lebanon: al-Maktab al-Islāmī, 1398 AH/1978 CE.

—. *al-Musnad,* Beirut, Lebanon: Muʾassasa al-Risāla, 1420 AH/1999 CE.

Aḥmad b. Zaynī al-Daḥlān, Sayyīd al-Ḥasanī al-Hāshimī al-Qurashī al-Makkī (1233–1304 AH), *Sīra al-Nabawiyya*, Beirut, Lebanon: Dār al-Fikr.

—. *Sīra al-Nabawiyya*, Beirut, Lebanon: Muʾassisa al-Kutub al-

Thaqāfiyya, 1421 AH/2001 CE.
Aḥmad Muṣṭafā, al-Marāghī, *Tafsīr al-Qur'ān al-Karīm*, Beirut, Lebanon: Dār al-Fikr, 1394 AH/1974 CE.
Aḥmad Riḍā b. Naqī ʿAlī Khān al-Qādirī (1272–1340 AH/1856–1921 CE), *Ḥadā'iq-e-Bakhshish*, Lahore, Pakistan: Muslim Kitābawī, 1420 AH/1999 CE.
—. *Iqāma al-qiyāma ʿalā ṭāʿin al-qiyām li-Nabī tihāma.*
—. *Nuṭq al-hilāl bi arkh wilādat al-Ḥabīb wa al-wiṣāl.*
Ibn Aḥmad Saʿīd, Shaykh Muhammad Maẓhar (d. 1301 AH/1884 CE), *al-Risāla al-Saʿīdiyya.*
Ibn Abī ʿĀṣim, Abū Bakr b. ʿAmr al-Ḍaḥḥāk b. Makhlad al-Shaybānī (287–206 AH/900–822 CE), *al-Sunna,* Beirut, Lebanon: al-Maktab al-Islāmī, 1400 AH.
Ibn ʿAjība, Abū al-ʿAbbās Aḥmad b. Muhammad b. Mahdī Ḥasanī (1224–1160 AH), *al-Baḥr al-madīd fī tafsīr al-Qur'ān al-ʿAẓīm*, Beirut, Lebanon: Dār al-Kutub al-ʿIlmīyya, 1423 AH/2002 CE.
ʿAjlūnī, Abū al-Fidā' Ismāʿīl b. Muhammad b. ʿAbd al-Hādī b. ʿAbd al-Ghanī al-Jarrāḥī al- (1162–1087 AH/1749–1676 CE), *Kashf al-Khifā' wa Muzīl al-Ilbās,* Beirut, Lebanon: Mu'assisa al-Risāla, 1405 AH/1985 CE.
Ibn ʿAllān, Muhammad ʿAlī al-Ṣiddiqī al-Makkī, *Mawrid al-ṣafā fī mawlid al-Muṣṭafā* ﷺ.
Ālūsī, Abū al-Faḍl Shihāb al-Dīn al-Sayyid Maḥmūd al- (–1217 1270 AH/1854–1802 CE), *Rūḥ al-Maʿānī*, Beirut, Lebanon: Dār al-Iḥyā' al-Turāth al-ʿArabī.
Anwar Shāh Kashmīrī, Muhammad Anwar b. Muhammad Muʿaẓẓam Kashmīrī (1352–1292 AH), *Fayḍ al-Bārī ʿalā Ṣaḥīḥ Bukhārī*, Cairo, Egypt: Maṭbaʿa Ḥijāzī, 1357 AH/1938 CE.
ʿAqqād, Muhammad b. ʿAlī b. Ḥasan al-Sālimī (d. 1202 AH), *Tadhkira ahl al-khayr fī al-mawlid al-Nabawī* ﷺ.
ʿĀrif Zaylī, Abū al-Thanā' Aḥmad b. Muhammad b. ʿĀrif Zaylī Rūmī Ḥanafī (d. 1006 CE), *Mawlid al-Nabī* ﷺ.
Ibn ʿAsākir, Abū al-Qāsim ʿAlī b. al-Ḥasan b. Hibat Allāh b. ʿAbd Allāh b. al-Ḥusayn al-Dimashqī (571–499 AH/1176–1105 CE), *Tārīkh Dimashq al-Kabīr,* generally known as *Tārīkh Ibn ʿAsākīr,* Beirut, Lebanon: Dar al-Fikr, 1995 CE.
—. *Tārīkh Dimashq al-Kabīr,* generally known as *Tārīkh Ibn*

ʿAsākīr, Beirut, Lebanon: Dār al-Iḥyāʾ al-Turāth al-ʿArabī, 1421 AH/2001 CE.

—. *al-Sīra al-Nabawiyya*, Beirut, Lebanon: Dār al-Iḥyāʾ al-Turāth al-ʿArabī, 1421 AH/2001 CE.

Ashraf ʿAlī Thānwī (1362–1280 AH/1943–1863 CE), *Imdād al-mushtāq ilā Ashraf al-akhlāq*, Lahore, Pakistan: Islamī Kutub Khāna.

—. *Khuṭbāt Mīlād al-Nabī*, Multan, Pakistan: Idāra Tālīfāt Ashrafiyya, 1426 AH/2005 CE.

—. *Nashr al-ṭīb fī dhikr al-Nabī al-Ḥabīb* ﷺ, Karachi, Pakistan: H. M. Saʿīd Company, 1989 CE.

Aṣīl al-Dīn al-Harawī, Sayyid ʿAbd Allāh b. ʿAbd al-Raḥmān al-Ḥusayn al-Shīrāzī (d. 883 AH), *Darj al-durar fī mīlād Sayyid al-bashar* ﷺ.

Ibn al-Athīr, Abū al-Ḥasan ʿAlī b. Muhammad b. ʿAbd al-Karīm b. ʿAbd al-Wāḥid al-Shaybānī al-Jazarī (630–555 AH/1233–1160 CE), *Usad al-Ghāba fī Maʿrifa al-Ṣaḥāba,* Beirut, Lebanon: Dār al-Kutub al-ʿIlmiyya.

—. *al-Kāmil fī al-tārīkh*. Beirut: Dār Ṣādir, 1979 CE.

Abū ʿAwāna, Yaʿqūb b. Isḥāq b. Ibrāhīm b. Zayd al-Naysabūrī (316–230 AH/928–845 CE), *al-Musnad,* Beirut, Lebanon: Dār al-Maʿrifa, 1998 CE.

ʿAynī, Badr al-Dīn Abū Muhammad Maḥmūd b. Aḥmad b. Mūsā b. Aḥmad b. Ḥusayn b. Yūsuf b. Maḥmūd al- (855–762 AH/–1361 1451 CE), *ʿUmdat al-Qārī Sharḥ ʿalā Ṣaḥīḥ al-Bukhārī,* Beirut, Lebanon: Dār al-Fikr, 1399 AH/1979 CE.

—. *ʿUmda al-Qārī Sharḥ ʿalā Ṣaḥīḥ al-Bukhārī,* Beirut, Lebanon: Dār al-Iḥyāʾ al-Turāth al-ʿArabī.

Azdī, Maʿmar b. Rāshid al- (d. 151 AH), *al-Jāmiʿ*, Beirut, Lebanon: al-Maktab al-Islāmī, 1403 AH.

ʿAẓīm Ābādī, Abū al-Ṭayyab Muhammad Shams al-Ḥaqq al-, *ʿAwn al-Maʿbūd Sharḥ Sunan Abī Dāwūd,* Beirut, Lebanon: Dār al-Kutub al-ʿIlmiyya, 1415 AH/1995 CE.

Azraqī, Abū al-Walīd Muhammd b. ʿAbd Allāh b. Aḥmad b. Muhammad b. al-Walīd b. ʿUqba al- (d. 223 AH), *Akhbār Makka wa mā jāʾa fīhā min al-āthār*, Makka, Saudi Arabia: Maktaba al-Thaqāfa, 1423 AH/2002 CE.

Bā ʿAlawī, ʿUmar b. ʿAbd al-Raḥmān b. Muhammad b. ʿAlī b.

Muhammad b. Aḥmad Haḍramī (d. 880 AH), *Kitāb Mawlid al-Nabī* ﷺ.

Baghawī, Abū Muhammad Ḥusayn b. Masʿūd b. Muhammad al-Farrāʾ al-. *Maʿālim al-Tanzīl*. Beruit: Dār al-Maʿrifa, 1407 AH/1987 CE.

—. *Sharḥ al-Sunna,* Beirut, Lebanon: al-Maktab al-Islāmī, 1983/1403 CE.

Bājūrī, Ibrāhīm b. Muhammad al-Shāfiʿī al-Miṣrī al- (1277–1198 AH), *Tuḥfa al-Bashar ʿalā Mawlid Ibn Ḥajar.*

Bājūrī, Ibrāhīm b. Muhammad al-Shāfiʿī al-Miṣrī al- (1277–1198 AH), *al-Mawāhib al-laduniyya ḥāshiya ʿalā al-Shamāʾil al-Muḥammadiyya*, Egypt: Maṭbaʿa Muṣṭafa al-Bābī al-Ḥalabī, 1375 AH/1956 CE.

Bakrī, Abū al-Ḥasan Aḥmad b. ʿAbd Allāh al-, *Kitāb al-anwār wa miftaḥ al-surūr wa al-afkār fī mawlid al-Nabī Muhammad* ﷺ.

Bakrī, Muhammad b. ʿAlī b. Muhammad b. ʿAllān al-Ṣiddīqī al-ʿAlawī al-Makkī al- (1647–1588 CE), *Mawrid al-ṣafā fī mawlid al-Muṣṭafā* ﷺ.

Barzanjī, Jaʿfar b. Ḥasan b. ʿAbd al-Karīm al-Ḥusaynī al-Madanī al- (d. 1177 AH), *ʿAqd al-Jawhar fī Mawlid al-Nabī al-Azhar* ﷺ, Kano, Nigeria: Dār al-Afrīqiyya li Ṭabāʿa wa al-Nashr.

—. *Naẓm mawlid al-Nabī* ﷺ, Beirut, Lebanon, Maktaba al-Thaqāfa.

Bāʿūniyya, ʿAʾishā b. Yūsuf al-Dimashqiyya al-Shāfiʿiyya (d. 922 AH), *Mawlūd al-Nabī* ﷺ.

Bayhaqī, Abū Bakr Aḥmad b. al-Ḥusayn b. ʿAlī b. ʿAbd Allāh b. Mūsā al- (458–384 AH/1066–994 CE), *Dalāʾil al-Nubuwwa wa Maʿrifa Aḥwāl Ṣāḥib al-Sharīʿa*, Beirut, Lebanon: Dār al-Kutub al-ʿIlmiyya, 1405 AH/1985 CE.

—. *Dalāʾil al-Nubuwwa wa Maʿrifa Aḥwāl Ṣāḥib al-Sharīʿa,* Beirut, Lebanon: Dār al-Kutub al-ʿIlmiyya, 2002/1423.

—. *al-Sunan al-Ṣughrā*, Medina, Saudi Arabia: Maktaba al-Dār, 1989/1410 CE.

—. *al-Sunan al-Ṣughrā*, Beirut, Lebanon: Dār al-Kutub al-ʿIlmiyya, 1412 AH/1992 CE.

—. *al-Sunan al-kubrā*, Mecca, Saudi Arabia: Maktaba Dār al-Bāz, 1414 AH/1994 CE.

—. *al-Sunan al-kubrā*, Multan, Pakistan: Nashr al-Sunna.

—. *Shuʿab al-Īmān*, Beirut, Lebanon: Dār al-Kutub al-ʿIlmiyya, 1410 AH/1990 CE.

—. *al-Madkhal ilā al-Sunan al-Kubrā,* Kuwait: Dār al-Khulafāʾ li al-Kitāb al-Islāmī, 1404 AH/1984 CE.

Bazzār, Abū Bakr Aḥmad b. ʿAmr b. ʿAbd al-Khāliq al-Baṣrī al- (292–210 AH/905–825 CE), *al-Baḥr al-Zukhār*, Beirut, Lebanon: Muʾassisa ʿUlūm al-Qurʾān, 1409 AH.

—. *al-Baḥr al-Zukhār*, Medina, Saudi Arabia: Maktaba al-ʿUlūm wa al-Ḥikam, 1424 AH/2003 CE.

Bhopālī, Ṣiddīq b. Ḥasan al-Qanūjī (1307–1248 AH), *al-Shamāma al-ʿAnbariyya min mawlid Khayr al-bariyya* ﷺ, Dehli, India, Maṭbaʿa al-Anṣārī.

Bukhārī, Abū ʿAbd Allāh Muhammad b. Ismāʿīl b. Ibrahīm b. Mughīra al- (256–194 AH/870–810 CE), *al-Adab al-Mufrad*, Beirut, Lebanon: Dār al-Bashāʾir al-Islāmiyya, 1409 AH/1989 CE.

—. *Khalq Afʿāl al-ʿIbād*, Riyad, Saudi Arabia: Dār al-Maʿārif al-Saʿūdiyya, 1398 AH /1978 CE.

—. *al-Ṣaḥīḥ*, Beirut, Lebanon, Dār Ibn Kathīr, al-Yamāma, 1407 AH/987 CE.

—. *al-Tārīkh al-Awsaṭ*, Beirut, Lebanon: Dār al-Maʿrifa, 1406 AH/1986 CE.

—. *al-Tārīkh al-Kabīr,* Beirut, Lebanon: Dār al-Kutub al-ʿIlmiyya, 1422 AH/2001 CE.

—. *al-Tārīkh al-Ṣaghīr,* Beirut, Lebanon: Dār al-Maʿrifa, Dār al-Maʿrifa, 1406 AH/1986 CE.

al-Būṣīrī, Abū ʿAbd Allāh Sharaf al-Dīn Muhammad (696–608 AH/1296–1212 or 1297 CE), *Qaṣīda al-Burda.*

Dāraquṭnī, Abū al-Ḥasan ʿAlī b. ʿUmar b. Aḥmad b. al-Mahdī b. Masʿūd b. al-Nuʿmān al- (385–306 AH/995–918 CE), *al-Sunan*, Beirut, Leba-non: Dār al-Maʿrifa, 1966/1386.

Dārimī, Abū Muhammad ʿAbd Allāh b. ʿAbd al-Raḥmān al- (–181 255 AH/869–797 CE), *al-Sunan*, Beirut, Lebanon: Dār al-Kitāb al-ʿArabī, 1407 AH.

Abū Dāwūd, Sulaymān b. Ashʿath b. Isḥāq b. Bashīr al-Sijistānī (275–202 AH/889–817 CE), *al-Sunan*, Beirut, Lebanon: Dār al-Fikr, 1414 AH/1994 CE.

Daylamī, Abū Shujāʿ Shīrawayh b. Shardār b. Shīrawayh al-Daylamī al-Hamdānī al- (509–445 AH/1053–1115 CE), *al-Firdaws bi maʾthūr al-khiṭāb,* Beirut, Lebanon: Dār al-Kutub al-ʿIlmiyya, 1406 AH/1986 CE.

—. *al-Firdaws bi maʾthūr al-khiṭāb,* Beirut, Lebanon: Dār al-Kutub al-ʿIlmiyya, 1407 AH/1987 CE.

Dhahabī, Shams al-Dīn Muhammad b. Aḥmad al- (748–673 AH/–1274 1348 CE), *al-Mūqiẓa fī ʿilm muṣṭalaḥ al-ḥadīth,* Beirut, Lebanon: Dār al-Bashāʾir al-Islāmiyya, 1405 AH.

—. *Siyar Aʿlām al-Nubalāʾ,* Beirut, Lebanon: Muʾassisa al-Risāla, 1413 AH.

—. *Siyar Aʿlām al-Nubalāʾ,* Beirut, Lebanon: Dār al-Fikr, 1418 AH/1997 CE.

—. *Tadhkirat al-Ḥuffāẓ,* Beirut, Lebanon: Dār al-Kutub al-ʿIlmiyya.

—. *Tārīkh al-Islām wa wafiyāt al-mashāhīr wa al-aʿlām,* Beirut, Lebanon: Dār al-Kitāb al-ʿArabī, 1409 AH/1989 CE.

Ibn Diḥya al-Kalbī, Abū Khaṭṭāb ʿUmar b. Ḥasan b. ʿAlī b. Muhammad (633–544 AH), *al-Tanwīr fī Mawlid al-Bashīr al-Nadhīr.*

Dimashqī, Ḥāfiẓ Shams al-Dīn Muhammad b. Nāṣir al-Dīn b. Abī Bakr ʿAbd Allāh Qīsī Shāfiʿī (842–777 AH), *Jāmiʿal-āthār fī mawlid al-Nabī al-Mukhtār* ﷺ.

—. *al-Lafẓ al-rāʾiq fī mawlid Khayr al-khalāʾiq* ﷺ.

—. *Mawrid al-ṣādī fī mawlid al-Hādī* ﷺ.

Dimyāṭī, Muhammad b. Muhammad al-, *Mawlid al-ʿazb.*

Diyār al-Bakrī, Ḥusayn b. Muhammad b. al-Ḥasan al- (d. 966 AH/1559 CE), *Tārīkh al-khamīs fī aḥwāl anfus nafīs,* Beirut, Lebanon: Muʾassasa al-Shuʿbān li-Nashr wa al-Tawzīʿ.

—. *Mawlid al-Nabī* ﷺ.

Dūlābī, Abū Bishr Muhammad b. Aḥmad b. Muhammad b. Ḥammād al- (310–224 AH), *al-Dhurriya al-Ṭāhira al-Nabawiyya,* Kuwait: Dār al-Salafiyya, 1407 AH.

Ibn Abī al-Dunyā, Abū Bakr ʿAbd Allāh b. Muhammad b. al-Qurashī (281–208 AH), *al-Munāmāt,* Cairo, Egypt: Maktaba al-Qurʾān.

Edward Van Dyck, *Iktifāʾal-Qanūʿ bimā huwa Maṭbūʿ.*

Ibn Fakhr, Shaykh Shams al-Dīn Abū al-Qāsim Muhammad b. Fakhr al-Dīn ʿUthmān Luʾluʾī al-Dimashqī al-Ḥanbalī (d. 867 AH), *al-Durr al-munaẓẓam fī mawlid al-Nabī al-Muʿaẓẓam* ﷺ.
Fākihī, Abū ʿAbd Allāh Muhammad b. Isḥāq b. ʿAbbās al-Makkī al- (217–275 AH), *Akhbār Makka fī Qadīm al-Dahr wa Ḥadīthi-hī*, Beirut, Lebanon: Dār Khiḍar, 1414 AH.
Fanānī, Zayn al-Dīn Makhdūm al-, *al-Bunyān al-marṣūṣ fī sharḥ al-mawlid al-manqūṣ*.
Farāhīdī, Abū ʿAbd al-Raḥmān al-Khalīl b. Aḥmad al- (175–100 AH), *Kitāb al-ʿayn*, Qom, Iran, Muʾassisa Dār al-Hijra, 1405 AH.
Farīdī, Khawāja Muhammad Yār (d. 1368 AH/ 1948 CE), *Dīwān Muḥammadī* known as *Anwār Farīdī*, Khānpūr, Pakistan: Darbār Muhammadiyya Garhī Sharīf, 1411 AH/1991 CE.
Faryābī, Abū Bakr Jaʿfar b. Muhammad b. al-Ḥasan al-(301–207 AH), *Kitāb al-qadr,* Saudi Arabia, Aḍwā al-Salaf, 1418 AH.
Fāsī, Muhammad Mahdī b. Aḥmad b. ʿAlī Yūsuf al- (1109–1033 AH/1698–1624 CE), *Maṭāliʿ al-masarrāt bi-jalāʾ dalāʾil al-khayrāt*, Faisalabad, Pakistan: Maktaba Nūriyya Riḍwiyya.
Fayrūzabādī, Abū Ṭāhir Muhammad b. Yaʿqūb al- (729–817 AH/1329–1414 CE), *al-Nafkha al-ʿanbariyya fī mawlid Khayr al-bariyya* ﷺ.
—. *al-Qāmūs al-muḥīṭ*, Beirut, Lebanon: Muʾassisa al-ʿArabiyya.
—. *al-Ṣalāt wa al-bishr fī al-ṣalā ʿalā Khayr al-bashr* ﷺ, Lahore, Pakistan: Maktaba Ishāʿat al-Qurʾān.
—. *Tanwīr al-miqbās min tafsīr Ibn ʿAbbās*, Beirut, Lebanon: Dār al-Kutub al-ʿIlmiyya.
Ghulām Dastagīr Rashīd, *Āthār Iqbāl*, Hyderabad Deccan, India: Sayyid ʿAbd al-Razzāq Tājir Kutub (Mālik Idāra Ishāʿat Urdu).
Hiba Allāh, Abū al-Faraj Muhammad b. ʿAbd al-Qādir b. Muhammad Ṣāliḥ Damishqī al-Shāfiʿī (d. 1311 AH), *Mawlid al-Nabī* ﷺ.
Ḥaḍramī, Muhammad b. ʿUmar Buḥrāq al-Shāfiʿī al- (930–869 AH) *Ḥadāʾiq al-anwār wa maṭāliʿ al-asrār fī sīra al-Nabī al-Mukhtār* ﷺ, Beirut, Lebanon: Dār al-Minhāj, 1419 AH/1998 CE.
Ibn Ḥajar al-ʿAsqalānī, Aḥmad b. ʿAlī b. Muhammad b. Muhammad b. ʿAlī b. Aḥmad al-Kinānī (773–852 AH/1372–1449 CE), *Fatḥ al-Bārī Sharḥ Ṣaḥīḥ al-Bukarī,* Lahore, Pakistan: Dār Nashr al-

Kutub al-Islāmiyya, 1401 AH/1981 CE.

—. *Fatḥ al-Bārī sharḥ Ṣaḥīḥ al-Bukhārī*. Beruit: Dār al-Maʿrifa, 1379 AH.

—. *al-Iṣāba fī Tamyīz al-Ṣaḥāba*, Beirut, Lebanon: Dār al-Jīl, 1412 AH/1992 CE.

—. *Nuzha al-naẓr bi-sharḥ nukhba al-fikr fī muṣṭalaḥ ḥadīth ahl al-āthār*. Cairo, Egypt: Maktaba al-Turāth al-Islāmī.

—. *al-Iṣāba fī Tamyīz al-Ṣaḥāba*, Beirut, Lebanon: Dār al-Fikr, 1421 AH/2001 CE.

—. *Taghlīq al-Taʿlīq ʿalā Ṣaḥīḥ al-Bukhārī*, Beirut, Lebanon: al-Maktab al-Islāmī & Oman, Jordan: Dār Ammār, 1405 AH.

—. *Tahdhīb al-tahdhīb*. Beirut: Dar al-Fikr, 1404 AH/1984 CE.

Ibn Ḥajar al-Haytamī, Abū al-ʿAbbās Aḥmad b. Muhammad b. Muhammad b. ʿAlī b. Muhammad b. ʿAlī b. Ḥajar (973–909 AH/1566–1503 CE), *Itmām al-Niʿma ʿalā al-ʿĀlam bi mawlid Sayyid walad Ādam* ﷺ.

Ibn Ḥajar al-Haytamī, Abū al-ʿAbbās Aḥmad b. Muhammad b. Muhammad b. ʿAlī b. Muhammad b. ʿAlī b. Ḥajar (973–909 AH/1566–1503 CE), *al-Jawhar al-munaẓẓam fī ziyāra al-qabar al-sharīf al-Nabawī al-Mukarram al-Muʿaẓẓam* ﷺ, Lahore, Pakistan: Idāra Markaziyya li Ishāʿa al-Qurʾān wa al-Sunna.

—. *Mawlid al-Nabī* ﷺ, Lahore, Pakistan: Markaz Taḥqīqāt Islāmiyya, 1400 AH/1980 CE.

—. *al-Ṣawāʿiq al-muḥriqa*, Jaddah, Saudi Arabia: Dār al-Minhāj li al-nashr wa al-Tawzīʿ, 1426 AH/2005 CE.

—. *Taḥrīr al-kalām fī al-qiyām ʿinda dhikr al-mawlid Sayyid al-anām* ﷺ.

—. *Tuḥfa al-akhyār fī mawlid al-Mukhtār* ﷺ.

—. *al-Tatāwā al-Ḥadīthiyya*, Beirut, Labanon: Dār Iḥyāʾ al-Turāth al-ʿArabī, 1419 AH/1998 CE.

Ḥājī Khalīfa, Muṣṭafā b. ʿAbd Allāh al-Qusṭunṭīnī al-Rūmī al-Ḥanafī (1067–1017 AH/1657–1609 CE), *Kashf al-ẓunūn ʿan usāmī al-kutub wa al-funūn*, Beirut, Lebanon: Dār al-Kutub al-ʿIlmiyya, 1413 AH.

Ibn al-Ḥājj al-Mālikī, Abū ʿAbd Allāh Muhammad b. Muhammad b. Muhammad b. ʿAbdarī al-Fāsī (d. 737 AH/1336 CE), *al-Madkhal ilā tanmiya al-aʿmāl bi taḥsīn al-niyyāt wa*

al-tanbīh ʿalā kathīr min al-bidʿ al-muḥdatha wa al-ʿawāʾid al-muntaḥala, Beirut, Lebanon, Dār al-Fikr, 1401 AH/1981 CE.
Ḥākim, Abū ʿAbd Allāh Muhammad b. ʿAbd Allāh b. Muhammad al- (405–321 AH/1014–933 CE), *al-Mustadrak ʿalā al-Ṣaḥīḥayn*, Beirut, Lebanon: Dār al-Kutub al-ʿIlmiyya, 1411 AH/1990 CE.
—. *al-Mustadrak ʿalā al-Ṣaḥīḥayn*, Mecca, Saudi Arabia: Dār al-Bāz.
Ḥakīm al-Tirmidhī, Abū ʿAbd Allah Muhammad b. ʿAlī b. Ḥasan b. Bashīr al- (360 AH), *Nawādir al-uṣūl fī aḥādīth al-Rasūl*, Beirut, Lebanon: Dār al-Jīl, 1992 CE.
Ḥalabī, Abū al-Futūḥ al-, *al-Fawāʾid al-bahiyya fī mawlid Khayr al-bariyya* ﷺ.
—. *Insān al-ʿuyūn fī sīra al-Amīn al-Maʾmūn (al-Sīra al-ḥalabiyya)*, Beirut, Lebanon: Maktaba al-Islāmiyya.
—. *Insān al-ʿuyūn fī sīra al-Amīn al-Maʾmūn (al-Sīra al-ḥalabiyya)*, Beirut, Lebanon: Dār al-Firk, 1400 AH.
—. *Insān al-ʿuyūn fī sīra al-Amīn al-Maʾmūn (al-Sīra al-ḥalabiyya)*, Beirut, Lebanon: Dār al-Kutub al-ʿArabiyya, 1427 AH/2006 CE.
—. *al-Kawākib al-durriyya fī mawlid Khayr al-bariyya* ﷺ.
—. *al-Kawākib al-munīr fī mawlid al-Bashīr al-Nadhīr* ﷺ.
Ḥassān b. Thābit, Ibn Mundhir al-Khazrajī (d. 54 AH/674 CE), *Dīwān*, Beirut, Lebanon: Dār al-Minhāj, 1419 AH/1998 CE.
Ḥamawī, Yāqūt b. ʿAbd Allāh al-Ḥamawī Abū ʿAbd Allāh al- (d. 626 AH), *Muʿjam al-Buldān*, Beirut, Lebanon: Dār al-Fikr.
Ḥārith, Ibn Abī Usāma al- (282–186 AH/895–802 CE), *Baghyat al-Bāḥith ʿan Zawāʾid Musnad al-Ḥārith*, Medina, Saudi Arabia: Markaz Khidma al-Sunna wa al-Sīra al-Nabawiyya, 1413 AH/1992 CE.
Ibn Abī Ḥātim al-Rāzī, ʿAbd al-Raḥmān b. Muhammad Idrīs (240–327 AH/854–938 CE), *Tafsīr al-Qurʾān al-ʿAẓīm*. Sayda: al-Maktaba al-ʿAṣriyya.
—. *al-Thiqāt*.
Hawārī, Ṣalāḥ al-Dīn al-, *al-Mawlid al-nabawī al-sharīf* ﷺ.
Haythamī, Nūr al-Dīn Abū al-Ḥasan ʿAlī b. Abī Bakr b. Sulaymān al- (807–735 AH/1405–1335 CE), *Majmaʿ al-zawāʾid wa manbaʿ al-fawāʾid*, Cairo, Egypt: Dār al-Riyān li al-Turāth & Beirut, Lebanon: Dār al-Kitab al-ʿArabī, 1407 AH/1987 CE.
—. *Mawārid al-Ẓamʾān ilā Zawāʾid Ibn Ḥibbān*, Beirut, Lebanon:

Dār al-Kutub al-ʿIlmiyya.
—. *Mawārid al-Ẓamʾān ilā Zawāʾid Ibn Ḥibbān,* Beirut, Lebanon & Damascus, Syria: Dār al-Thaqāfa al-ʿArabīyya 1411 AH/1990 CE.
Ibn Ḥayyān, ʿAbd Allāh b. Muhammad b. Jaʿfar b. Ḥayyan al-Aṣbahānī Abū Muhammad (369–274 AH), *al-ʿAẓama,* Riyad, Saudi Arabia: Dār al-ʿĀṣima, 1408 AH.
—. *al-Baḥr al-muḥīṭ,* Beirut, Lebanon: Dār al-Fikr, 1403 AH/1983 CE.
Ibn Ḥazm, Abū Muhammad ʿAlī b. Āḥmad b. Saʿīd b. Ḥazm al-Andalusī al-Zāhirī (456–383 AH/1064–993 CE), *al-Muḥallā,* Beirut, Lebanon: Dār al-Āfāq al-Jadīd.
Ibn Ḥibbān, Abū Ḥātim Muhammad b. Ḥibbān b. Aḥmad b. Ḥibbān (354–270 AH/965–884 CE), *al-Ṣaḥīḥ,* Beirut, Lebanon: Muʾassisa al-Risāla, 1414 AH/1993 CE.
—. *al-Thiqāt*, Beirut, Lebanon: Dār al-Fikr, 1395 AH/1975 CE.
Ḥimṣī, ʿAbd Allāh al-Shādhilī al-, *Mawlid al-Nabī* ﷺ.
Hindī, Ḥusām al-Dīn ʿAlāʾ al-Dīn ʿAlī al-Muttaqī al- (d. 975 AH), *Kanz al-ʿUmmāl fī Sunan al-Afʿāl wa al-Aqwāl,* Beirut, Lebanon: Muʾassisa al-Risāla, 1399 AH/1979 CE.
Ibn Hishām, Abū Muhammad ʿAbd al-Malik b. Hishām (d. 213 AH/828 CE), *al-Sīra al-Nabawiyya,* Beirut, Lebanon: Dār al-Jīl, 1411 AH.
—. *al-Sīra al-Nabawiyya,* Damascus, Syria: Dār Ibn Kathīr, 1424 AH/2003 CE.
Ḥumaydī, Abū Bakr Muhammad b. Isḥāq al- (834/219), *al-Musnad*, Beirut, Lebanon: Dār al-Kutub al-ʿIlmiyya.
Ibrāhm Muṣṭafā, *al-Muʿjam al-wasīṭ*, Beirut, Lebanon: Dār Iḥyāʾ al-Turāth al-ʿArabī, 1956 CE.
ʿIdrūsī, Muḥy al-Dīn ʿAbd al-Qādir b. Shaykh b. ʿAbd Allāh al- (1038–987 AH), *al-Muntakhab al-muṣaffā fī akhbār mawlid al-Muṣṭafā* ﷺ.
Iqbāl, Dr. Muhammad (1357–1294 AH/1938–1877 CE), *Kulliyāt (Persian)*, Lahore, Pakistan, Iqbāl Academy Pakistan, 1994 CE.
—. *Kulliyāt (Urdu)*, Lahore, Pakistan, Shaykh Ghulām Nabī & Sons, 1989 CE.
Iqlīshī, Abū al-ʿAbbās Aḥmad b. Maʿd b. ʿĪsā al-Andalūsī al- (d. 550

AH), *al-Durr al-munaẓẓam fī mawlid al-Nabī al-Aʿẓam* ﷺ.

ʿIrāqī, Ḥāfiẓ Abū al-Faḍl Zayn al-Dīn ʿAbd al-Raḥīm b. Ḥusayn b. ʿAbd al-Raḥmān Miṣrī al-ʿIrāqī al- (808–725 AH), *Mawrid al-hanī fī mawlid al-sunnī*.

ʿIrāqī, Abū Zurʿa Aḥmad b. ʿAbd al-Raḥīm al- (762–826 AH/1361–1423 CE), *Ṭarḥ al-tathrīb fī sharḥ al-Taqrīb*, Beirut, Lebanon: Dār Iḥyāʾ al-Turāth al-ʿArabī, n.d.

Ibn Isḥāq, Ismāʿīl al-Azdī al-Mālikī (199–282 AH), *Faḍl al-ṣalāt ʿalā al-Nabī* ﷺ, Beirut, Lebanon: al-Maktab al-Islāmī, 1397 AH.

Ibn Isḥāq, Muhammad b. Isḥāq b. Yasār al-Maṭlabī al-Madanī (85–151 AH), *al-Sīrat al-Nabawiyya*, Beirut, Lebanon: Dār al-Kutub al-ʿIlmiyya, 1424 AH/2004 CE.

Iskandarānī, Sayyid ʿAbd al-Qādir al-, *al-Ḥaqāʾiq fī qirāʾa mawlid al-Nabī* ﷺ.

Ismāʿīl al-Baghdādī, Ibn Muhammad Amīn b. Salīm Albānī (d. 1339 AH/1920 CE), *Hadiya al-ʿĀrifīn*.

—. *Īḍāḥ al-Maknūn fī al-dhayl ʿalā kashf al-ẓunūn ʿan usāmī al-kutub wa al-funūn*, Beirut, Lebanon: Dār Iḥyāʾ al-Turāth al-ʿArabī.

Ismāʿīl Ḥaqqī (1063–1137 AH/1652–1724 CE), *Tafsīr Rūḥ al-Bayān*, Quetta, Pakistan: Maktaba Islamia, 1450 AH/1985 CE.

Ismāʿīlī, Abū Bakr Aḥmad b. Ibrahīm b. Ismāʿīl al- (277–371 AH), *Muʿjam Shuyūkh Abī Bakr al-Ismāʿīlī*, Medina, Saudi Arabia, Maktaba al-ʿIlm wa al-Ḥikam, 1410 AH.

Ibn al-Jaʿd, Abū al-Ḥasan ʿAlī b. Jaʿd b. ʿUbayd Hāshimī (230–133 AH/845–750 CE), *al-Musnad*, Beirut, Lebanon: Muʾassisa Nādir, 1410 AH/1990 CE.

Abū Jaʿfar, Sayf al-Dīn ʿUmar b. Ayyūb b. ʿUmar b. al-Ḥumayrī al-Turkumānī al-Dimashqī al-Ḥanafī, *al-Durr al-naẓīm fī mawlid al-Nabī al-Karīm* ﷺ.

Jaʿfarī, Sayyid Muhammad b. Ḥusayn al-Madanī al-ʿAlawī al-Ḥanafī al- (1186–1149 AH), *Mawlid al-Nabī* ﷺ.

Ibn Abī Jarāda, Kamāl al-Dīn ʿUmar b. Aḥmad, *Bughya al-Ṭalab fī Tārīkh Ḥalab*, Beirut, Lebanon: Dār al-Fikr.

Jaṣṣāṣ, Aḥmad b. ʿAlī al-Rāzī Abū Bakr al- (370/305 AH), *Aḥkām al-Qurʾān*, Beirut, Lebanon: Dār al-Iḥyāʾ al-Turāth, 1405 AH.

Jawharī, Ismāʿīl b. Ḥamād (d. 393 AH), *al-Ṣiḥāḥ fī al-lugha wa*

al-ᶜulūm, Beirut, Lebanon: Dār al-Ḥaḍārah al-ᶜArabiyya.
Ibn al-Jawzī, Abū al-Faraj ᶜAbd al-Raḥmān b. ᶜAlī b. Muhammad b. ᶜAlī b. ᶜUbayd Allāh b. Ḥamādī al-Qurashī al-Ḥanbalī (510–579 AH/1116–1201 CE), *Bayān al-mīlād al-Nabawī* ﷺ.
—. *Mawlid al-ᶜurūs* ﷺ, Beirut, Lebanon: Dār al-Kutub al-ᶜIlmiyya.
—. *al-Muntaẓam fī Tārīkh al-Mumlūk wa al-Umam,* Beirut, Lebanon: Dār al-Kutub al-ᶜIlmiyya, 1415 AH/1995 CE.
—. *Ṣifa al-Ṣafwa,* Beirut, Lebanon: Dār Maᶜrifa, 1399 AH/1989 CE.
—. *al-Wafā bi-Aḥwāl al-Muṣṭafā* ﷺ, Beirut, Lebanon: Dār al-Kutub al-ᶜIlmiyya, 1408 AH/1988 CE.
—. *Zād al-Masīr fī ᶜIlm al-Tafsīr,* Beirut, Lebanon: al-Maktab al-Islāmī, 1404 AH/1984 CE.
Jazā'irī, Shaykh Abū Bakr Muhammad b. ᶜAbd Allāh b. Muhammad b. Muhammad b. Aḥmad al-ᶜAṭṭār al- (d. 707 AH), *al-Mawrid al-ᶜAdhb al-Maᶜīn fī Mawlid Sayyid al-Khalq Ajmaᶜīn* ﷺ.
Jazarī, Abū al-Khayr Shams al-Dīn Muhammad b. ᶜAbd Allāh al-Shāfiᶜī al- (d. 660 AH/1262 CE), *ᶜUrf al-Taᶜrīf bi al-Mawlid al-Sharīf.*
Jazūlī, Abū ᶜAbd Allah Muhammad b. Sulaymān (d. 870 AH), *Dalā'il al-khayrāt wa shawāriq al-anwār fī dhikr al-ṣalā ᶜalā al-Nabī al-Mukhtār*, Beirut, Lebanon: al-Maktaba al-ᶜAṣriyya, 1423 AH/2003 CE.
Kabbānī, Shaykh Muhammad Hishām, *al-Mawlid fī al-Islām bayna al-bidᶜa wa al-īmān.*
Kākūrawī, Muftī Muhammad ᶜInāyat Aḥmad al- (1279–1228 AH/1863–1813 CE), *Tawārīkh Ḥabīb Ilāh yaᶜnī sīrat Sayyid al-Mursalīn* ﷺ.
Kalāᶜī, Abū al-Rabīᶜ Sulaymān b. Mūsā al-Kalāᶜī al-Andulsī al- (634–565 AH), *al-Iktifā' fī Maghāzī Rasūl Allāh* ﷺ *wa la-Thalātha al-Khulafā'*, Beirut, Lebanon: ᶜAlim al-Kutub, 1997 CE.
Kāsānī, ᶜAlā' al-Dīn al- (d. 587 AH), *Badā'iᶜ al-Ṣanā'iᶜ*, Beirut, Lebanon: Dār al-Kutub al-ᶜArabī, 1982 AD.
Ibn Kathīr, Abū al-Fidā' Ismāᶜīl b. ᶜUmar (774–701 AH/–1301 1373 CE), *al-Bāᶜith al-ḥathīth sharḥ Ikhtiṣār ᶜulūm al-ḥadīth*, Baghdād, Iraq.
—. *al-Bidāya wa al-Nihāya,* Beirut, Lebanon: Dār al-Fikr, 1419 AH/1998 CE.

—. *al-Bidāya wa al-Nihāya*, Beirut, Lebanon: Maktaba al-Maʿārif.
—. *Dhikr mawlid Rasūl Allāh* ﷺ *wa raḍāʿihī*, Lahore, Pakistan, Markaz Taḥqīqāt Islāmīyya, 1400 AH/1980 CE.
—. *Tafsīr al-Qurʾān al-ʿAẓīm*. Beirut, Lebanon: Dar al-Fikr, 1401 AH.
Kāzarūnī, Saʿīd b. Masʿūd b. Muhammad al-, *Manāsik al-ḥijz al-muntaqā min siyar mawlid al-Muṣṭafā* ﷺ.
—. *Taʿrīb al-Mittaqā fī siyar mawlid al-Muṣṭafā* ﷺ.
Khafājī, Abū al-ʿAbbās Aḥmad b. Muhammad b. ʿUmar al- (979–1069/1571–1659), *Nasīm al-riyāḍ fī sharḥ Shifā al-Qāḍī ʿIyāḍ*, Beirut, Lebanon: Dār al-Kutub al-ʿIlmiyya, 1421 AH/2001 CE.
Khaṭīb al-Baghdādī, Abū Bakr Aḥmad b. ʿAlī b. Thābit b. Aḥmad b. al-Mahdī b. Thābit al- (463–393 AH/1071–1003 CE), *Tārīkh Baghdād*, Beirut, Lebanon: Dār al Kutub al-ʿIlmiyya.
Khaṭīb al-Tabrīzī (d. 741 AH), Walī al-Dīn Abū ʿAbd Allāh Muhammad b. ʿAbd Allāh al-, *Mishkāt al-Maṣābīḥ,* Beirut, Lebanon: Dār al-Kutub al-ʿIlmiyya, 1424 AH/2003 CE.
Khawārizmī, Abū ʿAbd Allāh Muhammad b. Aḥmad b. Yūsuf al- (d. 387 AH/997 CE), *Mafātīḥ al-ʿulūm*.
Khayyāṭ, Muhammad b. Muhammad Manṣūrī al-Shāfiʿī al- (1063–1137 AH/1652–1724 CE), *Iqtināṣ al-shawārid min mawārid al-mawārid*.
Khāzin, ʿAlī b. Muhammad b. Ibrāhīm al- (678–741 AH/1279–1340 CE) *al-Lubāb al-taʾwīl fī maʿānī al-Tanzīl*. Beruit: Dār al-Maʿrifa.
Khilāl, Aḥmad b. Muhammad b. Hārūn b. Yazīd al-Khilāl Abū Bakr al- (334–311 AH), *al-Sunna,* Riyad, Saudi Arabia, 1410 AH.
Khiṭābī, Abū Sulymān Aḥmad b. Muhammad b. Ibrāhīm al-Bustī al- (d. 388 AH), *Gharīb al-ḥadīth*, Makka, Saudi Arabia: Jāmiʿa Umm al-Qurā, 1402 AH.
Khusrū, D., Amīr (651–725 AH/1253–1325 CE), *Dīwān*.
Khazāʿī, Abū al-Ḥasan ʿAlī b. Maḥmūd b. Saʿūd al- (709–789 AH), *Takhrīj al-dalālāt al-samʿiyya ʿalā mā kāna fī ʿahd Rasūl Allāh min al-ḥarf*, Beirut, Lebanon: Dār al-Gharb al-Islāmī, 1405 AH.
Ibn Khuzayma, Abū Bakr Muhammad b. Isḥāq (311–223 AH/–838 924 CE), *al-Ṣaḥīḥ,* Beirut, Lebanon: al-Maktab al-Islāmī, 1390 AH/1970 CE.

Ibn Kīkladī, Abū Saʿīd Khalīl b. Kīkladī b. ʿAbd Allāh al-Aʿlāʿī al-Dimashqī al-Shāfiʿī (761–697 AH), *al-Durra al-sunniyya fī mawlid Khayr al-bariyya* ﷺ.

Kinānī, Aḥmad b. Abī Bakr b. Ismāʿīl al- (840–762 AH), *Miṣbāḥ al-Zujāja fī Zawaʾīd b. Māja,* Beirut, Lebanon: Dār al-ʿArabiyya, 1403 AH.

Kittānī, Abū ʿAbd Allāh Muhammad b. Jaʿfar b. Idrīs b. Muhammad al-Zamzamī al- (1345–1274 AH/1927–1857 CE), *al-Risāla al-mustaṭrifa li bayān mashūr kutub al-sunna al-musharrafa*, Beirut, Lebanon: Dār al-Bashāʾir al-Islāmīyya, 1406 AH/ 1986 CE.

Lālakāʾī, Abū al-Qāsim Hibat Allāh b. al-Ḥasan b. al-Manṣūr al- (d. 418 AH), *Sharḥ Uṣūl Iʿtiqād Ahl al-Sunna wa al-Jamaʿa min al-Kitāb wa al-Sunna aw Ijmāʿ al-Ṣaḥāba,* Riyadh, Saudi Arabia, Dār al-Ṭayba, 1402 AH.

Ludhyānwī, Muftī Rashīd Aḥmad, *Aḥsan al-fatāwā*, Karachi, Pakistan: H. M. Saʿīd Company.

Madābaghī, Ḥasan b. ʿAlī b. Aḥmad b. ʿAbd Allāh al-Manṭāwī (d. 1170 AH), *Risāla fī al-mawlid al-Nabawī* ﷺ.

Maghribī, Badar al-Dīn Yūsuf, *Fatḥ al-qadīr fī Sharḥ mawlid al-Dardīr* ﷺ.

Maghribī, Muhammad (d. 1240 AH), *al-Mawlid al-Nabawī* ﷺ.

Abū al-Mahāsin, Yūsuf b. Mūsā al-Ḥanafī, *al-Muʿtaṣar min al-Mukhtasar min Mashkal al-Āthār,* Beirut, Lebanon: ʿĀlim al-Kutub.

Maḥmūd Maḥfūẓ, al-Dimishqī al-Shāfiʿī, *Mawlid al-Nabī* ﷺ.

Ibn Mājah, Abū ʿAbd Allāh Muhammad b. Yazīd al-Qazwīnī (273–209 AH/887–824 CE), *al-Sunan,* Beirut, Lebanon: Dar al-Fikr.

Mālik, Ibn Anas b. Mālik b. Abī ʿĀmir b. ʿAmr b. Ḥārith al-Aṣbaḥī (179–93 AH /795–712 CE), *al-Muwaṭṭāʾ*, Beirut, Lebanon: Dār Iḥyāʾ al-Turāth al-ʿArabī, 1406 AH/1985 CE.

Manāwī, ʿAbd al-Rawf b. Tāj al-Ārifīn b. ʿAlī b. Zayn al-ʿAbidīn al- (1031–952 AH/1621–1545 CE), *Mawlid al-jalīl ḥusn al-shakl al-jamīl.*

—. *Mawlid al-Manāwī.*

Manṣūrpūrī, Qāḍī Muhammad Sulaymān (1349 AH/1930 CE),

Raḥmatan liʾl-ʿĀlamīn ﷺ.

Ibn Manẓūr, Muhammad b. Mukarram b. ʿAlī b. Aḥmad b. Abī Qāsim b. Ḥabqa al-Ifrīqī (711–630 AH/1311–1232 CE), *Lisān al-ʿArab,* Beirut, Lebanon: Dār Sādir.

Maqdisī, Abū ʿAbdullah Muhammad b. ʿAbd al-Wāḥid al-Ḥanbalī (569–643 AH/1173–1245 CE), *al-Aḥādīth al-mukhtāra.* Mecca, Saudi Arabia: Maktaba al-Nahḍa al-Ḥaditha, 1410 AH/1990 CE.

Maqdisī, Ibn Ṭāhir (d. 507 AH), *al-Bidʾ wa al-tārīkh,* Maktaba al-Thaqāfiyya al-Dīnīyya.

Maqrīzī, Abūu al-ʿAbbās Taqī al-Dīn Aḥmad b. ʿAlī b. ʿAbd al-Qādir b. Muhammad b. Ibrāhīm b. Muhammad b. Tamīm b. ʿAbd al-Ṣamad al- (845–769 AH/1441–1367 CE), *Imtāʿ al-asmāʿ bi mā li al-Nabī* ﷺ *min al-aḥwāl wa al-amwāl wa al-ḥafada wa al-matāʿ*, Beirut, Lebanon: Dār al-Kutub al-ʿIlmīyya, 1420 AH/1999 CE.

Mardāwī, ʿAlāʾ al-Dīn ʿAlī b. Sulaymān b. Aḥmad b. Muhammad (d. 885 AH), *al-Manhal al-ʿadhb al-qarīr fī mawlid al-Hādī al-Bashīr al-Nadhīr* ﷺ.

Marwazī, Muhammad b. Naṣr b. al-Ḥajjāj Abū ʿAbd Allāh al- (d. 294–202 AH), *al-Sunna,* Beirut, Lebanon: Muʾassisa al-Kutub al-Thaqāfiyya, 1408 AH.

—. *Taʿẓīm Qadr al-Ṣalāt,* Medina, Saudi Arabia, Maktaba al-Dār, 1406 AH.

Marzūqī, Sayyid Abū al-Fawz Aḥmad b. Muhammad b. Ramaḍān al-Makkī al-Mālikī (ca. 1281 AH/ 1864 CE), *ʿAqīda al-ʿawām.*

—. *Bulūgh al-marām li-bayān alfāẓ mawlid Sayyid al-anām fī sharḥ mawlid Aḥmad al-Bukhārī.*

Māwardī, ʿAlī b. Muhammad b. Ḥabīb al- (364–450 AH), *Aʿlām al-Nabuwwa*, Beirut, Lebanon: Dar Iḥyāʾ al-ʿUlūm, 1412 AH/1992 CE.

Mihrān al-Aṣbahānī (430–336 AH/1038–948 CE), *al-Musnad al-Mustakhraj ʿalā Ṣaḥīḥ al-Imām Muslim,* Beirut, Lebanon: Dār al-Kutub al-ʿIlmiyya, 1996 CE.

Mīrghanī, Muhammad ʿUthmān b. Muhammad Makkī al-Ḥanafī al- (1268–1208 AH/1852–1794 CE), *al-Asrār al-Rabbāniyya al-maʿrūf bi mawlid al-Nabī* ﷺ, Sudan: Maktaba Maḍwān.

Mizzī, Abū al-Ḥajjāj Yūsuf b. Zakī ʿAbd al-Raḥmān b. Yūsuf b.

ᶜAbd al-Malik b. Yūsuf b. ᶜAlī al- (742–654 AH/1341–1256 CE), *Tahdhīb al-Kamāl,* Beirut, Lebanon: Muʾassisa al-Risāla, 1400 AH/1980 CE.

Ibn al-Mubārak, Abū ᶜAbd al-Raḥmān ᶜAbd Allāh b. Wāḍiḥ al-Marwazī (181–118 AH/798–736 CE), *Kitāb al-Zuhd,* Beirut, Lebanon: Dār al-Kutub al-ᶜIlmiyya.

Mubārakpūrī, Muhammad ᶜAbd al-Raḥmān al-. (1283–1353 AH) *Tuḥfat al-aḥwadhī fī sharḥ Jāmiᶜ al-Tirmidhī.* Beirut: Dar al-Kutub al-Ilmiyah, n.d.

Muhājir al-Makkī, Ḥājī Imdād Allāh (1317–1233 AH/1899–1817 CE), *Fayṣala haft masʾala*, Kamāliyya, Pakistan: Idāra Islāmiyya.

Muhājir al-Makkī, Ḥājī Imdād Allāh (1317–1233 AH/–1817 1899 CE), *Shamāʾim imdādiyya*, Multān, Pakistan: Madanī Kutubkhāna, 1405 AH.

Muhammad ᶜAlawī, Sayyid Muhammad b. ᶜAlawī al-Makkī al-Ḥasanī (d. 1425 AH/ 2004 CE), *Minhaj al-salaf fī fahm al-nuṣūṣ bayn al-naẓriyya wa al-taṭbīq*, 1419 AH.

Muhammad Amīn, Muhammad Amīn al-Ḥasanī, *Nafḥ al-ṭayyib fī Madḥ al-Ḥabīb* ﷺ, Medina, Saudi Arabia: Dār al-Ṭabāᶜa al-Mutmīza.

Muhammad Riḍā, al-Miṣrī (d. 1369 AH/1950 CE), *Muhammad Rasūl Allāh* ﷺ, Beirut, Lebanon: Dār al-Kutub al-ᶜIlmīyya, 1409 AH/1988 CE.

Muḥibb al-Ṭabarī, Abū Jaᶜfar Aḥmad b. ᶜAbd Allāh b. Muhammad b. Abī Bakr b. Muhammad b. Ibrahīm (694–615 AH/1295–1218 CE), *Dhakhāʾir al-ᶜuqbā fī manāqib dhawī al-qurbā,* Jeddah, Saudi Arabia: Maktaba al-Ṣaḥāba, 1415 AH/1995 CE.

Muḥibī, Muhammad Amīn b. Faḍl Allāh b. Muḥibb Allāh b. Muhammad Muḥibb al-Dīn b. Abī Bakr b. Dawūd al-Dimishqī (1111–1061 AH/1699–1651 CE), *Khulāṣa al-athar fī tarājim aḥwāl al-qarn al-ḥādī ᶜashar*, Beirut, Lebanon: Dār Ṣādir.

Mujaddid Alf Thānī, Shaykh Aḥmad Sirhindī (d. 1134 AH), *Maktūbāt*, Delhi, India: Maṭbaᶜa Murtaḍawī, 1290 AH.

Mujaddidī, Shāh Aḥmad Saᶜīd Dihlawī (d. 1277 AH/1860 CE), *Ithbāt al-mawlid wa al-qiyām.*

Mujāhid, Abū al-Ḥujjāj Mujāhidīn Jubayr al-Tābiᶜī al-Makkī (104–21 AH), *Tafsīr Mujāhid*, Beirut, Lebanon: al-Manshūrāt

al-ʿIlmīyya.
Mullā ʿAlī al-Qārī (d. 1014 AH/1606 CE), *al-Mawrid al-rawī fī mawlid al-nabawī* ﷺ *wa nasabihi al-ṭāhir*, Cairo, Egypt: Maktaba al-Qurʾān & Lahore, Pakistan: Markaz Taḥqīqāt Islāmiyya, 1400 AH/1980 CE.
—. *Mirqāt al-mafātīḥ sharḥ mishkāt al-maṣābīḥ*, Mumbai, India: Aṣaḥḥ al-Maṭābiʿ.
—. *Sharḥ al-Shifā*, Beirut, Lebanon: Dār al-Kutub al-ʿIlmiyya, 1421 AH/2001 CE.
—. *Sharḥ sharḥ nukhba al-fikr*, Quetta, Pakistan, Maktaba al-Islāmiyya, 1397 AH.
Mullā ʿArab, al-Wāʿiẓ (d. 938 ah), *Mawlid al-Nabī* ﷺ.
Mundhirī, Abū Muhammad ʿAbd al-Aẓīm b. ʿAbd al-Qawī b. ʿAbd Allāh b. Salama b. Saʿd al- (656–581 AH/1258–1185 CE), *al-Targhīb wa al-Tarhīb,* Beirut, Lebanon: Dār al-Kutub al-ʿIlmiyya, 1417 AH.
Muqrī, ʿAbd al-Raḥmān b. Muhammad al-Naḥrāwī al-Miṣrī al-Muqrī al- (d. 1210 AH), *Ḥāshiyya ʿalā mawlid al-Nabī* ﷺ *li al-Madābighī.*
Muqriʾ, Abū ʿAmr ʿUthmān b. Saʿīd Dānī al- (444–371 AH/–981 1052 CE), *al-Sunan al-Wārida fī al-Fitan,* Riyadh, Saudi Arabia: Dār al-ʿĀṣima, 1416 AH.
Muslim, Ibn al-Ḥajjāj Abū al-Ḥasan al-Qushayrī al-Naysābūrī (261–206 AH/875–821 CE), *al-Ṣaḥīḥ,* Beirut, Lebanon: Dār al-Iḥyāʾ al-Turāth al-ʿArabī.
Nābalusī, Imām ʿAbd al-Ghanī al- (d. 1143 AH), *al-Mawlid al-Nabawī* ﷺ.
Nabhānī, Yūsuf b. Ismāʿīl b. Yūsuf al- (1350–1265 AH), *al-Anwār al-Muhammadiyya min al-mawāhib al-laduniyya*, Beirut, Lebanon: Dār Iḥyāʾ al-Turāth al-ʿArabī, 1417 AH/1997 CE.
—. *Jawāhir al-biḥār fī faḍāʾil al-Nabī al-Mukhtār* ﷺ, Beirut, Lebanon: Dār Kutub al-ʿIlmiyya, 1419 AH/1998 CE.
—. *Ḥujja Allāh ʿalā al-ʿālimīn fī muʿjazāt Sayyid al-mursalān* ﷺ, Faisalabad, Pakistan: Maktaba Nūriyya Riḍwiyya.
Ibn Nadīm, Abū al-Farj Muhammad b. Isḥāq (d. 385 AH), *al-Fihrist*, Beirut, Lebanon: Dār al-Maʿrifa, 1398 AH/1978 CE.
Najjār, Abū Bakr Aḥmad b. Sulaymān al- (348–253 AH), *al-Radd*

ʿalā man yaqūl al-Qurʾān makhlūq, Kuwait: Maktaba al-Ṣaḥāba al-Islāmiyya, 1400 AH.

Nasāʾī, Aḥmad b. Shuʿayb Abū ʿAbd al-Raḥmān al- (303–215 AH/915–830 CE), *ʿAmal al-Yawm wa al-Layla*, Beirut, Lebanon: Muʾassisa al-Risāla, 1407 AH/1987 CE.

—. *Faḍāʾil al-Ṣaḥāba*, Beirut, Lebanon: Dār al-Kutub al-ʿIlmiyya, 1405 AH.

—. *al-Sunan*, Beirut, Lebanon: Dār al-Kutub al-ʿIlmiyya, 1416 AH/1995 CE & Ḥalb, Syria: Maktaba al-Maṭbūʿāt al-Islamiyya, 1406 AH/1986 CE.

—. *al-Sunan*, Beirut, Lebanon: Dār al-Kutub al-ʿIlmiyya, 1411 AH/1991 CE.

Nasafī, ʿAbd Allāh b. Maḥmūd b. Aḥmad al- (d. 710 AH), *Madārik al-tanzīl*, Beirut, Labanon: Dār Iḥyāʾ al-Turāth al-ʿArabī.

Nawawī, Shaykh Muhammad Nūrī b. ʿUmar b. ʿArabī b. ʿAlī al-Shāfʿī al-, *Bughya al-ʿawwām fī sharḥ mawlid Sayyid al-anām* ﷺ.

—. *al-Ibrīz al-dānī fī mawlid Sayyidinā Muhammad al-ʿAdnānī* ﷺ.

—. *Tahdhib al-Asmāʾ wa al-Laughāt*, Beirut, Lebanon: Dār al-Fikr, 1996 CE.

Naysabūrī, ʿAbd al-Malik b. Abī ʿUthmān Muhammad b. Ibrahīm al-Kharkūshī al-Naysabūrī al- (d. 406 AH), *Sharaf al-Muṣṭafāʾ* ﷺ, Mecca, Saudi Arabia, Dār al-Bashāʾir al-Islāmiyya, 1424 AH/2003 CE.

Abū Nuʿaym, Aḥmad b. ʿAbd Allāh b. Aḥmad b. Isḥāq b. Mūsā b. Mihrān al-Aṣbahānī (430–336 AH/1038–948 CE), *Ḥilya al-Awliyāʾ wa Ṭabaqāt al-Aṣfiyāʾ*, Beirut, Lebanon: Dār al-Kitāb al-ʿArabī, 1405 AH/1985 CE.Abū Nuʿaym, Aḥmad b. ʿAbd Allāh b. Aḥmad b. Isḥāq b. Mūsā b. Mihrān al-Aṣbahānī (430–336 AH/1038–948 CE), *Dalāʾil al-Nubuwwa*, Beirut, Lebanon: Dār al-Nafāʾis, 1406 AH/1986 CE.

Ibn Nujaym, Zayn al-Dīn b. Ibrāhīm b. Muhammad b. Muhammad b. Muhammad b. Bakr al-Ḥanafī (926–970 AH), *al-Baḥr al-rāʾiq sharḥ kanz al-daqāʾiq*. Beirut, Lebanon: Dār al-Maʿrifa, n.d.

Nūrī, Abū Hāshim Muhammad Sharīf al-, *Iḥrāz al-maziyya fī mawlid al-Nabī Khayr al-bariyya* ﷺ.

Qāḍī ʿIyāḍ, Abū al-Faḍl ʿIyāḍ b. Mūsā b. ʿIyāḍ b. ʿAmr b. Mūsā b. ʿIyāḍ b. Muhammad b. Mūsā b. ʿIyāḍ al-Yaḥṣubī al- (544–476 AH/1149–1083 CE), *Ikmāl al-muʿlim bi fawāʾid Muslim*. Beirut, Lebanon: Dār al-Wafā, 1419 AH/1998 CE.

—. *al-Shifā bi taʿrīf ḥuqūq al-Muṣṭafā* ﷺ. Beirut, Lebanon: Dār al-Kitāb al-ʿArabī, n.d.

Ibn Qāniʿ, Abū al-Ḥusayn ʿAbd al-Bāqī b. Qāniʿ (351/265 AH), *Muʿjam al-Ṣaḥāba*, Medina, Saudi Arabia: Maktaba al-Ghurabāʾ al-Athariyya, 1418 AH.

—. *Muʿjam al-Ṣaḥāba*, Mecca, Saudi Arabia: Maktaba Naẓār al-Muṣṭafā al-Bāz, 1418 AH/1998 CE.

Qanūjī, Ṣiddīq b. Ḥasan al-Qanūjī al- (1307–1248 AH), *Abjad al-ʿUlūm al-Washiyy al-Marqūm fī Bayān Aḥwāl al-ʿUlūm*, Beirut, Lebanon: Dār al-Kutub al-ʿIlmiyya, 1978 AD.

Qāqūwjī, Sayyid Muhammad b. Khalīl al-Ṭarābulusī, *Mawlid al-Nabī* ﷺ.

Ibn Qāsim, Aḥmad Mālikī Bukhārī Ḥarīrī, *Mawlid al-Nabī* ﷺ.

Qasṭallānī, Abū al-ʿAbbās Aḥmad b. Muhammad b. Abī Bakr b. ʿAbd al-Malik b. Aḥmad b. Muhammad b. Muhammad b. Ḥusayn b. ʿAlī al- (923–851 AH/1517–1448 CE), *al-Mawāhib al-Laduniyya bi al-Minḥ al-Muhammadiyya*, Beirut, Lebanon: al-Maktab al-Islāmī, 1412 AH/1991 CE.

Ibn al-Qayyim, Abū ʿAbd Allāh Muhammad b. Abī Bakr Ayyūb al-Zarʿī (751–691 AH/1350–1292 CE), *Jalāʾ al-afhām fī al-ṣalāt wa al-salām ʿalā Khayr al-anām* ﷺ, Beirut, Lebanon: Dār al-Kutub al-ʿIlmiyya.

—. *Jalāʾ al-afhām fī al-ṣalāt wa al-salām ʿalā Khayr al-anām* ﷺ, Riyadh, Saudi Arabia: Maktaba Dār al-Bāz.

—. *Zād al-maʿād fī hudā Khayr al-ʿibād*, Beirut, Lebanon: Muʾassisa al-Risāla, 1407 AH/1986 CE.

—. *Zād al-maʿād fī hudā Khayr al-ʿibād*, Kuwait, Maktaba al-Manār al-Islāmiyya.

Qazwīnī, ʿAbd al-Karīm b. Muhammad Rāfiʿī al-, *al-Tadwīn fī Akhbār Qazwīn*, Beirut, Lebanon: Dār al-Kutub al-ʿIlmiyya, 1987 CE.

Ibn Qudāma, Abū Muhammad ʿAbd Allāh b. Aḥmad al-Maqdasī (d. 620 AH), *al-Mughnī fī Fiqh al-Imām Aḥmad b. Ḥanbal al-Shaybānī*,

Beirut, Lebanon: Dār al-Fikr, 1405 AH.

Qurṭubī, Abū ʿAbd Allāh Muhammad b. Aḥmad b. Muhammad b. Yaḥyā b. Mufarraj al-Umawī al- (d. 671 AH), *al-Jāmiʿ li-Ahkām al-Qurʾān,* Beirut, Lebanon: Dār al-Iḥyāʾ al-Turāth al-ʿArabī.

—. *al-Jāmiʿ li-Ahkām al-Qurʾān,* Cairo, Egypt: Dār al-Shuʿayb, 1372 AH.

—. *al-Tadhkira fī umūr aḥwāl al-mawtā wa umūr al-ākhira,* Cairo, Egypt: Maktaba al-Qaiyyima.

Quṭb al-Dīn, al-Ḥanafī al- (d. 988 AH), *Kitāb al-iʿlām bi-aʿlām bayt Allāh al-ḥarām fī tārīkh Makka al-musharrafa*, Mecca, Saudi Arabia: al-Maktaba al-ʿIlmīyya.

Ibn Rāhawayh, Abū Yaʿqūb Isḥāq b. Ibrahīm b. Makhlad b. Ibrahīm b. ʿAbd Allāh (237–161 AH/851–778 CE), *al-Musnad,* Medina, Saudi Arabia: Maktaba al-Īmān, 1412 AH/1991 CE.

Ibn Rajab al-Ḥanbalī, Abū al-Faraj ʿAbd al-Raḥmān b. Aḥmad (795–736 AH/1393–1336 CE), *Jāmiʿ al-ʿUlūm wa al-Ḥikam fī Sharḥ Khamsīn Ḥadīth min Jawāmiʿ al-Kalim,* Beirut, Lebanon: Muʾassisa al-Risāla, 1417 AH.

—. *Laṭāʾif al-maʿārif fīmā li-mawāsim al-ʿām min al-waẓāʾif,* Beirut, Lebanon & Damascus, Syria: Dār Ibn Kathīr, 1424 AH/ 2003 CE.

Rāzī, Fakhr al-Dīn Muhammad b. ʿUmar al-. *Mafātīḥ al-ghayb* (*al-tafsīr al-kabīr*). Beirut: Dār al-Kutub al-ʿIlmiyya, 1421 AH.

Rāzī, Muhammad b. Abī Bakr b. ʿAbd al-Qādir Ḥanafī (d. 660 AH) *Mukhtār al-Ṣiḥāḥ*, Beirut, Lebanon: Dār Iḥyāʾ al-Turāth al-ʿArabī, 1419 AH/ 1999 CE.

Rifāʿī, Shaykh Muhammad Hāshim, *Mawlid al-Nabī* ﷺ.

Ruyānī, Abū Bakr Muhammad b. Hārūn al- (d. 307 AH), *al-Musnad,* Beirut, Lebanon: Dār al-Kutub al-ʿIlmiyya, 1417 AH/1997 CE.

—. *al-Musnad,* Cairo, Egypt: Muʾassisa Cordoba, 1416 AH.

Rūzbihān, Abū Muhammad b. Abī Naṣr al-Baqlī al-Shīrāzī (d. 606 AH/1209 CE), *Arāʾis al-Bayān fī ḥaqāʾiq al-Qurʾān*, Kanpur, India: Maṭbaʿ al-ʿĀlī al-Maghribī Munshī Naw Lakshawr.

Ibn Saʿd, Abū ʿAbd Allāh Muhammad (230–168 AH/845–784 CE), *al-Ṭabaqāt al-Kubrā,* Beirut, Lebanon: Dār Beirut li al-Ṭabʿat wa al-Nashr, 1398 AH/1978 CE.

Saʿdī, Shaykh Musharaf al-Dīn b. Muṣliḥ al-Dīn (690–580

AH/1291–1184 CE), *Kulliyāt*, Iran: Nashr Ṭulūʿ, 1374 AH.
—. *Kulliyāt*, Tehran, Iran: Chāpkhāna Sapher, 1369.
Sahāranpūrī, Khalīl Aḥmad (1346–1269 AH), *al-Muhannad ʿalā al-Mufannad*, Lahore, Pakistan: Maktaba al-ʿIlm.
Ibn Saʿīd, Aḥmad b. ʿAlī, *Ẓill al-ghamāma fī mawlid Sayyid Tihāma* ﷺ.
Sakhāwī, Shams al-Dīn Muhammad b. ʿAbd al-Raḥmān al- (902–831 AH/1497–1428 CE), *al-Fakhr al-ʿalawī fī al-mawlid al-Nabawī* ﷺ.
—. *Kitāb al-Ghāya fī sharḥ al-hidāya fī ʿilm al-riwāya*, Medina, Saudi Arabia: Maktaba al-ʿUlūm wa al-Ḥikam, 1422 AH/2002 CE.
—. *al-Qawl al-badīʿ fī al-ṣalā ʿalā al-Ḥabīb al-Shafīʿ* ﷺ, Medina, Saudi Arabia: al-Maktaba al-ʿIlmiyya, 1397 AH/1977 CE.
—. *al-Tuḥfa al-laṭīfa fī tārīkh al-Madīna al-sharīfa*, Beirut, Lebanon: Dār al-Kutub al-ʿIlmiyya, 1414 AH/1993 CE.
Ṣāliḥī, Abū ʿAbd Allāh Muhammad b. Yūsuf b. ʿAlī b. Yūsuf al-Ṣāliḥī al-Shāmī al- (d. 942 AH/1536 CE), *Subul al-hudā wa al-rashād fī sīra khayr al-ʿibād* ﷺ, Beirut, Lebanon: Dār al-Kutub al-ʿIlmiyya, 1414 AH/1993 CE.
Samarqandī, Abū Ḥamd Muhammad b. Aḥmad al- (d. 539 AH), *Tuḥfat al-Fuqahāʾ*, Beirut, Lebanon: Dār al-Kutub al-ʿIlmiyya, 1405 AH/1984.
Samhūdī, Nūr al-Dīn Abū al-Ḥasan ʿAlī b. ʿAbd Allāh b. Aḥmad Ḥusaynī Shāfiʿī (911–844 AH), *al-Mawrid al-haniyya fī mawlid Khayr al-bariyya* ﷺ.
—. *Wafāʾ al-wafāʾ bi-akhbār dār al-Muṣṭafāʾ* ﷺ, Beirut, Lebanon: Dār Iḥyāʾ al-Turāth al-ʿArabī.
Samnūdī, Muhammad b. Ḥasan b. Muhammad b. Aḥmad b. Jamāl al-Dīn al-Khalwatī, *al-Durr al-thamīn fī mawlid Sayyid al-awwalīn wa al-ākhirīn* ﷺ.
Sarakhsī, Shams al-Dīn al- (d. 483 AH), *Kitāb al-Mabsūṭ*, Beirut, Lebanon: Dār al-Maʿrifa, 1398 AH/1978 AD.
Sayyid ʿAlī, Ibn Ibrāhīm b. Muhammad b. Ismāʿīl b. Ṣalāḥ al-Amīr al-Ṣanʿānī (1236–1171 AH), *Taʾnīs arbāb al-ṣafā fī mawlid al-Muṣṭafā* ﷺ.
Sayyid Māḍī, Abū al-ʿAzāʾim, *Bashāʾir al-akhyār fī mawlid al-*

Mukhtār, Cairo, Egypt: Dār al-Kitāb al-Ṣūfī, 1417 AH/1996 CE.
Shāh ʿAbd al-ʿAzīz, Muḥaddith al-Dihlawī, *Fatāwā*, Dehli, India: Maṭabbaʿ Mujtabāʾī, 1341 AH.
Shāh Walī Allāh, Muḥaddith al-Dihlawī (1174–1114 AH/–1703 1762 CE), *al-Durr al-thamīn fī mubashirāt al-Nabī al-Amīn* ﷺ, Lailpur, Pakistan: Sunnī Dār al-Ishāʿa al-ʿAlawiyya al-Riḍ awiyya, 1970 CE.
—. *Fuyūḍ al-Ḥaramayn*, Karachi, Pakistan: Qurʿān Maḥal.
Abū Shāma, ʿAbd al-Raḥmān b. Ismāʿīl (665–599 AH/1267–1202 CE), *al-Bāʿith ʿalā inkār al-bidʿa wa al-ḥawādith*, Cairo, Egypt: Dār al-Hudā, 1398 AH/1978 CE.
Shams al-Dīn, Ibn al-Shaykh Āq Ḥamd Allāh, *al-Mawlid al-jismānī wa al-mawrid al-ruḥānī*.
Shaʿrānī, Abū al-Mawahib ʿAbd al-Wahāb b. Aḥmad b. ʿAlī Shāfiʿī al- (973–898 AH), *al-Mīzān al-kubrā*, Cairo, Egypt, Maktaba Muṣṭafā al-Bānī, 1940 CE.
—. *al-Yawāqīt wa al-jawāhir fī bayān ʿaqāʾid al-akābir*, Beirut, Lebanon: Dār Iḥyāʾ al-Turāth al-ʿArabī.
Shalabī, Abū Shākir ʿAbd Allāh al-, *al-Durr al-munaẓẓam sharḥ al-kanz al-muṭalsam fī mawlid al-Nabī al-Muʿaẓẓam* ﷺ.
Shanwānī, Muhammad b. ʿAlī Miṣrī al-Azharī Shāfiʿī al- (d. 1233 AH), *al-Jawāhir al-sunniyya fī mawlid Khayr al-bariyya* ﷺ.
Shawkānī, Muhammad b. ʿAlī b. Muhammad al- (1173–1250 AH/1834–1760 CE), *Fatḥ al-Qadīr,* Beirut, Lebanon, Dār al-Fikr.
—. *Nayl al-Awtār Sharḥ Muntaqā al-Akhbār,* Beirut, Lebanon: Dār al-Fikr, 1402 AH/1982 CE.
—. *Nayl al-awṭār sharḥ Muntaqā al-akhbār.* Beirut: Dār al-Jīl, 1973 CE.
Ibn Abī Shayba, Abū Bakr ʿAbd Allāh b. Muhammad b. Ibrahīm b. ʿUthmān al-Kūfī (235–159 AH/850–776 CE), *al-Muṣannaf,* Riyadh, Saudi Arabia: Maktaba al-Rushd, 1409 AH.
Shaybānī, Ḥāfiẓ ʿAbd al-Raḥmān b. ʿAlī al-, *Mawlid al-Nabī* ﷺ.
Shaybānī, Abū ʿAbd Allāh Muhammad b. al-Ḥasan al- (189–132 AH), *Kitāb al-Ḥujja ʿalā Āhl al-Madīna*, Beirut, Lebanon: ʿal-Ālim al-Kutub, 1403 AH.
Shaybānī, Abū Bakr Aḥmad b. ʿAmr b. al-Ḍaḥḥāk b. Makhlad al- (287–206 AH/900–822 CE), *al-Āḥād wa al-Mathānī,* Riyadh,

Saudi Arabia: Dār al-Rāya, 1411 AH/1991 CE.

—. *al-Āḥād wa al-Mathānī,* Riyadh, Beirut, Lebanon: Dār al-Kutub al-ʿIlmiyya, 1424 AH/2003 CE.

Shirbīnī, Muhammad Khaṭīb al-. *Mughnī al-muḥtāj ilā maʿrifat maʿānī alfāẓ al-minhāj.* Beirut, Lebanon: Dār Iḥyāʾ al-Turāth al-ʿArabī, 1982 CE.

Shirwānī, ʿAbd al-Ḥamīd al-, *Ḥāshiyya ʿalā tuḥft al-muḥtāj bi-sharḥ al-minhāj*, Beirut, Lebanon: Dār Ṣādir.

—. *al-Ḥawashī*, Beirut, Lebanon: Dār al-Fikr.

Sidūsī, Abū Yūsuf Yaʿqūb b. Shayba (262–182 AH), *Musnad ʿUmar b. al-Khaṭṭab* ﷺ, Beirut, Lebanon: Muʾassisa al-Kutub, 1405 AH.

Subkī, Taqī al-Dīn Abū al-Ḥasan ʿAlī b. ʿAbd al-Kāfī b. ʿAlī b. Tammām b. Yūsuf b. Mūsā b. Tammām al-Anṣārī al- (756–683 AH/1355–1284 CE), *Shifāʾ al-Saqām fī Ziyāra Khayr al-Anām,* Hyderabad, India: Dāʾira Maʿārif Niẓāmmiyya, 1315 AH.

Suhaylī, Abū al-Qāsim ʿAbd al-Raḥmān b. ʿAbd Allāh b. Aḥmad b. Abū al-Ḥasan al-Khathmaʿī al- (581–508 AH), *al-Rawḍ al-unuf fī tafsīr al-sīrā al-Nabawiyya li-Ibn Hishām*, Beirut, Lebanon: Dār al-Kutub al-ʿIlmiyya, 1418 AH/1997 CE.

Sulamī, Abū ʿAbd al-Raḥmān Muhammad b. al-Ḥusayn b. Mūsā al-Azdī al- (d. 412 AH), *Ḥaqāʾiq al-tafsīr*, Beirut, Lebanon: Dār al-Kutub al-ʿIlmiyya, 1421 AH/2001 CE.

Sulaymān Barsawī al-Ḥanafī, Sulaymān b. ʿIwaḍ Bāshā b. Maḥmūd (d. 780 AH), *Wasīla al-najāh.*

Suwaydān, ʿAbd Allāh b. ʿAlī b. ʿAbd al-Raḥmān al-Damlījī al-Ḍarīr al-Miṣrī al-Shādhilī (d. 1234 AH), *Maṭāliʿ al-anwār fī mawlid al-Nabī al-mukhtār* ﷺ.

Suyūṭī, Jalāl al-Dīn Abū al-Faḍl ʿAbd al-Raḥmān b. Abī Bakr b. Muhammad b. Abī Bakr b. ʿUthmān al- (911–849 AH/1505–1445 CE), *al-Durr al-manthūr fī al-tafsīr bi al-maʾthūr.* Beirut: Dār al-Fikr, 1993 CE.

—. *al-Jāmiʿ al-Ṣaghīr fī Aḥadīth al-Bashīr al-Nadhīr,* Beirut, Lebanon: Dār al-Kutub al-ʿIlmiyya.

—. *al-Ḥāwī li al-Fatāwā,* Beirut, Lebanon: Dār al-Kutub al-ʿArabī, 1425AH/2005 CE.

—. *Ḥusn al-maqṣid fī ʿamal al-mawlid*, Beirut, Lebanon: Dār al-

Kutub al-ʿIlmiyya, 1405 AH/1985 CE.
—. *al-Khaṣāʾiṣ al-Kubrā*, Beirut, Lebanon: Dār al-Kutub al-ʿIlmiyya, 1985 CE.
—. *Manāhil al-ṣifā fī takhrīj aḥādīth al-Shifā*.
Ṭabarānī, Abū al-Qāsim Sulaymān b. Aḥmad b. Ayyūb b. Maṭīr al-Lakhmī al- (360–260 AH/971–873 CE), *al-Muʿjam al-awsaṭ*. Cairo: Dār al-Ḥaramayn, 1415 AH.
—. *al-Muʿjam al-Kabīr,* Cairo, Egypt: Maktaba Ibn Taymiyya.
—. *al-Muʿjam al-kabīr*. Mosul, Iraq: Maktaba al-ʿUlūm wa al-Ḥikam, 1404 AH/1983 CE.
—. *al-Muʿjam al-kabīr*. Mosul, Iraq: Matbaʿa al-Zahrāʾ al-Ḥadītha.
—. *al-Muʿjam al-ṣaghīr*. Beirut: al-Maktab al-Islāmī, 1405 AH/1985 CE.
—. *Musnad al-Shāmiyyīn*. Beirut: Muʾassasa al-Risāla, 1405 AH/1984 CE.
—. *Musnad al-Shāmiyyīn*. Doha, Qatar: Dār al-Thaqāfa, 1410 AH/ 1990 CE.
Ṭabarī, Abū ʿAbbās Aḥmad b. ʿAbd Allāh b. Muhammad b. Abī Bakr b. Muhammad b. Ibrahīm al- (694–615 AH/1295–1218 CE), *al-Riyāḍ al-Naḍra fī Manāqib al-ʿAshra,* Beirut, Lebanon, Dār al-Gharb al-Islāmī, 1996 CE.
Ṭabarī, Abū Jaʿfar Aḥmad Muhammad b. Jarīr b. Yazīd al- (–224 310 AH/923–839 CE), *Jāmiʿ al-Bayān fī tafsīr al-Qurʾān,* Beirut, Lebanon: Dār al-Fikr, 1405 AH.
—. *Tārīkh al-Umam wa al-Mulūk,* Beirut, Lebanon: Dār al-Kutub al-ʿIlmiyya, 1407 AH.
Ṭabarasī, Abū ʿAlī Faḍl b. Ḥasan, *Majmaʿ al-bayān fī tafsīr al-Qurʿān*, Qom, Iran: Maṭbaʿ al-ʿIrfān, 1403 AH.
Tabrīzī, ʿAfīf al-Dīn Muhammad b. Sayyid Muhammad b. ʿAbd Allāh al-Ḥusaynī al-Tabrīzī al-Shāfiʿī al- (d. 855 AH), *Mawlid al-Nabī* ﷺ.
Ṭaḥāwī, Abū Jaʿfar Aḥmad b. Muhammad b. Salama b. Salma b. ʿAbd al-Malik b. Salma al- (321–229 AH/933–853 CE), *Sharḥ Maʿānī al-Āthār,* Beirut, Lebanon: Dār al-Kutub al-ʿIlmiyya, 1399 AH.
—. *Sharḥ Maʿānī al-Āthār,* Beirut, Lebanon: Dār al-Kutub al-ʿIlmiyya, 1422 AH/2001 AH.
Tamām Rāzī, Abū al-Qāsim Tamām b. Muhammad (414–330 AH),

Kitāb al-Fawāʾid, Riyadh, Saudi Arabia: Maktaba al-Rushd, 1412 AH.

Ṭanṭāwī, Ibn Jawharī al-Miṣrī al- (1359–1287 AH/1939–1870 CE), *al-Jawāhir fī tafsīr al-Qurʾān al-kārīm*, Beirut, Lebanon: Dār al-Fikr, 1350 AH.

Ṭarābulusī, Ibrāhīm b. Sayyid ʿAlī al-Ḥanafī al- (d. 1308 AH), *Manẓūma fī mawlid al-Nabī* ﷺ.

Ṭayālisī, Abū Dāwūd Sulaymān b. Dāwūd al-Jārūd al- (133–204 AH/819–751 CE), *al-Musnad,* Beirut, Lebanon: Dār al-Maʿrifa.

Ibn Taymiyya, Aḥmad b. ʿAbd al-Ḥalīm b. ʿAbd al-Salām al-Ḥarānī (1328–1263/728–661), *Iqtiḍāʾ al-Ṣirāṭ al-Mustaqīm,* Beirut, Lebanon: Dār Ibn Ḥazm.

—. *Iqtiḍāʾ al-Ṣirāṭ al-Mustaqīm,* Riyadh, Saudi Arabia: Dār Ibn Ḥazm, 1424 AH/2003 CE.

Tirmidhī, Abū ʿĪsā Muhammad b. ʿĪsā b. Sūra b. Mūsā b. Ḍaḥḥāk Salmā al- (892–825/279–210), *al-Jāmiʿ al-Saḥīḥ*, Beirut, Lebanon: Dār Iḥyāʾ al-Turāth al-ʿArabī.

Abū ʿUbayd al-Andalusī, ʿAbd Allāh b. ʿAbd al-ʿAzīz b. Muhammad b. Ayūb b. ʿAmarw Bakrī (487–432 AH/1094–1070 CE), *Muʿjam mā istaʿjam min asmāʾ al-bilād wa al-mawāḍiʿ*, Beirut, Lebanon: ʿAlim al-Kutub, 1403 AH.

Ibn Abī Usāma, Abū al-Qāsim ʿAbd Allāh b. Muhammad b. ʿAbd al-ʿAzīz b. Marzbān al-Baghwī (213–317 AH), *al-Musnad*, Riyadh, Saudi Arabia: Dār al-Ḍiyāʾ, 1409 AH.

Veltori, Abū Muhammad, *Ibtighāʾ al-wuṣūl li ḥubb Allāh bi madḥ al-Rasūl* ﷺ.

Ibn Abī al-Wafāʾ, Burhān al-Dīn Abū al-Ṣafāʾ (d. 887 AH), *Fatḥ Allāh ḥasbī wa kafā fī mawlid al-Muṣṭafā* ﷺ.

Wafā al-Ṣiyādī, Shaykh Muhammad, *Mawlid al-Nabī* ﷺ.

Wahba al-Zuhaylī,, *al-Fiqh al-Islāmī wa adillatuhu*, Damascus, Syria: Dār al-Fikr, 1978 CE.

Wahīd al-Zamān (d. 1338 AH/1920 CE), *Hadya al-mahdī min al-fiqh al-Muḥammadī*, 1325 AH.

Ibn Wālidī, Shaykh Khālid, *Mawlid al-Nabī* ﷺ.

Ibn al-Wardī, Zayn al-Dīn ʿUmar b. Muẓaffar (d. 749 AH), *Tatimma al-mukhtaṣar fī akhbār al-bashar (al-Tārīkh)*, Beirut, Lebanon: 1417 AH/1996 CE.

Abū Yaʿlā, Aḥmad b. ʿAlī b. Mathnā b. Yaḥyā b. ʿĪsā b. al-Hilāl al-Mūṣilī al-Tamīmī (307–210 AH/919–825 CE), *al-Musnad*, Damascus, Syria: Dār al-Maʾmūn li al-Turāth, 1404 AH/1984 CE.

Yūsuf Uzbuk, ʿAlī Riḍā b. ʿAbd Allāh b. Aḥmad b. ʿAlī Riḍā, *Musnad ʿAlī Ibn Abī Ṭālib* ﷺ, Beirut, Lebanon & Damascus, Syria: Dār al-Maʾmūn li al-Turāth, 1416 AH/1995 CE.

Yūsuf Sarkīs, Yūsuf b. Ilyān b. Mūsā Dimishqī (1351–1272 AH/1932–1856 CE), *Muʿjam al-maṭbūʿāt al-ʿarabiyya wa al-muʿarraba*.

Yūsuf Zādah al-Rūmī, ʿAbd Allāh Ḥilmī b. Muhammad b. Yūsuf b. ʿAbd al-Mannān Rūmī Ḥanafī Muqrī (1167–1085 AH), *al-Kalām al-sanī al-muṣaffā fī mawlid al-Muṣṭafā* ﷺ.

Ibn Ẓahīra, Muhammad b. Jār Allāh b. Ẓahīra al-Qurashī (d. 986 AH/1587 CE), *al-Jāmiʿ al-laṭīf fī faḍl Makka wa ahlihā wa bināʾ al-bayt al-sharāf*, Beirut, Lebanon: al-Maktaba al-Shaʿbiyya, 1399 AH/1979 CE.

Zamakhsharī, Jār Allāh Abū al-Qāsim Maḥmūd b. ʿUmar al- (427–538 AH), *al-Kashshāf ʿan ḥaqāʾiq ghawāmiḍ al-Tanzīl*. Cairo, Egypt, 1373 AH/1953 CE.

Abū Zayd al-Qurashī, *Jamhara ashʿār al-ʿArab*.

Zaylaʿī, Abū Muhammad ʿAbd Allāh b. Yūsuf al-Ḥanafī al- (d. 762 AH/1360 CE), *Naṣb al-Rāya li-Aḥadīth al-Hidāya*, Egypt: Dār al-Ḥadīth, 1357 AH/1938 CE.

Zubaydī, Muḥibb al-Dīn Abū al-Fayḍ Muhammad b. Muhammad b. Muhammad b. ʿAbd al-Razzāq Murtaḍa Ḥusaynī Ḥanafī (1205–1145 AH/1791–1732 CE), *Tāj al-ʿurūs min jawāhir al-qamūs*, Beirut, Lebanon: Dār al-Fikr, 1414 AH/1994 CE.

Zurqānī, Abū ʿAbd Allāh Muhammad b. ʿAbd al-Bāqī b. Yūsuf b. Aḥmad b. ʿAlwān Egyptian Azharī Mālikī al- (1122–1055 AH/1710–1645 CE), *Sharḥ al-Mawāhib al-Laduniyya*, Beirut, Lebanon: Dār al-Kutub al-ʿIlmiyya, 1417 AH/1996 CE.

Indices

Index of Qur'ānic Verses

2:4 *And those who believe in (all) that which has been revealed to you* 17

2:30 *And (recall) when your Lord said to the angels: I am about to place My vicegerent on the earth* 101

2:47 *O Children of Yaʿqūb! Recall those favours that I bestowed upon you* 135, 167, 536

2:49 *And (also recall) when We delivered you from Pharaoh's people* 6, 135

2:57 *And (recall) when We cast the shade of clouds over you (in the Tīha valley)* 7

2:64 *So, had there not been Allah's bounty and His mercy upon you, you would have been wrecked indeed* 144, 157

2:117 *He is the One Who has originated the heavens and the earth* 544

2:125 *Make the place, where Ibrāhīm* ﷺ *stood, a place of Prayer* 51

2:130 *And who turns away from the religion of Ibrāhīm* 19

2:135 *And (the People of the Book) say: 'Become Jews or Christians, then you will be guided aright'* 19

2:151 *Likewise, We have sent you (Our) Messenger (blessings and peace be upon him) from amongst yourselves* 116

2:152 *So remember Me, I shall remember you. And always be thankful to Me* 8, 169

2:158 *Verily the hills of al-Ṣafā and al-Marwa are from amongst the signs* 54

2:185 *The month of Ramaḍān (is the month) in which the Qur'ān has been sent* 125

2:253 *Of all these Messengers (whom We sent) We have exalted some above others* 125

3:31 *(O Beloved!) Say: If you love Allah, follow me* 140

3:34 *Verily, Allah chose Ādam, and Nūḥ, and the family of Ibrāhīm* 105

3:35 *And (recall) when the wife of ʿImrān said: O my Lord, I vow purely to You*

what is in my womb 106
3:36 *So when she delivered a baby girl, she submitted: Lord, I have given birth but to a female child* 106
3:37 *So, her Lord graciously accepted her (Maryam) with excellent acceptance* 107
3:38 *At the same place, Zakariyyā supplicated his Lord. He submitted: 'O my Lord, bless me'* 108
3:42 *And (remember) when the angels said: O Maryam, surely Allah has chosen you* 107
3:43 *O Maryam! Obey your Lord consistently with utmost humbleness, prostrate yourself* 107
3:44 *(O Beloved!) These are the tidings of the unseen which We reveal to you* 107
3:45 *When the angels said: 'O Maryam, surely, Allah gives you glad tidings of a (particular) Word from Him named the Messiah* 112, 536
3:46 *And he will talk to the people (alike) both in the cradle and in ripe years* 112
3:47 *Maryam submitted: 'O my Lord, how shall I have a son when no man has ever touched me?'* 112
3:95 *Say: 'Allah has proclaimed the truth, so follow the Religion of Ibrāhīm* 19
3:103 *But call to mind the blessing of Allah upon you when you were enemies (one to another)* 14, 134
3:103 *Remember the favours of Allah upon you when you were disunited, so he joined your hearts in love* 167
3:164 *Indeed, Allah conferred a great favour on the believers that He raised amongst them (the most eminent) Messenger* 5, 117, 145, 165
3:191 *These are the people who, remembering Allah, remain standing (as the epitome of submissiveness)* 470, 492
4:64 *And We have not sent any Messenger but that he must be obeyed by the command of Allah* 410
4:80 *Whoever obeys the Messenger ﷺ obeys (but) Allah indeed* 411
4:83 *Had there not been Allah's favour to you and His mercy, certainly you would (all) have followed Satan except only a few* 144, 157
4:113 *And Allah has revealed*

to you the Book and Wisdom and has bestowed upon you all that knowledge 155
4:125 *And with regard to adopting the Religion, who can be better than the one who submits his whole being entirely to Allah* 20
4:163 *(O Beloved!) Indeed, We have sent Revelation to you as We sent it to Nūḥ and (other) Messengers after him* 22
4:170 O *humankind! Indeed, this Messenger (blessings and peace be upon him) has come to you* 117
5:3 *Today I have perfected your Dīn (Religion) for you* 191
5:15 O *People of the Book! Indeed there has come to you Our Messenger who (clearly) unfolds to you many such things* 117
5:15 *There has indeed come to you a light from Allah (i.e., Muhammad ﷺ) and an Enlightening Book (i.e., the Holy Qur'ān)* 117, 127
5:19 O *People of the Book! Indeed, Our (Last) Prophet has come to you (at the juncture) when (the chain of) Messengers succession is breaking off* 118
5:114 O *Allah, our Lord, send down to us from heaven the table spread (with bounties)* 7, 8, 133, 137, 171, 534
5:117 *I said to them nothing except (that) which You ordered me to say: Worship (only) Allah, Who is my Lord and your Lord (too)* 567
5:118 *If You torment them, they are only Your servants, and if You forgive them, You are indeed Almighty, All-Wise* 567
6:54 *And when those who believe in Our Revelations come to you, then say (affectionately): Peace be upon you!* 448
6:86 *And (We guided) Ismāʿīl, al-Yasaʿ, Yūnus and Lūṭ (too). And We exalted all of them* 92
6:87 *And also of their ancestors and descendants and their brothers* 92
6:101 *He is the One Who is the Originator of the heavens and the earth* 554
6:161 *Say: 'Verily, my Lord has guided me to the straight path.'* 20
6:162 *Say: My Prayer, my Ḥajj (Pilgrimage) and my sacrifice (together with the entire worship and*

servitude) and my life and my death 140
7:14 *If you are thankful, I shall certainly increase (My blessings on) you, and if you are ungrateful, then My torment is surely severe* 369
7:31 *O Children of Ādam! Dress up decently every time you offer Prayer* 560
7:46 *And they will call out to the people of Paradise: Peace be upon you* 451
7:72 *Then We emancipated him and those who were on his side by Our Mercy, and cut the roots of those who denied Our Revelations* 18
7:157 *(They are the people) who follow the Messenger, the Prophet (titled as) al-Ummī* 411
7:157 *And he removes from them their heavy burdens and yokes (i.e., shackles) weighing upon them* 13, 178
7:158 *Say: O humankind! I have (come) to all of you (as) the Messenger of Allah* 412
8:17 *And (O Glorious Beloved,) when you smote (them with pebbles), it was not you who smote them, but Allah* 412
8:33 *Allah shall not punish a people whilst you (the Prophet) are amongst them* 82
9:128 *Surely, a (Glorious) Messenger from amongst yourselves has come to you. Your suffering and distress (becomes) grievously heavy on him* 118, 412
10:58 *Say: (All this) is due to the bounty and mercy of Allah (bestowed upon you through raising Muhammad* ﷺ 139, 142, 160
10:58 *This is far better than (all that affluence and wealth) that they amass* 139, 163
11:69 *And indeed, Our deputed angels came to Ibrāhīm (Abraham), bearing glad tidings. They greeted him, saying: Peace (be on you)* 448
12:38 *And I follow the Religion of my father and forefathers: Ibrāhīm, Isḥāq and Yaʿqūb* 21
13:23 *(There) are evergreen gardens. They will enter them with the pious from amongst their ancestors* 451
13:24 *(Greeting, they will say:) Peace be upon you as a reward for your*

patience! 451
14:5 *And indeed, We sent Mūsā with Our signs: (O Mūsā), bring your people out of the darkness to the light* 532
14:7 *If you are thankful, I shall certainly increase (My blessings on) you* 5, 166
14:37 *O our Lord! Verily, I have settled my offspring (Ismāʿīl) in the barren valley (of Mecca)* 53
14:39 *All praise belongs to Allah alone, Who has bestowed upon me (two sons) in old age* 93
15:28 *And (recall) when your Lord said to the angels: I am about to create a human organism* 101
15:29 *So when I accomplish the perfection of his (physical) constitution into his real being* 101
15:30 *So, (no sooner did the light of Allah's effulgence illumine the human organism than) all the angels fell down in prostration together* 101
15:31 *except Iblīs. He refused to join those who prostrated themselves* 101
15:52 *When they came to Ibrāhīm (Abraham), they greeted (him with): Peace* 449
15:72 *(O Glorious Beloved!) By your (sacred) life, surely these people (too) are wandering astray, possessed by their lust* 412
16:32 *The angels take their lives whilst they are pure, clean, pleased and contented (due to obedience and piety* 451
16:123 *Then, (O Glorious Beloved,) We sent down Revelation to you: Follow the Religion of Ibrāhīm* 20
17:1 *Holy (i.e., free of any imperfection, weakness and insufficiency) is He Who took His (most beloved and intimate) Servant* 416
19:2 *This is an account of the mercy of your Lord (bestowed) upon His (chosen) servant Zakariyyā* 93, 109
19:3 *When he called upon his Lord in a low voice (charged with politeness and submissiveness)* 93, 110
19:7 *(Allah said:) 'O Zakariyyā, indeed We give you the good news of a son whose name shall be Yaḥyā* 536
19:13 *And (blessed him) with sympathy and tenderness*

and purity and virtuousness from Our kind presence 93, 111
19:15 *And peace be on Yaḥyā the day he was born* 100, 111, 447, 620
19:16 *And, (O My Esteemed Beloved,) recite the account of Maryam in the Book* 94, 114
19:17 *Then We sent towards her Our Spirit (the angel, Gabriel), who appeared before her in complete form of a human being* 502
19:33 *And peace be upon me on the day of my birth* 100, 115, 447, 620
19:41 *And recite the account of Ibrāhīm in the Book* 94
19:51 *And recite the account of Mūsā in (this Holy) Book* 94
19:54 *And recite the account of Ismāʿīl in (this) Book* 94
19:55 *And he used to enjoin on his family Prayer and Zakat* 94
19:56 *And mention in the Book the account of Idrīs* 95
19:57 *And We raised him to a lofty station* 95
20:1 *Ṭā-Ḥā (Only Allah and the Messenger a know the real meaning)* 413
20:2 *(O My Esteemed Beloved!) We have not revealed the Qurʾān to you that you land in distress* 413
21:35 *Every soul is to taste death and then to Us you will be returned* 370
21:50 *This (Qurʾān) is the Most Blessed Admonition which We have revealed. Do you deny it?* 95
21:51 *And surely, We awarded Ibrāhīm understanding and guidance* 95
21:72 *And We made all of them pious* 96
21:73 *And We made them the leaders (of mankind) who guided (people) by Our command* 96
21:84 *So We granted his prayer, and We removed the misery that was afflicting him* 96
21:85 *And (also recall) Ismāʿīl, and Idrīs and Dhū al-Kifl. They were all steadfast men of patience* 97
21:86 *And We admitted them to (the embrace of) Our mercy. Surely, they were of the pious* 97
21:90 *Surely, they (all) used to hasten in (doing) pious deeds and used to call on Us* 97
21:104 *The way We created*

(the universe) the first time, We shall repeat the same process of creation (after its extinction) 567
21:106 *Surely, there is for the devoted worshippers a guarantee and sufficient provision in this* 97
21:107 *And, (O Esteemed Messenger,) We have not sent you but as a mercy for all the worlds* 98, 119, 144, 154, 413
21:112 *(Our Beloved) submitted: My Lord, judge (between us) with truth* 98
22:27 *Enjoin people with the Pilgrimage and they shall flock to you, on foot and riding from every corner* 36
22:28 *Then eat of them yourselves and feed the distressed and the needy* 518
22:36 *Eat of it and (also) feed those who are sitting contented as well as the (needy) who beg* 518
22:36 *The animals of sacrifice have been prescribed as signs of Allah for you* 61
22:78 *And strive hard in the way of Allah (for the establishment of peace and human dignity) such a striving as is due to Him* 21
24:27 *O believers! Do not enter houses other than your own until you obtain their permission* 449
24:61 *Then, when you enter the houses, greet (the members of) your (family) with the greeting of peace and security* 449
24:63 *(O Muslims!) Do not regard the calling of the Prophet amongst you like your calling of one another* 413
27:59 *Say: All praise be to Allah, and peace be upon His Servants whom He has chosen (and exalted)* 448
28:3 *(O Esteemed Beloved!) We recite to you from the true account of Mūsā and Pharaoh* 103
28:76 *Verily, Allah does not like those who gloat* 160
33:6 *This (Esteemed) Prophet is nearer to and has a greater claim on the believers than their own souls and his (pure) wives are their mothers* 414
33:43 *He is the One Who sends peace and blessings on you and His angels as well* 498
33:44 *On the Day when they (the believers) will meet*

Him, their gift (of the meeting/greeting) will be: Peace 450
33:45 *O (Esteemed) Prophet! Surely, We have sent you as a Witness (to the truth and the creation)* 414
33:46 *And (as) an Inviter towards Allah by His command and as a Sun spreading Light* 414
33:53 *O believers! Do not enter the houses of the Holy Prophet (blessings and peace be upon him) unless permission is granted* 518
33:56 *Surely, Allah and (all) His angels send blessings and greetings on the Holy Prophet* ﷺ 410, 445, 453, 498
35:43 *And you will not find any amendment in Allah's Sunna* 446
36:1 *Yā-Sīn. (Only Allah and the Messenger a know the real meaning.)* 415
36:2 *By the Qurʾān, full of wisdom* 415
36:3 *You are indeed one of the Messengers* 415
36:58 *Peace (be upon you)! (This) greeting will be conveyed (to them) from the Ever-Merciful Lord* 450
37:103 *Ibrāhīm* عليه السلام *laid him down on his forehead* 63
37:104 *O Ibrāhīm! (How wonderfully) have you made your dream really true!* 63
37:180 *Holy is your Lord, the Lord of Honour, Transcendent above these (things) which they utter* 454
37:181 *And peace be upon (all) the Messengers* 448, 454
37:182 *And all praise be to Allah alone, the Lord of all the worlds* 454
38:48 *And (also) mention Ismāʿīl and al-Yasaʿ and Dhū al-Kifl. And all of them were of the chosen ones* 98
48:8 *Indeed, We have sent you as an eyewitness (of the actions and the state of affairs of Umma* 415
48:9 *So that, (O people,) you may believe in Allah and His Messenger* ﷺ 415, 446
48:10 *(O Beloved!) Indeed, those who pledge allegiance to you in fact pledge allegiance to Allah alone* 415
49:2 *O believers! Do not raise your voices above the voice of the Prophet* ﷺ 218, 416, 447
49:3 *Assuredly, those who*

keep their voices low in the presence of Allah's Messenger 416
49:13 *Surely, the most honourable amongst you in the sight of Allah is he who fears Allah the most* 126
53:1 *By the bright star (Muhammad ﷺ) when (he ascended during the Ascension Night in the twinkling of an eye and) descended* 417
56:91 *Then (it will be said to him:) Peace for you from those on the Right Hand!* 452
62:2 *He is the One Who sent a (Glorious) Messenger (blessings and peace be upon him) amongst the illiterate people* 119, 146
62:3 *And (He has sent this Messenger for purification and education amongst) others of them also who have not yet joined* 147
62:4 *This (arrival of the Holy Messenger ﷺ as well as his spiritual benevolence) is Allah's bounty* 147
68:4 *And assuredly, you are placed high on the Most Glorious and Exalted (seat of) character* 418
73:15 *Surely, We have sent towards you a Messenger (blessings and peace be upon him)* 119
76:8 *And they give (their own) food, in deep love of Allah, to the needy* 517
76:9 *We are feeding you only to please Allah. We do not seek any recompense from you* 517
90:1 *I swear by this city (Mecca)* 100, 116, 126, 418
90:2 *(O My Esteemed Beloved,) because you are residing in it* 100, 116, 126, 418
90:3 *(O My Esteemed Beloved!) by (your) father (Ādam or Ibrāhīm [Abraham])* 100, 116, 419
93:1 *By the growing morning bright (when the sun gains height and spreads its radiance)* 419
93:4 *Indeed, every following hour is a better (source of eminence and exaltation) for you* 168, 419
93:11 *And proclaim (well) the bounties of your Lord* 7, 169, 420
94:1 *Have We not broadened your breast for you (for the light of knowledge, wisdom and spiritual gnosis)?* 409
94:2 *And We have taken off*

the load (of grief of the Umma [Community]) from you 409
94:3 *(The load) which was growing heavier on your (holy) back* 409
94:4 *And We exalted for you your remembrance (by annexing it to Ours)* 168, 409, 493
97:1 *Surely, We sent down this (Holy Qur'ān) during the Night of Destiny* 125
97:3 *The Night of Destiny is better than a thousand months (in merit, blessings, reward and recompense)* 132
97:4 *The angels and the Spirit of Peace (Gabriel) descend by their Lord's command during this (night)* 450
97:5 *This (night) is (absolute) peace and security till daybreak* 450
105:1 *Have you not seen how your Lord dealt with those who had elephants?* 85
108:1 *Indeed, We have bestowed on you an infinite abundance (every kind of superiority, bliss and bounty)* 420
108:2 *So pray to your Lord and offer sacrifice (a token of gratitude)* 420
108:3 *Indeed, your enemy will remain childless and his race will be cut off* 420
111:1 *Perished be the two hands of Abū Lahab and be he perished himself (he has pointed his finger to Our Beloved)!* 208
111:2 *Neither His (inherited) wealth nor his earned riches have given him any benefit* 208
111:3 *Soon he will tumble into the Flaming Fire* 208
112:1 *(O Esteemed Messenger!) Proclaim: He is Allah, Who is the One* 140

Index of Hadith Reports and Narrations

A child is redeemed by its *ʿaqīqa*. A sacrifice should be performed on its behalf 202

A funeral procession passed by, and the Prophet ﷺ stood up for it 490

A truthful word, but its intent is mistaken 573

A women said to ʿĀʾisha ؓ, 'Uncover for me the grave of Allah's Messenger ﷺ' 364

ʿAbbās came and when the Prophet ﷺ saw him, he stood up for him 481

ʿAbd al-Muṭṭalib prepared a banquet for him (i.e., his *ʿaqīqa*) 202

Actions are valued according to the intentions 470, 545

Ādam ؑ circumambulated the house seven times 42

Ādam ؑ descended to India whilst Ḥawwāʾ to Jeddah 56

Ādam descended to the Indian Subcontinent and Ḥawwāʾ to Jeddah 57

Ādam performed the Pilgrimage and circumambulated the House seven times 41

Ādam used to circumambulate it, as the *ʿArsh* 41

Al-ʿAbbās came to Allah's Messenger ﷺ, for he seemed to have heard something 389

Allah has chosen Ismāʿīl from the children of Ibrāhīm. He has chosen the tribe of Kināna 391, 609

Allah will not unite my *Umma* (community) in agreement upon an error 594, 595

Allah's Messenger ﷺ (when he became aware of this) bade them (to dispose of that water) 77

Allah's Messenger ﷺ and his Companions ؓ performed the Visitation (*ʿumra*) 47

Allah's Messenger ﷺ ordered the Companions to pour away the water 76

Allah's Messenger ﷺ walked quickly around the House and between *al-Ṣafā* and *al-Marwa* 46

Allah's Messenger ﷺ was asked about fasting on Mondays 200

Among us is the Messenger of Allah, who recites His Book as the sun appears shining

at daybreak 425
And this is (also) the day when the ark settled (safely) on Mount Judi 185
Before you came to this world, you were excellent 429
Bilāl used to make the call to prayer. He would not recite the *iqāma* until the Prophet ﷺ came out 482
Do not enter the dwellings of those who wronged themselves 78, 81
Do not enter upon these people afflicted with punishment except in a tearful state 79
Do you know where you prayed? You prayed at Bethlehem 199
Do you not know what they invented after you: they shed the blood (of the Muslims) 570
Do you take men as arbitrators in the matter of Allah? There is no judgment, save God's alone 573
Everything became illuminated the day in which the Prophet ﷺ entered Medina 356
Friday is the day of ʿ*īd*. Do not make your day of ʿ*īd* a day of fasting 196
Hūd and Ṣāliḥ ﷺ passed by this valley, riding on young red camels 34
He continued until he reached to the valley of *Muḥassir*. Then he took to the reigns of his camel 86
How can I do something which the Messenger of Allah ﷺ did not do? 577
I am indeed holding you back from you casting yourselves into the Fire 565
I am the answer to my father Ibrāhīm's supplication and the glad-tidings of ʿĪsā 11
I am the first of them to come forth (from the enlightened grave) 402
I am your forerunner at the Basin [*al-Ḥawḍ*] 564, 566
I do not want a Medina void of Allah's Messenger. I cannot bear the Prophet's place empty of him 358
I do not wish to see any of you approach my Basin [*al-Ḥawḍ*] and then be dragged away from it 565
I have greater right to Mūsā ﷺ, and I have greater right to fast this day 176, 186
I have never seen Allah's Messenger ﷺ perform the prayer except at its prescribed time 59
I have not seen anyone closer in conduct and manners to the Messenger of Allah ﷺ, in regards to standing and sitting, than Fāṭima 475

I have not touched silk softer than the palms of Allah's Messenger ﷺ 355

I hear the invocations of (blessings recited by) my lovers and I recognise the 461

I heard your discourse and your amazement that Ibrāhīm is Allah's Sincere Friend 393

I killed eight of them with my very hands 574

I know full well that you are just a stone. You do not harm nor benefit anyone. Had I not seen the Prophet ﷺ kiss you, I would never do so 49

I know the day in which the verse, "*Today I have perfected your Dīn for you*" was revealed 74

I never saw Sayyida Fāṭima laugh after the Prophet's passing away 353

I only loved those eyes of mine because I was able to see the Messenger of Allah ﷺ 363

I passed by Mūsā whilst he was reciting ṣalāt in his tomb! 495

I performed the ritual prayer behind ʿUmar ؓ. He recited *Sūra Yūsuf* 87

I saw ʿĪsā b. Maryam standing reciting ṣalāt 501

I saw Ibrāhīm standing reciting ṣalāt 501

I saw myself in the company of the prophets. There was Mūsā standing reciting ṣalāt 500

I swear by Him in whose hand lies my soul! None of you truly believes until I am more beloved to him than his parents and children 547

(I was a prophet, when the creation of) Ādam was between the spirit and the body 388

I was present with Āmina ؓ at the moment of the birth of Allah's Messenger ﷺ 10

I was sitting with Abū Hurayra ؓ when a man came to him and said, 'You forbade people from fasting on Fridays.' 196

I was with the Prophet ﷺ in Mecca, so we set out in one of its directions, and no mountain and tree on his way came to pass 613

I will be at the Basin [al-Ḥawḍ] until I will be waiting for you 568

I will be at the Basin [al-Ḥawḍ] waiting for you to be conveyed to me 569

I will be the first for whom the earth will split 403

I will be the leader of the children of Ādam on the

Day of Resurrection 403
Ibn ʿUmar never mentioned Allah's Messenger ﷺ except that he wept 362
Ibrāhīm ﷺ performed four cycles of prayer upon being blessed with Isḥāq ﷺ in the afternoon 26
Ibrāhīm ﷺ turned around and saw a beautiful, large-eyed, white ram 63
Ibrāhīm ﷺ, the intimate friend of Allah, stood upon a rock and exclaimed, 'O people! The Pilgrimage has been prescribed upon you' 38
If I am remembered, you are remembered with Me 493
If someone introduces a good custom into Islam, he is entitled to its reward 589
If someone invents in our *Dīn* (Religion) something which does not belong to it 561
If someone invents in our Dīn (Religion) something which has no root in it 561
If someone performs a practice which is not commanded by us, it is rejected 561
If you are unable to weep, then endeavour to weep fearing that what afflicted them may afflict you 80
If you see the funeral procession, stand 489-490
Increase the invocation of blessings upon me on Friday; for it is a day of attestation witnessed by the angels 460
Increase your invocations of blessings upon me on Friday 464
Indeed, Allah ﷻ has declared the bodies of the prophets forbidden to the earth 198
Indeed, I know in which day the verse, "*Today I have perfected your Dīn (Religion) for you*" 192
Indeed, this is the day of *ʿīd*. Allah made it for the Muslims. Whoever goes for the Friday (congregational prayers), let him bathe 195
Indeed, we know that day, and the place in which it was revealed 190
Instruct your children in three things: love of your Prophet ﷺ, love of his family 541
Invoke blessings and send salutations of peace upon me, wherever you may be 457
Invoke blessings upon me. Surely, your invocation reaches me wherever you may be 458
Invoke blessings upon me. Surely, your invocations reach me wherever you may be 459,
Ismāʿīl's ransom was the

slaughtering of a big, healthy ram at *Thabīr* Valley (Mount Mecca) 60
It is as though I am looking at Mūsā b. ʿImrān ﷺ in this valley 33
It was revealed on a day of two ʿĪds: on a Friday and the day of ʿArafa 193-194
Listen! I am indeed the Beloved of Allah [Ḥabīb Allāh] and that is no boast! 393
Mūsā ﷺ would remind his nation of the days of Allah. The days of Allah are His trials and tribulations 533
My life is good for you because you get new matters (regarding the religion) and we bring new matters for you 367
Men and women climbed on the top of houses. Children and servants ran in the streets, proclaiming: 'O Muhammad!' 525
My *Umma* (community) shall certainly split into 73 groups 594
My *Umma* (community) will not agree (collectively) upon an error 592
None of you will truly believe until I am dearer to him than his offspring and his father, and the people altogether 547
O Abū Bakr! If you bought me only for yourself, then stop me; and if you freed me only for the sake of Allah, then leave me 358
O Allah! Take away my eyesight so that I may come to know no one except my Beloved Muhammad ﷺ 363
O Allah, were it not for You, we would not have been guided nor given charity nor prayed! 427
O Anas! How could you endure to bury Allah's Messenger ﷺ by placing dust over him? 351
O Anas! How could you endure to bury Allah's Messenger ﷺ in the earth whilst you yourselves return? 351
O Bilāl! We desire to hear the call to prayer from you which you used to make for the Messenger of Allah 361
O Bilāl! What type of loyalty is this? Will you not come to visit me? 360
O Ḥassān! Respond on behalf of Allah's Messenger. O Allah, assist him with the Holy Spirit 423
(O Ḥassān) scorn the polytheists through satiric poetry and Jibrāʾīl is with you 424
O Messenger of Allah ﷺ!

If only you would take *Maqām Ibrāhīm* as a place of prayer 50
O Messenger of Allah, how will the blessing we invoke be presented to you after your demise? 198
O Messenger of Allah, I have eulogised Allah with a hymn and eulogised you with another 424
O Messenger of Allah, when was prophethood bestowed upon you? 387
O Messenger of Allah, when was Prophethood made incumbent upon you? 610
O people! Spread the greetings of peace, feed others, and offer your ritual prayer when others are asleep 519
O the full white moon rose over us; From the valley of *al-Wadā*ᶜ 434, 526
On the expedition to Tabūk, Allah's Messenger ﷺ stopped at *al-Ḥijr* 75
On the night when I was transported on the Heavenly Ascension, I passed by Mūsā at the red sandbank 495
On this day, Ādam ﷺ was created 197
One day Allah's Messenger ﷺ visited the ground of Uḥud and prayed as if he was praying the funeral prayer 394
One day when Allah's Messenger ﷺ was sitting, his foster-father arrived 480
One of the Prophet's Companions lost his eyesight so the Companions went to console him 363
Prophet Mūsā ﷺ performed Pilgrimage on a red camel 34
Prophets ᶜUzayr ﷺ and Dāwūd ﷺ were granted forgiveness at sunset 26
Seventy Prophets have trodden the mountainous path of *al-Rawḥā* 33
Seventy-five Prophets performed the Pilgrimage; all of them circumambulated the House 41
So he came to Maymūna and she took out for him the Prophet's mirror 364
So when he proclaimed, 'Allah is the greatest; Allah is the Greatest', there was an echo in Medina 361
Stand for your master (or the best among you) 474
Surely, Allah will support Ḥassān with the Holy Spirit, as long as he glorifies and defends Allah's Messenger 421
Surely, the (*qiyām* of the) ritual prayer used to be held for

the Prophet ﷺ 488
Surely, your salutations of peace reach me wherever you may be 458
The best amongst you is the one who feeds others and who replies to the greeting of peace 520
The cause of Abū Bakr's death was his bereavement for the Prophet ﷺ 346
The cause of Abū Bakr's death was the (grief he felt at the) Prophet's passing away 345
The Children of Israel split into 71 groups; the Christians split into 72 groups 593
The finest of your days is the Day of Congregation (Friday), on which Ādam ﵇ was created 195
The first person to be clothed will be Ibrāhīm 567
The first person to lay the foundation of the *Kaʿba* 40
The first person to perform the *ʿishā* prayer—the final ritual prayer of the day—was our Prophet Muhammad 27
The Holy Spirit will not cease to support you, as long as you defend Allah and His Messenger 422
The hypocrites assume that the Prophet ﷺ has passed away, but the Prophet has not died 346
The inhabitants of Khaybar used to fast on *Yawm ʿĀshūrā'* taking it as a day of *ʿīd* 181
The *iqāma* for the ritual prayer had been recited, so we straightened our rows before the Messenger of Allah ﷺ came out to us 485
The Jews replied, 'This is a great day. On this day, Allah liberated Mūsā ﵇ and his people 177
The Jews used to consider *Yawm ʿĀshūrā'* as an *ʿīd* 180
The Messenger of Allah used to sit with us in the mosque and converse with us 479
The most esteemed Prophet ﷺ saw the women and children coming—I think Anas said, 'from a wedding' 476
The noble Companions asked the most esteemed Prophet ﷺ, 'Should we continue this action after you pass away?' 460
The people would take to their rows before the Prophet ﷺ stood in his place of prayer 488
The Prophet ﷺ came to Medina and saw the Jews fasting on *Yawm ʿĀshūrā'* 176
The Prophet ﷺ entered (Mecca) and circumambulated the

House seven times 42
The Prophet ﷺ got up for him with his body uncovered, dragging his cloth 478
The Prophet ﷺ is my elder, but I was born before him 603
The Prophet ﷺ offered the *ẓuhr* and *ʿasr* ritual prayers, with one *ādhān* and two *iqāmas*, at ʿArafāt 59
The Prophet ﷺ ordered them (i.e., the Companions) to perform three circuits haughtily 45
The Prophet ﷺ performed an *ʿaqīqa* for himself 201
The Prophet ﷺ performed the *ṭawāf* with *iḍṭibāʿ*, wearing a green cloak 47
The Prophet ﷺ sheltered himself with his cloak 81
The Prophet's she-camel did not eat or drink anything until she died 366
The Quraysh searched intensively for the Messenger of Allah 603
The Quraysh used to fast *Yawm ʿĀshūrāʾ* during the days of ignorance 187
The second call to prayer on Friday was ordered by ʿUthmān 580
There are angels of Allah, who roam through the earth relaying to me the salutations of peace 463
There is a stone in Mecca which used to recite salutations upon me 613
There is a verse in your Holy book which you recite, had it been revealed upon us, the Jews 190
There is no one who sends salutations of peace upon me except that Almighty Allah returns to me my soul 462
There is not a Muslim in the east or the west who sends salutations of peace upon me 462
There is not a night except that I see my Beloved ﷺ 356
They (the Arabs) used to fast *ʿĀshūrāʾ* prior to the obligation of *Ramaḍān* 187
To feed others and to spread the greeting of peace 519
Two are better than one, three are better than two, and four are better than three 593
ʿUmar ؓ lead us in the *fajr* prayer. He recited *Sūra Yūsuf*, until he reached to the verse 87
ʿUmar sat and cried and continued crying until eventually he knocked on the old woman's door 348
ʿUzayr ؑ was resurrected (after a century) and was asked: 'How long did you remain

(in this state)?' 26
Whatever the true believer regards as a good thing is a good thing in the sight of Allah 588
Whatever the true believers regards as a bad thing is a bad thing in the sight of Allah 588
When Ādam's ﷺ repentance was accepted at dawn, he offered two cycles of ritual prayer 25
When Abū Lahab died, some of his family members saw him (in a dream) in a dire state 208
When Allah intends a mercy for a Community, He takes the Prophet before it 368
When he (the chief of the created beings, the Holy Prophet ﷺ), appeared, a light was emitted 12
When he reached to the Prophet's court, the Prophet ﷺ was delighted and got up for him 477
When I gave birth to him, I witnessed light emanating from me 510
When Ibrāhīm ﷺ completed the construction of the *Kaʿba* 37, 39
When Ibrāhīm ﷺ was ordered to carry out the rites of Pilgrimage, Jibrāʾīl ﷺ took him to *Jamra al-ʿAqaba* 62
When Ibrāhīm ﷺ, the intimate friend of Allah, completed the construction of the Sanctified House 42
When Jaʿfar came (to Medina) from the migration to Abyssinia, the Prophet ﷺ got up to receive him 476
When Sayyida Fāṭima was in the last stage of her illness, I used to take care of her 354
When she gave birth, a light emitted from her 509
When the birth of Allah's Messenger ﷺ was approaching 511
When the Companions returned from burying the Prophet ﷺ 352
When the *iqāma* is recited, do not stand until you see me 485, 487
When the Prophet ﷺ came to Medina, he found the Jews fasting on *Yawm ʿĀshūrāʾ* 177
When the Prophet ﷺ entered Mecca, he circumambulated the House seven times 43
When the Prophet ﷺ had passed away, Bilāl made the call to prayer 358
When the Prophet ﷺ was born, ʿAbd al-Muṭṭalib sacrificed a ram on his behalf 202
When we heard that the

Prophet ﷺ left Mecca, we began anticipating his arrival 376
Whenever ᶜAbd al-Raḥmān b. al-Qāsim would remember the Holy Prophet ﷺ, the colour of his face would change 365
Whenever he heard a hadith, his state would change and he would weep bitterly 364
Whenever the Prophet ﷺ would enter her company, she would stand from her place and then kiss him 475, 480
Wherever you may be, invoke blessings upon me. For indeed, your invocations reach me 459
Whoever eats of these vegetables (i.e., onions and garlic) should not approach our mosques 560
Whoever feeds his brother bread until he is satisfied and gives him to drink until he is quenched 520
Whoever invokes blessings upon me on Friday and its (preceding) night one hundred times, Allah will fulfil for him one hundred of his needs 463
Whoever invokes blessings upon me once, Allah will invoke blessings on him in exchange of it ten times 498
Whoever is pleased that people should stand for him let him make his abode in the Hellfire 505
Worship the Most Merciful Almighty Allah, feed others, and spread the greetings of peace 520
Yawm ᶜĀshūrāʾ is not the day which people presume. It is only the day in which the Kaᶜba is covered 188
Yawm ᶜĀshūrāʾ was a day venerated by the Jews; they took this day as an *ᶜīd* 180
You are merely a stone. Had I not seen Allah's Messenger ﷺ kiss you, I would never do so 49
You must therefore invoke blessings upon me frequently on that day 195, 197
You ridiculed Muhammad, so I returned it to you on his behalf and with Allah be the recompense for that 422
You shall indeed be resurrected barefoot and naked 567

General Index

ʿAbbās b. ʿAbd al-Muṭṭalib 208, 214, 216, 217, 243, 282, 355, 389, 390, 392, 428, 436, 437, 481
Abbasid 581
ʿAbd al-ʿAzīz b. Muhammad 335
ʿAbd al-Ghanī al-Nābalusī 327
ʿAbd al-Ḥaqq Muḥaddith al-Dihlawī 84, 86, 129, 212, 272, 274, 284, 301, 319, 365
ʿAbd al-Ḥayy Lakhnawī 131, 212, 284, 626
ʿAbd al-Karīm al-Adrantawī 325
ʿAbd Allāh b. ʿAbbās 34, 36, 37, 38, 40, 41, 45, 47, 50, 52, 53, 54, 56, 57, 61, 62, 149, 153, 154, 155, 176, 192, 194, 195, 202, 533, 566, 569, 605, 622
ʿAbd Allāh b. ʿAbd al-Muṭṭalib 121, 122, 215
ʿAbd Allāh b. Abī Sulaymān 42
ʿAbd Allāh b. al-Mubārak 348
ʿAbd Allāh b. ʿAmr 519, 520
ʿAbd Allāh b. Khabbāb 573
ʿAbd Allāh b. Masʿūd 33, 59, 367, 463, 498, 564, 587, 588, 592
ʿAbd Allāh b. Qays 572
ʿAbd Allāh b. Rawāḥa 425, 426, 436, 438
ʿAbd Allāh b. Salām 519
ʿAbd Allāh b. ʿUmar 34, 75, 76, 79, 80, 81, 345, 594, 595
ʿAbd Allāh b. Zayd 362
ʿAbd al-Muṭṭalib 9, 202, 203, 204, 257
ʿAbd al-Qādir al-Rāzī al-Ḥanafī 602
ʿAbd al-Raḥmān b. ʿAbd al-Qārī 579
ʿAbd al-Raḥmān b. al-Qāsim 365
ʿAbd al-Raḥmān b. Dabīʿ al-Shaybānī 216
ʿAbd al-Raḥmān b. ʿUwaym 376
ʿAbd al-Razzāq al-Ṣanʿānī 217
Abraha 84, 85
Abū ʿAbd Allāh al-Mālikī 233, 236, 319
Abū ʿAbd Allāh b. Abī al-Nuʿmān 263, 313
Abū ʿAbd al-Raḥmān al-Ṣaqlī 238
Abū al-Dardāʾ 460, 564, 570
Abū al-Ḥasan al-Mardawī

323
Abū al-Khaṭṭāb b. Diḥya al-Kalbī 227, 240, 245, 275, 296
Abū al-Rajā᾽ 435
Abū al-Shaykh 154
Abū al-Ṭayyab al-Sabtī al-Mālikī 240, 275, 314
Abū al-Thanā᾽ Aḥmad al-Ḥanafī 326
Abū Awbar 196
Abū Ayyūb al-Anṣārī 377
Abū Bakr al-Ḥajjār 263
Abū Bakr al-Ṣiddīq 34, 345, 346, 357, 358, 359, 365, 564, 567, 569, 571, 577, 578, 623
Abū Bakr b. Muhammad al-Ḥalabī 324
Abū Bilāl [Kharijite] 572
Abū Dāwūd 474, 505
Abū Dharr 593
Abū Ḥamw Mūsā 296, 297
Abū Ḥanīfa 348
Abū Ḥayyān al-Andalusī 151, 154, 314
Abū Hurayra 38, 44, 65, 73, 185, 196, 387, 403, 423, 425, 458, 462, 479, 485, 488, 500, 547, 610
Abū Lahab 3, 184, 189, 207, 208, 210, 212, 214, 216, 217, 228, 243, 250, 258, 264, 270, 273, 279, 280, 282, 284, 289, 295
Abū Mūsā al-Ashᶜarī 32, 180, 368
Abū Mūsā al-Zarhūnī 263
Abū Nuᶜaym al-Aṣbahānī 318
Abū Qatada 200, 485, 487
Abū Qubays, Mount 36
Abū Saᶜd Kharkūshī al-Nīsābūrī 319
Abū Saᶜīd al-Khudrī 473, 493
Abū Saᶜīd al-Muẓaffar 226, 227, 230, 238, 240, 242, 243, 244, 246, 275, 296, 310, 312, 535
Abū Saᶜīd Khalīl 321
Abū Salama b. ᶜAbd al-Raḥmān 485
Abū Shāma 229, 295, 310
Abū Ṭālib 204, 437
Abū Ṭufayl 46
Abū Umāma 11, 464, 593
Abū Wā᾽il 622
Ādam, Prophet 25, 27, 40, 56, 57, 64, 100, 101, 105, 116, 121, 122, 195, 197, 199, 234, 237, 249, 388, 393, 402, 403, 404, 419, 429, 531, 610, 611, 613
Adfuwī, al- 314, 320
Aḥmad b. Ḥanbal 73, 185, 196, 249, 351, 491
Aḥmad Ḥasan Amrūhī 298
Aḥmad Muṣṭafā al-Marāghī 152
Aḥmad Riḍā Khān 168, 333, 461, 618
ᶜĀ᾽isha al-Ṣiddīqa 186, 364, 421, 423, 436, 437, 475, 477, 480, 561
ᶜĀ᾽isha b. Yūsuf

Bāʿūniyya 324
Ajyad fortress 308
ʿAlī al-Qārī, Mullā 247, 268, 269, 292, 303, 311, 325, 326, 335, 369, 374, 584, 585
ʿAlī b. Abī Ṭālib 85, 352, 353, 354, 365, 457, 458, 572, 574, 613
ʿAlī b. Ḥusayn 457
Ālūsī, al- 152, 154, 363
ʿAmar b. Sāʾib 480
Āmina, Sayyida 10, 12, 88, 121, 122, 208, 215, 404, 509, 510, 543
ʿĀmir b. Akwaʿ 427, 428
ʿĀmir b. Rabīʿa 489
ʿAmmār b. Abī Ammār 192, 604
ʿAmr b. al-ʿĀṣ 572
Anas b. Mālik 9, 50, 199, 201, 203, 350, 351, 355, 356, 402, 426, 463, 476, 495, 547, 592
Andalusia 296, 315, 320
ʿaqīqa 9, 201, 202, 203, 204, 256, 257
ʿArsh 41
Asad b. Zanīm 436
ʿAsfān 34
Ashʿath b. Qays 572
ʿĀshiq Ilāhī Mirathī 299
Ashraf ʿAlī Thānwī 156, 285, 292, 294, 299, 334
Aṣīl al-Dīn al-Harawī 323
Asmāʾ b. Abī Bakr 568, 569
ʿAsqalānī, al- 601
Aswad b. Sarīʿ, al- 424
Aswad b. ʿUnzah al-ʿAnsi 571
ʿAwf b. Mālik 593
ʿAwn b. Ḥujayfa 476
Aws 526
Aws b. Aws 194
Ayyūb, Prophet 96
ʿAzīz al-Raḥmān 299
Azraqī, al- 33
Badr al-Dīn al-ʿAynī 215, 484
Badr, Battle of 378
Baghawī, al- 214, 217
Banū Hāshim 389, 391
Banū Qurayẓa 473
Bāqir, al- 59
Barāʾ b. ʿĀzib, al- 424
Barsawī, al-Ḥanafī 321, 330
Barzanjī, al- 328
Basant 538, 539
Bā-Yazīd al-Bustāmī 371
Bayḥaqī, al- 201, 203, 213, 217, 257, 318, 615
Bayjūrī, al- 330, 331
Bayram Khān 317
Bethlehem 199
Bilāl b. Rabāḥ 357, 358, 359, 360, 482, 484
Black Stone 31, 45, 48, 49, 116
Bosra 12
British Raj 135
Bukhārī, al- 50, 52, 180, 181, 186, 190, 205, 207, 208, 210, 216, 217, 348, 350, 351, 390, 487, 489, 491, 505, 569, 580, 614
Burhān al-Dīn Abū al-Ṣafāʾ

323
Burhān al-Dīn b. Jamāʿa 247, 311
Burhānī al-Shāfiʿī, al- 303
Burrāq 199, 496, 499
Buṣīrī, Sharaf al-Dīn 170, 434, 436
Children of Israel 5, 6, 12, 72, 102, 103, 134, 176, 177, 178, 185, 534, 535, 593, 605
Ḍaḥḥāk, al- 57, 153
Dardīr 330
Dāwūd, Prophet 26, 27, 96
Deobandi 156, 282, 285, 292, 298, 299, 334
Dhahabī, al- 238, 323, 615
Dhū al-Ḥijja 31, 32, 56, 58, 84
Dhū al-Kifl 96, 98
Ḍimār 436
Ḍiyāʾ al-Maqdisī 201
Eden, Garden of 226
Faḍl b. ʿAbbās 84, 355
Fakhr al-Dīn al-Rāzī 159
Fāṭima b. ʿAbd Allāh 509, 510
Fāṭima, Sayyida 349, 350, 351, 352, 353, 354, 437, 475, 480
Ghassān b. ʿIbād 621
Ḥafṣa, Sayyida 578
Ḥajar, Sayyida 31, 32, 52, 55
Ḥājī Imdād Allāh Muhājir al-Makkī 285, 286, 292
Ḥājī Khalīfa 322, 323, 606
Ḥākim, al- 570
Ḥalīma al-Saʿdiyya 121, 122, 404, 543
Hamābūn Bādshāh 317
Hamān 103
Ḥamza b. ʿAbd al-Muṭṭalib 437
Ḥarra 376
Hārūn, Prophet 115
Ḥasan al-Baṣrī 60
Ḥasan b. ʿAlī 459
Ḥasan b. Ḥasan b. ʿAlī 459
Ḥasan b. Ḥusayn 459
Ḥasan b. Sahl 621
Ḥassān b. Thābit 421, 423, 436, 438, 442
Ḥawwāʾ, Sayyida 56, 57
Haytham b. Abī Sanān 425
Hellfire
people of 44
Ḥijr, al- 76
Ḥudaybiyya 44, 45
Hūd, Prophet 34
Ḥusayn b. ʿAlī 360
Ḥusayn b. Khārija 570
Iblīs *see* Satan
Ibn ʿAbd al-Barr 570
Ibn ʿĀbidīn 27, 333
Ibn Abī Mulayka 568, 569
Ibn Abzī 87
Ibn al-ʿArabī 497
Ibn al-Athīr 319, 615
Ibn al-Ḥājj al-Mālikī 236, 275
Ibn al-Jawzī 226, 284, 296, 300, 319, 436, 606, 615
Ibn al-Jazarī 259, 270, 273, 290, 311
Ibn al-Wardī 616

Ibn ʿAsākir 154, 217, 319, 359
Ibn ʿAwn 604
Ibn Dībaʿ 325
Ibn Diḥya al-Kalbī 320, 535
Ibn Ḥajar al-ʿAsqalānī 57, 73, 182, 183, 184, 185, 187, 191, 203, 251, 252, 269, 325, 553, 570, 604, 623
Ibn Ḥajar al-Haythamī 264, 325, 333, 335, 336
Ibn Ḥajar al-Makkī 586
Ibn Ḥibbān 196
Ibn Hishām 318, 614
Ibn Isḥāq 318, 614
Ibn Jamāʿa 248, 269
Ibn Jawzī 212, 217, 225
Ibn Kathīr 151, 217, 242, 243, 245, 247, 319, 321, 335, 601, 616
Ibn Mājah 195, 350
Ibn Manẓūr 497, 553, 602
Ibn Nāṣir al-Dīn al-Dimashqī 322
Ibn Qāniʿ 431
Ibn Quful 224, 313
Ibn Rajab al-Ḥanbalī 555
Ibn Saʿd 56, 217, 318, 614
Ibn Taymiyya 232
Ibn Ẓahīra al-Ḥanafī 304
Ibn Ẓufar 262, 313
Ibrāhīm al-Bayjūrī 357
Ibrāhīm b. Muhammad b. Sulaymān 359
Ibrāhīm, Prophet 11, 31, 32, 36, 37, 38, 39, 42, 48, 50, 52, 53, 60, 61, 62, 63, 65, 92, 94, 95, 100, 116, 122, 235, 249, 391, 393, 419, 448, 453, 540, 570, 609
  Maqām 50, 116, 305
  Religion of 19, 21
ʿĪd al-waṭanī, al- 379, 537
Idrīs, Prophet 95, 96
ʿIkrima 477
ʿImrān 105, 106
Iqbāl, Muhammad 127, 290, 364, 405, 546, 548
Iqlīshī al-Andalūsī, al- 319
ʿIrbāḍ b. Sāriya 249
ʿĪsā b. Maryam 8, 11, 100, 105, 109, 112, 113, 114, 115, 120, 137, 138, 171, 199, 249, 393, 404, 447, 501, 535, 536, 540, 605, 620
Isḥāq, Prophet 93, 95
Ismāʿīl al-Haqqī 241, 277
Ismāʿīl, Prophet 31, 42, 50, 52, 55, 60, 61, 63, 92, 93, 94, 96, 98, 122, 391, 609
ʿIyāḍ, Qāḍī 365, 390, 483
ʿIzz al-Dīn b. ʿAbd al-Salām 583, 584
Jābir b. ʿAbd Allāh 43, 50, 51, 58, 292, 490, 568
Jābir b. Samura 482, 613
Jaʿfar 476
Jaʿfar al-Kattānī 334
Jaʿfar al-Ṣādiq 59
Jalāl al-Dīn al-Rūmī 327
Jamāl al-Dīn al-ʿAjamī 224, 313
Jamāl al-Dīn al-Ḥanafī 265

Jamāl al-Dīn al-Kattānī 261
Jarīr b. ʿAbd Allāh 589
Jawharī, al- 602
Jawzī, al- 150, 153
Jazāʾirī, al- 320
Jazarī, al- 210, 320
Jews 13, 72, 176, 177, 178, 179, 180, 181, 183, 185, 186, 189, 252
Jibrāʾīl 42, 48, 57, 62, 63, 113, 114, 120, 199, 351, 352, 421, 424, 450, 452, 493, 502
Jinnah, Muhammad Ali 618
Jiʿrāna 47
Jūdī, Mount 73, 185
Junayd al-Baghdādī 371
Jundub 574
Kaʿba 34, 35, 36, 37, 39, 40, 41, 42, 50, 51, 52, 84, 186, 187, 188
Kaʿb al-Aḥbār 40, 73, 74, 191
Kaʿb b. Mālik 436, 438
Kaʿb b. Zuhayr 430, 431
Kākūrawī, al- 281, 282, 302, 375
Kalbī, al- 64
Kamāl al-Dīn al-Adfawī 240
Kāzarūnī, al- 320
Khadīja, Sayyida 204
Khālid b. Walīd 572
Khalīfatī, al- 327
Kharīm b. Aws 428
Khaṭīb, al- 154
Khaṭīb al-Shurbīnī, al- 326
Khaybar 181
Khāzin, al- 151
Khazraj 526
Khindif 429
Khomeini 542
Kināna 391
Kirmānī, al- 215, 357
kiswa 267
Layla al-Qadr 4, 125, 126, 128, 132, 237, 272, 450
Lenin, Vladimir 542
Luʾluʾ b. al-Fakhr, al- 322
Lūṭ, Prophet 92, 95
Maḥmūd al-Ḥasan 285, 298
Manāwī, al- 326
Manṣūr al-Nashhār 263
Mao Zedong 541
Maqrīzī, al- 615
Marwa, al- 31, 52, 54, 116
Marwazī, al- 217
Maryam, Sayyida 94, 105, 106, 107, 108, 112, 114, 115, 120, 502
mawlūd 91, 102, 281, 324, 328, 334
Maymūna 364
Mehr ʿAlī Shāh al-Golarwī 285
Minā 31, 57, 61, 84
Muʿāwiya 432, 505, 572
Muhammad al-Kharkūshī 615
Muhammad b. ʿAbd al-Wahhāb 279
Muhammad b. ʿĀʾisha 25
Muhammad b. ʿAlawī al-Mālikī 335
Muhammad b. al-Fayḍ 359
Muhammad b. Allān

al-Ṣiddīqi 327
Muhammad b. al-Nuʿmān 224
Muhammad b. Isḥāq 40, 42, 430
Muhammad b. Muslima 604
Muhammad b. Sīrīn 436
Muhammad b. Yaʿqūb Fayrūzābādī 322
Muhammad b. Yūsuf 567
Muhammad b. Yūsuf al-Ṣāliḥī 263, 319
Muhammad Jār Allāh al-Ḥanafī 511
Muhammad Maẓhar Allāh al-Dihlawī 295, 375
Muḥassir 84, 85
Muḥy al-Dīn ʿAbd al-Qādir al-ʿĪdrūsī 326
Muʿīn al-Dīn al-Mallā 224
Mujaddid Alf Thānī 271
Mujāhid 533
Mujāhid b. Jubayr 34, 41, 63
Mullā ʿArab al-Wāʿiẓ 324
Murtaḍā al-Zabīdī 602
Mūsā b. Muhammad al-Taymī 358
Mūsā, Prophet 12, 33, 34, 72, 94, 102, 103, 104, 105, 176, 177, 178, 179, 183, 184, 253, 346, 393, 494, 495, 496, 499, 500, 532, 605
Musaylama al-Kadhdhāb 571, 577
Muslim, Imam 45, 79, 180, 181, 200, 390, 491, 609, 612
Muthannā b. Saʿīd 356
Muṭṭalib b. Abī Wadāʿa 388
Muttaqī al-Hindī, al- 325
Muzdalifa 31, 57, 60, 84
Nabhānī, al- 129, 131, 288, 301, 319, 334, 390
Nābigha al-Jaʿdī 432, 433, 440
Najdis 618
Nasafī, al- 150
Nasāʾī, al- 491
Naṣīr al-Dīn b. al-Ṭabbākh 260
Nāṣir al-Dīn Maḥmūd b. al-ʿImād 240, 314
Nawāb Ṣiddīq Ḥasan Khān Bhopalī 285, 332
Nawāb Waḥīd al-Zamān 288
Nawawī, al- 56, 229, 295, 310, 322, 555
New Year's Day 539
Nile, River 6
Nūḥ, Prophet 73, 96, 105, 185
Nūr al-Dīn ʿAlī b. Ibrāhīm al-Ḥalabī 271, 326
Nūr al-Dīn al-Samhūdī 324
Ottoman Empire 540
Pakistan 135, 379, 537, 538, 557, 618
Pharaoh 6, 12, 72, 102, 103, 105, 135, 176, 177, 178, 183, 185, 253, 533
Qāsim al-Nanotwī 285
Qāsim b. Muhammad 363
Qasṭallānī, al- 129, 258, 260, 301, 390, 615

Qatāda 50, 364
Qibla al-Farānīsh 266, 305
Qubāth b. Ashyam 603
Qubayṣa b. ʿUqba 567, 569
Quraysh 186, 188, 389, 391
Qurṭubī, al- 56, 215
Quṭb al-Dīn al-Ḥanafī 266, 305, 513, 544
Rabīʿa Khātūn 243, 246
Rashīd Aḥmad Gangohī 285
Rashīd Aḥmad Ludhyānawī 212, 294
Rawḥā, al- 33, 34
Riḍā al-Miṣrī 295
Rūyānī, al- 526
Saʿd b. Muʿādh 473, 474
Ṣadr al-Dīn Mawhūb 230
Ṣafā, al- 31, 52, 54, 116
Sahāranpūrī 282, 298
Sakhāwī, al- 254, 296, 301, 302, 323, 500
Saladin 238, 243, 246, 535
Salafi 285, 288, 332
Ṣāliḥ, Prophet 34, 74, 77
Salma b. Akwaʿ 427
Samra b. Jundub 202
Ṣarṣarī al-Ḥanbalī, al- 241
Satan 62, 63, 106, 145, 226, 311, 339
Saudi Arabia 379
Shāfiʿī, al- 582
Shāh ʿAbd al-ʿAzīz Muḥaddith al-Dihlawī 278
Shāh ʿAbd al-Raḥīm al-Dihlawī 276, 550, 627
Shāh Aḥmad al-Dihlawī 280
Shāh Walī Allāh Muḥaddith al-Dihlawī 277, 278, 307, 550, 582, 626
Shams al-Dīn al-Dimashqī 211, 250
Shams al-Dīn al-Jazarī 227
Shaʿrānī, al- 499
Shawkānī, al- 57, 323, 326
Shayba 623
Sibṭ al-Jawzī 240, 245, 535
Sidra al-muntahā 499
Sufyān al-Thawrī 622
Ṣuhayb 520
Suhaylī, al- 214, 217
Sulaymān Barsūnī 321
Sulaymān Manṣūrpūrī, Qāḍī 348
Sulaymān, Prophet 27, 96
Sulṭān Bāyazīd ʿUthmānī 321
Sūq al-Layl 267, 303, 306, 544
Suyūṭī, al- 9, 152, 154, 182, 183, 203, 204, 216, 251, 255, 275, 277, 324, 371, 601
Syria 52
Ṭabarānī, al- 188, 352, 570
Ṭabarī, al- 56, 319, 534, 601, 615
Table-spread 9, 137, 171, 172
Ṭabrasī, al- 150, 155
Tabuk 74, 76
Ṭaḥāwī, al- 25, 131, 178, 180, 491
Tāj al-Fākahānī, al- 275
Ṭanṭāwī, al- 153
Taqī al-Dīn al-Subkī 241, 623

Thabīr Valley 60
Thamūd 74, 76, 80, 81, 82, 83
Thaniya 53
Thuwayba 189, 208, 209, 211, 213, 214, 228, 243, 250, 259, 264, 270, 273, 279, 282, 289
Tībī, al- 48
Tilimsān 296
Tirmidhī, al- 318, 322, 390, 505, 601, 609, 610, 612, 614
Torah 9
Ṭulayḥa al-Asadī 571
Ubayy b. Kaᶜb 533, 578
Uḥud 394
ᶜUmar Bā ᶜAlawī Haḍramī 323
ᶜUmar b. al-Khaṭṭāb 9, 40, 42, 48, 49, 50, 51, 73, 74, 87, 189, 191, 194, 345, 346, 347, 348, 426, 520, 565, 577, 578, 579, 582, 622
Umayya b. Khalaf 604
Umayyad 581
Umm Faḍl 481
ᶜUqba b. ᶜĀmir 393
ᶜUrwa b. Adaya 572
ᶜUrwa b. Masᶜūd 501
Usāma b. Zayd 571
ᶜUthmān b. Abī al-ᶜĀṣ 10, 509, 510
ᶜUthmān b. ᶜAffān 280, 570, 577, 578, 580, 603
ᶜUzayr 26
Valentine's Day 539
Walī al-Dīn al-ᶜIrāqī 249
Wāthila b. Asqaᶜ 391, 609
Yaḥyā, Prophet 27, 99, 106, 108, 109, 111, 120, 447, 536, 620
Yaᶜlā b. Umayya 47
Yamānī, al- 321
Yaᶜqūb Fayrūzābādī 359
Yaᶜqūb, Prophet 27, 88, 95, 111, 135
Yāqūt al-Ḥamawī 57
Yasaᶜ, al- 92, 98
Yūnus, Prophet 92, 97
Yūsuf al-Ḥajjār 224, 313
Yūsuf b. ᶜAlī 262, 263
Yūsuf, Prophet 21
Yūsuf Zādah 328
Zāhid al-Kawtharī 334
Zāhir al-Dīn al-Taznatī 231
Zakariyyā al-Miṣrī 325
Zakariyyā, Prophet 93, 97, 106, 107, 108, 109, 111, 120, 536
Zamakhsharī, al- 149
Zayd b. Aslam 347
Zayd b. Ḥāritha 477
Zayd b. Thābit 188, 577
Zaynab b. Abī Salama 208
Zayn al-Dīn ᶜAbd al-Bāsiṭ 624
Zayn al-Dīn al-ᶜIrāqī 321
Zayn al-Dīn Maḥmūd al-Hamadānī 317
Zaynī al-Daḥlān 283
Ziyād b. Ḥanẓala 346
Ẓufar al-Makkī 223
Zurqānī, al- 129, 274, 319

Also available by Shayh-ul-Islam Dr Muhammad Tahir-ul-Qadri

Title: The Glorious Qur'ān
Format: Hardback, 1100 pages 4 colour [Gold embossed Cover]
Date of publication: September 2011
ISBN–13: 978–1–908229–00–7
Price: £24.99 or $39.95 [+ P&P]

Title: Prophetic Virtues & Miracles
Format: Hardback, 384 pages
Date of publication: January 2012
ISBN–13: 978–1–908229–01–4
Price: £29.99 or $45.95 [+ P&P]

Title: Righteous Character & Social Interactions
Format: Hardback, 640 pages
Date of publication: January 2012
ISBN–13: 978–1–908229–02–1
Price: £34.99 or $49.95 [+ P&P]

Title: Fatwa on Terrorism & Suicide Bombings
Format: Hardback, 512 pages
Date of publication: January 2011
ISBN–13: 978–0–95518–889–3
Price: £24.99 or $39.95 [+ P&P]